Progressions and Innovations in Model–Driven Software Engineering

Vicente García Díaz
University of Oviedo, Spain

Juan Manuel Cueva Lovelle
University of Oviedo, Spain

B. Cristina Pelayo García–Bustelo
University of Oviedo, Spain

Oscar Sanjuán Martínez
University of Carlos III, Spain

A volume in the Advances in Systems Analysis, Software Engineering, and High Performance Computing (ASASEHPC) Book Series

An Imprint of IGI Global

Managing Director:	Lindsay Johnston
Editorial Director:	Joel Gamon
Production Manager:	Jennifer Yoder
Publishing Systems Analyst:	Adrienne Freeland
Development Editor:	Christine Smith
Assistant Acquisitions Editor:	Kayla Wolfe
Typesetter:	Christina Barkanic
Cover Design:	Jason Mull

Published in the United States of America by
Engineering Science Reference (an imprint of IGI Global)
701 E. Chocolate Avenue
Hershey PA 17033
Tel: 717-533-8845
Fax: 717-533-8661
E-mail: cust@igi-global.com
Web site: http://www.igi-global.com

Library of Congress Cataloging-in-Publication Data

Progressions and innovations in model-driven software engineering / Vicente Garcia Diaz, Juan Manuel Cueva Lovelle, Begona Cristina Pelayo Garcia-Bustelo, and Oscar Sanjuan Martinez, editors.
    pages cm
  Includes bibliographical references and index.
  Summary: "This book investigates the most recent and relevant research on model-driven engineering, identifying opportunities and advantages, and complexities and challenges, inherent in the future of software engineering"--Provided by publisher. ISBN 978-1-4666-4217-1 (hardcover) -- ISBN 978-1-4666-4219-5 (print & perpetual access) -- ISBN 978-1-4666-4218-8 (ebook) 1. Software engineering. I. Garcia Diaz, Vicente, 1981- editor of compilation. II. Cueva Lovelle, Juan Manuel, editor of compilation. III. Pelayo Garcia-Bustelo, Begona Cristina, 1971- editor of compilation. IV. Sanjuin Martinez, Oscar, editor of compilation.
  QA76.758.P77 2013
  005.1--dc23
                                    2013009692

This book is published in the IGI Global book series Advances in Systems Analysis, Software Engineering, and High Performance Computing (ASASEHPC) (ISSN: 2327-3453; eISSN: 2327-3461)

British Cataloguing in Publication Data
A Cataloguing in Publication record for this book is available from the British Library.

Advances in Systems Analysis, Software Engineering, and High Performance Computing (ASASEHPC) Book Series

Vijayan Sugumaran
Oakland University, USA

ISSN: 2327-3453
EISSN: 2327-3461

MISSION

The theory and practice of computing applications and distributed systems has emerged as one of the key areas of research driving innovations in business, engineering, and science. The fields of software engineering, systems analysis, and high performance computing offer a wide range of applications and solutions in solving computational problems for any modern organization.

The **Advances in Systems Analysis, Software Engineering, and High Performance Computing (ASASEHPC) Book Series** brings together research in the areas of distributed computing, systems and software engineering, high performance computing, and service science. This collection of publications is useful for academics, researchers, and practitioners seeking the latest practices and knowledge in this field.

COVERAGE

- Computer Graphics
- Computer Networking
- Computer System Analysis
- Distributed Cloud Computing
- Enterprise Information Systems
- Metadata and Semantic Web
- Parallel Architectures
- Performance Modeling
- Software Engineering
- Virtual Data Systems

IGI Global is currently accepting manuscripts for publication within this series. To submit a proposal for a volume in this series, please contact our Acquisition Editors at Acquisitions@igi-global.com or visit: http://www.igi-global.com/publish/.

Titles in this Series

For a list of additional titles in this series, please visit: www.igi-global.com

Service-Driven Approaches to Architecture and Enterprise Integration
Raja Ramanathan (Independent Researcher, USA) and Kirtana Raja (Independent Researcher, USA)
Information Science Reference • copyright 2013 • 411pp • H/C (ISBN: 9781466641938) • US $195.00 (our price)

Progressions and Innovations in Model-Driven Software Engineering
Vicente García Díaz (University of Oviedo, Spain) Juan Manuel Cueva Lovelle (University of Oviedo, Spain) B. Cristina Pelayo García-Bustelo (University of Oviedo, Spain) and Oscar Sanjuán Martínez (University of Oviedo, Spain)
Engineering Science Reference • copyright 2013 • 352pp • H/C (ISBN: 9781466642171) • US $195.00 (our price)

Knowledge-Based Processes in Software Development
Saqib Saeed (Bahria University Islamabad, Pakistan) and Izzat Alsmadi (Yarmouk University, Jordan)
Information Science Reference • copyright 2013 • 318pp • H/C (ISBN: 9781466642294) • US $195.00 (our price)

Distributed Computing Innovations for Business, Engineering, and Science
Alfred Waising Loo (Lingnan University, Hong Kong)
Information Science Reference • copyright 2013 • 369pp • H/C (ISBN: 9781466625334) • US $195.00 (our price)

Data Intensive Distributed Computing Challenges and Solutions for Large-scale Information Management
Tevfik Kosar (University at Buffalo, USA)
Information Science Reference • copyright 2012 • 352pp • H/C (ISBN: 9781615209712) • US $180.00 (our price)

Achieving Real-Time in Distributed Computing From Grids to Clouds
Dimosthenis Kyriazis (National Technical University of Athens, Greece) Theodora Varvarigou (National Technical University of Athens, Greece) and Kleopatra G. Konstanteli (National Technical University of Athens, Greece)
Information Science Reference • copyright 2012 • 330pp • H/C (ISBN: 9781609608279) • US $195.00 (our price)

Principles and Applications of Distributed Event-Based Systems
Annika M. Hinze (University of Waikato, New Zealand) and Alejandro Buchmann (University of Waikato, New Zealand)
Information Science Reference • copyright 2010 • 538pp • H/C (ISBN: 9781605666976) • US $180.00 (our price)

www.igi-global.com

701 E. Chocolate Ave., Hershey, PA 17033
Order online at www.igi-global.com or call 717-533-8845 x100
To place a standing order for titles released in this series, contact: cust@igi-global.com
Mon-Fri 8:00 am - 5:00 pm (est) or fax 24 hours a day 717-533-8661

Table of Contents

Chapter 13

Detailed Table of Contents

Chapter 1

Kevin Lano, King's College London, UK
Shekoufeh Kolahdouz-Rahimi, King's College London, UK

Model-Based Development (MBD) has become increasingly used for critical systems, and it is the subject of the MBDV supplement to the DO-178C standard. In this chapter, the authors review the requirements of DO-178C for model-based development, and they identify ways in which MBD can be combined with formal verification to achieve DO-178C requirements for traceability and verifiability of models. In particular, the authors consider the implications for model transformations, which are a central part of MBD approaches, and they identify how transformations can be verified using formal methods tools.

Chapter 2

Vahid Garousi, University of Calgary, Canada
Shawn Shahnewaz, University of Calgary, Canada
Diwakar Krishnamurthy, University of Calgary, Canada

Performance is critical to the success of every software system. As a sub-area of software engineering, Software Performance Engineering (SPE) is a systematic and quantitative discipline to construct software systems that meet performance objectives. A family of SPE approaches that has become popular in the last decade is SPE based on models developed using the Unified Modeling Language (UML), referred to as UML-Driven Software Performance Engineering (UML-SPE). This particular research area has emerged and grown since late 1990s when the UML was proposed. More than 100 papers have been published so far in this area. As this research area matures and the number of related papers increases, it is important to systematically summarize and categorize the current state-of-the-art and to provide an overview of the trends in this specialized field. The authors systematically map the body of knowledge related to UML-SPE through a Systematic Mapping (SM) study. As part of this study, they pose two sets of research questions, define selection and exclusion criteria, and systematically develop and refine a systematic map (classification schema). In addition, the authors conduct bibliometric, demographic, and trend analysis of the included papers. The study pool includes a set of 90 papers (from 114 identified papers) published in the area of UML-SPE between 1998 and 2011. The authors derive the trends in terms of types of papers, types of SPE activities, and types of evaluations. They also report the demographics and bibliometrics trends in this domain and discuss the emerging trends in UML-SPE and the implications for researchers and practitioners in this area.

Chapter 3

Requirements engineering is a process of constantly changing worlds of intentions, goals, and system models. Conventional semantics for goal specifications is synchronous. Semantics of conventional system modeling techniques is asynchronous. This semantic mismatch complicates requirements engineering. In this chapter, we propose a new method EXTREME that exploits similarities in semantics of goal specification and executable protocol models. In contrast with other executable modelling techniques, the semantics of protocol modelling is based on a data extended form of synchronous CSP-parallel composition. This synchronous composition provides advantages for relating goals and system models, reasoning on models, requirements management, and evolution.

Chapter 4

By consideration of scientific paradigm shifts, in this chapter the authors evaluate possible parallels in the evolution of modelling, and particularly metamodelling and modelling language construction, as a basis for evaluating whether or not the time is ripe for a similar change of direction in model language development for software engineering. Having identified several inconsistencies and paradoxes in the current orthodoxy, they then introduce a number of ideas from outside software engineering (including language use, philosophy, and ontology engineering) that seem to solve many of these issues. Whether these new ideas, together, are sufficient to create a shift in mindset or whether they are simply the stimulus for others to create new and orthogonal ideas remains to be seen. The authors urge the modelling and metamodelling communities to search out that new orthodoxy (i.e. instigate a paradigm shift) that will, necessarily, ensure that the science will offer simpler and more satisfying solutions in the years to come.

Chapter 5

Geographically distributed organizations face unique challenges to effectively implement shared information services across the enterprise. Traditional solutions require options such as establishing large centralized application and database servers, which simplifies some data integration issues but involves higher associated centralization risks with potential scalability limitations, or establishing multiple decentralized application servers optionally arranged in hierarchical hubs, requiring significant customization and data migration functions to be developed, reducing the level of risk but incurring additional expenditure on data integration and transfer. Our ongoing development of a distributed temporal metadata framework for Enterprise Information Systems (EIS) applications seeks to overcome these issues with the application logic model supporting the capability for direct integration with similar distributed application instances to readily provide: data replication, transfer, and transformations; centralized authorization and distribution of core identity data; sharing and deployment of modified logic model elements; and workflow integration between application instances.

Chapter 6

This chapter shows how Model Driven Engineering (MDE) can contribute to the production of Crop models. The ITK firm works in agronomy; it designs digital models and Decision Support Systems for croppers. Common model development at ITK relies on a dual implementation. The first one in Matlab® is usually proposed by agronomists, but for industrial purposes, software engineers translate this model in Java. This leads to double implementation, maintenance, and heavy production costs. To deal with this efficiency problem, the authors use a MDE approach to produce a Crop Model Factory (CMF). For this factory they propose a DSML (Domain Specific Modeling Language) formalized by a metamodel. In this chapter, the authors present this DSML, the concrete syntax retained for the factory, and its implementation in a tool enabling automatic code generation. The resulting Crop Model Factory (CMF) prototype is the fruit of an interdisciplinary collaboration, and they also present feedback on this working experience.

Chapter 7

The chapter explores the development of a specific process e-Commerce metamodel for reuse and interoperability, which is proposed to obtain the taxonomy of e-business processes. It defines a specific ontology and semantics of independent processes platform. This is achieved with the help of the principles proposed by the Model Driven Engineering (MDE), specifically the proposal for the OMG, Model Driven Architecture (MDA), enabling it to minimize the time and effort required to create ecommerce solutions.

Chapter 8

The development of systems consisting of hardware and software is a challenging task for the system architect. On the one hand, he has to consider an increasing number of system requirements, including the dependencies between them for designing the system architecture; on the other hand, he has to deal with a shortened time-to-market period and requirements changes of the customers up to the implementation phase. This chapter presents a process that enables the architect to validate the system architecture against the architecture-relevant requirements. The process is part of the system design phase and can be integrated in the iterative design of the system architecture. In order to keep track of all requirements, including their dependencies, the architect clusters the requirements according to architecture-specific aspects, the so-called validation targets. For each target he defines examinations processes and check criteria to define the validation status. If all targets are valid, i.e., all check criteria are met by the result of the examination processes, the system architecture itself is valid. Instead of formal validation techniques like model checking, the approach prefers simulations for the examination processes. The approach uses model-based documentation based on the Unified Modeling Language (UML). All data required for the simulations is part of an UML model and extracted to configure and run the simulations. Therefore, changes in the model affect the validation result directly. The process supports the architect in building a system architecture that fulfills the architecture-relevant requirements, and it supports the architect in analyzing the impacts after requirements or architecture changes. A tool facilitates the work effort of the architect by partly automating the major process steps.

Chapter 9

Abdelilah Kahlaoui, École de Technologie Supérieure, Canada

Alain Abran, École de Technologie Supérieure, Canada

Domain Specific Languages (DSLs) provide interesting characteristics that align well with the goals and mission of model-driven software engineering. However, there are still some issues that hamper widespread adoption. In this chapter, the authors discuss two of these issues. The first relates to the vagueness of the term DSL, which they address by studying the individual terms: domain, specificity, and language. The second is related to the difficulty of developing DSLs, which they address with a view to making DSL development more accessible via processes, standards, and tools.

Chapter 10

Tony Clark, Middlesex University, UK

Balbir Barn, Middlesex University, UK

Modern organizations need to address increasingly complex challenges including how to represent and maintain their business goals using technologies and IT platforms that change on a regular basis. This has led to the development of modelling notations for expressing various aspects of an organization with a view to reducing complexity, increasing technology independence, and supporting analysis. Many of these Enterprise Architecture (EA) modelling notations provide a large number of concepts that support the business analysis but lack precise definitions necessary to perform computer-supported organizational analysis. This chapter reviews the current EA modelling landscape and proposes a simple language for the practical support of EA simulation including business alignment in terms of executing a collection of goals against prototype execution.

Chapter 11

Guillermo Infante Hernández, Universidad de Oviedo, Spain

Aquilino A. Juan Fuente, Universidad de Oviedo, Spain

Benjamín López Pérez, Universidad de Oviedo, Spain

Edward Rolando Núñez-Valdéz, Universidad de Oviedo, Spain

Software platforms for e-government transactions may differ in developed functionalities, languages and technologies, hardware platforms, and operating systems that support them. Those differences can be found among public organizations that share common processes, services, and regulations. This scenario hinders interoperability between these organizations. Hence, to find a technique for integrating these platforms becomes a necessity. In this chapter, a rule-based domain-specific modeling environment for public services and process integration is suggested, which consists of common identified public service elements and a set of process integration rules. This approach provides the needed integration or interoperability pursued in this domain. Furthermore a service and process model is proposed to formalize the information needed for integration of both. A set of integration rules is also presented as part of the modeling environment. This set of integration rules completes the proposed model to meet the business requirements of this domain.

Modernization of legacy systems is a new research area in the software industry that is intended to provide support for transforming an existing software system to a new one that satisfies new demands. Software modernization requires technical frameworks for information integration and tool interoperability that allow managing new platform technologies, design techniques, and processes. The new OMG (Object Management Group) initiative for modernization aligned with this requirement is Architecture-Driven Modernization (ADM). Reverse engineering techniques play a crucial role in system modernization. In this chapter, the authors describe the state-of-the-art in the model-driven modernization area, reverse engineering in particular, and discuss about existing tools and future trends. In addition, they describe a framework to reverse engineering models from object-oriented code that distinguishes three different abstraction levels linked to models, metamodels, and formal specifications. As an example, this chapter shows how to reverse engineering use case diagrams from Java code in the ADM context focusing on transformations at metamodel level. The authors validate their approach by using Eclipse Modeling Framework.

Despite significant research efforts in the last decade, UML has not reached the status of being a high-confidence modeling language. This is due to unsound foundations that result from the insufficiently formal structuring of metamodels that define the MOF/UML Infrastructure. Nowadays, UML-related metamodels are implemented in computing environments (e.g., EMF) to play the role of metadata when one seeks adaptation at runtime. To properly instrument metamodel-based adaptation, this chapter re-formalizes the core of the MOF/UML Infrastructure along with giving formal proofs that avoid ambiguities, contradictions, or redundancies. A (meta-)class creation mechanism (either by instantiation or inheritance) is based on inductive types taken from the constructive logic. Inherent proofs based on the Coq automated prover are also provided. This chapter's contribution is aligned with a previously established metamodeling framework named "Matters of (meta-)modeling."

Foreword

Software Model Engineering has a long tradition of practice and innovation, probably as old as Program Engineering itself. The history of program engineering (in short programming) is more documented by excellent books and papers for several reasons. Since the first computers, one knows what a programming language is, and starting from early assembly languages, it is relatively easy to draw multiple maps of the evolution of these thousands of programming languages, insisting on various properties and various traceability and influence links. Unfortunately, the situation is not so clear when we look at the history of modeling languages. There is no unique banner under which we could classify the huge number of modeling formalisms that accompanied executable programming languages since the beginning. One easily remembers flowcharts used to prepare or to understand programs in the ages when these programs were still full of goto instructions. One could also talk about non-executable specifications, problem statement languages, structured analysis and design, formal and semi-formal methods, CASE formalisms, formal specifications, requirement languages, QOS formalisms, and many more. Today, we have a clearer view of all these modeling languages, mainly because we came to realize that they usually correspond to multiple Domain Specific Languages (DSLs). We can much easier understand the lineages linking PSL/PSA, JSD, SADT, HOOD, OMT, and many others. Understanding the history of modeling languages is of paramount importance to the present organization of research in the field. It allows us to understand when we are progressing, how we build on previous results, and where we could/should put additional efforts. This history is made of different phases, the last ones being the Object-Oriented Analysis and Design multiple proposals, the UML unification and standardization, the MDA initiative, and the MDE generalization. Each period has emphasized some specific features. The net result of this long evolution is probably that we have not yet reached the ultimate goal of having models everywhere in the software development cycle, but the demonstration of the tremendous potential of software modeling has now been firmly established. We are currently midstream, and it is particularly exciting to observe the constant flow of contributions that are offered to evolve and consolidate this important research field. This book *Progressions and Innovations in Model-Driven Software Engineering* is a typical illustration of this phenomenon. It not only shows the important number of projects going on in MDSE, but it also illustrates their high diversity. They apply to most moments of the software lifecycle from requirements, architecture, and code generation through validation and runtime until maintenance and evolution. They cover many application fields from electronic commerce and e-government to agricultural engineering. They address several techniques like standardization, performance evaluation, DSL development, executable requirements, metamodeling, and many more. They offer a typical snapshot of current MDSE initiatives and are a perfect illustration of the dynamism and diversity of research activities in this field. Keeping in mind the continuous and rapid evolution of software modeling theory and practices, it is a very pleasant and enriching reading experience that we are being offered by all chapters of this book.

Jean Bézivin is industry consultant in software modeling and emeritus professor of Computer Science at the University of Nantes. He previously created AtlanMod, a research team common to INRIA and Ecole des Mines de Nantes. He got his Master degree from the University of Grenoble and Ph.D. from the University of Rennes. He has been research assistant in 1972 at the Queen's University of Belfast and in 1973 at the Concordia University of Montreal. Since 1980 he has been very active in Europe in the object-oriented and in the model-driven communities, helping to initiate several research conferences like ECOOP, TOOLS, UML/MODELS, ICMT, etc. He founded in 1979, at the University of Nantes, one of the first Master programs in Software Engineering entirely devoted to Object Technology (Databases, Concurrency, Languages and Programming, Analysis and Design, etc.). His research interests include model-driven engineering and more especially the techniques of model transformation applied to data engineering and to software forward and reverse engineering. He has published many papers and organized tutorials and workshops in the domains of concurrency, simulation, object-oriented programming, and model-driven engineering. On the subjects of model-driven engineering and MDA™, he has been leading the OFTA industrial group in France, co-animating a CNRS specific action, and a Dagstuhl seminar. He is a member of the ECOOP, TOOLS, MODELS, and ICMT steering committees. He was co-chair of the ECOOP 2006 conference organized in Nantes and program chair of TOOLS Europe 2007 held in Zurich in June 2007. He is currently interested in the broadening relations between software engineering and engineering software and in the multiple applications of software modeling to various domain engineering fields.

Jean Bézivin
University of Nantes, France

Preface

A common problem in recent years is the growth of software development complexity due to customer demand for more features and fewer errors. Furthermore, due to recent advancements in technology, it has become necessary to utilize software in multiple domains and professional areas. This leads to problems such as development teams becoming experts in one particular area, necessitating an adjustment period when the team starts new projects in other professional areas.

However, software engineering continually offers new tools that, when properly used, can help in the difficult task of developing software complying with the triple constraint of project management (scope, time, and cost) that is cited in numerous sources. Thus, a relatively new software development approach called Model-Driven Engineering (MDE) has appeared.

MDE is an important and emerging approach in software engineering to increase the level of abstraction of the development tasks. In recent years, Model-Driven Engineering has become a critical area of study, as companies and research institutions have started to emphasize the importance of using model as first-class artifacts in the software development process of complex systems.

The mission of this book is to bring researchers, practitioners, and students to one of the most promising fields in computer science, helping all to understand the current state of the art and to know what the future will bring. The objectives include:

- Bringing together the most relevant research on model-driven engineering.
- Updating the scientific literature on model-driven engineering.
- Identifying and address the complexities encountered in the application of model-driven engineering technologies.
- Identify the most important issues to be addressed by scientists in the coming years.

The target audience of this book will be composed of professionals and researchers working in the field of model-driven software engineering in various disciplines. Moreover, the book will also be a reference for researchers, professionals, and students in computer science and related fields. The book will provide a much needed reference on the state-of-the-art of advanced tools and techniques that are either available or under development to support the maximization of the efficacy and efficiency of model-driven software development. It will also provide foundations to professionals, researchers, and academics on the underlying theory and current applications for use in the future advancement of the existing body of knowledge. This combination of theory, applications, and success stories will provide the reader with an important and detailed view of recent developments in the field and lay the background for future research.

Regarding the distribution of chapters, they are distributed as follows:

- Chapter 1 focuses on the implications of the DO-178C standard for model transformations, which are a central part of Model-Driven Engineering approaches.

- Chapter 2 focuses on Software Performance Engineering (SPE), a sub-area of software engineering. In particular, in SPE based on models developed using the Unified Modeling Language (UML).
- Chapter 3 focuses on requirements engineering, a process of constantly changing intentions, goals, and system models, proposing a new method that exploits similarities in semantics of specifications and executable models.
- Chapter 4 focuses on the evaluation of possible parallels to know whether or not the time is ripe for a change of direction in model language development for software engineering.
- Chapter 5 focuses on the development of a distributed temporal meta-data framework for Enterprise Information Systems (EIS) applications to overcome traditional solutions issues.
- Chapter 6 focuses on the production of crop models for the ITK firm. For that, a Domain-Specific Modeling Language has been formalized by a metamodel to create a Crop Model Factory (CMF) prototype.
- Chapter 7 focuses on an e-Commerce metamodel for reuse and interoperability through the use of the Model-Driven Architecture (MDA) standard proposed by the Object Management Group (OMG).
- Chapter 8 focuses on a process, which enables the software architect to validate the system architecture against the architecture-relevant requirements in the development of complex systems.
- Chapter 9 focuses on some issues that hamper widespread adoption of Domain-Specific Languages (DSLs) with particular emphasis on the vagueness of the term DSL and the difficulty of developing DSLs.
- Chapter 10 focuses on modeling notations for expressing various aspects of modern organizations (Enterprise Architecture) with a view to reducing complexity, increasing technology independence, and supporting analysis.
- Chapter 11 focuses on platforms for e-government transactions and suggests a rule-based Domain-Specific Modeling Environment for public services and process integration, avoiding the lack of interoperability of traditional methods.
- Chapter 12 focuses on modernization of legacy systems, intended to provide support for transforming an existing software system to a new one that satisfies new demands. This is done with reverse engineering and models.
- Chapter 13 focuses on the core of the Unified Modeling Language (UML), which is reformalized to avoid ambiguities, contradictions, or redundancies to properly instrument metamodel-based adaptation.

As a conclusion, we think that the book can be used to learn the challenges related to software modeling and new lines of research in which we will work in the coming years regarding the Model-Driven Engineering.

Vicente García Díaz
University of Oviedo, Spain

Begoña Cristina Pelayo García-Bustelo
University of Oviedo, Spain

Juan Manuel Cueva Lovelle
University of Oviedo, Spain

Oscar Sanjuán Martinez
University of Carlos III, Spain

Acknowledgment

We would like to thank all the people who have contributed to this book. A special thanks to the Editorial Advisory Board Members and the reviewers for their great work. Also to Professor Jean Bézivin who has kindly written the prologue, and Christine Smith, Development Editor for IGI Global who has helped us at any moment. Similarly, we would like to thank all the other people who have participated in this project but have not been mentioned in this text.

Chapter 1
High-Integrity Model-Based Development

Kevin Lano
King's College London, UK

Shekoufeh Kolahdouz-Rahimi
King's College London, UK

ABSTRACT

Model-Based Development (MBD) has become increasingly used for critical systems, and it is the subject of the MBDV supplement to the DO-178C standard. In this chapter, the authors review the requirements of DO-178C for model-based development, and they identify ways in which MBD can be combined with formal verification to achieve DO-178C requirements for traceability and verifiability of models. In particular, the authors consider the implications for model transformations, which are a central part of MBD approaches, and they identify how transformations can be verified using formal methods tools.

INTRODUCTION

Model-based development is the engineering of software systems using models, which may be graphical or textual in nature, but which should conform to some precise language definition. MBD is contrasted to traditional software development in which informal natural language text or low-level program code were the only artifacts. The formal nature of modelling languages used in MBD permits the definition of analysis and transformation tools which operate on models. In particular, *model transformations* are considered to be an essential part of model-based development, and they enable the automation of many operations on models:

- Mapping a model at one level of abstraction to a model at a different level (refinement, abstraction or reverse engineering).
- Comparing two models for differences or for consistency with respect to some relation (eg., different views of the same system).
- Generating code or other text from a model, such as test cases.
- Propagating changes from one model to another linked model.
- Migrating models from one version of a modelling language to another version.

Model-based development offers many advantages, including the ability to reuse models, to facilitate communication with non-software experts, and to reduce implementation costs by automating code generation.

DOI: 10.4018/978-1-4666-4217-1.ch001

For these reasons, MBD has had increasing uptake across many industry sectors, including high-integrity and safety-critical application domains such as avionics. In consequence, standards for these domains, such as RTCA DO-178 (RTCA, 2012), have begun to incorporate guidance on the use of MBD for critical systems.

The undisciplined use of models may actually decrease software reliability, if the models are developed without higher-level requirements (so that required functionality is omitted from the models) or without precise model analysis (so that the meaning of the model, when converted to code, is insufficiently understood). Therefore, DO-178C defines rigorous procedures for the use and validation of models. In this chapter, we will consider the requirements of the DO-178C standard in detail, and provide techniques for MBD which aim to satisfy these requirements.

BACKGROUND

DO-178C is the successor to the RTCA/EURO-CAE DO-178B standard "Software Considerations in Airborne Systems and Equipment Certification" (1992). DO-178C was published in 2012 and represents a significant extension and update of DO-178B. In particular, four supplements are added, giving detailed guidance on:

- Model-based development and verification.
- Object-oriented technology.
- Formal methods.
- Tool qualification.

Like DO-178B, DO-178C remains primarily a 'process' standard, whose intent is to define necessary properties of the software development process which ensure that (i) all required functionality of the software is correctly implemented, and (ii) that no unintended functionality is implemented.

For MBD this implies that all models should be derived from, traced back to, and verified against higher level requirements. Models themselves can be at different levels of abstraction, such as specification models (expressing high-level requirements) and design models (expressing low-level requirements).

The key attribute of a model in DO-178C is that it should be *unambiguous*. This means that the modelling language itself must have a well-defined syntax, and that a precise semantics exists which gives an unambiguous denotation to every syntactically valid model.

Tracing between models is of critical importance, in particular developers should ensure that automated transformations which derive one model from another (and source code from models) are able to provide detailed tracing information defining how elements in the target model are derived from elements in the source model. Tracing ultimately should relate model elements to some original system requirements, and source code elements to model elements.

DO-178C differentiates *Specification Models* (high-level requirements models) from *Design Models* (low-level requirements models): the former are unambiguous descriptions of the externally observable properties of the software system or component, such as its functional, performance and safety characteristics. They should not define internal software design details such as particular algorithms. In contrast, design models may define internal data structures, architectures and algorithms of a component. Models that are used to synthesise source code are considered to be design models.

Design models may be derived from specification models, and from additional (non-model) specification text. Alternatively, even the low level requirements may be expressed partly in design models and partly in non-model forms, and used together to produce source code.

The following verification relationships should exist between models: model *coverage* is the property that a model at a lower level of abstraction contains only functionality derived from a higher-level model, with no additional functionality. Model *compliance* ensures that the lower level model does satisfy the higher level model requirements. Model *consistency* ensures that a model is internally consistent.

Figure 1 shows the typical software artifacts and verification and validation activities considered by DO-178C.

These verification activities were traditionally carried out using manual inspection and review of source code, and by testing. The use of precise models at more stages of the development process increases, potentially, the scope for formal analysis at these stages.

The formal methods supplement of DO-178C permits the use of such formal analysis, but requires that tools and techniques used for formal analysis must meet the condition of *soundness*: that the analysis does not assert properties to be true when they may not be true. Soundness applies particularly to the way that the analysed system and its models are represented in the formalism. Every property derivable from such formal representations should also be true for the original system. Additionally, the formal representations of system requirements must be shown to be *conservative*

representations: to accurately express the exact intent of the informal requirements.

Therefore, if we attempt to prove some property P about a model M, by means of a formal analysis using formal representations CSem(P) and Sem(M), which are conservative and sound representations, respectively, then the result that CSem(P) is true for Sem(M) allows us to conclude that M does satisfy P.

We can summarise the requirements of DO-178C for the use of MBD and formal methods as:

- Models must be expressed in an unambiguous notation.
- Models must be derived from a preceding level of abstraction.
- Verification of models against preceding models or specifications is necessary, to ensure model coverage and compliance.
- Verification of the internal consistency of models is also necessary. Tracing relationships should exist between successive models.
- Formal analysis applied directly to the models must be sound.
- Formal representations (verification models) of the models must be sound representations, and formal representations of their requirements must be conservative.

The following sections define a particular approach for high-integrity software development, using UML and MBD. We show how this approach satisfies the requirements of DO-178C. We give a case study of specification and verification using the approach and describe implementation and transformation techniques for the approach. We evaluate the approach, and survey related approaches.

Figure 1. Models and verification in DO-178C

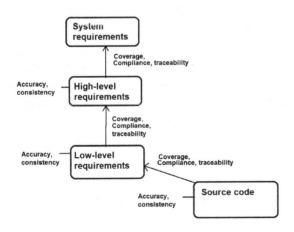

SATISFYING DO-178C FOR MODEL-BASED DEVELOPMENT

In this section we define a particular approach for high-integrity software development, using UML (OMG, 2009) and MBD. We consider UML because it is the most widely-used software modelling language, and it is the basis of most MBD approaches. UML consists of several different modelling notations, including use case models, class diagrams, state machine diagrams, activity models, sequence diagrams, deployment diagrams, and the Object Constraint Language (OCL). However, other modelling languages can also be used for MBD conforming to DO-178C, provided that the language has a well-defined syntax and semantics.

The syntax of a modelling language consists of both *concrete syntax*, the graphical/textual elements that form the human-readable representation of a model, and *abstract syntax*, the formal representation of the model as a collection of elements in its language.

For example, Figure 2 shows the concrete syntax of a model of a simple directed graph. The visual elements are nodes and directed edges, both of which have names.

The modelling language abstract syntax can be formally defined by a *metamodel* in a metamodelling language such as MOF (OMG, 2006). Figure 3 shows a MOF metamodel for the graph language.

In addition to the definition of model element types *Edge* and *Node*, this metamodel defines that each edge has a source and target, and that edges are uniquely named, likewise so are nodes.

Figure 2. Graph model

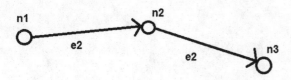

Figure 3. Graph metamodel

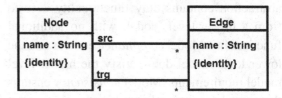

It can be mechanically checked that a given model is a correct instance of the modelling language of Figure 3. The abstract syntax representation of Figure 2 is shown in Figure 4.

The modelling language semantics can be given by a mapping from the models of the language to a suitable semantic domain, such as a domain of mathematical structures. In this example, nodes could be represented by the string of their name, and edges represented as triples (src.name, trg.name, name) of the source and target names and the edge name. A model is then represented as a set of such elements, ie., a pair in the mathematical domain

Set(String) * Set(String * String * String)

In our MDB approach, UML-RSDS (Lano, 2009), we only use UML and OCL constructs which have a precise and unambiguous mathematical semantics. Notations such as sequence diagrams, which have an excessively complex and unclear semantics (Cengarle and Knapp, 2009), are therefore excluded.

We use class diagrams, restricted to avoid multiple inheritance, qualified associations, composition associations and association classes, and state machines without nested states. Our subset of OCL omits the general 'iterate' construct of OCL, but includes the usual specific cases of this such as the *select*, *collect* and *reject* operators.

Use cases are used to define top-level capabilities or services of a software system, and are made precise by specifying their functionality using pre and post conditions expressed in OCL.

Figure 4. Graph model abstract syntax

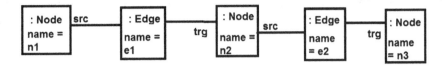

Our MBD process can be summarised as follows:

- The software system requirements are formalised at a high level of abstraction as use-case diagrams and class diagrams. These models should avoid platform-specific and algorithmic detail and instead specify requirements by means of logical constraints (in OCL). We term these models *Computation-Independent Models* (CIMs). They correspond to high-level requirements models (specification models) in DO-178C. An *architecture model* may be defined to identify high-level system components and their inter-relationships.
- The design model (*platform independent model*, PIM) can refine the CIM by defining explicit algorithms for operations and for use cases, as UML activities. In our approach the PIM can usually be automatically derived from the CIM. The PIM corresponds to low-level requirements (design models) in DO-178C. Each component in a software architecture model of the system is defined by its own PIM.
- Executable code is automatically synthesised from the PIMs and the architecture model.

Figure 5 shows the process, together with the DO-178C verification relationships between models which can be established by our approach.

Model coverage and compliance in the sense of DO-178C are ensured between the CIM and PIMs by this process: the design model satisfies the data and behavioural requirements of the specification model, and only contains functionality derived from the specification model. Likewise, the executable code synthesised from the design is correct by construction, and corresponds element-by-element with the design.

Verification of the internal consistency and correctness of the models is necessary in order that a functionally correct implementation is produced. These checks are carried out by using a formal method, B (ClearSy, 2012), to prove properties of the models. The UML models are translated into *verification models* in B, which express their mathematical semantics, and which can be analysed using type checking and theorem-proving in B.

The translation from UML to B (described in the following section) satisfies the *soundness* requirement of the formal methods supplement of DO-178C: the assertions that B tools prove about the B representation of a UML model also hold

Figure 5. MBD process

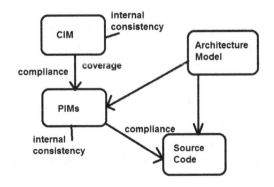

true for the model itself. The representation is conservative because it expresses only the formal semantics of the model, together with essential axioms of UML.

We assert also that B is a sound method: it does not prove false properties. This assertion depends upon the correct construction of the B tools. Proofs derived using B can also be submitted for proof checking by an independent tool, to gain higher assurance of their correctness.

CIM models of a software system are specified in UML-RSDS by UML class diagrams, which define the structure and properties of the data of the system, and by use cases which operate on the data of the class diagram, and which define the functionalities of the system.

Use cases are specified by four OCL predicates (Lano and Kolahdouz-Rahimi, 2011a):

- Assumptions *Asm* on the system state at the start of the use case: these are essentially the preconditions of the use case.
- Ensured conditions *Ens* on the system state at termination of the use case.
- Invariant conditions *Inv* which should be maintained during the use case.
- A sequence of constraints *Cons* defining the completed effect of the use case.

Ens and *Cons* together define the use case postcondition. The difference between these predicates is that each *Cons* constraint *Cn* should have a procedural interpretation *stat(Cn)* as a UML activity. These interpretations will be used to construct the procedural refinement of the use case in the design model. In contrast, *Ens* can be of any form. *Inv* expresses that certain properties are preserved during the use case execution, these properties can then be used to deduce *Ens* at termination. *Inv* also plays an important role in ensuring model coverage: it can be used to limit the functional effect of the use case to only those changes permitted by a higher-level specification.

The *syntactic correctness* of a use case is the condition that *Cons* ensures *Ens*, assuming *Asm*, *Inv*, and the theory *Th(S)* of the class diagram *S* of the system:

$$Th(S) \vdash Asm \ \& \ Inv' \ \& \ Cons' => Ens'$$

where features and entities which are updated in *Cons* are postfixed with ' in *Cons'* and *Ens'*. Features/entities postfixed with @pre in *Cons* (denoting the value of the data at the start of the use case execution) have this postfix removed in *Cons'*.

Semantic correctness is the condition that the implementation *stat(Cons)* ensures *Cons*, assuming *Asm* and the system language theory:

$$Th(S) \vdash Asm => [stat(Cons)]Cons$$

where *[act]P* is the weakest precondition of activity *act* with respect to *P*.

In addition, *Inv* should be true initially, and should be preserved by each step *d* of *stat(Cons)*:

$$Th(S) \vdash Asm => Inv[E/E@\text{pre}, f/f@\text{pre}]$$

and

$$\vdash Inv => [d]Inv$$

Other important verification properties of a use case are:

- **Termination:** the implementation always terminates and establishes the postcondition in a finite number of steps.
- **Confluence:** the state at termination is the same regardless of the ordering of individual steps.

To prove termination and confluence properties, we identify *variant functions Q_C: NAT* for each *Cons* constraint *C*, which are decreased by each application of *C*, and which are bounded below (eg., by 0). Termination follows from the existence of such a variant. Confluence follows if there is a unique state (reachable from the initial state by an iteration of a minimal set of algorithm steps) for which *Q_C* attains its minimal value.

Use cases may *extend* other use cases, to provide additional functionality to the extended use case, or *include* other use cases to invoke their functionality as a subroutine (OMG, 2009).

The architecture model of a system consists of components and their client-supplier relations. Each component is defined by a class diagram and the use cases that operate on this diagram: the use cases define the services offered by the component. When a use case of one component invokes (by inclusion) the use case of another component, this identifies that the first component has a client-supplier dependency on the second.

FORMALISATION OF UML AND OCL

In order to semantically analyse UML models, we need to express the semantics of the models in a mathematical formalism. We use first order logic and set theory as a suitable formalism, following the semantics of Richters and Gogolla (1998), Lano (2009b) for UML and OCL. In this chapter, we use the FOL notation of B.

Table 1 shows the semantic interpretation of entities, attributes, associations, and generalisations.

One distinction between B and OCL is that B integers are of bounded (32 bit) size, whereas OCL uses the idealised unbounded set of integers: to ensure soundness and conservativeness, bounded integers should also be adopted in the UML/OCL models. Real numbers should not be used as these cannot be represented in B.

In addition, a two-valued logic is used for B and should be adopted for OCL, ie., there should be no use of undefined values. Optional association ends (ie, of 0..1 multiplicity) are modelled as being sets of size 1 (when the end is defined) or of size 0 (when the end is undefined).

Table 1. Mapping of UML to FOL

UML model element	FOL (B) interpretation
Integer type	INT
Boolean type	BOOL
String type	STRING
Real type	no interpretation
Entity E (as a type)	Set E_OBJ
E.allInstances()	Set es
Attribute att: T of E	Map att: es --> T' where T' is B type for T
Primary key att: T of E	Map att: es >-> T'
Role r: F of E	Map r: es --> fs
Role r: Set(F) of E	Map r: es --> FIN(fs)
Role r: Sequence(F) of E	Map r: es --> seq(fs)
F is subclass of E	fs <: es

<: is the subset operator.

Table 2 shows the mapping of some OCL expressions into FOL in B.

These are exact (conservative) representations of the semantics of the OCL expressions, when 2-valued logic and bounded integer domains are adopted for OCL.

Table 2. Interpretation of OCL expressions

OCL expression e	FOL (B) interpretation e'
obj.f	f'(obj')
s->at(i)	s'(i')
P and Q	P' & Q'
P or Q	P' or Q'
P implies Q	P' => Q'
not(P)	not(P')
e->exists(x | P)	#x.(x: e' & P')
e->forAll(x | P)	!x.(x: e' => P')
Integer.subrange(a,b) a'	b'
Set{ x1, ..., xn }	{ x1', ..., xn' }
Sequence{ x1, ..., xn }	[x1', ..., xn']
s->includes(x)	x': s'
s->including(x)	s' \/ { x' }

CASE STUDY

We will illustrate the UML-RSDS MBD process using an example of a system which computes all non-empty paths through a directed graph. A path is a sequence of distinct edges connected nose to tail.

This computation operates on the data of a model of Figure 6.

For the use case defining the path-finding system, we take *Asm* as assertions that the starting model satisfies the restrictions of the language of Figure 6, ie, that it is a valid model of this metamodel. Name1 and name2 are asserted to be primary keys: Node->isUnique(name1) and Edge->isUnique(name2). In addition, at the start of the computation, there are assumed to be no paths:

(Asm): Path = {}

The end model should also be a valid model of the language, and all created paths should be valid paths of the graph:

```
(Ens): Path->forAll(p | p.elements-
>isUnique(self) and
     Integer.subrange(1,
p.elements.size - 1)->forAll(i |
     p.elements[i].trg =
p.elements[i+1].src))
```

s->isUnique(e) is true if the elements of s have distinct e values. This *Ens* predicate could also be used as the definition of *Inv*: each path p as it is created must satisfy the quantified predicate.

The Cons conditions define that first, a basic path is created for each edge in the graph, consisting of only that edge:

```
(C1): Edge->forAll(e | Path->exists(p
| p.elements = Sequence{ e }))
```

Figure 6. Graph system metamodel

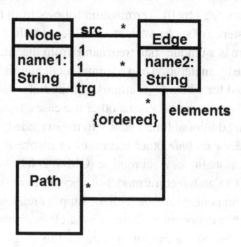

More complex paths are built up from simpler ones by extending them by any edge (not already in the path) that follows the end of the original path:

```
(C2): Edge->forAll(e | Path->forAll(p
| e /: p.elements and
e.src = p.elements.last.trg implies
Path->exists1(p1 | p1.elements =
p.elements ^ Sequence{ e })))
```

The metamodel, together with the *Asm, Ens, Inv* and *Cons* constraints, form a CIM or specification model of the system.

This specification model can be analysed for consistency by UML tools such as USE (Gogolla et al., 2005), which will check if the combination of *Asm* and the language constraints *Th(S)* is consistent, ie, that there is some non-empty model satisfying both. Likewise for the combination of *C1, C2* and *Ens* with the language constraints.

The semantics of the class diagram model and constraints of the system can also be mathematically expressed in first order logic and set theory using the B formal method (Lano et al., 2012).

For example, the B verification model corresponding to this system has the form:

```
MACHINE Specification
SEES SystemTypes, String_TYPE
VARIABLES
  edges, paths, nodes, src, trg,
name1, name2, elements
INVARIANT
  edges <: Edge_OBJ & paths <: Path_
OBJ &
  nodes <: Node_OBJ &
  src: edges --> nodes & trg: edges
--> nodes &
  name1: nodes >-> STRING & name2:
edges >-> STRING &
  elements: paths --> iseq(edges) &
  /* Ens, Inv: */
  !p.(p: paths =>
   !ii.(ii: 1..(card(elements(p))-1)
=>
    trg(elements(p)(ii)) =
src(elements(p)(ii+1))))
INITIALISATION
  nodes, edges, paths, src, trg,
name1, name2, elements:=
    {}, {}, {}, {}, {}, {}, {}, {}
OPERATIONS
  create_Node(name1x) =
  PRE nodes /= Node_OBJ & name1x:
STRING & paths = {} &
    name1x /: name1[nodes]
    THEN
     ANY nodex WHERE nodex: Node_OBJ
- nodes
    THEN
     nodes:= nodes \/ { nodex } ||
     name1(nodex):= name1x
    END
  END;


C1_op(edgex) =
  PRE edgex: edges & paths /= Path_
OBJ &
   not(#pathx.(pathx: paths &
elements(pathx) = [edgex]))
```

```
  THEN
   ANY pathx WHERE pathx: Path_OBJ -
paths
  THEN
   paths:= paths \/ { pathx } ||
   elements(pathx):= [edgex]
  END
 END;


END
```

The data of this module represents the entities and features of the class diagram of the system. These are expressed as sets and maps of various types. >-> denotes the type of total injective functions, iseq(edges) denotes the type of injective sequences of edges, ie., sequences without duplicates. The machine formally expresses the theory *Th(S)* of the system class diagram. The *Ens* and *Inv* properties of the use case are also expressed as invariants of the module.

The operations of the module are either (1) constructors of elements of the system, and other operations to modify its data prior to the application of the use case, or (2) operations representing the steps of the use case.

Operations (1) must not violate the assumptions *Asm*, and can assume that the transformation has not been started (paths = { }). Operations (2) must not violate *Inv*. Tools for B, such as ClearSy Atelier B, automatically generate internal proof obligations for B modules which include the correctness proof obligations for these operations. Specifically, that the initialisation establishes the invariant, and that each operation maintains the invariant if executed when its precondition is true.

create_Node maintains the property that node names are unique, because the precondition name1x /: name1[nodes] implies that the name of the new node has not already been assigned to an existing node. Likewise, C1_op ensures that the elements sequence of the new path pathx is injective, by construction of this sequence as a singleton sequence.

Internal consistency proof therefore establishes the correctness of individual steps of the implementation of the use case, and proves that *Ens* is invariant and holds at termination of the use case, ie., that the use case only generates paths that satisfy the specification of the system.

For *C1*, a suitable variant function to establish termination is:

```
Edge->select(e | not(Path->exists(p |
p.elements = Sequence{ e })))->size()
```

Each application of C1_op can be proved to strictly reduce this.

For *C2*, a variant function can be defined as the number of possible paths which are not already in Path:

```
(OrderedSet(Edge)->select(s | s-
>size() >= 1 and
    Integer.subrange(1,(s->size()
- 1))->forAll(i | s->at(i).
trg = s->at(i+1).src)) - Path-
>collect(elements))->size()
```

Each application of *C2* creates a new path and therefore reduces this quantity. It is bounded below by the number of possible paths, so termination follows.

For confluence of *C1*, the variant function first reaches 0 when each edge has been processed exactly once, and the corresponding paths have been created. The resulting state is unique, with Path consisting of exactly the card(Edge) derived paths of length 1. The order of creation of these paths does not affect their values.

For *C2*, the variant function reaches its minimal value when all possible paths have been created, that is, Path consists of all non-empty chained sequences of edges in the graph. Again, this is a unique state which is independent of the order in which the paths were created.

Formal proof of termination and confluence can be carried out in B, by using the concept of refinement.

Refinement establishes that a more detailed version of a system satisfies the behaviour of an abstracted version. In this case, the abstracted version contains only the system class diagram data, without path data, together with operations to initialise this data, and variables q1, q2, ... to represent the variant functions. Operations representing the steps of the system computations are also included.

For our system, the abstraction module has the form:

```
MACHINE Abstraction
SEES SystemTypes, String_TYPE
VARIABLES
  edges, nodes, name1, name2, q1, q2
INVARIANT
  edges <: Edge_OBJ &
  nodes <: Node_OBJ &
  name1: nodes >-> STRING & name2:
edges >-> STRING &
  q1: NAT & q2: NAT
INITIALISATION
  nodes, edges, name1, name2:= {},
{}, {}, {} || q1, q2:= 0, 0
OPERATIONS
  create_Node(name1x) =
  PRE nodes /= Node_OBJ & name1x:
STRING &
    name1x /: name1[nodes]
  THEN
    ANY nodex WHERE nodex: Node_OBJ -
nodes
  THEN
  nodes:= nodes \/ { nodex } ||
  name1(nodex):= name1x
  END
END;
```

```
C1_op =
 PRE q1 > 0
 THEN
  q1:: 0..(q1-1) || q2:: 0..(q2-1)
 END;
END
```

In the refined module, q1 and q2 are explicitly defined:

```
REFINEMENT Refinement
REFINES Abstraction
SEES SystemTypes, String_TYPE
VARIABLES
 edges, nodes, paths, src, trg,
name1, name2
INVARIANT
 edges <: Edge_OBJ &
 nodes <: Node_OBJ & paths <: Path_
OBJ &
 src: edges --> nodes & trg: edges
--> nodes &
 name1: nodes >-> STRING & name2:
edges >-> STRING &
 elements: paths --> iseq(edges) &
 q1 = card({ ee | ee: edges & [ee]
/: elements[paths] }) &
 q2 = card({ ss | ss: iseq(edges) &
card(ss) >= 1 &
   !ii(ii: NAT & ii >= 1 & ii
< card(ss) => trg(ss(ii)) =
src(ss(ii+1))) } -
     elements[paths])
INITIALISATION
 nodes, edges, paths, src, trg,
name1, name2, elements:=
   {}, {}, {}, {}, {}, {}, {}, {}
OPERATIONS
 create_Node(name1x) =
 PRE nodes /= NODE_OBJ & name1x:
STRING &
  name1x /: name1[nodes]
 THEN
  ANY nodex WHERE nodex: Node_OBJ -
nodes
```

```
  THEN
   nodes:= nodes \/ { nodex } ||
   name1(nodex):= name1x
  END
 END;
```

```
 C1_op =
  PRE #edgex.(edgex: edges & [edgex]
/: elements[paths])
   THEN
    ANY edgex, pathx
    WHERE edgex: edges & [edgex] /:
elements[paths] &
     pathx: Path_OBJ - paths
    THEN
     paths:= paths \/ { pathx } ||
     elements(pathx):= [edgex]
   END
  END;

END
```

The proof obligations for refinement include that each refined version of an operation has a weaker (or equivalent) precondition to the abstract version, and a stronger or equivalent postcondition. This means that within the domain of the abstract postcondition, any behaviour exhibited by the refined operation obeys the specification of the abstract operation. In terms of DO-178C this means that it exhibits no unintended behaviour within this domain.

In the above example, the refined precondition of C1_op is clearly equivalent to q1 > 0 by the definition of q1. The effect of the operation also clearly reduces both q1 and q2, so it establishes the abstract postcondition.

Modelling using B includes the implicit assumption that operations of the system are executed sequentially, in particular, that the postcondition constraints of a use case are implemented as a sequence of applications of a basic operation step such as C1_op in the above example.

IMPLEMENTATION

Specific design and implementation strategies are used for the *Cons* constraints of use cases, as defined in Table 3. *Ante* denotes the antecedent of the constraint, *Succ* the succedent. The choice of strategy depends upon the internal data dependencies of the constraint *Cn*: if the constraint modifies a disjoint collection *wr(Cn)* of model features (entities and their features) to the collection *rd(Cn)* of model features that it reads, then it can be implemented by a bounded loop. Otherwise a fixpoint iteration is required, which applies the constraint until it is established.

Code is generated initially as UML activities, expressed in a pseudocode language with assignment, conditionals, sequencing, bounded and unbounded loops. This also serves as an intermediate language from which executable code in a number of languages can be generated. Currently Java is supported. The resulting code has a close structural correspondence with the specification: each use case is implemented by a corresponding system-level operation with the same name, and each use case constraint is implemented by an operation of the principal class that it operates upon. UML classes are mapped 1-1 to same-named Java classes, and their features also directly correspond to Java features of the implementing classes. This structural congruence between the specification and code provides tracing, and helps to ensure model coverage and compliance of the implementation.

In our case study, *C1* is a type 1 constraint, and is implemented by a for loop

```
for e: Edge do e.op1()
```

where in Edge we include an operation of the form:

```
op1()
```

Table 3. Implementation choices for constraints

Data dependencies	Implementation choice
Type 1 wr(Cn) ∧ rd(Cn) = { }	for loop
Type 2 Succedent Succ has wr(Succ) ∧ rd(Succ) /= { } but wr(Succ) ∧ rd(Ante) = { }	while-iteration of for loop
Type 3 wr(Succ) ∧ rd(Ante) /= { }	while iteration of search-and-return loop

```
post:

  Path->exists(p | p.elements = Se-
quence{ self })
```

C2 is of type 3 and is implemented by a loop of the form

while (some source element s satisfies a constraint lhs) do

select such an s and apply the constraint

This can be explicitly coded as:

```
running:= true;
while running do
  running:= search()
```

where:

```
search(): Boolean
  (for e: Edge do
    for p: Path do
      if e /: p.elements and e.src =
p.elements.last.trg
        then
          (e.op2(p); return true));
  return false
```

and where op2 has postcondition

Path->exists1(p1 | p1.elements = p.elements ^ Sequence{ self })

MODEL TRANSFORMATIONS

Model transformations can be specified by use cases operating on instances of metamodels, in the same manner as for general software systems. Source and target models and metamodels may be distinguished: the source model is an instance of the source metamodel, and the use case creates a target model as a transformed version of the source model. The target model is an instance of the target metamodel. For *update-in-place* transformations, the target model is formed by modifying the source model.

The specification, design, synthesis, and verification of model transformations follows the same process defined in the previous sections. Indeed the path computation example can be considered to be an update-in-place transformation.

The role of the invariant *Inv* in ensuring coverage of the target model compared to the source is particularly important when transformations are used as part of a high-integrity MBD process. The invariant expresses that the intermediate and final models produced by the transformation satisfy some constant relationship to the initial models, and hence *Inv* can be used to ensure that no extraneous elements or structures are present in the transformed models. In our example, *Inv* was used to ensure that the elements of Path were all derived from the source graph.

The formalised development and verification process provides the capability to assure the correctness of model transformations to the same standard as other critical software systems, and therefore to assure model-based development processes that use the transformations.

EVALUATION

Several developments have been carried out using UML-RSDS:

- Software engineering tools, such as state machine slicers (Lano and Kolahdouz-Rahimi, 2011b).
- Refinement transformations, including the UML to relational database transformation (Lano and Kolahdouz-Rahimi, 2011a) and UML to J2EE and to Java (incorporated into the UML-RSDS tools).
- Re-expression transformations, including a mapping from state machines to activity diagrams (Lano and Kolahdouz-Rahimi, 2010b) and other migration examples (Lano and Kolahdouz-Rahimi, 2011c, 2011d).
- Quality-improvement transformations, including the removal of multiple inheritance and removal of duplicated attributes (Kolahdouz-Rahimi, et al., 2012).

Complex computations such as the calculation of maximum inheritance depth in a class diagram (Chimia-Opoka et al., 2008), or transformations involving nested updates (Rensink and Kuperus, 2009) can be concisely and declaratively specified in UML-RSDS.

The largest metamodels considered were those for the state machine to activity diagram mapping (31 source entities and features, 35 target entities and features). This is an actual industrial problem, as is the GMF migration example of (Lano and Kolahdouz-Rahimi, 2011d), which involves a complex restructuring and a combination of update-in-place and input-preserving transformation mechanisms. The class diagram rationalisation problem (Kolahdouz-Rahimi et al., 2012) also involves complex restructuring of models. A comparison of the UML-RSDS solution with the Kermeta and QVT-R solutions identified that our solution is simpler and more modular than these solutions.

UML-RSDS also provides efficient implementations. In a comparison using the test cases of (Amstel et al., 2011) on the UML to relational database case study, the generated Java implementation from the UML-RSDS specification was substantially more efficient on test cases of all sizes, compared to the ATL, QVT-R and QVT-O implementations. On the largest test case, with 50,000 source model elements, the UML-RSDS version executed in 0.156 second, compared with 60 seconds for ATL, and over 100 seconds for QVT.

Together, these case studies have demonstrated that the constraint-based specification approach of UML-RSDS is versatile and applicable to a wide range of software systems.

Alternative verification techniques which could be applied to UML-RSDS specifications are proof of syntactic correctness and semantic correctness using a theorem-prover such as HOL (Brucker and Wolff, 2008) or Coq (Poernomo and Terrell, 2010), or using SMT solvers such as Z3 (Microsoft, 2012) or Yices (SRI, 2012). At present, the B approach seems more effective, due to the decomposition of verification which it supports (the verification model machine is structured to express the procedural effect of separate constraints as separate operations, and the proof of universally-quantified *Inv* properties is automatically decomposed into an induction), and because of the implicit frame axioms of B modules.

We have carried out a comparison of B and Z3 for model transformation verification (Lano et al., 2012). The conclusions were that Z3 has advantages for automated proof of specifications, provided these satisfy the restrictions of being expressed in a decidable subset of first order logic, however B is more generally applicable, and provides a more expressive language in which OCL constraints can be directly encoded.

The UML-RSDS tools, together with examples of transformation specification and implementation, are available at: http://www.dcs.kcl.ac.uk/staff/kcl/uml2Web/.

RELATED WORK

Other standards for high-integrity systems are IEC 61508 (IEC, 2012) and UK DEF-STAN 00-55 (MOD, 1997). These are focussed on the 'product' produced by a software development process, rather than the process itself. They mandate different levels of formal analysis and verification for systems depending on the risks identified for the system controlled by the software, and the corresponding safety integrity level (SIL) of the software. Formal verification is mandated for the highest category, 4, of SIL. The techniques described in this paper are usable in principle for such verification.

Verification of model-based development has primarily focused on the checking of the internal consistency of models, by techniques which exhibit counter-examples to intended invariants of models. Tools such as the USE environment (Gogolla et al., 2005) or UMLtoCSP (Cabot et al., 2007) operate on UML class diagrams to perform such checks. Translation to Alloy has also been used for such model checking (Anastasakis et al., 2010). These techniques are however not applicable for demonstrating model coverage.

Previous work in the verification of model transformations has been hindered by the general lack of high-level transformation specifications, with most transformation development focussing upon the implementation level (Guerra et al., 2010). The verification model approach to transformation verification has been the main focus of recent work. In (Cabot et al., 2010), specifications in OCL are derived from model transformation implementations in triple graph grammars and QVT-Relations, in order to analyse properties of the transformations, such as definedness and determinacy. Specific work on syntactic correctness includes formalisation and proof of target model constraints in MAUDE (Egea and Rusu, 2010), the use of bounded satisfaction solvers in (Buttner et al., 2011), and the graph-theory approach of (Baar and Markovic, 2007). Our approach using

B has the advantage that syntactic correctness corresponds directly to internal consistency in B, and that the set-theoretic formalisation of metamodels, constraints and transformations in B can be directly related to standard set-theoretic semantics for UML and OCL (Lano, 2009b; Richters and Gogolla, 1998). Both B and OCL derive from the Z notation, so that they are relatively closely related (both are based on first order classical logic and ZF set theory). This enables traceability between the transformation specification and the B verification model, and supports modular verification (for example, only a small part of a transformation may affect a given target language constraint, so that a machine to verify the constraint needs only to formalise that part). Our approach additionally considers termination and confluence, extending previous verification model approaches.

In Guerra et al. (2010), a general method *transML* for model transformation development is described, using multiple levels of description (requirements, specification, high-level design and low-level design). Our specification predicates *Asm*, *Cons*, *Inv* and *Ens* play the same role as the pattern-based specification language of (Guerra et al., 2010). In comparison to transML, our approach is more lightweight, utilising only UML and OCL notations, and avoiding the explicit construction of designs. Instead, designs and implementations are generated from specifications, which are made the focus of transformation development activities.

We have adopted B for formal verification of system and transformation properties, as it has strong tool support, and a relatively simple mathematical basis which is appropriate for software verification. It can support verification of most forms of verification properties, however it lacks support for analysis of satisfiability properties, such as checking that some rule is applicable, or for the instantiation of metamodels with counterexamples to properties, and other tools, such as the USE environment (Gogolla et al., 2005) or UMLtoCSP (Cabot et al., 2007) could be applied instead to carry out such analysis.

CONCLUSION

In this chapter, we have described the requirements of the DO-178C standard for model-based development and verification, and we have defined an MBD approach which can be used to satisfy these requirements.

REFERENCES

Anastasakis, K., Bordbar, B., Georg, G., & Ray, I. (2010). On challenges of model transformation from UML to alloy. *Software Systems Modelling, 9*(1).

Baar, T., & Markovic, S. (2007). A graphical approach to prove the semantic preservation of UML/OCL refactoring rules. [LNCS]. *Proceedings of the Perspectives of Systems Informatics, 4378*, 70–83. doi:10.1007/978-3-540-70881-0_9.

Brucker, A., & Wolff, B. (2008). HOL-OCL: A formal proof environment for UML/OCL. In *Proceedings of FASE 2008* (LNCS), (vol. 4961). Berlin: Springer.

Buttner, F., Cabot, J., & Gogolla, M. (2011). On validation of ATL transformation rules by transformation models. In Proceedings of MoDeVVa 2011. MoDeVVa.

Cabot, J., Clariso, R., Guerra, E., & De Lara, J. (2010). Verification and validation of declarative model-to-model transformations through invariants. *Journal of Systems and Software.* doi:10.1016/j.jss.2009.08.012.

Cabot, J., Clariso, R., & Riera, D. (2007). UMLtoCSP: A tool for the verification of UML/OCL models using constraint programming. [ACM Press.]. *Proceedings of Automated Software Engineering, 07*, 547–548.

Cengarle, M., & Knapp, A. (2009). Interactions. In Lano, K. (Ed.), *UML 2 Semantics and Applications*. New York: Wiley.

Chimia-Opoka, J., Felderer, M., Lenz, C., & Lange, C. (2008). Querying UML models using OCL and prolog: A performance study. [IEEE Press.]. *Proceedings of ICSTW, 2008*, 81–88.

ClearSy. (2012). *Atelier B*. Retrieved from http://www.atelierb.eu

Egea, M., & Rusu, V. (2010). Formal executable semantics for conformance in the MDE framework. *Innovations in System Software Engineering, 6*(1-2), 73–81. doi:10.1007/s11334-009-0108-1.

Gogolla, M., Bohling, J., & Richters, M. (2005). Validating UML and OCL models in USE by automatic snapshot generation. *Software & Systems Modeling, 4*(4), 386–398. doi:10.1007/s10270-005-0089-y.

Guerra, E., de Lara, J., Kolovos, D., Paige, R., & Marchi dos Santos, O. (2010). transML: A family of languages to model model transformations. In *Proceedings of MODELS 2010* (LNCS), (vol. 6394). Berlin: Springer-Verlag.

IEC. (2012). *IEC 61508: Functional safety of electrical/electronic/programmable electronic safety-related systems*. IEC.

Kolahdouz-Rahimi, S., Lano, K., Pillay, S., Troya, J., & Van Gorp, P. (2012). Goal-oriented measurement of model transformation methods. *Science of Computer Programming*.

Lano, K. (Ed.). (2009). *UML 2 semantics and applications*. New York: Wiley. doi:10.1002/9780470522622.

Lano, K. (2009). A compositional semantics of UML-RSDS. *SoSyM, 8*(1), 85–116. doi:10.1007/s10270-007-0064-x.

Lano, K., & Kolahdouz-Rahimi, S. (2010a). Specification and verification of model transformations using UML-RSDS. In *Proceedings of IFM 2010* (LNCS), (vol. 6396, pp. 199-214). Berlin: Springer.

Lano, K., & Kolahdouz-Rahimi, S. (2010b). Migration case study using UML-RSDS. In *Proceedings of TTC 2010*. Malaga, Spain: TTC.

Lano, K., & Kolahdouz-Rahimi, S. (2011a). Model-driven development of model transformations. In *Proceedings of ICMT 2011*. ICMT.

Lano, K., & Kolahdouz-Rahimi, S. (2011b). Slicing techniques for UML models. *Journal of Object Technology, 10*, 1–49. doi:10.5381/jot.2011.10.1.a11.

Lano, K., & Kolahdouz-Rahimi, S. (2011c). Specification of the hello world case study. In *Proceedings of TTC 2011*. TTC.

Lano, K., & Kolahdouz-Rahimi, S. (2011c). Specification of the GMF migration case study. In *Proceedings of TTC 2011*. TTC.

Lano, K., Kolahdouz-Rahimi, S., & Clark, T. (2012). Comparison of verification techniques for model transformations. In *Proceedings of Modevva Workshop, MODELS 2012*. MoDeVVa.

Microsoft. (2012). *Z3 theorem prover*. Retrieved from http://research.microsoft.com/en-us/um/redmond/projects/z3/

Ministry of Defence. (1997). Defence standard 00-55: Requirements for safety-related software in defence equipment. Ministry of Defence.

Object Management Group. (2006). *Meta-object facility (MOF) core specification*. OMG document formal/06-01-01.

Object Management Group. (2009). *UML superstructure, version 2.3*. OMG document formal/2010-05-05.

Orejas, F., Guerra, E., de Lara, J., & Ehrig, H. (2009). Correctness, completeness and termination of pattern-based model-to-model transformation. [CALCO.]. *Proceedings of CALCO, 2009*, 383–397.

Poernomo, I., & Terrell, J. (2010). Correct-by-construction Model Transformations from Spanning tree specifications in Coq, *ICFEM 2010*.

Rensink, A., & Kuperus, J.-H. (2009). Repotting the geraniums: On nested graph transformation rules. In *Proceedings of GT-VMT 2009*. EASST.

Richters, M., & Gogolla, M. (1998). On formalising the UML object constraint language OCL. In *Proceedings of the 17th International Conference on Conceptual Modelling* (LNCS). Berlin: Springer.

RTCA. (2012). *RTCA/EUROCAE DO-178C standard software considerations in airborne systems and equipment certification*. RTCA.

SRI. (2012). *Yices SMT solver*. Retrieved from http://yices.csl.sri.com/

van Amstel, M., Bosems, S., Kurtev, I., & Pires, L. F. (2011). Performance in model transformations: Experiments with ATL and QVT. In *Proceedings of ICMT 2011* (LNCS), (vol. 6707, pp. 198-212). Berlin: Springer.

Chapter 2
UML–Driven Software Performance Engineering:
A Systematic Mapping and Trend Analysis

Vahid Garousi
University of Calgary, Canada

Shawn Shahnewaz
University of Calgary, Canada

Diwakar Krishnamurthy
University of Calgary, Canada

ABSTRACT

Performance is critical to the success of every software system. As a sub-area of software engineering, Software Performance Engineering (SPE) is a systematic and quantitative discipline to construct software systems that meet performance objectives. A family of SPE approaches that has become popular in the last decade is SPE based on models developed using the Unified Modeling Language (UML), referred to as UML-Driven Software Performance Engineering (UML-SPE). This particular research area has emerged and grown since late 1990s when the UML was proposed. More than 100 papers have been published so far in this area. As this research area matures and the number of related papers increases, it is important to systematically summarize and categorize the current state-of-the-art and to provide an overview of the trends in this specialized field. The authors systematically map the body of knowledge related to UML-SPE through a Systematic Mapping (SM) study. As part of this study, they pose two sets of research questions, define selection and exclusion criteria, and systematically develop and refine a systematic map (classification schema). In addition, the authors conduct bibliometric, demographic, and trend analysis of the included papers. The study pool includes a set of 90 papers (from 114 identified papers) published in the area of UML-SPE between 1998 and 2011. The authors derive the trends in terms of types of papers, types of SPE activities, and types of evaluations. They also report the demographics and bibliometrics trends in this domain and discuss the emerging trends in UML-SPE and the implications for researchers and practitioners in this area.

DOI: 10.4018/978-1-4666-4217-1.ch002

1. INTRODUCTION

Performance is critical to the success of every software system. Many software products fail to meet their performance objectives after they are released. Fixing these problems late in the software development life-cycle is costly and causes schedule delays, cost overruns, damaged customer relations, missed market windows, lost revenues, and a host of other difficulties (Liu, 2011).

To avoid such costs, a system's performance characteristics must be considered throughout the whole software development life-cycle. Software Performance Engineering (SPE) is a systematic and quantitative discipline which provides a collection of methods to assure appropriate performance-related product quality throughout the entire development process (Liu, 2011).

The Unified Modeling Language (UML) is a standardized general-purpose modeling language in software engineering. Since UML's inception in late 1990's (Object Management Group [OMG]), many researchers have benefitted from powerful structural and behavioral modeling features of UML to model, test, analyze and predict software performance, and as a result, a joint area between UML and SPE has emerged, which is referred to as UML-driven Software Performance Engineering (UML-SPE) in this study.

More than 100 papers have appeared since 1998 in the area of UML-SPE. As this research area matures and the number of related papers increases, it is important to systematically classify the current state-of-the-art and to provide an overview of the trends in this specialized field (Kitchenham, et al., 2009; Kitchenham & Charters, 2007; Petersen, et al., 2008). Such categorized results provide many benefits to the broader community. For example, they are valuable resources for new researchers (e.g., PhD students) aiming to identify open research areas needing further work and/or to conduct additional *secondary studies* (Kitchenham, et al., 2009; Kitchenham & Charters,

2007; Petersen, et al., 2008). A secondary study is defined as a study of studies (Jill, et al., 2011).

We systematically analyze and classify the body of knowledge related to UML-SPE through a systematic mapping (SM) study (Petersen, et al., 2008). As part of this study, we pose two sets of research questions, define selection and exclusion criteria, and systematically develop and refine a systematic map (classification schema). In addition, we conduct a bibliometric and trend analysis of the included papers, to analyze the annual trend of papers, and identify the active researchers and most cited studies (a smaller-scale version of larger studies such as (Garousi & Varma, 2010; Tse, et al., 2006; W. Eric, et al., 2011)).

After a careful selection process (Section 4), our study pool includes a set of 90 papers (from the set of 114 identified papers) published in the area of UML-SPE between 1998 and 2011. The full version of our mapping data is available through a publicly-accessible online repository (Garousi, et al., Last accessed: Sept. 5, 2012). We derive the trends for instance in terms of types of papers (types of contribution and research facets), types of SPE activities (e.g., modeling, model transformation, and testing), and types of metrics and evaluations used in papers.

The main contributions of this article are four-fold:

- A systematic map (Section 5) developed for the area of UML-SPE which could be used for other secondary studies (e.g., surveys, systematic mappings or systematic literature reviews) in this field.
- Systematic mapping of the existing research in this area (Sections 6).
- An online article repository which has been created during this SM (Garousi, et al., Last accessed: Sept. 5, 2012).
- Bibliometric, trends and demographics data of the UML-SPE field (Section 7).

The remainder of paper is organized as follows. Section 2 discusses background and related work. In Section 3, we describe our research method, including the overall SM process, the goal and research questions tackled in this study. Section 4 discusses the article selection process. Section 5 presents the systematic map which has been built through an iterative selection and synthesis process. Section 6 presents the results of the systematic mapping. Bibliometrics, trends and demographics data are presented in Section 7. Section 8 summarizes and discusses implications of the SM results for researchers (both new and established) and also practitioners in UML-SPE. Finally, Section 9 concludes this study and states the future work directions. The reference section at the end of the paper is divided into two parts: primary studies of the SM are listed first and then the other references used in this study.

2. BACKGROUND AND RELATED WORK

In this section, a brief introduction to UML-driven software performance engineering is provided first. We then give a brief introduction to systematic mapping studies, bibliometric and demographics studies in software engineering. Related works are discussed next.

2.1. UML-Driven Software Performance Engineering

An overview of UML-SPE is shown as a UML activity diagram in Figure 1. The UML models of the software system under analysis or test is taken as input. Both types of UML models (structural and behavioral) (Object Management Group [OMG]) are usually needed for SPE purposes, since both structural and behavioral aspects of a system impact its performance. Examples of structural models include class and deployment diagrams. Examples of behavioral models include state-chart, sequence and activity diagrams. There are in general three types of SPE activities (Cortellessa Vittorio, et al., 2011): (1) modeling (specifying) the performance properties (e.g., workload, inter-arrival time distribution) on UML models, (2) model transformation, (3) testing, and (4) analysis and prediction.

After UML models are annotated with performance information, a type of model transformation approach is utilized. There are different types of model transformation approaches which transform UML models to performance models or other types of models, e.g., test models (e.g., concurrent control flow graphs (Vahid, et al., 2008)) or simulation models (to be fed to different simulation tools). Common types of performance models include: Queuing Network (QN) models and

Figure 1. An overview of UML-driven software performance engineering (UML-SPE), as a UML activity diagram

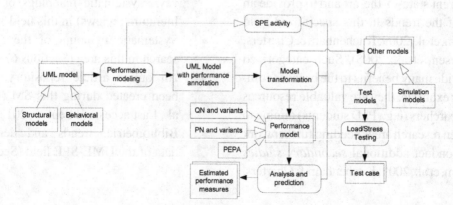

variants, Petri Net (PN) models and variants, and Performance Evaluation Process Algebra (PEPA). The output of analysis and prediction activities are usually estimated performance measures, e.g., response time and throughout. When the type of SPE activity is performance testing (e.g., load or stress testing), the outputs are test cases which are then executed on the software under test.

2.2. Secondary Studies in Software Engineering

Research proceeds by learning from and being inspired by existing work. When a research area grows and owns a large number of existing studies, it requires a substantial effort to read all the literature before conducting new research. Summarizing the existing literature and providing an overview for a certain area is helpful for new researchers (e.g., new Master or PhD students), since such summaries identify research trends and shed light on future directions.

Secondary studies are common in software engineering. Secondary study is defined as a study of studies (Jill, et al., 2011), i.e., a review of individual studies (each of which is called a primary study). Examples of secondary studies include: survey papers, systematic mapping (SM) studies and Systematic Literature Reviews (SLR). A SM study is a defined method to build a classification scheme and structure a research field of interest. A SLR is a means of evaluating and interpreting all available research relevant to a particular research question, topic area, or phenomenon of interest. SLRs aim to present a fair evaluation of a research topic by using a trustworthy, rigorous, and auditable methodology. A SLR study often includes a SM study as part of it, and is thus more comprehensive than a SM

Similar to many other research fields, software engineering has its methodologies for conducting secondary studies. Petersen et al. (Petersen, et al., 2008) presented a guideline paper on how to conduct systematic mapping (SM) studies in software engineering. The guideline paper by Petersen et al. (Petersen, et al., 2008) provides insights on building classification schemes and structuring a particular sub-domain of interest in software engineering. Kitchenham et al. also presented in (Kitchenham & Charters, 2007) detailed guidelines for performing SLR studies in software engineering, most of which could also be used for a SM study. The guidelines described by Petersen et al. (Petersen, et al., 2008) and also Kitchenham et al. (Kitchenham & Charters, 2007) were followed in our SM study. Justification to follow the guidelines from those two papers is that they are treated as the most comprehensive guidelines to conduct SLR/SM in software engineering and have been used by many other researchers conducting and reporting SLRs and SMs in software engineering, e.g., (Ali, et al., 2010; Elberzhager, et al., 2012; Garousi, 2011).

2.3. Bibliometric and Demographics Studies in Software Engineering

Bibliometric and demographics studies have been popular in software engineering (e.g., Fabrício Gomes & Jerffeson Teixeira, 2011; Garousi & Varma, 2010; Tse, et al., 2006; Eric, et al., 2011). For example, the series of 12 papers by Glass and Chen (e.g., Glass, 1995; Glass & Chen, 2001, 2002; Tse, et al., 2006) have been an ongoing annual series of studies that have identified the top 15 scholars and institutions for five-year periods in systems and software engineering. The rankings are based on the number of papers published in the leading journals within the field. In another work (Garousi & Varma, 2010), our team members conducted a recent study in 2010 which ranked the Canadian software engineering scholars and institutions from 1996-2006.

The benefits of bibliometric assessments include the following:

- They reveal outstanding institutions and scholars, allowing graduate students and researchers to better choose where they want to study or work.

- They can allow employers to recruit the most qualified potential graduate students/ researchers, and also industrial firms to choose the most promising academic research teams for collaboration.
- They identify for new researchers the top venues for publication so they can submit papers to and also attend them.

We conduct a small-scale bibliometric and demographics assessment in the area of UML-SPE in this study (Section 7).

2.4. Related Works

Focusing on the area of UML-SPE, we were able to find eight secondary studies (Di Marco & Mirandola, 2006; Evgeni, et al., 2002; José & Javier, 2003; Reiner, et al., 2001; Schmietendorf

& Dimitrov, 2001; Simonetta, et al., 2004; Simonetta & Marta, 2011; Cortellessa Vittorio, et al., 2011) in this field. A summary of these works are shown in Table 1 (sorted by year of publication). In essence, Table 1 can be viewed as a brief "ternary" look at this field, where a "ternary" study is defined as a study of secondary studies.

Three of these eight secondary studies are surveys (José & Javier, 2003; Simonetta, et al., 2004; Simonetta & Marta, 2011) (as explicitly identified by the authors themselves) and the others are either books (Reiner, et al., 2001) (collection of papers on UML-SPE), overview papers discussing capabilities of UML for SPE purposes (Evgeni, et al., 2002; Schmietendorf & Dimitrov, 2001), taxonomy (Di Marco & Mirandola, 2006), or summary papers (Cortellessa Vittorio, et al., 2011).

Table 1. Summary of related works (secondary studies in UML-SPE)

Reference	Year	Title	Publication Type	Type of secondary study	SPE Approach(es)	Number of primary studies
(Simonetta & Marta, 2011)	2001	On transforming UML models into performance models	Conference paper	Survey	Model transformation	12
(Reiner, et al., 2001)	2001	Performance engineering: state of the art and current trends	Book of invited papers	Collection of papers	Modeling, analysis, practical experience	11 chapters about UML-SPE
(Schmietendorf & Dimitrov, 2001)	2001	Possibilities of Performance modeling with UML	Book chapter	Overview of capabilities	Modeling, Tool support, process	9
(Evgeni, et al., 2002)	2002	UML-based performance engineering possibilities and techniques	Magazine article	Overview of capabilities	Modeling, Tool support,	9
(José & Javier, 2003)	2003	Software performance modeling using UML and Petri nets	Conference paper	Survey	Modeling, Model transformation, analysis	27
(Simonetta, et al., 2004)	2004	Model-based performance prediction in software development: a survey	Journal article	Survey	Modeling, Model transformation, analysis	15
(Di Marco & Mirandola, 2006)	2006	Model transformation in software performance engineering	Conference paper	Taxonomy	Model transformation, Tool support,	8
(Cortellessa Vittorio, et al., 2011)	2011	Model-Based Software Performance Analysis	Book	Summary of state of the art	Modeling, Model transformation, analysis and prediction	32

We were not able to find any SM or SLR studies in this area. The recent book (Cortellessa Vittorio, et al., 2011), entitled "Model-Based Software Performance Analysis" and published in 2011, is a good summary of state of the art in UML-SPE and is the closest to our SM study. Our work differs from (Cortellessa Vittorio, et al., 2011) in the following aspects: (1) our SM study systematically maps all the 90 papers in this area, while (Cortellessa Vittorio, et al., 2011) only reviews 32 papers, and (2) our SM study is a SM, while (Cortellessa Vittorio, et al., 2011) is only an overview and does not present trends and implications as we report in this paper. Essentially, one could say that our work and (Cortellessa Vittorio, et al., 2011) are two complementary pieces of work, in that our study lays down a classification of the field and the 190-page book on the topic (Cortellessa Vittorio, et al., 2011) goes into depth on technical details.

The number of primary studies in the eight secondary studies (Di Marco & Mirandola, 2006; Evgeni, et al., 2002; José & Javier, 2003; Reiner, et al., 2001; Schmietendorf & Dimitrov, 2001; Simonetta, et al., 2004; Simonetta & Marta, 2011; Cortellessa Vittorio, et al., 2011) listed in Table 1 have varied between 8 and 32 papers. Our SM study considers all the 90 papers in this field, which have passed our inclusion criteria (Section 4).

3. RESEARCH METHOD

In the following, an overview of our research method and then the goal and research questions of our study are presented.

3.1. Overview

This SM is carried out based on the guidelines provided by Petersen et al. (Kitchenham & Charters, 2007; Petersen, et al., 2008). In designing the methodology for this SM, methods from several other SMs such as (Ali, et al., 2010; Elberzhager, et al., 2012; Garousi, 2011) were also incorporated. The process that lies at the basis of this SM is outlined in Figure 2, which includes four phases described in Sections 4-7. The Research Questions (RQs) 1 and 2 appearing in Figure 2 are discussed in the next section.

3.2. Goal and Research Questions

The goal of this study is to systematically map (classify) the state-of-the-art in the area of UML-SPE, to explore the bibliometrics trends in this area, to identify opportunities for future research, and to find out the recent trends and directions in this field from the point of view researchers and practitioners in this area.

We also want to understand how the research has evolved over time with regards to the above research attributes. Based on the above goal, the following Research Questions (RQs) are raised. To extract detailed information for each of the questions, each question is divided into sub-questions.

- **RQ 1 - Systematic mapping:** What is the research space of UML-SPE? This question aims at conducting a systematic mapping (classification) in the area.
  - **RQ 1.1 – Mapping of studies by contribution facet:** How many studies present UML-SPE methods, techniques, tools, models, metrics, or processes? Petersen et al. (Petersen, et al., 2008) proposed the above types

Figure 2. The research process used to conduct this SM study

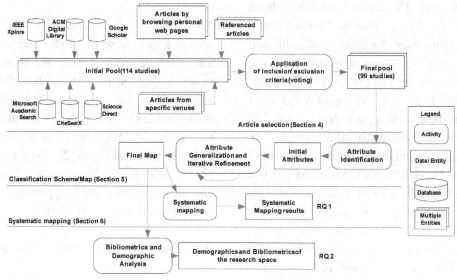

of contributions to enable systematic mapping of studies in software engineering.

○ **RQ 1.2 – Mapping of studies by research facet:** What type of research methods are used in the studies in this area? Some studies only propose solutions without extensive validations, while some other studies present in-depth evaluation of their approach. Petersen et al. (Petersen, et al., 2008) has also proposed guidelines to classify the research approach of papers, which we will use to answer this RQ.

○ **RQ 1.3 – Types of SPE approach:** What types of SPE activities have been presented in the literature (e.g., performance modeling, model transformation, and testing), and which types are more popular than others?

○ **RQ 1.4 – Type of performance metrics used and evaluated:** What performance metrics (e.g., response time, utilization) have been used for evaluation of approaches in the litera-

ture, and which ones are more popular than others?

○ **RQ 1.5 – Input UML diagrams:** Which type of UML diagrams are used as inputs for SPE activities, and which ones are more widely used than others?

○ **RQ 1.6 – Output:** Which types of outputs are generated using the approaches presented in the literature (e.g., performance models, test cases and analysis results)?

○ **RQ 1.7 – Model annotation languages:** Which UML annotation languages (e.g., the UML SPT profile (OMG), or the MARTE profile (OMG) are used to annotate the input UML diagrams? Which ones are more popular than others?

○ **RQ 1.8 – Application domains:** Which application domains have received most of the focus by the papers? Examples include: real-time systems, embedded systems, and mobile devices.

- **RQ 1.9 – Methods of evaluation:** Which types of evaluation methods (e.g., comparing the predicted measures with actual measures) are used in the papers, and which ones are more widely used than others?
- **RQ 1.10 – Attributes of the software systems under analysis:** What are the attributes of the software systems under analysis in the studies? What ratios of studies have used open-source, commercial, or academic experimental systems for evaluation?
- **RQ 1.11 – Tools presented in papers:** How many SPE tools have been proposed in the studies? Are they available for download and/or purchase?
- **RQ 2 - Bibliometric data and demographics:**
  - **RQ 2.1 - Publication count by year:** What is the annual publication count in this area?
  - **RQ 2.2 - Publication count by venue type:** What is the annual publication count in different types of venues (conference, journals, etc.)?
  - **RQ 2.3- Citation count by year:** What is the citation count for studies from different years? Do older papers necessarily receive more citations?
  - **RQ 2.4–Top-cited studies:** What are the top-cited studies in this area?
  - **RQ 2.5- Top venues:** Which venues have published most of the studies in this area?
  - **RQ 2.6– Citation count by venue type:** What is the average citation count for different publication venue types? Do journal papers in this area necessarily receive more citations than workshop and conference papers?

- **RQ 2.7- Top authors:** Which authors have been most active in terms of number of papers?
- **RQ 2.8- Author affiliation** What ratios of the authors are from academia or industry? How many papers have been jointly authored by people from academia and industry? This RQ will show the extent of academia- industry collaborations in this field.
- **RQ 2.9- Top countries:** Which countries have been more active in terms of number of papers?

4. ARTICLE SELECTION

Let us recall from our SM process (Figure 2) that the first phase of our study is article selection. For this phase, we followed the following steps in order:

- Source selection and search keywords (Section 4.1).
- Inclusion and exclusion criteria and application of voting mechanism (Section 4.2).
- Finalizing the pool of articles and the online repository (Section 4.3).

4.1. Source Selection and Search Keywords

Based on the SM guidelines (Kitchenham & Charters, 2007; Petersen, et al., 2008), to find relevant studies, we searched the following six major online search academic article search engines: (1) IEEE Xplore[1], (2) ACM Digital Library[2], (3) Google Scholar[3], (4) Microsoft Academic Search[4], (5) CiteSeerX[5], and (6) Science Direct[6].

In order to ensure that we included as many relevant publications as possible in the pool of selected studies, we identified all potential search keywords regarding the focus of each of our research questions. The search keywords were:

- UML performance engineering.
- UML performance modeling.
- UML performance testing.
- UML load testing.
- UML performance prediction.
- UML stress testing.

We searched for the above keywords another time by replacing the word "UML" with "model". In terms of the search time-window, only publications available in the above search engines by early September 2012 (the time of this writing) were included in our pool.

To decrease the risk of missing relevant publications, similar to previous SM studies and SLRs, we searched the following potential publication venues manually:

- Personal Web pages of active researchers in the field of interest: We extracted the names of active researchers from the initial set of papers found in the above search engines.
- References found in publications already in the pool.
- Specific venues: We extracted the names of those venues from the initial set of papers found in the above search engines.

Specific venues included the International Conference on Performance Engineering (ICPE), which has recently been established as a joint event of the ACM Workshop on Software and Performance (WOSP) and the SPEC International Performance Evaluation Workshop (SIPEW). We searched the proceedings of ICPE, WOSP, and SIPEW for all the available years.

All publications found in the additional venues that were not yet in the pool of selected publications but seemed to be candidates for inclusion were added to the initial pool. With the above search strings and search in specific venues, we found 114 publications which we considered as our initial pool of potentially-relevant publica-

tions (also depicted in Figure 2). At this stage, papers in the initial pool were ready for the voting mechanism described next.

4.2. Inclusion/Exclusion Criteria and Application of Voting Mechanism

In our study, the inclusion criteria were properties of papers based on which we would include or exclude them in our study, such as topic (UML-SPE), and the extensiveness of the study. If multiple papers with the same title by the same author(s) were found, the most recent one was included and the rest were excluded. Only papers written in English language and only the ones which were electronically available were included. If a conference paper had a more recent journal version, only the latter was included.

To apply the inclusion/exclusion criteria to the initial pool, the authors of this article inspected the studies in the initial pool and assigned a vote on a 9-point scale to each study, with '9' indicating a strong opinion in favor of not excluding a study, and '1' indicating a strong opinion in favor of excluding a study. Thus, the maximum vote on a study could be 45 marks. We decided to use a threshold of 25 marks for the decision on study exclusion, i.e., studies with cumulative votes of less than 25 marks were excluded.

To vote on each study, we reviewed its title, abstract and keywords. If not enough information could be found in those sources, a more in-depth evaluation was conducted. Based on the results of the joint voting, the size of the pool of selected studies decreased from 114 to 90. Works reported in (Hayat Khan & Heegaard, 2010; Vahid, et al., 2005) are two examples of the studies that were excluded, since the former (Vahid, et al., 2005) had a more recent corresponding journal paper (Vahid, et al., 2009), and the latter (Hayat Khan & Heegaard, 2010) was a very short paper (only 2 pages) with no evaluation section (or even an example).

4.3. Final Pool of Articles and the Online Repository

After the initial search and the follow-up analysis for exclusion of unrelated and inclusion of additional studies, the pool of selected studies was finalized with 90 studies. The reader can refer to Section 9.1 for the full reference list of all 90 primary studies. The final pool of selected publications has also been published in an online repository using Google Docs system, and is publically accessible online at (Garousi, et al., 2012). The classifications of each selected publication according to the classification scheme described in Section 5 are also available in the online repository.

5. DEVELOPMENT OF THE SYSTEMATIC MAP (CLASSIFICATION SCHEME)

Iterative development of our systematic map is discussed in Section 5.1. Section 5.2 presents the final systematic map. Section 5.3 discusses our data-extraction approach.

5.1. Iterative Development of the Map

To develop our systematic map, as it is shown in Figure 2, we analyzed the studies in the pool and identified the initial list of attributes. We then used attribute generalization and iterative refinement to derive the final map. To increase the preciseness of our systematic map, we utilized the "observer triangulation" method (Runeson, et al., 2012) in designing the systematic map.

As studies were identified as relevant to our research project, we recorded them in a shared spreadsheet (hosted in the online Google Docs spreadsheet [Garousi, et al., 2012]) to facilitate further analysis. The following information was recorded for each paper: (1) paper title, (2) authors, (3) publication venue (e.g., IEEE Software), (4) year of publication, (5) authors' country of affili-

ation, and (6) type of institution authors are affiliated with (academic, industry or a combination).

With the relevant studies identified and recorded, our next goal was to categorize the studies in order to begin building a complete picture of the research area. Though we did not a-priori develop a categorization scheme for this project, we were broadly interested in: (1) types of SPE approaches, and (2) types of performance models used and developed in studies.

We refined these broad interests into a systematic map using an iterative approach that involved all the authors of this paper. The first author of this paper conducted an initial pass over the data, and based on (at least) the title, abstract and introduction of the studies created a set of initial categories and assigned studies to those categories. As a group we discussed and reviewed the results of this first analytic pass and refined the categorization. Next the rest of the researchers conducted a second pass over the data, to revisit the categorization. When the assignment of studies to categories could not be clearly determined just based on the title, abstract and introduction, more of the paper was considered. In this process both the categories and the assignment of studies to categories were further discussed and refined.

5.2. Final Systematic Map

Table 2 shows the final classification scheme that we developed after applying the process described above. In the table, column 1 is the list of RQs, column 2 is the corresponding attribute/aspect. Column 3 is the set of all possible values for the attribute. Finally, column 4 determines whether the particular attribute can take multiple-choice values from the set of values or it is an exclusively single-choice value. In another words, the last column indicates for an attribute whether multiple selections can be applied. For example, for RQ 1.2 (Research type), the corresponding value in the last column is 'S' (Single). It indicates that one study can be classified under only one research type (e.g., solution proposal, validation research, or evaluation research), which are discussed next. In contrast, for RQ 1.1 (Contribution type), the corresponding value in the last column is 'M' (Multiple). It indicates that one study can contribute more than one type of options (e.g. method, tool, etc.).

We utilized the following techniques to derive the list of categories for each attribute: attribute generalization, clustering and aggregation. If there were choices under "other" which were more than three instances, we grouped them to create new categories, e.g., this was the case for the "Performance Evaluation Process Algebra (PEPA)"

category for output performance models (RQ 1.6 in Table 2). We believe most of the categories in Table 2 are self explanatory, except for those for contribution and research types (RQ 1.1 and RQ 1.2) which are explained in the next two sub-sections. All the attributes and categories will be reviewed in detail in Section 5 (results).

For RQ's 2.x (bibliometrics and demographics), there was no systematic mapping required. We essentially extracted the necessary data, e.g., for RQ 2.1 (publication count by year) and RQ 2.2 (publication count by venue type), we extracted the publication year and venue of each paper.

Table 2. Systematic map developed and used in our study

RQ	Attribute/Aspect	Categories	(M)ultiple/ (S)ingle
1.1	Contribution type	{Method (technique), Tool, Metric, Process, Other }	M
1.2	Research type	{Solution Proposal, Validation Research, Evaluation Research, Experience Papers, Philosophical Papers, Opinion Papers, Other}	S
1.3	Type of SPE approach	{Modeling, Model Transformation, Testing, Analysis and prediction, Other}	M
1.4	Type of performance metrics used and evaluated	{Execution (response) Time, Utilization, Throughput, Other}	M
1.5	Input UML diagrams	{Activity diagram, Class diagram, Collaboration Diagram, Deployment Diagram, Sequence Diagram, States Machine, Use-case diagram, Other}	M
1.6	Outputs	{Performance model, test cases, other} Performance model ∈ {queuing network (QN) and variants, Petri net (PN) and variants, Performance Evaluation Process Algebra, other}	M
1.7	Annotation languages	6. {UML Profile for Schedulability, Performance and Time (SPT), UML Profile for Modeling and Analysis of Real-Time and Embedded Systems (MARTE), other/custom}	M
1.8	Application domains	{ Real-time systems, Embedded Systems, Mobile/handheld, Other, Generic}	M
1.9	Methods of evaluation	{ Feasibility, Comparing with tests from operational profile, Comparing predicted measures with actual measures, Performance prediction, Other}	M
1.10	Attributes of the software systems under analysis	# of systems/ examples: integer SUT/example names: array of strings Type of system(s) ∈ {Open-source, Commercial, Government, Academic experimental} LOC of system(s): integer	M
1.11	Attributes of the tool(s) presented in the paper (if any)	Name: array of strings Available for download: Boolean URL to download: string	

5.2.1. Type of Paper: Contribution Facet

The first set of categories in our scheme is related to the contribution facet of the study. It donates the type of contributions each study provided. Petersen et al. (Petersen, et al., 2008) proposed the classification of contributions into: method/technique, tool, model, metric and process. These types were adapted in our context. We also added another type: survey or empirical results, since we found that many studies contribute such results. If a study could not be categorized into any above-mentioned types, it would be placed under "Other".

5.2.2. Type of Paper: Research Facet

The second set of categories in our scheme deal with the nature of the research reported in each paper. These categories were influenced by categories described by Petersen et al. (2008) and our aim is to provide insights into the empirical foundation being developed by the body of research. The "research type" categories include:

- **Solution Proposal:** A paper in this category proposes a solution to a problem. The solution can be either novel or a significant extension of an existing technique. The potential benefits and the applicability of the solution are shown only by a small example or a good line of argumentation.
- **Validation Research:** A paper in this category provides preliminary empirical evidence for the proposed techniques or tools. These studies either proposed a novel technique/approach and its limited application in a certain context to demonstrate its effectiveness, or conducted a survey or interview among a certain number of participants to answer a particular research question. More formal experimental methods (e.g., hypothesis testing, control experiment) or results are further needed to build relevant theories.

- **Evaluation Research:** These studies go further than papers of type "Validation research" by using strict and formal experimental methods (e.g., hypothesis testing, control experiment) in evaluating novel techniques or tools in practice. Hence, these studies provide more convincing empirical evidence and are helpful to build theories.
- **Experience Studies:** Experience studies explain how something has been done in practice, based on the personal experience of the author(s).
- **Philosophical Studies:** These studies sketch a new way of looking at existing things by structuring the area in form of a taxonomy or conceptual framework.
- **Opinion Studies:** These studies express the personal opinion of the author(s) around whether a certain technique is good or bad, or how things should been done. They do not significantly rely on related work or research methodologies.
- **Other:** A catchall category in the event that the work reported in a paper does not fit into any of the above research types.

5.3. Data Extraction

To extract data, the studies in our pool were reviewed with the focus of each RQ and the required information was extracted. To increase the preciseness of our classification scheme, we utilized the "observer triangulation" method (Runeson, et al., 2012) in data extraction and mapping phases, in which the consensus of all the authors were taken into account.

7. RESULTS OF SYSTEMATIC MAPPING (RQ 1)

Results of the systematic mapping are presented in this section from Section 6.1 to 6.11.

6.1. Mapping of Studies by Contribution Facet (RQ 1.1)

Figure 3 shows the distribution of the total and also annual breakdown of studies by contribution facet for all the primary studies. Exact paper references have also been provided under the figure. The top three contribution facets are: method (also referred to as technique or approach), tool and model, which have appeared in 73 studies (81%), 28 studies (31%), and 11 studies (12%), respectively.

Based on their contributions, some studies were classified under more than one facet. For example, the work by Woodside et al. (Murray, et al., 2005) makes three contributions: (1) a performance analysis method, (2) a tool architecture called PUMA, and (3) an intermediate behavioural model called Core Scenario Model (CSM).

One paper (Vahid, et al., 2009) contributed a new performance metric called Resource Usage Measure. Three papers (Jose, et al., 2000b; Mathias, et al., 2008; Vahid, 2010b) proposed new SPE processes. The work in (Jose, et al., 2000b) proposed a SPE process called *Performance Requirements for OO design Patterns*. Garousi (Vahid, 2010b) proposed a specific stress-test performance engineering process for stress testing purposes. Fritzsche et al. (Mathias, et al., 2008) discussed a case study for performance analysis of business processes.

Four studies (Bennett, 2004; Jose, et al., 2000b; Merseguer & Campos, 2003; Vahid, 2008b) have made "other" types of contributions which are mostly in-depth case-studies, e.g., empirical results from a SPE case study (Vahid, 2008b), and an exploratory study (Merseguer & Campos, 2003).

The annual trend of contribution facets is also shown in Figure 3. Note that since many studies were classified under more than one contribution facet, this stack chart cannot be used as the annual trend of number of studies (that trend will be presented in Section 7.1). We can see that across different years, different contribution facets have been studied, and no clear trend change is observable.

6.2. Mapping of Studies by Research Facet (RQ 1.2)

Based on the scheme described in Section 5, we classified the studies into five categories. Figure 4 shows the classification of the all primary studies according to the type of research method they have followed and reported. Recall that, for the research facet type, each study was categorized under a single category.

The ranking of research facets are: solution proposal (47 studies), validation research (38 studies), evaluation research (3 studies), opinion papers (3 studies), and experience reports (3 studies). It seems that the UML-SPE field as a whole is leaning more towards to solution proposals and semi-formal validations. Thus, we view the application of more formal evaluation methods (e.g., controlled experiments) as a worthy endeavour to pursue in future research in this area.

Notable findings: Based on the annual trend of research facets (in Figure 4), the following notable observations can be made: (1) in recent years (after 2008), mix of the facets are more diverse than earlier years, and (2) opinion and experience papers are starting to appear in recent years.

Similar to other SM studies (e.g., Petersen, et al., 2008), it would also be interesting to review the number of studies by research facet versus contribution facet. As a scatter plot, Figure 5 shows that information. As we can observe, a large ratio of the primary studies are positioned in the bottom-left corner. 40 of the 90 studies (44%) have contributed new UML-SPE techniques and are "solution proposals" in terms of research facet. There is comparatively fewer number of studies in the top part of the XY plot. This denotes an opportunity for future research to explore empirical studies involving the UML-SPE solution proposals developed thus far.

Figure 3. Mapping of studies by contribution facet

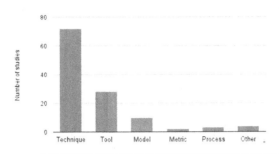

Technique:	(Ahmad, 2004; Alexander, et al., 2006; Andre & Paolo, 2007; Andrea, 2005; Andrew J. Bennett, et al., 2004; Canevet, et al., 2004; Canevet, et al., 2003; Christoph, et al., 2002; Dorina, 2000; Gu Gordon & Petriu, 2005; Hassan & A., 2000; Hui & C., 2005; James & Wolfgang, 2003, 2004; Jing, et al., 2003; Jose, et al., 2000a, 2000d; Jose, et al., 2002; Coopera Kendra, et al., 2004; Cooper Kendra, et al., 2003; Lukas, et al., 2009; Mathias, et al., 2009; Mirco & Stephen, 2008; Murray, et al., 2005; López-Grao Juan Pablo, et al., 2004; Pete & Rob, 2000; Peter & Rob, 2000; Petri, et al., 2005; D. C. Petriu & Hui, 2002; D. C. Petriu & Xin, 2000; Ping & C., 2003; QuYang, et al., 2006; Rasha & Dorina, 2008; Sabri & Thomas, 2002a; Sacha, et al., 2006; Simona & Jose, 2007; Simona, et al., 2002; Simonetta & Moreno, 2005; Smith, et al., 2005; Spiteri, 2008; Vahid, 2008a, 2010b, 2011; Vahid, et al., 2009; Cortellessa Vittorio, et al., 2005; Cortellessa Vittorio & Maurizio, 2004; Cortellessa Vittorio & Raffaela, 2000)(Anil & M., 2000; Bertolino, et al., 2002; Distefano, et al., 2005; Dorin & Murray, 2002; Fried, 2000; Gu Gordon & C., 2002; Mathias, et al., 2008; Oliveira, et al., 2007; Pekka, 2001; Raffaela & Vittorio, 2000; Rob, 1998; Sabri & Thomas, 2002b; Simonetta, et al., 2003; Simonetta & Moreno, 2003b; Steffen, et al., 2008; Theelen, et al., 2003; Vahid, 2008c, 2010c; Vahid, et al., 2006, 2008; Vincenzo & Raffaela, 2001, 2002; Cortellessaa Vittorio & Raffaela, 2002; Wet & Pieter, 2005)
Tool:	(Alexander, et al., 2006; Canevet, et al., 2003; Distefano, et al., 2005; Dorin & Murray, 2002; Gomez-Martinez Elena & Jose, 2005; Gómez-Martínez Elena & José, 2006; Fried, 2000; Lukas, et al., 2009; Mathias, et al., 2009; Mathias & Jendrik, 2008; Mirco & Stephen, 2008; Moreno & Simonetta, 2004; Murray, et al., 2005; Nariman, et al., 2008; Oliveira, et al., 2007; Lopez-Grao Juan Pablo, et al., 2002; López-Grao Juan Pablo, et al., 2004; Sabri & Thomas, 2005; Simonetta & Moreno, 2003b; Steffen, et al., 2008; Stephen & Leila, 2005; Theelen, et al., 2003; Vahid, 2008b, 2010a, 2011; Vahid, et al., 2008; Cortellessa Vittorio, et al., 2004; Wet & Pieter, 2005)
Model:	(Hassan & A., 2000; Miguel, et al., 2000; Pekka, 2001; D. B. Petriu & Murray, 2004, 2007; Salvatore, et al., 2004; Smith, et al., 2005; Vahid, 2008a; Vahid, et al., 2009; Cortellessa Vittorio & Maurizio, 2004)
Metric:	(Vahid, et al., 2009)
Process:	(Jose, et al., 2000b; Mathias, et al., 2008; Vahid, 2010b)
Other:	(A. J. Bennett & J., 2004; Jose, et al., 2000b; Merseguer & Campos, 2003; Vahid, 2008b)

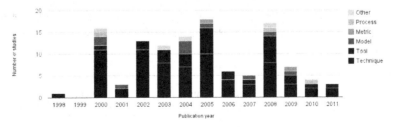

Figure 4. Mapping of studies by research facet

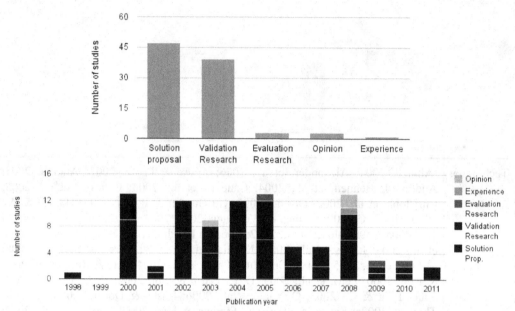

Solution proposal:	(Alexander, et al., 2006; Andre & Paolo, 2007; Andrea, 2005; Canevet, et al., 2004; Dorin & Murray, 2002; Dorina, 2000; Gomez-Martinez Elena & Jose, 2005; Gómez-Martínez Elena & José, 2006; Fried, 2000; Gu Gordon & C., 2002; Gu Gordon & Petriu, 2005; James & Wolfgang, 2003, 2004; Jose, et al., 2000a, 2000b; Jose, et al., 2002; Mathias, et al., 2009; Mathias, et al., 2008; Miguel, et al., 2000; Mirco & Stephen, 2008; Nariman, et al., 2008; Oliveira, et al., 2007; López-Grao Juan Pablo, et al., 2004; Pekka, 2001; Pete & Rob, 2000; D. B. Petriu & Murray, 2004; D. C. Petriu & Hui, 2002; D. C. Petriu & Xin, 2000; Ping & C., 2003; Rasha & Dorina, 2008; Rob, 1998; Sabri & Thomas, 2002a, 2002b; Salvatore, et al., 2004; Simona, et al., 2002; Simonetta, et al., 2003; Simonetta & Moreno, 2003b, 2005; Smith, et al., 2005; Spiteri, 2008; Vahid, 2008a; Vincenzo & Raffaela, 2001; Cortellessa Vittorio, et al., 2004; Cortellessa Vittorio & Raffaela, 2000; Wet & Pieter, 2005)
Validation research:	(Ahmad, 2004; Andre & Paolo, 2007; A. J. Bennett & J., 2004; Andrew J. Bennett, et al., 2004; Canevet, et al., 2003; Christoph, et al., 2002; Hassan & A., 2000; Hui & C., 2005; Jing, et al., 2003; Jose, et al., 2000b, 2000d; Coopera Kendra, et al., 2004; Cooper Kendra, et al., 2003; Murray, et al., 2005; Oliveira, et al., 2007; Lopez-Grao Juan Pablo, et al., 2002; Peter & Rob, 2000; Petri, et al., 2005; D. B. Petriu & Murray, 2007; QuYang, et al., 2006; Sabri & Thomas, 2002b, 2005; Sacha, et al., 2006; Simona & Jose, 2007; Simonetta & Moreno, 2003a; Steffen, et al., 2008; Theelen, et al., 2003; Vahid, 2008b, 2008c, 2010b, 2011; Vahid, et al., 2006, 2008, 2009; Vincenzo & Raffaela, 2002; Cortellessa Vittorio, et al., 2005; Cortellessa Vittorio & Maurizio, 2004)
Evaluation research:	(Lukas, et al., 2009; Stephen & Leıla, 2005; Vahid, 2010a)
Experience papers:	(Mathias & Jendrik, 2008)
Opinion papers:	(Mathias & Jendrik, 2008; Mathias, et al., 2008; Merseguer & Campos, 2003)

6.3. Type of SPE Activities (RQ 1.3)

Figure 6 shows the mapping of the studies in terms of the SPE activities they have proposed. As we can see, the top three SPE activities in order are: (1) model transformation, (2) analysis and prediction, and (3) modeling, which have appeared in 55 studies (61%), 42 studies (47%), and 32 studies (36%), respectively. It is surprising that UML-based performance testing has been investigated in only 10 studies, while it is a very important topic.

Three works (Jing, et al., 2003; QuYang, et al., 2006; Vahid, 2010b) have conducted other types of SPE activities. Garousi reported (Vahid, 2010b) a performance tuning approach, i.e., the study proposed guidelines to fix performance problems when performance testing has identified performance issues in a software under test. Jari et al. (QuYang, et al., 2006) reported a performance simulation approach. Xu et al. (Jing, et al., 2003) reported a performance improvement (tuning) approach as well.

Notable findings: Based on the annual trend of SPE activities (in Figure 6), we can see that, in recent years (after about 2006), mix of the facets are more diverse than earlier years.

Figure 5. Number of studies by research facet versus contribution facet (as an XY plot)

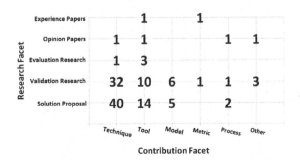

6.4. Type of Performance Metrics Used and Evaluated (RQ 1.4)

Figure 7 shows the breakdown of type of performance metrics used and evaluated. The top three performance metrics are: response time (32 studies), utilization (16 studies), and throughput (10 studies). 11 studies used other types of performance metrics, e.g., queue length (Bennett, 2004; Wet & Pieter, 2005), sojourn time (Simona & Jose, 2007) (amount of time it takes for an object to leave the system), probability of missing a deadline (Jing, et al., 2003), and network transfer rate (Lopez-Grao Juan Pablo, et al., 2002).

6.5. Input UML Diagrams (RQ 1.5)

The UML specification (from its earlier versions in 1990's to its latest version 2.4.1 in 2011 (OMG, 2012) has proposed various types of structural and behavioral UML diagrams (models). Different studies have used different types of UML diagrams as inputs to their UML-SPE approaches. Figure 8 shows the total and also annual breakdown of input UML diagrams.

The top three input UML diagrams are: sequence diagrams (49 studies), activity diagrams (35 studies), and deployment diagrams (34 studies). 6 studies used other types of UML diagrams, e.g., component diagrams (Alexander, et al., 2006; Hui, 2005; Steffen, et al., 2008), and composite-structure diagrams (Lukas, et al., 2009); or extended UML diagrams such as: use-case maps (Dorin & Murray, 2002).

Notable findings: Based on the annual trend of input UML diagrams used in studies (in Figure 8), we can see that, regardless of the issue that the number of papers have declined in recent years, a semi-balanced mix of different input UML diagrams have been used across different years.

Figure 6. Types of SPE activities proposed in the studies

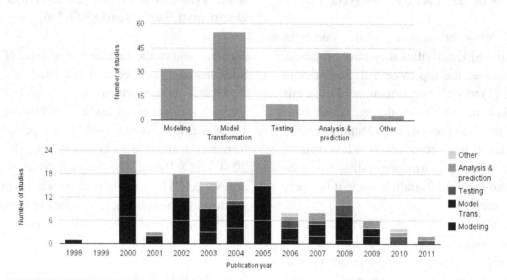

Modeling:	(Ahmad, 2004; Andre & Paolo, 2007; A. J. Bennett & J., 2004; Bertolino, et al., 2002; Christoph, et al., 2002; Distefano, et al., 2005; Hassan & A., 2000; James & Wolfgang, 2003; Jing, et al., 2003; Jose, et al., 2000a, 2000b, 2000d; Coopera Kendra, et al., 2004; Lukas, et al., 2009; Mathias, et al., 2009; Merseguer & Campos, 2003; Miguel, et al., 2000; Pete & Rob, 2000; Peter & Rob, 2000; Petri, et al., 2005; D. B. Petriu & Murray, 2004, 2007; D. C. Petriu & Hui, 2002; Sabri & Thomas, 2002a, 2002b, 2005; Smith, et al., 2005; Steffen, et al., 2008; Stephen & Leila, 2005; Cortellessaa Vittorio & Raffaela, 2002; Wet & Pieter, 2005)
Model Transformation:	(Alexander, et al., 2006; Andrea, 2005; Anil & M., 2000; Andrew J. Bennett, et al., 2004; Canevet, et al., 2004; Canevet, et al., 2003; Distefano, et al., 2005; Dorin & Murray, 2002; Dorina, 2000; Gomez-Martinez Elena & Jose, 2005; Gómez-Martínez Elena & José, 2006; Gu Gordon & Petriu, 2005; Hassan & A., 2000; Hui & C., 2005; Jing, et al., 2003; Jose, et al., 2000b, 2000d; Jose, et al., 2002; Cooper Kendra, et al., 2003; Lukas, et al., 2009; Mathias, et al., 2009; Mathias & Jendrik, 2008; Mathias, et al., 2008; Mirco & Stephen, 2008; Murray, et al., 2005; Nariman, et al., 2008; Oliveira, et al., 2007; Lopez-Grao Juan Pablo, et al., 2002; López-Grao Juan Pablo, et al., 2004; Pekka, 2001; Pete & Rob, 2000; Peter & Rob, 2000; Petri, et al., 2005; D. B. Petriu & Murray, 2004, 2007; D. C. Petriu & Xin, 2000; Ping & C., 2003; Raffaela & Vittorio, 2000; Rasha & Dorina, 2008; Sacha, et al., 2006; Salvatore, et al., 2004; Simona & Jose, 2007; Simona, et al., 2002; Simonetta, et al., 2003; Simonetta & Moreno, 2005; Smith, et al., 2005; Spiteri, 2008; Vincenzo & Raffaela, 2001; Cortellessa Vittorio & Raffaela, 2002)(Fried, 2000; Gu Gordon & C., 2002; Rob, 1998; Theelen, et al., 2003; Cortellessa Vittorio, et al., 2004)
Testing:	(Oliveira, et al., 2007; Sacha, et al., 2006; Vahid, 2008b, 2008c, 2010a, 2010b, 2011; Vahid, et al., 2006, 2008; Cortellessa Vittorio & Maurizio, 2004)
Analysis and prediction:	(Ahmad, 2004; Alexander, et al., 2006; Andre & Paolo, 2007; A. J. Bennett & J., 2004; Bertolino, et al., 2002; Christoph, et al., 2002; Distefano, et al., 2005; Fried, 2000; Hui & C., 2005; James & Wolfgang, 2003, 2004; Jing, et al., 2003; Jose, et al., 2000a, 2000d; Coopera Kendra, et al., 2004; Cooper Kendra, et al., 2003; Lukas, et al., 2009; Mathias, et al., 2008; Moreno & Simonetta, 2004; Murray, et al., 2005; Nariman, et al., 2008; Lopez-Grao Juan Pablo, et al., 2002; Pekka, 2001; Petri, et al., 2005; D. C. Petriu & Hui, 2002; Ping & C., 2003; Raffaela & Vittorio, 2000; Rasha & Dorina, 2008; Sabri & Thomas, 2005; Simona & Jose, 2007; Simona, et al., 2002; Simonetta & Moreno, 2003a, 2003b; Steffen, et al., 2008; Stephen & Leila, 2005; Theelen, et al., 2003; Vahid, 2008a, 2010c; Vincenzo & Raffaela, 2002; Cortellessa Vittorio, et al., 2005; Cortellessa Vittorio & Raffaela, 2000; Wet & Pieter, 2005)
Other:	(Jing, et al., 2003; QuYang, et al., 2006; Vahid, 2010b)

Figure 7. Type of performance metrics used and evaluated

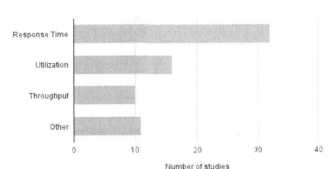

Response time:	(Alexander, et al., 2006; Andre & Paolo, 2007; A. J. Bennett & J., 2004; Bertolino, et al., 2002; Hassan & A., 2000; Hui & C., 2005; James & Wolfgang, 2004; Jing, et al., 2003; Jose, et al., 2000b, 2000d; Coopera Kendra, et al., 2004; Lukas, et al., 2009; Murray, et al., 2005; Lopez-Grao Juan Pablo, et al., 2002; Petri, et al., 2005; Ping & C., 2003; Rasha & Dorina, 2008; Sabri & Thomas, 2005; Sacha, et al., 2006; Simona & Jose, 2007; Steffen, et al., 2008; Theelen, et al., 2003; Vahid, 2008a, 2008b, 2008c, 2010a, 2010b, 2011; Vahid, et al., 2006, 2008; Vincenzo & Raffaela, 2002; Cortellessa Vittorio, et al., 2005; Cortellessa Vittorio & Maurizio, 2004)
Utilization:	(A. J. Bennett & J., 2004; Andrew J. Bennett, et al., 2004; Bertolino, et al., 2002; Christoph, et al., 2002; Distefano, et al., 2005; Fried, 2000; Hui & C., 2005; Jing, et al., 2003; Coopera Kendra, et al., 2004; Murray, et al., 2005; Ping & C., 2003; QuYang, et al., 2006; Simonetta & Moreno, 2003a, 2003b; Vahid, et al., 2009; Cortellessaa Vittorio & Raffaela, 2002)
Throughput:	(Distefano, et al., 2005; Hassan & A., 2000; Pekka, 2001; Peter & Rob, 2000; Ping & C., 2003; Raffaela & Vittorio, 2000; Simona & Jose, 2007; Simonetta & Moreno, 2003a, 2003b; Cortellessaa Vittorio & Raffaela, 2002)
Other:	(A. J. Bennett & J., 2004; Bertolino, et al., 2002; Gomez-Martinez Elena & Jose, 2005; Gómez-Martínez Elena & José, 2006; Jing, et al., 2003; Lopez-Grao Juan Pablo, et al., 2002; Simona & Jose, 2007; Simona, et al., 2002; Stephen & Leila, 2005; Vahid, et al., 2009; Wet & Pieter, 2005)

6.6. Output Models and Artifacts (RQ 1.6)

Each UML-SPE approach usually takes a sub-set of input UML diagrams and generates as output either: QN, PN, or PEPA performance models (52 studies), test cases (10 studies), or other type of artifacts (e.g., simulation models) (13 studies). Figure 9 shows this breakdown. It is clear that QN, PN or PEPA performance models dominate and since a few papers only focus on testing, the number of studies which generate test-cases is relatively small.

13 studies proposed techniques to generate other output models and artifacts, e.g., simulation models (Mathias & Jendrik, 2008; Moreno & Simonetta, 2004; QuYang, et al., 2006; Sabri & Thomas, 2005; Simonetta, et al., 2003; Simonetta & Moreno, 2003a, 2003b; Steffen, et al., 2008), models in an architectural description language called *Rapide* (Cooper Kendra, et al., 2003), (3) performance failure probability (Cortellessa Vittorio, et al., 2005), or (4) domain-specific models in languages such as the Multi-agent Software Engineering (MaSE) language (Nariman, et al., 2008).

Figure 8. Input UML diagrams used for SPE

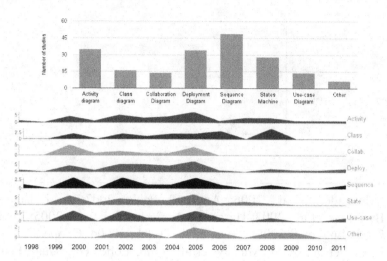

Activity diagram:	(Andre & Paolo, 2007; Andrea, 2005; Canevet, et al., 2004; Christoph, et al., 2002; Distefano, et al., 2005; Dorina, 2000; Gomez-Martinez Elena & Jose, 2005; Fried, 2000; Gu Gordon & C., 2002; Gu Gordon & Petriu, 2005; Mathias, et al., 2009; Mathias, et al., 2008; Mirco & Stephen, 2008; Moreno & Simonetta, 2004; Murray, et al., 2005; Oliveira, et al., 2007; López-Grao Juan Pablo, et al., 2004; Pekka, 2001; Peter & Rob, 2000; D. C. Petriu & Hui, 2002; Ping & C., 2003; QuYang, et al., 2006; Raffaela & Vittorio, 2000; Rob, 1998; Sabri & Thomas, 2002a, 2002b; Salvatore, et al., 2004; Simona & Jose, 2007; Simonetta & Moreno, 2003a, 2003b, 2005; Spiteri, 2008; Theelen, et al., 2003; Vahid, 2010c; Wet & Pieter, 2005)
Class diagram:	(Ahmad, 2004; Alexander, et al., 2006; Hassan & A., 2000; Coopera Kendra, et al., 2004; Cooper Kendra, et al., 2003; Miguel, et al., 2000; Nariman, et al., 2008; Petri, et al., 2005; QuYang, et al., 2006; Rasha & Dorina, 2008; Sabri & Thomas, 2002a, 2002b; Vahid, 2008c; Vahid, et al., 2006, 2008; Wet & Pieter, 2005)
Collaboration diagram:	(Anil & M., 2000; Distefano, et al., 2005; Fried, 2000; Gu Gordon & Petriu, 2005; Hassan & A., 2000; Murray, et al., 2005; López-Grao Juan Pablo, et al., 2004; Peter & Rob, 2000; D. C. Petriu & Xin, 2000; Ping & C., 2003; Simona, et al., 2002; Vincenzo & Raffaela, 2001, 2002; Wet & Pieter, 2005)
Deployment diagram:	(Ahmad, 2004; Andrea, 2005; Bertolino, et al., 2002; Distefano, et al., 2005; Dorina, 2000; Fried, 2000; Gu Gordon & Petriu, 2005; Hui & C., 2005; James & Wolfgang, 2003; Jing, et al., 2003; Moreno & Simonetta, 2004; Murray, et al., 2005; Pekka, 2001; D. B. Petriu & Murray, 2004; D. C. Petriu & Hui, 2002; Ping & C., 2003; Raffaela & Vittorio, 2000; Rob, 1998; Sabri & Thomas, 2002a; Salvatore, et al., 2004; Simonetta & Moreno, 2003a, 2003b, 2005; Theelen, et al., 2003; Vahid, 2008c, 2010b, 2011; Vahid, et al., 2006, 2008, 2009; Vincenzo & Raffaela, 2002; Cortellessa Vittorio, et al., 2005; Cortellessa Vittorio & Raffaela, 2000; Cortellessaa Vittorio & Raffaela, 2002; Wet & Pieter, 2005)
Sequence diagram:	(Ahmad, 2004; Alexander, et al., 2006; A. J. Bennett & J., 2004; Andrew J. Bennett, et al., 2004; Bertolino, et al., 2002; Distefano, et al., 2005; Dorina, 2000; Fried, 2000; James & Wolfgang, 2003, 2004; Jing, et al., 2003; Jose, et al., 2000b, 2000d; Coopera Kendra, et al., 2004; Cooper Kendra, et al., 2003; Merseguer & Campos, 2003; Moreno & Simonetta, 2004; Nariman, et al., 2008; Lopez-Grao Juan Pablo, et al., 2002; López-Grao Juan Pablo, et al., 2004; Pekka, 2001; Peter & Rob, 2000; D. B. Petriu & Murray, 2004, 2007; D. C. Petriu & Xin, 2000; Ping & C., 2003; Rasha & Dorina, 2008; Rob, 1998; Sabri & Thomas, 2005; Sacha, et al., 2006; Salvatore, et al., 2004; Simona & Jose, 2007; Simona, et al., 2002; Smith, et al., 2005; Vahid, 2008a, 2008b, 2008c, 2010a, 2010b, 2010c, 2011; Vahid, et al., 2006, 2008, 2009; Vincenzo & Raffaela, 2001, 2002; Cortellessa Vittorio, et al., 2005; Cortellessa Vittorio & Raffaela, 2000; Cortellessaa Vittorio & Raffaela, 2002)
State diagram:	(Anil & M., 2000; Canevet, et al., 2003; Christoph, et al., 2002; Distefano, et al., 2005; Gomez-Martinez Elena & Jose, 2005; Gómez-Martínez Elena & José, 2006; Hui & C., 2005; Jose, et al., 2000a, 2000d; Jose, et al., 2002; Cooper Kendra, et al., 2003; Merseguer & Campos, 2003; Moreno & Simonetta, 2004; Oliveira, et al., 2007; Lopez-Grao Juan Pablo, et al., 2002; López-Grao Juan Pablo, et al., 2004; Pekka, 2001; Pete & Rob, 2000; Peter & Rob, 2000; Petri, et al., 2005; Raffaela & Vittorio, 2000; Rasha & Dorina, 2008; Sabri & Thomas, 2005; Salvatore, et al., 2004; Simona & Jose, 2007; Simona, et al., 2002; Stephen & Leila, 2005; Wet & Pieter, 2005)
Use-case diagram:	(Distefano, et al., 2005; Fried, 2000; Jose, et al., 2000d; Merseguer & Campos, 2003; Lopez-Grao Juan Pablo, et al., 2002; López-Grao Juan Pablo, et al., 2004; Rasha & Dorina, 2008; Sacha, et al., 2006; Simonetta & Moreno, 2003a, 2005; Vincenzo & Raffaela, 2002; Cortellessa Vittorio, et al., 2005; Cortellessaa Vittorio & Raffaela, 2000)
Other:	(Alexander, et al., 2006; Dorin & Murray, 2002; Hui & C., 2005; Lukas, et al., 2009; Simonetta, et al., 2003; Steffen, et al., 2008)

Figure 9. Types of output models generated

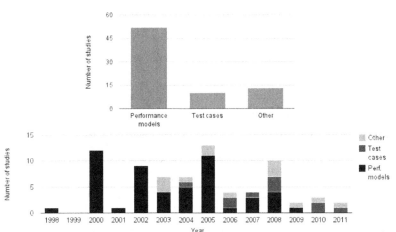

Performance models:	(Ahmad, 2004; Andre & Paolo, 2007; Andrea, 2005; Anil & M., 2000; Bertolino, et al., 2002; Canevet, et al., 2004; Canevet, et al., 2003; Distefano, et al., 2005; Dorin & Murray, 2002; Dorina, 2000; Gomez-Martinez Elena & Jose, 2005; Gómez-Martínez Elena & José, 2006; Fried, 2000; Gu Gordon & Petriu, 2005; Hassan & A., 2000; Hui & C., 2005; James & Wolfgang, 2003; Jing, et al., 2003; Jose, et al., 2000a, 2000b, 2000d; Jose, et al., 2002; Cooper Kendra, et al., 2003; Lukas, et al., 2009; Mathias, et al., 2008; Mirco & Stephen, 2008; Murray, et al., 2005; Oliveira, et al., 2007; Lopez-Grao Juan Pablo, et al., 2002; López-Grao Juan Pablo, et al., 2004; Pekka, 2001; Pete & Rob, 2000; Peter & Rob, 2000; Petri, et al., 2005; D. B. Petriu & Murray, 2004; D. C. Petriu & Hui, 2002; D. C. Petriu & Xin, 2000; Raffaela & Vittorio, 2000; Rasha & Dorina, 2008; Rob, 1998; Simona & Jose, 2007; Simona, et al., 2002; Simonetta & Moreno, 2005; Smith, et al., 2005; Spiteri, 2008; Stephen & Leila, 2005; Vincenzo & Raffaela, 2002; Cortellessa Vittorio & Raffaela, 2000; Cortellessaa Vittorio & Raffaela, 2002; Wet & Pieter, 2005)(Gu Gordon & C., 2002; Cortellessa Vittorio, et al., 2004)
Test cases:	(Oliveira, et al., 2007; Sacha, et al., 2006; Vahid, 2008b, 2008c, 2010a, 2010b, 2011; Vahid, et al., 2006, 2008; Cortellessa Vittorio & Maurizio, 2004)
Other:	(Cooper Kendra, et al., 2003; Mathias & Jendrik, 2008; Moreno & Simonetta, 2004; Nariman, et al., 2008; QuYang, et al., 2006; Sabri & Thomas, 2005; Simonetta, et al., 2003; Simonetta & Moreno, 2003a, 2003b; Steffen, et al., 2008; Vahid, et al., 2009; Cortellessa Vittorio, et al., 2005)

Focusing on performance models as output artifacts, different types of performance models have been used and/or proposed (as shown in Figure 10). The top three performance models are: (1) Queuing Network (QN) and variants, (2) Petri Net (PN) and variants, and (3) Performance Evaluation Process Algebra (PEPA).

Various variants of QN included: layered QN (LQN) (e.g., Andrea, 2005), Multi-Class QN (MCQN) (Lukas, et al., 2009; Simonetta & Moreno, 2005), Extended QN Model (EQNM) (Vincenzo & Raffaela, 2002; Cortellessa Vittorio & Raffaela, 2000; Cortellessaa Vittorio & Raffaela, 2002), and Augmented QN (AQN) (Pekka, 2001). Various variants of PN included: Stochas-

tic PN (SPN), Generalized Stochastic PN (GSPN) (Gomez-Martinez Elena & Jose, 2005; Gómez-Martínez Elena & José, 2006; Jose, et al., 2002; Peter & Rob, 2000; Simona & Jose, 2007), Labelled Generalized Stochastic PN (LGSPN) (López-Grao Juan Pablo, et al., 2004; Simona, et al., 2002), Colored PN (CPN) (Spiteri, 2008), and Object PN (OPN) (Anil, 2000).

The "other" types of performance models include: a custom-built time model (Vahid, 2008a), Core Scenario Model (CSM) (Petriu & Murray, 2004, 2007), Finite-State Processes (FSP) (Bennett, 2004), Generalized Semi-Markov Process (GSMP) (Christoph, et al., 2002), and Program

Figure 10. Types of performance models generated

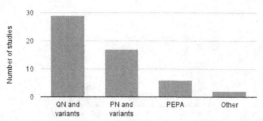

Queuing Network (QN) and variants:	(Ahmad, 2004; Andre & Paolo, 2007; Andrea, 2005; Bertolino, et al., 2002; Dorin & Murray, 2002; Dorina, 2000; Fried, 2000; Gu Gordon & C., 2002; Gu Gordon & Petriu, 2005; Hassan & A., 2000; Hui & C., 2005; James & Wolfgang, 2003; Jing, et al., 2003; Cooper Kendra, et al., 2003; Lukas, et al., 2009; Mathias, et al., 2008; Murray, et al., 2005; Pekka, 2001; D. B. Petriu & Murray, 2004; D. C. Petriu & Hui, 2002; D. C. Petriu & Xin, 2000; Raffaela & Vittorio, 2000; Rasha & Dorina, 2008; Simonetta & Moreno, 2005; Smith, et al., 2005; Vincenzo & Raffaela, 2002; Cortellessa Vittorio, et al., 2004; Cortellessa Vittorio & Raffaela, 2000; Cortellessaa Vittorio & Raffaela, 2002)
Petri Net (PN) and variants:	(Anil & M., 2000; Distefano, et al., 2005; Gomez-Martinez Elena & Jose, 2005; Gómez-Martínez Elena & José, 2006; Jose, et al., 2000a, 2000b, 2000d; Jose, et al., 2002; Murray, et al., 2005; Oliveira, et al., 2007; Lopez-Grao Juan Pablo, et al., 2002; López-Grao Juan Pablo, et al., 2004; Peter & Rob, 2000; D. B. Petriu & Murray, 2004; Simona & Jose, 2007; Simona, et al., 2002; Spiteri, 2008)
Performance Evaluation Process Algebra (PEPA):	(Canevet, et al., 2004; Canevet, et al., 2003; Mirco & Stephen, 2008; Pete & Rob, 2000; Rob, 1998; Stephen & Leila, 2005)
Other:	(Petri, et al., 2005; Wet & Pieter, 2005)

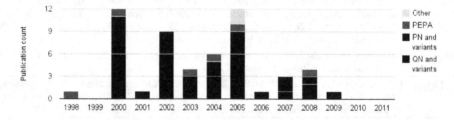

Evaluation and Review Technique (PERT) models (Vahid, 2010c).

Notable findings: Based on the annual trend of output models generated used in studies (shown in Figure 10), we can see that, in recent years, mix of the facets are more diverse than earlier years. Both QN and PN family of models have been used across all the years.

6.7. Model Annotation Languages (RQ 1.7)

To specify various performance-related properties on UML models (e.g., workload and timing of a message in a sequence diagram), which will be provided as inputs to UML-SPE techniques, studies have used either standard UML annotation languages (i.e., UML profiles) or have proposed custom-made annotation languages. Figure 11 shows the breakdown of the model annotation languages used in the studies.

Figure 11. Types of model annotation languages

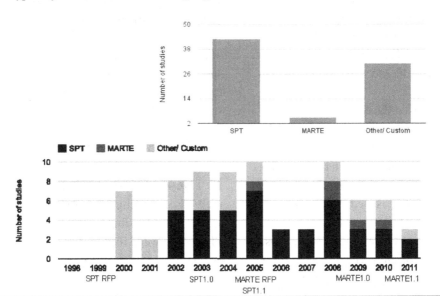

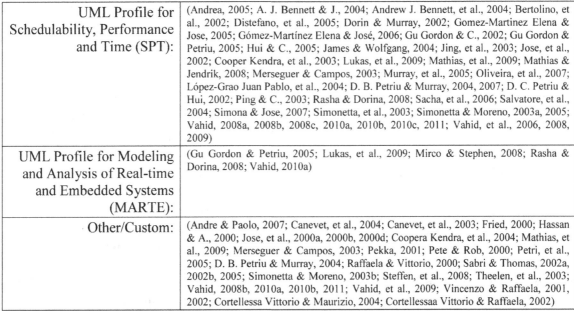

UML Profile for Schedulability, Performance and Time (SPT):	(Andrea, 2005; A. J. Bennett & J., 2004; Andrew J. Bennett, et al., 2004; Bertolino, et al., 2002; Distefano, et al., 2005; Dorin & Murray, 2002; Gomez-Martinez Elena & Jose, 2005; Gómez-Martínez Elena & José, 2006; Gu Gordon & C., 2002; Gu Gordon & Petriu, 2005; Hui & C., 2005; James & Wolfgang, 2004; Jing, et al., 2003; Jose, et al., 2002; Cooper Kendra, et al., 2003; Lukas, et al., 2009; Mathias, et al., 2009; Mathias & Jendrik, 2008; Merseguer & Campos, 2003; Murray, et al., 2005; Oliveira, et al., 2007; López-Grao Juan Pablo, et al., 2004; D. B. Petriu & Murray, 2004, 2007; D. C. Petriu & Hui, 2002; Ping & C., 2003; Rasha & Dorina, 2008; Sacha, et al., 2006; Salvatore, et al., 2004; Simona & Jose, 2007; Simonetta, et al., 2003; Simonetta & Moreno, 2003a, 2005; Vahid, 2008a, 2008b, 2008c, 2010a, 2010b, 2010c, 2011; Vahid, et al., 2006, 2008, 2009)
UML Profile for Modeling and Analysis of Real-time and Embedded Systems (MARTE):	(Gu Gordon & Petriu, 2005; Lukas, et al., 2009; Mirco & Stephen, 2008; Rasha & Dorina, 2008; Vahid, 2010a)
Other/Custom:	(Andre & Paolo, 2007; Canevet, et al., 2004; Canevet, et al., 2003; Fried, 2000; Hassan & A., 2000; Jose, et al., 2000a, 2000b, 2000d; Coopera Kendra, et al., 2004; Mathias, et al., 2009; Merseguer & Campos, 2003; Pekka, 2001; Pete & Rob, 2000; Petri, et al., 2005; D. B. Petriu & Murray, 2004; Raffaela & Vittorio, 2000; Sabri & Thomas, 2002a, 2002b, 2005; Simonetta & Moreno, 2003b; Steffen, et al., 2008; Theelen, et al., 2003; Vahid, 2008b, 2010a, 2010b, 2011; Vahid, et al., 2009; Vincenzo & Raffaela, 2001, 2002; Cortellessa Vittorio & Maurizio, 2004; Cortellessaa Vittorio & Raffaela, 2002)

The UML Profile for Schedulability, Performance and Time (SPT) (OMG, 2005) was the first effort by the world-wide UML consortium, the Object Management Group (OMG), to enable UML users to specify time and performance-related properties on UML models. The request for proposal (RFP) asking for the UML SPT profile for was issued by the Analysis and Design Platform Task-Force of the OMG In March of 1999 (OMG, 1999). Two versions of SPT were released in response to that RFP so far, version 1.0 (OMG, 2003) on September 2003 and version 1.1 (OMG, 2005) on January 2005.

The UML Profile for Modeling and Analysis of Real-Time and Embedded Systems (MARTE) (OMG, 2011) has been another effort by the

OMG for performance modeling and several other purposes. The Request For Proposal (RFP) for MARTE was issued in 2005 (OMG, 2005). Two versions of MARTE have been released so far: version 1.0 on November 2009 and version 1.1 on June 2011.

43 studies have used the SPT profile as their annotation languages, while 5 studies have used the MARTE profile, likely because it is more recent than SPT. In the annual trend shown in Figure 11, we have specified also the times when the requests for proposals (RFP) were issued and also release time of each version of SPT and MARTE to assess whether there is any correlation among those dates and the number of studies using each profile.

31 studies used other custom-made types of model annotation languages, e.g., the Performance-enabled Web-Service Definition Language (P-WSDL) (Andre & Paolo, 2007), annotations using PEPA (Canevet, et al., 2004), Business Process Modeling Notation (BPMN) (Mathias, et al., 2009), performance analysis profile for UML (pa-UML) (Merseguer & Campos, 2003), and real-time UML (RT-UML) (Cortellessa Vittorio & Maurizio, 2004).

Notable findings: The observations are the followings: (1) several (five) papers appeared in 2002 even before the first version (1.0) of SPT was released, and (2) usage of SPT continues through the years.

6.8. Application Domains (RQ 1.8)

As Figure 12 shows, most studies have discussed methods for "generic" application domains (i.e., not specific to any specific domain). For studies focusing on specific domains, the following three domains were the most frequent, in order: real-time systems (in 12 studies), mobile/handheld (in 4 studies), and embedded systems (in 2 studies). The following "other" domains have also been studied: parallel and distributed applications (Pekka, 2001; Raffaela & Vittorio, 2000; Sabri & Thomas, 2002a, 2002b, 2005), agent-based systems (Jose,

et al., 2000d), and enterprise information systems (James & Wolfgang, 2004).

Notable findings: While generic application domains are dominating, the following three specific domains have also received noticeable focus: real-time systems, mobile/handheld (in 4 studies), and embedded systems.

6.9. Methods of Evaluation (RQ 1.9)

As Figure 13 shows, to evaluate the proposed methods and techniques, most papers (71%) assessed the "feasibility" of the proposed ideas. 11 studies went further and used the following evaluation methods:

- Comparing the test results with results of testing based on operational profiles (Vahid, 2008b, 2008c, 2010a, 2011; Vahid, et al., 2006, 2008).
- Comparing the predicted measures with actual measures (Lukas, et al., 2009; Sabri & Thomas, 2005; Vahid, et al., 2009).
- Prediction of performance properties (Jose, et al., 2000b; Stephen & Leıla, 2005).

As mentioned previously, due to the mature nature of the UML-SPE area in terms of the proposed techniques and approaches, it is fair to expect more studies in the future that would use methods similar to the above three approaches.

Notable findings: Most studies used the "feasibility" approach (perhaps the easiest way possible) as their methods of evaluation.

6.10. Type/Scale of the Software Systems Under Analysis (RQ 1.10)

We next classified the primary studies by the type/scale of the software systems under analysis. Results are shown in Figure 14. It is clear that experimental systems developed in the academia are the majority (used in 62 studies). 9 and 8 studies, respectively, used open-source or commercial

Figure 12. Application domains

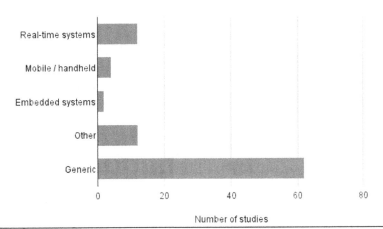

Real-time systems:	(Bertolino, et al., 2002; Vahid, 2008a, 2008b, 2008c, 2010a, 2010b, 2010c, 2011; Vahid, et al., 2006, 2008, 2009; Cortellessa Vittorio & Maurizio, 2004)
Mobile/handheld:	(Lukas, et al., 2009; Simonetta & Moreno, 2003b; Vincenzo & Raffaela, 2001, 2002)
Embedded systems:	(Lukas, et al., 2009; Petri, et al., 2005)
Other:	(Bertolino, et al., 2002; Jose, et al., 2000b, 2000d; Cooper Kendra, et al., 2003; Mathias, et al., 2008; Nariman, et al., 2008; Pekka, 2001; Peter & Rob, 2000; Raffaela & Vittorio, 2000; Sabri & Thomas, 2002b, 2005; Cortellessa Vittorio, et al., 2005)
Generic:	(Ahmad, 2004; Alexander, et al., 2006; Andre & Paolo, 2007; Andrea, 2005; A. J. Bennett & J., 2004; Andrew J. Bennett, et al., 2004; Canevet, et al., 2004; Canevet, et al., 2003; Christoph, ct al., 2002; Distefano, et al., 2005; Dorin & Murray, 2002; Dorina, 2000; Gomez-Martinez Elena & Jose, 2005; Gómez-Martínez Elena & José, 2006; Gu Gordon & Petriu, 2005; Hassan & A., 2000; Hui & C., 2005; James & Wolfgang, 2003; Jing, et al., 2003; Jose, et al., 2000a; Jose, et al., 2002; Coopera Kendra, et al., 2004; Cooper Kendra, et al., 2003; Mathias, et al., 2009; Mathias & Jendrik, 2008; Merseguer & Campos, 2003; Mirco & Stephen, 2008; Murray, et al., 2005; Oliveira, et al., 2007; Lopez-Grao Juan Pablo, et al., 2002; López-Grao Juan Pablo, et al., 2004; Pete & Rob, 2000; D. B. Petriu & Murray, 2004, 2007; D. C. Petriu & Hui, 2002; D. C. Petriu & Xin, 2000; Ping & C., 2003; QuYang, et al., 2006; Rasha & Dorina, 2008; Sacha, et al., 2006; Simona & Jose, 2007; Simona, et al., 2002; Simonetta & Moreno, 2003a, 2005; Smith, et al., 2005; Spiteri, 2008; Steffen, et al., 2008; Cortellessa Vittorio, et al., 2005; Cortellessa Vittorio & Raffaela, 2000; Cortellessaa Vittorio & Raffaela, 2002)(Anil & M., 2000; Fried, 2000; Gu Gordon & C., 2002; Miguel, et al., 2000; Moreno & Simonetta, 2004; Rob, 1998; Salvatore, et al., 2004; Simonetta, et al., 2003; Steffen, et al., 2008; Theelen, et al., 2003; Cortellessa Vittorio, et al., 2004; Wet & Pieter, 2005)

software for evaluation of their methods. We feel this opens up a fertile opportunity for future work to evaluate the UML-SPE techniques proposed on large-scale commercial software systems.

The following open-source software are several examples used in studies: the server-side POP3 protocol (used in López-Grao Juan Pablo, et al., 2004), MPEG-4 decoder library (used in QuYang, et al., 2006), an MP3 library (QuYang,

et al., 2006), Domain Name Service (DNS) (Cooper Kendra, et al., 2003), and SCAPS (a SCADA-based Power System) (Vahid, 2008a, 2008b, 2008c, 2010a, 2010b; Vahid, et al., 2006, 2008, 2009).

The following commercial software systems or protocols have been used in the studies: Digital Broadcasting Video (DVB) protocol (used in Lukas, et al., 2009), Siemens medical solutions

Figure 13. Methods of evaluation

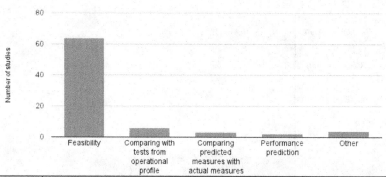

Feasibility:	(Ahmad, 2004; Alexander, et al., 2006; Andre & Paolo, 2007; Andrea, 2005; A. J. Bennett & J., 2004; Andrew J. Bennett, et al., 2004; Bertolino, et al., 2002; Canevet, et al., 2004; Canevet, et al., 2003; Christoph, et al., 2002; Dorina, 2000; Gu Gordon & Petriu, 2005; Hassan & A., 2000; Hui & C., 2005; James & Wolfgang, 2003, 2004; Jing, et al., 2003; Jose, et al., 2000a, 2000d; Jose, et al., 2002; Coopera Kendra, et al., 2004; Cooper Kendra, et al., 2003; Mathias & Jendrik, 2008; Mirco & Stephen, 2008; Murray, et al., 2005; Oliveira, et al., 2007; Lopez-Grao Juan Pablo, et al., 2002; López-Grao Juan Pablo, et al., 2004; Pete & Rob, 2000; Peter & Rob, 2000; Petri, et al., 2005; D. B. Petriu & Murray, 2004, 2007; D. C. Petriu & Hui, 2002; D. C. Petriu & Xin, 2000; QuYang, et al., 2006; Rasha & Dorina, 2008; Sabri & Thomas, 2002a; Sacha, et al., 2006; Simona & Jose, 2007; Simona, et al., 2002; Simonetta & Moreno, 2005; Smith, et al., 2005; Spiteri, 2008; Vahid, 2008a; Vincenzo & Raffaela, 2002; Cortellessa Vittorio, et al., 2005; Cortellessa Vittorio & Maurizio, 2004; Cortellessa Vittorio & Raffaela, 2000; Cortellessaa Vittorio & Raffaela, 2002)(Anil & M., 2000; Bertolino, et al., 2002; Distefano, et al., 2005; Dorin & Murray, 2002; Fried, 2000; Gu Gordon & C., 2002; Mathias, et al., 2008; Pekka, 2001; Rob, 1998; Sabri & Thomas, 2002b; Simonetta & Moreno, 2003b; Theelen, et al., 2003; Vahid, 2010c; Wet & Pieter, 2005)
Comparing with tests from operational profile:	(Vahid, 2008b, 2008c, 2010a, 2011; Vahid, et al., 2006, 2008)
Comparing predicted measures with actual measures:	(Lukas, et al., 2009; Sabri & Thomas, 2005; Vahid, et al., 2009)
Performance prediction:	(Jose, et al., 2000b; Stephen & Leıla, 2005)
Other:	(Mathias, et al., 2009; Ping & C., 2003; Steffen, et al., 2008; Vahid, 2010b)

(used in Sacha, et al., 2006), a hierarchical cellular network (Stephen & Leıla, 2005), alternating bit protocol (Peter & Rob, 2000), NASA's Earth Observing System (EOS) (Cortellessa Vittorio, et al., 2005), Quake2 3D game (QuYang, et al., 2006), an efficient short remote operations (ESRO) transport protocol (Wet & Pieter, 2005), and a telecom application (Fried, 2000).

6.11. Tools Presented in Papers (RQ 1.11)

For this RQ, we wanted to know the number of tools presented in the papers. Note that if a paper had only "used" an existing tool and had not presented a new tool, it was not counted for this RQ. 28 studies (31%) presented (new) tools. It was important to know how many tools were

Figure 14. Type/scale of the software systems under analysis

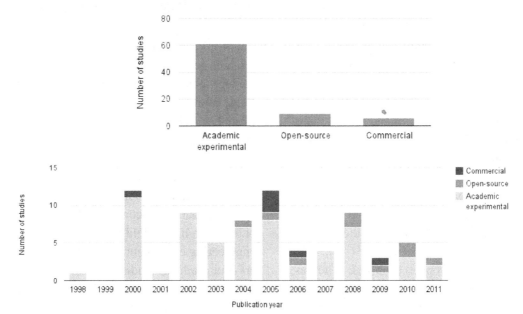

Academic experimental:	(Ahmad, 2004; Alexander, et al., 2006; Andre & Paolo, 2007; A. J. Bennett & J., 2004; Andrew J. Bennett, et al., 2004; Bertolino, et al., 2002; Canevet, et al., 2003; Christoph, et al., 2002; Distefano, et al., 2005; Dorin & Murray, 2002; Dorina, 2000; Gu Gordon & Petriu, 2005; Hassan & A., 2000; Hui & C., 2005; Jing, et al., 2003; Jose, et al., 2000b, 2000d; Coopera Kendra, et al., 2004; Cooper Kendra, et al., 2003; Murray, et al., 2005; Oliveira, et al., 2007; Pete & Rob, 2000; Petri, et al., 2005; D. B. Petriu & Murray, 2004, 2007; D. C. Petriu & Hui, 2002; D. C. Petriu & Xin, 2000; Rasha & Dorina, 2008; Sabri & Thomas, 2005; Salvatore, et al., 2004; Simona & Jose, 2007; Simona, et al., 2002; Simonetta & Moreno, 2003a, 2003b, 2005; Smith, et al., 2005; Spiteri, 2008; Steffen, et al., 2008; Vahid, 2008a, 2008b, 2008c, 2010a, 2010b, 2011; Vahid, et al., 2006, 2008; Vincenzo & Raffaela, 2002; Cortellessa Vittorio & Maurizio, 2004; Cortellessa Vittorio & Raffaela, 2000; Cortellessaa Vittorio & Raffaela, 2002)(Anil & M., 2000; Fried, 2000; Gu Gordon & C., 2002; Miguel, et al., 2000; Pekka, 2001; Raffaela & Vittorio, 2000; Rob, 1998; Sabri & Thomas, 2002b; Salvatore, et al., 2004; Theelen, et al., 2003; Vahid, 2010c)
Open-source:	(López-Grao Juan Pablo, et al., 2004; QuYang, et al., 2006; Vahid, 2008a, 2008b, 2010a, 2010b, 2011; Vahid, et al., 2009; Cortellessa Vittorio, et al., 2005)
Commercial:	(Lukas, et al., 2009; Peter & Rob, 2000; Sacha, et al., 2006; Stephen & Leila, 2005; Cortellessa Vittorio, et al., 2005; Wet & Pieter, 2005)

available for download for usage by other researchers. Only 20 of those 28 tools were available for download (either free or commercial license). The exact URL to download each of those tools have been recorded in our online repository (Garousi, et al., 2012). Among the most notable tools are the followings:

- UML-PSI (Moreno & Simonetta, 2004; Simonetta & Moreno, 2003a, 2003b): UML performance simulator.
- U2Q (Lukas, et al., 2009): a tool to covert UML models to queuing network models.
- ArgoSPE (Gomez-Martinez Elena & Jose, 2005) and ArgoPerformance (Distefano, et al., 2005): two UML-SPE plug-ins for the popular ArgoUML tool.

- GARUS (Genetic Algorithm-based test Requirement tool for real-time distribUted Systems) (Vahid, 2008a, 2008b, 2008c, 2010a, 2010b; Vahid, et al., 2006, 2008, 2009): a tool to generate performance test cases from UML models.
- SysXplorer (Alexander, et al., 2006): a tool for performance analysis and simulation of UML/SysML models for embedded systems and systems-on-chip.
- UML/PEPA Bridge (Mirco & Stephen, 2008): a tool for automatic extraction of PEPA performance models from UML activity diagrams annotated with the MARTE profile.
- Performance Prophet (Sabri & Thomas, 2005): a tool for performance prediction of parallel and distributed applications on cluster and grid architectures.
- UML2AnyLogic (Mathias & Jendrik, 2008): a tool to covert UML models to models to be fed into the *AnyLogic* simulation software tool.
- SHESim (Theelen, et al., 2003): a tool for UML-based performance modeling.

8. TRENDS, BIBLIOMETRICS, AND DEMOGRAPHICS (RQ 2)

This section presents results related to our second research question (RQ 2). It aims at characterizing demographics and bibliometrics of the UML-SPE field. Bibliometrics comprises a set of methods to analyze scientific and technological literature (Soloway, et al., 1988). In particular, it utilizes quantitative analysis and statistics to describe patterns of publication within a given field or body of literature. Bibliometric data such as the ranking of authors according to the number of their publication in the field of software performance engineering can potentially be used by researchers and graduate students as an entry point for literature search and establishing promising contacts and, perhaps, collaborations. The answers to sub-questions under RQ 2 are described in the following one by one.

7.1. Publication Count by Year (RQ 2.1)

Figure 15 shows the annual publication trend of the primary studies. It is interesting to point out that we have also published another SM study on UML books recently (Garousi, 2011), from which we have extracted the publication trend of UML books and have also shown it in Figure 15 for comparison purposes.

Figure 15. Publication count by year

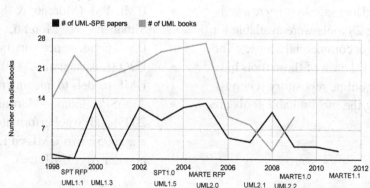

Similar to what was done in Section 6.7 (Model Annotation Languages, RQ 1.7), in the annual trend shown in Figure 15, we have also specified the release times of major versions of the UML specification and also its SPT and MARTE profiles. The rationale is to assess whether there is any correlation among those dates and the number of studies in those certain times.

Notable findings: The annual trend of number of papers has had a decline in recent years. This is brining the question that whether there is very little left in the field to be "solved". It is quite alarming that number of UML books is also decreasing in recent years. We will discuss the implications of this observation in Section 8.1.

7.2. Publication Count by Venue Type (RQ 2.2)

Figure 16 shows the distribution of the 90 selected publications over types of publication venues. More than half of the selected publications are conference (34 studies, 37%) and workshop (32 studies, 35%) papers, followed by journal articles (15 studies, 16%). Other publication types include five symposium papers, two books, one paper in forums, and one technical report.

To put the distribution shown in Figure 16 into context, we are showing in Figure 17 the frequency of studies per venue type from two recent SM studies, one in the area of Web-application testing (Garousi, et al., 2012) and the other in the area of graphical user interface (GUI) testing (Banerjee, et al., 2012). We can notice slight differences between the distribution of Figure 16 and the two distributions shown in Figure 17. It

Figure 16. Frequency of studies per venue type

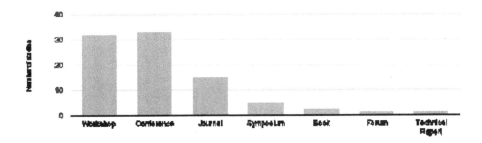

Figure 17. Frequency of studies per venue type from two other recent SM studies

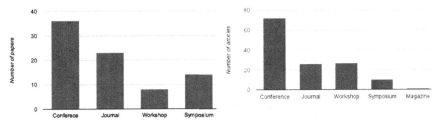

SM of Web-application testing (Garousi, et al., 2012)

SM of graphical user interface (GUI) testing (Banerjee, et al., 2012)

seems in the current SM (UML-SPE), the ratio of workshop papers are more than the two other selected topics. This is most probably due to the fact that a large ratio of papers in UML-SPE has been published in the International Workshop on Software and Performance (WOSP), to be discussed further in Section 7.5.

Notable findings: Conference and workshop papers are the majority. This is inline with what one would expect informally since conference and workshop venues are considered the quickest way to disseminate research results.

7.3. Citation Count vs. Publication Year (RQ 2.3)

RQ 2.3 is intended to identify the citation count by year and evaluate the hypothesis that whether older papers necessarily receive more citations. The citation numbers were extracted on July 25, 2012 from the Google Scholar online service. We considered two types of metrics for this analysis: (1) absolute (total) value of number of citations,

and (2) normalized number of citations that, for a given paper p, is defined as follows:

$$NormalizedCitations(p) = \frac{TotalCitations(p)}{2012 - PublicationYear(p)}$$

For example, the study (Simona, et al., 2002) has 255 total citations as of this writing and was published in 2002. Thus, its normalized citations are calculated as:

$$NormalizedCitations([37]) = \frac{255}{2012 - 2002} = 25.5$$

Compared to the absolute value, the normalized metric essentially returns the average number of citations of a paper per year, since its publication year. Figure 18 visualizes the absolute (total) citation count, in both regular and log scales, and also the normalized citation count of each paper versus its publication year. Each point in these two figures corresponds to a single primary study.

Figure 18. Citation count vs. publication year of primary studies

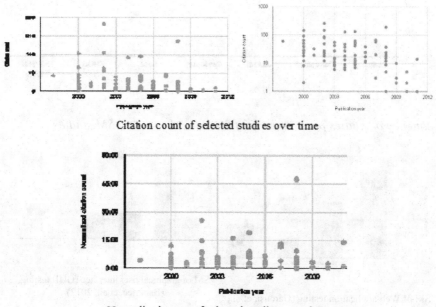

Citation count of selected studies over time

Normalized count of selected studies over time

To analytically assess the above hypothesis that whether older papers necessarily receive more citations, we calculated the Pearson correlation coefficient for both data sets. The correlation coefficients for absolute and normalized citation count are -0.25 and 0.06, respectively, which denote that there is a weak support for the above hypothesis using the absolute citation count metric, while there is almost no correlation support using the normalized citation count metric.

Notable findings: Using the absolute citation count metric, we found that, to some extent, older papers in this domain receive more citations.

7.4. Top-Cited Studies (RQ 2.4)

The list of top 10 cited papers are shown in Table 3 (ordered by absolute number of citations). The mapping of each article based on our classification scheme (Section 5.1) is also shown. We can see that most of the top-cited papers are solu-

tion proposals and contribute SPE techniques (methods). The first-highly cited paper is a 2002 paper (Simona, et al., 2002). It is a "solution proposal" which proposed a method that translates UML sequence diagrams and state-charts into analyzable Petri-net models. The second-highly cited paper (with 109 citations) is a 2008 paper (Steffen, et al., 2008). In this paper, the Palladio Component Model (PCM) is used to represent the component-based software architectures in a parametric way. The third-highly cited paper (145 citations) is a 2002 paper (Petriu & Hui, 2002). This paper reports a new graph-grammar-based method for transformation of UML models into Layered Queuing Network models.

Notable findings: According to Figure 18, the top 10 papers have significantly more citations than the rest of the papers.

Table 3. Top 10 cited papers

Article	Number of citations	Publication year	Research type	Type of Paper-Contribution Facet	Type of SPE approach
(Simona, et al., 2002)	255	2002	Solution proposal	Method	Model Transformation
(Steffen, et al., 2008)	190	2008	Validation research	Method	Model Transformation
(D. C. Petriu & Hui, 2002)	145	2002	Solution proposal	Method	Modeling, Analysis and prediction
(Cortellessa Vittorio & Raffaela, 2000)	144	2000	Solution proposal	Method	Model Transformation, Analysis and prediction
(Murray, et al., 2005)	132	2005	Validation research	Method, model	Model Transformation, Analysis and prediction
(López-Grao Juan Pablo, et al., 2004)	128	2004	Solution proposal	Method, tool	Model Transformation
(Peter & Rob, 2000)	91	2000	Validation research	Method, tool	Modeling, Model Transformation
(Cortellessaa Vittorio & Raffaela, 2002)	86	2002	Validation research	Method, tool	Model Transformation
(Anil & M., 2000)	89	2000	Solution proposal	Method, tool	Model Transformation
(Gu Gordon & C., 2002)	78	2002	Solution proposal	Method, tool	Model Transformation

Figure 19. Citation count of selected studies distributed over venues with at least two publications

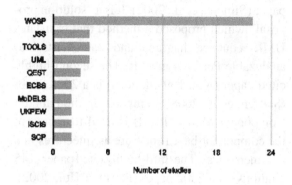

7.5. Top Venues (RQ 2.5)

Figure 19 shows the list of top publication venues based on their number of publications. Only venues with at least two publications are shown. The most popular publication venue is the International Workshop on Software and Performance (WOSP), which is the venue of 22 papers (24%) in our study. Although WOSP focuses on different performance engineering topics, a good number of UML-SPE studies have been published in that venue. The other top venues are the Journal of Systems and Software (JSS), the International Conference on Modeling Techniques and Tools for Computer Performance Evaluation (TOOLS), International Conference on the Unified Modeling Language (UML), and International Conference on the Quantitative Evaluation of Systems (QEST).

Notable findings: WOSP by far has been the main venue for papers in this area.

7.6. Average Citation Count by Venue Type (RQ 2.6)

In this RQ, we analyze the relationship between average citation count for different venue types (e.g., conferences, journals and workshops). The rationale to analyze these data is to evaluate the hypothesis that whether there is a difference in number of citations to studies appearing in different venue types. Figure 20 shows that data.

Workshop publications have the highest average citation count, followed by journals, conference papers and books. Publications in workshops have the highest total citation numbers. It seems that the reason for this observation is due to the fact that the WOSP workshop has published a large ratio of the papers in this area (22 studies) and those studies have been cited on average more than other studies.

It would also be interesting to analyze the number of studies by venue type versus average citation count for each study (publications), by combining data from Section 7.2 (RQ 2.2) and this section. The data have been visualized as a scatter plot in Figure 21. We can see that books and papers published in forums (only one) have the highest relative average citation count, with 11.75 and 11.0 average citations, respectively. On the other hand, conference and workshop papers

Figure 20. Average citation count by venue type

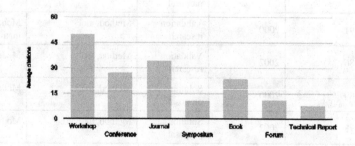

Figure 21. Scatter plot of number of studies by venue type versus average citation count for each study

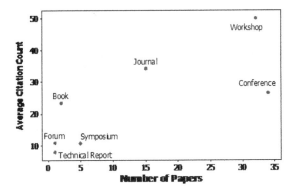

have the lowest relative average citation count, with 0.78 and 1.56 average citations, respectively.

Notable findings: There are wide differences among the number of studies by venue type and average citation count for each study in the each venue type.

To put the distribution shown in Figure 20 into context, we are showing in Figure 22 the average citation count per venue type from two recent SM studies, one in the area of Web-application testing (Garousi, et al., 2012) and the other in the area of Graphical User Interface (GUI) testing (Banerjee, et al., 2012).

Similar to the comparison conducted in Section 7.2, we can again notice slight differences between the distribution of Figure 20 and the two distributions shown in Figure 22. It seems in the current

SM (UML-SPE), the average citation count for workshop papers are more than the two other selected topics. This is most probably due to the fact that a large ratio of papers in UML-SPE has been published in the International Workshop on Software and Performance (WOSP), and those papers have received relatively high citations.

7.7. Top Authors (RQ 2.7)

Figure 23 shows the ranking of researchers who have authored (or co-authored) two or more of the primary studies. Dorina Petriu, affiliated with the Carleton University (in Canada) is the most active author with a total of thirteen publications (Dorin & Murray, 2002; Dorina, 2000; Gu Gordon & C., 2002; Gu Gordon & Petriu, 2005; Hui, 2005; Jing, et al., 2003; Murray, et al., 2005; Petriu & Murray, 2004, 2007; Petriu & Hui, 2002; Petriu & Xin, 2000; Ping, 2003; Rasha & Dorina, 2008). The 2nd ranked author is Jose Merseguer with 12 publications (Gomez-Martinez Elena & Jose, 2005; Gómez-Martínez Elena & José, 2006; Jose, et al., 2000a, 2000c, 2000d; Jose, et al., 2002; Merseguer & Campos, 2003; Murray, et al., 2005; Lopez-Grao Juan Pablo, et al., 2002; López-Grao Juan Pablo, et al., 2004; Simona & Jose, 2007; Simona, et al., 2002) from the Universidad de Zaragoza (in Spain).

Notable findings: Authors from different nations have ranked in the top authors list.

Figure 22. Average citation count by venue type from two other recent SM studies

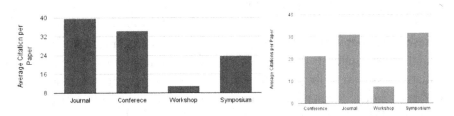

SM of Web-application testing (Garousi, et al., 2012)

SM of graphical user interface (GUI) testing (Banerjee, et al., 2012)

Figure 23. Top authors (with at least two publications)

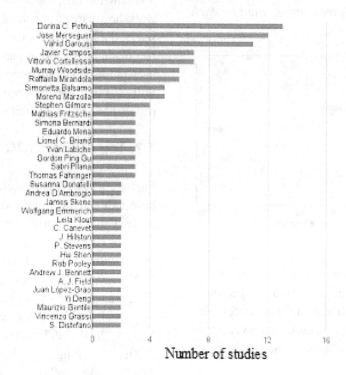

Number of studies

Figure 24. Types of author affiliations

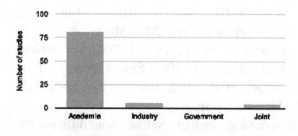

7.8. Author Affiliations (RQ 2.8)

Figure 24 shows the distribution of author affiliations. We defined four categories of affiliations: (1) universities, (2) industrial practitioners, (3) governmental research groups, and (4) collaborative work (joint research published by groups of authors affiliated with two or three different categories). Figure 24 indicates that publications where all authors are affiliated with academia (81 studies) are the most frequent in our set of selected studies. 4 studies were the result of academia-industry joint collaborations. None of the authors had affiliations with governmental R&D centers. Building critical academia-industry collaborations and applying UML-SPE techniques in industrial contexts is thus an exciting future area of pursuit worthy of consideration by existing and new researchers.

Notable findings: Academics are dominating the UML-SPE community. There is a need for involvement of more industrial researchers and practitioners.

7.9. Top Countries (RQ 2.9)

Figure 25 shows the ranking of the top country (based on author affiliations). If a study had authors from several countries, all those countries were counted. Since authors of a study can have affiliations from different countries, the sum of the numbers shown in the bar chart is larger than 90. As Figure 25 indicates, papers in this area have originated from only 16 countries across the

Figure 25. Researchers' affiliations by country

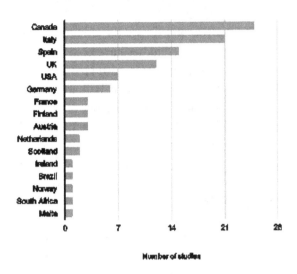

globe. Canada, Italy and Spain are the top three contributing countries, followed by UK, USA, Germany, Finland, Austria, Netherlands and Scotland. The majority of publications originate from North American and European countries generally. In this regard, our sample may be biased as we only searched for publications written in English.

Notable findings: North American and European nations are dominating the UML-SPE community.

We wanted to also know the extent of international collaborations in this area. Thirteen studies (14% of studies) were the result of international collaborations between the following countries:

- Spain, Italy (Jose, et al., 2002; Simona & Jose, 2007; Simona, et al., 2002).
- Germany, Ireland (Sacha, et al., 2006).
- France, Scotland (Stephen & Leila, 2005).
- France, UK (Mathias, et al., 2009).
- USA, Italy (Cortellessa Vittorio, et al., 2005; Cortellessa Vittorio & Raffaela, 2000).
- Canada, UK (Andrew J. Bennett, et al., 2004).
- USA, Italy, Spain (Smith, et al., 2005).

- Canada, Spain (Murray, et al., 2005).
- UK, Germany (Mathias & Jendrik, 2008).
- Canada, Norway (Vahid, et al., 2006).

9. DISCUSSIONS

Section 8.1 discusses the summary of findings, summary of trends, and implications of our SM. Section 8.2 discusses the potential threats to the validity of our study and steps we have taken to minimize or mitigate them.

8.1. Summary of Findings, Trends, and Implications

For RQ 1 (SM study), we answered eleven research questions (RQ 1.1 to RQ 1.11). For RQ 2 (trends, bibliometric and demographics), we answered nine research questions (RQ 2.1 to RQ 2.9). Below we summarize the main results of each RQ and discuss the implications of the findings for the research community and also practitioners:

- **RQ 1 (mapping of studies by contribution facet):** In terms of contribution facet, most of the primary studies (81%) proposed new techniques or improved an existing one. Only 1 and 3 studies presented new metrics and new processes, respectively. This denotes that either (1) there is a need for more work in these areas, or (2) the existing metrics and processes in this area are adequate to address the needs and challenges. To evaluate the latter, a more-in-depth SLR study is needed.
- **RQ 2 (mapping of studies by research facet):** In terms research approach, 47 papers were of type solution proposals, while 38 and 3 studies were classified under validation research and evaluation research) 3 studies have applied formal evaluation research techniques (e.g., controlled experiments). In keeping with similar efforts

in the software engineering research community (e.g., [124-126]), we view the more extensive application of such techniques as a worthy endeavour to pursue in future research in this area.

- **RQ 1.3 (types of SPE approach):** The ranking of proposed SPE activities in order were: (1) model transformation (61% of studies), (2) analysis and prediction (47%), (3) modeling (36%), (4) testing (10%), and (5) other (3%), e.g., performance tuning. While UML-based performance testing is an important and promising field of study (Vahid, 2008c, 2010b; Vahid, et al., 2008), this particular area has not received the deserved attention and focus in the community, and thus needs more work by the research community and practitioners.

- **RQ 1.4 (types of performance metrics used and evaluated):** The top three performance metrics used were: response time (32 studies), utilization (16 studies), and throughput (10 studies).

- **RQ 1.5 (input UML diagrams):** The top three input UML diagrams used were: sequence diagrams (49 studies), activity diagrams (35 studies), and deployment diagrams (34 studies).

- **RQ 1.6 (output models and artifact):** The top three types of output models and artifact were: performance models (58% of studies), test cases (11%), and other types (13%), e.g., performance failure probability. Since a small ratio of studies has focused on testing, the number of studies which generate test-cases is relatively small. Focusing on performance models as output artifacts, the ranking of the performance models were: (1) Queuing Network Models (QNM) and variants (32% of the studies), (2) Petri Net (PN) and variants (19%), (3) Performance Evaluation Process Algebra (PEPA) (7%), and (4) other (16%).

- **RQ 1.7 (model annotation languages):** 43 studies have used the UML SPT profile (OMG, 2005) as their annotation languages, while 5 studies have used the UML MARTE profile (OMG, 2011). The annual usage trend analysis reveals that usage of SPT continues through the years.

- **RQ 1.8 (application domains):** The following three application domains were the most frequent, in order: real-time systems (13% of studies), mobile/handheld (4%), and embedded systems (2%). Most studies (69%), however, have proposed methods for "generic" application domains (i.e., not particular to any specific domain). It would be logical to expect more domain-specific UML-SPE approaches in the coming years, as the challenges of different application domains are quite different from each other.

- **RQ 1.9 (methods of evaluation):** To evaluate the proposed methods and techniques, most papers (71%) assessed the "feasibility" of the proposed ideas. 11 studies went further and used the following evaluation methods:
  ◦ Comparing the test results with results of testing based on operational profiles.
  ◦ Comparing the predicted measures with actual measures.
  ◦ Prediction of performance properties.

Due to continuously maturing nature of the UML-SPE area, it is fair to expect a larger fraction of studies in the future that use methods similar to the above three approaches.

- **RQ 1.10 (type/scale of the software systems under analysis):** Our results showed that prototype or experimental systems developed in the academia are the majority (used in 62 studies). 9 and 8 studies used open-source or commercial software for evaluation of their methods. We feel this opens up a fertile opportunity for future work to evaluate the UML-SPE techniques proposed on large-scale commercial software systems.

- **RQ 1.11 (tools presented in papers):** Tool support is an important issue in all sub-fields of the software engineering. A "healthy" ratio of the primary studies (31%) presented 28 (new) tools. Only 20 of those 28 tools were available for download (either free or commercial license). Certainly, the authors encourage more efforts on developing additional industry-scale UML-SPE tools and also technology transfer of those tools to the industry.

- **RQ 2.1 (publication count by year):** The annual trend of number of papers has had a decline in recent years. This is brining the question that whether there is little left to be "solved" in the field. Recall from Section 7.1 that we also compared the annual trend of UML-SPE papers' count with that of UML books, adapted from another SM study (Garousi, 2011). It is quite alarming that number of UML books is also decreasing in recent years (see Figure 15). One potential root cause for these trends is that the popularity of UML is slowly fading away. UML was introduced in late 1990's with "lot of promise," but it seems that it did not deliver some of its promises. Interested reader is referred to online postings such as (Daniel, 2012; Guy, 2012) for further details, since the discussion of UML's popularity is out of this paper's scope. In the SM study of UML books (Garousi, 2011), we found a strong similarity of the trend of UML books to classical *Hype* cycles (Jackie, 1995), denoting the rise and fall of UML. In summary, no one can be for sure forecast the future state of the UML and UML-SPE fields. The future of these fields is in hand of researchers and practitioners who may or may not use UML for SPE purposes in industrial contexts.

- **RQ 2.2 (publication count by venue type):** 34 conference papers, 32 workshop papers, 15 journal articles, five symposium papers, two books, one paper in forums, and one technical report were included in our pool.

- **RQ 2.3 (citation count by year):** We raised the following hypothesis: Do older papers necessarily receive more citations? Based on analytical evaluations, we found that there is a weak support (correlation coefficients=-0.25) for the above hypothesis using the absolute citation count metric, while there is almost no correlation support (correlation coefficients=0.06) using the normalized citation count metric.

- **RQ 2.4 (top-cited studies):** The three top cited papers are Simona, et al. (2002), Steffen, et al. (2008), and Petriu and Hui (2002).

- **RQ 2.5 (top venues):** The top three venues of publications are (1) the International Workshop on Software and Performance (WOSP), (2) Journal of Systems and Software (JSS), and (3) the International Conference on Modeling Techniques and Tools for Computer Performance Evaluation (TOOLS).

- **RQ 2.6 (citation count by venue type):** We wanted to analyze the relationship between average citation count for different venue types (e.g., conferences, journals and workshops). The rationale was to evaluate the hypothesis that whether there is a difference in number of citations to studies appearing in different venue types. We found that workshop publications (mostly published in the WOSP workshop) have the highest average citation count, followed by journals, conference papers and books.

- **RQ 2.7 (top authors):** The top two authors are Dorina Petriu (with 13 publications in UML-SPE) and Jose Merseguer (12 publications).

- **RQ 2.8 (author affiliation):** 81 studies were authored by academic researchers, while 5 studies were authored by practitioners (authors with industry affiliations). 4 studies were the result of academia-industry joint collaborations. Applying UML-SPE techniques in industrial contexts is thus an exciting future area of pursuit worthy of consideration by existing and new researchers.

- **RQ 2.9 (publication count by country):** The top three countries contributing to this field are Canada, Italy and Spain.

In closing, as the final summary of trends and implications, we would like to highlight that RQs 1.3, 1.6, 1.9, and 2.1 are among the most important items that would help the reader to derive implications from our results. As we discussed in detail, the above former three questions raise the need for additional focus on testing and evaluation methods for UML-SPE works in near future. Also, results from RQ 2.1 could lead to a major issue in near future as the annual number of studies in this area is slowly decreasing and one might feel the impression that the UML-SPE area might slowly be getting less popular. Papers appearing in this area in the next few years will show us how this area continues to grow and shape itself, and also to what extent the results of our SM is going to help researchers in this area.

8.2. Threats to Validity

The discussion of threats to validity is important to judge the strengths and limitations of our SM study with regard to the validity of the results. For our study, the following issues may induce threats to validity: selection of search databases, definition of search terms and time frame, researcher bias with regards to exclusion/inclusion, and incorrect data extraction (classification). Using the standard classification scheme of validity threats suggested in (Wohlin, et al., 2000), we discuss these issues in relation to four types of threats to validity: (1) conclusion validity, (2) construct validity, (3) internal validity, and (4) external validity.

8.2.1. Conclusion Validity

In Section 4, we presented the article selection process. Information including search terms and databases was provided in detail. Also, the process of exclusion/inclusion of relevant publications was described in the same section. This enables us to present results that can be reproduced.

One problematic part lies in the inclusion/exclusion criteria which relied on the researchers' judgment and experience. Personal bias could be introduced during this process. To mitigate this issue, we applied strategies to increase the reliability of our decisions. First each of the authors examined candidate publications independently and followed the voting process described in Section 4. With regards to data extraction, each piece of data, extracted by an author, was carefully reviewed by another author. In case of disagreement about a specific classification decision, in-person discussions were made. In all cases, this procedure yielded consensus.

With these procedures in place, we trust that a replication of our SM study will not result in a significantly different set of relevant publications nor do we expect major deviations from our classification decisions.

8.2.2. Construct Validity

The construct validity issue in this study is related to what extent the object of study really represents what we intended to investigate regarding our research question. To obtain a relatively complete set of relevant publications in this area, we chose the search terms chosen with scrutiny. Our strategy is, by using a systematic procedure, we attempted to be as inclusive as possible to construct various terms for UML-SPE. As discussed in Section 4, a number of false positives were discovered during the process and we removed them manually. It is believed that we did not miss relevant publications.

Another threat to construct validity lies in the categorization scheme for the data extraction. As discussed in Section 5, our categorization scheme went through several reviews by all the authors. In such a way, the defined schemes were ensured to be unambiguous in terms of terminology.

8.2.3. Internal Validity

Internal validity issue occurs when drawing incorrect conclusions about causal relationships between study treatment and result. The fact that this paper mainly presents descriptive results makes us believe that few threats to internal validity exist.

8.2.4. External Validity

External validity is concerned with to what extent we can generalize the results of our SM study. As described in Section 4, our selected literature under study was all written in English language. Publications written in other languages were excluded. The issue lies in whether our selected works can represent all types of literature in the area of UML-SPE. For these issues, we argue that relevant literature we selected in our pool contained sufficient information to represent the knowledge reported by previous researchers or professionals.

Also, note that our findings in this study are mainly within the field of UML-SPE. Beyond this field, we had no intention to generalize our results. Therefore, few problems with external validity are worthy of substantial attention.

10. CONCLUSION AND FUTURE WORK

In this paper, we presented a first systematic mapping of the papers in the area of UML-Driven Software Performance Engineering (UML-SPE), published between 1998 and 2011. Our initial search retrieved 114 papers of which 90 were included in this study using a selection strategy. We incrementally derived a classification scheme by analyzing the included papers and used that scheme to conduct the mapping. In addition, we presented a first bibliometrics analysis of the domain to gain an understanding of the publication trend per year, citations, active researchers and venues in the area, etc. Our study indicates that UML-SPE has been an active area of research, however the number of studies in recent years are starting to decline. Our mapping shows the state-of-the-art in UML-SPE, what areas have been studied and by what means. It provides a guideline to assist researchers in planning future work by spotting the areas that need more attention. For instance, some topics that need additional investigation include UML-based performance testing and investigation of existing UML-SPE proposals in large scale industrial settings.

As future work, based on this study, we intend to conduct a systematic literature review of the field to analyze the evidence for different UML-SPE techniques and their effectiveness.

ACKNOWLEDGMENT

Vahid Garousi was supported by the Discovery Grant no. 341511-07 provided by the Natural Sciences and Engineering Research Council of Canada (NSERC). Shawn Shahnewaz was supported by the Collaborative Research and Development (CRD) grant #CRDPJ414157-11 provided by the NSERC and the software industry.

REFERENCES

Ahmad, A. (2004). *A performance analysis approach based on the UML class diagram.* Paper presented at the International Workshop on Software and Performance. New York, NY.

Alexander, V., Timo, S., Oliver, B., & Wolfgang, R. (2006). *Formal performance analysis and simulation of UML/SysML models for ESL design.* Paper presented at the e Conference on Design, Automation and Test in Europe. London, UK.

Ali, S., Briand, L. C., Hemmati, H., & Panesar-Walawege, R. K. (2010). A systematic review of the application and empirical investigation of search-based test-case generation. *IEEE Transactions on Software Engineering, 36*(6), 742–762. doi:10.1109/TSE.2009.52.

Andre, D. A., & Paolo, B. (2007). *A model-driven approach to describe and predict the performance of composite services.* Paper presented at the 6th International Workshop on Software and Performance. New York, NY.

Andrea, D. A. (2005). *A model transformation framework for the automated building of performance models from UML models.* Paper presented at the 5th International Workshop on Software and Performance. New York, NY.

Anil, S. J. (2000). *UML diagrams to object Petri net models: An approach for modeling and analysis.* Paper presented at the 12th International Conference on Software Engineering and Knowledge Engineering. Chicago, IL.

Banerjee, I., Nguyen, B., Garousi, V., & Memon, A. (2012). Graphical user interface (GUI) testing: Systematic mapping and repository. *Information and Software Technology.*

Bennett, A. J. (2004). *Performance engineering with the UML profile for schedulability, performance and time: A case study.* Paper presented at the IEEE Computer Society's 12th Annual International Symposium on Modeling, Analysis, and Simulation of Computer and Telecommunications Systems. New York, NY.

Bennett, A. J., & Murray, W. C. (2004). *Experimental evaluation of the uml profile for schedulability, performance, and time.* Paper presented at the International Conference on the Unified Modeling Language. New York, NY.

Bertolino, A. (2002). *Real-time UML-based performance engineering to aid manager's decisions in multi-project planning.* Paper presented at the 3rd International Workshop on Software and Performance. Rome, Italy.

Canevet, C. (2003). Performance modelling with the unified modelling language and stochastic process algebras. *IEE Proceedings. Computers and Digital Techniques, 150*(2), 107–120. doi:10.1049/ip-cdt:20030084.

Canevet, C. (2004). *Analysing UML 2.0 activity diagrams in the software performance engineering process.* Paper presented at the 4th International Workshop on Software and Performance. New York, NY.

Christoph, L., Axel, T., Alexander, K., & Marco, L. (2002). *Performance analysis of time-enhanced UML diagrams based on stochastic processes.* Paper presented at the 3rd International Workshop on Software and Performance. Rome, Italy.

Daniel, P. (2012). *13 reasons for UML's descent into darkness.* Retrieved from http://littletutorials.com/2008/05/15/13-reasons-for-umls-descent-into-darkness/

Di Marco, A., & Mirandola, R. (2006). *Model transformation in software performance engineering*. Paper presented at the International Conference on Quality of Software Architectures. New York, NY.

Distefano, S. (2005). *Software performance analysis in uml models*. Paper presented at the Workshop on Techniques, Methodologies and Tools for Performance Evaluation of Complex System. New York, NY.

Dorin, P., & Murray, W. (2002). *Software performance models from system scenarios in use case maps*. Paper presented at the 12th International Conference on Computer Performance Evaluation, Modelling Techniques and Tools. London, UK.

Dorina, P. D. (2000). *Deriving performance models from UML models by graph transformations*. Paper presented at the Tutorials, Workshop on Software and Performance. New York, NY.

Elberzhager, F., Münch, J., & Nha, V. T. N. (2012). A systematic mapping study on the combination of static and dynamic quality assurance techniques. *Information and Software Technology*, *54*, 1–15. doi:10.1016/j.infsof.2011.06.003.

Elena, G.-M., & Jose, M. (2005). *A software performance engineering tool based on the UML-SPT*. Paper presented at the International Conference on the Quantitative Evaluation of Systems. New York, NY.

Elena, G.-M., & José, M. (2006). *ArgoSPE: Model-Based software performance engineering*. Paper presented at the International Conference on Applications and Theory of Petri Nets and Other Models of Concurrency. New York, NY.

Eric, W., Robert, L., & Victor, R. (2011). An assessment of systems and software engineering scholars and institutions (2003–2007 and 2004–2008). *Journal of Systems and Software*, *84*(1), 162–168.

Evgeni, D., Andreas, S., & Reiner, D. (2002). UML-based performance engineering possibilities and techniques. *IEEE Software*, *19*(1), 74–83. doi:10.1109/52.976944.

Fabrício Gomes, D. F., & Jerffeson Teixeira, D. S. (2011). *Ten years of search based software engineering: A bibliometric analysis*. Paper presented at the International Symposium on Search-Based Software Engineering. New York, NY.

Fried, H. (2000). *Using UML models for performance calculation*. Paper presented at the 2nd International Workshop on Software and Performance. Ottawa, Canada.

Garousi, V. (2011). Classification and trend analysis of UML books (1997-2009). *Journal on Software & System Modeling*.

Garousi, V., Krishnamurthy, D., & Shahnewaz, S. (2012). *UML-driven software performance engineering: A systematic mapping*. Paper presented at the http://www.softqual.ucalgary.ca/projects/SM/UML_SPE

Garousi, V., Mesbah, A., Betin-Can, A., & Mirshokraie, S. (2012). A systematic mapping of web application testing. *Information and Software Technology*.

Garousi, V., & Varma, T. (2010). A bibliometric assessment of Canadian software engineering scholars and institutions (1996-2006). *Canadian Journal on Computer and Information Science*, *3*(2), 19–29.

Glass, R. L. (1995). An assessment of systems and software engineering scholars and institutions (1993-1994). *Journal of Systems and Software*, *31*(1), 3–6. doi:10.1016/0164-1212(95)00058-9.

Glass, R. L., & Chen, T. Y. (2001). An assessment of systems and software engineering scholars and institutions (1996-2000). *Journal of Systems and Software*, *59*(1), 107–113. doi:10.1016/S0164-1212(01)00052-8.

Glass, R. L., & Chen, T. Y. (2002). An assessment of systems and software engineering scholars and institutions (1997-2001). *Journal of Systems and Software, 64*(1), 79–86. doi:10.1016/S0164-1212(02)00023-7.

Gu Gordon, P. (2002). *XSLT transformation from UML models to LQN performance models.* Paper presented at the 3rd International Workshop on Software and Performance. Rome, Italy.

Gu Gordon, P., & Petriu, D. C. (2005). *From UML to LQN by XML algebra-based model transformations.* Paper presented at the International Workshop on Software and Performance. New York, NY.

Guy, W. (2012). *Ranting about UML tools.* Retrieved from http://www.cs.bgu.ac.il/~gwiener/software-engineering/ranting-about-uml-tools-part-1/

Hassan, G. (2000). Performance engineering of component-based distributed software systems. In *Performance Engineering, State of the Art and Current Trends* (pp. 40–55). London: Springer-Verlag.

Hayat Khan, R., & Heegaard, P. E. (2010). *Translation from UML to SPN model: A performance modeling framework.* Paper presented at the International Conference on Computer Design and Applications. New York, NY.

Hui, S. (2005). *Performance analysis of UML models using aspect-oriented modeling techniques.* Paper presented at the 8th International Conference on Model Driven Engineering Languages and Systems. Montego Bay, Jamaica.

Jackie, F. (1995). *When to leap on the hype cycle.* Gartner Inc..

James, S., & Wolfgang, E. (2003). *A model-driven approach to non-functional analysis of software architectures.* Paper presented at the 18th IEEE International Conference on Automated Software Engineering. New York, NY.

James, S., & Wolfgang, E. (2004). *Model driven performance analysis of enterprise information systems.* Paper presented at the International Workshop on Test and Analysis of Component Based Systems. Warsaw, Poland.

Jill, J., Lydia, M., & Fiona, L. (2011). *Doing your literature review: Traditional and Systematic techniques.* Thousand Oaks, CA: SAGE Publications.

Jing, X., Murray, W., & Dorina, P. (2003). *Performance analysis of a software design using the uml profile for schedulability, performance, and time.* Paper presented at the 13th International Conference on Modelling Techniques and Tools for Computer Performance Evaluation. Urbana, IL.

José, M., & Javier, C. (2003). Software performance modeling using UML and petri nets. In Calzarossa, M. A. G. (Ed.), *Performance Tools and Applications to Networked Systems (LNCS)* (*Vol. 2965*, pp. 265–289). Berlin: Springer.

Jose, M., Javier, C., & Eduardo, M. (2000a). *A pattern-based approach to model software performance.* Paper presented at the 2nd International Workshop on Software and Performance. Ottawa, Canada.

Jose, M., Javier, C., & Eduardo, M. (2000b). *A Pattern-based approach to model software performance using UML and Petri nets: Application to agent-based systems.* Paper presented at the International Workshop on Software and Performance. New York, NY.

Jose, M., Javier, C., & Eduardo, M. (2000c). *A pattern-based approach to model software performance using UML and Petri nets: Application to agent-based systems*. Paper presented at the 2nd International Workshop on Software and Performance. Ottawa, Canada.

Jose, M., Javier, C., & Eduardo, M. (2000d). *Performance evaluation for the design of agent-based systems: A Petri net approach*. Paper presented at the Workshop on Software Engineering and Petri Nets, within the 21st International Conference on Application and Theory of Petri Nets. Aarhus, Denmark.

Jose, M., Javier, C., Simona, B., & Susanna, D. (2002). *A compositional semantics for UML state machines aimed at performance evaluation*. Paper presented at the Sixth International Workshop on Discrete Event Systems. New York, NY.

Kendra, C., Lirong, D., & Yi, D. (2004). Performance modeling and analysis of software architectures: An aspect-oriented UML based approach. *Science of Computer Programming*, *57*(1), 89–108.

Kendra, C., Lirong, D., Yi, D., & Jing, D. (2003). *Modeling performance as an aspect: A UML based approach*. Paper presented at the 4th AOSD Modeling With UML Workshop. San Francisco, CA.

Kitchenham, B., Brereton, O. P., Budgen, D., Turner, M., Bailey, J., & Linkman, S. (2009). Systematic literature reviews in software engineering – A systematic literature review. *Information and Software Technology*, *51*(1), 7–15. doi:10.1016/j.infsof.2008.09.009.

Kitchenham, B., & Charters, S. (2007). *Guidelines for performing systematic literature reviews in software engineering*. Evidence-Based Software Engineering.

Liu, H. H. (2011). *Software performance and scalability: A quantitative approach*. New York: John Wiley & Sons. doi:10.1002/9781118135532.

Lukas, P., Simon, S., Michael, G., Peter, M., & Volker, D. (2009). A practical approach for performance-driven UML modelling of handheld devices – A case study. *Journal of Systems and Software*, *82*(1), 75–88. doi:10.1016/j.jss.2008.03.065.

Mathias, F., Hugo, B., & Bert, V. (2009). *Applying megamodelling to model driven performance engineering*. Paper presented at the IEEE International Conference and Workshop on the Engineering of Computer Based Systems. New York, NY.

Mathias, F., & Jendrik, J. (2008). Putting performance engineering into model-driven engineering: Model-driven performance engineering. In Giese, H. (Ed.), *Models in Software Engineering* (pp. 164–175). Berlin: Springer-Verlag.

Mathias, F., Wasif, G., Christoph, F., Ivor, S., Peter, K., & John, B. (2008). *Towards utilizing model-driven engineering of composite applications for business performance analysis*. Paper presented at the 4th European Conference on Model Driven Architecture: Foundations and Applications. Berlin, Germany.

Merseguer, J., & Campos, J. (2003). *Exploring roles for the UML diagrams in software performance engineering*. Paper presented at the International Conference on Software Engineering Research and Practice. New York, NY.

Miguel, D., Thomas, L., Mehdi, H., Stéphane, B.-B., & Sophie, P. (2000). *UML extensions for the specification and evaluation of latency constraints in architectural models*. Paper presented at the 2nd International Workshop on Software and Performance. Ottawa, Canada.

Mirco, T., & Stephen, G. (2008). *Automatic extraction of PEPA performance models from UML activity diagrams annotated with the MARTE profile*. Paper presented at the International Workshop on Software and Performance. New York, NY.

Moreno, M., & Simonetta, B. (2004). *UML-PSI: The UML performance simulator.* Paper presented at the Quantitative Evaluation of Systems, First International Conference. Torino, Italy.

Murray, W., Hui, S., Toqeer, I., & Jose, M. (2005). *Performance by unified model analysis (PUMA).* Paper presented at the 5th International Workshop on Software and Performance. Palma, Spain.

Nariman, M., & Vahid, G. (2008). *A UML-based conversion tool for monitoring and testing multi-agent systems.* Paper presented at the IEEE International Conference on Tools with Artificial Intelligence. New York, NY.

Object Management Group (OMG). (1999). *RFP for scheduling, performance, and time.* OMG document number ad/99-03-13.

Object Management Group (OMG). (2003). *UML profile for schedulability, performance and time (SPT), version 1.0.* Retrieved from http://www.omg.org/spec/SPTP/1.0/

Object Management Group (OMG). (2005a). *RFP for UML profile for modeling and analysis of real-time and embedded systems (MARTE).* OMG document: realtime/05-02-06.

Object Management Group (OMG). (2005b). *UML profile for schedulability, performance and time (SPT), version 1.1.* Retrieved from http://www.omg.org/spec/SPTP/1.1/

Object Management Group (OMG). (2011). *UML profile for MARTE: Modeling and analysis of real-time embedded systems, version 1.1.* Retrieved from http://www.omg.org/spec/MARTE/1.1

Object Management Group (OMG). (2012). *UML meta-model superstructure specification.* Retrieved from http://www.omg.org/spec/UML/2.4.1/Superstructure/PDF

Oliveira, F. M. (2007). *Performance testing from UML models with resource descriptions.* Paper presented at the Brazilian Workshop on Systematic and Automated Software Testing. Sao Paolo, Brazil.

Pablo, L.-G. J., Jose, M., & Javier, C. (2002). *Performance engineering based on UML & SPN's: A software performance tool.* Paper presented at the 7th International Symposium on Computer and Information Sciences. Orlando, FL.

Pablo, L.-G. J., José, M., & Javier, C. (2004). *From UML activity diagrams to stochastic Petri nets: Application to software performance engineering.* Paper presented at the International Workshop on Software and Performance. New York, NY.

Pekka, K. (2001). UML-based performance modeling framework for component-based distributed systems. In *Performance Engineering, State of the Art and Current Trends* (pp. 167–184). London: Springer-Verlag.

Pete, M., & Rob, H. (2000). *PEPA performability modelling using UML statecharts.* Paper presented at the UK Performance Engineering Workshop. Durham, UK.

Peter, K., & Rob, P. (2000). *Derivation of Petri net performance models from UML specifications of communications software.* Paper presented at the International Conference on Computer Performance Evaluation: Modelling Techniques and Tools. New York, NY.

Petersen, K., Feldt, R., Mujtaba, S., & Mattsson, M. (2008). *Systematic mapping studies in software engineering.* Paper presented at the 12th International Conference on Evaluation and Assessment in Software Engineering (EASE). New York, NY.

Petri, K., & Marko, H. (2005). *Performance modeling and reporting for the UML 2.0 design of embedded systems.* Paper presented at the International Symposium on System-on-Chip. Tampere, Finland.

Petriu, D. B., & Murray, W. (2004). *A metamodel for generating performance models from UML designs.* Paper presented at the 7th International Conference on Modelling Languages and Applications. New York, NY.

Petriu, D. B., & Murray, W. (2007). An intermediate metamodel with scenarios and resources for generating performance models from UML designs. *Journal of Software and Systems Modeling,* 6(2), 163–184. doi:10.1007/s10270-006-0026-8.

Petriu, D. C., & Hui, S. (2002). *Applying the UML performance profile: Graph grammar-based derivation of LQN models from UML specifications.* Paper presented at the International Conference on Computer Performance Evaluation, Modelling Techniques and Tools. New York, NY.

Petriu, D. C., & Xin, W. (2000). *From UML descriptions of high-level software architectures to LQN performance models.* Paper presented at the International Workshop on Applications of Graph Transformations with Industrial Relevance. New York, NY.

Ping, G. G. (2003). *Early evaluation of software performance based on the UML performance profile.* Paper presented at the Conference of the Centre for Advanced Studies on Collaborative Research. New York, NY.

Qu Yang. K. J., Juha-Pekka, S., & Kari, T. (2006). *Layered UML workload and SystemC platform models for performance simulation.* Paper presented at the International Forum on Specification and Design Languages. Darmstadt, Germany.

Raffaela, M., & Vittorio, C. (2000). *UML-based performance modeling of distributed systems.* Paper presented at the 3rd International Conference on the Unified Modeling Language. York, UK.

Rasha, T., & Dorina, P. (2008). *Integrating performance analysis in the model driven development of software product lines.* Paper presented at the International Conference on Model Driven Engineering Languages and Systems. New York, NY.

Reiner, D., Claus, R., Andreas, S., & Andre, S. (Eds.). (2001). *Performance engineering: State of the art and current trends.* Berlin: Springer.

Rob, P. (1998). *Using UML to derive stochastic process algebra models.* Paper presented at the 15th UK Performance Engineering Workshop, Department of Computer Science. Bristol, UK.

Runeson, P., Runeson, P., Rainer, A., & Regnell, B. (2012). *Case study research in software engineering: Guidelines and examples.* New York: John Wiley & Sons. doi:10.1002/9781118181034.

Sabri, P., & Thomas, F. (2002a). *On customizing the UML for modeling performance-oriented applications.* Paper presented at the 5th International Conference on The Unified Modeling Language. Dresden, Germany.

Sabri, P., & Thomas, F. (2002b). *UML-based modeling of performance oriented parallel and distributed applications.* Paper presented at the Winter Simulation Conference. San Diego, CA.

Sabri, P., & Thomas, F. (2005). *Performance prophet: A performance modeling and prediction tool for parallel and distributed programs.* Paper presented at the 2005 International Conference on Parallel Processing Workshops. Oslo, Norway.

Sacha, R., Andreas, M., & Klaus, P. (2006). *A reuse technique for performance testing of software product lines.* Paper presented at the International Workshop on Software Product Line Testing. New York, NY.

Salvatore, D., Daniele, P., Antonio, P., & Marco, S. (2004). *UML design and software performance modeling*. Paper presented at the 19th International Symposium on Computer and Information Sciences. Kemer-Antalya, Turkey.

Schmietendorf, A., & Dimitrov, E. (2001). Possibilities of performance modeling with UML. In *Performance Engineering, State of the Art and Current Trends* (pp. 78–95). Berlin: Springer.

Simona, B., & Jose, M. (2007). Performance evaluation of UML design with stochastic well-formed nets. *Journal of Systems and Software, 80*(11), 1843–1865. doi:10.1016/j.jss.2007.02.029.

Simona, B., Susanna, D., & Jose, M. (2002). *From UML sequence diagrams and statecharts to analysable petri net models*. Paper presented at the International Workshop on Software and Performance. New York, NY.

Simonetta, B., Di Marco, A., & Inverardi, P. (2004). Model-based performance prediction in software development: A survey. *IEEE Transactions on Software Engineering, 30*(5), 295–310. doi:10.1109/TSE.2004.9.

Simonetta, B., & Marta, S. (2011). *On transforming UML models into performance models*. Paper presented at the Workshop on Transformations in the Unified Modeling Language. Genova, Italy.

Simonetta, B., Mattia, G., & Moreno, M. (2003). *Towards simulation-based performance modeling of UML specifications* (Technical Report CS-2003-2). Mestre, Italy: Dipartimento di Informatica, Universit`a Ca' Foscari di Venezia.

Simonetta, B., & Moreno, M. (2003a). *A simulation-based approach to software performance modeling*. Paper presented at the European Software Engineering Conference. Berlin, Germany.

Simonetta, B., & Moreno, M. (2003b). *Towards performance evaluation of mobile systems in UML*. Paper presented at the The European Simulation and Modelling Conference. Naples, Italy.

Simonetta, B., & Moreno, M. (2005). *Performance evaluation of UML software architectures with multiclass queueing network models*. Paper presented at the 5th International Workshop on Software and Performance. Palma, Spain.

Smith, C. U., Vittorio, C., & Di, M. A. (2005). *From UML models to software performance results: An SPE process based on XML interchange formats*. Paper presented at the International Workshop on Software and Performance. New York, NY.

Soloway, E., Lampert, R., Letovsky, S., Littman, D., & Pinto, J. (1988). Designing documentation to compensate for delocalized plans. *Journal of Communication of the ACM, 31*(11), 1259–1267. doi:10.1145/50087.50088.

Spiteri, S. T. (2008). *Intuitive mapping of UML 2 activity diagrams into fundamental modeling concept Petri net diagrams and colored Petri nets*. Paper presented at the 15th IEEE International Conference and Workshops on the Engineering of Computer-Based Systems. Seoul, Korea.

Steffen, B., Heiko, K., & Ralf, R. (2008). The Palladio component model for model-driven performance prediction. *Journal of Systems and Software, 82*(1), 3–22.

Stephen, G., & Leıla, K. (2005). A unified tool for performance modelling and prediction. *Reliability Engineering & System Safety, 89*(1), 17–32. doi:10.1016/j.ress.2004.08.004.

Theelen, B. D., & der, P. P. H. A. v. (2003). *Using the SHE method for UML-based performance modeling*. Paper presented at the Forum on Specification and Design Language. Marseille, France.

Tse, T. H., Chen, T. Y., & Glass, R. L. (2006). An assessment of systems and software engineering scholars and institutions (2000-2004). *Journal of Systems and Software*, *79*(6), 816–819. doi:10.1016/j.jss.2005.08.018.

Vahid, G. (2008a). *A formalism for arrival time analysis of real-time tasks based on UML models.* Paper presented at the Canadian Conference on Electrical and Computer Engineering. Toronto, Canada.

Vahid, G. (2008b). *Empirical analysis of a genetic algorithm-based stress test technique for distributed real-time systems.* Paper presented at the Annual Conference on Genetic and Evolutionary Computation. New York, NY.

Vahid, G. (2008c). *Traffic-aware stress testing of distributed real-time systems based on UML models in the presence of time uncertainty.* Paper presented at the International Conference on Software Testing, Verification, and Validation. Lillehammer, Norway.

Vahid, G. (2010a). A genetic algorithm-based stress test requirements generator tool and its empirical evaluation. *IEEE Transactions on Software Engineering*, *36*(6), 778–797. doi:10.1109/TSE.2010.5.

Vahid, G. (2010b). Experience and challenges with UML-driven performance engineering of a distributed real-time system. *Information and Software Technology*, *52*(6), 625–640. doi:10.1016/j.infsof.2010.01.003.

Vahid, G. (2010c). *UML model-driven detection of performance bottlenecks in concurrent real-time software.* Paper presented at the IEEE International Symposium on Performance Evaluation of Computer Telecommunication Systems. Ottawa, Canada.

Vahid, G. (2011). Fault-driven stress testing of distributed real-time software based on UML models. *Software Testing. Verification & Reliability*, *21*(2), 101–124. doi:10.1002/stvr.418.

Vahid, G., Briand, L. C., & Yvan, L. (2005). *A unified approach for predictability analysis of real-time systems using UML-based control flow information.* Paper presented at the GHHS. New York, NY.

Vahid, G., & Yvan, L. (2006). *Traffic-aware stress testing of distributed systems based on UML models.* Paper presented at the 28th International Conference on Software Engineering. Shanghai, China.

Vahid, G., & Yvan, L. (2008). Traffic-aware stress testing of distributed real-time systems based on UML models using genetic algorithms. *Journal of Systems and Software*, *81*(2), 161–185. doi:10.1016/j.jss.2007.05.037.

Vahid, G., & Yvan, L. (2009). A UML-based quantitative framework for early prediction of resource usage and load in real-time systems. *Journal of Software and System Modeling*, *8*(2), 275–302. doi:10.1007/s10270-008-0099-7.

Vincenzo, G., & Raffaela, M. (2001). *UML modelling and performance analysis of mobile software architectures.* Paper presented at the 4th International Conference on The Unified Modeling Language, Modeling Languages, Concepts, and Tools. New York, NY.

Vincenzo, G., & Raffaela, M. (2002). *PRIMAmob-UML: A methodology for performance analysis of mobile software architectures.* Paper presented at the 3rd International Workshop on Software and Performance. Rome, Italy.

Vittorio, C., Antinisca, D. M., & Paola, I. (2011). *Model-based software performance analysis.* Berlin: Springer.

Vittorio, C., Katerina, G.-P., & Kalaivani, A., R., Ahmed, H., Rania, E., et al. (2005). Model-based performance risk analysis. *IEEE Transactions on Software Engineering, 31*(1), 3–20. doi:10.1109/TSE.2005.12.

Vittorio, C., & Maurizio, G. (2004). *Performance modeling and validation of a software system in a RT-UML-based simulative environment.* Paper presented at the International Symposium on Object-Oriented Real-Time Distributed Computing. Vienna, Austria.

Vittorio, C., Michele, G., & Marco, P. (2004). *Xprit: An XML-based tool to translate uml diagrams into execution graphs and queueing networks.* Paper presented at the Quantitative Evaluation of Systems, First International Conference. Enschede, The Netherlands.

Vittorio, C., & Raffaela, M. (2000). *Deriving a queueing network based performance model from UML diagrams.* Paper presented at the International Workshop on Software and Performance. New York, NY.

Vittorio, C., & Raffaela, M. (2002). PRIMA-UML: A performance validation incremental methodology on early UML diagrams. *Science of Computer Programming, 44*(1), 101–129. doi:10.1016/S0167-6423(02)00033-3.

Wet, N. D., & Pieter, K. (2005). Using UML models for the performance analysis of network systems. *The International Journal of Computer and Telecommunications Networking - Telecommunications and UML Languages, 49*(5), 627-642.

Wohlin, C., Runeson, P., Höst, M., Ohlsson, M. C., Regnell, B., & Wesslén, A. (2000). *Experimentation in software engineering: An introduction.* Dordrecht, The Netherlands: Kluwer Academic Publishers. doi:10.1007/978-1-4615-4625-2.

ENDNOTES

[1] http://ieeexplore.ieee.org
[2] http://dl.acm.org
[3] http://scholar.google.com
[4] http://academic.research.microsoft.com
[5] http://citeseerx.ist.psu.edu
[6] http://www.sciencedirect.com

Chapter 3

EXTREME:
EXecuTable Requirements Engineering, Management, and Evolution

Ella Roubtsova
Open University of The Netherlands, The Netherlands

ABSTRACT

Requirements engineering is a process of constantly changing worlds of intentions, goals, and system models. Conventional semantics for goal specifications is synchronous. Semantics of conventional system modeling techniques is asynchronous. This semantic mismatch complicates requirements engineering. In this chapter, we propose a new method EXTREME that exploits similarities in semantics of goal specification and executable protocol models. In contrast with other executable modelling techniques, the semantics of protocol modelling is based on a data extended form of synchronous CSP-parallel composition. This synchronous composition provides advantages for relating goals and system models, reasoning on models, requirements management, and evolution.

INTRODUCTION

It is "reasonably well known that requirements will never be totally complete, finished, and finalized as long as a system is in service and must evolve to meet the changing needs of its customers and users" (Firesmith, 2005). However, there is a temporary notion of adequate completeness at some moment in time when the stakeholders are agreed on requirements. Adequate completeness of requirements is needed to estimate the development costs and to avoid incorrect assumptions for implementation decisions.

One of the powerful instruments to get adequately complete requirements is executable system modeling. Psychology studies show that people's thinking is context related (Tversky & Simonson, 1999). For requirements engineering this means that stakeholders can identify missing or tacit requirements at the moment they see the behaviour of the system model. Hence, the executable models offer to stakeholders the contextual basis for identification of incompleteness. The semantics of executable modelling should be consistent with the semantics of goals.

In practice there is a semantic mismatch. The semantics of goals is synchronous. The conventional executable system modeling techniques are asynchronous. Asynchronous execution of the

DOI: 10.4018/978-1-4666-4217-1.ch003

models gives birth to states that are not expressed by the goals. In such states, stakeholders do not understand the execution of the models and cannot properly evaluate the models and reason on them.

In this chapter we propose a new method EXTREME that exploits similarities in semantics of goal specification and executable protocol models in order to simplify executable requirements engineering, management and evolution. Protocol models use a data extended form of synchronous CSP-parallel composition. The combination of protocol models and goal-oriented approaches semantically coherent, all states can be goal interpreted and this eases reasoning on models in terms of goals, goal refinement and identification of missing requirements.

Before showing the EXTREME method, we first remind elements of goal modelling. Then we remind elements of protocol modeling and show how to create protocol models corresponding to goals. The process is illustrated with a case from the insurance domain. We discuss the semantic elements of Protocol modelling that make it suitable for combination with goal-oriented modeling.

GOAL MODELLING

Goal-Oriented Requirements Engineering (GORE) is a well-established group of approaches (Kavakli, 2002; van Lamsweerde, 2004; Darimont & Lemoine, 2006; Regev & Wegmann, 2012). The aim of a goal-oriented approach is to justify requirements by linking them to higher-level goals.

The notion of a goal is used as a partial description of a *system state* being a result of an execution of the system. The authors of the GORE methods emphasize the similarity between goals, requirements, and concerns and propose to combine them in one tree structure. Goals are refined by requirements and concerns. The goal models are used to keep the business motivation in mind of requirement engineers and to elaborate the strategic goals with requirements and concerns.

An example of a goal tree is shown in Figure 1. The top nodes of Figure 1 present business goals of a simplified system supporting insurance business. The goals are:

- A product is composed.
- A policy is bought by a registered customer.
- A claim of a client with a bought policy is handled.

Each parent goal (the one pointed to by the arrow) is refined with a list of sub-goals and requirements. The leaves of the tree present system requirements. Business and strategic goals are expressed using concepts of the stakeholders' vocabulary. Lower-level goals are typically expressed using words from the stakeholders' vocabulary as well as specific technical terms introduced in the model on purpose and where necessary (Respect-IT, 2007).

Identifying goals is not proceeding exclusively from either a top-down or a bottom-up approach. In most cases the two approaches are used at the same time. Refining goals in a goal model often follows a so-called "milestone approach" (although there are many other decomposition approaches). Milestone goals represent goals as intermediate states in a process aimed to achieve the top goals. For example, the goal *"A product is composed"* (Figure 1) is refined by goals *"There is a list of medical procedures"*, *"Medical procedures are combined into groups"*, *"Each group corresponds to a NoLimit(Coverage) or MaxCoverage"*.

GORE trees are also used to relate goals and structural elements of the: Entities, Agents, and Operations. Entities represent passive objects in contrast with Agents that represent active objects. Agents are either human beings or automated components that are responsible for achieving requirements. The goals of this level assigned to the humans are called expectations. Software agents are responsible for requirements. Agents, Entities and their Relations are captured in an

Figure 1. Goal tree of an insurance business

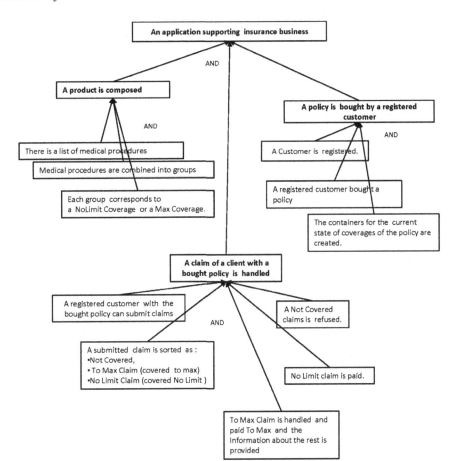

object model. Often goals are assigned to several agents rather than a single one.

In order to achieve goals software agents perform operations. The operation model in GORE sums up all the behaviors that agents need to have to fulfill their requirements. Behaviors are expressed in terms of operations performed by agents. Those operations work on objects (entities and agents) described in the object model: they can create objects, provoke object state transitions or trigger other operations through the send and receive events.

GORE operation diagrams are either data flow or control flow diagrams. Data flow and control flow diagrams have asynchronous semantics. This is the place where the operation model introduces

states that cannot be related to goals. Even if the operational model is executable, not all of its states can be related to goals. A simple example is asynchronous arriving of two data items to reach a state expressed with a goal. In the asynchronous model the items arrive one after another and produce intermediate state when one item has arrived and the other has not arrived yet. This state cannot be interpreted from the goal perspective and may be seen by stakeholders as an evidence of wrong model behaviour. Letier et al. (2008) note that in order to be semantically equivalent to the synchronous goal models, the operation models need to refer explicitly to timing events. It seems that the object and operation models present the abstraction level that is lower than the level needed for the requirement analysis by the stakeholders. GORE methods need synchronous compositional executable behavioural models corresponding to goals.

PROTOCOL MODELLING

Protocol models have elements of synchronization needed to present the system behavior at the higher level of abstraction than the operation diagrams. We propose to relate goals to protocol machines instead of class and operation diagrams. Synchronously composed protocol machines form together the protocol model corresponding to goals. In Figure 2 a dashed arrow is drawn from a box presenting a protocol machine to the box presenting the corresponding requirement. In this section, we discuss the elements of protocol models and the advantages of using them in goal–oriented approaches.

Protocol Modelling approach was developed by McNeile and Simons (2006). This approach can be viewed as a combination of object life-cycle modelling and the data-extended synchronous CSP-parallel composition. The initial ideas of this composition technique were borrowed from the process algebra of Communicating Sequential Processes (Hoare, 1985) and then extended in order to enable composition of models with data. In this part we present main elements of Protocol Modelling. We also show that this approach produces the system models, all states of which can be related to goals.

A protocol machine is a state-transition structure with data storage that defines ability of a system to interact with the environment by accepting events from environment or refusing events. A protocol machine can be seen like an object that exists even without its creation in its initial state. An object goes into its active state with a creating event.

For example, the protocol machine *Medical Procedure* defines *the attributes* and *stored states*

of the life cycle and transitions of every object of type *Medical Procedure*. Transitions define the interactions with the environment recognized by the object.

```
OBJECT Medical Procedure
  NAME Name
  ATTRIBUTES Name: String, MPGroup:MPGroup
  STATES created, added
  TRANSITIONS
      new*Create Medical Procedure=created
      created*AddMPintoGroup=added.
      added*Submit Claim=added.
```

The named interactions are specified as event types. Event types are presented as data structures. The attributes of event types are used as data containers for the data exchange with the environment.

For example, the definition of event *Create Medical Procedure* shown below tells that this event is used by the protocol machine *Medical Procedure* and it takes a string from environment to name this medical procedure.

```
EVENT Create Medical Procedure
ATTRIBUTES
    Medical Procedure: Medical Procedure,
Name: String
```

Being in a state specified by a transition, the protocol machine accepts the event of this transition. If the protocol machine is not in the state where a given event causes a transition, this event is refused even if the event is recognized by the protocol machine. If an event has been accepted, it is processed until the quiescent state of the protocol machine. During this processing the other events are refused. This behavior of protocol machines is different from behavior of state machines. The UML state machines accumulate all recognized events in a queue so that they may cause a transition in the future (UML2.OMG, 2007). Accumulating events in the queues causes extra states of the

Figure 2. Goals and corresponding protocol machines

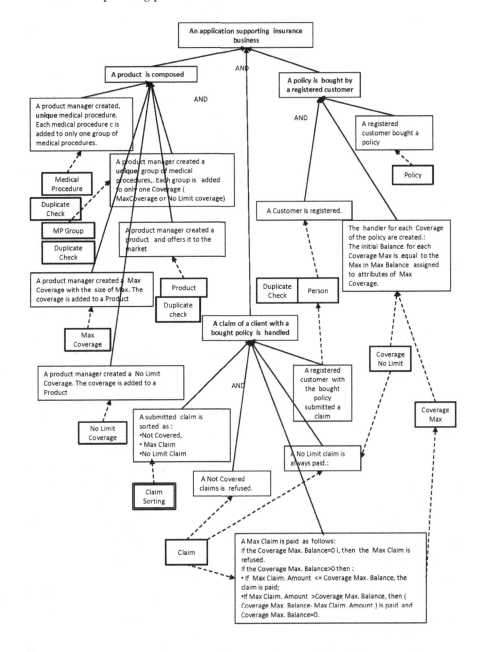

model and non-determinism in behavior of state machines. Protocol machines are deterministic.

A protocol model is a synchronous CSP parallel composition of all protocol machines in the model (McNeile & Simons, 2006). The composition is used to compose different views on the system expressed as protocol machines. Protocol machines work synchronously resulting in observable behavior. That is why an event is only accepted by the model if all protocol machines recognizing this event accept it. Otherwise the event is refused. This is the core of the CSP parallel composition.

For example, event *AddMPintoGroup* synchronizes two protocol machines *Medical Procedure* and MPGroup:

```
EVENT AddMPintoGroup
ATTRIBUTES
  Medical Procedure: Medical Procedure,
MPGroup:MPGroup
```

We say that there is a CSP parallel composition: *Medical Procedure || MPGroup*.

Event *Submit Claim* synchronizes protocol machines *Claim, Polis* and *Medical Procedure* and takes from the environment the *Claim Number* and its *Amount*.

```
EVENT Submit Claim
ATTRIBUTES
  Claim:Claim, Polis:Polis, Medical
Procdure: Medical Procedure,
  Claim Number:String, Amount:
Currency
```

The result of synchronization is the CSP parallel composition: *Claim || Polis || Medical Procedure.*

The complete protocol model in our insurance case is the CSP parallel composition the instances of 12 protocol machines. The number of instances is not restricted and depends on the interactive process of model execution. The meta-code of the model is given in the appendix.

The data extension of the initial CSP parallel composition semantics concerns with the ability of protocol machines to read but not alter the state of other protocol machines, so that the state causing accepting or refusing events can be formulated using states and local storages of all protocol machines in the model and the data from events.

Another consequence of the data extension of the CSP composition is the ability of protocol machines to derive own states from the states of other protocol machines. Derived states are calculated from the values of the stores states

specified for protocol machines. A derived state extends the state space of the system model and used to generalize the state of different protocol machines for a specific system view. For example, if all medical procedures have been included into a group, the state "the group has been completed" can be derived. Having derived states we can separate stored state space and derived state space for reasoning and analyses.

The updating of the stored space of a protocol model is restricted by accepting one event at a time and handing it until the new quiescent state of the model. Only quiescent states visible from the environment are included into protocol models. As only quiescent states are specified in the goals, the semantics of protocol model corresponds to the semantics of goal specification.

A protocol machine called *Behaviour* may be included into another protocol machine. This means that an instance of the *Behaviour* is automatically created with the instance of the including protocol machine.

Behaviours are equally CSP parallel composed with other protocol machines.

Deriving state and updating state of several protocol machines demand some search of instances of protocol machines and their attributes. These search commands are specified in small java files using a set of search functions built into the Modelsope tool. There are three types of search functions:

1. Function *selectByRef("Behaviour_Name", "Attribute_Name")* returns an array of instances, all of which include the specified behaviour (or object) and have the specified attribute referencing this.
2. Function *selectInContext ("Behaviour_Name", "Event_Name")* returns an array of instances, all of which include the specified behaviour and have the specified event with the specified subscript in context.

3. Function *selectInState ("Behaviour_ Name", "State")* returns an array if instances, all of which include the specified behaviour.

The data extension of the CSP parallel composition for protocol machines makes protocol models flexible in presentation of any modeling abstraction, such as objects and crosscutting concerns (see details in McNeile & Roubtsova, 2008, 2010) and adopting any model change as a separate protocol machines. The experimental studies demonstrate scalability and change adoptability on the applications of industrial size (Verheul & Roubtsova, 2011).

Events are identified in the goal-oriented approaches, but they are not used for object communication and do not contain data. Events in the goal-oriented approaches trigger operations. Protocol models work at the higher level than the level of operations. Protocol machines communicate with environment accepting or refusing events and by generating events to the environment. Dealing with events with data in protocol machines allows abstracting from the send-receive-operations and avoiding the non-determinism caused by them. The use of operations is an implementation decision which the protocol models avoid as "requirements have to describe what the system does, not how its does it (Zave & Jackson, 1997).

Protocol models are directly executable in the Modelscope tool (McNeile & Simons, 2011). The tool provides a generic interface for execution of any protocol model allowing submitting events and observation of results, protocol machine, and their attributes. The interface generated by the Modelscope tool for this model is shown in Figure 3.

Local Reasoning on Protocol Machines

Protocol Models are unique in the sense that they possess the property of local reasoning on each protocol machine about the behavior of the whole system. The local reasoning on protocol machines was proven in McNeile and Roubtsova (2008), and it was discussed in detail in McNeile and Roubtsova (2010) and Roubtsova (2011).

Local reasoning in Protocol Modelling is based on a property of CSP composition.

Figure 3. Execution of the protocol model

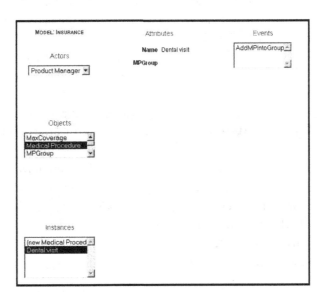

- Let us take a sequence, *S*, of events that is accepted by the CSP parallel composition of protocol machines (*M1* || *M2*) of the two machines *M1* and *M2*.
- Then let us take the subsequence, *S0*, of *S* obtained by removing all events in *S* that are not recognized by the protocol machine *M1*.
- *S0* will be accepted by the machine *M1* by itself.

In other words, composing *M1* with another machine with cannot "break its trace behavior of *M1*. We can use this property to support local reasoning on each protocol machine about the behaviour of the whole model. If by removing all events in *S* that are not recognized by *M1*, we have got a sequence *S0* that were not acceptable to *M1* or *M2*, then the original sequence *S* could not have been acceptable to *(M1* || *M2)*.

Each protocol machine has usually 1-5 states (Figure 4). The set of its sequences is observable. The loops can produce infinite traces, but testing of the finite set of traces for each simple protocol machine is sufficient to test one protocol machine. This means that verification of any requirement may be reduced to testing of a finite set of traces of relevant protocol machines. The testing of goals means that for each goal there is a reachable state and there are no states that do not correspond to one or another intermediate or final goal leading to the final state.

PROTOCOL MODEL CORRESPONDING TO THE GOAL MODEL

The state-transition part of protocol models can be presented graphically. Graphical presentation of CSP composition is possible but not necessary. The CSP parallel composition is comparable with an interpreter that executes the model interacting with its environment.

The graphical presentation of our case is shown in Figure 4. States of any protocol machine are ellipses, events are labels on arcs and transitions are triples of two ellipses and a labeled arc between them. The graphical presentation does not allow adequate specification of data.

We discuss this correspondence of goals and protocol machines goal by goal.

Goal "A Product is Composed"

Defining the goal *"A product is composed"* via sub-goals and requirements we identify *concepts Medical procedure, MPGroup, NoLimit Coverage, Max Coverage* and *Product*. Each of the concepts is specified as a protocol machine.

In order to create an instance of a *Product* the concept *Medical procedure* is populated with instances. Chosen instances of *Medical Procedure* are combined in one *MPGroup* and this group is assigned to a *NoLimit Coverage* instance. Another group is assigned to *Max Coverage*.

Several instances of *Max Coverage* can be defined with different attribute *Max Balance*. A completely composed product is offered to the market. Acceptance of the event *Offer Product* transits the instance of a *Product* to state *offered*. If a product is in the state *offered* (Figure 4), it is available for clients willing to buy a policy. At this moment the actor *Client* may submit events to the model.

Almost all events recognized by described protocol machines are submitted to the system by the actor called *Product Manager* and this is described in the meta-code in the Appendix. The specification of an actor selects protocol machines visible to a particular interacting actor from the actor specification and metacode of corresponding protocol machines the *Modelscope* tool generates the *Product Manager* interface to test the model.

Figure 4. Protocol model

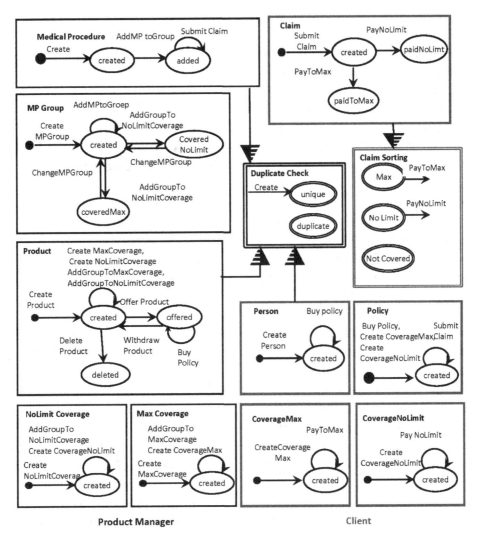

Product Manager   **Client**

Unfolding Hidden Requirements

Very often during the execution of the life cycle events, a stakeholder may recognize a tacit requirement.

For example, a stakeholder executes the model and creates two medical procedures with the same name. The stakeholder decides that this is not what he wants and any *Medical procedure*; any *MPGroup* and any *Product* should be unique in the system. To achieve this crosscutting requirement a protocol machine that controls the duplication can be added and CSP composed with the model. The meta-code of the protocol machine *Duplicate Check* is presented below and in Figure 4. This protocol machine allows proceeding of event *Create* only if the created instance does not exist.

```
BEHAVIOUR !Duplicate Check
    STATES unique, duplicate
    TRANSITIONS @any*Create =unique
```

Graphical presentation of protocol machines with derived states demands particular attention.

We depict derived states as double line ellipses. The function of state derivation is specified in a java file and it is not presented in the Figure 4.

Derived states should not form pairs to a specify transition. A derived state constraints the acceptance of an event. If a derived state presents a pre-state of an event then an outgoing arc is labeled with this event. If a derived state presents a post-state of an event then an ingoing arc is labeled with this event.

If the event recognized by the machine with derived states is accepted by the model then the resultant state is defined by protocol machines with stored states accepting this event.

The behaviour *Duplicate Check* is a cross-cutting concern, as it is included into protocol machines *Medical Procedure*, *MP Group* and *Product*. This means that an instance of *Duplicate Check* is created with any instance of *Medical Procedure*, *MP Group* and *Product* and CSP composed with the model.

The exclamation symbol in the metacode *BEHAVIOUR !Duplicate Check* means that there is a java code corresponding to the protocol machine. The java code is shown below. It finds all instances of the hosting protocol machine and checks if there is an instance with the same name and the same identification. The *Duplicate Check* protocol machine with the corresponding code is used for modelling the uniqueness constraint. The user does not see the java code but she executes the model and is able to create and use only unique instances.

```
package Insurance;
import com.metamaxim.modelscope.callbacks.*;

public class DuplicateCheck extends
Behaviour {
public String getState() {
        String myName=getString("Name");
        Instance[] existingIns = this
selectInState(this.getObjec
Type(), "@any");
        for (int i = 0; i < existingIns.
length; i++)
```

```
    if(existingIns[i].getString("Name").
equals(myName)&& !existingIns[i].
equals(this))
        return "duplicate";
        return "unique";
    }
    }
```

Goal "A Policy is Bought by a Registered Customer"

For this goal concepts *Person* and *Policy* have been recognized and the corresponding protocol machines have been specified. A person and a policy should be unique, so the *Duplicate Check* is included into the protocol machines *Person* and *Policy*.

Goal "A Claim of a Client with a Bought Policy is Handled"

Unfolding Hidden Requirements

1. Concept Claim is identified from this goal. A claim can be paid without limit or paid to maximum. This specification hides the need of classification of claims.

2. Buying a policy means some obligations for the insurance business to create containers for coverages for handling the policy limits. When the payment takes place the corresponding "container" is updated. Creating containers are expressed in requirements. The rules of these updates are not presented in the requirements.

3. We improve the situation with tacit requirements about the claim classification by adding a protocol machine *Claim Sorting* included into protocol machine *Claim*. The behaviour *Claim Sorting* checks if the medical procedure of the submitted claim belongs to the group assigned to the *NoLimit Coverage* or one of the Max *Coverages* in the policy of the client. If the medical procedure is not assigned to a group, it is not covered. If

it is assigned, then correspondingly state *Max* or *NoLimit* is derived for protocol machines *Claim Sorting* (Figure 4). In state *Max* event *PayToMax* is allowed. In state *NoLimit* event *Pay NoLimit* is allowed.

4. We improve the situation with the specification of claim handling. We have identified that we need concepts of "containers" that will be updated with claim handling. To support modeling of claim handling from the point of view of the insurance business we create protocol machines CoverageNoLimit and *CoverageMax*. We put java file *BuyPolicy* into correspondence to event *Buy Policy*, so that this event generates events *createCoverageMax* and *createCoverageNoLimit* and submits them to the environment. Protocol machines *CoverageMax* and *CoverageNoLimit* accept these events and create the instances. All coverages of the product are found in the *Product* protocol machine and collected in an array *Instance[] myMaxCoverages*. For each coverage a creating event is generated (for example Event *createCoverageMax* and all attributes are filled in with the data. The presented code does not specify any implementation; it translates the event *BuyPolicy* to the concepts of protocol machines *CoverageMax* and *CoverageNoLimit*. The Modelscope tool finds the java file with the same name *Buy Policy* and executes it, so that the stakeholder executes the model and tests her requirements.

```
package Insurance;
import com.metamaxim.modelscope.callbacks.*;
public class BuyPolicy extends Event {
 public void handleEvent() {
        this.submitToModel();
        //Add the associated CoveragesProce-
dures to the Policy
        Instance myProduct= this=
getInstance("Product");
```

```
        String myProductName=myProduct.
getString("Product Name");
        Instance[] myMaxCoverages =
        this.getInstance("Product")
selectByRef("MaxCoverage", "Product");
        for (int i = 0; i < myMaxCoverages.
length; i++) {
        String myName=myMaxCoverages[i].
getString("MaxCoverage Name");
        int myMax=myMaxCoverages[i].
getCurrency("MaxBalance");
        Event createCoverageMax = this
createEvent("Create CoverageMax");
        createCoverageMax.
setNewInstance("CoverageMax", "Coverage-
Max");
        createCoverage-
Max.setInstance("MaxCoverage",
myMaxCoverages[i]);
        createCoverageMax.
setString("CoverageMax Name", myName);
createCoverageMax.setCurrency("Balance",
myMax);
        createCoverageMax.submitTo-
Model();
}
        Instance[] myNoLimitCoverages =
        this.getInstance("Product").
selectByRef("NoLimitCoverage", "Product");
        for (int i = 0; i < myNoLimitCover-
ages.length; i++) {
        String
myNoLimit=myNoLimitCoverages[i].
getString("NoLimitCoverage Name");

        Event createCoverageNoLimit = this.
createEvent("Create CoverageNoLimit");
        createCoverageNoLimit.setNewInstance("
CoverageNoLimit", "CoverageNoLimit");
        createCoverageNoLimit.
setInstance("NoLimitCoverage",
myNoLimitCoverages[i]);
        createCoverageNoLimit.
setString("CoverageNoLimit Name", myNoLim-
```

```
it);
        createCoverageNoLimit.submitToMod-
el();
            }
        }
    }
```

5. Handling of claims means updating containers. The given requirements of these updates are not precise enough for executable modelling. For example, the goal *"A Max-claim is paid to Max" is* ambiguous. The executable model demands refinement of this goal formulation to a simple algorithm on how to calculate the payment and the rest of the coverage. This algorithm is presented in the state-function of the protocol machines *CoverageMax*:

```
package Insurance;
import com.metamaxim.modelscope.callbacks.*;

public class CoverageMax extends Behaviour {
public void
processPayToMax(Event event, String sub-
script) {

int newBalance=this.getCurrency("Balance");
int newAmount=
event.getInstance("Claim").
getCurrency("Amount");

int newPayment=0;
    if (newBalance >= newAmount) {
        newBalance=newBalance-newAmount;
        newPayment=newAmount;
    }    else {
        newPayment=newBalance;
        newBalance=0;
        }
    this.setCurrency("Balance", newBalance);
    this.setCurrency("PaymentToMax", newPay-
ment);
```

```
}
}
```

We can see that as a result of executable modeling we have refined initial requirements to the point that they may be executed. Even our simple case shows that the initial goal specification is refined because the executable protocol model demands more precision to be executed.

DISCUSSION

EXTREME is a New Method for EXecuTable Requirements Engineering, Management, and Evolution

If the ideas of a collection of methods used together produces more knowledge then each of combined methods, this collection presents a new method.

Our collection of methods combines the ideas of goal-oriented methods and protocol modeling.

Goal-oriented modeling methods along suggest strategic structuring of wishes of stakeholders as goals and refinement of the goals to requirements up to structural elements of system implementation: classes, their attributes and operations. In the absence of system implementation, verification of the produced specification demands methods of model checking. The properties are specified in a formal logic. Goal–oriented methods do not give instructions for transformation of requirements into formal properties. The properties are specified by an analyst, which is an error prone process. Then the state space specified by classes and attributes is built and the sequences of operation calls are generated to verify the truth of specified properties or the false of negations of properties.

The results of model checking need to be interpreted to stakeholders who specified goals. The interpretation may be misunderstood and the feedback of stakeholders may be lost at this stage. In this case the knowledge about correspondence between the specifications to the wishes of stakeholders will be fully identified only at the implementation stage.

Protocol modeling along allows producing executable models of requirements with any possible decomposition; however, this method does not answer the question how the protocol models should be built from system requirements. Tracing requirements and management of requirements is not addressed in protocol modeling.

Business practice needs methods that consider requirements engineering, evolution and management as parts of one process. Using model-checking techniques in this process (with specification of system properties and interpretation of results to requirements engineers) is not effective. This is like an extra step of translating to model checking after every change in requirements and translating the results of model checking back to requirements. Requirements engineers should be able to fulfill the self-validation of their requirements. By executing requirements on the protocol model in EXTREME, they are able to do this.

EXTREME replaces refinement of goals to the specification of classes, attributes, and operations with refinement of goals to protocol models. Being compositional in nature, the protocol models contain protocol machines directly corresponding to requirements. Protocol models possess the property of local reasoning described in section 3. Local reasoning means that properties of each protocol machine are preserved in the behaviour of the whole protocol model. That is why building and analyzing of large state space of the system by model checking may be replaced with execution of a limited number of protocol machines collaboratively responsible for the tested requirement.

The tested requirements should not be transformed into formal property. Each requirement usually describes the sequential steps of a protocol machine or update of local storage of a protocol machine. This means that a requirement is directly visible in one of protocol machines. The execution of the protocol model in de Modelscope tool shows the protocol machines responsible for the

requirement. The requirements implemented as a protocol machine is preserved in the CSP parallel composition of protocol machines. The presence or absence of a requirement is an additional indication of the correctness of model evolution.

The user and requirements engineer provide their feedback as many times as needed by looking at model execution. In such a way EXTREME produces the knowledge about the correspondence of requirement specification to the wishes of stakeholders before the implementation of the system and more knowledge is produced than in original goal-oriented methods.

The improvement of the requirement engineering process means

- Producing adequately complete requirements.
- Enabling easy management of requirements including easy changing.
- Enabling local reasoning on parts of the model about the behavior of the whole.

Producing Adequately Complete Requirements

Protocol Modelling of requirements results in a refined goal tree shown in Figure 2. Contextual playing with executable requirements caused recognizing tacit requirements.

- We have extended initial requirements with uniqueness of instances. For example, *any Medical Procedure, Medical Procedure Group, Product* and *Person* should be unique. This concern is specified as a separate protocol machine *Duplicate Check*. This protocol machine accompanied with the corresponding call-back function is included into each of the named protocol machines and CSP composed with them. *Duplicate check* is a good example of a crosscutting concern. Protocol models provide the necessary flexibility for presentation of crosscutting concerns and other refinements of requirements (McNeile,A., Roubtsova E. (2010)).

- We have completed the requirements needed for claim handling by adding containers of coverages for each policy and by specification of updating procedure of those containers.

As we can see the ambiguities of the first definitions of claim handling and product definition are resolved by adding new protocol machines and CSP composing them with the protocol machines representing life cycle of identified objects. In fact each protocol machine is a presentation of a requirement that can be tested. If a requirement cannot be presented as a protocol machine it has to be refined. An executable protocol model if requirements indicate their adequate completeness.

Enabling Easy Management of Requirements Including Easy Changing

Goals have a clear tree structure and combining of them with protocol models puts protocol machines as leaves of the goal tree. The tree structure is good for search of goals and corresponding protocol machines. It is easy to delete an existing goal (protocol machine) and add a new goal (protocol machine).

The only problem with the trees is the accommodation of crosscutting concerns. In a tree structure, the crosscutting requirement and the corresponding protocol machine will inevitable appear several times.

In order to solve this inconvenience, the name of the protocol machine in the tree may contain a link to the place of the metadata specifying this protocol machine in the textual document. Modification of a requirement (goal) will result in search of the corresponding protocol machine in order to correct it.

In other methods combining of goal and operation models (Respect-IT (2007), Van, H.T. et.al. (2004)), refinement of requirements usually results in remodeling. The crosscutting concerns cause a lot of error prone remodeling activities. This is explained by the composition techniques used in operation models, namely, the sequential composition and the hieratical composition. If a concern is added, the sequences have to destroyed and built again. The change of the hierarchy usually causes complete remodeling. Example of these problems in conventional operation models are shown in McNeile,A., Roubtsova.E. (2007).

ENABLING LOCAL REASONING ON PARTS OF THE MODEL ABOUT THE BEHAVIOR OF THE WHOLE

EXTREME inherits the property of local reasoning from Protocol Modelling enabling also direct relations with the requirements for local reasoning.

Let us take a requirement "A submitted claim is sorted as: *Not Covered, Max Claim No Limit Claim.*"

This requirement corresponds to the protocol machine *Claim Sorting*. We see that this machine has the specified states: *Not Covered, Max, No Limit. Claim Sorting* is included into protocol machine *Claim*.

The state of the protocol machine *Claim Sorting* is derived when the protocol machine *Claim* accepts event *Submit Claim*. Event *Submit Claim* contains information about *Medical Procedure*. If this *Medical Procedure* has been included into a group for Max *Coverage*, then the claim should be sorted as *Max Claim*. The behaviour of *Claim and Claim Sorting* is tested locally without analysis of the complete state space of the model. The proposed tests are the Submit *Claim* eventwith a medical procedure from the group *Max Coverage* and the check if it is sorted as *Max Claim*.

FUTURE RESEARCH DIRECTIONS

Modeling of More Abstract Business Concepts

Controllable development of business is impossible without monitoring of its state, capacities, calculating key performance indicators and making decisions for correct and timely investment. Such monitoring happens both at the level of enterprises, enterprise departments and educational institutions, but also at the level of ministries and government. The major problem with monitoring and decision support is different interpretation of state, capacities, and key performance indicators. This problem has an objective reason as even businesses of the same branch have different variations. Ambiguity and different understanding of state, capacities and key performance indicators cause problems for management in making right decisions and for employees in directing their efforts. Cloud technologies and mobile technologies introduce new indicators that need to be unambiguously understood.

Our preliminary studies show that conceptual models of business capacities and KPIs lead to unambiguous definitions. EXTREME allows for building conceptual models of abstract business concepts and key performance indicators using ideas of goal-oriented approaches and protocol modelling. Analysis of KPIs models may result in useful standardisation of operational KPIs. The classified KPIs and business capacities will speed up solution of many business intelligence tasks, lead to easy building of business analytics into information systems and eventually will result in better decision support for business and better decisions.

At the moment performance indicators are not included into system models, but maintaining of high performance is always a goal of a system. The compositional nature of Protocol Models used in our method to make requirements operational gives the opportunity to raise the level of abstraction in models and relate many complex business concepts to behavioral models. Such concepts as business capabilities, Key Performance Indicators (KPIs) and motivation models may extend behavior models.

For example, let us see the monitoring of KPIs as a new goal *"The numbers of submitted and paid claims per year are calculated."*

Figure 5. KPI: Submitted and paid claims per year

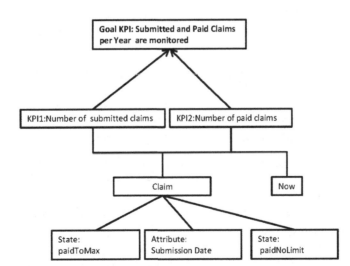

These KPIs are conceptually related to the concept *Claim*, its attribute *Submission Date*, the time concept *Now* and two values of the concept *State, namely* the state value *paidToMax and* the state value *paidNoLimit*. The conceptual model is shown in Figure 5. The claims that have these values of their *State* concept are paid.

In order to calculate *KPI1: Number of submitted claims,* the date *oneYearAgo* from the value of Now is calculated. Then the claim instances with the value of the attribute *Submission Date* after *oneYearAgo* are found and the *KPI1: NumberOfClaims* is calculated (see function *getNumberOfClaims()*).

In order to calculate *KPI2:Number of paid claims,* the claims situated in the state *paidToMax* or *paidNoLimitthat* submitted after the *Submission Date* are found and their number is calculated (function *getNumberOfPaidClaims()*).

The ability to derive states makes it possible to calculate KPIs in Protocol Models. The metacode of the Protocol Model and the corresponding java code calculating the number of claim instances is shown below.

> OBJECT *CounterNumberOfClaims*
>
> NAME *Name*
>
> ATTRIBUTES *Name: String, !NumberOfClaims:Integer,*
> *!NumberOfPaidClaims:Integer*
>
> STATES *created*
>
> TRANSITIONS *@new*GetNumberOfClaims=created*
>
> EVENT *GetNumberOfClaims*
>
> ATTRIBUTES *CounterNumberOfClaims:CounterNumberOf*
> *Claims, Name:String*
>
> #---

```java
package Insurance;
import com.metamaxim.modelscope.callbacks.*;
import java.util.*;

public class CounterNumberOfClaims extends
Behaviour {
    public int getNumberOfClaims() {
        int NumberOfClaims=0;
        Date d = new Date();
        Calendar cal = Calendar.getIn-
stance();
        cal.add(Calendar.YEAR, -1);
        Date oneYearAgo = cal.getTime();
        Instance[] existingIns =
selectInState("Claim", "@any");
        for (int i = 0; i < existingIns.
length; i++) {
        Date SD=existingIns[i].
getDate("SubmissionDate");
            if (SD.compareTo(oneYearAgo)>0)
            NumberOfClaims=NumberOfClaims+1;
    }
            return NumberOfClaims;
    }
    public int getNumberOfPaidClaims() {
        int NumberOfPaidClaims=0;
        Date d = new Date();
        Calendar cal = Calendar.getIn-
stance();
        cal.add(Calendar.YEAR, -1);
        Date oneYearAgo = cal.getTime();
        Instance[] PaidToMaxIns =
selectInState("Claim", "paidToMax");
        for (int i = 0; i < PaidToMaxIns.
length; i++) {
        Date SD=PaidToMaxIns[i].
getDate("SubmissionDate");
            if (SD.compareTo(oneYearAgo)>0)
            NumberOfPaidClaims=NumberOfPaidC
laims+1;
    }
    Instance[] PaidNoLimitIns =
selectInState("Claim", "paidNoLimit");
        for (int i = 0; i < PaidNoLimi-
tIns.length; i++) {
        Date SD=PaidNoLimitIns[i].
getDate("SubmissionDate");
            if (SD.compareTo(oneYearAgo)>0)
            NumberOfPaidClaims=NumberOfPaidCla
ims+1;
```

```
       }
              return NumberOfPaidClaims;
       }
       }
```

It is possible that during the modelling and execution the stakeholder will decide that the date of KPI monitoring is fixed and this concept *Fixed Monitoring Date* will replace concept *Now* in the conceptual model.

The discovery of patterns of protocol models of different KPIs and other abstract business concepts is one of directions for future work.

Tool Support for Traceability of Requirements in Models

The goals and requirements are naturally kept in a tree structure. From this tree structure is possible to generate a textual document for metadata of protocol machines. The goals and requirements may be presented in this document as comments following the hierarchy of requirements in the goals tree. The meta-code of each protocol machine may be written then under own requirements as we have presented in the appendix. In case of crosscutting concerns, the meta-code of a protocol machine may have a link to the requirement in the tree structure and the description of the relevant requirements from the branch of the goal tree may be generated in its comments when necessary. This means that the problem of traceability of requirements in protocol models will be solved. The traceability of requirements in protocol models needs to be supported with a tool in near future.

CONCLUSION

The correspondence between the strategic and the operational levels of a business is a success factor of the business. In this chapter, we have presented a new method EXTREME that combines the ideas of the goal models at the strategic level with the executable protocol models at the operational level. The uniqueness of the proposed combination is in synchronous semantics both at the strategic and the executable levels that easies both the goal refinement and the executable modeling.

The name of the method EXTREME can be associated with Extreme Programming (Cockburn, 2001b). The associating is not wrong as the ideas of Extreme Programming to improve a software project on the basis of five essential principles; communication, simplicity, feedback, respect, and courage are present in the method EXTREME. The difference is that the EXTREME can be also used for modeling of businesses, not necessarily for programming software, and the five principles are used already at the stage of requirements engineering before the implementation phase.

The extended CSP parallel composition used in Protocol Modelling gives extra decomposition flexibility and ability to reason locally avoiding the state space explosion at the stage of analysis.

The goal-orientation brings the order and simplicity into decomposition, testing and evolution. New goals are refined as requirements and corresponding new protocol machines and CSP composed with the rest of the model. The existing model parts are not changed and preserve their behaviour in the growing model. Synchronous nature of protocol models does not add any states that cannot be explained by goals and their refinement. Therefore the execution of models can be easily controlled from the goal perspective by the stakeholders.

The method has been tested for insurance products in Oracle Nederland (Verheul & Roubtsova, 2011). Currently there is a running experiment in two companies that want to improve requirements management of product releases by application of the EXTRIME method.

REFERENCES

Alsumait., et al. (2003). Use case maps: A visual notation for scenario-based requirements. In *Proceedings of the 10th International Conference on Human-Computer Interaction*. IEEE.

Cockburn, A. (2001a). *Writing effective use cases*. Reading, MA: Addison-Wesley.

Cockburn, A. (2001b). *Agile software development*. Reading, MA: Addison-Wesley Professional.

Dardenne, A., van Lamsweerde, A., & Fickas, S. (1991). Goal-directed requirements acquisition. *Science of Computer Programming, 20*(1-2), 3–50. doi:10.1016/0167-6423(93)90021-G.

Darimont, R., & Lemoine, M. (2006). Goal-oriented analysis of regulations. In *Proceedings of the International Workshop on Regulations Modelling and their Validation and Verification, REMO2V'06*, (pp. 838-844). REMO2V.

Firesmith, D. G. (2005). Are your requirements complete? *Journal of Object Technology, 4*(1), 27–43. doi:10.5381/jot.2005.4.1.c3.

Harel, D., & Kugler, H. (2002). Synthesizing state-based object systems from LSC specifications. *Foundation of Computer Science, 13*(1), 5–51. doi:10.1142/S0129054102000935.

Hoare, C. (1985). *Communicating sequential processes*. New York: Prentice-Hall International.

ITU. (2008). *Formal description techniques (FDT) – User requirements notation recommendation Z.151 (11/08)*. Retrieved September 3, 2012, from http://www.itu.int/rec/T-REC-Z.151-200811-I/en

Jensen, K. (1997). *Coloured Petri nets: Basic concepts, analysis methods, and practical use*. Berlin: Springer Verlag. doi:10.1007/978-3-642-60794-3.

Kavakli, E. (2002). Goal-oriented requirements engineering: A unified framework. *Requirements Engineering, 6*(4), 237–251. doi:10.1007/PL00010362.

Letier, E. et al. (2008). Deriving event-based transition systems from goal-oriented requirements models. *Automated Software Engineering, 15*(2), 175–206. doi:10.1007/s10515-008-0027-7.

McNeile, A., & Roubtsova, E. (2007). Protocol modelling semantics for embedded systems. In *Proceedings of the Special Session on Behavioural Models for Embedded Systems at the IEEE Second International Symposium on Industrial Embedded Systems, SIES'2007*. Lisbon, Portugal: IEEE.

McNeile, A., & Roubtsova, E. (2008). CSP parallel composition of aspect models. In *Proceedings of the International Workshop on Aspect-Oriented Modelling, AOM'08*. ACM Press.

McNeile, A., & Roubtsova, E. (2010). Aspect-oriented development using protocol modeling. *Transactions on Aspect-Oriented Software Development, 7*, 115–150.

McNeile, A., & Simons, N. (2006). Protocol modelling: A modelling approach that supports reusable behavioural abstractions. *Software & Systems Modeling, 5*(1), 91–107. doi:10.1007/s10270-005-0100-7.

McNeile, A., & Simons, N. (2011). *Modelscope*. Retrieved September 3, 2012, from http://www.metamaxim.com

Regev, G., & Wegmann, A. (2011). Revisiting goal-oriented requirements engineering with a regulation view. *Lecture Notes in Business Information Processing, 109*.

Respect-IT. (2007). *A KAOS-tutorial*. Retrieved September 3, 2012, from http://www.objectiver.com/fileadmin/download/documents/KaosTutorial.pdf

Roubtsova, E. E. (2011). Reasoning on models combining objects and aspects. *Lecture Notes in Business Information Processing, 109*, 1–18. doi:10.1007/978-3-642-29788-5_1.

Tversky, A., & Simonson, I. (1993). Article. *Management Science, 39*(10), 1179–1189. doi:10.1287/mnsc.39.10.1179.

UML2.OMG. (2007). *Unified modeling language: Superstructure version 2.1.1*. Formal/2007-02-03.

Van, H. T., et al. (2004). Goal-oriented requirements animation. In *Proceedings of RE'04: 12th IEEE International Requirements Engineering Conference*, (pp. 218-228). IEEE.

van Lamsweerde, A. (2004). Goal-oriented requirements engineering: A roundtrip from research to practice. In *Proceedings of the 12th IEEE International Requirements Engineering Conference*. Kyoto, Japan: IEEE.

Verheul, J., & Roubtsova, E. (2011). An executable and changeable reference model for the health insurance industry. In *Proceedings of the 3rd International Workshop on Behavioural Modelling - Foundations and Applications*. ACM.

Yu, E. (1995). *Modelling strategic relationships for process reengineering*. (Ph.D. Thesis). Dept. of Computer Science, University of Toronto, Toronot, Canada.

Zave, P., & Jackson, M. (1997). Four dark corners of requirements engineering. *ACM Transactions on Software Engineering and Methodology, 6*(1), 1–30. doi:10.1145/237432.237434.

KEY TERMS AND DEFINITIONS

Adequate Completeness of Requirements: Requirements are adequately complete if all specified requirements are met by an executable system model and the model can be used to reason about the system.

CSP Parallel Composition: Is an algorithm of constructing sequences of events accepted by the abstracting from data. Processes P and Q must both be able to perform event before that event can occur. Processes communicate via synchronous message passing. $(a \rightarrow P) \,|\, [\{a\}] \,|\, (a \rightarrow Q)$.

CSP Parallel Composition Extended for Machines with Data: Is an algorithm of constructing sequences of events accepted by the modeled system including data storages and state spaces.

Event: A recognized happening in an environment that can be expressed as a data structure. One element of this data structure is an event type.

Goal: A general name of a piece of system functionality; a description of a system state being a result of an execution of the piece of system functionality.

Goal Tree: A tree the root of which is a system, the next nodes is the system goals; the goals are refined to requirements.

Protocol Machine: Is a state-transition construction with data storage that defines ability of a system to accept events from environment. If a pre-event or a post-event constraint on the data storage is not met then the machine refuses the event.

Requirement: A description of system reactions on related events.

APPENDIX

Meta Code of a Protocol Model of an Insurance Business

MODEL Insurance
#--
#Product is composed.
#A product manager created, unique medical procedure. Each medical procedure c is added to only one
#group of medical procedures.

```
OBJECT Medical Procedure
    NAME Name
    INCLUDES Duplicate Check
        ATTRIBUTES Name: String, MPGroup:MPGroup
        STATES created, added
        TRANSITIONS         @new*Create Medical Procedure=created,
                            created*AddMPintoGroup=added,
                            added*Submit Claim=added,

BEHAVIOUR !Duplicate Check
    STATES unique, duplicate
        TRANSITIONS @any*Create =unique
```

#A product manager created a unique group of medical procedures, Each group is added to only #one
#Coverage (MaxCoverage or No Limit coverage.

```
OBJECT MPGroup
    NAME Name
    INCLUDES Duplicate Check
    ATTRIBUTES
        Name: String,
        !CurrentState:String,
        MaxCoverage:MaxCoverage,
        NoLimitCoverage:NoLimitCoverage
        STATES created, coveredMax,
        coveredNoLimit
    TRANSITIONS @new*Create MPGroup=created,
            created*AddMPintoGroup=created,
            reated*!AddGroupToNoLimitCoverage=coveredNoLimit,
            created*!AddGroupToMaxCoverage= coveredMax,
            coveredMax*ChangeMPGroup=created,
            coveredNoLimit*ChangeMPGroup=created,
```

#A product manager created a Max Coverage with the size of Max. The coverage is added to a #Product.

```
OBJECT MaxCoverage
     NAME Name
     ATTRIBUTES
          Name: String,
          MaxBalance:Currency,
          Product:Product,
          Product Name:String
          STATES created,
TRANSITIONS @new*Create MaxCoverage =created,
               created*AddGroupToMaxCoverage= created,
               created*Create CoverageMax= created,
```

#A product manager created a No Limit Coverage. The coverage is added to a Product.

```
OBJECT NoLimitCoverage
NAME Name
     ATTRIBUTES
     Name: String,
     Product:Product,
     Product Name:String
     STATES created,
     TRANSITIONS @new*Create NoLimitCoverage =created,
               created*AddGroupToNoLimitCoverage= created,
               created*Create CoverageNoLimit= created,
```

#A product manager created a product and offers it to the market.

```
OBJECT Product
     NAME Name
     INCLUDES Duplicate Check
     ATTRIBUTES Name:String
     STATES created, offered
     TRANSITIONS @new*Create Product=created,
               created* Create MaxCoverage=created,
               created*Create NoLimitCoverage=created,
               created*AddGroupToMaxCoverage=created,
               created^AddGroupToNoLimitCoverage=created,
               created*Offer Product=offered,
               offered*Buy Policy=offered

EVENT Create MaxCoverage
ATTRIBUTES    MaxCoverage:MaxCoverage,
                Name: String,
                MaxBalance:Currency,
                Product:Product
EVENT Create NoLimitCoverage
ATTRIBUTES    NoLimitCoverage:NoLimitCoverage,
                Name:String,
                Product:Product
```

```
EVENT AddMPintoGroup
ATTRIBUTES    Medical Procedure: Medical Procedure,
                 MPGroup:MPGroup
EVENT Create Medical Procedure
ATTRIBUTES    Medical Procedure: Medical Procedure,
                 Name:String
EVENT Create MPGroup
ATTRIBUTES    Name: String, MPGroup:MPGroup
EVENT AddGroupToNoLimitCoverage
ATTRIBUTES    MPGroup:MPGroup,
              NoLimitCoverage:NoLimitCoverage,
              Product:Product
EVENT AddGroupToMaxCoverage
ATTRIBUTES    MPGroup:MPGroup,
                 MaxCoverage:MaxCoverage,
                 Product:Product
EVENT ChangeMPGroup
ATTRIBUTES    MPGroup:MPGroup

EVENT Create Product
ATTRIBUTES    Product:Product,
                 Name:String

EVENT Offer Product
ATTRIBUTES    Product:Product

GENERIC Create
MATCHES Create Medical Procedure,Create Product,Create MPGroup
```

#A policy is bought by a registered customer.
#A Customer is registered.

```
OBJECT Person
NAME Name
INCLUDES Duplicate Check
     ATTRIBUTES
     Name: String,Policy: Policy
     STATES created
     TRANSITIONS @new*Create Person=created,
                 created*Buy Policy=created,
```

#A registered customer bought a policy.

```
OBJECT Policy
    NAME Name
    INCLUDES Duplicate Check
    ATTRIBUTES Name: String, Product:Product, Person:Person
        STATES created, deleted, offered
    TRANSITIONS @new*Buy Policy=created,
            created*Submit Claim=created,
              created*Create CoverageMax=created,
                created*Create CoverageNoLimit=created
```

#The handler for each Coverage of the policy are created.
#The initial Balance for each Coverage Max is equal to the Max in Max Balance assigned to #attributes
#of Max Coverage.

```
OBJECT CoverageMax
NAME CoverageMax Name
    ATTRIBUTES CoverageMax Name: String,MaxCoverage:MaxCoverage,
       Balance:Currency PaymentToMax:Currency, Policy:Policy
            STATES created
            TRANSITIONS @new*Create CoverageMax =created,
                        created*!PayToMax=created,


OBJECT CoverageNoLimit
NAME CoverageNoLimit Name
    ATTRIBUTES CoverageNoLimit Name:String,PaymentNoLimit:Currency,
Policy:Policy
            STATES created
        TRANSITIONS @new*Create CoverageNoLimit=created,
                created*!PayNoLimit=created,


EVENT !Buy Policy
ATTRIBUTES Policy:Policy, Policy Number:String, Person:Person, Product:Product
#-------------------------------------------------------------------------
```

#A Claim of a client with a bought policy is handled.
#A registered customer with the bought policy submitted a claim.

```
OBJECT Claim
    NAME Name
    INCLUDES Duplicate Check,Sorting Claim,
    ATTRIBUTES Name: String, Policy:Policy, Medical Procedure: Medical
Procedure,
            Amount:Currency, SubmissionDate:Date,
            CoverageMax:CoverageMax, CoverageNoLimit:CoverageNoLimit,
    STATES created, paidToMax, paidNoLimit
    TRANSITIONS @new*Submit Claim=created,
            created*PayToMax=paidToMax,
            created*PayNoLimit=paidNoLimit
```

#A submitted claim is sorted as:
#Not Covered,
#Max Claim
#No Limit Claim
    #A Max Claim is paid as follows:
    #If the Coverage Max. Balance=0 I, then the Max Claim is refused.
    #If the Coverage Max. Balance>0 then:
    #If Max Claim. Amount <= Coverage Max. Balance, the claim is paid;
    #If Max Claim. Amount >Coverage Max. Balance, then (
    #Coverage Max. Balance- Max Claim. Amount) is paid and
    #Coverage Max. Balance=0.

    #A Not Covered claims is refused.
    #A No Limit claim is always paid.

```
BEHAVIOUR !Sorting Claim
         ATTRIBUTES
     STATES Max, NoLimit, NotCovered
     TRANSITIONS Max*PayToMax=@any,
              NoLimit*PayNoLimit=@any


EVENT PayToMax
ATTRIBUTES CoverageMax:CoverageMax, Claim: Claim


EVENT PayNoLimit
ATTRIBUTES CoverageNoLimit:CoverageNoLimit, Claim:Claim



EVENT Create CoverageMax
ATTRIBUTES CoverageMax:CoverageMax, Policy:Policy, CoverageMax Name:String,
Balance:Currency, MaxCoverage:MaxCoverage


EVENT Create CoverageNoLimit
ATTRIBUTES CoverageNoLimit:CoverageNoLimit, Policy: Policy, CoverageNoLimit
Name: String, NoLimitCoverage:NoLimitCoverage


EVENT Submit Claim
ATTRIBUTES Claim:Claim, Policy:Policy, Claim Number:String, Medical Procedure:
Medical Procedure, Amount:Currency, SubmissionDate:Date


EVENT Create Person
ATTRIBUTES Person:Person, Name: String
#----------------------------------------------------------------------------
```

```
ACTOR Product Manager
      BEHAVIOURS Medical Procedure, MPGroup,
                MaxCoverage, NoLimitCoverage,
                Product, CounterNumberOfClaims
      EVENTS Create Medical Procedure,
             Create MPGroup,AddMPintoGroup,
             Create MaxCoverage, Create NoLimitCoverage,
             AddGroupToNoLimitCoverage, AddGroupToMaxCoverage,
             ChangeMPGroup, Create Product,
             Offer Product, GetNumberOfClaims
#----------------------------------------------------------------------------


ACTOR Client
BEHAVIOURS Claim, Person,
Sorting Claim,
Policy, CoverageMax, CoverageNoLimit
EVENTS Submit Claim,
     Buy Policy,
             PayToMax,
             PayNoLimit,
             Create Person
#----------------------------------------------------------------------------
```

#*Performance Indicator: Number of Claims and Paid Claims during one year.*

```
OBJECT CounterNumberOfClaims
NAME Name
      ATTRIBUTES Name: String, !NumberOfClaims:Integer,
!NumberofPaidClaims:Integer
          STATES created
       TRANSITIONS @new*GetNumberOfClaims=created
EVENT GetNumberOfClaims
ATTRIBUTES Name:String, CounterNumberOfClaims:CounterNumberOfClaims
#----------------------------------------------------------------------------
```

Chapter 4
Ptolemaic Metamodelling?
The Need for a Paradigm Shift

Brian Henderson-Sellers
University of Technology, Australia

Owen Eriksson
Uppsala University, Sweden

Cesar Gonzalez-Perez
Spanish National Research Council (CSIC), Spain

Pär J. Ågerfalk
Uppsala University, Sweden

ABSTRACT

By consideration of scientific paradigm shifts, in this chapter the authors evaluate possible parallels in the evolution of modelling, and particularly metamodelling and modelling language construction, as a basis for evaluating whether or not the time is ripe for a similar change of direction in model language development for software engineering. Having identified several inconsistencies and paradoxes in the current orthodoxy, they then introduce a number of ideas from outside software engineering (including language use, philosophy, and ontology engineering) that seem to solve many of these issues. Whether these new ideas, together, are sufficient to create a shift in mindset or whether they are simply the stimulus for others to create new and orthogonal ideas remains to be seen. The authors urge the modelling and metamodelling communities to search out that new orthodoxy (i.e. instigate a paradigm shift) that will, necessarily, ensure that the science will offer simpler and more satisfying solutions in the years to come.

1. INTRODUCTION

Model-Driven Engineering (MDE) focuses on models and model transformations. At the very heart of modelling is the need for models to be depicted in some way by using modelling languages (e.g. Selic, 2011), typically specified by

a metamodel (e.g. Sanchez Cuadrado, de Lara, & Guerra, 2012). Metamodels are thus a (or maybe the) core element in MDE – current and future metamodelling approaches are the topic of this chapter.

The scientific approach to knowledge creation and acquisition has been the topic of many books and papers. It embodies a combination of theory building and theory testing and the ability to re-

DOI: 10.4018/978-1-4666-4217-1.ch004

place old theories when newer data and/or newer theories offer a more consistent and scientific explanation of the topic under consideration. The framework in which the theory resides also implies a philosophical underpinning, a paradigmatic choice that is seldom discussed or even appreciated. This interaction between theory and empirically obtained data for testing that theory is crucial in science and, hence also, in all branches of computing (e.g. Genova, 2010). Notwithstanding, there is an unfortunate trend in journal reviewing of software engineering research to reject papers that have little or no empirical support (as observed by Genova, 2010). Indeed, Broy (2011) observes that "in the long run, software engineering cannot be established without a solid body of scientific theory." When scientific frameworks are totally reconstructed, often because they have degraded to a point where their coherence is challenged, it is said that a paradigm shift has occurred (Kuhn, 1962).

In this chapter, we focus on models and metamodels. Models have a long history in scientific research: "If you want to understand some aspect of the Universe, it helps if you simplify it as much as possible, and include only those properties and characteristics that are essential to understanding. If you want to determine how an object drops, you don't concern yourself with whether it is new or old, is red or green, has an odour or not. You eliminate those things and thus do not needlessly complicate matters. The simplification you can call a model or a simulation and you can present it either as an actual representation on a computer screen, or as a mathematical relationship" (Asimov, 1988). However, even with this illustrious and lengthy history, Ritchey (2012) argues that there is still no general theory of modelling.

Here, we take a largely theoretical approach, where our evaluation approach uses examples taken from considering the real world and asking whether each model provides a good or a better appreciation of the target problem domain. In

order to create such a comprehensive modelling approach, we integrate knowledge from various sub-fields of computing: software engineering, modelling (especially the use of UML and, more generally, conceptual modelling), as well as considering research knowledge from outside the traditional context of computing: ontology engineering, philosophy, mathematics, language use (especially speech acts) and cognitive linguistics. For the non-computing fields, we note that each has its own conferences and journals and, importantly, their own communities, which tend often to be 'clubs' or 'closed shops' with their own internal terminology immediately understandable by members of the club but unintelligible to those outside (e.g. Kuhn, 1962). To improve our models and our modelling axioms and constraints, we need to break into each and every of these clubs.

In this chapter, we will argue that the time is ripe for a paradigm shift in software language engineering and in particular in the model we use to understand multilevel metamodel architectures, especially relevant for MDE. Firstly, we will outline a parallel in the history of science: that of the Copernican Revolution (Section 2.1). In Section 2.2, we will give a brief overview of the history of software engineering metamodelling. Whilst Section 2 describes some of the problems and some of the fixes made at a high level, Section 3 delves into the detail of each of these proposed solutions. In particular, we explore the generalization[1] and instantiation relationships, the potential value of powertypes, and how ontology engineering and language use can add value to the creation and use of modelling languages. Despite these new additions to software language engineering, problems remain; in Section 4 we propose that the time is ripe for a minor revolution in thinking with respect to the relative positioning of metamodels, modelling languages and multilevel frameworks.

2. DRAWING PARALLELS WITH HISTORY

This section will thus set the scene for our argument that current 'solutions' to the various issues identified and agreed upon in contemporary software modelling languages and, especially, metamodelling are more akin to the Ptolemaic model with its many 'fixes' and lead into our proposal that what is needed for this important topic in modern-day modelling is a brand-new approach i.e. a new approach that results from a conceptual deconstruction and reconstruction (Kuhn, 1962).

2.1. History: From Ptolemy to Copernicus (Science)

In ancient Greece, despite Pythagoras[2]'s argument that the Earth and other heavenly bodies moved around a 'central fire', a rough consensus emerged (e.g. by Plato ca. 428-347 BC) that the Earth was the centre of the universe and that all the other astronomical bodies revolved in circular orbits around the Earth – as observed by the naked eye. Aristotle (384-322 BC) (see Stocks, 1922), Plato's student, argued for a crystal sphere carrying each such astronomical body where the gaps between spheres were filled with solid aether, the spheres themselves being concentric. Less predictable movements of nearby planets required an embedded sphere to account for their more erratic observed behaviour. Ptolemy (150) removed this constraint of concentricity, introducing a second sphere for each planet. Each planet moved around this sphere (actually a circle as shown in Figure 1). This is called an epicycle, formalized by Ptolemy but used much earlier by e.g. Apollonius of Perga and Hipparchus of Rhodes in the second century BC. The centre of this circle moves around a central point that is displaced from the Earth itself, the motion again being circular, the circle being known as the deferent. Its centre (cross in Figure 1) is halfway between the Earth and a point known

Figure 1. Ptolemy's geocentric model showing the deferent (large dashed circle), the epicycle (smaller dashed circle) with the cross marking the centre of the deferent and the large dot denoting the equant (public domain image, author Fastfission: http://en.wikipedia.org/wiki/File:Ptolemaic_elements.svg)

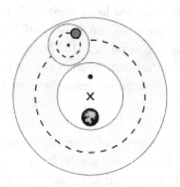

as the equant, introduced by Ptolemy to account for variations in velocities of the planets (see also Peurbach & Regiomontanus, 1496). The system model required of the order of 30-40 epicycles and was standard for around a thousand years until heliocentric models became accepted.

The idea that the Sun and not the Earth was the centre of our solar system was first proposed by Aristarchus of Samos (310-ca. 230 BC) but was then abandoned until resurrected in the 16th century by Nicolaus Copernicus (1473-1543) (Figure 2) after a careful and detailed analysis of planetary models (Swerdlow & Neugebauer, 1984). However, his initial models, whilst removing the contentious equant, needed additional epicycles, creating a system of greater complexity than that of Ptolemy[3]. Indeed, it was not until Johannes Kepler replaced Copernicus's circular orbits by elliptical ones that observations, especially those by Tycho Brahe, and theory (as developed by Newton (1687), based to a large degree on the work of Kepler) became both aligned and less complicated.

Despite Copernicus's continued use of epicycles, his change of mindset (paradigm shift)

Figure 2. Copernicus's house in Gdansk

from a geocentric to a heliocentric solar system model is usually taken to denote the beginnings of a revolution and of modern astronomy (Copernicus, 1543). After his death, his work was denigrated as foolish and with no solidity by Tolosani in 1544 (in an appendix to the treatise *On the Truth of Holy Scripture*). Indeed, it could be argued that the paradigm shift was not completed until a combination of Brahe's (1546-1601) observation of the Great Comet of 1577, which condemned the idea of solid celestial spheres[4], Kepler's (1571-1630) use of Brahe's observations, from which he deduced the elliptical nature of orbits (Kepler, 1596, 1609, 1617-21, 1627) and predicted the transit of Venus, first observed by Jeremiah Horrocks in 1639, and, finally, Galileo Galilei (1564-1642), who recognized that, with the recent advent of the telescope, the cytherean phases could not be accommodated in the Ptolemaic system (Galilei, 1610, 1632), thus providing observa-

tional support for the heliocentric model of Copernicus[5]. Together, the work of Galilei and Copernicus became the "dangerous idea" responsible for the overthrow of nearly 2000 years of Aristotelian physics. According to Bhathal (2012), Butterfield (1957) argues for the new scientific revolution "in which experiment and measurement are the arbiters of truth" – following in the steps of Husserl who advocated the prime importance of empiricism above a positivistic orientation of science and philosophy of his day (Wikipedia, 2012).

Similarly, although we will not pursue equivalent detail here, is the story of the development of Darwin's masterpiece *On the Origin of Species* (Darwin, 1859). Other contemporary scientists had very similar insights, especially Alfred Russel Wallace (Wallace, 1855). Beddall (1968) documents in detail the interactions between these two scientists, noting that Patrick Matthew and William Wells were also contenders for the discovery of the theory of natural selection. As with the Copernican revolution, Darwin, as Copernicus before him, built on the knowledge already created[6], for instance by Sir Joseph Dalton Hooker (1817-1911), Sir Charles Lyell (1797-1875), and Asa Grey as well as conducting many conversations and communications with these contemporary thinkers. He read widely, including influential works by Lamarck (1809), Paley (1809), and Chambers (1844). But it was the ability of Darwin to synthesis all this on a large and fully integrated scale that created the paradigm shift. However, such a change in mindset does not/did not occur overnight. Indeed, as late as 1862, the presidential address of George Bentham to the Linnean Society was hugely negative on the topic, as was Thomas Bell's presidential address three years earlier (see Beddall, 1968, p304), the latter at the meeting on 1 July 1858 at which Darwin and Russell first published their theories in a joint presentation (Darwin & Wallace, 1858).

2.2. History: Multilevel Architectures, Strict Metamodelling, and an Ontological Viewpoint (Modelling Languages)

Whilst modelling has an extensive history, extending back over several millennia, its application in computing sciences did not begin until the 1970s (e.g. Wieringa, 2011). However, prior to the introduction of object-oriented modelling languages in the early 1990s, formal definition in terms of metamodels[7] were rare (but see CDIF standards as a counterexample, e.g. Flatscher, 2002) although formalizations equivalent to metamodels, such as the schemata used in creating ER models (for recent examples, see Pastor, Levin, Celma, Casamayor, Virrueta, & Eraso, 2011), had indeed been widely used. Nevertheless, here we devote our historical study to begin with the introduction into object modelling techniques of metamodels used to underpin and even define such modelling languages as OML (Firesmith, Henderson-Sellers, & Graham, 1997) and UML™ (OMG, 2011a, 2011b)[8]. We begin with the supposition, as a basic 'axiom', of the *type-instance relationship*. This was taken over from (typed) object-oriented programming languages as an initial framework and turns out to be both a fundamental basis and also a fundamental challenge in the introduction of a multilevel architecture that occurred in the mid to late 1990s.

The type-instance axiom is also fundamental to ontological thinking and of language use (see later discussion for additional detail) and tightens up the class-object relationship prevalent in early published OO modelling examples. Liskov (1987) stressed that the use of types (rather than classes) permits type substitution in a truly object-oriented framework – and hence polymorphism, seen by many as a cornerstone of the object-oriented paradigm. Although polymorphism is primarily implementation-related, the underpinning notion of types and relationships between types has been adopted without change into modelling and metamodelling. The utility and validity of such adoption is part of our exploration and analysis herein.

2.2.1. The Four-Level Metamodelling Hierarchy

The use of metamodels for OO modelling languages was first promoted in 1994 (Henderson-Sellers, 1994; Carmichael, 1994; Monarchi, Booch, Henderson-Sellers, Jacobson, Mellor, Rumbaugh, & Wirfs-Brock, 1994) and consequently realized in Henderson-Sellers and Bulthuis (1998) in their creation of metamodels for 14 out of a list of 22 identified (then extant) modelling languages (at that time often mis-called methodologies). Around 1997, the OMG first publicized their strict metamodelling hierarchy (OMG, 1997) apparently based on theoretical suggestions of Colin Atkinson, not published until a little later (Atkinson, 1997, 1999). The need for a multiple level hierarchy (Figure 3), thus extending the two level type-instance model, was seen as necessary in order to (1) provide a clear means by which elements in the (then emergent) modelling language of UML could be themselves defined i.e. an M3 level[9] and (2) acknowledge the existence at the M0 level of individual (instances) of the classes designed at the M1 level – although for the OMG/UML world these were seen as less important because such instances only exist as 'data' within the computer program and, in general, do not appear within the modelling process.

Figure 3 uses as its basis the arguments embodied in 'strict metamodelling'; strict metamodelling states that these four layers (of the OMG architecture seen in Figure 3) are linked by an instanceOf relationship and, furthermore, that instanceOf can only occur *between* layers and never within a layer (e.g. Atkinson, 1997; Atkinson & Kühne, 2000a). A corollary is that no other relationship between layers is permissible. It should be noted that these constraints impose an artificiality on the framework that is not sup-

Figure 3. OMG four-level metamodelling hierarchy based on strict metamodelling (after Henderson-Sellers & Unhelkar, 2002) © Pearson Education Limited

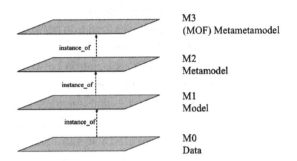

Figure 4. An example of metamodelling – note that not all instanceOf relationships are shown (after OMG, 2010)

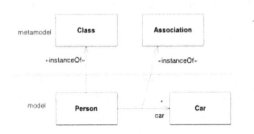

ported by traditional philosophical or ontological reasoning. Indeed, it should be noted that there is no obvious intent to give the four levels of Figure 3 an ontological verisimilitude.

Notwithstanding this four-level architecture, in modelling languages such as the Unified Modeling Language (UML), it is the two-level type-instance relationship[10] that is the main focus (e.g. Atkinson, 1999). Each entity at a given Mx layer is regarded as an instance of a corresponding entity in the layer immediately above it i.e. M(x+1) i.e. in one philosophical terminology, a thing that 'exemplifies' a universal (in modelling, the notion of an object as an instance of a type has a similar intent). This refers to both classes and relationships. There are, however, two schools of thought: (a) one that insists on relationships in a 'type' model (i.e. M1 model in Figure 3) being defined by classes in a metamodel (as shown in Figure 4) and (b) one that permits one to describe a model-level relationship as being an instance of a similar relationship in the metamodel (as in Figure 5). Although both these figures are from UML documentation (OMG, 2010), the annotations of <<instanceOf>> and <<snapshot>> in Figure 5 are said to be informal and not part of the model (Selic, 2012a); UML uses the class-based infrastructure of Figure 4 for all its model-level relationships. This is just one example of ambigu-

ous modelling/metamodelling that is implicated in the need to continually add 'fixes' to the UML. In Figure 4, Person is an instanceOf Class and the association between Person and Car is an instance of a class called Association in the metamodel. Hence, at one level higher, we can observe that association relationships between classes in the (M2) metamodel are in effect instances of a class in the metametamodel (M3) (i.e. atomic 'particulars') and cannot therefore have any instances in the model (M1). Figure 5, showing all four Mx layers, illustrates one well-known concern with

Figure 5. An example of the OMG four-layer metamodel hierarchy (after OMG, 2010)

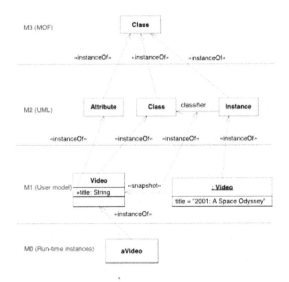

UML: the existence and location (within the Mx layers) of the Instance class. In earlier versions of UML this was named Object, which led to paradoxical situations of the need to have instances of Object at M0 when the framework dictates that all instances of M2 classes exist at level M1 (e.g. Atkinson & Kühne, 2001a).

To appreciate these issues in more detail, a diagram like that in Figure 6 can be drawn. In this diagram, we consider the details of a model (centre) and compare it to a typical representation (left hand side using UML's notation) and ask what the defining metamodel fragment should look like (right hand side). The model states that a particular dog, called Rover, is an instance of a class of Dogs. Of what this class Dog is an instance of is left undefined. The attributes on any class are arguably (see discussion below) incorrect (dependent upon whether they are part of the ontological commitment and philosophical paradigm adopted) and can be shown as explicit links to other classes. This is shown in the middle column where we can see that the typed attributes are themselves

instances of classes. The metamodel aspect is depicted in the right hand column, which shows that a class has one or more attributes; that objects are typed by classes; and that objects have values that are in turn typed by their corresponding attribute class. The instanceOf association between f:Dog and Dog in the left hand column is a representation of the isTypeOf association between Object and Class in the metamodel. This also ties in with foundational ontologies and language use (Section 3) where we can equate an object (of type Object) with a Particular, which is an instance of a Universal (here equated to a Class).

This analysis of a modelling language infrastructure recommends the infrastructure of Figure 5 over that of Figure 4; yet it is the class-focussed architecture of Figure 4 upon which all versions of UML rely. The all-critical instanceOf relationship is shown (in Figure 6) to conform to the isTypeOf *association* between Object and Class in the modelling language infrastructure. This is very similar to using an association to model relationships such as Person Owns House or

Figure 6. Mappings between model and modelling language infrastructure (here as a metamodel fragment) showing the usual UML-style representation of the model together with a more detailed exposition (middle column) to illustrate how both classes, objects, and attributes are all defined by classes and relationships in the modelling language infrastructure itself

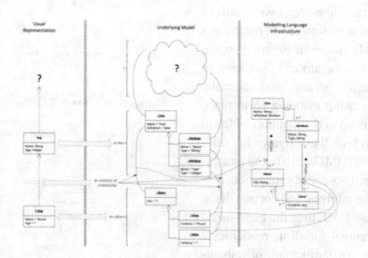

Computer Runs Application. Thus, when we instantiate the model (centre), we obtain instances of Class (actual classes) and Object (actual objects), which are connected by links that are instances of IsOfType. This is analogous to having instances of Person (actual persons) and House (actual houses) connected by links that are instances of Owns. The IsOfType links in the centre column are depicted as plain solid lines (i.e. with no arrowhead) connecting ": Object" and ": Class", for example. What happens (and here is the twist) is that IsOfType links are usually called "instance-of" relationships in OO (and especially UML) modelling, and depicted in diagrams by using a special notation, as shown in the left-hand side column of the figure (the UML-ish dashed line with an arrowhead). This makes the Object IsOfType Class association a bit special and different from, say, Person Owns House; but it is still a plain association from the metamodel's viewpoint.

One problem with UML's choice of a class to represent a relationship as part of the modelling language infrastructure is that this needs associations to link the RelationshipClass to the Class and Object classes in the M2 model, which in turn need classes in the M3 model to represent these relationships – recursively, ad infinitum (see also discussion in Graham, Bischof, & Henderson-Sellers, 1997).

2.2.2. Ptolemaic Fixes to the Four-Level Architecture

From the strict metamodelling definition and its widespread adoption as *the* fundamental architecture mechanism (e.g. Atkinson, Gutheil, & Kennel, 2009) flow the modifications that we here draw as parallels to the Copernican revolution discussed in Section 2.1.

2.2.2.1. Attributes and the Potency Fix

An additional concern is that of the existence or otherwise of attributes as components of entities rather than relationships, common in modelling languages like UML (see, e.g., discussion in Shan & Zhu, 2012) and in ontologies (e.g. the property of Bunge, 1977, 1979 and Wand & Weber, 1993, 1995; see also Opdahl & Henderson-Sellers, 2004) but eschewed in some contemporary philosophy (Partridge, 2012, p.c. – see also Swoyer & Orilia, 2011 for a detailed philosophical discussion on properties).

Attributes (often called, alternatively, properties[11] or, sometimes, qualities or characteristics e.g. Searle, 1969, p105) are assigned to particulars (typically instances of natural kinds) by means of predication (in language use – see Section 3.4). They were originally identified with 'substance' (e.g. Partridge, 1996, chapter 4), an idea that was strongly attacked by both Locke (1690) and Hume (1739). This resulted in a shift from a substance paradigm to an extension paradigm (e.g. Descartes, 1637, 1644), along with which came a shift (in philosophical thinking) from attributes to logical classes and tuples (e.g. Partridge, 1996, page 94). However, this necessary realignment of attributes as extensions (e.g. the red attribute of an object is turned into a member of a class of RedThings[12]) brings its own challenges and contradictions, which we explore in Section 3.5. Based on Searle (1969, pp. 113–118) who shows that you cannot understand the meaning of "red" in the speech act "the rose is red" as a type that has the extension of all red things, e.g. roses. Neither can it be seen as a reference to the universal redness. It is simply an attribute ascribed to the rose.

However, in the following we retain the notion of attribute since this is all-pervasive in the software and conceptual modelling and metamodelling literature to date. Furthermore, since we use set theory as our basic mathematical reference (as outlined in Section 3.1 below), we note that the predicate used to specify set membership defines the common property of all members of that set (Denning, Dennis, & Qualitz, 1978, p. 13).

In the years following the OMG adoption (and consequently widespread industry adoption) of the 4-layer architecture of Figure 3, attention was turned to its application for process modelling and the depiction of lifecycle methodologies. Whilst some authors (Kent, Evans, & Rumpe, 1999; Halpin & Bloesch, 1999; Álvarez, Evans, & Sammut, 2001) have questioned the poor semantics of UML in general, Atkinson & Kühne (2001b) identified two major problems particularly relevant to process modelling: firstly, that in many cases, an attribute of an M2 class did not require a (slot) value to be determined until instantiated to an M0 instance. Since strict metamodelling enshrines two-level type-instance semantics, this is not possible because the M2 attribute has a value at M1 not M0. (Alternatively, one could define the attribute at M1 giving the required slot value at M0; but this is not acceptable since it is desired to have the standard at M2 not M1.) Their solution was to invent a tag on the attribute that could be used to override such type-instance semantics by specifying at what level beneath the definition the attribute could acquire its value. This is called deep instantiation using tags known as potency (see Figure 7 and the further detailed discussion in Section 3.1) – our first serious Ptolemaic fix!

2.2.2.2. The Alignment of Product and Process in a Methodology Fix

Secondly, a work product such as a (UML) Class Diagram is clearly an artefact that exists at the (OMG) M1 level. However, if processes and methodologies are being modelled, this is no longer true since work products are the inputs and outputs of elements of process (typically of tasks that form the overall process). They are created

Figure 7. The use of deep instantiation and potency to permit a value to be assigned two "levels" below its definition

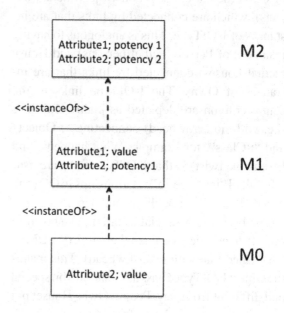

by people working on projects. When characterized in terms of a multilevel architecture for the methodology domain (Figure 8), one can see that the 'M1' level describes the methodology a.k.a. process model – that is equivalent to a methodology[13] described in a book or on a collection of Webpages – while the actual process 'enactment'

Figure 8. The "layers" of process and method terminology (modified from Henderson-Sellers, 2006)

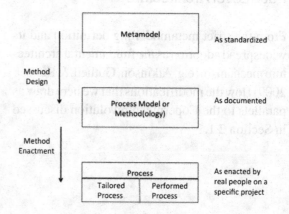

occurs at the equivalent of the OMG level M0. It is at this level that work products are created and used. This is in effect a contradiction (or at least a challenge) since work products are now expected to be in both the M1 level (if viewed as UML design diagrams) but at M0 when one considers how they are actually created by real people on real projects (e.g. Gonzalez-Perez & Henderson-Sellers, 2006). In the series of papers by Atkinson and Kühne (2001b, 2003, 2005), a number of alternative fixes are described based on the assumption that strict metamodelling MUST be adhered to. If, on the other hand, it is permissible to abandon the strict metamodelling constraints, then other solutions become possible (as we will discuss below).

Furthermore, as seen in Figure 8 and pointed out by McBride and Henderson-Sellers (2011), there is actually a static and a dynamic discrimination at the process enactment (M0) level: the process model individualized for a particular project (the 'tailored process') and its dynamic progress in calendar time (the 'performed process').

As part of the proposed reformulation of the UML from Version 1 to Version 2, Álvarez, Evans, and Sammut (2001) proposed the Meta-Modeling Language (MML). Whilst deviating from strict metamodelling, they argue it fulfils the mandatory requirements for UML 2.0 (OMG, 2000) by ensuring that exactly one element of a model conforms to a single element in a model at a higher level. Their deviation is that sometimes that higher level is one level higher and sometimes two levels (Figure 9). This is essentially the same idea as that of deep instantiation, in that it provides a mechanism for instantiation across multiple levels. Whilst a formal proposal based on these ideas was made to the OMG for UML Version 2.0 (OMG, 2002), it was not included in the standard (OMG, 2006); although it presages proposals for a single level model alluded to in Section 4. This is arguably, as it stands (but not as argued in Section 4), also a Ptolemaic fix!

Figure 9. Instantiation of the MML metamodel (after Álvarez, Evans, & Sammut, 2001) (with kind permission of Springer Science+Business Media)

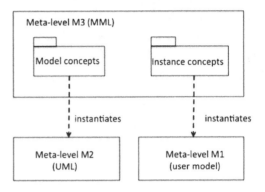

2.2.2.3. The Clabject Fix

The next problem that can be identified with Figure 3 is the sole use of instanceOf between layers, which immediately leads to a chain of instanceOf relationships. The problem here is that, when we take the normal modelling interpretation of instance as an (atomic) individual or particular, we see that instanceOf strictly relates to a pair of layers *only*. This means that it is an intransitive relationship that creates an instance (an object) from a type (e.g. an OO class); since this instance is indeed an individual it cannot then be further instantiated. This is consistent with the basically two-layer model embedded within the four-layer architecture of Figure 3. Whilst it is of course possible to view a class (or type) as an individual, this is not anticipated within the OMG modelling architecture. The consequence of such an extended instanceOf chain would be the need to consider its mathematical representation in terms of sets of sets – an approach that deserves future attention but which has historically not been considered.

However, what is often required is such a chain of entities linked by instanceOf relationships, as shown in the left hand side of Figure 10. The modeller here wishes to state firstly that Prancer is a Horse, so that it is appropriate to model the idea of a Horse as a class but that we also wish

Figure 10. On the left-hand side, horse is shown as a class that is also an instance of class, which is impossible within the conventional object-oriented paradigm. On the right-hand side, horse is shown as a class that is specified by the objects obj1 through a forward-looking isotypical interpretive mapping (depicted as a solid arrow).

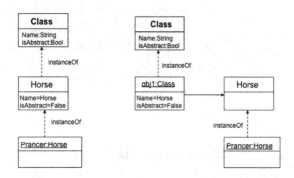

to connect the Horse class to the definition of Class in the metamodel – this leads to the need for conformance of that Horse class to an entity in the defining metamodel, here the class named Class. As noted above, however, this double instanceOf chain must be invalid by virtue of the essentially two-layer nature of the traditional OO modelling approach (as discussed above). In our preliminary investigations (Gonzalez-Perez and Henderson-Sellers, 2007), we suggest that what must happen, as depicted on the right hand side of Figure 10, is that the developer automatically inserts a mapping from <u>obj1:Horse</u> (the object conformant to class Class) to a class of the same name, Horse, from which individual horses, such as Prancer, can be instantiated in the model. Another interpretation is that the middle level entity is neither wholly a class nor wholly an object. It is an amalgam of class and object, an entity named 'clabject' by Atkinson (1999). Introduction of these clabjects into the four level strict metamodelling hierarchy clearly represents another Ptolemaic 'fix'.

2.2.2.4. The Powertype "Fix"

The fourth problem results from a confusion between, and consequent misapplication of, the generalization relationship and the instantiation (instanceOf) relationship. This is most clearly seen when simple set theoretic representations of types/classes and their instances are depicted using Euler or Venn diagrams[14]. If we represent each class as a set, then the instances of that class (objects) are members of that set (Figure 11) – the allocation of a particular instance to a class (set) being called classification (for an interesting discussion of classification and categorization, although not ontology-related, see Lakoff [1987]; a more recent detailed discussion of generalization compared to classification in the software modelling language context is to be found in Kühne [2009]). A collection of a limited number of these members creates a subset (in OO terms, a subclass or subtype – see also Cardelli, 1988), which is represented in an OO modelling language by a generalization/specialization relationship (Figure 12). As seen in Figure 12, any individual member of the subset **A** is also a member of the set **B** but the subset **A** is NOT itself necessarily a member of set **B**. On the other hand, if all the individual members of set **B** are grouped into a finite number of partitions, then each partition can be visualized as a member of a set – but this set

Figure 11. Simple set membership representation useful for OO classes and their instances (after Henderson-Sellers, 2012) (with kind permission of Springer Science+Business Media)

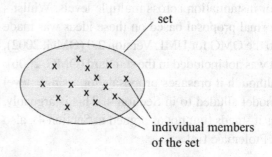

Figure 12. Representation of a subset as an Euler diagram (upper) and as a UML model (lower)

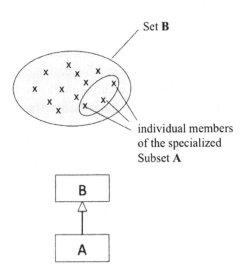

(as shown in Figure 13) is NOT the set **B**. This subtle distinction between the two different uses of an Euler diagram showing topological inclusion (physical containment on the two-dimensional plane) highlights a common confusion when depicting generalization and instantiation using essentially the same graphical means and trying to make logical deductions from the visualizations alone (see also later discussion).

Such mathematical representations have been in use in simple form for many years (e.g. Martin & Odell, 1992) but only by a limited set of authors discussing (object-oriented) modelling. In the last

Figure 13. Representation of each subset of set B as an element in a new set, C

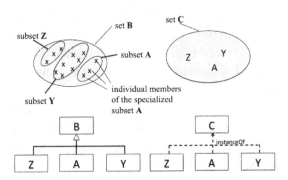

decade, with the rise of the acceptance of metamodelling as a formality for modelling languages, more extensive use of set theory (together with a promise of category theory) has been made (e.g. Whitmire, 1997; Henderson-Sellers, 2012) – see more detailed discussion in Section 3.1.

A solution to the generalization and instantiation (instanceOf) relationship misapplication has been explored in series of papers by Henderson-Sellers & Gonzalez-Perez (2005, 2006); Gonzalez-Perez & Henderson-Sellers (2006) using the mathematical ideas of powertypes (e.g. Cardelli, 1988) - introduced into software modelling first by Odell (1994) (see detailed discussion in Section 3.1 below). Whether powertypes provide our next Ptolemaic fix (as suggested by Atkinson, Gutheil, & Kennel, 2009) or whether they are the progenitors of a modelling revolution remains to be assessed.

2.2.2.5. The "Orthogonal Classification Architecture Fix"

The next concern that arose in the literature (Atkinson & Kühne, 2003) led to the creation of two sorts of metamodelling: linguistic and ontological. Figure 14 shows the 'Orthogonal Classification Architecture' that these authors proposed. It has three linguistic layers: the top L3 layer being the layer in which a Metaclass is defined. Instances of this (in the L2 layer) are entities such as Class and Object (although often objects are considered to be in the L0 layer since they are instances of classes in the L1 layer[15] – a well known UML paradox, e.g. Atkinson & Kühne, 2001a). Since this L2 layer provides the 'metamodel' or, arguably (see discussion below), the 'modelling language' then the model (as created by software developers) contains entities representing concepts and things in the real world (e.g. Lakoff, 1987, p. 8) (or at least the domain under consideration). In this example, these are Rover (an individual), Collie (a concept or class of dogs) and Breed. The

Figure 14. Linguistic versus ontological metamodelling (slightly modified from Henderson-Sellers, 2012) (with kind permission of Springer Science+Business Media)

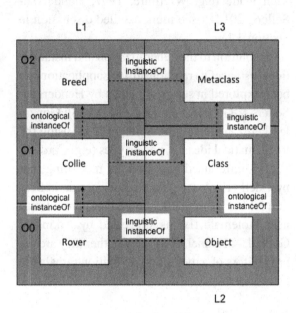

argument proposed by these authors is that there is a close parallel between Rover-Collie-Breed (left hand side of Figure 14) and Object-Class-Metaclass (right hand side) and thus one should deduce that Breed is in some way a metaclass. Clearly this is not a metaclass in the way that Class or Metaclass are on the right hand side of this diagram since obviously one would not expect to find a Breed entity in any standard definition (at the 'M2' level of Figure 3) of a general purpose modelling language (whether or not one could expect it in a domain-specific modelling language is another question that we do not address here). The authors therefore conclude that what is needed is a second kind of multilevel modelling hierarchy in which Breed, Collie, and Rover can co-exist whilst, at the same time, be described using instanceOf relationships and hence some kind of multilevel architecture that looks highly similar to the OMG architecture of Figure 3. To facilitate this, the notion of 'ontological instanceOf' is introduced as distinct from the linguistic

instanceOf that links elements in the real world to defining classes in the modelling language's metamodel. Thus, it is argued that, even though strict metamodelling forbids instanceOf within a layer, this is now understood to mean linguistic instanceOf. In other words, ontological instanceOf is permitted within such a single linguistic layer e.g. L1, but, conversely, is not to be used between linguistic layers

A number of authors have tried to extend these ideas further in the search for a 'Level-Agnostic Language (LAL)' (e.g. Atkinson, Kennel, & Goß, 2011a). Other authors (e.g. Seidewitz, 2003) have argued for instanceOf within a layer based on the assumption that such a single layer is formally a 'theory', which, by definition, permits instanceOf relationships within it i.e. within a single layer and not between layers – effectively a contradiction of the assumptions underpinning strict metamodelling.

An associated discussion is exemplified by the challenge of modelling products and product categories. A typical example is that of cars, their brands (e.g. Toyota), models of a given brand (e.g. Prius, Camry, Corolla) and variants on those models (e.g. Prius, Prius c, Prius v). Suggestions can be found in the early OO literature and, more recently, in Atkinson and Kühne (2008) and Neumayr, Schrefl, and Thalheim (2011). These latter authors compare several means by which multi-level modelling (i.e. not multilevel metamodelling as we focus on in this chapter) can be accomplished by means of powertypes[16] (two versions), deep instantiation and materialization, evaluating these approaches with several functional characteristics including accidental complexity, a topic discussed more by Atkinson and Kühne (2008). In both these studies, however, all classes and instances belong to the L1 domain of Figure 14 albeit at a range of ontological (Ox) levels. These studies, although interesting applications of deep instantiation and powertypes, do not consider language definitions nor linguistic metamodels and so will not be discussed further here.

2.2.3. The Need for a Copernican-Style Revolution in Metamodelling

The conclusion one must make is that several Ptolemaic fixes have already been applied to a general purpose modelling language ensconced in a multi-layer framework. To improve these modelling languages further, other avenues have been explored – in particular suggestions to incorporate foundational ontologies and insights from language use.

Over the past few years, such collaborations and technology transfer have been attempted between ontology engineering and software engineering, specifically software modelling languages. For example, using the Unified Foundational Ontology (UFO) (Guizzardi, 2005), Guizzardi, Wagner, Guarino, and van Sinderen (2004) make some suggestions regarding the incorporation of ontological classes into the UML metamodel. Such contributions reflect a slightly different mindset in domain ontologies – that of a single inheritance tree and precious few other relationships – as compared to an object modeller who will minimize the depth of inheritance hierarchies and, conversely, populate their UML models with a range of relationships such as associations and aggregations. Linking ontologies, metamodels and modelling languages has been explored, for instance, by Aßmann, Zschaler, and Wagner (2006) and Henderson-Sellers (2011a). A coalescence of these ideas together with set theory is explored in Henderson-Sellers (2012) and in further detail in Section 3.4.

Even more recently, the disciplinary area of language use (e.g. Austin, 1962) and, especially, speech acts (e.g. Searle, 1969) have begun to be considered in the modelling and metamodelling literature. Eriksson, Henderson-Sellers, and Ågerfalk (2013) show how these ideas can be fully integrated into a modelling language whilst in his introduction to the book *The Evolution of Conceptual Modeling*, Kaschek (2011) uses not only the term speech act but also refers to 'language games' with reference to Wittgenstein. To date, the direct influence of philosophers is limited. However, it is becoming clear that conceptual modelling has a Lockean basis – Locke's (1690) ideas (see also Armstrong, 1989) now generally having been replaced by philosophical thoughts of, for Brentano (1874) and Peirce (1898). Such recent and pending influences need to be discussed in detail and evaluated in terms of their potential applicability to conceptual modelling, potentially offering more revolutionary ideas to the discipline of software language engineering (paper in preparation).

Notwithstanding, the ontological/linguistic debate continues, linked strongly to the assertion that strict metamodelling should be maintained *at all costs* (e.g. Atkinson, Gutheil, and Kennel [2009], who state that "Without this principle, the definition of model levels becomes somewhat arbitrary"). This need to retain strict metamodelling is at the core of many of the 'Ptolemaic fixes' that have occurred in software language engineering since the mid-1990s. In summary, these are:

- The potency fix.
- The product and process alignment fix of methodology.
- The clabject fix.
- The powertype fix.
- The 'Orthogonal Classification Architecture' fix.

It is as yet unclear whether powertypes constitute a 'Ptolemaic fix' or whether they are the harbingers of a new mindset in conceptual modelling and metamodelling – a quandary we will attempt to resolve in the latter part of this chapter.

The challenge (that we address below) is therefore the need to identify a formal (mathematical) underpinning that permits (1) standardization (i.e. not accessible to developers), (2) modelling languages (used by software developers) for both product and process, and (3) a means to represent the static and dynamic aspects of process enactment. Clearly the axioms currently used in strict metamodelling are not helpful for contemporary product and process modelling (i.e. we need, at least, to be able to link the attribute definitions of a class at 'M2' to the slot values of a corresponding instance at 'M0': Figure 15) as well as for linking methodologies to ontologies. We suggest here that too many Ptolemaic fixes have been made already; a Copernican revolution is needed to sweep away the old and introduce a new metamodelling mindset.

As a critical part of that impending revolution, the equivalency of modelling language and metamodel needs to be challenged; the underpinning philosophy tenets of conceptual modelling need to be investigated and a new paradigm needs to be identified, developed and adopted. We suggest that it is time for a Kuhnian (1962) paradigm shift from our current Ptolemaic (read strict metamodelling) way of thinking to a new Copernican model of our particular software universe (software language engineering and conceptual modelling).

Figure 15. The challenge of retaining a class-instance relationship for contiguous pairs of layers and identifying an appropriate mathematical link between OMG levels M0 and M2 in particular

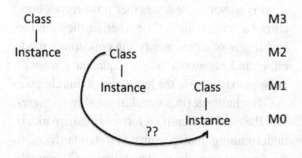

3. EVOLUTION: ADDITION OF SAFETY HARNESSES IN MODELLING

The history of computing is that of adding increasing usability and safety. Early programming required significant knowledge and technical ability in coding in machine code. Later developments led first to assembler and then to procedural languages such as COBOL and FORTRAN that were nearer to a human's mode of speech – although still stilted. Such an innovation at the same time makes coding easier, making it harder to make 'stupid mistakes' in the binary code (now to be generated) but at the same time denies the ability of the good programmer some flexibility. The next innovation, object technology, added additional safety by enforcing a significant degree of modularization and information hiding (Parnas, 1972). The interfaces of the program chunks (now objects, previously subroutines) are minimized *by default*. Nevertheless, it is still quite possible to do excellent modular programming in an older, non-object-oriented language such as FORTRAN but it requires some attention to detail and additional work on the part of the programmer. With an object-oriented programming language such as Eiffel (Meyer, 1988) it is not possible to violate these modularization principles.

Similar comments apply to the evolution (and potential evolution) of modelling languages and their incarnations in the form of drawing and CASE (computer aided software engineering) tools. A drawing tool like Visio™ is able to support the drawing of all the symbols of UML but has no knowledge of the semantics of the modelling language. A CASE tool that embodies the language rules will ensure that the modeller does not violate the rules of the modelling language, perhaps by greying out inappropriate selections. With such a contemporary CASE tool, one could quite easily draw the two model fragments shown in Figure 16. They could readily be understood as saying (a) that there are several kinds of customer, especially

Figure 16. Two ontologically incorrect examples, both of which are valid UML models

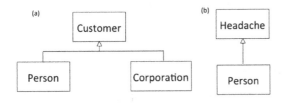

persons and corporations; and (b) that a person is a special kind of headache. In this chapter, we will argue that both of these are ontologically invalid, despite them being syntactically valid UML models – suggesting therefore that UML itself is incomplete insofar as it permits such invalid diagram fragments to be drawn.

In the following subsections, we explore in detail some of the several solutions proposed in respect to the issues raised in Section 2. We first explore the double instanceOf relationship embodied in much of the strict metamodelling literature and how powertypes appear to offer at least a partial solution, contrasting this approach with deep instantiation plus potency. We then introduce foundational ontologies and examine their support for various characteristics (notably adjectival properties using a moment universal and temporary properties captured in the notion of a role) that can be said to embellish a basic class in a conceptual model.

In Sections 3.4 and 3.5, we describe the recent contributions that have resulted from an examination of language use its incorporation, along with foundational ontologies, into the definition of a software modelling language.

3.1. Metamodelling Basics

As noted in Section 2, the type-instance relationship has been, for many years, taken as axiomatic in contemporary software modelling languages. This leads naturally, as we have seen, to representation of classes and types as sets with members

of those sets representing individuals or instances (Figure 11). The term 'meta' is then often used to refer to the type layer relative to the instance layer (e.g. Atkinson, 1999).

Whilst this type-instance model works well across two-layers, as we have seen, software language engineering requires more than two layers, especially for modelling processes. We can thus depict not only M0 instances of an M1 type but also M1 instances of an M2 type (Figure 17) or even M2 instances of an M3 type (not shown here). Thus the members of an M2 level class are in fact types/classes representable as sets. Furthermore, it is generally accepted that, while sets have members, these only form the *extension* of the set. To create a type, we need to add some semantics in the form of rules that determine whether a candidate member does or does not belong to the set. Such rules are generally in the form of a predicate, *p(x),* and are said to be the *intension* of the set. Kühne (2009) notes that this approach uses ideas from Carnap (1947): a pupil of Frege who extended the ideas on Wittgenstein (1921) and developed the notion of a 'concept' as being the entity represented by a mathematical set or, with an intension, a type (e.g. Frege, 1892b); although such categorization may not always be consistent with a single set of unalterable and readily identifiable properties (Wittgenstein, 1953, pp. 6-71)[17]. This notion of 'concept' was also a key in the work of Martin and Odell (1992) in explaining the theoretical ideas behind object-oriented modelling. However, the idea of concept has more recently been challenged on philosophical grounds – another indication that a revolution in metamodelling thinking is due. Smith (2004) identifies significant ambiguity in the use of the term and recommends its avoidance, particularly in the context of domain ontologies. Indeed, Searle (1969) recommends that we should abandon the use of the word concept in our current context.

Figure 17 illustrates two type-instance relationships (as seen also in Figure 15). It is tempting, but incorrect, to link these in a 'double instanceOf'

Figure 17. Using set theory to represent instanceOf

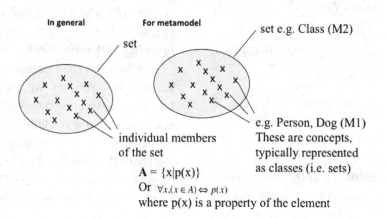

chain (Figure 18) and continue to assert that this remains valid according to the basic type-instance axiom. Figure 18 shows an individual dog (Rover) as an instance of a Dog set combined with, supposedly, the statement that a Dog (now a class) is an instance of the UML (M2) class called Class (i.e. a Fregian concept). The problem here is simply that Dog as a set with members such as Rover is NOT the same as the Dog class, when considered as an instance of the M2 Class. This is readily seen when we consider the attributes of Dog as a class and Dog as an instance in the model. As an object, Dog might have attributes (instantiated from the UML V2.4 class Class) of $isActive=F$; $isAbstract=F$; isFinalSpecialization=F; whilst Dog as a class is likely to have attributes such as name, height, colour.

The only acceptable and simplistic mathematical description of data such as that in Figure 17

Figure 18. An often seen double instanceOf chain purportedly to represent both rover as an instance of a dog class and, at the same time, dog as an instance of class

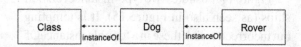

or Figure 18 is that of a set of sets. In other words, in Figure 18 we could say that Class is a set containing a number of members, all of which are themselves sets (e.g. the Dog set, the Cat set, the BankAccount set). Then the Dog set has many members, one of which is Rover. Whilst traditional (OMG) metamodelling has focussed on pairs of levels (simple set membership), this revision to sets of sets may provide an improved multilevel architecture of the future, remembering that one aim is to standardize elements at the M2 level such that appropriate attributes and their values occur at the correct level (M1 or M0). However, it does not provide an ability to transmit attributes from their specification in M2 to an attribute value at M0 i.e. a set of sets model effectively decouples the M0 and M2 levels.

Another mathematical construction in set theory, closely aligned but potentially confused with set of sets, is the powerset. A powerset is defined as a set composed of all possible subsets – a very simple example is shown in Figure 19. In software engineering, a similar notion was introduced by Odell (1994) and named, perhaps a little inappropriately, 'powertype' since this software version does not contain *all* subsets but only sufficient subsets to partition the original set. Strictly, this is called a 'family of sets' in mathematics – although for historical and continu-

Figure 19. A powerset D contains elements of all subsets of the original set C

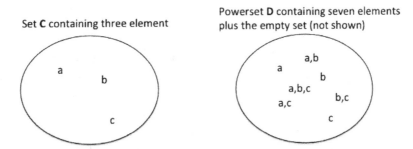

ity reasons we will continue to utilize the name 'powertype' for this.

Indeed, as noted in Section 2, there is a possibility of confusion when we re-look at the members in a set and partition them into subsets. Figure 20 shows one such example in the software methodology domain. We can model various activities within a methodology, grouping some of these as Design-type activities, some as Code-linked activities and the remainder as Testing activities (left hand side of Figure 20). This grouping creates, in this example, three partitions such that each partition in the Euler diagram can be represented in OO fashion as one class (named Activity) with three subclasses/subtypes as shown. This model also uses the UML generalization

Figure 20. Comparison of generalization and instantiation for the same data set (modified from Henderson-Sellers, 2011b) (with kind permission of Springer Science+Business Media)

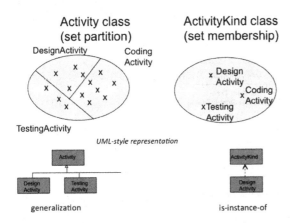

relationship to link subtypes and (super)type. If we now consider each partition as a single entity (right hand side of Figure 20), then we can construct a new set representation which has three members only: DesignActivity, CodingActivity and TestingActivity. Clearly this must represent a different class/type from the Activity class since, obviously, there is a large disparity in the number of elements in each of these two sets, the one on the left being our original Activity class/set and the one on the right with a new appellation of ActivityKind. The relationship between ActivityKind and, for example, DesignActivity is that of instanceOf. Confusion can often arise because the name 'Coding Activity' can be interpreted as both the name of the sector (Figure 20 left hand side) and the name of an instance (Figure 20 right hand side). We could also say 'a coding activity' meaning an individual member of the Coding Activity sector in the left hand diagram of Figure 20.

Further inspection of Figure 20 leads to the identification of, for example, DesignActivity as both a subtype of the type called Activity and as an instance of a type called ActivityKind. Furthermore, the members of the set ActivityKind each represent one of the partitions of the set called Activity. We can thus redraw this information as a powertype pattern as shown in Figure 21. Note that this also means that DesignActivity etc. are in fact clabjects. Thus, they have not only an object facet but also a class facet so that, from this class facet, further instantiation can take place.

Figure 21. Representation of the data of Figure 20 as a traditional powertype pattern

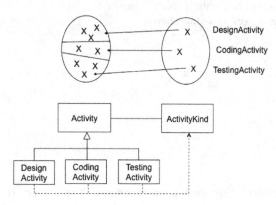

If we now (at least loosely) place Activity and ActivityKind in the OMG architecture's M2 level, then DesignActivity, CodingActivity and Testing Activity are at the M1 level (i.e. they are part of the process model a.k.a. methodology – see discussion of Figure 8 above) and a project-specific (instanceOf) DesignActivity, say called Brian's design activity can be created at the M0 level. If, for the sake of argument, we wanted this M0 level instance to have an attribute value of 2 days for an attribute called Duration whilst acknowledging that all instances of DesignActivity needed a managerial signoff, then we can represent this as shown in Figure 22. Although this is current state-of-the-art, in Section 2 we concluded that clabject and powertypes were (probably) Ptolemaic fixes. This is a major target of the revolution proposed in Section 4 below.

Gonzalez-Perez and Henderson-Sellers (2008) argued that powertypes have value in software engineering metamodelling – whether this is valid or whether powertypes are a current Ptolemaic fix such that they should be replaced remains an open question. However, we do note that some other authors have reservations about the use of powertypes – although this relates more to their use in modelling than in metamodelling. For instance, Halpin (2005) argues that for most modelling examples he can devise (see also modelling ex-

amples in Martin & Odell, 1998), there are better ways of accomplishing the same result without using either powertypes or the very similar ideas of materialization (Pirotte, Zimányi, Massart, & Yakusheva, 1994; Dahchour & Pirotte, 2002). For many modelling situations, this is undoubtedly true but for the specific multilevel issue of declaring an attribute at the metamodel/standardized level that should not be given a value until two 'levels' lower (as discussed above), there is no simple alternative, other than potency, which, as we discuss below, appears to have less theoretical foundation than powertypes although at the same time being easier to implement.

As noted above, Figure 22 shows how the use of powertypes, themselves mathematically based (as discussed above), can lead to a solution to the challenge of defining attributes in the metamodel but refraining from allocating values until the endeavour level (i.e. at enactment). The result is not dissimilar to the result achieved by the more pragmatic use of potency and deep instantiation (Figure 7) – a visual comparison of these two approaches is shown in Figure 23. In this approach, each attribute of a class has an associated potency value. Each time the responsible class is instantiated, the potency value of all its attributes

Figure 22. An illustration of the use of a powertype to support attribute values at both M1 and M0 level

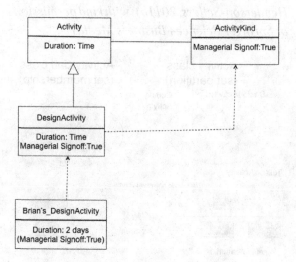

Figure 23. Comparison of potency and powertype approaches (after Gonzalez-Perez & Henderson-Sellers, 2006) (with kind permission of Springer Science+Business Media)

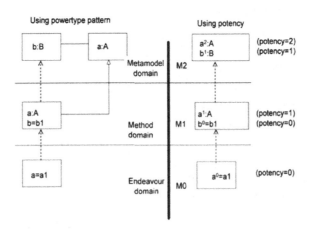

is decremented. When the potency has a value of zero, a value *must* be assigned.

The deep instantiation plus potency approach was invented in order to permit multilevel modelling of processes and methodologies; particularly to permit standardization at OMG level M2 for methodology elements that had attributes that need to have their value allocated at OMG level M0 i.e. *two* levels below the metamodel standard. Type-instance semantics is unable to provide such support; this newer potency approach is, although the underlying theory is either arcane or unavailable.

These issues are also discussed in detail in Atkinson, Gutheil, and Kennel (2009) although in that case the context is that of insisting that a solution fits within the strict metamodelling hierarchy of Figure 3 (which deep instantiation does but which powertypes do not). Indeed, the use of powertypes necessitates a new multilevel architecture, as shown in Figure 24. In this architecture, devised initially for use in the International Standard ISO/IEC 24744 (ISO/IEC, 2007), the 'levels' (here renamed 'domains') are defined in terms of what is observed in practice viz. people work on endeavours (in the Endeavour Domain), they use tools, methodologies etc. in the Method Domain, all of which are defined by a metamodel

Figure 24. Multi-level architecture based on powertypes rather than strict metamodelling (after Henderson-Sellers, 2006)

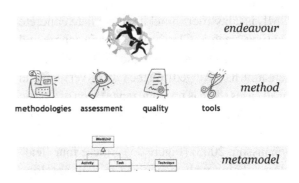

(which thus defines the scope of the Metamodel Domain).

Gonzalez-Perez and Henderson-Sellers (2008) note that the potency approach has the advantage of having one less class to consider and that the potency idea is not limited to the three layers that we have used in this example. However, the use of an additional class in the powertype approach allows an explicit differentiation between the two very different classes (xxx and xxxKind: as we shall see later, these are a base type and a universal – see Figure 20), that are by necessity convoluted in the potency approach. Secondly, in the potency approach there is an *implicit* introduction of a generalization relationship (as noted above), hidden within the instance-of relationship overlain by a potency decrement whereas in the powertype approach the necessary generalization relationship (which after all is responsible for the ability of either of these approaches to transmit attributes unchanged) is explicit. According to these two aspects, it could be argued that the powertype approach allows for a more faithful and explicit representation of the SUS.

3.2. The UML Metamodel: Improving Its Modelling Language Contribution

As noted above, the current UML needs a degree of developer discipline and expertise to use it to its fullest potential. It is, nevertheless, still possible to draw ontologically incorrect diagrams such as those introduced earlier e.g. Figure 16. This is because the finest grained ontological concept in UML is Classifier[18] (and its immediate concrete subtypes such as Class). Although instances and classes are differentiated in the UML, their representation has changed over the various versions and in all cases there is no cognizance taken of a basic discriminant used in some schools of ontology engineering: that of endurants and perdurants (e.g. Johansson, 2005) (Figure 25) – these four 'leaf' classes being well recognized in both ontology (e.g. Guizzardi, 2005; Laarman & Kurtev, 2010) and philosophy (e.g. Aristotle in translation, 1984; Smith, 1997; Lowe, 2001; Partridge, 2002); noting that in some philosophical approaches (e.g. Quine, 1960; Lewis, 1971; Sider, 2003), only perdurants are recognized (see also http://plato.stanford.edu/entries/temporal-parts).

Foundational ontologies contain a much richer classification hierarchy, subtypes of the four 'leaf' classes of Figure 25. For example, Figure 26 shows the hierarchy proposed by Guarino and Welty (2000) and Figure 27 depicts a similarly scoped proposal by Guizzardi (2005) known as the Unified Foundational Ontology or UFO. It is this latter that we will use in our subsequent

Figure 25. Basic structure of a foundational ontology

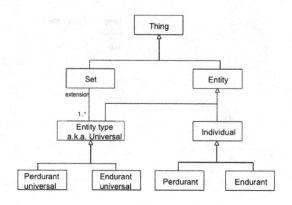

Figure 26. A formal foundational ontology as devised by Guarino and Welty (2000)

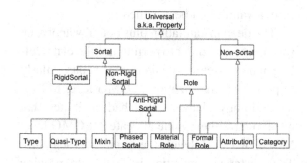

Figure 27. A formal foundational ontology as devised by Guizzardi (2005)

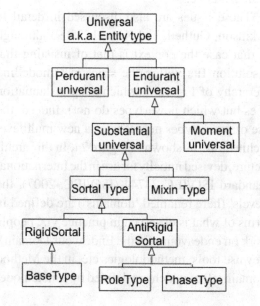

discussion since the context of its derivation was closest to our context of modelling languages and metamodels (e.g. Guizzardi, Wagner, Guarino, & van Sinderen, 2004; Guizzardi & Wagner, 2005), although as part of our ongoing philosophical and ontological analysis of metamodelling approaches we intend to provide an improved foundational ontology (paper in preparation). In particular, we will utilize instances of MomentUniversal and RoleType, the definitions for which are given by Guizzardi and Wagner (2005) as:

Definition 1: A MomentUniversal is a kind of EndurantUniversal that cannot exist by itself; that is, it depends on other EndurantUniversals that are not among its parts

Definition 2: A RoleType is a "sortal type that is anti-rigid and for which there is a relationship type such that it is the subtype of a base type formed by all instances participating in the relationship type."

Guizzardi and Wagner (2005) give as an example of RoleType that of Student. This is clearly anti-rigid since it can have instances (e.g. John) that are presently members of the extension of the Student class but could easily (at a later time) leave i.e. remove themselves from such set membership. (A similar notion is depicted by Martin and Odell [1995] – see Figure 28). However, since we are depicting these ontological categories in terms of set theory, the concern arises that sets

do not change membership (Partridge, 2012, pers. comm.) since the set and its membership are inextricably linked. In other words, if the membership changes then the set is no longer the same set. Figure 29 shows how roles could be represented in this way, ostensibly as sets. Thus, whilst the set B is well-defined at time t and also at time t' (since it contains the same members at all times), the subset A that contains member y at time t must be replaced by a different subset A' that does not contain y as a member at time t'. In other words, the mathematics of roles cannot be represented simply by set theory and, furthermore, can be aligned with neither classification nor instantiation as discussed further below. Thus it is not possible to use set theory to depict a role. Indeed, the difficulty of adequately representing such temporal change is recognized by Smith (2004) who proposes the following modification to the definition of subsumption:

Definition 3: A is-a B if and only if:

1. A and B are universals.
2. For all times *t*, if anything instantiates universal A at *t* then that same thing must instantiate also the universal B at *t*.

*Figure 29. An individual playing a role may do so at time t (and hence be a member of the subset **A**) but at a later time t' may be a member of the set **B** but this means that the set **A** must be replaced by a totally different set **A'***

Figure 28. The Brian object takes on roles at different stages in his life – depicted here as suggested in Martin and Odell (1995)

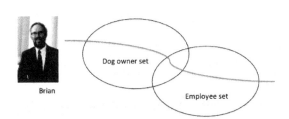

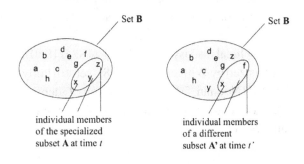

Other important leaf classes in the UFO, to which we will refer later, are BaseType and MixinType. The definitions for these are given by Guizzardi & Wagner (2005) as:

Definition 4: A BaseType is a SortalType that is rigid (all its instances are necessarily its instances) and that supplies an identity criterion for its instances

Person is given as an example of a BaseType. It is easily seen that all instances of Person (as a class) – e.g. Brian, Owen – are necessarily instances of Person and that each instance has an identity criterion, as defined by the Person class.

Definition 5: A MixinType is an entity type that is not a sortal type and can be partitioned into disjoint subtypes which are sortal types (typically role types) with different identity criteria. Since a mixin is a non-sortal it cannot have direct instances.

Mixins tend to describe characteristics that are 'adjectival' i.e. they are concepts existentially dependent upon a substantial universal. Examples might be RedObject, which might refer to an apple, a shirt or a car) and Product (television, car, wine bottle). Interestingly, Customer can also be said to be a mixin as it could refer to a person or an organization – although some authors use Customer as a prime exemplar of the RoleType (a digression that we will not address here). Arguably, mixins provide yet another Ptolemaic fix, worthy of further analysis using a well-founded philosophy of modelling (paper in preparation).

An important element of the above five definitions is the notion of identity. Introduced into philosophical discussions by Frege (1884, 1950), emphasized by Wittgenstein (1958), yet still hotly debated (Noonan, 2011), the criterion of identity is used to determine whether two things are the same or not.

To augment a modelling language, like UML, with a broader ontological basis, one could 'hang' a hierarchy such as that in Figure 27 beneath a leaf class in the UML by making Universal (entity type) a direct subtype of Class (and transitively of Classifier) (Figure 30) - together with new subtypes of the Dependency Relationship and Association and introducing new meronymic relationships into the extant UML metamodel.

Such a new availability of metalevel classes (quasi M2) such as MixinType and, especially, MomentUniversal, offers extended modelling capability that allows for much greater quality modelling in the sense that no longer does everything have to be a base type (since in current UML, base types are essentially the only kind of class available to the modeller). Thus, for example, moment universals such as 'headache' or 'dog breed', which are concepts that are existentially dependent on other concepts, can be modelled directly. Figure 31 shows a simple association

Figure 30. The addition of a foundational ontology into a standard modelling language like UML

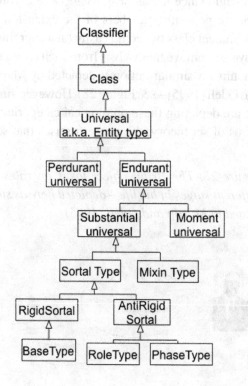

Figure 31. The use of a moment universal to depict existentially dependent characteristic of base types

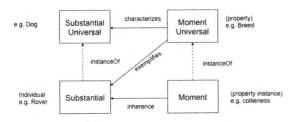

that attaches Headache to Brian (not shown) or Collieness to Rover.

Recognition of the availability of moment universals now also permits a re-evaluation of the double-instanceOf conundrum as seen in the literature and as exemplified earlier here in Figures 10 and 18. One recent example was identified in the literature (Atkinson, Gutheil, & Kennel, 2009) as a major running example in their evaluation of potency as compared to powertype modelling. An analogous example is given in Figure 32.

As well as the obvious double instanceOf, there are several other concerns in Figure 32.

- A type (e.g. MedicalPractitioner) cannot be an instance of another type (e.g. Profession), see the "powertype fix" above[19]. If MedicalPractitioner *were* an instance of Profession, then it is an object (an individual) that cannot be further instantiated (to Peter) – unless we extend traditional modelling to include types of types (sets of sets).
- Peter is an instance of a base type, Person, which is not included in the model.

Figure 32. An example of a double instanceOf chain of three linked classes

MedicalPractitioner is not a base type, it is a property name (Searle, 1969).

- MedicalPractitioner cannot be an instance of Profession – either MedicalProfession is an instance of Profession or MedicalPractitioner is an instance of Professional.

Figure 33 underlines some of these concerns graphically, with the third of the four corrections above now incorporated i.e. Profession moderated to be Professional. Remembering that a diagram such as this can easily confound set membership with set partition, we can see that this is exactly what is happening with respect to the UML double instanceOf diagram on the left hand side of this diagram. On the right hand side we see in the Euler diagrammatic representation that Peter is an individual instance of the MedicalPractitioner set and, secondly, that the Professional set contains (at least) three subsets (partitions), here exemplified as the Civil Engineer, the Medical Practitioner and the ITProfessional. To reprise earlier discussions, we see that although Peter is an instance of MedicalPractitioner and MedicalPractitioner is a member of Professional, we CANNOT conclude that Peter is a member of Professional.

For a better quality model, we can utilize the ideas of moment universals as shown in Figure 31,

Figure 33. Slight revision of the double instanceOf chain of Figure 32 together with a depiction in terms of an Euler diagram

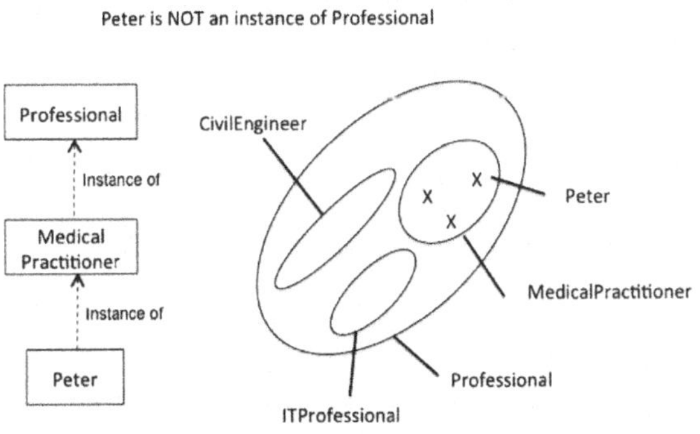

since Profession is actually a moment universal as it complies with Definition 1 above. Consequently, Figure 34 offers a more accurate model diagram than Figure 32. The base type of Person has a Profession (a moment universal) and then an instance of each is taken to represent the fact that Peter (an instance of Person) has a profession, which happens to be the MedicalProfession. Alternatively, we show this more mathematically as a function that maps instances of the Person set into instances of the Profession set (Figure 35) (the use of mathematical functions or mappings in this context is explored in more detail in Henderson-Sellers, 2012).

Figure 34. A revised version of Figure 32 using the moment universal as depicted in Figure 31

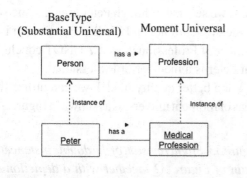

Figure 35. Alternative representation of the data in Figure 34 using mathematical functions (mappings) between sets

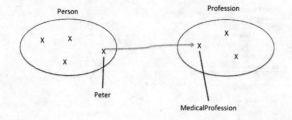

3.3. The Challenges of Role Modelling

Roles, which are one example where the qualities of a particular may change with time, have been long regarded as important in conceptual modelling and, especially, in agent models. The availability of RoleType in the UFO, once added to a modelling language, makes available a direct representation of roles rather than having to create them as stereotypes of a UML class (or similar) as is presently the case. These are shown in Figures 26 and 27 where they are depicted using UML generalization relationships. This generalization relationship is defined in UML.

A classifier can only specialize classifiers of a valid type. This valid type is defined by an operation maySpecializeType:

```
Classifier::maySpecializeType(c:
Classifier): Boolean;
maySpecializeType = self.
oclIsKindOf(c.oclType)
```

Thus, a classifier may only specialize classifiers of the same or a more general type e.g. an association cannot specialize a class or vice versa since "neither of the Association or Class metaclasses is a specialization of the other" (Seidewitz, 2012).

Consequently, a base type can specialize a rigid sortal but not an anti-rigid sortal (e.g. phase type, role type). This means that generalization relationships between instances of two 'leaf' classes is not permitted. Thus, by incorporating a foundational ontology (here Figure 27; itself interpreted as a UML class diagram) into a modelling language like UML and, as a consequence, necessarily adopting the rules of UML, we can immediately see that the two models proposed in Figure 16 are invalid. A person cannot be a customer since the former is (an instance of) a base type while the latter is a role type. Similarly, a headache is a moment universal. In both cases, the metaclass to which these classes (in Figure 16) are conformant are not related in any way (other than having a common ancestor). And intuitively, in the first case, we would not wish a person to be modelled as a kind of customer since there are many people, we would argue, that in a given context are NOT customers and, in the second case, a person being a headache is nonsensical.

However, appealing to common sense and intuition[20] identifies one problem that is worthy of discussion: whether it is valid to have a class representing a role as a subtype of a base type – a typical example is shown in Figure 36. Guizzardi & Wagner (2005) insist that commonsense should permit this – whilst not permitting the inverse i.e. Person as a kind of Student. In order to do this, they add a textual 'override' in their definition of RoleType in Figure 27 as given in Definition 2 above. In essence, they are adding an association in the UFO between RoleType and BaseType as

Figure 36. A typical generalization relationship between a role type and a base type

Figure 37. The necessary introduction of a Sub-TypeOf relationship linking RoleType to BaseType in the UFO

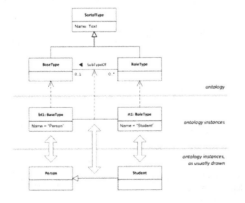

shown in Figure 37. Arguably another 'Ptolemaic fix'!

In fact, it is not even clear that the RoleType should be the focus of our attention. Rather than depicting a Person as moving in and out of Roles, an alternative is to consider Person as having a set of states, one of which is Student (Partridge, 2012, pers. comm.).

One reason for wishing to validate a diagram such as Figure 36 is the need for identity. In the UFO, only a base type (such as Person) can *supply* an identity criterion. Clearly an instance of Student also needs an identity but, being a role type, can only carry identity and not supply it (Guizzardi & Wagner, 2005). By making Student a subtype of Person, it can acquire the ability to create identity. Our concern is that this introduces a contradiction since, at heart, Student is a role type that CANNOT create identity. We suggest that another means for Student to acquire an identity criterion should be sought (as we do below).

Somewhat in contradiction to the common-sense notion that a student should be a subtype of person, Wieringa, de Jonge, and Spruit (1995) propose an alternative model in which they require a role instance to have identity independently of the base type playing that role i.e. that RoleType is a RigidSortal (in contradiction to Figure 27). In other words, in this approach, instances of Student obey a different principle of identity compared to instances of Person e.g. Masolo, Guizzardi, Vieu, Bottazzi, and Ferrario (2005). Guizzardi (2006) suggests, instead, that the conceptualization of role in Wieringa, de Jonge, and Spruit (1995) more closely accords with the notion of a qua-individual (Masolo, Guizzardi, Vieu, Bottazzi, & Ferrario, 2005)[21] in which the two participating entities (base type and role type in Figure 27) are constrained by one or more externally dependent qualities – for example, John-qua-husband involves a set of rights and responsibilities flowing from his participation (with Mary) in a marriage event. Bock and Odell (1994) note that a qua-type is "a convenient way of referring to subtypes that are created solely due to a relationship with another object type" – although often a qua-type is used for states i.e. types that change over time (Partridge, 2012, pers. com.)

Steimann (2000) also notes that a role is meaningful only in the context of a relationship i.e. he argues that it must be existentially dependent[22] upon a base type (or natural type as he calls it). Indeed, Masolo, Guizzardi, Vieu, Bottazzi, & Ferrario (2005) summarize their approach as follows: "students existentially specifically depend on persons but they are not persons (i.e. the instances of Student obey a different principle of identity than the instances of Person)". If Steimann's role model is accepted, then this statement in itself immediately precludes the generalization relationship between Person and Student as shown in Figure 36.

In order to discriminate between these various role models, Guizzardi (2006) proposes a harmonization of the two approaches, calling the notion of role as a moment universal (when the role is represented as a set of properties possessed by the substantial individual playing the role) 'qua individual type', whilst reserving the name 'role' for when the role is itself regarded as a substantial universal. Perhaps yet another Ptolemaic fix?

Although there is, as noted above, significant discussion in the literature about roles, especially in terms of the 'counting problem' (Wieringa, de Jonge, & Spruit, 1995; Steimann, 2000; Guizzardi, 2006), which will not concern us here, another major aspect of roles is their temporary nature. In Section 2.2 above (see Figure 29), we saw that the use of Euler diagrams could be confusing when representing generalization (classification and subtyping) as opposed to instantiation (set membership). Set theory, per se, is essentially time-independent; roles, by their very nature are context dependent (time and space).

Whilst following intuition and commonsense (according to Guizzardi, 2011-2012, pers. comm.), we need to ask if this Ptolemaic fix (of a textual override to permit an instance of RoleType to be

a subtype of an instance of BaseType), whilst being pragmatically useful, is really necessary – or whether there is a more theoretically useful means of achieving the same result. The analysis that follows focusses on the portion of Figure 27 that describes RoleType as an Anti-Rigid SortalType and BaseType as a Rigid SortalType. We investigate the validity of the hypothesis depicted by the exemplar model in Figure 36 (i.e. that Student is a subtype of Person).

If we use the mathematical ideas of Figure 17, then this portion of the UFO can be depicted using an Euler diagram as shown in Figure 38 (which for completeness also includes PhaseType although we will not include this in the following discussion). In this diagram, we note that one member of the SortalType is Person; whilst Student is a member of the RoleType partition. These partitions (and the inheritance structure of Figure 27) are all non-overlapping so that it is obvious that Person and Student are distinct types. If we now include the relationships of Figure 36 and depict the result using types and instances, we might deduce from Figure 39 that Brian is both a student and a person (Figure 40) but, more importantly for our discussion, that Student is an instance of both RoleType and BaseType. We might therefore

Figure 38. Euler diagram depicting the three types of Sortals. For each subtype (each disjoint partition), several instances are depicted. SortalType is a set with members that are themselves sets, i.e. SortalType is a set of sets (after Henderson-Sellers, 2012) (with kind permission of Springer Science+Business Media).

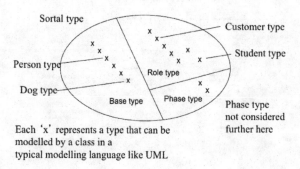

Each 'x' represents a type that can be modelled by a class in a typical modelling language like UML

Figure 39. UML diagram based on the UFO for the example of student (assumed to be a subtype of person – Figure 36)

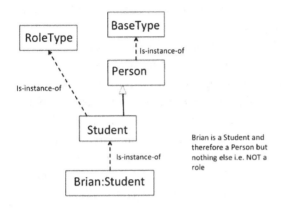

Figure 40. UML and Euler diagram representations of brian, the student and the person

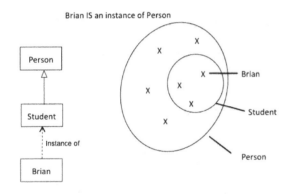

Figure 41. Intersecting sets: RoleType and BaseType purporting to show student as belonging to both sets

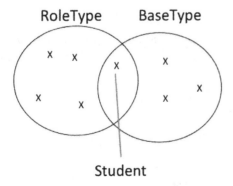

conclude that this means that RoleType and BaseType in fact overlap (Figure 41) and, since our original assertion was that these two types were in fact non-overlapping, we have a contradiction. Hence our original assumption – that Figure 36 is valid – is negated.

Whilst this argument is initially appealing, we will now demonstrate that it is in fact fallacious.

Figure 39 shows that Brian is a student i.e. he is a member of the Student class. Now, this Student class is a specialization of Person (according to this graphical depiction) so that we can also conclude that Brian is a Person. However, Student is an instance of RoleType so that a diagrammatic representation such as the right hand side of Figure 17 is valid i.e. we have no knowledge of the internalities of this 'point' in the Euler diagram (see also Figure 38 wherein student is just one element in the set RoleType). Conversely, since Student is shown in Figure 39 to be a subtype of Person, then a graphical representation such as that in Figure 12 is appropriate (Figure 40). This representation permits us to state that an individual student (here 'Brian') is a member of the Student subset and consequently also a member of the Person set. However, it is the Person set that is a member of the BaseType set. In this case, Person is effectively a 'point' (a particular) insofar as it is not possible to perceive or represent any internal details of Person in the representation of Figure 38 i.e. we can make no statement linking the Student subset (Figure 40) to BaseType, thus negating any apparent validity of Figure 41. We have thus used an Euler diagram in two different topological ways (as discussed earlier with respect to Figures 11 and 12), but not kept these two ways separate – as we must.

The only way to extend this set-based argument is to invoke sets of sets and interpret a 'M2' type as a set of sets. In this case, BaseType in Figure 38 would be interpreted as a set containing a number of sets, one of which is Person, one Dog and so on. Then we could invoke Figure 40 to show that Person is a set with instances of Student etc. But, once again, Student remains a 'point' since we are using type-instance semantics, which is orthogonal to the type-subtype semantics of Figure 40, only the latter of which could permit us to represent Brian as both a student and a person. Thus, with this revised understanding, we not only show that Figure 41 is fallacious but we still fail to establish a valid link between Student and Person i.e. we cannot yet validate Figure 36.

Rather than a set-based argumentation, we offer the following, based on consideration of the practicalities of the application in real life of permitting Student to be a subtype of Person. If a role, like Student, is permissible as a subtype of Person, then so equally are other roles, such as Customer, BankTeller, Athlete and so on. Many instances will in fact wish to take on multiple

roles such that multiple generalization is required, leading rapidly to a combinatorial explosion. Such modelling approaches have long been regarded with suspicion in the object-oriented modelling literature (e.g. McGregor & Korson, 1993; Henderson-Sellers & Edwards, 1994).

Consequently, a more accurate representation of what is happening here is shown in Figure 42, in which Student as an instance and Student as a class are clearly differentiated. We therefore suggest that a model more akin to the ontological approach would not attempt to link (instances of) roles and base types using generalization but using associations. Although the notion of role type needs further elaboration, a simplified generic model of such a usage is shown in Figure 43, a model that could also be extended to other pairs of

Figure 42. A more accurate representation of student and person in the context of BaseType and RoleType

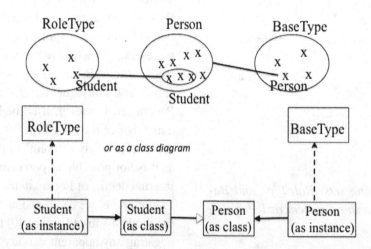

Figure 43. A template for roles, as played by base types: (upper) expressed using UML anonymous object notation and (lower) for a particular example using UML's stereotype notation, where the definitions of the stereotype are undertaken via the hierarchy of Figure 27 (the UFO or an equivalent foundational ontology)

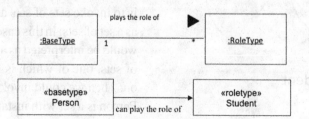

ontological sortal types – or even at a higher level in the UFO between pairs of endurant universals.

Figure 31 showed how associations between base types and non-base types can often give a more mathematically acceptable solution than some of the 'Ptolemaic fixes' that we have been discussing. Indeed, this 'pattern' is also useful for role modelling. Since Person is an instance of BaseType and Student is an instance of RoleType, then, using the template of Figure 43 (upper), the example of Figure 40 can equivalently be depicted as shown in Figure 44, analogous to Figure 34. As before (Figure 35), we can alternatively represent the information in Figure 44 as a mapping between two sets (Figure 45). Representing roles by relationships is also advocated in the description logics approach of Baader and Nutt (2002).

Figure 16(a) presented an ontologically poor model of customers, people and corporations. If we now permit the override that allows instances

of RoleType to be able to be subtypes of instances of a BaseType, then (so Guizzardi and Wagner, 2005 argue) the ontological correct version of this modelled domain is as shown in Figure 46. This introduces two more concerns: now, the class Customer, often used as a typical example of a RoleType, is represented as a mixin type; secondly, Figure 46 uses two examples of multiple specialization, generally regarded in the OO modelling literature of the late 1990s as a bad idea.

From Figure 46 we deduce that:

- The class Person is an instance of the BaseType class.
- The class PersonalCustomer is an instance of the RoleType class.
- The class Customer is an instance of the MixinType class.
- The class PersonalCustomer is a subtype of Person.
- The class PersonalCustomer is a subtype of Customer.
- And so on.

If we now interpret Figure 46 in terms of an Euler diagram for the UFO but neglecting PhaseType in Figure 27 (as shown in Figure 47), then we can observe the following facts:

- The set representing the class Person is an instance of the BaseType set.

Figure 44. Application of Figure 43's template to the link between person and student

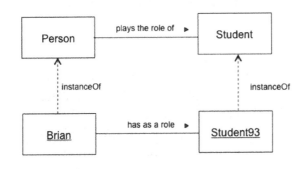

Figure 45. Mapping between members of the set person and the set student

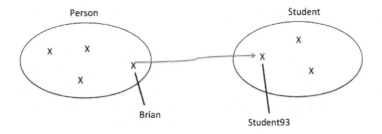

Figure 46. Example from the literature showing an arguably ontologically correct model (after Guizzardi & Wagner, 2005) (with kind permission of Springer Science+Business Media)

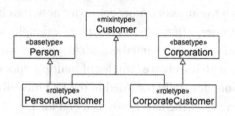

Figure 47. Set representations of the classes shown in Figure 46

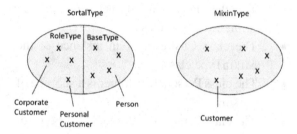

- The set representing the class PersonalCustomer is an instance of the RoleType set.
- The set representing the class Customer is an instance of the MixinType set.

For PersonalCustomer to be a subtype of Person and of Customer, we again need to invent a relationship that permits generalization between RoleType and BaseType (as in Figure 36) but additionally between RoleType and MixinType. Whilst not impossible, such overrides (as shown in Figure 37) could quickly proliferate, thus making the 'clean' structure of Figure 27 somewhat messy. We could again label these 'additions' as Ptolemaic fixes.

However, if we avoid the textual override to permit role types to specialize base types, we can utilize the template shown in Figure 43 to good effect. Figure 48 shows the resultant model, which

Figure 48. Revision of Figure 46 using the template of Figure 43

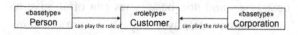

contains only three classes to replace the five-class structure of Figure 46.

Another Ptolemaic fix is offered by Guarino and Welty (2001) who state that the property of rigidity (a property of a base class) is not inherited by its subtypes. Thus, when trying to ensure that a diagram such as Figure 36 is ontologically valid, the anti-rigid nature of a class like Student does not conflict with an (inherited) rigidity from a base class such as Person. However, this does violate not only Liskov-style substitutability but also the AI guidelines of Brachman (1985).

3.4. Addition of Language Use Theory

A major motivation for our analysis of metamodelling, as here, is its participation in the definition of modelling languages. The literature offers two distinct connections:

1. The metamodel is (defines) the language. [This is seen in much of the OO metamodelling literature (e.g. Gonzalez-Perez & Henderson-Sellers 2007) and in OMG and ISO standards like the UML.] Similarly, the metamodel defines (or represents) the ontology underlying the language (e.g. Shan & Zhu, 2012).
2. The metamodel is a model of the language (e.g. Seidewitz 2003; Favre 2004).

(This is also seen in statements such as 'language is the set of all 'sentences' [models] that are conformant to the metamodel [e.g. Aßmann, Zschaler, & Wagner, 2006, p. 261; Favre & Nguyen, 2005].)

From a modelling language viewpoint, it therefore seems apposite to investigate the utility of incorporating ideas from the language use, philosophy of language and linguistics communities.

In the late nineteenth century, Frege (1892a) pondered over the assertion that the meaning of a sentence derives solely from the words that constitute the sentence. His example, much quoted, is "The morning star [Venus] is identical to the evening star [Venus]"[23]. He was the first to make the distinction between 'concept' and 'object' (Frege, 1892b) wherein the grammatical subject of a sentence signifies an object i.e. an individual or a particular[24] and the predicate signifies a concept (although this latter was not accepted by Husserl). This leads to the conclusion that grammatical subject refers to something in reality, either a singular entity (a particular) or to a more abstract and collective notion (a universal): the referent. The predicate is often said to be 'assigning a property' (e.g. Searle, 1969, p101) rather than signifying a concept because, according to Searle (i) Frege uses the term 'concept' in two incompatible ways, leading to the much quoted "The concept horse is not a concept" (see e.g. discussion in MacBride, 2011) that is an inevitable conclusion of Frege; and (ii) the normal usage of the word concept is more like a universal in the sense of being collective in nature than a single property – the "idea of the attributes common to a class of thing" (OED, 1942). Similarly, a generalized, broadbrush definition (Margolis & Laurence, 2012) is that "Concepts are the constituents of thought" which may be identified with (a) mental representations (dating back to Locke, 1690 and Hume, 1739), (b) abilities (Wittgenstein, 1953) or (c) Fregean senses (e.g. Peacocke, 1992). Of these, it would appear that the first has had the greatest influence on the field of conceptual modelling and on ontology engineering. Indeed, in ontology engineering, Ogden's triangle (Ogden & Richards, 1923; Ullmann, 1972) is often utilized – although this is not without its critics in some philosophy researchers. Indeed, this confusion leads Searle

(1969) to recommend that we abandon the whole idea of 'concept'. In a similar vein, Smith (2004) notes the ambiguities in the literature regarding the term 'concept', in particular describing its interpretation and use in linguistics, engineering and ontology. His most important conclusion is that universals and particulars that exist in reality should be our focus, particularly in developing domain ontologies, not the mental constructs that are typically used in such situations.

This suggests that particulars and universals (both substantial and non-substantial universals), derived from language use analysis, therefore relate to reality whilst objects and classes to software models (Figure 49). As shown in this figure, may then choose to formalize these in set theory terms using members (to depict objects that represent particulars in reality) and sets (to depict universals). Furthermore, it is generally accepted that there are three kinds of universals: type (a.k.a. kind), property, and relationship.

Notwithstanding Searle's recommendation above, it is also worth noting that Frege went on to suggest that the meaning of a concept (or of a sign) has two components: sense and reference, where reference links the concept to reality and

Figure 49. A depiction of elements in the software domain and how they represent elements of reality and how we might represent them mathematically

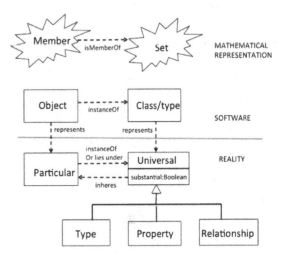

sense provides cognitive significance or meaning to this reference by relating it to other concepts in that specific context (Figure 50). Husserl (1900, 1901, 1939), working independently of Frege but his contemporary, concerned himself with the differences between meaning and object, identifying those names that express a meaning and refer to the same object (as with the Venus example), proper names with no meaning but designate an individual (e.g. 'Brian') and those 'universal' names that refer to a variety of objects – these denote a 'concept' and, since they are said to refer to a number of similar objects that form the extension (Wikipedia, 2012), this suggests to software modellers the use of set theory in which universals become classes (or sometimes types) and particulars are objects in the object-oriented design and implementation (see e.g. Martin & Odell, 1995). The blurring of mental representations, software representations (classes/types and objects) and the real-life referents (that are often ignored in software models makes undertaking a detailed and formal description of modelling and metamodelling in software engineering a serious challenge.

Much later, a classic discussion of the use of language, said to replace the term 'meaning',

is found in Austin (1962) in which an utterance (verbal for the moment) plus its immediate context formulate this speech act. Typically, this is a rhetic act (Austin, 1962, p. 93). Indeed, speaking a language is performing an act (viz. a speech act) according to a set of rules (Searle, 1969, p. 37,38). Speech acts become the central tenet in Searle (1969) who combined three accepted elements (which are that the utterance of sentence (a) indicates that an act is performed, (b) is an indication of what the speaker means, and (c) addresses an audience who are within communication range) to consolidate the illocutionary acts of Austin. Figure 51 is an initial attempt to model these ideas using a UML-like modelling language. A speech-act (an utterance) is composed by a propositional act and an illocutionary act (Searle, 1969, p. 24). As noted above, the propositional act can be further divided into a reference and a predicate act. A speech act is governed by a number of pragmatic use rules (page 40) that the speaker must comply to in order to succeed with his speech act. These are rules (general functions) for (1) referencing, (2) predication, and (3) the illocutionary component of the speech act. The illocutionary function (3) is further divided into five different subtypes (p. 31).

Figure 50. Venus's meaning map (after Partridge, 1996). Searle (1969, p. 171) comments that since morning star and evening star are not strictly proper names, Frege was possibly marginally misled by this example

Figure 51. Partial OO model of the main elements proposed by Austin and Searle that constitute speech acts

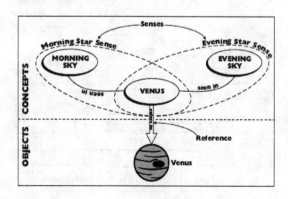

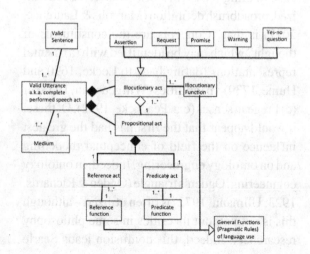

In Searle (1969) he makes an analysis that shows the important difference between the reference and predication functions of language. He quotes Frege (1884, p. 73) as stating that "only in the context of a sentences do words have reference" and discusses at length the many roles of predication in language. He also concludes (Searle, 1969, p. 122) that "the tendency to construe predication as a kind of, or analogous to, reference is one of the most persistent mistakes in the history of Western philosophy."

However, speech act theory is not without its critics: in addition to critics cited by Searle himself – and refuted – Dörge (2004) argues that the term is poorly defined and ambiguous such that authors often use their own idiosyncratic meaning of the term.

Austin's (1962) study of the way words are used is enhanced by Pennebaker, Mehl, and Niederhoffer (2003) study of how this usage is individualistic to the speaker. That suggests that, in our modelling language context where words (especially nouns) are replaced by visualized concepts, class names and hence structural aspects of class diagrams, for instance, may also be highly idiosyncratic. It therefore seems vital to ensure that, in any standardized modelling language, each symbol is clearly and tightly defined in terms of either a social/institutional entity or a physical thing.

Guizzardi (2005) stresses the need for an 'ontological commitment', citing Quine (1969) and Guarino (1998); although Searle (1969, chapter 5.3) has demonstrated that the notion of an ontological commitment as proposed and discussed by Quine (1953, 1960), for example, is untenable. His notion of 'commitment', with which he concludes his book, is either to a set of brute facts (i.e. scientific and real-world concrete entities) or to a social construct (see also Searle, 1995) such that this commitment is bound tightly into the meaning of the speech acts themselves.

Eriksson, Henderson-Sellers, and Ågerfalk (2013) undertake an extensive analysis of conceptual modelling based on language use and

speech act theory and conclude that these two approaches can be reconciled by realizing that one definition describes 'language definition' (following authors such as Kühne, 2006) whereas the alternative definition is based on a Chomsky view of language (Chomsky, 1956, 1959) focussing instead on language use – as utilized in software engineering by Favre (2004). As indicated above, a more elaborate view of language use is that represented by speech act theory (Austin, 1962; Searle, 1969; Habermas, 1979) where language use is conceived of as the performance of speech acts, thus emphasising the pragmatic meaning of sentences in use. This is depicted graphically in Figure 52 focussing on language use in terms of 'a set of speech acts' and in more detail in Figure 53 in which we also see in the language use section the 'ontology rectangle' as introduced above in Figure 30, suggesting that when we use language we use both types and instances (in the modelling sense discussed in Section 2). Indeed, when we expand the natural language use concepts and link them to definitions versus examples, as shown in Figure 54, we can superpose on this natural language metamodel/model framework the observation

Figure 52. Reconciliation of the two apparently disparate definitions of a modelling language

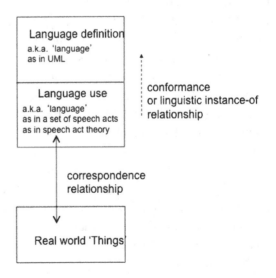

Figure 53. Complete multilevel framework based on language use – to replace the strict metamodelling architecture of Figure 3 when modelling in information systems development and software engineering (after Henderson-Sellers, 2012) (with kind permission of Springer Science+Business Media)

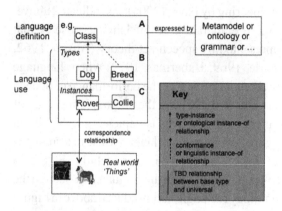

Figure 54. Depicting natural language constituents as a 'M2' level metamodel together with natural language as used by individual persons ('M1' level example nouns and verbs forming valid sentences). Further details of the complete performed speech acts are in Figure 51.

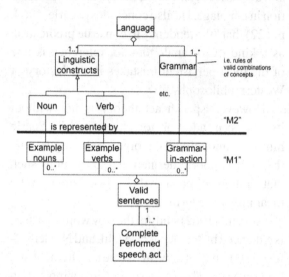

that language use suggests that at the 'M1' level of example nouns (for instance), common nouns (person, city, animal, etc.) denote classes whilst proper nouns (Brian, Cesar, London, Sydney, Rover, etc.) denote instances (see also Searle, 1969, p. 171; Lakoff, 1987, p. xiii). In natural language use, we often use both type names and instance names in the same sentence, primarily the former (Lakoff, 1987, p xiii). Similarly, Smith (2004) describes, from a philosophical standpoint, the differences between 'particulars' (individuals, tokens – here proper nouns) and 'non-particulars' (kinds, types – here common nouns) a.k.a. universals, where a universal is defined (Smith, 2004) as 'anything that is instantiated' i.e. something that has instances that fall under it. Brute facts relate to things that exist in the real world (facts in the world) whereas the existence of universals depends upon the meaning of words (Searle, 1969, p. 105, 116, 184). Thus, finally, we can translate Figure 54 into terminology useful for modelling languages as opposed to natural languages, with Class replacing Noun and Relationship replacing Verb (Figure 55).

Figure 55. Translation of Figure 54 into the modelling language domain

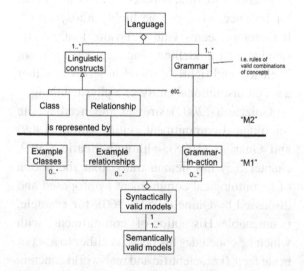

If we now focus on natural language syntax as being a set of rules plus a set of symbols used to reify them, then valid utterances conform to these rules and are depicted using a set of sym-

Figure 56. Natural language definition

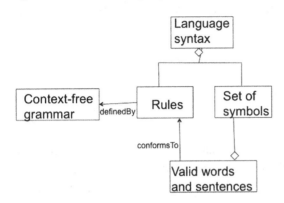

bols. The rules, in turn, are defined in terms of a context-free grammar (Figure 56). We now translate this from a natural language context into a (software) modelling language context (Figure 57) – where these two diagrams could be called 'megamodels' as proposed[25] by Bézivin, Joualt, and Valduriez (2004).

If we now incorporate Figure 57 as the modelling language definition in Figure 53 and combine it with a 'use' of language, then we have a definition of Modelling Language as shown in Figure 58. Acknowledging language use implies that we have to consider also the pragmatic functions of language when defining a modelling grammar.

Figure 57. Translation of the concepts in Figure 56 from their natural language domain into the domain of modelling languages

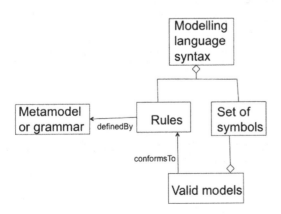

Figure 58. A megamodel of modelling language showing not only that it is a combination of definitional elements (syntax and semantics) but also of its use. In addition a proposed linkage between the rules component of the ML to a metamodel or grammar is made explicit

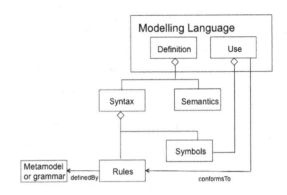

Restricting the analysis of language to syntax and semantics alone without considering pragmatic language use functions leaves unresolved the question as to whether a dictionary definition of a concept is a definition of the class or of objects belonging to that class or indeed perhaps merely a description of same. It is reasonable to argue, based on the analysis presented here, that the answer may be 'both, but don't bother about the bread' (Milne, 1926). If that assumption is valid, then one should deduce that such a dictionary definition could be interpreted as that of a clabject. Language use theory, on the other hand, vehemently denies the existence of clabjects. For example, Searle (1969) views speech acts in terms of reference and predication such that reference maps to individuals[26] (in his principle of identification, page 85) and predication typically involves categorization i.e. the use of universals, which are used to assign properties (Figure 49) to the individual concerned (assuming that properties are part of the prevalent philosophy, e.g. Partridge, 1996). As can be seen in Figures 30 and 49, universals in speech act/language theory as well as in ontology can be represented by types and classes ('concepts') in UML-style modelling (see also

Selic, 2011). Since reference and predication are orthogonal, such that a predicate cannot refer to an identifiable individual as does the subject of the speech act (although it may denote a relationship (Figure 49) that involves an identifiable particular), we can conclude that language use is either to an individual or a category/class/concept but not both simultaneously (see also Searle, 1969, p. 100). The functions of reference and predication convey completely different meanings when they are used together in a speech act. Thus, the modelling notion of a clabject (Atkinson, 1999) is contrary to current understanding of language use and hence is evidently a Ptolemaic fix, see further discussion below.

Finally, it is important to note that one of the missing elements in almost all OMG/UML style modelling is the omission of the real world i.e. the referent to which our software objects refer. In Figure 53 the object Rover (either as a software representation or a language symbol) has a correspondence relationship to the referent of Rover, the flesh and blood dog. We should also note that there is philosophical debate regarding whether types (universals) such as Dog and Breed also have referents in the real world. Despite these being conceptual and not substantial, we will take the view, implicit in software modelling, that both instances and types in software have (real-world) referents – while noting that other philosophies and ontological commitments are possible and used in other circles.

3.5. Utilizing Both Language Use and Foundational Ontologies for Multilevel Modelling

Following the introduction of foundational ontologies (Sections 3.2 and 3.3) and language use and speech acts (Section 3.4), we can now turn once again to the so-called 'linguistic/ontological metamodelling paradox'. From Figure 14, we can extract the ontological layers (Figure 59). Note that, although this diagram is visually identical

Figure 59. A typical example found in the literature to explain ontological metamodelling (cf. Figure 14)

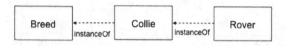

in form to that of Figure 18, the semantics of the concepts depicted in the three class 'boxes' is very different. In the earlier diagram, the left hand instance of purported to link an M1 level class with an M2 level class. Thus, arguably, the former instanceOf is a linguistic instanceOf whereas in Figure 32 the Collie-Breed relationship is an ontological instanceOf since both Rover and Collie belong to the M1 layer (see Figure 14 and associated discussion). Furthermore, in this example, all three classes belong to the M1 level. Secondly, in Figure 18 Rover was (correctly) instantiated from a base type whereas here in Figure 32 it is incorrectly instantiated from a moment universal (see also Eriksson, Henderson-Sellers, & Ågerfalk, 2013).

We have noted earlier (Figure 10) that an initial fix was to 'invent' a mapping between Collie as an object and Collie as a class (Figure 60). However, there is in fact a more important observation: there is no base class in this diagram. We have discovered that Collie relates to an instance of

Figure 60. Recognition of collie as a clabject that needs replacing by an object to class mapping

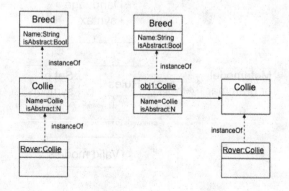

a Moment Universal named Breed. If Rover is to be an instance of Collie it would appear to be able to access collieness characteristics[27] but not those defining characteristics of what it means to be a dog. For example, a dictionary definition of the concept "Collie" is "any of a breed of large, long-haired dog with a long, narrow head: first bred in Scotland for herding sheep" (Webster's, 2010). However, we must also know implicitly or explicitly the meaning of "dog", for example by agreeing on a definition such as "any of a large and varied group of domesticated canines (Canis familiaris) often kept as a house pet or used for hunting, guarding people or property, etc." (Webster's, 2010) With this recognition of the missing Dog class, we can improve on Figure 60 as shown in Figure 61. In other words, with this restricted approach, we view Rover as an instance of Collie, itself a subtype of Dog. Although this redrawn diagram (Figure 61) introduces the base class Dog it violates the restrictions derived from speech-act theory that Collie must be an instance of Breed, and that Rover must be an instance of Dog . In Section 3.4, we showed, in Figure 53, how Breed and Dog together with instances of Collie and Rover form an ontologically sound

model, also acceptable within the constraints of language use.

We can now compare this solution (Figure 53) that utilizes ideas from foundational ontologies and speech act theory with one based on powertypes, as advocated by, for instance, Gonzalez-Perez and Henderson-Sellers (2006, 2008). In Figure 62 we see the base type of Dog associated to the Breed class, which essentially provides the partitioning rule for the Dog class. In this example, we just show three subclasses of the Dog class – in both set and OO notations. This suggests that any subtype of Dog, e.g. Collie, is not only a class/type but also an instance (of Breed); in other words, it is a clabject with a class facet and an object facet (right hand side of Figure 63).

Figure 62. Traditional powertype representation of the same problem domain as in Figures 61 and 51

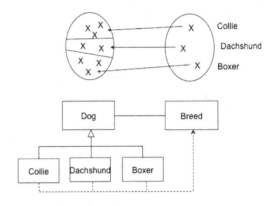

Figure 63. Collie as a clabject representation compared to the ontological "square" of Figures 31 and 51

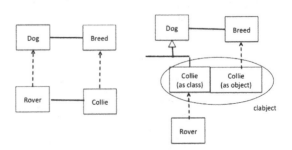

Figure 61. Further recognition of the lack of a base class. Here the class dog is inserted into Figure 60 to rectify this omission.

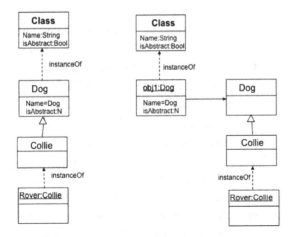

Although at first sight the language use pattern to the left and the powertype pattern (software pattern) to the right in Figure 63 may appear to convey the same meaning, closer inspection reveals that they are indeed fundamentally different. This is illustrated in Figures 64 and 65.

Figure 64 depicts the powertype pattern in which Collie appears to be a subclass of the superclass Dog, and the object Rover is an instance of the subclass Collie with three own attributes: dog name = Rover, dog height = 50, dog colour = black, which can access three breed level attributes: breed name = collie, breed height=45–55, breed colour=(black, tri-coloured, sable) via the association to Collie (thus equating attributes and associations as is commonly done in OO modelling). All these attributes are used to represent the physical dog and the properties it inheres (cf. Figure 49).

The meaning of Figure 65 that depicts a language-use pattern is described below, focusing on the relationships a, b, c and d:

a.   Depicts a type-instance relationship between Rover as an object (instance) and its type Dog. Rover, the dog name, is an identifier

Figure 64. The meaning of the powertype pattern in Figure 63

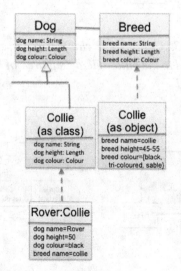

Figure 65. The meaning of the language use pattern in Figure 63

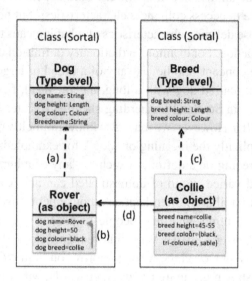

and Dog is the class type name. We use the notion of class to represent the sortal i.e. both the intension and extension of the class. From a language-use perspective, the Dog class can be used to communicate about dogs (at both type and instance level, i.e. the intension and extension of the class Dog) using speech acts. For example, the speech act "Rover is a dog" is used to instantiate the Rover object in the Dog class if no such object exists, and to refer to a dog named Rover if such a dog has already been instantiated by a previous speech act.

b.   Depicts the predicate relationship between the identifier and the attributes. The identifier (dog name) is used to uniquely refer to the object, and the attributes: dog height, dog colour and breed are used to ascribe attribute values to dog objects. In the speech act "Rover is a Collie," Collie is used as an attribute value that is assigned to Rover, not as a class name (Dog is the class type name) that instantiates Rover. This is in line with how the notion of predication is described in speech act theory. There is no type-instance relationship between the language constructs

Collie and Rover because Collie is simply used as an attribute value in this speech act, in the same way that 50 is used as a dog height attribute value, and "black" is used as a dog colour attribute value. Rover cannot access (it is not the possible software implementation of Rover that is of interest at this stage) and does not inherit the three Collie attributes: breed name = collie, breed height=45-55, breed colour=(black, tri-coloured, sable).

c. Depicts the type-instance relationship between Collie as an object and its type Dog Breed. The speech act "Collie is a dog breed" is used to instantiate Collie in the Dog Breed class if no such object exists, and to refer to a dog breed named Collie if such a breed has already been instantiated by a previous speech act. Here Collie is used to represent the meaning of Collie(ness) and need not have anything to do with the object Rover, or any other particular dog object. Thus we can talk about the collieness of dogs without ascribing it as an attribute to any particular dog object. The word Collie is hence used with a completely different meaning compared to (b).

d. Depicts a partition relationship between Collie and Dog. Collie is used to partition Dog objects which are identified and instantiated with the Dog class. Collie provides a rule for the partitioning of dog objects, which means that Collie essentially is a partition of Dog objects. and the definition of Collie see below provides a partitioning rule for a number of dog objects (c.f. Figure 21).

The analysis above shows that the powertype software pattern is a Ptolemaic fix, because it is based on the idea of clabject (which we already have showed in Section 3.4 to be a Ptolemaic fix). For example, the definition of the concept "Collie" as "any of a breed of large, long-haired dog with a long, narrow head: first bred in Scotland for herding sheep" leaves unresolved the question

as to whether Collie is used as a type, an object, a predicate, or a partition. This is homonymous until we specify the rules for how it could be used in the particular language system under scrutiny. To maintain that Collie is a clabject, which suggests that it could be used both as an object and a type in the same language system does not explain the meaning of "Collie". On the contrary, it further obscures the meaning of "Collie" because, according to speech act theory, Collie is used as a predicate in relationship to already instantiated dog objects (relationship b), and as a predicate it cannot be used to instantiate dog objects (relationship a). Predication (relationship b) is orthogonal to instantiation (relationship a). Neither does predication (relationship b) mean referring to a collie object via an association to Collie, which would equate attributes and associations as is commonly undertaken in OO modelling. If this were the case, then Rover must also be considered an instance of the attribute values "dog height 50" and "dog colour black". Searle (1969, pp. 113–118) argues strongly and convincingly against such an understanding of predication – we cannot, for example, use the attribute red to refer to redness, in the speech act "the rose is red"; red is merely an attribute predicated to a rose, and not a reference to the universal redness, considering the universal an object. We believe that much of the confusion surrounding these issues is due to a mix-up in the understanding of "is a" as signifying inheritance/ subclassification (e.g. Dog is a Mammal), instantiation (Rover is a Dog) and predication (Rover is a Collie) – essentially confusing the latter with one or both of the former.

The language use analysis also shows that restricting modelling to syntax and semantics alone without considering the pragmatic language use functions of reference and predication leaves the meaning of concept definitions unresolved. In a modelling situation, it is important to clarify the meaning of basic concepts such as "Collie" and, if we do not clarify how the word Collie can be used - as a type, an object, a predicate or a partition

- "Collie" becomes a misused homonym as in the models shown in Figures 59, 60, 61, 63, and 64.

Thus, we suggest that powertypes is a 'Ptolemaic fix' according to speech act theory and that the incorporation of ontological thinking together with language use insights should give an improved quality solution. However, whilst being theoretically invalid, the powertype fix does provide a solution *within the constraints imposed by the multilevel architectures currently in use* (e.g. Figures 3 and 24). Consequently, powertypes can be regarded as a temporary solution until all the ramifications of our proposals of Section 4 for a paradigm shift are universally adopted. If the revolution proves to be successful, and we do not see any logical-theoretical reasons that it should not (albeit perhaps political ones), then this would no longer have to be the case. Modellers would then be trained to see that the Earth is indeed circling the Sun, and the "geocentric view of metamodelling" (Ptolemaic metamodelling, as we call it) will eventually only be mentioned in passing as a historical anecdote. It is always easier to learn the right thing from the beginning than having to unlearn. As John Maynard Keynes is known to have said, "The difficulty lies, not in new ideas, but in escaping from the old ones, which ramify, for those brought up as most of have been, into the corners of our minds."

3.6. Other Related Research

Although we have endeavoured to include all relevant research work so far in this section (3.1-3.5), there are other contributions that might be considered to be in the same sphere of interest.

A large number of authors criticize UML or MOF. We do not aim to collect them all here as they span a large compass in both scale and temporality. One with an obvious title is "Errors in the UML Metamodel?" by Fuentes, Quintana, Llorens, Génova, and Prieto-Diaz (2003). These authors identified 450 errors in the UML V1.5 metamodel (OMG, 2003); although they do not

challenge the basic structure or architecture of a metamodel-based language like UML, rather likening the UML standard to a 'bible'.

Song and Baik (2003) recognize that nowhere in the OMG's documents nor spin-off books is the question addressed "Which UML diagrams should be used in each of the SDLC phases?" These authors propose three phases, which they call conceptual, specific, and concrete. For each phases they consider use cases, class models, state charts and activity models and argue that each combination requires an individual metamodel that are later integrated.

The topic of the paucity of behavioural support in UML is widely discussed. One such example is the discussion by Gargantini, Riccobene, and Scandurra (2009) who propose a semantic framework, in an MDE context, that uses translational mappings together with weaving and a technique called semantic hooking. This approach is compatible with a basic assumption that the abstract syntax of a modelling language is defined in terms of a metamodel (see also discussion in Henderson-Sellers, 2012). Modelling and metamodelling in an MDE environment is a topical and an interesting research area exemplified by papers such as those of Kühne (2007) and Kleppe (2007). Another emerging area, often linked to MDE, is that of domain-specific languages and, especially in our context here, of Domain Specific Modelling Languages (DSMLs) (e.g. Selic, 2011). These allow users to work directly with a set of concepts closely related to their domain-specific knowledge (e.g. Kühne, 2007; Gargantini, Riccobene, & Scandurra, 2009), often expressed as a domain ontology (Falbo, Guizzardi, & Duarte, 2002; Kurtev, Bézivin, Joualt, & Valduriez, 2006).

Most recently, Shan and Zhu (2012) ask 'What is the exact meaning of the instanceOf relationship between an Mx model and an M(x+1) model (in the context of Figure 3). They propose four equally acceptable alternative understandings from the UML specification documents for the case of a simple class diagram with a single class labelled A:

- There is only one class in the system and it is named A.
- There is at least one class named A in the system (which may have other classes).
- There is only one class in the system and its name does not matter.
- There is at least one class in the system and its name does not matter.

These authors seek a uniform semantics for models in all pairs of metalevels. They undertake this research by mapping UML models to predicate calculus.

4. REVOLUTION: MAKE LANGUAGE USE NOT MODELS THE FOCUS

The history of the evolution of modelling languages and conceptual modelling more generally has, over the last decades, depended significantly on the multilevel architecture of Figure 3. This multilevel stack is of 'models' viz. model, metamodel, metametamodel etc. ad infinitum (but closed off in the OMG version with a topmost level of metametamodel). This architecture, as we (and others) have shown, leads to many significant problems. Since many authors recognize the problems inherent in the four-level architecture of the OMG (Figure 3), there have been attempts made to circumvent these by investigating alternative m-level architecture (m>=1). As a smooth evolution from earlier ideas by Colin Atkinson and Thomas Kühne (e.g. Atkinson & Kühne, 2000a, and see earlier discussion), the Pan Level Model (PLM) and Level-agnostic Modelling Language (LML) have emerged (Atkinson, Kennel, & Goß, 2011). We propose here that it is time for a revolution to replace the evolution with a new Kuhnian paradigm. Our discussion is intended to provide a stimulus for the modelling community to develop a new mindset – whether or not our proposals here become the core of such a revolution remains to be seen. We encourage community debate once

the realization of the need for a paradigm shift has been accepted (as we hope it has after reading our treatise here).

In practical terms, adoption of a language-focussed paradigm for modelling means that individual developers no longer need understand non-standard 'Ptolemaic fixes' such as potency or powertypes, which not only add complexity to the modelling environment but also run the risk of being interpreted differently by different people. With this newly proposed emphasis on modelling languages rather than multi-level modelling hierarchies, the tacit knowledge of each developer, as a natural language speaker, matches smoothly with the underlying theories of language use and speech acts, thus turning the conceptual modelling environment from an artificial one to a more natural one. In addition, correct utilization of the various ontological types (for instance, whether role types can or cannot be linked directly to base types) will not only avoid incorrect models but will also permit tool vendors to enforce these additional foundational ontological classes in a seamless manner thus supporting the developer in creating useful and high quality models– much as object technology itself removed from the software developer the need to concentrate hard on how to insist on information hiding and correctly bundle together state and behaviour: the new default (in OO).

We saw in Figure 53 a first indication of how a restructured multi-level architecture might be envisaged. Rather than have the 'M2' level being the metamodel, instead it is the 'Language Definition' with 'M1' being the type part of language use and 'M0' being the instance part of language use. A straight incorporation of these observations into Figure 3 suggests that the replacement architecture looks like that in Figure 66. However, Figure 66 cannot be the whole story since, as we see in Figure 53, we also need to incorporate real world entities. These are not M0 since M0 are the modelled instances that *correspond* to things in the real world. Indeed, the correspondences seen

Figure 66. First revision of the OMG multi-level architecture of Figure 3 to place the modelling language and not the metamodel at the 'M2' level in the multilevel stack (now restricted to three levels with a linkage to a second multilevel stack – here shown as having only two levels)

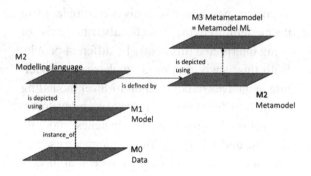

in this diagram are what Searle (1969, p. 82) calls 'fully consummated references'. Secondly, as seen in Figure 53, both types and instances are part of our everyday use of language i.e. any modelling distinction between types and instances could be regarded as both artificial and unnecessary – in the sense that as we speak and write (language use) we do NOT continually assess whether the morphemes denote instances or types (i.e. references or predication). We do not differentiate between types and instances in natural language

usage suggesting that this combination could constitute what we have previously called the 'M1' level (Figure 67). In this diagram is also shown the representation of Dog and Breed as tables suitable for a database (for full discussion see Eriksson, Henderson-Sellers, & Ågerfalk, 2013).

With these changes, Figure 66 is revised as shown in Figure 68, noting in addition that the "M2 metamodel" of Figure 66 is equivalent to an "ontological commitment" that is formalized in terms of a foundational ontology. However, even Figure 68 still has a basic influence (and indeed aim) of creating an OMG-like architecture. We have seen that an alternative architecture is the multi-level model of Figure 24. In this alternative structure, the real world was called the Endeavour Domain, the M1/M0 model level of Figure 68 becomes the Method Domain but the Metamodel Domain of Figure 24 needs to be replaced by the Definitional Domain (which includes the modelling language definition and also the metamodel of the 'M2' level and the metametamodel 'M3' level of Figure 68). Remodelling Figure 68 along these lines leads to our final suggestion of Figure 69. In this diagram, we suggest including both design models (including process models or methodologies) and enactment models (previously M0 models) in a single "Model" domain (or layer). The lowest layer is then distinct from models and

Figure 67. Type and instance level as the new 'M1' level. The key at the base is not only a key but an implicit metamodel to which all elements in the new 'M1' level must conform.

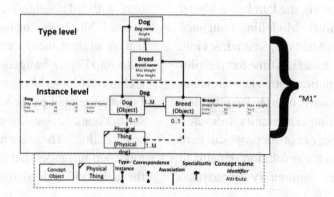

Figure 68. Revision of Figure 66 to incorporate the ideas depicted in Figure 53

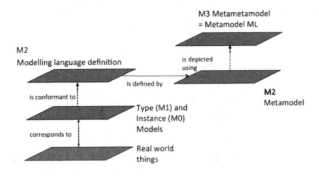

Figure 69. Revision of Figure 68 to incorporate the ideas of Figure 24

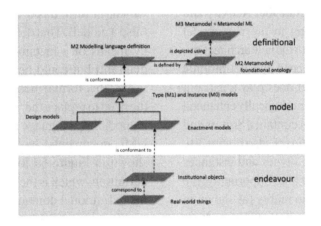

only refers to real world entities, method following actions etc,. This approach aligns with Ågerfalk and Fitzgerald's (2006) notion of methods as action knowledge and also provides an architecture compatible with reduced-level approaches. Note that "real world entities" include systems specifications (models) that are produced and used during systems development as part of communication/design activities concerned with the system to be constructed. They are what Eriksson and Ågerfalk (2010) refer to as institutional objects. It is not their status of their being models that is in focus at this level. Instead, they are included by virtue of being used in method-following speech acts – such as in coming to an agreement on system requirements. For example, if the subject of study (SUS) in the systems developing project is a Ken-

nel club, the model depicted in Figure 67 could be a part of such an agreement. The enactment model describes the design activities. Hence, a specific design activity such as "Brian's design activity" (cf. Section 3.1 above) is part of the model layer in Figure 69. It is also important to recognize that the enactment model can be both prescriptive and descriptive in relation to real world modelling activities (Ågerfalk & Fitzgerald, 2006). For example, if Brian gets a managerial signoff for a 2 day duration on his design activity, it is a commitment (institutional object) that should be complied with. Similarly, the method prescription that such a signoff should be agreed is a directive represented in the Enactment model that may or may not result in the institutional object. Post facto analysis of the situation may result in descriptive models that can be compared with such prescriptions to assess conformance. This means that the deep instantiation plus potency approach, which was suggested in order to permit multilevel modelling of processes and methodologies, can be avoided.

As an example to aid understanding, we compare this new language-use-based architecture as applied to the standardization for methodologies with the current status as exemplified in Figure 22 earlier. Figure 70 compares the essence of Figure 22 with its equivalent in the new architecture (of Figure 69). In Figure 22, the multilevel constraints of Figure 3 or Figure 24 dictate that Activity and ActivityKind MUST belong to the metamodel level (OMG's M2 level). With the new architecture, the metamodel layer is replaced by a definitional layer in which a metamodel does play a part but more along the lines of the ontologically enhanced structure of Figure 27, e.g. it contains, Sortals and Moment Universals *inter alia* (cf. also Figure 30). As shown in Figure 67, both types and instances can co-exist in the M1 layer and, importantly, the M0 layer now relates only to reality (as shown in Figures 53 and 69). This means that (1) standard-

izing a general purpose modelling language, such as the UML, still occurs at the definitional layer but that (2) a DSML (Domain Specific Modelling Language), much as the name suggests, as well as a methodology (meta)model like ISO/IEC 24744 (ISO/IEC 2007) are now defined at the type level within the model layer. Finally, a standard like ISO/IEC 12207 (ISO/IEC, 1995) is identified with the instance level of M1 as shown in Figure 67.

Figure 71 stresses that, in fact, models occur in all three 'domains' of Figure 24 and of Figure 69. All three kinds of model use a modelling language (often the same language, e.g. Shan & Zhu, 2012), which, in turn, has a specification or definition (also a model). That definition is frequently made by means of a metamodel (depicted as a class diagram) but could be by a textual grammar or some other formal means. Figure 71 also stresses the need to replace the 'metamodel' as a key focus in modelling language design (as currently in the UML documents) by 'modelling language' (as shown in Figure 69 for instance in terms of its definition, which is the main connection between the definitional domain and the model domain).

Figure 70. An architectural multi-level view of Figure 67 compared to the current multi-level architecture exemplified by Figure 22

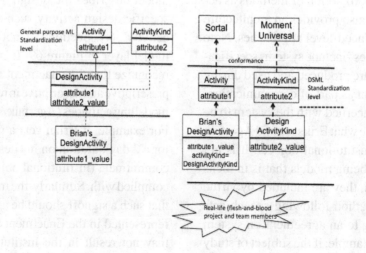

Figure 71. There are three main kinds of model used in software engineering, all of which are depicted using a modelling language. That language needs to be specified (defined), which can be accomplished by one of several means e.g. metamodel, grammar.

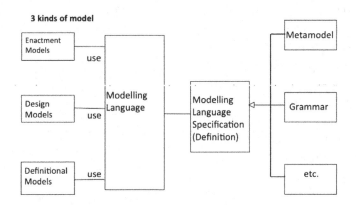

5. CONCLUSION: FUTURE NEEDS

Science progresses partly by small additions to knowledge and partly due to paradigm shifts (Kuhn, 1962). Often the seeds for the revolution are sown earlier, scattered throughout the literature and may, or may not, be recognized as harbingers of an impending paradigm shift. We saw how the early ideas leading to both the Copernican revolution in astronomy and the Darwinian exposition of natural selection were present in earlier writings of other researchers prior to the paradigm shift occurring and the establishment, sometimes after many decades, of the new orthodoxy.

In this chapter, we have considered parallels from scientific revolutions as a basis for evaluating whether or not the time is ripe for a similar change of direction in metamodelling for software engineering, especially in the context of MDE (or in its new guise of MBE: model-based engineering (Selic 2012b)). We have introduced a number of ideas that seem to solve many of the inconsistencies and paradoxes of the current orthodoxy. Although what we have presented in this chapter may at first sight appear to be complex, it is in fact far less complex than suggested alternatives, such as the OMG multi-level architecture. Metamodelling is indeed a complex task that requires somewhat

intricate tools, although we also recall and superpose the so-called Einstein's Razor (Borkar, 1998, p. 42): "Everything should be made as simple as possible, but not simpler."

Essentially what we suggest is a change in mindset similar to the "pragmatic turn" in philosophy (Egginton & Sandbothe, 2004; Bernstein, 2010). Our focus as modellers needs to shift from models to language, and by extension to how language is used to achieve pragmatic outcomes (Ågerfalk, 2010). Eriksson & Ågerfalk (2010) showed the implications of such a turn for information infrastructures and for conceptual modelling of information systems. In this chapter we have laid the groundwork for a similar revolution to the practices of metamodelling.

And being even more pragmatic, we argue that practitioners and software developers in industry will find metamodelling, and modelling in general, a much more affordable domain. In the age of agile development, where focus is often on code, a pragmatic and simpler approach like the one proposed here is most likely to be well received and adopted by the community.

Whether what we have presented, together, are sufficient to create a shift in mindset or whether they are simply the stimulus for others to create new and orthogonal ideas remains to be seen. We urge the modelling and metamodelling communities to search out that new orthodoxy that will, necessarily, ensure that our science will offer simpler and more satisfying solutions in the years to come.

Our future work is aimed at analysing various possible philosophical and ontological underpinnings for modelling and metamodelling. There are a number of accepted but contrasting paradigms discussed in the contemporary philosophical literature including those dating back to the late 19th century (e.g. Frege, 1892a,b), those focussed on speech acts (e.g. Austin, 1962 and Searle, 1969) and some specifically aimed at supporting object-oriented analysis and design (Partridge, 1996). These need to be evaluated for our metamodelling context but also augmented by a revised and improved version of a foundational ontology like the UFO that was used earlier in this chapter.

ACKNOWLEDGMENT

B. Henderson-Sellers wishes to acknowledge the support of the Australian Research Council through grant DP0878172. This is contribution 12/07 of the Centre for Object Technology Applications and Research within the Human-Centred Technology Design Centre at the University of Technology, Sydney.

We wish to thank Chris Partridge for his insightful comments on an earlier draft of this manuscript. We also wish to acknowledge, with thanks, discussions over the years with, in alphabetical order, Colin Atkinson, Tony Clark, Sergio DeCesare, Giancarlo Guizzardi, Thomas Kühne, and Graham Low.

REFERENCES

Ågerfalk, P. J. (2010). Getting pragmatic. *European Journal of Information Systems, 19*(3), 251–256. doi:10.1057/ejis.2010.22.

Ågerfalk, P. J., & Fitzgerald, B. (2006). Exploring the concept of method rationale: A conceptual tool for method tailoring. In Siau, K. (Ed.), *Advanced Topics in Database Research* (*Vol. 5*). Hershey, PA: Idea Group. doi:10.4018/978-1-59140-935-9.ch004.

Álvarez, J., Evans, A., & Sammut, P. (2001). Mapping between levels in the metamodel architecture. In M. Gogolla, & C. Kobryn (Eds.), *Proc. UML 2001 – The Unified Modeling Language: Modeling Languages, Concepts and Tools* (LNCS), (vol. 2185, pp. 34-46). Berlin: Springer-Verlag.

Aristotle. in Translation. (1984). Complete works. (J. Barnes, Ed.). Princeton, NJ: Princeton University Press.

Armstrong, D. M. (1989). *Universals: An opinionated introduction*. Westview Press.

Asimov, I. (1988). *Prelude to foundation*. London: Grafton Books.

Aßmann, U., Zschaler, S., & Wagner, G. (2006). Ontologies, meta-models, and the model-driven paradigm. In Calero, C., Ruiz, F., & Piattini, M. (Eds.), *Ontologies for Software Engineering and Software Technology*. Berlin: Springer. doi:10.1007/3-540-34518-3_9.

Atkinson, C. (1997). Metamodelling for distributed object environments. In *Proceedings of the First International Enterprise Distributed Object Computing Workshop (EDOC'97)*. Brisbane, Australia: IEEE Computer Society.

Atkinson, C. (1999). Supporting and applying the UML conceptual framework. In Bézivin, J., & Muller, P.-A. (Eds.), *The Unified Modeling Language «UML» 1998: Beyond the Notation (LNCS)* (*Vol. 1618*, pp. 21–36). Berlin: Springer-Verlag. doi:10.1007/978-3-540-48480-6_3.

Atkinson, C., Gutheil, M., & Kennel, B. (2009). A flexible infrastructure for multilevel language engineering. *IEEE Transactions on Software Engineering*, *35*(6), 742–755. doi:10.1109/TSE.2009.31.

Atkinson, C., Kennel, B., & Goß, B. (2011). The level-agnostic modeling language. In Malloy, B., Staab, S., & van den Brand, M. (Eds.), *SLE 2010 (LNCS)* (*Vol. 6563*, pp. 269–275). Berlin: Springer-Verlag.

Atkinson, C., & Kühne, T. (2000a). Strict profiles: why and how. In *Proceedings Third International Conference on the Unified Modeling Language*, (LNCS), (vol. 1939, pp. 309-322). Berlin: Springer-Verlag.

Atkinson, C., & Kühne, T. (2001a). The essence of multilevel metamodelling. In Gogolla, M., & Kobryn, C. (Eds.), *UML»2001 – The Unified Modeling Language. Modeling Languages, Concepts and Tools, (LNCS)* (*Vol. 2185*, pp. 19–33). Berlin: Springer-Verlag. doi:10.1007/3-540-45441-1_3.

Atkinson, C., & Kühne, T. (2001b). Processes and products in a multi-level metamodelling architecture. *International Journal of Software Engineering and Knowledge Engineering*, *11*(6), 761–783. doi:10.1142/S0218194001000724.

Atkinson, C., & Kühne, T. (2003). Model-driven development: a metamodelling foundation. *IEEE Software*, *20*, 36–41. doi:10.1109/MS.2003.1231149.

Atkinson, C., & Kühne, T. (2005). Concepts for comparing modeling tool architectures. In *Model Driven Engineering Languages and Systems, (LNCS)* (*Vol. 3713*, pp. 398–413). Berlin: Springer-Verlag. doi:10.1007/11557432_30.

Atkinson, C., & Kühne, T. (2008). Reducing accidental complexity in domain models. *Software & Systems Modeling*, *7*(3), 345–359. doi:10.1007/s10270-007-0061-0.

Austin, J. L. (1962). *How to do things with words*. Oxford, UK: Oxford University Press.

Baader, F., & Nutt, W. (2002). Basic description logics. In Baader, F., Calvanese, D., McGuinness, D. L., Nardi, D., & Patel-Schneider, P. F. (Eds.), *Description Logic Handbook*. Cambridge, UK: Cambridge University Press.

Beddall, B. G. (1968). Wallace, Darwin, and the theory of natural selection. *Journal of the History of Biology*, *1*(2), 261–323. doi:10.1007/BF00351923.

Bernstein, R. J. (2010). *The pragmatic turn*. Cambridge, UK: Polity Press.

Bézivin, J. (2004). In search of a basic principle for model-driven engineering. *Upgrade*, *5*(2), 21–24.

Bézivin, J., Joualt, F., & Valduriez, P. (2004). On the need for megamodels. In *Proceedings of Workshop on Best Practices for Model-Driven Software Development at the 19th Annual ACM Conference on Object-Oriented Programming, Systems, Languages, and Applications*. ACM Press.

Bhathal, R. (2012). Australia and the transit of Venus. *Astronomy & Geophysics*, *53*(3), 3.22-3.24.

Bock, C., & Odell, J. J. (1994). A foundation for composition. *Journal of Object-Oriented Programming*, *7*(6), 10–14.

Borkar, V. S. (1998). There's no such thing as a free lunch: The bias-variance dilemma. *Resonance -. Journal of Science Education*, *3*(6), 40–51.

Brachman, R. J. (1985). I lied about the trees' or, defaults and definitions in knowledge representation. *AI Magazine*, *6*(3), 80–93.

Brentano, F. (1874). *Psychologie vom empirischen standpunkt*. Leipzig, Germany: Verlag von Duncker & Humblot.

Broy, M. (2011, October). Can practitioners neglect theory and theoreticians neglect practice? *IEEE Software*, 19–24.

Bunge, M. (1977). Treatise on basic philosophy: *Vol. 3. Ontology I: The furniture of the world*. Boston: Reidel.

Bunge, M. (1979). Treatise on basic philosophy: *Vol. 4. Ontology II: A world of systems*. Boston: Reidel.

Butterfield, H. (1957). *The origins of modern science, 1300-1800*. London: G. Bell.

Cardelli, L. (1988). Structural subtyping and the notion of power type. In J. Ferrante, & P Mager (Eds.), *Proceedings Fifteenth Annual ACM Symposium on Principles of Programming Languages*. ACM Press.

Carmichael, A. (1994). Towards a common object-oriented meta-model for object development. In Carmichael, A. (Ed.), *Object Development Methods* (pp. 321–333). New York: SIGS Books.

Carnap, R. (1947). *Meaning and necessity: A study in semantics and modal logic*. Chicago, IL: University of Chicago Press.

Chambers, R. (1844). *Vestiges of the natural history of creation*. London, W: R Chambers.

Chomsky, N. (1956). Three models for the description of language. *I.R.E. Transactions on Information Theory, 2*(3), 113–124. doi:10.1109/TIT.1956.1056813.

Chomsky, N. (1959). On certain formal properties of grammars. *Information and Control, 2*(2), 137–171. doi:10.1016/S0019-9958(59)90362-6.

Copernicus, N. (1543). *De revolutionibus orbium coelestium*. Nuremburg.

Dahchour, M., & Pirotte, A. (2002). Materialization and its metaclass implementation. *IEEE Transactions on Knowledge and Data Engineering, 14*(5), 1078–1094. doi:10.1109/TKDE.2002.1033775.

Darwin, C. (1859). *On the origin of species*. London: John Murray.

Darwin, C., & Wallace, A. R. (1858). On the tendency of species to form varieties, and on the perpetuation of varieties and species by natural means of selection. *Journal of the Proceedings of the Linnean Society of London Zoology, 3*, 46–50. doi:10.1111/j.1096-3642.1858.tb02500.x.

Denning, P. J., Dennis, J. B., & Qualitz, J. E. (1978). *Machines, languages, and computation*. Englewood Cliffs, NJ: Prentice-Hall.

Descartes, R. (1637). *Discours de la méthode*.

Descartes, R. (1644). *Principia philosophiae*.

Dörge, F. C. (2004). *Illocutionary acts: Austin's account and what Searle made of it. Inaugural-Dissertation zur Erlangung des Grades eines Doktors der Philosophie*. Eberhard-Karls-Universität Tübingen.

Egginton, W., & Sandbothe, M. (2004). *The pragmatic turn in philosophy: Contemporary engagements between analytic and continental thought*. State Albany, NY: University of New York Press.

Eriksson, O., & Ågerfalk, P. J. (2010). Rethinking the meaning of identifiers in information infrastructures. *Journal of the Association for Information Systems, 11*(8), 433–454.

Eriksson, O., Henderson-Sellers, B., & Ågerfalk, P. J. (2013). *Ontological and linguistic metamodelling revisited – A language use approach*. Unpublished.

Falbo, R., Guizzardi, G., & Duarte, K. C. (2002). An ontological approach to domain engineering. In *Proceedings of the International Conference on Software Engineering and Knowledge Engineering SEKE'02*. Ischia, Italy: ACM Press.

Favre, J.-M. (2004). Foundations of meta-pyramids: Languages vs. metamodels: Episode II: Story of Thotus the baboon. In *Proceedings of Dagstuhl Seminar 04101 "Language Engineering for Model-Driven Software Development"*. Dagstuhl.

Favre, J.-M., & NGuyen, T. (2005). Towards a megamodel to model software evolution through transformations. *Electronic Notes in Theoretical Computer Science, 127*(3), 59–74. doi:10.1016/j.entcs.2004.08.034.

Firesmith, D., Henderson-Sellers, B., & Graham, I. (1997). *OPEN modeling language (OML) reference manual*. New York: SIGS Books.

Flatscher, R. G. (2002). Metamodeling in EIA/CDIF – Meta-metamodel and metamodels. *ACM Transactions on Modeling and Computer Simulation, 12*(4), 322–342. doi:10.1145/643120.643124.

Frege, G. (1884). *Die grundlagen der arithmetik*. Breslau.

Frege, G. (1892a). Über sinn und bedeutung. In Zeitschrift für Philosophie und philosophische Kritik, 100, 25-50.

Frege, G. (1892b). Über begriff und gegenstand. In Vierteljahrsschrift für Wissenschaftliche Philosophie, 16, 192-205.

Frege, G. (1950). *The foundations of arithmetic* (Austin, J. L., Trans.). Oxford, UK: Basil Blackwell.

Fuentes, J. M., Quintana, V., Llorens, J., Génova, G., & Prieto-Diaz, R. (2003). Errors in the UML metamodel? *ACM SIGSOFT Software Engineering Notes, 28*(6), 3. doi:10.1145/966221.966236.

Galilei, G. (1610). *Sidereus nuncius*.

Galilei, G. (1632). *Dialogue concerning the two chief world systems*.

Gargantini, A., Riccobene, E., & Scandurra, P. (2009). A semantic framework for metamodel-based languages. *Journal of Automated Software, 16*(3-4), 415–454. doi:10.1007/s10515-009-0053-0.

Genova, G. (2010). Is computer science truly scientific? *Communications of the ACM, 53*(7), 37–39. doi:10.1145/1785414.1785431.

Gonzalez-Perez, C., & Henderson-Sellers, B. (2006). A powertype-based metamodelling framework. *Software & Systems Modeling, 5*(1), 72–90. doi:10.1007/s10270-005-0099-9.

Gonzalez-Perez, C., & Henderson-Sellers, B. (2007). Modelling software development methodologies: A conceptual foundation. *Journal of Systems and Software, 80*(11), 1778–1796. doi:10.1016/j.jss.2007.02.048.

Gonzalez-Perez, C., & Henderson-Sellers, B. (2008). *Metamodelling for software engineering*. Chichester, UK: John Wiley & Sons.

Graham, I. M., Bischof, J., & Henderson-Sellers, B. (1997). Associations considered a bad thing. *Journal of Object-Oriented Programming, 9*(9), 41–48.

Guarino, N. (1998). Formal ontology and information systems. In N. Guarino (Ed.), *Formal Ontology in Information Systems: Proceedings of the International Conference on Formal Ontology and Information Systems (FOIS)*. IOS Press.

Guarino, N., & Welty, C. (2000). A formal ontology of properties. In R. Dieng & O. Corby (Eds.), *Proceedings 12th International Conference on Knowledge Engineering and Knowledge Management,* (LNCS), (vol. 1937, pp. 97-112). Berlin: Springer-Verlag.

Guarino, N., & Welty, C. (2001). Identity and subsumption: LADSEB-CNR internal report 01/2001. In Green, R., Bean, C. A., & Myaeng, S. H. (Eds.), *The Semantics of Relationships: An Interdisciplinary Perspective*. Dordrecht, The Netherlands: Kluwer.

Guizzardi, G. (2005). *Ontological foundations for structural conceptual models*. CTIT PhD Thesis Series, No. 05-74, Enschede, The Netherlands.

Guizzardi, G. (2006). Agent roles, qua individuals and the counting problem. In Garcia, Choren, Pereira de Lucena, Giorgini, Holvoet, & Romanovky (Eds.), Software Engineering for Multi-Agent Systems IV, Research Issues and Practical Applications (LNCS), (vol. 3914, pp. 143-160). Berlin: Springer-Verlag.

Guizzardi, G., & Wagner, G. (2005). Towards ontological foundations for agent modelling concepts using the unified foundational ontology (UFO). In Bresciani, P., Giorgini, P., Henderson-Sellers, B., Low, G., & Winikoff, M. (Eds.), *Agent-Oriented Information Systems II (LNAI)* (*Vol. 3508*, pp. 110–124). Berlin: Springer-Verlag. doi:10.1007/11426714_8.

Guizzardi, G., Wagner, G., Guarino, N., & van Sinderen, M. (2004). An ontologically well-founded profile for UML conceptual models. In A. Persson & J. Stirna (Eds.), *16th International Conference on Advances in Information Systems Engineering (CAiSE'04)*, (LNCS), (vol. 3084, pp. 122-126). Berlin: Springer-Verlag.

Habermas, J. (1979). What is universal pragmatics? In Habermas, J. (Ed.), *Communication and the Evolution of Society* (McCarthy, T., Trans.). London: Heinemann.

Halpin, T. (2005). Higher order types and information modeling. In Siau, K. (Ed.), *Advanced Topics in Database Research*. Hershey, PA: Idea Group. doi:10.4018/978-1-59140-471-2.ch010.

Halpin, T., & Bloesch, A. (1999). Data modeling in UML and ORM: A comparison. *Journal of Database Management, 10*(4), 4–13. doi:10.4018/jdm.1999100101.

Henderson-Sellers, B. (1994). Methodologies - Frameworks for OO success. *American Programmer, 7*(10), 2–11.

Henderson-Sellers, B. (2006). Method engineering: theory and practice. In Karagiannis, D., & Mayr, H. C. (Eds.), *Information Systems Technology and its Applications (LNI)*. Bonn: Gesellschaft für Informatik.

Henderson-Sellers, B. (2011a). Bridging metamodels and ontologies in software engineering. *Journal of Systems and Software, 84*, 301–313. doi:10.1016/j.jss.2010.10.025.

Henderson-Sellers, B. (2011b). Random thoughts on multi-level conceptual modelling. In Delcambre, L., & Kaschek, R. (Eds.), *The Evolution of Conceptual Modeling (LNCS)* (*Vol. 6520*, pp. 93–116). Berlin: Springer-Verlag. doi:10.1007/978-3-642-17505-3_5.

Henderson-Sellers, B. (2012). *On the mathematics of modelling, metamodelling, ontologies and modelling languages*. Berlin: Springer. doi:10.1007/978-3-642-29825-7.

Henderson-Sellers, B., & Bulthuis, A. (1998). *Object-oriented metamethods*. New York: Springer. doi:10.1007/978-1-4612-1748-0.

Henderson-Sellers, B., & Edwards, J. M. (1994). booktwo of object-oriented knowledge: The working object. New York: Prentice-Hall.

Henderson-Sellers, B., & Gonzalez-Perez, C. (2005). The rationale of powertype-based metamodelling to underpin software development methodologies. *Australian Conferences in Research and Practice in Information Technology, 43*, 7-16.

Henderson-Sellers, B., & Gonzalez-Perez, C. (2006). On the ease of extending a powertype-based methodology metamodel. In Proceedings of Meta-Modelling and Ontologies WoMM 2006. WoMM.

Henderson-Sellers, B., & Unhelkar, B. (2000). *OPEN modeling with UML*. Reading, MA: Addison-Wesley.

Hume, D. (1739). *A treatise of human nature*. Oxford, UK: Oxford University Press.

Husserl, E. (1900). *Logische untersuchungen: Erster teil: Prolegomena zur reinen logik*.

Husserl, E. (1901). *Logische untersuchungen: Zweiter teil: Untersuchungen zur phänomenologie und theorie der erkenntnis*.

Husserl, E. (1939). Erfahrung und urteil: Untersuchungen zur genealogie der logik (experience and judgment). (J.S. Churchill & K. Amerika, Trans.). Lodnon: Routledge.

ISO/IEC. (1995). *Software life cycle processes ISO/IEC 12207*. Geneva: International Standards Organization/ International Electrotechnical Commission.

ISO/IEC. (2007). *Software engineering - Metamodel for development methodologies, ISO/IEC 24744*. Geneva: International Organization for Standardization/International Electrotechnical Commission.

Johansson, I. (2005). Qualities, quantities, and the endurant-perdurant distinction in top-level ontologies. In Althoff, K.-D., Dengel, A., Bergmann, R., Nick, M., & Roth-Berghofer, T. (Eds.), *WM 2005: Professional Knowledge Management Experiences and Vision*. DFKI.

Kaschek, R. (2011). Introduction: Issues of a conceptual modeling agenda. In Kaschek, R., & Delcambre, L. (Eds.), *The Evolution of Conceptual Modeling (LNCS)* (Vol. 6520, pp. ix–xv). Berlin: Springer. doi:10.1007/978-3-642-17505-3.

Kent, S., Evans, A., & Rumpe, B. (1999). UML semantics FAQ. In Moreira, A., & Demeyer, S. (Eds.), *ECOOP '99 Workshops (LNCS)* (Vol. 1743, pp. 33–56). Berlin: Springer-Verlag.

Kepler, J. (1596). *Mysterium cosmographicum*.

Kepler, J. (1609). *Astronomia nova*.

Kepler, J. (1617-1621). *Epitome of Copernican astronomy*.

Kepler, (1627). *Rudolphine tables*.

Kleppe, A. (2007). *A language description is more than a metamodel*. Paper presented at ATEM2007 (part of MoDELS2007). IEEE.

Kuhn, T. (1962). *The structure of scientific revolutions*. Chicago, IL: University of Chicago Press.

Kühne, T. (2006). Matters of (meta-)modeling. *Software & Systems Modeling*, 5, 369–385. doi:10.1007/s10270-006-0017-9.

Kühne, T. (2007). *Making modeling languages fit for model-driven development*. Paper presented at ATEM2007 (part of MoDELS2007). IEEE.

Kühne, T. (2009). Contrasting classification with generalization. In M. Kirchberg & S. Link (Eds.), *Proceedings of the Sixth Asia-Pacific Conference on Conceptual Modelling*, (pp. 71-78). IEEE.

Kurtev, I., Bézivin, J., Joualt, F., & Valduriez, P. (2006). Model-based DSL frameworks. In *Proceedings of OOPSLA'06: Companion to the 21st ACM SIGPLAN Conference on Object-Oriented Programming Systems, Languages, and Applications*. ACM.

Laarman, A., & Kurtev, I. (2010). Ontological metamodelling with explicit instantiation. In van den Brand, M., Gašević, D., & Gray, J. (Eds.), *SLE2009 (LNCS)* (Vol. 5969, pp. 174–183). Berlin: Springer-Verlag.

Lakoff, G. (1987). *Women, fire, and dangerous things: What categories reveal about the mind.* Chicago, IL: University of Chicago Press. doi:10.7208/chicago/9780226471013.001.0001.

Lamarck, J.-B. (1809). *Philosophie zoologique, ou exposition des considérations relatives à l'histoire naturelle des animaux.* Paris.

Lewis, D. (1971). Counterparts of persons and their bodies. *The Journal of Philosophy, 68,* 203–211. doi:10.2307/2024902.

Liskov, B. (1987). Data abstraction and hierarchy. In *Addendum to the Proceedings OOPSLA (Addendum).* ACM.

Locke, J. (1975). *An essay concerning human understanding.* Oxford, UK: Oxford University Press.

Lowe, E. J. (2001). *The possibility of metaphysics: Substance, identity and time.* Oxford, UK: Oxford University Press. doi:10.1093/0199244995.001.0001.

MacBride, F. (2011). Impure reference: A way around the concept *horse* paradox. *Philosophical Perspectives, 25*(1), 297–312. doi:10.1111/j.1520-8583.2011.00217.x.

Margolis, E., & Laurence, S. (2012). Concepts. In E. N. Zaltz (Ed.), *The Stanford Encyclopedia of Philosophy.* Retrieved from http://plato.stanford.edu/archives/fall2012/entries/concepts/

Martin, J., & Odell, J. J. (1992). *Object-oriented analysis and design.* Englewood Cliffs, NJ: Prentice-Hall.

Martin, J., & Odell, J. J. (1995). *Object-oriented methods: A foundation.* Upper Saddle River, NJ: Prentice Hall.

Martin, J., & Odell, J. J. (1998). *Object-oriented methods: A foundation.* Upper Saddle River, NJ: Prentice Hall.

Masolo, C., Guizzardi, G., Vieu, L., Bottazzi, E., & Ferrario, R. (2005). Relational roles and qua-individuals. In *Proceedings AAAI Fall Symposium on Roles, an Interdisciplinary Perspective,* (pp. 103-112). AAAI.

McBride, T., & Henderson-Sellers, B. (2011). A method assessment framework. In Ralyté, J., Mirbel, I., & Deneckère, R. (Eds.), *Engineering Methods in the Service-Oriented Context.* Berlin: Springer. doi:10.1007/978-3-642-19997-4_7.

McGregor, J. D., & Korson, T. (1993). Supporting dimensions of classification in object-oriented design. *Journal of Object-Oriented Programming, 5*(9), 25–30.

Meyer, B. (1988). *Object-oriented software construction.* Hemel Hempstead, UK: Prentice-Hall.

Milne, A. A. (1926). In which pooh goes visiting and gets into a tight place. In *Winnie-the-Pooh.* London: Methuen & Co. Ltd., London.

Monarchi, D., Booch, G., Henderson-Sellers, B., Jacobson, I., Mellor, S., Rumbaugh, J., & Wirfs-Brock, R. (1994). Methodology standards: help or hindrance? *ACM SIGPLAN, 29*(10), 223–228. doi:10.1145/191081.191115.

Neumayr, B., Schrefl, M., & Thalheim, B. (2011). Modeling techniques for multi-level abstraction. In Kaschek, R., & Delcambre, L. (Eds.), *The Evolution of Conceptual Modeling, (LNCS) (Vol. 6520,* pp. 68–92). Berlin: Springer. doi:10.1007/978-3-642-17505-3_4.

Newton, I. (1687). *Philosophiæ naturalis principia mathematica.*

Noonan, H. (2011). Identity. In E. N. Zaltz (Ed.), *The Stanford Encyclopedia of Philosophy.* Retrieved from http://plato.stanford.edu/archives/win2011/entries/identity/

Odell, J. (1994). Power types. *Journal of Object-Oriented Programming, 7*(2), 8–12.

OED. (1942). *The pocket oxford dictionary of current English* (Fowler, F. G., & Fowler, H. W., Eds.). 4th ed.). Oxford, UK: Clarendon Press.

Ogden, C. K., & Richards, I. A. (1923). *The meaning of meaning*. New York: Harcourt, Brace and World.

OMG. (1997). *UML notation: Version 1.1*. OMG document ad/97-08-05.

OMG. (2000). *Request for proposal: UML 2.0 infrastructure RFP*. OMG Document Number ad/2000-08-08.

OMG. (2002). *Unambiguous UML (2U) submission to UML 2 infrastructure RFP*. OMG Document number ad/2002-06-07.

OMG. (2003). *Unified modeling language specification*. OMG document formal/03-03-01.

OMG. (2006). *Unified modeling language: Infrastructure: Version 2.0*. OMG Document Number formal/05-07-05.

OMG. (2010). *OMG unified modeling language™ (OMG UML): Infrastructure version 2.3*. OMG Document Number formal/2010-05-03.

OMG. (2011a). *OMG unified modeling language™ (OMG UML): Infrastructure version 2.4.1*. OMG Document Number: formal/2011-08-05.

OMG. (2011b). *OMG unified modeling language™ (OMG UML): Superstructure version 2.4.1*. OMG Document Number: formal/2011-08-06.

Opdahl, A., & Henderson-Sellers, B. (2004). A template for defining enterprise modelling constructs. *Journal of Database Management, 15*(2), 39–73. doi:10.4018/jdm.2004040103.

Paley, W. (1809). *Natural theology: Or, evidences of the existence and attributes of the deity* (12th ed.). London: Printed for J. Faulder.

Parnas, D. L. (1972). A technique for software module specification with examples. *Communications of the ACM, 15*(5), 330–336. doi:10.1145/355602.361309.

Partridge, C. (1996). *Business objects: Re-engineering for re-use*. Oxford, UK: Butterworth Heineman.

Partridge, C. (2002). *Note: A couple of meta-ontological choices for ontological architectures*. Technical Report 06/02, LADSEB-CNR, Padova, Italy.

Pastor, O., Levin, A. M., Celma, M., Casamayor, J. C., Virrueta, A., & Eraso, L. E. (2011). Model-based engineering applied to the interpretation of the human genome. In Kaschek, R., & Delcambre, L. (Eds.), *The Evolution of Conceptual Modeling, (LNCS) (Vol. 6520*, pp. 306–330). Berlin: Springer. doi:10.1007/978-3-642-17505-3_14.

Peacocke, C. (1992). *A study of concepts*. Cambridge, MA: MIT Press.

Peirce, C. (1898). *Reasoning and the logic of things: The Cambridge conference lectures of 1898*. Harvard.

Pennebaker, J. W., Mehl, M. R., & Niederhoffer, K. G. (2003). Psychological aspects of natural language use: Our words, our selves. *Annual Review of Psychology, 54*, 547–577. doi:10.1146/annurev. psych.54.101601.145041 PMID:12185209.

Peurbach, G., & Regiomontanus, J. (1496). *Epitome of Ptolemy's almagest*.

Pirotte, A., Zimányi, E., Massart, D., & Yakusheva, T. (1994). Materialization: A powerful and ubiquitous abstraction pattern. In J. Bocca, M. Jarke, & C. Zaniolo (Eds.), *20ᵗʰ International Conference on Very Large Data Bases* (pp. 630-641). Academic Press.

Ptolemy, C. (150). *Almagest, originally entitled mathematike syntaxis*.

Quine, W. V. O. (1953). *From a logical point of view*. Boston: Harvard University Press.

Quine, W. V. O. (1960). *Word and object*. Cambridge, MA: MIT Press.

Quine, W. V. O. (1969). *Ontological relativity and other essays*. New York: Columbia University Press.

Ritchey, T. (2012). Outline for a morphology of modelling methods: Contributions to a general theory of modelling. *Acta Morphologica Generalis*, *1*(1), 1–20.

Sanchez Cuadrado, J., de Lara, J., & Guerra, E. (2012). Bottom-up meta-modelling: An interactive approach. In R.B. France, J. Kazmeier, R. Breu, & C. Atkinson (Eds.), *Model Driven Engineering Languages and Systems: 15th International Conference, MODELS 2012*, (LNCS), (vol. 7590, pp. 3-19). Berlin: Springer-Verlag.

Searle, J. R. (1969). *Speech acts: An essay in the philosophy of language*. Cambridge, UK: Cambridge University Press. doi:10.1017/CBO9781139173438.

Searle, J. R. (1995). *The construction of social reality*. New York: The Free Press.

Seidewitz, E. (2003). What models mean. *IEEE Software*, *20*, 26–31. doi:10.1109/MS.2003.1231147.

Selic, B. (2011). The theory and practice of modeling language design for model-based software engineering – A personal perspective. In Fernandes, J. M., Lämmel, R., Visser, J., & Saraiva, J. (Eds.), *Generative and Transformational Techniques in Software Engineering III International Summer School, GTTSE 2009, (LNCS)* (*Vol. 6491*, pp. 390–321). Berlin: Springer-Verlag. doi:10.1007/978-3-642-18023-1_7.

Selic, B. (2012b). What will it take? A view on adoption of model-based methods in practice. *Software & Systems Modeling*, *11*, 513–526. doi:10.1007/s10270-012-0261-0.

Shan, L., & Zhu, H. (2012). Unifying the semantics of models and meta-models in the multi-layered UML meta-modelling hierarchy. *International Journal of Software Informatics*, *6*(2), 163–200.

Sider, T. (2003). *Four dimensionalism: An ontology of persistence and time*. Oxford, UK: Oxford University Press.

Smith, B. (1997). On substances, accidents and universals: In defence of a constituent ontology. *Philosophical Papers*, *27*, 105–127. doi:10.1080/05568649709506558.

Smith, B. (2004). Beyond concepts: Ontology as reality representation. In A. Varzi & L. Vieu (Eds.), *Proceedings FOIS 2004: International Conference on Formal Ontology and Information Systems*. IOS Press.

Song, C.-Y., & Baik, D.-K. (2003). A layered metamodel for hierarchical modeling in UML. *International Journal of Software Engineering and Knowledge Engineering*, *13*(2), 191–214. doi:10.1142/S0218194003001263.

Steimann, F. (2000). On the representation of roles in object-oriented and conceptual modelling. *Data & Knowledge Engineering*, *35*, 83–106. doi:10.1016/S0169-023X(00)00023-9.

Stocks, J. L. (1922). *Translation of Aristotle's De Caelo*.

Swerdlow, N., & Neugebauer, O. (1984). *Mathematical astronomy in Copernicus's de revolutionibus*. New York: Springer-Verlag. doi:10.1007/978-1-4613-8262-1.

Swoyer, C., & Orilia, F. (2011). Properties. In E. N. Zalta (Ed.), *The Stanford Encyclopedia of Philosophy*. Retrieved from http://plato.stanford.edu/archives/win2011/entries/properties/

Ullmann, S. (1972). *Semantics: An introduction to the science of meaning*. Oxford, UK: Basil Blackwell.

Wallace, A. R. (1855). On the law which has regulated the introduction of new species. *Annals & Magazine of Natural History*, *16*, 184–196. doi:10.1080/037454809495509.

Wand, Y., & Weber, R. (1993). On the ontological expressiveness of information systems analysis and design grammars. *Journal of Information Systems*, *3*, 217–237. doi:10.1111/j.1365-2575.1993.tb00127.x.

Wand, Y., & Weber, R. (1995). On the deep structure of information systems. *Information Systems Journal*, *5*, 203–223. doi:10.1111/j.1365-2575.1995.tb00108.x.

(2010). *Webster's New World College Dictionary*. Cleveland, OH: Wiley Publishing, Inc..

Whitmire, S. A. (1997). *Object oriented design measurement*. New York: John Wiley & Sons, Inc..

Wieringa, R. (2011). Real-world semantics of conceptual models. In Kaschek, R., & Delcambre, L. (Eds.), *The Evolution of Conceptual Modeling (LNCS)* (*Vol. 6520*, pp. 1–20). Berlin: Springer. doi:10.1007/978-3-642-17505-3_1.

Wieringa, R., de Jonge, W., & Spruit, P. (1995). Using dynamic classes and role classes to model object migration. *Theory and Practice of Object Systems*, *1*(1), 31–83.

Wikipedia. (2012). *Edmund Husserl*. Retrieved from http://www.en.wikipedia.org/wiki/Edmund_Husserl

Wittgenstein, L. (1921). *Tractatus logico-philosophicus*. London: Routledge and Kegan Paul.

Wittgenstein, L. (1953). *Philosophical investigations*. New York: Macmillan.

Wittgenstein, L. (1958). *Philosophical investigations* (2nd ed.). Oxford, UK: Basil Blackwell.

ENDNOTES

[1] Generalization as in subtype relation between types (as discussed by e.g. Frege), not as in abstracting away detail (as discussed by e.g. Locke).

[2] Pythagoras: ca. 560-480 BC or possibly ca. 570-495 BC.

[3] Although the addition of epicycles was not solely the province of Ptolemy (ca. 90-ca. 168), it is to Ptolemy that the name is most closely associated. In this paper, we will denote this idea, of continually adding detail in order to give further explanation without any backing theory a 'Ptolemaic fix'.

[4] Despite his observations, Brahe's concerns about parallax meant he could not accept a geocentric view, leading to his creation of a hybrid or Tychonic model.

[5] However, it was not the heliocentric model that proved most controversial; it was in 1632 that Galileo's *Dialogue Concerning the Two Chief World Systems* led directly to his trial for heresy, the crime being that lay people were not allowed to interpret Biblical writings.

[6] A deconstruction/reconstruction approach discussed earlier (Kuhn, 1962).

[7] Here, taken loosely as a type model of user-defined models (but see later discussion).

[8] UML seems to have been trademarked only from version 2.3. We acknowledge that trademark but in all other references omit it as being assumed.

[9] Although this approach gives rise to an infinite number of levels, in the OMG standards there is an arbitrary truncation at the M3 level (e.g., Selic, 2011), thus creating the four levels shown in Figure 3.

[10] It has been argued (e.g., Bézivin, 2004) that instanceOf is an incorrect name for this relationship and that conformantTo is more accurate.

11   From a philosophical viewpoint, attributes may be considered either as part of the entity or as a relation to a property. Thus, from this viewpoint, these terms may or may not be synonyms as suggested by Searle.

12   Compare this with the representation of a 'redness' quality of an object as an instance of a MixinType in a foundational ontology such as the UFO (Section 3.2).

13   Here, we take method and methodology as synonyms.

14   The corresponding algebraic descriptions (equations) are to be found in Henderson-Sellers (2012). We choose not to repeat them here but rely instead on Venn and Euler diagrams for illustrative purposes.

15   Thus, here, Rover could be considered to be in the L0 layer as well as the O0 layer.

16   Powertypes, deep instantiation and materialization are discussed in detail in Section 3.1 below.

17   The example given is that of 'game' which may or may not be competitive; may or may not use long-term strategies; may or may not involve skill in the participants (Lakoff, 1987, p. 16).

18   An abstract class.

19   Of course, all types can be viewed as instance of the type Type (a singleton). This provides the parallel to Class:Class in Figure 3 and ultimately resolves to a case akin to Russell's Paradox (e.g. similar to Frege's 'The concept horse is not a concept' as discussed earlier) – see also MacBride (2011).

20   Commonsense and intuition are, of course, poor measures of scientific validity.

21   Although this source is cited as the origin of the term qua-individual, the use of the word 'qua' in this same context dates back to (at least) early object-oriented design, e.g. Bock and Odell (1994).

22   More correctly, this should be a relational dependence if Student is taken as a rigid sortal – it becomes an existential dependence only if Student is an instance of a Moment Universal (Guizzardi, 2011).

23   A conclusion reached first by Pythagoras.

24   Note that these two terms are not strictly synonyms because it is possible to construe junk particulars, i.e. Instance is a subtype of Particular.

25   Bézivin, Joualt, and Valduriez (2004) define a megamodel as ''a model of which at least some elements represent and/or refer to models or metamodels.''

26   Whilst Searle acknowledges that a subject can also refer to a universal under certain circumstances, his treatise focuses on singular definite reference (Searle, 1969, p. 72).

27   Searle (1969, p. 120) notes importantly that collieness can only be construed as a characteristic if and only if we understand the predicate 'is a collie dog.'

Chapter 5
Runtime Integration Capability for Distributed Model Driven Applications

Jon Davis
Curtin University, Australia

ABSTRACT

Geographically distributed organizations face unique challenges to effectively implement shared information services across the enterprise. Traditional solutions require options such as establishing large centralized application and database servers, which simplifies some data integration issues but involves higher associated centralization risks with potential scalability limitations, or establishing multiple decentralized application servers optionally arranged in hierarchical hubs, requiring significant customization and data migration functions to be developed, reducing the level of risk but incurring additional expenditure on data integration and transfer. Our ongoing development of a distributed temporal metadata framework for Enterprise Information Systems (EIS) applications seeks to overcome these issues with the application logic model supporting the capability for direct integration with similar distributed application instances to readily provide: data replication, transfer, and transformations; centralized authorization and distribution of core identity data; sharing and deployment of modified logic model elements; and workflow integration between application instances.

INTRODUCTION

Large and geographically distributed organizations need to resolve unique challenges to effectively implement Enterprise Information System (EIS) scale shared information services across their entire organization. Multiple architecture options exist with great variability on the ultimate scalability, expense, functionality, and risk of the final solution.

A common approach is to establish very large centralized application and database servers with appropriate wide area network links to all remote business units to centrally service all users across the organization from a single virtual instance of the corporate applications. This option may simplify some data integration issues by centralizing the availability of all corporate data but requires additional costs to ensure adequate network accessibility is maintained. There are higher associated

DOI: 10.4018/978-1-4666-4217-1.ch005

centralization risks with this option due to the need for high network availability and failover with the potential for scalability concerns of the underlying applications to ensure they can service an expanding organization.

A potentially less risky option is to establish multiple de-centralized application and database servers to service individual or clusters of business units. Depending on the geographical user base and optionally arranged in hierarchical hubs serviced with appropriate wide area network links, each application instance provides services to all local regional users. This option typically requires significant customization and data migration functions to be developed in order to transfer the required transactions data or transaction summaries between the separate application and database instance tiers that simulate a suitable logical or functional corporate organizational hierarchy, to satisfy the information requirements of both corporate management and of each business unit. The overall level of operational risk is reduced from the previous centralized option but at the cost of incurring additional expenditure on architecture environment, and customizing data integration and transfer functions to implement the information transfers.

A common additional problem to both scenarios is that it is rare that the out-of-the-box functionality of an EIS application will satisfy all the functional requirements of an organization's business units, requiring additional customization and maintenance expense. The cost and availability of customizations can be variable but often extensive for either architecture option.

While the technologies for application development, layer separation and deployment, data transfer and network accessibility continue to change dramatically bringing continually improving functionality and access capability, these scenarios for core application (de)centralization options and their associated risks and costs have not been fundamentally altered in terms of their basic complexity or requirements. Emerging cloud based technologies can alter the technical landscape in terms of scalability and cost of ownership but are currently primarily leveraging platform and hardware efficiencies rather than solving any underlying data and application integration issues, although multi-tenanted SaaS options are evolving as maturing candidates.

Model Driven Architecture (MDA) options or more specifically what we term as Meta-Data based Enterprise Information Systems (MDEIS), as a variant of MDA, can directly provide the capability to substantially simplify the hierarchical or indeed any organizational topology of structured information, data and application logic integration requirements for widespread geographically de-centralized organizations. We rely on the Distributed Components (DC) within the MDEIS application model and a supporting framework to seamlessly provide advanced integration services such as: data replication, transfer and transformations; centralized authorization and distribution of core identity data; sharing and deployment of modified logic model elements; and workflow integration between application instances.

How do we define MDEIS applications? Firstly, we consider the class of EIS applications that we summarize as visual and interactive applications that prompt for the entry of appropriate transaction data and user events from the application users, use rules based workflow sequences and actions and utilize database transactions in a (relational) database environment to complete the actions (Davis, 2004). They are typically structurally repetitive and tend to be a technically simpler subset of possible software applications. They generally consist of EIS and Enterprise Resource Planning (ERP) style applications such as; logistics, human resource, payroll, project costing, accounting, customer relationship management and other general database applications. The collective application design requirements are stored and available in a suitable meta-model structure and supported by an execution framework that will allow the EIS application models to be executed automatically and directly from the model, thus the transformation to the MDEIS application.

The MDEIS model title can also pre-fixed with temporal and distributed; the former represents the transaction tracking nature of the application data and meta-data to permit rollback or rollforward through any time period, regardless of the application logic version (the correct state of which is always maintained); the latter refers to the distributed operations as described in this chapter.

The benefits of an associated MDEIS application lifecycle can be shown to approach an order of magnitude reduction over a specific development for an individual application for a single organization employing multiple efficient MDEIS customizations, expanding to multiple orders of magnitude when scaled to the commercial environment of vendors supplying hundreds or thousands of individual customer organizations (Davis, 2011a).

A key aspect of the MDEIS application model offers a direct solution to the information sharing and integration problems facing large and geographically distributed enterprises. The distributed components of the MDEIS model simplify the need to customize the de-centralized EIS application, in this case a MDEIS application, to implement enterprise wide information sharing and access and minimize the need to develop specific data transfer, integration and processing features across each separate instance within the enterprise. The MDEIS distributed components will implement the required data exchange and processing functionality with minimal additional logic definition (note these are not customizations) and without the need for additional or specific data transfer and processing utilities.

A MDEIS runtime environment will achieve this by the implementation of identical or similar core meta-data application logic at every distributed site across the enterprise - analogous to the installation of common application software for each site. This does not limit local MDEIS application instances to only maintaining identical

meta-data logic at each site (just the core application meta-data) as Variant Logic can be locally defined and applied as required at each site's MDEIS application instance to provide for any specific localized logic differences. Variant Logic provides the capability for third parties and end users to define and create their own application logic to supplement or replace a vendor's pre-defined MDEIS application logic to become an alternate variation of the application logic (Davis, 2011b).

The distributed components would then be invoked at any site's MDEIS application instance by defining any of the following types of Distribution Execution Requests (DER) that will then operate between any groups of MDEIS application instances:

- **Data Replication (DR):** Defines the automated transfer of transaction or summary data between MDEIS instances.
- **Key Authorization (KA):** Defines a distributed schema for obtaining key, identifier or sequence based data from a pseudo master MDEIS instance simulating a distributed authorization hierarchy or other virtual topology of MDEIS instances.
- **Logic Variant (LV):** Defines the transferring of a locally defined Logic Variant to other MDEIS instances for local execution.
- **Workflow Trigger (WT):** Defines a pseudo master MDEIS instance to automatically escalate defined application workflow objects requiring transaction authorization beyond local authorization limits.

Any combination of these DERs with each requiring only minimal definition at each of the involved MDEIS instance nodes, denoted the Master and Slave nodes, will be executed automatically by the MDEIS runtime components of each MDEIS instance. Any organizational topology can be represented by the overall combinations of Master and Slave node pairs and defined DERs.

A Master node is the MDEIS instance that defines the requirement via the definition of a DER type and transfers it to any group of Slave nodes for their local execution and possible transfer of information back to and between the Master node. Each Master and Slave node pair must first be granted mutual privileges to accept DERs from the other node with each specific DER from the Master node optionally requiring specific authorization approval from the Slave node.

This chapter will expand upon the capabilities of the MDEIS application and its distributed components, by reviewing comparative traditional and emerging distribution and integration technologies, examining the operation of each of the Distribution Execution Request types in detail, and provide examples demonstrating the practical application of each DER.

BACKGROUND

Developing and improving methods for how software applications interact with each other is a key research and industry concern. Implementing practical solutions in response to business requirements for sharing data, processes and workflows between different sites, applications, levels of management or operations, supports a network of developers, system integrators, business analysts, and system and application administrators to tie together an often complex Web of technologies for each individual solution instance.

We review the following related issues of applications integration and technologies that have guided the ongoing development of integration options and subsequently to assist in defining the distributed component capabilities of the temporal meta-data framework for EIS applications.

Distributed vs. Centralized Applications

There are two basic options for implementing enterprise wide applications; centralized or distributed, or a hybrid of the two. Centralized implementations offer a degree of simplification by utilizing large single application instances but also attract higher networking costs to ensure access with redundancy, greater system administration effort to ensure higher availability, and higher risks of ensuring ongoing scalability of the centralized solution. De-centralized or distributed implementations minimize these aspects but at the additional cost of execution environment duplication, operations and maintenance, and often requiring data migration and workflow integrations to be developed to provide integration between different application instances. (Gaynor, 2004) provides a network topology analysis methodology which in combination with the application-centric analysis of (Schuff, 2001) can be used to assess an enterprise's centralized vs. de-centralized options.

One hybrid option can be how the enterprise topology of de-centralized application instances is arranged, where each instance services an appropriate geographical area comprising both local and remote users. Emerging cloud based options also represent a hybrid approach as they can abstract the physical infrastructure away from the ultimate end-users – a key factor that contributes to the level of abstraction is the geographical distribution of end-users overlaid with the geographical distribution and internal redundancy of each critical access point of the cloud based solution – the more distributed the end-users then the less risk of overall service loss assuming there are adequate redundant and internal pathways and components utilized by the cloud provider. Current cloud based options tend to operate on a macro scale providing access to servers or multiple servers, and now supporting multi-tenanted Software as a Service (SaaS) variable software instances with their inherent software or platform capability (Sengupta, 2011).

The distributed components of the MDEIS application framework currently apply primarily to providing integration capability between application instances in a de-centralized or distributed environment.

Data Transfer and Sharing between Distributed Applications

In a centralized application or database environment, it can usually be assumed that each application already has secure access to all of the data managed within its application environment, although this can be more complicated in some legacy application environments. The primary data transfer problem is usually inter-application or inter-database.

In a distributed application architecture each application instance is typically an island of data, some with only local relevance but some data will be of crucial enterprise importance particularly when data needs to be processed on an enterprise wide basis such as sales, costs, performance etc. The key requirement for each identified data integration then becomes how to identify the data, extract the data, transport the data, access the data and process the data into a cohesive schema. (Sovran, 2011) addresses geo-replication of data as a generic middleware solution although replication of data is a standard feature of many database management systems. However, in our distributed solution we only need to consider specific subsets of data replication on a needs basis. The traditional solution to each of these aspects of data integration may require any combination of third party utilities, custom developments or manual procedures to be implemented to achieve the required result. The distributed components of the MDEIS application framework will replicate, summarize and perform the transfer of many data integrations directly based on simple model based definitions and without any additional tools or utilities.

Workflow between Distributed Applications

The options for providing application workflow vary greatly between software applications; some do not offer any workflow options, some offer only fixed logic transactional workflows, some may provide workflow options for only some transactions and some may provide for interaction with third party workflow applications.

When applications are executing in a distributed environment there is a requirement for workflow options particularly for transactions that may be generated in the local application instance but need a higher level of authorization that might only be provided by users from another site's application instance such as in a higher tier of an organizations hierarchy or management. (Weiping, 2009) examines the general workflow requirements for distributed applications as should be built-in for optimal functionality, while (Eugster, 2004) reviews the general difficulties in developing safe general purpose distributed applications.

A technically simpler but administratively inefficient solution that is often used is to provide senior authorizers from other sites with local accounts on all application instances that may require their authorization, often problematic in terms of communicating the workflow and with users successfully managing access to multiple instances.

Otherwise, these workflow authorizations require either the application or a third party solution to resolve the communications and workflow between the distributed application instances. If the application does not directly support the remote instance workflow capability, and few do, then a third party workflow integration is required to be implemented, if the specific transaction can be supported by the originating application. (Wu, 2011) provides such an alternative SaaS based workflow middleware reference model.

Every transaction and logical object of the application model of the MDEIS application framework will be accessed by third party applications via Web service commands. The distributed components will also manage the workflows between MDEIS application instances transparently with the workflow component and associated data distributed to the required MDEIS application instance for authorization automatically based on simple model based definitions and without any additional tools or utilities.

Application Integration and Customization

Modifying a software application by engaging the vendor, authorized third parties or internal development teams to develop specific customizations can be an expensive option requiring highly specialized skills and knowledge but may be required in a distributed application environment to provide for different local operating procedures. Subsequently deploying any customizations to multiple application instances and maintaining suitable version control over potentially disparate sites, applications and variable local requirements can add further complexity to maintaining the overall execution environment.

Customizations to EIS software systems require developers fluent in the development languages and in the detailed structure of the application logic and structure and depending on the scale can become significant software engineering exercises. (Hui, 2003) provides a model to optimize capturing the requirements for any major customizations. Ongoing review and potential re-engineering is also required for each customization whenever the EIS is upgraded or updated by the OEM to ensure ongoing compatibility of the customizations, which adds often considerable further time and expense to each upgrade.

As a MDEIS application is based purely on defined meta-data of the application model, any application logic customizations are modifications to the meta-data model and all of the data and logic objects will be available for remote access via Web service commands – it is a key example of a Service Oriented Architecture offering complete modularization (Papazoglou, 2007). Any aspect of the MDEIS application will be available for authorized modification by Logic Definers who only require business process and model knowledge rather than the full technical knowledge suite required by EIS application developers.

OMG, MDA, and MDE

The aim of the Object Management Group (OMG) is to "provide an open, vendor-neutral approach to the challenge of business and technology change." The OMG represent one of the largest proponent groups for Model Driven Engineering (MDE) with the goal for their Model Driven Architecture (MDA) initiative to "separate business and application logic from underlying platform technology" (OMG, 2012).

The OMG approach is predicated on the design of platform independent models defined primarily with Unified Modeling Language (UML), which can be rendered into a platform specific model with interface definitions to describe how the base model will be implemented on the target platform. A primary goal of the OMG is interoperability and the tools and technologies are primarily aimed at highly technical analysts and developers. The OMG supports industry developers of supporting toolsets as well as users developing with the technologies.

A key alternative to the common process of hard coded application logic is provided by on-going Model Driven Engineering (MDE) which is a generic term for software development that involves the creation of an abstract model and how it is transformed to a working implementation (Schmidt, 2006). Zhu (2009) takes a strong model generation approach that seeks to identify customizations to a base model but then implements and maintains each new customized model as separate models executed as individual application instances. In France (2007) they argue for future MDE research to focus on runtime models, where these executing models can also be used to modify the models in a controlled manner. Such a direction provides not only more manageable change control but also necessarily shifts the target of the change agent closer to the knowledgeable business end user rather than relying solely on the technical programmer.

Such a model is the goal of our distributed temporal meta-data framework for EIS applications. This framework concept is based on our assertion that performance of the analysis and efficient collection of this information can also perform the bulk of the design phase for an EIS application largely as a simultaneous activity. With the collective design requirements stored and available in a meta-model structure, MDEIS applications can be executed automatically from the model with the availability of the framework runtime components. It not only seeks to separate the application logic from the technology platform but to also make the application logic accessible to a less technically skilled base of application modelers that we define as Logic Definers. Specifically we aim to reduce the competency entrance for EIS style application development from technical programmers down to knowledgeable power users, to around the level of competency of medium to advanced spreadsheet creators.

Configuration, Customization, and Variant Logic

Most applications will provide some level of user configuration, whereby some aspects of the application can be readily defined by authorized users that will modify some application behavior. However there is no common or minimum capability for which user configuration options are provided in applications. Some applications may provide extensive configuration options whilst others may provide minimal flexibility options. While varying in complexity the generally available configurable content for end users tends to be limited to simplistic features (Rajkovic, 2010) with application customization being required for more advanced features. (Hagen, 1994) long ago identified the need to focus on more configurable software to benefit users and developers as a joint initiative of software development to merge configuration and customization aspects. (Nitu,

2009) extends the configuration options to multi-tenanted SaaS systems.

The scope of the typical end user to extend functionality changes beyond that permitted by the commonplace user configuration capabilities is typically quite minimal, however every feature of the meta-data EIS application from the simple to the complex can be optionally configured by authorized users and specified to apply to only specific users or user groups – analogous to (Bezemer, 2010) who describes code isolation for customizations of multi-tenant SaaS applications from discrete user groups. Simple features require only basic knowledge to configure whilst more complex features will require a necessarily deeper understanding of function and capability. The self-documentation capability of the MDEIS application satisfies much of the required architecture description that (Goethals, 2004) recommends to provide a suitable application knowledge base.

All features of a MDEIS application can be permitted to be customized by authorized end users, acting as Logic Definers, aiming at the knowledgeable business user or power user rather than solely restricted to technical experts. Defining complex or new application segments will require a correspondingly higher understanding of MDEIS functionality which a technical programmer can certainly fulfill as can a knowledgeable power user. The framework will provide the capability for any end user to define and create their own application logic to supplement or replace a vendor's pre-defined MDEIS application logic as what we term Variant Logic - to become an alternate variation of the application logic (Davis, 2011a).

Variant Logic can be applied to any object defined in a meta-data EIS application model whether visual objects, logical processing objects, or as data structures objects. Variant Logic can be defined by any authorized user acting as a Logic Definer via additional object definition in the model and can be assigned for execution to any user as an alternative to the original application logic

Software Version Management

Version control is the goal of software configuration management, to ensure the controlled change or development of the software system (De Alwis, 2009), to track the development of the components and manage the baseline of software developments (Ren, 2010) including throughout the various phases of a project as (Kaur, 2009) provides for.

In traditional software development, the atomic level to which version control can be applied varies on the version control systems used but can be as high as individual source code files or database table definitions. The atomic level to apply version control for a MDEIS application model is each individual object's attribute definition within the MDEIS application model. Meta-data version control needs to be managed at the lowest levels as it is also fundamentally tied to maintaining model integrity and permitting direct dynamic execution as (Koegel, 2010) demonstrates with their graph-based conflict detection algorithms.

Version control in an MDEIS application is an automatic function closely related to the management and support of the temporal execution capability of the framework (Davis, 2011c) which maintains the temporal status of data and meta-data to support the rollback and rollforward execution to any point in time. An associated technique for identifying changes between versions of software (Steinholtz, 1987) is a classical key approach when applied to the meta-data model and combined with the runtime version control of distributed components of (Ma, 2011) is instrumental to allowing an automated update approach to be applied to MDEIS applications and for determining model element compatibility when deploying Logic Variants between MDEIS instances. The MDEIS application framework will process the automatic updates as a sequence of new meta-data update commands.

Software Update and Deployment

Software updates for applications have traditionally been released in a form of hard media that is distributed to the end user although this has largely been superseded by electronic distribution via the Internet. For smaller consumer and utility software systems the update often consists of a specific update program and instructions, or alternatively a replacement program that uninstalls the previous version and installs the latest version. Both will operate largely automatically with minimal user input required.

Larger EIS/ERP style systems tend to utilize either the version update process or otherwise install the new version cleanly and attempt to migrate the data and configuration from the previous version installation. The larger and more complex a system is the less likely that automated updates will complete successfully as less effort and quality assurance seems to be expended on producing each specific update program than on the primary software product (Jansen, 2008), exacerbating existing common issues with system development quality assurance (Brown, 2009). Managers of EIS upgrades attest to the often extensive projects required for particularly major version EIS upgrades which can require months of effort and considerable expense.

MDEIS applications can be automatically updated as each update is a stream of individual meta-data commands – there is no need for specialist update applications (Davis, 2011d). Updates can even be performed on a live operating application although prudence would suggest performing updates in an offline state as some updates may involve individually lengthy executions e.g. where schema changes occur in large data tables. Where Variant Logic modifications have been made there may be the potential for some logic conflict with updates to the core application meta-data – any potential conflicts will be precisely identified for focused consideration and otherwise where no conflicts are identified the Variant Logic can be immediately available in the updated system with no additional verification required.

DISTRIBUTED EXECUTION IN META-DATA EIS APPLICATIONS

Why are De-Centralized EIS Applications Difficult and Expensive to Integrate?

Many of the concerns of traditional implementations of distributed software systems and required integrations have been previewed in the previous section. Specific primary problems that need to be resolved to streamline enterprise wide implementations of efficiently interoperating, de-centralized and distributed EIS applications include:

Variable Distribution Topology: A network topology will not necessarily mimic an organizational authorization structure so cannot be simply overlaid as a de-facto instance or authorization topology. Nor will every required enterprise-wide data flow or workflow transaction necessarily follow identical pathways as organizational business units can be located amongst any combination of physical locations. The distributed components of the MDEIS application operate under a set of Master / Slave node pairs which can collectively simulate any authorization structure that is required - analogous to the traditional bus, star, tree in any combination.

Solution Architecture Visibility: In a distributed Web of applications across many sites where many of the applications are provided by different vendors there will be a great variety in the style and implementation of data transfers and application integrations. Some common application modifications can be carefully controlled and managed across the sites, data middleware can be used to replicate or transfer much of the accessible data,

and third party workflow applications may be compatible with some applications. However it is unlikely that any solution or set of solutions will readily satisfy all information sharing requirements due to the disparity of application technologies most often employed, usually requiring some level of other ad-hoc integrations. Overall, implementing, understanding and managing the entire set of enterprise wide integrations can become a very complicated process. In a MDEIS application environment all data and application logic is open and available (via appropriate authorization) as are all of the Distributed Execution Requests so all data transfers and application integrations are defined within the same overall environment and can be readily extracted as self-documenting guides.

Consistent Authorization and Control: Similarly to above, the variety of and disparity in execution and authorization of integration methods will mean that some integrations are easily managed with high level utility support while others are performed as lower level tasks requiring more detailed technical knowledge for implementation, maintenance and execution. In a large enterprise this can involve a variety of staff, roles, technologies and authorization mechanisms. The distributed components of the MDEIS framework will provide consistent access and authorization to each of the authorized Distributed Execution Requests within the same overall security access structure.

Distributed Application Execution: The vast majority of applications are not designed with any particular distribution or de-centralization functionality as a core design factor – they are standalone applications with possibly some level of integration capability. Executing these applications enterprise wide becomes more a case of standardizing the application setup and configuration to provide a more consistent general operation mode for each instance, using common customizations or specific integrations to achieve any cohesive distributed functionality such as sharing data or workflows. When similar or identical

MDEIS applications are in use at multiple sites they are executing from the same underlying application model logic and data structures. Any instance can be defined to become a source or destination of any required information such as centralizing a common data source for all instances or automatically replicating data or summaries between instances, or for integrating workflow authorizations.

Data Transfer Integrity: In traditional applications the database may be open and supported by high quality documentation, accessible transactions or APIs, although for many applications there may be either minimal schema knowledge or direct access to managed interfaces. It can become a high risk option to make unguaranteed assumptions about third party application data schemas and applying independent import or export transactions against these assumptions - an occurrence that is not infrequent particularly for users of applications that are considered to be less open. Major risks include missing or misunderstanding of extracted data, posting incomplete or partial transactions, up to damaging the internal integrity of a database when importing external data. MDEIS applications provide a complete model of data and transactions with a runtime environment providing full remote access to the data and transactions using secure Web service commands allowing full import, export and transaction control.

Application and Workflow Integration: Most traditional applications are the result of compiled code often utilizing a combination of multiple technologies and legacy components, providing only the integration options that have been specifically programmed in. The ability to integrate with these applications at the application logic layer is often very low unless they have been developed to offer a level of component accessibility. Where available the integration options may include; an API for direct access, integration with major workflow middleware applications, or simple access to the database (as above). The development of various

"screen scraper" technologies to extract data from user displays was a virtual act of desperation to try to extract useful data from inherently closed applications. MDEIS applications also provide a complete model of the application logic and every aspect of the model will be able to be defined, manipulated and executed remotely via secure Web service commands permitting unlimited application logic and workflow integration.

Customization Sharing and Deployment: In a well managed software environment some application customizations or integrations that are developed for use at a site may also be able to be redeployed to other enterprise instances with only minor configuration changes or customizations required. MDEIS applications individually permit the definition of Logic Variants throughout the application model where any authorized third party or user is able to securely supplement or replace parts of the application logic, without coding. When similar or identical MDEIS applications are in use at multiple sites any Logic Variant defined at a site can be deployed directly to other instances for immediate availability of the new functionality.

Version Control and Compatibility: To successfully maintain an enterprise collection of integrated applications and instances across multiple sites requires IT administration rigor and discipline. Any modifications to applications whether upgrades, fixes, integrations, customizations or configuration changes must be carefully tested against each versioned set of candidate application instances to ensure compatibility. Each change may also have different implementation requirements in terms of the compatibility with specific application versions and combinations, the automation of the installation, and the technical requirement for and capability of the installers and testers. In a complex enterprise application architecture each potential change can become an arduous and resource consuming task often resulting in the decision to skip some lesser important or non-mandatory updates and thus the organization may miss out or have delayed many useful efficiency improvements. MDEIS applications update automatically based on a stream of individual updates to the application model, greatly simplifying the update. All updates are precisely defined and automatically documented to inform application administrators and users of the changes. Where any Logic Variants, analogous to customizations in traditional software, have been defined the update will determine if there are any potential conflicts with any existing Logic Variants and highlight exactly where in the model a logic definer may need to review. Logic Variants that are not affected will be clearly identified and do not require any other confirmation testing. Any Distributed Execution Requests will require that any other candidate MDEIS application Slave instances will maintain the application model components to a level of compatibility that will be determined by analysis of all of the DER's referenced model objects. The details of any incompatibility will be advised if unable to be implemented pending local update of the application model.

These major issues are a natural consequence of complex IT and application architectures particularly where the heterogeneous nature of applications developed by different vendors, to different standards, aimed at mainly single instances, with different technologies over a long time span work against the corporate desire to maintain a simplified homogeneous environment. The solution requires a significant improvement in reducing commercial and technological barriers and opening up the functionality of applications to permit greater logic and workflow sharing. The operation of the distributed components of MDEIS style solutions is a sound candidate model for solving many of these problems.

Distributed Components of MDEIS Applications Provide Instant Integration

Our ongoing development of a distributed temporal meta-data model for EIS applications seeks to remove the need for hard coding by technical developers (other than in the creation of the runtime engine and meta-data editors), and instead transform the responsibility of defining application logic to business analysts, knowledge engineers and even business end users.

Once the MDEIS application logic has been defined as meta-data and stored as a model, the model is then used for direct execution by a runtime engine. The model allows the application logic to be defined as a set of high-level objects (which provide the greatest functionality from the smallest definition) through to allowing for low-level functions such as mathematical expressions. The model is abstracted away from any underlying framework code and relies on specifying the relationships between defined application objects and the required actions.

When deploying MDEIS applications across a large enterprise the same primary architecture options exist for MDEIS applications as for traditional applications – centralized vs. distributed. In the centralized option a single MDEIS application instance is implemented and scaled to service all usage, with a probable larger number of customizations implemented as Variant Logic. In the distributed architecture option the distributed components of the MDEIS framework become of prime importance and are the ongoing focus of this chapter. Variant Logic will continue to play a major role in the applications' lifecycle as well as an important aspect of the distributed components that we will now review.

As in traditional application management where software version control is a key requirement for success the analogy in the MDEIS environment is the implementation of similar MDEIS instances at multiple sites. Each instance will have the same MDEIS application models installed for use although they do not strictly need to maintain the exact version at each site. As in much of technology the closer the similarity of the version the more effective will be the execution of the distributed components. As version control in the MDEIS model occurs at the object level the framework can review the compatibility of all individual objects for each DER that is generated providing a direct compatibility result and overall higher frequency of compatibility than traditional batch based version control.

The next consideration is the overall commu-nication, authorization, and distribution topology of the application instance network. Ultimately, the distributed network will be any connected graph of sites and DERs but implementing a basic topology is the logical starting point for defining the distributed authorizations.

The overall authorization topology is com-posed of pairs of MDEIS instances called Master and Slave nodes relative to each defined DER. A Master node is the MDEIS instance that defines the requirement via the definition of a DER type and sends it to a Slave node for its local execu-tion and possible transfer of information back to and between the Master node. Each Master and Slave node pair must first be granted mutual privileges to accept DERs from the other node. The classification of whether an instance is a

Master or Slave node is a term relative to each DER transaction authorization - any instance can be both a Master and Slave node, both mutually and to other instances.

Figure 1 depicts a simple hierarchical or tree authorization topology that might be the initial set of Master and Slave nodes established for an organization executing MDEIS application instances in the Head Office, Regional Offices down to Local Offices, for a particular set of similar DERs.

The initial DERs in Figure 1 would typically be established to implement the common standards required throughout the enterprise. This might include options such as the sharing of centralized information from the head office out to all in-stances, as well as the returning of local transac-tion data from local sales offices back to the re-gional and head offices.

Over time as other enterprise and local shar-ing requirements emerge additional DERs will be defined and authorized between sites to satisfy those requirements. There is no limit to the level of DERs that can be established between sites or which sites can be involved other than access policies implemented by the security or applica-tion administrators to manage the authorization structures.

Figure 2 illustrates where a few additional DERs have subsequently been authorized between

Figure 1. Example initial authorization nodes for a de-centralized organization

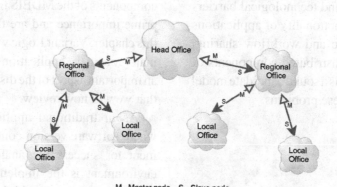

M - Master node   S - Slave node

Figure 2. Example multiple ad-hoc authorization nodes for a de-centralized organization

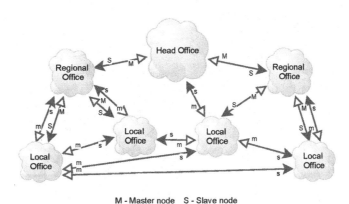

M - Master node   S - Slave node
m,s subsequent additional DERs

any required sites acting as either the Master or Slave node as required. Ultimately such a DER mapping could be based on hundreds or thousands of individual DERs across a large enterprise.

Defined Distributed Execution Requests

The distributed components are integral to the design of the MDEIS application model. They are specifically designed to provide additional distribution execution modes to the operation of similar MDEIS application instances so that organizations choosing to operate in a distributed architecture will be able to closely emulate and also achieve many of the benefits of a comparative centralized application implementation. For other heterogeneous distributed access to and sharing of the data, application logic and workflows of different MDEIS applications there would be standard remote access to all data and logic components via Web service commands.

The following types of DERs can currently be defined to operate between similar MDEIS instances:

- **Data Replication (DR):** Defines the automated transfer of transaction or summary data between MDEIS instances.

- **Key Authorization (KA):** Defines a distributed schema for obtaining key, identifier or sequence based data from a pseudo master MDEIS instance simulating a distributed authorization hierarchy or other virtual topology of MDEIS instances.

- **Logic Variant (LV):** Defines the transferring of a locally defined Logic Variant to other MDEIS instances for local execution.

- **Workflow Trigger (WT):** Defines a pseudo master MDEIS instance to automatically escalate defined application workflow objects requiring transaction authorization beyond local authorization limits.

Publication limitations on the display size and available commentary in this chapter naturally prevent describing the hundreds of classes and how they interact in the MDEIS model. Figure 3 is a highly condensed overview of how the distributed components are modeled.

The distributed components use the following major classes to model the definition of the Distribution Execution Requests, no detail of attributes or methods can be displayed on the small diagram. Note that these distributed components classes are depicted in the middle area of the diagram between the spaced lines:

Figure 3. Overview class diagram of the Distribution Execution Requests model objects

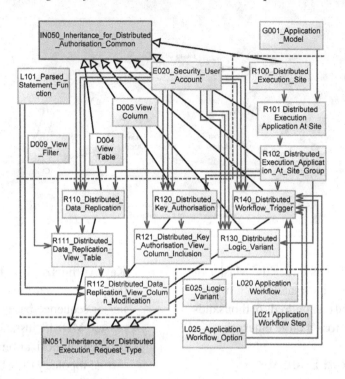

Distributed Execution Site: Lists each of the known sites implementing MDEIS application instances that this site is aware of and authorized to potentially share DER transactions (including the host site). Only these sites can ever be authorized for distributed execution with the host site.

Distributed Execution Application At Site: Is the combination of sites / applications that have been authorized to potentially share DER transactions. Not all applications from each site will be enabled for DER access.

Distributed Execution Application At Site Group: When defining a DER as a Master node to multiple Slave nodes, a set of the above sites / applications can be grouped to broadcast the DER to multiple sites.

Distributed Data Replication: Is a DER type defining the automated transfer of transaction or summary data between MDEIS instances.

Distributed Data Replication View Table: Part of defining the Data Replication DER. Lists the specific View Table(s) (analogous to updateable database views) that are required to be replicated for this Data Replication.

Distributed Data Replication View Column Modification: Part of defining the Data Replication DER. Lists the specific View Column(s) (analogous to data table columns) of the View Tables that are required to be either; transformed, not replicated or require a summary calculation for this Data Replication.

Distributed Key Authorization: Is a DER type defining a distributed schema for obtaining key, identifier or sequence based data from a pseudo master MDEIS instance simulating a distributed authorization hierarchy or other virtual topology of MDEIS instances.

Distributed Key Authorization View Column Inclusion: Part of defining the Key Authorization DER. Lists the specific View Column(s) that are required to be included and replicated for this Key Authorization. Each View Column may also have separately defined lists of data or generation rules that a particular site must use when creating a new View Column entry locally (see Figure 6 later).

Distributed Logic Variant: Is a DER type defining the transferring of a locally defined Logic Variant to other MDEIS instances for local execution.

Distributed Workflow Trigger: Is a DER type defining a pseudo master MDEIS instance to automatically escalate defined application workflow objects requiring transaction authorization beyond local authorization limits.

Inheritance for Distributed Authorization Common: Is a common inheritance for major distributed execution runtime classes used to define enabling and authorization options. This is shown at the top of the diagram.

Inheritance for Distributed Execution Type: Is a common inheritance for distributed execution request type classes used to define runtime options. This is shown at the lower left area of the diagram.

Figure 3 also references multiple other standard model classes that provide additional core functionality. These classes are depicted in the upper left and lower right of the diagram outside of the central area bounded by the spaced lines:

Parsed Statement Function: Are any specific defined Functions that are used here to either calculate the summary result for a Data Replication DER when individual records are not being replicated, or to transform how a View Column is replicated for a Data Replication DER.

View Filter: Is a defined data filter for a View Table to determine the selection of data records, used here to determine data selection for a Data Replication DER.

View Table: Is any combination of View Columns combined to become a new View Table which becomes the primary reference for data within the MDEIS application and provides similar functionality to common updateable database views although with additional capability. The composition of the View Columns and their

underlying relationships to Virtual Columns and Virtual Tables (the physical table objects) automatically determines the final data transactions, an abstraction that is managed by the runtime engine.

View Column: Is a discrete column reference as either an alias to another View Column or as a direct reference to a Virtual Column (the physical column object). A View Column becomes a key source of data within the MDEIS application. Key data integrity issues such as validation rules and input masks can also be defined and additional data abstraction can apply alternate compatible naming, formats and transformations to the View Column.

Security User Account: Is the list of users that are defined in the application runtime execution environment. These users may be granted individual access.

Application Model: Represents the ultimate common identifier for each application model (and component object) that is installed or available for the instance.

Logic Variant: Is an identifier that groups all of the individual logic model changes together into a specific set as an instance of Variant Logic as an alternative logic pathway.

Application Workflow: Provides a more targeted focus on defining the specific pathways and steps that are required to achieve a required outcome and specifying the appropriate logic that defines how those requirements will be achieved.

Application Workflow Option: Are the possible individual branches that a workflow may be required to proceed through in order to succeed. A Function will determine the conditional execution of the appropriate option.

Application Workflow Step: Are the individual steps that a workflow may be required to proceed through in order to succeed. Multiple parallel steps for a particular workflow option may be undergoing independent authorization concurrently.

These DERs enabled by the distributed components of the MDEIS application framework offer powerful in-built functionality that will be configured directly without the need for any additional coding or external utilities. Each of the DER types will now be reviewed in more detail to examine its operation.

Data Replication Distributed Execution Request

The Data Replication DER is used to define an automated transfer of data from the Slave node back to the Master node. The required data for each DR can be either a copy of each transaction record or a calculated summary of data records based on a defined collation function. The incoming replicated data will be treated by the incoming instance as authentic data - simply sourced via a special batch process rather than by individual user entry.

Recalling that DERs only operate between identical or similar MDEIS application instances then the data structures and application model are expected to be either identical or similar enough in both instances (refer to the section for Verifying the Compatibility of Distributed Execution Requests for how this is determined at runtime). This means that the data structures and other constraints already exist in both Master and Slave node instances requiring only that we need to define what data needs to be replicated and then rely on the MDEIS framework runtime engine to then handle all future data replications once the DER is authorized.

The DR operates primarily on a View Table basis, which is a collection of View Columns, although multiple View Tables can be nominated in a single DR. For each selected View Table the dimensions of the data replication will be determined from these options:

- Select whether data records are to be replicated or if only a single summary record is to be created and updated. If only a single summary record is selected then a Function must be defined for each included

View Column to determine the value to be updated.

- The DR performs an update based on only the data that has changed since the last replication event which can be based on choosing to replicate after each host record update or on a defined frequency or period basis. A View Filter can also be defined to limit the available data selection.

- Select if any modifications are required for any View Columns which can be; to not include a View Column in the replication, or to specify a transformation Function to apply to the View Column value.

- A common option for any DER type include whether to rollback either the entire DER or just the failed DER component (such as a single View Table out of multiple) on a replication error.

The DR can be used to automatically effect distributed operations such as posting sales transactions from point of sale sites to a regional head office or posting transaction summaries from local offices to head office without the need to modify or customize the underlying MDEIS application logic or code.

One important constraint on the effective operation of the Data Replication DER is that a Master node will now be replicating data from another instance or site. In most cases this new data will need to be identifiable with an appropriate Application Site Identifier to correctly separate and identify the new remote site's data from the current site's data – this Application Site Identifier must be defined as part of the application logic, either explicit to the data design (preferred) or defined as a View Column transformation (exercise caution). Internally, all local data (and model meta-data) will be identified with an Internal Site Identifier to differentiate data that is local and thus treated as authentic application data by the instance, compared to other supporting or related data that has been replicated from another MDEIS instance or site which therefore will be identified by setting the Internal Site Identifier to indicate its source as the external site. See Figure 4 for an illustration of the difference between an Application Site Identifier and the Internal Site Identifier.

As the incoming replicated View Table data will be treated as genuine transactional data by the Master node instance (i.e. its Internal Site Identifier will be set to the local Master node site identifier while the Application Site Identifier will be some transformation or alias of the external Slave node site identifier) then all data related to the replicated View Tables must also be replicated as needed to ensure data integrity is maintained on the Master node instance. However, this related data is not treated in exactly the same way – the related data is recorded in the associated Master node View Tables (which already exist due to the similar or identical application models involved in the DER) but with the Internal Site Identifier set to the external Slave node site identifier – all internal schema relationships will also inherit the Internal Site Identifier attribute as a hidden dependency to support replicated site data. These additional transactions to replicate the related data from the external Slave node site onto the local Master node site will be performed automatically and directly as all of the related data has already been authenticated on the

external Slave node site instance. Sounds complicated but the user doesn't need to worry about it as the distributed components of the runtime engine will manage all of the processing.

In Figure 4 the DR View Table is the SALE_TRANSACTION which has the basic sales history from a site that is desired to be replicated at a Master node instance. If the SALE_LOCATION entity did not exist then the DR would simply replicate the sales transaction into the SALE_TRANSACTION View Table on the Master node instance potentially mixing and conflicting the sales transactions with those from the local Master node instance and possibly from other Slave node instances. To avoid this problem the application logic needs some form of Application Site Identifier to be applied to the original View Table which should be applied at every application instance – in this case the SALE_LOCATION entity via a mandatory foreign key – which could either be defined as part of the original core application logic or applied later as an example of a Logic Variant (which could itself be an example of a DER).

Note that Figure 4 also depicts an inherited Distributed_Execution_Site to all application entities – this is the Internal Site Identifier that is automatically applied to all data and meta-data within the data and model structures to support the co-existence of replicated distributed data whilst

Figure 4. Illustration of internal site identifier and application site identifier

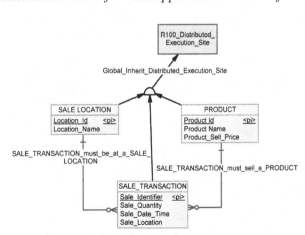

maintaining overall application data integrity. Hence the SALE_TRANSACTION data will be replicated on the Master node instance with the Internal Site Identifier set to the Master node instance and the Application Site Identifier copied as already set by the Slave node instance to the Slave node instance's Application Site Identifier. As the DR must also replicate data related to the target View Table (SALE_TRANSACTION) then the related data from SALE_LOCATION and PRODUCT are also replicated but these will have the Internal Site Identifier set to the originating Slave node instance to avoid conflict with either the Master node or other replicated Slave node data.

Now consider the following similar DR example: an organization operates the same sales and accounting MDEIS application installed at dozens of local sites and multiple regional offices (managing groups of local sites), all reporting to a single head office.

Between each local site and its regional office the Sale_Transaction View Table is defined with a Data Replication DER to replicate each sales transaction record to its regional office MDEIS instance. As the standard Sale_Transaction View Table already maintains an Application Site Identifier in this example then no specific transformation function is required and all associated related data objects are also replicated by the DER allowing the regional office to perform full local sales analyses on all of their local sites' data (now replicated in their instance) as they may require. The DR is set to be updated on a daily basis.

An additional Data Replication DER to replicate the sales transaction summaries from a Sales_Summary View Table from each regional office to the head office MDEIS instance is also defined. In this Sales_Summary View Table the record data (one for the regional office plus one each of its local sites) is calculated and updated by the standard application logic as based on transactions as they occur. The DR is also set to be updated on a daily basis following the previous DR to ensure the latest results are provided. Of course a higher update frequency could be defined for a more regular update.

Once the DERs are defined and submitted on their respective Master nodes any authorizations must be obtained on both the Master and Slave nodes before the DERs will execute on the Slave nodes.

In this example depicted in Figure 5 the entire regional organization's sales data will always be available in full detail for analysis at regional offices without the need for any specialized data processing and migration, while the entire organization's sales summaries are always available at head office for overall corporate analysis. The full sales transactions could also be replicated at head office if they were required in detail.

Figure 5. Example multiple Data Replication DER in a hierarchical de-centralized organization

M - Master node   S - Slave node

Figure 6. Overview of generic View Column generation options

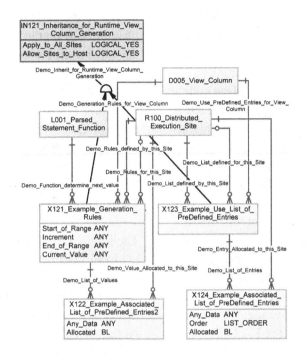

Key Authorization Distributed Execution Request

The Key Authorization DER defines a distributed schema for obtaining key, identifier or sequence based data from a pseudo master MDEIS instance simulating a distributed authorization hierarchy or other virtual topology. The KA provides the ability for a Master node to become the distributed source of data for some key data columns to selected Slave nodes. This source of this key data can be defined on the Master node on the basis of pre-prepared lists of data or generation rules to be used for each Slave node. When the Slave node's MDEIS application requires a new value for the nominated key data, instead of generating or entering the data locally on the Slave node a distributed request back to the Master node will be performed to retrieve or generate the required data.

The KA operates on a View Column basis and would typically be defined only for important identifiers, unique values, or high security data that the organization requires to be served from a centralized (or at least remote) MDEIS source instance to other MDEIS instances. The KA data from the Master node is provided to any requesting Slave node which treats the data as though it were entered or defined directly at or by the requesting Slave node.

The Master node will either serve existing predefined data or will utilize standard MDEIS auto-generation Functions to provide the rules governing the creation of any new data for the defined View Columns. This utilizes a standard feature of the MDEIS application framework whereby any View Column can be allocated these generation rules (see Figure 6):

- An auto-generation Function to determine the ongoing values to be applied.
- A defined range to select the next value from.
- A pre-defined list of values that will be sequentially applied.

These View Column generation options can be defined on a global basis to apply to all sites, including the host site, or can be created individually for specific sites.

When the KA is authorized the option exists for the rules to be distributed to the Slave node's MDEIS instance for both performance efficiency and optional network failure continuance. This option is only available if the rules are site specific – global (or shared) rules always require runtime distributed authorization from the Master node.

The KA can be used to establish hierarchical or centralized definition, management, distribution and allocation of pre-defined identifier data such as; employee identifiers, serial numbers, sequence or transaction identifiers, or other high security data without the need to modify or customize the underlying MDEIS application logic or code in any way, other than defining the KA DER.

Consider the following KA example: an organization operates the same accounting and payroll management MDEIS application installed at every manufacturing site including the largest site which also hosts the head office. Each site has the local authority to hire staff and manage their own payroll but the head office wants to manage and allocate employee numbers throughout the enterprise.

The head office MDEIS instance, acting as the Master node, defines a Key Authorization DER on the Employee Number View Column of the Employee View Table to apply to all other sites as Slave nodes. Using standard functionality (for any View Column) the Employee Number is defined to be created via a Function that concatenates two digits of the current year to an annual 4 digit sequential number to determine the Employee Number.

When the DER is authorized on each Slave node, whenever a new Employee record is created instead of allowing a manual entry for the Employee Number the Slave node instance will invoke the distributed call to the Master node to obtain the next Employee number.

For completeness, it would be straightforward for the head office to then also create a Data Replication DER on the Employee View Table (and any other useful related information) to each site to request the replication of the full Employee record at the head office - if the head office had a requirement to perform any other processing based on Employee data e.g. provide government employment statistics.

Logic Variant Distributed Execution Request

The Logic Variant DER defines the transferring of a locally defined Logic Variant to other MDEIS instances for local execution. Recall that a Logic Variant is alternate application logic that supplements or replaces the original application logic. As the MDEIS application instances are identical or similar then the defined Logic Variant from the Master node will be expected to execute on other Slave node MDEIS application instances to provide the identical functionality. The MDEIS application model provides the capability to define Logic Variants (as customizations) throughout the application model, the LV DER provides the ability to share and deploy these customizations with other instances executing the same MDEIS application.

The LV operates on a defined Logic Variant that would be expected to have already been utilized and verified in the current Master node instance. When authorized to be deployed to Slave nodes the Logic Variant definition will be copied to each Slave node for either global usage or on a Roles basis. Once installed locally at the Slave nodes the Logic Variant can then also be assigned to other local users as required although it cannot be modified locally on the Slave node. Any subsequent modifications to the original Logic Variant at the Master node would be broadcast to each Slave node defined in the DER.

The LV can be used to share and distribute any Logic Variant customization between MDEIS application instances where the new application logic segment serves a useful or mandatory purpose (in the case where Logic Variants that are applied globally to all users). A Logic Variant can provide any defined functionality.

Consider the following LV example: an international services organization operates the same project management, timesheet and billing MDEIS application installed at all regional offices where there can be multiple regional offices in some countries. Larger local sites access the MDEIS applications from their regional office while smaller remote local sites submit documents and information for processing to regional offices by fax and email.

A data entry clerk at a regional office has to transcribe the contents of hundreds of timesheets that are sent from their smaller local offices. The latest format of the timesheets does not match the order of entry on the MDEIS application screens plus there is some new additional information that is now required to be supplied from remote offices. A new Logic Variant is created for or by the user that re-arranges the user interface objects on the entry screens to better suit the manual update procedure including resizing the objects to their most common entry size. New View Columns are created to record the latest information requirements and updated validation functions are defined to help minimize the occurrence of data entry miss-keying on both existing and new data entry objects. This Logic Variant has been assigned to all other clerks at that regional office who are entering the remote timesheets.

The internal user group for this MDEIS application has been advised of that Logic Variant improvement and included an article detailing the changes in their regular newsletter. Sites in other regions that are now using the same updated timesheet format ask the author of the Logic Variant to provide them with the change. Acting as a Master node the Logic Variant author site defines a Logic Variant DER on that Logic Variant for the requesting sites, as Slave nodes, which would then deploy the Logic Variant automatically for use to those sites.

Workflow Trigger Distributed Execution Request

The Workflow Trigger DER defines a pseudo master MDEIS instance to automatically escalate application workflow objects requiring transaction authorization beyond local authorization limits. The appropriate element of the workflow will then be transferred to and executed on the Master node returning the result back to the Slave node for further processing and execution of any remaining workflow elements.

The WT operates on an Application Workflow basis (analogous to any commonly defined workflow capability that may be available to an application) although it is embedded as a core capability in the MDEIS framework. Application Workflows can be triggered off any condition based on defined Functions and associated with any data objects in the MDEIS instance. The distributed components will allow for the execution of the Application Workflow element in the Master node to partially or fully replace the normal execution of the same Application Workflow element on the Slave node. There are three options to define the escalated alternate execution on the Master node for the defined Application Workflow elements:

Application Workflow: Completely replaces execution of the Application Workflow onto the Master node. Only the triggering objects are supplied to the Master node as the subject of the workflow. No workflow execution occurs on the Slave node. Only the final result is returned from the Master node and used by the Slave node as the Application Workflow result.

Application Workflow Option: An Application Workflow is composed of one or multiple Application Workflow Options – only one option will ever be executed for a trigger instance based on a conditional test. This WT option transfers the execution of one Application Workflow Option to the Master node if it is required based on the conditional test, with the result returned from the Master node and used by the Slave node as the Application Workflow Option result. The Slave node then finalizes the workflow completion using that result.

Application Workflow Step: An Application Workflow Option is composed of one or multiple Application Workflow Steps – the set of Steps representing any serial or multi-path parallel sequence. This WT option transfers the execution of one Application Workflow Step to the Master node when it would otherwise be executed on the Slave node, with the result returned from the Master node and used by the Slave node as the Application Workflow Step result. Execution then continues on the Slave node for any remaining Application Workflow Steps.

If multiple Application Workflows, Options or Steps were required to be transferred to a Master node for execution then additional WT DERs would need to be defined separately, one for each object.

An important consideration though is how the Master node knows what object from the Slave node is the triggering subject of the original workflow, plus how the Master node provides the result and decision tracking information back to the Slave node. Note that the Application Workflow already exists on both the Master and Slave nodes as they are executing the same MDEIS application, as do all of the application data structures. Recall also the mechanism that the Data Replication DER utilizes to replicate all related data between the Slave and Master nodes to provide for full supporting transaction data and maintain data integrity. The identical replication process utilizing the Internal Site Identifier will be used to replicate related data for the WT DER.

Firstly the triggering object on the Slave node and related data will be replicated to the Master node, as well as any other data objects that are referenced by the relevant workflow element object. This data is required as background reference for the nature of the workflow authorization to be made available to the nominated authorizers on the Master node. The workflow element will

then be executed on the Master node and the result recorded.

Finally the result of the workflow element plus all associated workflow tracking and audit data (including the authorized users and their decisions) from the Master node must be replicated back to the Slave node. The result from the Master node is then integrated into any remaining workflow elements on the Slave node and the workflow execution continues to its ultimate conclusion on the Slave node. Any workflow tracking and audit data from the Master node will become available for Slave node access as though the workflow element were executed on the Slave node. Figure 7 illustrates the execution pathways and replications that occur on the Slave and Master nodes during the execution of a Workflow Trigger DER that replaces an Application Workflow Step.

To clarify, tracking and results data that are created due to the normal execution of the workflow element on both the Slave and Master nodes will be processed (as standard) as genuine data on the local MDEIS instance i.e. the Internal Site Identifier is set to the executing instance. Replicated data from another MDEIS instance that supports the execution of the workflow has the Internal Site Identifier set to the originating instance to maintain local data integrity.

The WT can be used to establish a selective hierarchical authorization of Application Workflows such as; high value financial transactions that require a higher regional or head office authorization, or key policy document amendments or any form of important information to be routed through higher corporate review workflows, without the need to modify or customize the underlying MDEIS application logic or code.

Consider the following WT example: an organization operates the same financial management and procurement MDEIS application installed at every site, including regional offices and head office. Initially all offices were established with an Application Workflow that locally managed

Figure 7. Workflow Trigger DER executing an application workflow step

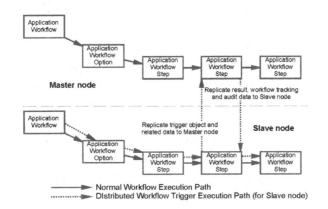

authorizations for all purchases; <$10K, up to $100K, and >$100K with a manual authorization process required with the next level of management for purchases over $500K – the latter being a policy decision to be followed manually as it is currently without any application workflow support.

Poor expenditure management throughout the organization have caused the authorization limits to be tightened and a better understanding of the distributed components of their MDEIS application permit the following changes to be readily applied throughout the enterprise:

- The current Application Workflow is redesigned at Head Office, as an example of a Logic Variant, to reflect the new authorization levels that will now be applied; <$10K, up to $50K, up to $250K, >$250K.
- A Logic Variant DER is created with Head Office as the Master node and all other sites as Slave nodes to now receive this Logic Variant as a replacement for the previous workflow.
- A Workflow Trigger DER is created with Head Office as the Master node and all other sites as the Slave nodes – defining the ">$250K" Application Workflow Option

i.e. this Option when required will invoke distributed execution on the Head Office MDEIS application for their authorization.

- Another Workflow Trigger DER is created at each Regional Office (with each Regional Office as the Master node) to all other local sites of the Regional Office as the Slave nodes – defining the "up to $250K" Application Workflow Option i.e. this Option when required will invoke distributed execution on each Regional Office's MDEIS application for their authorization.

After completing these steps a full hierarchical enterprise wide financial authorization workflow will have been implemented whereby local sites have limited expenditure authorization, automatically escalating to Regional Offices and Head Office as required.

This example is fairly simplistic. If a further level of review were required e.g. if expenditure ">$250K" were preferably first reviewed at the Regional Office for either veto or preliminary approval rather than escalating directly to Head Office, then defining finer control through modification and creation of DERs specifying the Application Workflow Step sequences would readily provide an option with greater flexibility.

Verifying the Compatibility of Distributed Execution Requests

We have referred to two pre-requisites for creating DERs; that the same core Application Model is executing at both the Master and Slave node MDEIS instances, and that the Application Model needs to be identical or similar (enough). Clearly, an identical Application Model would have no differences at all in any model elements – it would be analogous to an identical versioned set of executable applications and configurations in the traditional sense – and DERs would readily deploy and execute between these identical instances. But how similar is similar enough? First we need to understand a little about how the version control operates.

Version control in the MDEIS application model will occur at two levels. Internally, every model object and attribute change will be subject to audit tracking and each change is precisely known and identifiable – this is objective version control. At the human level manual version control is based on a decision to be made to identify and name the state of a subset of the application model at one point in time compared with the changed state of the application model at an earlier point in time – this is subjective version control.

While self-imposed policies may enforce rigidity across an enterprise preventing unsynchronized application model changes in application model instances, analogous to a strict subjective version control, this will not be the necessity for MDEIS applications that is often the recommended practice for managing traditional distributed application environments.

For the MDEIS application every model object will be individually tracked with every sequential change that has occurred throughout the model's existence. When subjective version control is applied only the model objects that have been altered since the previous version are candidates for inclusion in the new version - the final update set will be based on this selected subset of the model plus any other updated related model objects which must also be included. Thus subjective version control can be a modular Web of versions when considering the occurrence of partial application or module updates. Full application updates will include all updated model objects.

High level pseudo code for the version checking of DERs when they are submitted by a Master node to a Slave node occurs as follows:

- FOR each Master node DER model object M_i:
  - IF (M_i NOT EXIST in Slave) THEN slave_early++; IF (upgrade_slave < minimum_subjective_version_of_ current Master M_i) THEN upgrade_ slave = minimum_subjective_version_of_current Master M_i
  - ELSEIF (internal_version_of Master M_i == internal_version_of Slave M_i) THEN ok++
  - OTHERWISE
    - IF (internal_version_of Master M_i < internal_version_of Slave M_i) THEN slave_later++; IF (upgrade_master < minimum_ subjective_version_of_current Slave M_i) THEN upgrade_master = minimum_subjective_version_of_current Slave M_i
    - ELSE slave_early++; IF (upgrade_slave < minimum_subjective_version_of_current Master M_i) THEN upgrade_ slave = minimum_subjective_version_of_current Master M_i
    - IF (attribute_type Master M_i <> attribute_type Slave M_i) THEN error++
- IF (error > 0) THEN "Cannot Implement DER: fatal model mismatch"
- IF (slave_later > 0) THEN "Recommend Upgrade Master to version: " & upgrade_master

- IF (slave_early > 0) THEN "Recommend Upgrade Slave to version: " & upgrade_slave

Any clear syntactic mismatches between any of the required model objects would abort the DER due to incompatibility. However, it is not so clear to be able to always guarantee semantic compatibility - it is possible, due to valid module or partial application model updates, that there can be some model objects in the Slave node that are of a later subjective version than the Master node and some that are of an earlier subjective version, and vice versa simultaneously. The verification process would also advise if either or both the Slave and Master nodes are recommended to be upgraded for a greater likelihood of semantic compatibility.

While updating MDEIS applications is another subject again (Davis, 2011d), the updates will consist of a stream of meta-data commands that can always be applied automatically by the runtime update engine, greatly simplifying the upgrade process. Logic Variants may represent a potential source of incompatibility from the update however the potential incompatibilities could be precisely identified, and where there are no conflicts the Logic Variants can be immediately classified as fully verified and therefore compatible.

In this brief view of model object version control we can clearly verify compatible model objects, plus identify any incompatibilities and precisely log them for specific reference. Absolutely identifying semantic compatibility when there are minor object changes is itself a major ongoing research area.

Authorization Framework for Distributed Execution Requests

Traditional application integration options may require any combinations of internal application configurations, third party data or workflow middleware, custom developed scripts or software, or operating system utilities to facilitate the data or application integration requirements. This disparate set of technologies typically results in a cooperative Web of components that are authorized by multiple disjoint groups, including application administrators and system administrators, and executed in multiple environments.

Relying only on the common network infrastructure the MDEIS application framework model will support all definition and execution of its distributed components within one secure environment. Figure 8 provides an overview of the authorization classes for the distributed components of the MDEIS application model which allows for assigning authorizations to generate or approve individual DERs as well as in establishing and approving the inter-instance relationships.

The distributed components authorization in Figure 8 use the following classes to model site and DER authorizations. Note that these authorization classes are depicted in the left and lower area of the diagram separated by the spaced line:

Distributed Execution Request Role: Are the individual groups or roles that can be assigned to designate specific authorizations. The role is the basis of assigning access to users for the purpose of generating or authorizing Master or Slave distributed transactions, as well as the ability to manage other Distributed Execution Request Roles. Note that these roles are separate from but related to Security Roles, which grant access to the application model objects.

Manage Distributed Execution Request for Site: Provides the ability to manage authorization capability (and for other users in the role) for each external Site instance that is permitted to execute DERs with the host site.

Manage Distributed Execution Request for Application At Site: Provides the ability to manage authorization capability (and for other users in the role) for each combination of external Site instance and an implemented MDEIS application at that Site, that are permitted to execute DERs with the same MDEIS application at the host site.

Figure 8. Overview class diagram of distributed components authorization

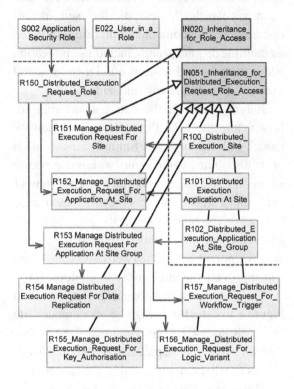

Manage Distributed Execution Request for Application At Site Group: Provides the ability to manage authorization capability (and for other users in the role) for groups of combinations of external Site instance and an implemented MDEIS application at that Site, that are permitted to execute DERs with the same MDEIS application at the host site. This allows a single DER to be defined for multiple Slave nodes (sites) and represents the common DER identifier used for each DER object. The remaining classes in this list all provide further control over the DER types that are defined for the group of external Site / Application combinations.

Manage Distributed Execution Request for Data Replication: Provides the ability to manage authorization capability (and for other users in the role) for all Data Replication DER access and authorization for a group of external Site / Application combinations with the host site.

Manage Distributed Execution Request for Key Authorization: Provides the ability to manage authorization capability (and for other users in the role) for all Key Authorization DER access and authorization for a group of external Site / Application combinations with the host site.

Manage Distributed Execution Request for Logic Variant: Provides the ability to manage authorization capability (and for other users in the role) for all Logic Variant DER access and authorization for a group of external Site / Application combinations with the host site.

Manage Distributed Execution Request for Workflow Trigger: Provides the ability to manage authorization capability (and for other users in the role) for all Workflow Trigger DER access and authorization for a group of external Site / Application combinations with the host site.

Inheritance for Role Access: Is a common inheritance for all of the role based authorizations in the MDEIS model to grant role and user management access. This is shown at the top right of the diagram.

Inheritance for Distributed Execution Request Role Access: Is a common inheritance for distributed execution roles used to grant Master and Slave authorizations. This is shown at the top of the diagram.

Figure 8 also references multiple other standard and previously described distributed model classes. These classes are depicted in the upper and right area of the diagram outside of the central area bounded by the spaced lines:

Application Security Role: Is the list of the available application roles. A Distributed Execution Request Role may be assigned a default Security Role to provide the appropriate access.

User in a Role: Is the list where Users are assigned to any of the Role types defined in the MDEIS model.

Distributed Execution Site: Lists each of the known sites implementing MDEIS application instances that this site is aware of and authorized to potentially share DER transactions (including the host site). Only these sites can ever be authorized for distributed execution with the host site.

Distributed Execution Application at Site: Is the combination of sites / applications that have been authorized to potentially share DER transactions. Not all applications from each site will be enabled for DER access.

Distributed Execution Application at Site Group: When defining a DER as a Master node to multiple Slave nodes, a set of the above sites / applications can be grouped to broadcast the DER to multiple sites.

The DER authorization structure allows for enabling any authorization topology between distributed MDEIS instances. It also allows multi-level authorization capability from allowing complete access, such as may be dictated by a higher authority location, down to manual authorization of each DER as it is raised. There is a neat simplicity of authorizing all distributed activity within a single process when compared to the potential multi-environment options of traditional application integrations.

Implementation and Execution of Distributed Execution Requests

The features as described for these Distributed Components have been defined and modeled as part of our original MDEIS application framework (Davis, 2004) which has undergone major enhancements to add the temporal and distributed capability to the core model to become what we now refer to as the distributed temporal MDEIS application framework.

Having the distributed components embedded into a modeling and execution framework provides the features as a virtually instantaneous capability to define and execute the Distributed Execution Requests. Distributed application modelers and administrators would have to follow these steps to establish and maintain the overall distributed execution environment:

Deploy Multiple De-Centralized MDEIS Applications: Use of the DERs requires that multiple (minimum of two) separate MDEIS application instances are established with at least one pair of identical or similar application models executed amongst the sites to act as candidate Master and Slave nodes. Standard network communications supporting Web services are required to transmit the distributed communications.

Establish Instance Authorizations: Initial authorizations must be established to permit each paired site and application model to interact, based on accepting DERs. Authorization options allow DERs to be accepted carte blanche or on a selective DER basis for each request.

Assign DER Role Authorizations: Local users at each participating MDEIS instance need to be assigned appropriate authorization to be able to define or create new DERs, or to accept DERs from another MDEIS instance for local execution. These authorizations are additional to any other Security Access or Logic Definer roles that users may have.

Define DERs: Authorized users in any participating MDEIS instance define the required new DERs (and the designated Slave nodes) using the runtime editor functionality for each defined DER type. The DER definers may need to consider the need for any other preparatory local logic redefinition (defined as Logic Variants) that may be required in advance of DER definition to support the ongoing DER execution.

Authorize DERs: A MDEIS instance may have chosen to pre-authorize some incoming DERs from some sites to be accepted and executed automatically. Otherwise based on the defined DER role authorizations any new DERs will require manual authorization to be provided by an authorized local user on an ad-hoc basis as each DER is received at each Slave MDEIS instance.

DER Execution: Once authorized, each authorized DER will automatically execute on the basis of its defined criteria. Automatic batch level rollback of failed DER transactions can be performed along with automatic re-execution. Continuous or multiple failures will require manual intervention as notified.

As described the simplistic nature of the DERs, from the point of view of application users, is that DERs can be readily defined by authorized users for acceptance and execution on the defined Slave nodes. All subsequent distributed execution and transfer of the DERs is performed automatically by the runtime framework.

FUTURE RESEARCH DIRECTIONS

The majority of distributed execution application research revolves around distributed workflow execution (and the development of distribution aware components), and the distributed processing of subsets of large data sets. Distributed workflow execution has some overlap with the works presented in this chapter although tend towards how to componentize applications into sufficiently small or logically useful segments to participate in a workflow along with a management layer for communications and integration between differing application and systems – these aspects will be largely catered for in MDEIS applications by the direct availability of the application model and the support of the distributed components. Large scale data processing is not a core feature that has been pursued for candidate MDEIS applications although there is no fundamental reason why this could not be a future consideration for optimization.

The DER options of the distributed components of the MDEIS application framework as reviewed here are a unique aspect of this particular variant example of Model Driven Engineering. They are also a recent enhancement of the MDEIS application model hot from the laboratory. Application specific workflows are a key design feature of the model and are currently limited to execution within the application model instance although the openness of the framework will provide the

opportunity for third party workflow middleware to operate any aspect of the MDEIS application via Web service commands.

This solution for the distributed components has also paved the way for what we believe will be reasonably minor changes to the model structure and runtime engine design to then extend the standard workflow functionality to define fully inter-application and inter-instance workflows. Much of the design difficulty has now been overcome in how the remote application's and site's data needs to be replicated and presented securely to maintain local data integrity and provide full local audit tracking of all transactions.

In order to take full advantage of these distributed components plus the other major benefits of the MDEIS application framework, such as Variant Logic and its accessibility to any end user, requires that the technologies are operated on a sufficiently widespread basis to ensure ongoing momentum and development of the framework in terms of providing; multiple and full model development environments, multiple platform layer options to leverage maximum accessibility, performance optimization of model execution, integration options for interaction with legacy applications and alternate models, and ongoing support and collaborative enhancement.

A final aspect of improvement has considerable potential in both the implementation of DERs and the automatic update of MDEIS applications with respect to optimizing the determination of the compatibility of Variant Logic with the underlying core application logic. Currently the fine grain version control as broadly described seeks to identify an appropriate pseudo-syntactic compatibility in determining and identifying potential Variant Logic and DER compatibility at an atomic model level. As the entire application model will be available, further effort on providing semantic compatibility through functional analysis of the model and application intention would provide a higher level of expected compatibility and correspondingly lower rate of potential conflict identification allowing for greater disparity between separate application model instances. The relative simplicity of the automated update process for MDEIS applications may really reduce this issue over time as there becomes less reason not to upgrade to the latest model, although application instances with very high usage of Variant Logic would receive direct benefit of semantic analysis improvements.

CONCLUSION

The Distributed Execution Request capability of the MDEIS application model provides some unique benefits to organizations that choose to operate similar applications throughout the enterprise in a distributed execution topology. By using these DERs as directly available from an execution framework the enterprise can directly achieve the following capability without additional environment expense or complexity:

- **Data Replication:** Automatically transfer and replicate any data between application instances.
- **Key Authorization:** Share and distribute key identifier or sequence based data or high security tokens centrally or via an authorization hierarchy.
- **Logic Variant:** Share the workflow and process optimization benefits of defined Logic Variants with users from other sites.
- **Workflow Trigger:** Incorporate other sites into aspects of standard application workflow execution to achieve distributed or centralized transaction authorizations.

Each of these DERs will be implemented directly between sites' MDEIS application instances through simple definition of the runtime DER model logic, requiring no additional combinations of third party utilities, middleware or custom programming, and are managed within a single

definition and authorization context, the MDEIS application instances.

Collectively the usage of these distributed components provide for:

- **Simple Environment:** All definitions for the DERs are maintained within the MDEIS application model – there is no need for combining or integrating multiple or additional technologies.
- **Ready Deployment:** The DERs operate as part of the intrinsic MDEIS application instance - no additional modules or software needs to be deployed to each site.
- **Any Enterprise:** Any authorization or sharing topology can be modeled based on sets of node pairs to combine to simulate any traditional bus, star or tree combination.
- **Open Definition:** DERs can be defined by the same target set of users as for Variant Logic, including business analysts, power and end users.
- **Functionality:** The DERs provide the functional coverage to share; data, application logic and workflow execution.
- **Minimal Expense:** No additional costs need to be incurred for hardware or software. Suitable network communications links are required between sites, and minimal additional knowledge is required to define DERs, similar in nature to that required for simple Variant Logic examples.

The defined DERs provide a very useful functional coverage in three main areas sharing key and transactional data, application logic segments, and application workflow execution between distributed instances of a similar MDEIS application. By providing these distributed components directly as part of the function of the installed MDEIS application instances, the enterprises can receive these benefits immediately and with minimal additional definition and setup involved, greatly reducing the comparative data and workflow integrations that would otherwise be required using traditional applications.

REFERENCES

Bezemer, C., & Zaidman, A. (2010). Multi-tenant SaaS applications: Maintenance dream or nightmare? In *Proceedings of the Joint ERCIM Workshop on Software Evolution (EVOL) and International Workshop on Principles of Software Evolution (IWPSE) (IWPSE-EVOL '10)*, (pp. 88-92). New York: ACM.

Brown, A. (2004). Oops! Coping with human error in IT. *ACM Queue – System Failures, 2*(8), 34-41.

Davis, J., & Chang, E. (2011a). Lifecycle and generational application of automated updates to MDA based enterprise information systems. In *Proceedings of the Second Symposium on Information and Communication Technology (SoICT '11)*, (pp. 207-216). ACM.

Davis, J., & Chang, E. (2011b). Variant logic meta-data management for model driven applications applications - Allows unlimited end user configuration and customization of all meta-data EIS application features. In *Proceedings of the 13th International Conference on Enterprise Information Systems (ICEIS 2011)*, (pp. 395-400). SciTePress.

Davis, J., & Chang, E. (2011c). Temporal meta-data management for model driven applications - Provides full temporal execution capabilities throughout the meta-data EIS application lifecycle. In *Proceedings of the 13th International Conference on Enterprise Information Systems (ICEIS 2011)*, (pp. 376-379). SciTePress.

Davis, J., & Chang, E. (2011d). Automatic application update with user customization integration and collision detection for model driven applications. In *Proceedings of the World Congress on Engineering and Computer Science 2011*, (pp. 1081-1086). Newswood Limited.

Davis, J., Tierney, A., & Chang, E. (2004). Meta data framework for enterprise information systems specification - Aiming to reduce or remove the development phase for EIS systems. In *Proceedings of the 6th International Conference on Enterprise Information Systems (ICEIS 2004)*, (pp. 451-456). SciTePress.

De Alwis, B., & Sillito, J. (2009). Why are software projects moving from centralized to decentralized version control systems? In *Proceedings of the 2009 ICSE Workshop on Cooperative and Human Aspects on Software Engineering*, (pp. 36-39). IEEE Computer Society.

Eugster, P. T., Damm, C. H., & Guerraoui, R. (2004). Towards safe distributed application development. In *Proceedings of the 26th International Conference on Software Engineering (ICSE '04)*, (pp. 347-356). IEEE Computer Society.

France, R., & Rumpe, B. (2007). Model-driven development of complex software: A research roadmap. In *Proceedings of Future of Software Engineering (FOSE 2007)*, (pp. 37-54). IEEE Computer Society.

Gaynor, M., & Bradner, S. (2004). A real options framework to value network, protocol, and service architecture. *SIGCOMM Computer Communications Review, 34*(5), 31–38. doi:10.1145/1039111.1039121.

Goethals, F., Vandenbulcke, J., & Lemahieu, W. (2004). Developing the extended enterprise with the FADEE. In *Proceedings of the 2004 ACM Symposium on Applied Computing (SAC '04)*, (pp. 1372-1379). ACM.

Hagen, C., & Brouwers, G. (1994). Reducing software life-cycle costs by developing configurable software. In *Proceedings of the Aerospace and Electronics Conference,* (vol. 2, pp. 1182-1187). IEEE Press.

Hui, B., Liaskos, S., & Mylopoulos, J. (2003). Requirements analysis for customisable software: A goals-skills-preferences framework. In *Proceedings of the 11th IEEE International Requirements Engineering Conference,* (pp. 117-126). IEEE Press.

Jansen, S., Brinkkemper, S., & Helms, R. (2008). Benchmarking the customer configuration updating practices of product software vendors. In *Proceedings of the 7th International Conference on Composition Based Software Systems* (pp. 82-91). IEEE Computer Society.

Kaur, P., & Singh, H. (2009). Version management and composition of software components in different phases of the software development life cycle. *ACM Sigsoft Software Engineering Notes*, *34*(4), 1–9. doi:10.1145/1543405.1543416.

Koegel, M., Herrmannsdoerfer, M., von Wesendonk, O., & Helming, J. (2010). Operation-based conflict detection. In *Proceedings of the 1st International Workshop on Model Comparison in Practice (IWMCP '10),* (pp. 21-30). ACM.

Ma, X., Baresi, L., Ghezzi, C., Panzica, V., Manna, L., & Lu, J. (2011). Version-consistent dynamic reconfiguration of component-based distributed systems. In *Proceedings of the 19th ACM SIGSOFT Symposium and the 13th European Conference on Foundations of Software Engineering (ESEC/FSE '11)* (pp. 245-255). ACM.

Nitu. (2009). Configurability in SaaS (software as a service) applications. In *Proceedings of the 2nd India Software Engineering Conference (ISEC '09)* (pp. 19-26). ACM.

OMG. (2012). OMG model driven architecture. *The Architecture of Choice for a Changing World.* Retrieved May 13, 2012, from http://www.omg.org/mda/

Papazoglou, M. P., & Heuvel, W. J. (2007). Service oriented architectures: approaches, technologies and research issues. *The VLDB Journal*, *16*(3), 389–415. doi:10.1007/s00778-007-0044-3.

Rajkovic, P., Jankovic, D., Stankovic, T., & Tosic, V. (2010). Software tools for rapid development and customization of medical information systems. In *Proceedings of 12th IEEE International Conference on e-Health Networking Applications and Services* (pp. 119-126). IEEE Computer Society.

Ren, Y., Xing, T., Quan, Q., & Zhao, Y. (2010). Software configuration management of version control study based on baseline. In *Proceedings of 3rd International Conference on Information Management, Innovation Management and Industrial Engineering,* (Vol. 4, pp. 118-121). IEEE Press.

Schmidt, D. (2006). Introduction: Model-driven engineering. *IEEE Computer Science*, *39*(2), 25–31. doi:10.1109/MC.2006.58.

Schuff, D., & St. Louis, R. (2001). Centralization vs. decentralization of application software. *Communications of the ACM*, *44*(6), 88–94. doi:10.1145/376134.376177.

Sengupta, B., & Roychoudhury, A. (2011). Engineering multi-tenant software-as-a-service systems. In *Proceedings of the 3rd International Workshop on Principles of Engineering Service-Oriented Systems (PESOS '11),* (pp. 15-21). ACM.

Sovran, Y., Power, R., Aguilera, M. K., & Li, J. (2011). Transactional storage for geo-replicated systems. In *Proceedings of the Twenty-Third ACM Symposium on Operating Systems Principles (SOSP '11),* (pp. 385-400). ACM.

Steinholtz, B., & Walden, K. (1987). Automatic identification of software system differences. *IEEE Transactions on Software Engineering, 13*(4), 493–497. doi:10.1109/TSE.1987.233186.

Weiping, L. (2009). An analysis of new features for workflow system in the SaaS software. In *Proceedings of the 2nd International Conference on Interaction Sciences: Information Technology, Culture and Human (ICIS '09)*, (pp. 110-114). ACM.

Wu, B., Deng, S., Li, Y., Wu, J., & Yin, J. (2011). Reference models for SaaS oriented business workflow management systems. In *Proceedings of the 2011 IEEE International Conference on Services Computing (SCC '11)*, (pp. 242-249). IEEE Computer Society.

Zhu, X., & Wang, S. (2009). Software customization based on model-driven architecture over SaaS platforms. In *Proceedings of International Conference on Management and Service Science* (pp. 1-4). CORD.

ADDITIONAL READING

Albrecht, J., Tuttle, C., Braud, R., Dao, D., Topilski, N., Snoeren, A. C., & Vahdat, A. (2011). Distributed application configuration, management, and visualization with plush. *ACM Transactions on Internet Technology, 11*(2). doi:10.1145/2049656.2049658.

Asadi, M., Mohabbati, B., Kaviani, N., Gašević, D., Bošković, M., & Hatala, M. (2009). Model-driven development of families of service-oriented architectures. In *Proceedings of the First International Workshop on Feature-Oriented Software Development (FOSD '09)*, (pp. 95-102). ACM.

Basin, D., Clavel, M., & Egea, M. (2011). A decade of model-driven security. In *Proceedings of the 16th ACM Symposium on Access Control Models and Technologies (SACMAT '11)*, (pp. 1-10). ACM.

Bonakdarpour, B., Bozga, M., Jaber, M., Quilbeuf, J., & Sifakis, J. (2010). From high-level component-based models to distributed implementations. In *Proceedings of the Tenth ACM International Conference on Embedded Software (EMSOFT '10)*, (pp. 209-218). ACM.

Cicchetti, A., Ciccozzi, F., Leveque, T., & Pierantonio, A. (2011). On the concurrent versioning of metamodels and models: Challenges and possible solutions. In *Proceedings of the 2nd International Workshop on Model Comparison in Practice (IWMCP '11)*, (pp. 16-25). ACM.

Corrêa, C. K. F. (2011). Towards automatic consistency preservation for model-driven software product lines. In *Proceedings of the 15th International Software Product Line Conference*. ACM.

Czarnecki, K., Grünbacher, P., Rabiser, R., Schmid, K., & Wąsowski, A. (2012). Cool features and tough decisions: A comparison of variability modeling approaches. In *Proceedings of the Sixth International Workshop on Variability Modeling of Software-Intensive Systems (VaMoS '12)*, (pp. 173-182). ACM.

Das, S., Agrawal, D., & El Abbadi, A. (2010). G-store: A scalable data store for transactional multi key access in the cloud. In *Proceedings of the 1st ACM Symposium on Cloud Computing (SoCC '10)*, (pp. 163-174). ACM.

Dearle, A. (2007). Software deployment, past, present and future. In *Proceedings of the 2007 Future of Software Engineering (FOSE '07)*, (pp. 269-284). IEEE Computer Society.

Fang, Y., & Neufeld, D. J. (2006). The pendulum swings back: Individual acceptance of re-centralized application platforms. *SIGMIS Database, 37*(2-3), 33–41. doi:10.1145/1161345.1161352.

Lammari, N., Bucumi, J., Akoka, J., & Comyn-Wattiau, I. (2011). A conceptual meta-model for secured information systems. In *Proceedings of the 7th International Workshop on Software Engineering for Secure Systems (SESS '11)*, (pp. 22-28). ACM.

Li, G., Muthusamy, V., & Jacobsen, H. (2010). A distributed service-oriented architecture for business process execution. *ACM Transactions on Web, 4*(1).

Mailloux, M. (2010). Application frameworks: How they become your enemy. In *Proceedings of the ACM International Conference Companion on Object Oriented Programming Systems Languages and Applications Companion (SPLASH '10)*, (pp. 115-122). ACM.

Mei, H., Zhang, L., & Yang, F. (2001). A software configuration management model for supporting component-based software development. *SIGSOFT Software Engineering Notes, 26*(2), 53–58. doi:10.1145/505776.505790.

Midtgaard, J. (2012). Control-flow analysis of functional programs. *ACM Computing Surveys, 44*(3). doi:10.1145/2187671.2187672.

Mietzner, R., Metzger, A., Leymann, F., & Pohl, K. (2009). Variability modeling to support customization and deployment of multi-tenant-aware software as a service applications. In *Proceedings of the 2009 ICSE Workshop on Principles of Engineering Service Oriented Systems (PESOS '09)*, (pp. 18-25). IEEE Computer Society.

Morin, B., Mouelhi, T., Fleurey, F., Le Traon, Y., Barais, O., & Jezequel, J. (2010). Security-driven model-based dynamic adaptation. In *Proceedings of the IEEE/ACM International Conference on Automated Software Engineering (ASE '10)*, (pp. 205-214). ACM.

Nguyen, T. N. (2006). Model-based version and configuration management for a web engineering lifecycle. In *Proceedings of the 15th International Conference on World Wide Web (WWW '06)*, (pp. 437-446). ACM.

Shrivastava, S. K., & Wheater, S. M. (1998). A transactional workflow based distributed application composition and execution environment. In *Proceedings of the 8th ACM SIGOPS European Workshop on Support for Composing Distributed Applications (EW 8)*, (pp. 74-81). ACM.

Trujillo, S., Zubizarreta, A., Mendialdua, X., & de Sosa, J. (2009). Feature-oriented refinement of models, metamodels and model transformations. In *Proceedings of the First International Workshop on Feature-Oriented Software Development (FOSD '09)*, (pp. 87-94). ACM.

Truyen, E., Cardozo, N., Walraven, S., Vallejos, J., Bainomugisha, E., & Günther, S. … Joosen, W. (2012). Context-oriented programming for customizable SaaS applications. In *Proceedings of the 27th Annual ACM Symposium on Applied Computing (SAC '12)*, (pp. 418-425). ACM.

Tu, Z., Zacharewicz, G., & Chen, D. (2011). Harmonized and reversible development framework for HLA-based interoperable application. In *Proceedings of the 2011 Symposium on Theory of Modeling & Simulation: DEVS Integrative M&S Symposium (TMS-DEVS '11)*, (pp. 51-58). San Diego, CA: Society for Computer Simulation International.

KEY TERMS AND DEFINITIONS

Distributed Components: Components of the MDEIS application framework that provide the distributed execution capability.

Distributed Execution Request: Specific instance types of distributed transactions that are supported by the Distributed Components.

Distributed Temporal MDEIS Application Framework: Refers to major features of the framework. Distributed refers to the distributed operations as described in this chapter. Temporal relates to audit processes that manage the ongoing change of all meta-data and data to enable temporal execution of MDEIS applications i.e. the framework then permits full application and data rollback and rollforward execution throughout the entire history to maintain the exact application and database state at any point.

Enterprise Information System (EIS): Large scale computing system that offers high quality of service, managing large volumes of data and capable of supporting large organizations.

Logic Variant: A specific instance of Variant Logic as an identified selection of associated logic changes.

Meta-Data: Computing information that is held as a description of stored data.

Meta-Data based Enterprise Information Systems (MDEIS) Application Framework: It is an example of a MDA based application modeling and execution environment for EIS applications.

Meta-Model: Defines the language and processes from which to form a model.

Model Driven Architecture (MDA): Is an initiative of the Object Management Group to "separate business and application logic from underlying platform technology."

Objective Version Control: The automatic audit tracking of every model object and attribute change.

Subjective Version Control: Manual version control based on human decisions identifying and naming the state of a subset of the application model at one point in time compared with the changed state of the application model at an earlier point in time.

Variant Logic: The overall concepts supporting allowing supplemental application logic changes to be managed within the MDEIS application framework.

Chapter 6

CMF:
A Crop Model Factory to Improve Scientific Models Development Process

Guillaume Barbier
ITK, France & Blaise Pascal University, France

Véronique Cucchi
ITK, France

François Pinet
Irstea, France

David R. C. Hill
Blaise Pascal University, France

ABSTRACT

This chapter shows how Model Driven Engineering (MDE) can contribute to the production of Crop models. The ITK firm works in agronomy; it designs digital models and Decision Support Systems for croppers. Common model development at ITK relies on a dual implementation. The first one in Matlab® is usually proposed by agronomists, but for industrial purposes, software engineers translate this model in Java. This leads to double implementation, maintenance, and heavy production costs. To deal with this efficiency problem, the authors use a MDE approach to produce a Crop Model Factory (CMF). For this factory they propose a DSML (Domain Specific Modeling Language) formalized by a metamodel. In this chapter, the authors present this DSML, the concrete syntax retained for the factory, and its implementation in a tool enabling automatic code generation. The resulting Crop Model Factory (CMF) prototype is the fruit of an interdisciplinary collaboration, and they also present feedback on this working experience.

INTRODUCTION

In an agronomical context, the Decision Support System (DSS) proposed by the ITK firm rely on mechanistic models. They represent the different biological processes occurring during the plant growth and in the field. Such models help identifying management options and are a precious aid for decision makers. However, ITK usually develops models in two steps. First, agronomists use specialized programming languages such as Matlab or R to prototype their crop models. Second, software engineers implement these models in Java or C++/C# for industrial use. This double

DOI: 10.4018/978-1-4666-4217-1.ch006

development is time consuming and error-prone. In order to overcome this issue, this chapter shows how Model Driven Engineering can be used by providing a Domain Specific Modeling Language (DSML) for agronomists. This DSML is dedicated to the representation and automatic implementation of crop models. This solution experimented by the ITK company allows agronomists to define and experiment their models with a specific graphical user interface and to produce directly Java code.

Domain-specific modeling is a software engineering methodology for the conception and implementation of systems. It implies the use of languages dedicated to particular domains (i.e., DSML) to represent models. DSMLs require less effort for modelers to specify a particular type of system than general purpose languages, such as UML (Unified Modeling Language). Code generation techniques can be also used to automate the production of source code directly from the models.

In order to implement our language and our "crop model factory", we have retained the Eclipse platform and the Graphical Modeling Framework (GMF) plugin. The tool we propose provides a Java code generator. In our work, we took inspiration from the contribution presented in (Hill and Gourgand, 1993; Hill, 1996) where graphical specifications led to simulation code generation and from the proposal of (deLara and Vangheluwe, 2004) where the syntax and the semantics of visual notations are based on metamodeling.

The present chapter will introduce the characteristics of crop models and will show how Model Driven Engineering (MDE) can contribute in their development. Our DSML will be presented and formalized by a metamodel. Then, the concrete syntax of our model factory will be shown as well as its implementation in a tool providing automatic code generation. Future research directions will be also described.

BACKGROUND

Crop Models Characteristics

To understand—as much as to build—a domain-specific approach, it is essential to provide enough information about the given domain. The following information results from a preliminary analysis led to identifying the main characteristics of crop models (Barbier, Pinet, & Hill, 2011). These were recovered from ITK legacy and from the study of various published models (Bouman, Van Keulen, van Laar, & Rabbinge, 1996; Brisson, Launay, & Beaudoin, 2009). Vine, wheat, and cotton are among the biological systems studied by ITK to provide DSS: modeling is focused on plant growth according to environmental conditions and cultural practices. The scientific modeling of these plants growth was inspired by (Jallas, 1998; Jamieson, Semenov, Brooking, & Francis, 1998; Louarn, 2009).

As stated by Bézivin and Gerbé (2001), "a model is a simplification of a system built with an intended goal in mind" (p. 274). This definition may be applied as much to the model-driven world as to the modeling and simulation one, and therefore to crop modeling. In crop models, the system studied consists of a plant or a plant population and in most cases of the soil on which it grows. The simplification is orientated towards using mathematical equations to represent biophysical processes (e.g. light interception, potential and actual transpiration or soil-water transfer dynamics) which seem of importance to the modeler given his/her goals. These processes use as inputs external information (e.g. weather data) and/or data produced by other processes to render one or more outputs using parameterized equations. They can also interact with a data structure describing the soil-plant system. Depending on the model, the plant description may range from considering the plant as a single big leaf to having an explicit description of the plant topology (e.g. individualized stems and leaves). We would like to highlight that in the latter case the data structure is dynamic, which means that processes will add new organs to it. The nature of the processes taken into account and the soil-plant system data structure are constrained by:

- The model main objectives (e.g. yield assessment, hydric stress or disease exposure estimation).
- The expected accuracy of the model.
- The actual knowledge of the biological system.
- **The available data:** These could be field data used for model calibration, or environmental data used for simulation runs.

In a crop-modeling context at least, modelers naturally adopt a logical decomposition of their models. They consider large biophysical concepts and divide them into sub-models until they obtain the simplest processes. At simulation time, the processes are taken into account sequentially, it is important to understand that there may be different time scales depending on data availability or the more or less fine representation of the processes.

MDE to the Rescue

The Modeling and Simulation (M&S) world is already overwhelmed by M&S tools. However, none seems to correspond to both our needs in modeling specificities and requirements for an industrial use.

Indeed, tools like Matlab® or R have general purpose, but in our context do not enable us to obtain Java code for our JEE platform. Others are specifically dedicated to agronomy.: This latter category is mostly composed of tools built by research teams, they are committed to be federative approach for knowledge sharing like OpenAlea (Pradal, Dufour-Kowalski, Boudon, Fournier, & Godin, 2008), the Record platform (Bergez et al.,

2013) or the ModCom platform (Hillyer, Bolte, van Evert, & Lamaker, 2003). Though dedicated to modeling in our domain of interest, they require software engineers for model implementation or to train modelers in using a general purpose language, like Python or C++.

Model-driven initiatives have also been developed in the field of M&S. However they are intended to be multi-domain M&S tools as is the case for OpenModelica (Jagudin, Remar, Pop, & Fritzson, 2006) or AToM[3] (deLara & Vangheluwe, 2002), these multi-domain approaches offer a lot of different formalisms which are not adapted to agronomists nor to crop modeling specificities. Finally, SimStudio (Touraille, Traoré, & Hill, 2011) is another interesting tool as is MDD4MS (Cetinkaya, Verbraeck, & Seck, 2011) but they are focused on discrete-event systems which is too constraining given the crop model sequential nature.

In this context, it seemed the best move was to build our own crop model design tool. Relying on the Model Driven Engineering (MDE) concepts, we aimed at producing a Domain Specific Model Language (DSML) suited to our users' needs and able to generate Java code. This code should be effortlessly integrated into our decision support systems.

Building this DSML required to identify, from the crop models main characteristics listed above, the specificities, and possible genericity in crop modeling and simulation. This approach also needed to have an understanding of the domain-specialists knowledge and practice.

TAILORING A DSML FOR CROP MODELLING

Domain-Specific Difficulties

As explained above the processes taken into account vary depending on the goal of the modeler. It is therefore impossible to have an *a priori* definition of which biological processes should be included in a model. It is essential that the modeler remains free to choose the processes which fit to her/his needs. Considering this statement, genericity in our approach can not be reached by considering the biological semantic of the processes but by focusing on the way they are defined regardless of biology. A similar point of view is adopted with regards to the data structure describing the soil-plant system. We made an analogy between this structure and the notion of blackboard as referred to by (Dalle, Ribault, & Himmelspach, 2009). The way the plant and soil are decomposed, whether their structure is dynamic or not depends on the modeler needs and choices. It is not possible to constrain their definition and/or biological or physical meaning.

Our approach is not only focused on obtaining an environment for designing crop models and generating Java code. Reusability is also a key concern of our work. Some processes, like light interception, are often represented with the same set of representations. Keeping in mind to improve productivity, it is thus essential for the modeler to have the possibility to save a subset of a model in a specific database. Any modeler willing to reuse this subset would just have to import it from the shared database. Reusability raises the question of model linking, since different time scales and different data units and/or dimension may be involved. Model linking should be addressed without modifying the internal behavior of the processes involved in it.

The choice of the processes included in the model, the definition of the blackboard structure and the flow of information between processes is made during the conceptual modeling phase. (Robinson, 2008) defines a conceptual model as *'a non-software specific description of the computer simulation model ..., describing the objectives, inputs, outputs, content, assumptions and simplifications of the model.'* The reader will notice the slight difference between conceptual modeling from a M&S point of view and its general meaning in the software engineering world. Furthermore

the non-software specific description is close to the concept of model from an MDE standpoint and the conceptual model content is defined using the M&S semantic. It seems that using a DSML is just what is needed for overcoming the lack of conceptual model design software as stressed by (Robinson, 2007).

In the crop modeling context, the conceptual model is often designed on paper as a flowchart as is the case in (Hakojarvi et al., 2010). The flowchart representation is focused on a general description of the model (nature of the process, data flows and model sequence) however it does not address the mathematical description of the involved processes. It is most probably due to the fact that there is no proper – or well-known – software for defining the conceptual model. Our approach allows us to obtain such software: a graphical concrete syntax could be defined to design the general model features and, in the end, a textual concrete syntax to design the mathematical model description.

C3M: A Crop Model Metamodel

In our context, we have proposed C3M (Crop Model MetaModel), a metamodel on which our DSML abstract syntax relies. It has been defined and refined from the reverse engineering and refactoring of the legacy models already used in DSS as advised by (Favre, Bézivin, & Bull, 2006). It is (almost) completely defined in Figure 1 and has been refined since our previous publications (Barbier, Flusin, Cucchi, Pinet, & Hill, 2013; Barbier et al., 2011).

The logical decomposition of the crop model with regards to its hierarchy and the biophysical processes is handled by the use of the *Composite* design pattern. The *CompositeModel* is used to define the crop model hierarchy, the terminal elements of this tree-like hierarchy are *ExecutableModel*s. The latter are intended to withhold the mathematical logic of the crop model.

Figure 1. UML class diagram of the crop model metamodel as used in CMF

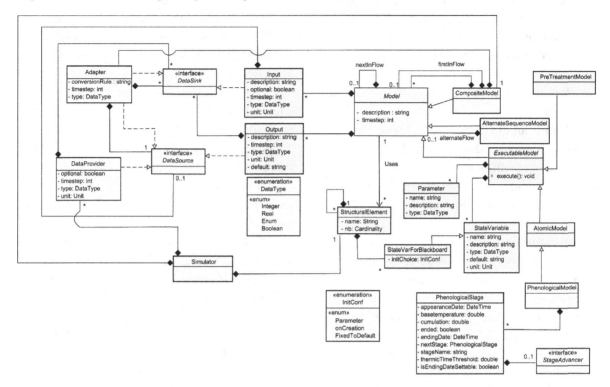

The simulation sequence—the order by which *ExecutableModels* are processed at simulation time—is determined by:

- The *firstInFlow* and *nextInFlow* relationships (respectively pertaining to the *CompositeModel* and the *Model* classes).
- The respective timescales of the models (*timestep* attribute of the *Model* class).
- The exact nature of the *ExecutableModel*, whether it is an *AtomicModel* or a *PretreatmentModel*.
- The use of an *AlternateSequenceModel* which permits the defining of alternative sequences depending on a given logical condition.

One of the possible conditions for defining an alternate sequence may rely on the phenological stage of the plant. The plant phenology determines

major changes into its functioning: new organs are created and/or some other behaviors are altered. For example, the fruiting stage corresponds to the transformation of flowers into fruits, which implies significant changes in the plant carbon allocation patterns. The phenological model can be seen as a simple state machine. This specific construct was integrated into the metamodel to ease its design by crop modelers.

With regards to data exchanges, two types of behavior can be identified: entities providing data (*DataSource*) or consuming data (*DataSink*). Data are provided either by model *Outputs*, by *DataProviders* linked to external data sources (e.g., weather database) or by *Adapters*. *Adapters* also act as data consumers, as do model *Inputs*. *Adapters* are the answer to the model linking issue. Adapters can be classified into four different subtypes (not detailed on Figure 1):

- **Aggregator:** To connect several data sources to a single data source (by default summing the different sources).
- **TimeAdapter:** To decompose or aggregate data in the case the sinks consumes information at a different scale it is produced by the source.
- **ConditionalAdapter:** To choose the actual source feeding a sink depending on certain conditions.
- **Convertor:** To ensure conversion in case the units of the source and the sink differ.

Separating the processes description from the soil-plant data structure was an early choice in our work (Barbier et al., 2011) and is consistent with other works on ontologies for modeling in agronomy like (Martin-Clouaire & Rellier, 2009). The blackboard, as defined above, is composed of *StructuralElement*s in a broad sense a structural element corresponds to a plant organ - like a leaf - or a soil compartment, like a layer. A structural element can own several - in type and number - other structural elements. As an example, the main stem of a plant has several leaves and possibility secondary stems. Any structural element can be described by a set of state variables like leaf area or nitrogen concentration for a soil compartment.

From the metamodel obtained, it was possible to define a graphical concrete syntax for crop model visual-design. This graphical concrete syntax has been integrated into a prototype of our Crop Model Factory (CMF). The expressivity of this concrete syntax has been tested empirically by defining the vine and wheat legacy models.

CMF and Its Concrete Syntax

As stated above CMF is designed for crop modelers, it must therefore propose graphical syntax close to the formalisms they naturally use. This syntax is inspired by flowcharts representations and is close to any graphical syntax used in M&S tools (Pradal et al., 2008; Quesnel, Duboz, &

Ramat, 2009). However, even if some concepts are common with other M&S, the semantics associated with our syntax is specific to our domain and may differ from other simulation domains. The visual syntax of CMF is dedicated to providing general description of crop models. It is not intended to define how modelers will formalize the mathematical and logical inner-description of the processes. We believe that the most suitable syntax to define the inner logic of the processes should be textual. Crop modelers already have knowledge of algorithms and it is easier to type mathematical equations than to type bloc diagrams to define it. The formalization of the required textual syntax for CMF—even if not achieved yet—has already started and will be treated in future research.

The prototype of CMF has been built relying on the Eclipse Modeling Framework (EMF), the Graphical Modeling Framework (GMF) and EuGENia (Kolovos, et al., 2010). Figure 2 shows a screen caption of CMF while the vine model is being edited. The open diagram corresponds to a subpart of the vine model. This part is dedicated to computing the daily actual evapotranspiration, representing the actual loss of water by the soil-plant system. Effective computation is done by the *AtomicModel* computeETR (1). This requires the reference evapotranspiration ETP (2)—which is loss of water by soil-plant if there were an unlimited amount of accessible water—as an input. However ETP data cannot always be provided by weather station. In this case, the ETP must be computed, thus an *AlternateSequenceModel* (3) is used. The alternative sequence consists in computing the quantity of sunrays received by the earth (4) and then using the result to compute the ETP (5). A *ConditionalAdapter* (6) is then needed to determine which of the computed ETP or the provided ETP should be used as an input for the computeETR model.

The diagram presented above is typical of the representations used to define the different processes involved in the crop model. As formerly

Figure 2. Screenshot of CMF: vine model design

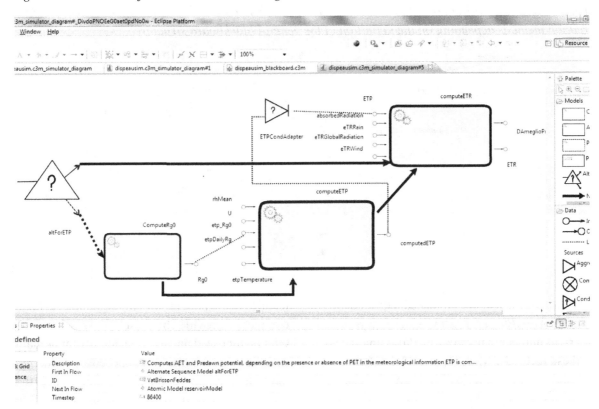

stated, the processes have to interact with a data structure describing the soil-plant system state, which is managed by the blackboard. In their usual scientific development environment, the crop modelers would use structures in addition to arrays or matrices to describe the blackboard. Therefore, representing the blackboard editor in a tree-like manner seemed the best choice. The current editor proposed by CMF relies on a simple editor obtained from the Eclipse Modeling Framework and the property tab for editing the different attributes of the blackboard elements. This is why Figure 3 presents two schematic representations of a blackboard instance as defined in the vine model.

Structural elements in the blackboard are just described by an id and cardinality. On Figure 3.A, the first element is the main stem of the plant, there is only one stem element to describe the main stem. The main stem is composed of one or more phytomere—a section of shoot—each one having a leaf and a possible stem element, which stands for ramification. Below the stem element, the height state variable represents the height of the main stem. It is a real number value expressed in centimeters whose initial value is defaulted to zero.

Cardinality and the way the state variables initial value is defined point to an interesting feature that Figure 3b helps understand. The "1…n" cardinality for phytomere means that there will be a process dedicated to creating new phytomeres, requiring a method on the stem element: *addPhytomere*. This method will instantiate a new phytomere and will add it to the stem phytomere collection. As the leaf element is mandatory and its area state variable is initialized on creation, the *addPhytomere* method should be parameterized with the initial value of the newly created leaf area. Depending on the modeler's choice, a blackboard

Figure 3. Conceptual representation of the CMF blackboard interface: a) decomposition in structural elements and state variables (main stem of the plant); b) use case showing the necessity to generate creation methods depending on the definition of the general blackboard structure

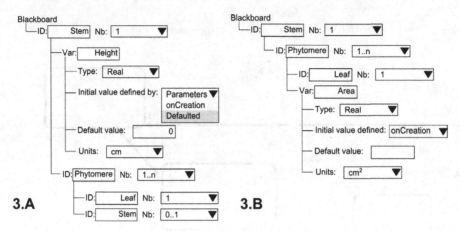

structural element can be enhanced with a various number of *addElement* method which may receive a various number of parameters. Providing access to these methods, when the modeler is textually editing processes behavior, would greatly improve the user experience and avoid errors or repeated operations. However generating these operations raises issues as will be discussed in the future research section.

Other features have been included in CMF; they are aimed at avoiding cumbersome operations for the users. Considering two specialists of the same domain having a discussion, they will tend to express concepts in a shortened manner thereby avoiding the use of long and hard-to-grasp sentences. We argue that a DSML-based environment should be able to do the same. It should permit the domain specialist to use a shortened sentence using concrete syntax elements from which the underlying formal sentence should be inferred. As formerly stated adapters have been introduced in the metamodel to handle the model linking issue. When a modeler links a data sink to a data source, CMF proposes automatically to create an adapter when it is needed. Moreover, a simple drag and drop of a given output to a model creates an input in the latter and automatically links the input to the output. The enrichment of the GUI with these

features could be seen as being equivalent to code completion provided by most IDE. With them the GUI is improved and exhibits intelligent domain specific behavior. MDE is supposed to be centered upon the domain specialists. Understanding the specialists' shortened expressions and integrating them as a DSML environment tooling is therefore essential to gain users' acceptance.

As it is, the Crop Model Factory has been tested to express the general structure of two of ITK legacy models (vine and wheat). There has been no limitation detected with our chosen formalism. Both models were expressed without having to resort to any circumventing construct. From this point, it was possible to handle Java code generation from the serialized models.

Generating Crop Model and Simulator Codes

In order to generate Java code, we worked with GMF generated editors, as it provides an *ad hoc* serialization feature relying on XMI files (XML Metadata Interchange). CMF then uses this file with Acceleo (http://www.eclipse.org/acceleo/) to generate the code. Acceleo is part of the Eclipse Model to Text (M2T) project and implements the Object Management Group Model to Text

Language specification. It relies on templates and Object Constraint Language (OCL) to produce efficient code generation.

Within the Crop Model Factory, the code generation uses a framework obtained from legacy models reengineering. This permits us to limit the amount of code being generated. Figure 4 exhibits an excerpt of the framework. The framework presents elements directly derived from some of the metamodel ones (model composition, blackboard). Some others are specific constructs for a better handling of the simulation execution: the *Workflow* class is dedicated to handling the simulation sequence depending on the current time step; the time flow is delegated by the *Simulator* to the *Clockwork* class. This class implements the *IClockworkAccess* interface: it permits any model to have access to various time representations (e.g. Julian date, hour of day, date comparisons).

Data flows are ensured by the *DataLinker* class: when the simulator is initialized, this class links various data sources. The effective linking is done by sharing a common reference to the same data representation (a primitive type wrapper). The outputs of the simulation are entirely configurable. To run the simulation the expected outputs have to be specified. A class implementing the *IResultsHandler* interface will register observers on the corresponding data sources. This feature is required to permit the scientific model validation, and then adapt the simulation outputs to the targeted DSS needs, without modifying the source code of the model and/or the simulator.

Implementing code generation was greatly eased by the tree-like structure of our models. Indeed it permits an easy parsing of the hierarchical model without having to ponder over possible circular cross-references. Currently the Java code generation is almost complete. Even if the features regarding the definition of the processes (mathematics and logics) have not yet been implemented, we have already obtained the essential parts of the code: structure, models, blackboard, data sources, and data sinks; all these classes are fully generated. The linking of sources and sinks is done and the simulation sequence is defined in a *Workflow* class. Considering the current rewriting of crop model prototypes into Java code, the resultant code generation covers the most error-prone part of the process. Only the inner logic of the executable models has to be rewritten; this logic is directly available in functions written in the Matlab prototype. So, even if CMF is still incomplete and will require further enhance-

Figure 4. Framework on which relies the Java code generated by CMF

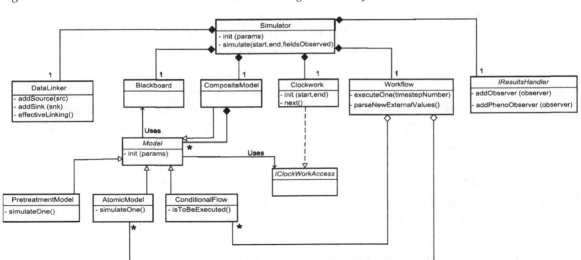

ments, a step has already been done in obtaining an environment for improving productivity and diminishing the risk of code disjunction between our prototype and in-production models.

FUTURE RESEARCH DIRECTIONS

CMF prototype is already providing interesting features with regards to the issues which lead to its design. However, it remains incomplete and the feasibility of several new features has to be tested. Priority will be given to the definition of a textual concrete syntax to define the executable models behavior. Though there is a rising interest in hybrid (textual and graphical) Domain-Specific Languages (DSL) there is no *ad hoc* tooling for their design. Hybrid DSLs we are aware of are designed by weaving graphical editors and textual obtained separately (Scheidgen, 2008) but progress has still to be made to obtain fully fledged hybrid DSLs design environment (Völter, 2011).

With regards to CMF, the textual syntax will offer a limited number of instructions to define simple algorithms. Domain-specific elements will have specific roles; for example, inputs will only be used on the right-hand side of an expression whereas outputs will only be used on the left-hand side of expressions. These examples are simple, other expected features for the textual syntax will be harder to achieve. First the definition of the operations to add new elements to the black-board, as stated above these operations signature will vary depending on the cardinalities defined for the structural elements and the way the state variables should be initialized. This means that the textual syntax should be flexible enough to permit operations call with arguments as deduced from the blackboard definition. The modeler may also want the blackboard to provide synthetic data from its underlying data structure. As an example, each leaf of the blackboard possesses an area state variable; the modeler may require access to the total leaf area s/he would need to

define an operation parsing the whole structure and summing the leaves area.

Another issue arises when considering built-in functions like the ones exposed by the clockwork. Though those could be included in the metamodel definition with the use of action languages as offered by KerMeta (Muller, Fleurey, & Jézéquel, 2005); one may not pretend to have full coverage of the users' needs with regards to the functions provided. This raises the question of how one must consider evolution of the metamodel content without jeopardizing the already developed tool and models obtained from it as observed by (Mohagheghi et al., 2011). This question is one the model-driven community has to answer should it want MDE to reach its full potential (DenHaan, 2008). Another possible way to reach end-users new requirements or unforeseen needs would be to permit them to enhance themselves their design environment by defining new built-in functions. But this kind of approach may hinder a generative process relying on a predefined framework.

As stated previously, reusability is key concern in our environment. The modeler should have the possibility to save a subpart of the model for later reuse by her/himself or another modeler. This feature would be on a shared knowledge-database. Though tools like Bonita Open Solution® (www. bonitasoft.com) offer a templating feature it does not meet our requirements and to our knowledge there is no MD tooling offering this kind of functionality. In the context of CMF, we can use the XMI serialization file to extract the nodes corresponding to the model subparts which we want to reuse and insert them in a new serialization file. However this is not a user-friendly operation and it would become even more cumbersome when a modeler has too many achieved models and thus an overwhelming number of serialization files. Moreover sharing knowledge between modelers will require electronic transmission of the model subparts. We think we could offer better than this by using model slicers. As defined by (Blouin, Combemale, Baudry, & Beaudoux,

2011) model slicers are "tools that extract a subset from a model, for a specific purpose" (p. 62). The specific purpose in this case is to achieve slice persistence. Slicing techniques aiming at model subsets persistence should be still considered in our problem, but integrating such features in MD tooling would probably be of interest.

Consistency checking of the designed models is also of concern for CMF, for instance, avoiding loops in the simulation flow or input definition without an output or a data provider feeding data to it. Object Constraint Language (OCL) is well integrated into EMF and GMF for model checking and should prove easy to handle. Validation of the generative approach is more of a concern and is still actively discussed in the model-driven community (Kornecki & Johri, 2006; Merilinna & Pärssinen, 2010). A first empirical validation has been done with CMF by comparing code for the vine and wheat models with the refactored legacy ones. However future generated models cannot be validated that way. Model executability plays a central-role for that matter. By delivering a model-driven crop model designer enabling simulation runs, we would provide the modelers with a way to evaluate their model at design-time and define simulation scenarios. These scenarios and obtained outputs would be used to validate the simulation results produced by the generated code and thus to validate the generative approach. As model compilation would take too long to be accepted by modelers used to standard M&S software, the model execution should rely on model interpretation. However, with regards to model executability, the current tooling does not offer fully fledged solutions to the industry as stressed by (Selic, 2012).

CONCLUSION

With regards to CMF, one striking thing about the formalisms retained for its DSML is that, apart from the phenological model, it does not contain any biological specific construct. This means that our formalism could well be used in other M&S fields. However, there would be some restrictions. There is for instance a strict sequential nature in the models CMF permits to define. There is no parallelized execution of models and no possibility to define loops in the simulation sequence. Another restriction is that the simulations are run from a given day to another; this gives our models an apparent time step of a day which for sure will be unsuited for many M&S applications and domains. Slight adaptations to CMF would permit to widen its domain to the process-based modeling one. As previously stated, the Crop Model Factory prototype already enables productivity gain and risk reduction by covering the most error-prone part of the Matlab to Java translation process. We do believe that MDE was the best way to address this specific problem and that, once fully matured; CMF will be a great improvement in our crop model production process.

This model-driven experience proved to be a good way to assess the strengths and weaknesses of Model-Driven Engineering. Providing domain-specialists with a way to define their models and obtain satisfactory program is the main objective of MDE. In this regard, the fulfillment can be considered as partial. Indeed, we identified two main drawbacks to MDE adoption. First of all, the entry barrier to MDE is quite high, integrating the theory and navigating among different levels of abstraction is a tricky challenge for one's mind. With practice, one gains in familiarity with this kind of exercise. The second drawback seems far more important, the model-driven community has been provided with a lot of different MD-tools, they are not all equivalent, some are dedicated to specific tasks. This abundance can be confusing for newcomers when they will have to decide which tool to adopt. This choice is made harder by the too-often observed lack of documentation. This raises the entry level to a higher point. (Kelly & Pohjonen, 2009) state that, for a DSML to succeed, documentation and training are required to gain acceptance by the modelers and that long-term resistance may be faced should the developers fail to deliver enough documentation and support on time. The same problem exists with MD tool, documentation and training materials are scarce. Should the model-driven community, actively developing MD tooling, be unable to produce these items it may jeopardize MD approaches broad acceptance and limit its use in the industry as noticed by (Selic, 2012). The problem seems worse when considering weaving different MD-tools like GMF-obtained editors and XText editors. This kind of activity relies too much on craftsmanship while one could expect full integrations of the tools shipped into the Eclipse Modeling Project for instance. We hope that in the future a federative approach will be adopted by the Eclipse community in this regard. In spite of the limits and difficulties observed, we are convinced that the Model Driven Engineering community will soon produce sound and reliable processes enabling the 'industrial' assembly of software applications conforming to metamodel specifications and following rigorous software engineering methods.

REFERENCES

Barbier, G., Flusin, J., Cucchi, V., Pinet, F., & Hill, D. R. C. (2013). *Vine model design using a domain-specific modeling language.* Paper presented at the European Simulation and Modeling Conference. Essen, Germany.

Barbier, G., Pinet, F., & Hill, D. R. C. (2011). MDE in action: First steps towards a crop model factory. In *Proceedings of the ESM 2011 European Simulation and Modeling Conference* (pp. 130-137). Guimarães, Portugal: ESM.

Bergez, J.-E., Chabrier, P., Gary, C., Jeuffroy, M. H., Makowski, D., & Quesnel, G. et al. (2013). An open platform to build, evaluate and simulate integrated models of farming and agro-ecosystems. *Environmental Modelling & Software*. doi:10.1016/j.envsoft.2012.03.011.

Bézivin, J., & Gerbé, O. (2001). Towards a precise definition of the OMG/MDA framework. In *Proceedings of the 16th IEEE International Conference on Automated Software Engineering (ASE 2001)* (pp. 273-280). San Diego, CA: IEEE Computer Society.

Blouin, A., Combemale, B., Baudry, B., & Beaudoux, O. (2011). *Modeling model slicers.* Paper presented at the MODELS 2011. New York, NY.

Bouman, B. A. M., Van Keulen, H., van Laar, H. H., & Rabbinge, R. (1996). The 'school of de wit' crop growth simulation models: A pedigree and historical review. *Agricultural Systems*, *52*(2/3), 171–198. doi:10.1016/0308-521X(96)00011-X.

Brisson, N., Launay, M., & Beaudoin, N. (2009). *Conceptual basis, formalisations and parameterization of the STICS crop model.*

Cetinkaya, D., Verbraeck, A., & Seck, M. S. (2011). *MDD4MS: A model driven development framework for modeling and simulation.* Paper presented at the 2011 Summer Computer Simulation Conference. Hague, Netherlands.

Dalle, O., Ribault, J., & Himmelspach, J. (2009). Design considerations for M&S software. In M. D. Rosseti, R. R. Hill, B. Johansson, A. Dunkin, & R. G. Ingalls (Eds.), *Proceedings of the WSC 2009 Winter Simulation Conference* (pp. 944-955). Austin, TX: WSC.

deLara, J., & Vangheluwe, H. (2002). AToM3: A tool for multi-formalism and meta-modelling. In Kutsche, R.-D., & Weber, H. (Eds.), *Fundamental Approaches to Software Engineering* (pp. 174–188). Berlin: Springer.

DenHaan, J. (2008). *8 reasons why model-driven aproaches (will) fail.* Retrieved September, 2012, from http://www.infoq.com/articles/8-reasons-why-MDE-fails

Favre, J. M., Bézivin, J., & Bull, I. (2006). Evolution, rétro-ingénierie et IDM: Du code aux modèles. In *L'ingénierie dirigée par les modèles* (pp. 185–215). Hermes Science.

Hakojarvi, M., Hautala, M., Ahokas, J., Oksanen, T., Maksimow, T., & Aspiala, A. et al. (2010). Platform for simulation of automated crop production. *Agronomy Research*, *8*(1), 797–806.

Hillyer, C., Bolte, J., van Evert, F., & Lamaker, A. (2003). The ModCom modular simulation system. *European Journal of Agronomy*, *18*, 333–343. doi:10.1016/S1161-0301(02)00111-9.

Jagudin, E., Remar, A., Pop, A., & Fritzson, P. (2006). OpenModelica MDT eclipse plugin for modelica development, code browsing, and simulation. In *Proceedings of the 47th Conference on Simulation and Modelling*. Helsinki, Finland: IEEE.

Jallas, E. (1998). *Improved model-based decision support by modeling cotton variability and using evolutionary algorithms. (Unpublished PhD)*. Mississippi: Mississippi State University.

Jamieson, P. D., Semenov, M. A., Brooking, I. R., & Francis, G. S. (1998). Sirius: A mechanistic model of wheat response to environmental variation. *European Journal of Agronomy*, *8*, 161–179. doi:10.1016/S1161-0301(98)00020-3.

Kelly, S., & Pohjonen, R. (2009). Worst practices for domain-specific modeling. *Software*, *26*(4), 22–29. doi:10.1109/MS.2009.109.

Kolovos, D. S., Rose, L. M., Abid, S. B., Paige, R. F., Polack, F. A. C., & Botterweck, G. (2010). EuGENia: Taming EMF and GMF using model transformation. In *Proceedings of the 13th International Conference, MODELS 2010, Model Driven Engineering Languages and Systems* (pp. 211-225). Oslo, Norway: Springer.

Kornecki, A. J., & Johri, S. (2006). Automatic code generation: Model-code semantic consistency. In H. R. Arabnia & H. Reza (Eds.), *Proceedings of the 2006 International Conference on Software Engineering and Practice SERP'06* (pp. 191-197). Las Vegas, NV: SERP.

Louarn, G. (2009). Analyse et modélisation de l'organogénèse et de l'architecture d'un rameau de vigne (vitis vinifiera l.). (Unpublished PhD). Ecole nationale supérieure agronomique de Montpellier, Montpellier, France.

Martin-Clouaire, R., & Rellier, J.-P. (2009). Modelling and simulating work practices in agriculture. *International Journal of Metadata. Semantics and Ontologies*, *4*(1/2), 42–53. doi:10.1504/IJMSO.2009.026253.

Merilinna, J., & Pärssinen, J. (2010). *Verification and validation in the context of domain-specific modelling.* Paper presented at the DSM'10 10th Workshop on Domain-Specific Modelling. Reno, NV.

Mohagheghi, P., Gilani, W., Stefanescu, A., Fernandez, M. A., Nordmoen, B., & Fritzsche, M. (2011). Where does model-driven engineering help? Experiences from three industrial cases. *Software & Systems Modeling*, 1–21.

Muller, P.-A., Fleurey, F., & Jézéquel, J.-M. (2005). *Weaving executability into object-oriented metalanguages.* Paper presented at the MODELS 2005. Montego Bay, Jamaica.

Pradal, C., Dufour-Kowalski, S., Boudon, F., Fournier, C., & Godin, C. (2008). OpenAlea: A visual programming and component-based software for plant modeling. *Functional Plant Biology*, *35*(9-10), 751–760. doi:10.1071/FP08084.

Quesnel, G., Duboz, R., & Ramat, E. (2009). The virtual laboratory environment - An operational framework for multi-modelling, simulation and analysis of complex dynamical systems. *Simulation Modelling Practice and Theory*, *17*(4), 641–653. doi:10.1016/j.simpat.2008.11.003.

Robinson, S. (2007). Editorial: The future's bright the future's... conceptual modelling for simulation! *Journal of Simulation*, *1*, 149–152. doi:10.1057/palgrave.jos.4250026.

Robinson, S. (2008). Conceptual modelling for simulation part I: Definition and requirements. *The Journal of the Operational Research Society, 59*(3), 278–290. doi:10.1057/palgrave.jors.2602368.

Scheidgen, M. (2008). *Textual modelling embedded into graphical modelling*. Paper presented at the ECMDAFA'08 4th European Conference on Model Driven Architecture - Foundations and Applications. London, UK.

Selic, B. (2012). What will it take? A view on adoption of model-based methods in practice. *Software & Systems Modeling*, 1–14.

Touraille, L., Traoré, M. K., & Hill, D. R. C. (2011). A model-driven software environment for modeling, simulation and analysis of complex systems. In *Proceedings of the Spring Simulation Multiconference - Symposium on Theory of Modeling and Simulation (TMS/DEVS)*, (pp. 229-237). Boston: TMS.

Völter, M. (2011). MD/DSL best practices [from http://www.voelter.de/publications/index.html]. *Update*, (March): 2011. Retrieved September 27, 2012

ADDITIONAL READING

Bézivin, J. (2005). On the unification power of models. *Software & Systems Modeling, 4*(2), 171–188. doi:10.1007/s10270-005-0079-0.

Bézivin, J. (2012a). *History and context of MDE*. Retrieved from http://www.nii.ac.jp/userimg/lectures/20120117/Lecture1.pdf

Bézivin, J. (2012b). *Theory and basic principles of MDE*. Retrieved from http://www.nii.ac.jp/userimg/lectures/20120117/Lecture2.pdf

Bézivin, J. (2012c). *Applications of MDE*. Retrieved from http://www.nii.ac.jp/userimg/lectures/20120117/Lecture3.pdf

Bézivin, J. (2012d). *Where will be MDE in 2030?* Retrieved from http://www.nii.ac.jp/userimg/lectures/20120117/Lecture4.pdf

Booch, G., Brown, A., Iyengar, S., Rumbaugh, J., & Selic, B. (2004). *An MDA manifesto*. Retrieved September 13, 2012, from http://www.bptrends.com/publications.cfm

deLara, J., & Vangheluwe, H. (2004). Defining visual notations and their manipulation through meta-modelling and graph transformation. *Journal of Visual Languages and Computing, 15*(3-4), 309–330. doi:10.1016/j.jvlc.2004.01.005.

Diskin, Z., & Dingel, J. (2006). A metamodel independent framework for model transformation: Towards generic model management patterns in reverse engineering. In *Proceedings of the 3rd International Workshop on Metamodels, Schemas, Grammars, and Ontologies (ATEM '06)*. Genoa, Italy: ATEM.

Favre, J. M., Estublier, J., & Blay-Fornarino, M. (2006). *L'Ingénierie dirigée par les modèles: Au-delà du MDA*. Hermes Science.

France, R., & Rumpe, B. (2007). Model-driven development of complex software: A research roadmap. In *Proceedings of FOSE'07 Future of Software Engineering* (pp. 37-54). FOSE.

Greenfield, J., & Short, K. (2003). Software factories assembling applications with patterns, models, frameworks and tools. [Anaheim, CA: OOPSLA.]. *Proceedings of OOPSLA, 03*, 16–27.

Gronback, R. C. (2009). Graphical modeling framework runtime. In *Eclipse Modeling Project: A Domain-Specific Language (DSL) Toolkit* (pp. 353–502). New York: Pearson Education, Inc..

Hemel, Z., Kats, L. C. L., & Visser, E. (2008). Code generation by model transformation: A case study in transformation modularity. []. Berlin: Springer.]. *Software & Systems Modeling, 9*, 183–198.

Hill, D. R. C. (1996). *Object-oriented analysis and simulation*. Reading, MA: Addison-Wesley Longman.

Hill, D. R. C., & Gourgand, M. (1993). A multi-domain tool for object-oriented simulation. In *TOOLS 10* (pp. 181–195). Versailles, France: Prentice Hall.

Kelly, S., & Tolvanen, J.-P. (2008). *Domain-specific modeling: Enabling full code generation*. New York: Wiley - IEEE Computer Society Press. doi:10.1002/9780470249260.

Minsky, M. (1965). *Matter, mind and models*. Cambridge, MA: MIT Press.

Russel, N., terHofstede, A. H. M., van der Aalst, W. M. P., & Mulyar, N. (2006). *Workflow control-flow patterns: A revised view*. BPM center Report BPM-06-22.

Steinberg, D., Budinsky, F., Paternostro, M., & Merks, E. (2008). *EMF: Eclipse modeling framework* (2nd ed.). Reading, MA: Addison-Wesley Professional.

Zeigler, B. P. (1976). *Theory of modelling and simulation*. New York: John Wiley.

KEY TERMS AND DEFINITIONS

Abstract Syntax: It corresponds to the concepts associated to the specific domains the language is built for. In a model driven approach, it consists in a metamodel and a set of constraint rules defining the way the different concepts can be associated one to another.

Concrete: Syntax: This syntax is used by the modeler to define a model with respect to the abstract syntax as defined above, this concrete syntax may be either textual and/or graphical.

Crop Model: Mechanistic model with a rather simple representation of the biophysical processes and plant data structures as opposed to Functional Structural Plant Models (FSPM).

Domain Specific Language/Domain Specific Modeling Language (DSL/DSML): Some authors distinguish the former by being limited to textual languages, from the latter which should be focused on graphical languages. We consider that the difference made between DSL and DSML is irrelevant since it only relies on different syntactic presentations. Combining graphical and textual syntax is useful in our case and could be used in many application domains. This leads to the notion of "hybrid DSL."

Model: A model is an abstraction representing a system. The simplification level and choices of the modeling process are guided by the modeler objectives. We also propose the following definition by Marvin Minsky from a paper that can be found in the additional reading section: *To an observer B, an object A* is a model of an object A to the extent that B can use A* to answer questions that interest him about A. The model relation is inherently ternary* (Minsky, 1965, p. 45).

Simulation: *Simulation consists in bringing about the evolution of model in time in order to assist in understanding the operation and behaviour of the system and to apprehend some of its dynamic characteristics with a view to evaluating various decisions* (Hill, 1996, p. 276).

Software Factory: The term factory refers to the industrialization process of artifacts production. Industrialization of software production conforming to validated specifications is among the main goals of Model Driven Engineering. By raising the abstraction level of software design gain should be made on productivity and manufacturing costs. Crop Model Factory is a software factory dedicated to crop model production.

Chapter 7
Model–Driven Engineering for Electronic Commserce

Giovanny Mauricio Tarazona Bermúdez
Distrital Francisco José de Caldas University, Colombia

Luz Andrea Rodríguez Rojas
University of Oviedo, Spain

ABSTRACT

The chapter explores the development of a specific process e-Commerce metamodel for reuse and interoperability, which is proposed to obtain the taxonomy of e-business processes. It defines a specific ontology and semantics of independent processes platform. This is achieved with the help of the principles proposed by the Model Driven Engineering (MDE), specifically the proposal for the OMG, Model Driven Architecture (MDA), enabling it to minimize the time and effort required to create ecommerce solutions.

INTRODUCTION

The competitive scenario in which operate business organizations are forced to create value as a condition of sustainability, the rapid development of Information Technology and Communications (ICT) make necessary to incorporate the modernization of business processes

within framework strategic organizational and technological. The boom in e-commerce as technology has had on the global industry and its impact on the organizational structure, has led to the development of multiple solutions in parallel to the traditional trade.

Enterprises are forced to implement changes in your organization to maximize the opportunities offered by electronic commerce, otherwise are going into bankruptcy. Therefore, the effective implementation of the strategy for e-business transformation turns out to be a critical factor for sustainable competitive advantage (Qingfeng, Wenbo, & Lihua, 2008).

BACKGROUND

Electronic commerce is the buying and selling of products or services over electronic means such as the Internet and other computer networks, its implementation offers advantages to buyers and sellers; the use of electronic commerce facilitates sellers to access narrow market segments that are widely distributed while buyers can benefit from access to global markets with greater availability of products from a variety of offers at reduced costs, this situation improves product quality and

DOI: 10.4018/978-1-4666-4217-1.ch007

the creation of new forms of business(Grandon & Pearson, 2004).

Originally, the term applies to the execution of transactions through electronic transactions, such as electronic data interchange. However, with the arrival of the Internet in the mid-90s, began referring mainly to the sale of products and services on the Internet through e-payment. The amount of trade conducted electronically has grown extraordinarily since the spread of the Internet. A wide variety of commerce is conducted in this way, spurring the creation and use of innovations such as electronic funds transfer, management of the supply chain, marketing on the Internet, online transaction processing, electronic data interchange, system inventory management and automated data collection (Carmona et al., 2012).

Electronic commerce is also defined as the purchase of products from suppliers and selling to customers using ICT. There are several models of e-commerce, Business to Business (B2B) Business to Consumer (B2C), Business and Government (B2G). Broadly, electronic business (e-business) covers all kinds of collaborations with partners, using ICT, and provides for legal purposes. A business interaction is the electronic exchange of business documents or a message containing a business document vital in a business process, these activities play a key role in the collaboration. Since the late 1960s, enterprises have used information systems for electronic data exchange with trading partners.

Electronic integration has led to dramatic changes in the definition of an enterprise, with the emergence of virtual enterprises whose capabilities to offer their products to market are defined largely by their ability to organize and maintain a network of business relationships in rather than for their ability to produce a product or provide a service. To understand an individual company, you need to study business networks in which it is immersed (Zwass, 1996).

Electronic commerce is a guiding strategic decisions in the domain business to business

(B2B), this is a favorable impact on the Internet. There is consensus on the influence on the Internet as a platform for development of alternative channels and / or complementary distribution. The proliferation of electronic commerce can be related to multiple business processes (Faroughian, Kalafatis, Ledden, Samouel, & Tsogas, 2012).

Faced with the evidence that Web proved to be an effective channel for trade, have suggested different views on how companies should develop an e-commerce strategy. Sung-Chi and others define a structure of building e-commerce Web sites with four major areas to break down the core technology that provide the functions that allow to conduct e-commerce activities (Chu et al. 2007) in Figure 1 shows the four areas with representative examples.

Comunications: For any of the parties involved in electronic commerce activities must establish a virtual channel.

Information Presentation and Representation: This specifies the presentation of information (format) and how to organize the exchange (plain text, graphic images, sound and video, or a combination).

Language: Precise and logical steps for handling data and computing resources is the critical

Figure 1. The core technology areas

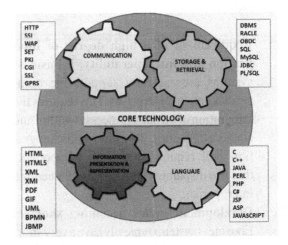

component that forms the foundation of the intelligence capability of a Web Site.

Storage and Retrieval: Precise and logical steps for handling data and computing resources is the critical component that forms the foundation of the intelligence capability of a Web Site.

Integration and Interoperability of Electronic Commerce Platforms

There are multiple platforms that provide e-commerce solutions, just as enterprises develop their own Websites according to their particular requirements. Upon selecting an e-commerce solution some essential feature is the integration with reporting tools, recommender systems, e-CRM, ERP, multimedia repositories, Marketing tools, category trees, shopping purchase, backoffice, multilanguage, multicurrency payment gateways, security, email alerts, among others. Each solution addressing these processes develops minimum standards that limit the reuse and interoperability.

During the last decade, e-business systems have gained rapid evolved from simple and static systems on the Web, where provided information and promoted products, to highly complex systems and dynamic applications that support business processes and transactions between companies.

Consequently, the development of e-commerce has become more complex applications systems. Some of the challenges business processes and technology have are:

1. **Requirement of a high degree of integration and interoperability:** E-business systems are radically support the competitiveness of enterprises. This requires the integration of business processes within and across companies. To achieve this integration will require distributed components that use disparate technologies that need to interoperate.

2. **Development cycles becoming shorter:** Ebusiness systems typically have a very short time to build. The development cycle of these applications should be reduced considerably to meet changing requirements.

3. **Quality:** Despite the fulfillment of e-business system gives the required functionality, the system must also meet the quality requirements must be reliable and efficient in their use.

4. **Technology changes:** In many ways, the technologies are the cause of the changes. A clear separation of business logic and technology will make the e-business systems more resistant to change.

5. **Shortage of qualified staff:** The complexity of e-business systems generates great demand on the skills of the developers and these demands are difficult to meet due to the shortage of architects and developers experienced e-business.(Zhao, Macaulay, Adams, & Verschueren, 2008).

Moreover, the analysis of e-business models is a complex process that involves selecting and implementing the most appropriate model to facilitate business transformation. After that a company has chosen an appropriate e-business model, should ensure a steady development enough to survive in the intense global competition. The right model is the first important question to consider and has enormous potential for business transformation but not enough if not focuses its improvement (Zou & Deng, 2011).

Automating the sales process achieved way online transactions, reduce the global burden of support staff (Soto & Meroño, 2009). The Website is the portal through which most electronic transactions are carried out, the degree of automation of the sales process will be influenced by the emphasis on the integration of the business with the e-commerce model implemented. Therefore, the performance of the company may be influenced by the features and orientations of e-business.

When the data is processed and automatically communicating, processing time is reduced.

Therefore, automated business interactions, using ICT, can be faster and less error-prone manual business interactions using email, phone calls, or faxes. Unfortunately, they are not easy to automate business processes and their interactions. Information systems are not interoperable due to differences between the companies. There would be fewer problems in electronic commerce if all companies use the same information systems, the meanings of the terms and the same modes of operation (Nurmilaakso & Kotinurmi, 2004).

If information systems are not interoperable, human intervention is necessary to prepare the data to be processed. Differences in technology infrastructure between enterprises are unavoidable, implementation costs forcing use despite the difficulties of interoperability. Fortunately, the rules may provide a way to reduce these costs. The rules put in order of complexity and uncertainty by reducing the variety. The standardization of business documents and business processes promotes interoperability by harmonizing the meanings of the terms and modalities of operations. Enterprises can streamline their information systems, as long as use the same kind of business documents, business processes and optimize their messaging interfaces. (Nurmilaakso, 2008).

Future research should be directed to fund new e-commerce standards to determine the contribution of value to a group of companies and check whether the proposed rules live up to of your expectations and sustainability in context (Kauremaa, Nurmilaakso, & Kari, 2010).

For Qingfeng and other criteria such as income and position in the value chain, interaction and integration of value chain patterns, functional integration and degree of innovation; core activities and price, economic control and value integration and supply suggest using different frameworks closely defined taxonomy of e-business models (Qingfeng et al., 2008). These criteria are essential to define the metamodel.

The accumulated knowledge in the field of engineering design and usability is not sufficiently organized and structured in terms of their representation to facilitate the construction of e-commerce applications. This is one of the factors hampering the proper use of ontologies in the analysis and domain to develop e-commerce software. From the identification of critical variables such as business goals and user characteristics, it is possible to infer that the formalization of knowledge through ontologies can be successfully incorporated into the development of such solutions (Bakaev & Avdeenko, 2010). Standards are required in order to develop successful business models and thus evaluate the strategy to ensure maximization of impact (Huang, Tzeng, & Ho, 2011).

Currently, there is an effort in creating information systems based on ontologies and is based on domain-specific ontologies including using the representation of processes in information sharing and annotation of resources. The characteristics of the representation languages Web-oriented, such as OWL ontologies, facilitate generic conceptualizations that can be used in several domains, facilitating the creation of systems based Web portals with ability to automate business processes (Garcia, Ruiz, Lopez, & Gonzalez, 2011).

Gonzalez and others propose a solution that begins with the generation of an ontology and then with the modeling of the processes of e-commerce standard, using the Model Driven Engineering (MDE) to achieve the transformation of the models proposed so as to permit go of the most general (Requirements) to the particular (Deploying the Solution) through the conversion of these models. (González et al., 2011)

METAMODEL OF PROCESSES ELECTRONIC COMMERCE

The following describes the methodology that leads to the specification proposed metamodel. We present advances in the taxonomy of e-business processes, subprocess of an integrated e-commerce, the study of existing e-commerce platforms, selection and evaluation criteria, the proposed ontology scheme and preliminary specification metamodel.

Approach to Taxonomy Processes of Electronic Commerce

Taxonomy of e-commerce processes to define a feasible business model to be automated with an MDE tool, then seeks in this section define the processes and sub-processes that interact with business e-commerce solutions.

Initially describes the enterprise system then processes listed by subsystem in which e-commerce solution can impact favorably. For the modeling of business processes that interact with e-commerce is required to analyze the company with an integrated approach like general systems theory.

All companies follow a particular business model. A business model describes the design and architecture of the mechanisms of value creation, selection, and hiring of employees and business sustainability. The essence of a business model is that crystallizes customer needs and ability to pay, defines how the company responds and delivers value to customers, applying innovation (Teece, 2010).

Analyze the company as open system has been proposed by various authors, based on the precepts of the biologist Ludwig von Bertalanffy (2006) to define the remarkable at the same time improbable permanent equilibrium process and increased level of organization of living systems and many of the social, economic and industrial man-made could not be explained from the perspective of increasing entropy. The reason should be sought in the fact that these systems interact with their environment: are open systems. These systems exchange with its environment flows of matter, energy and information and these flows make essential differences with closed systems (Sarabia, 1995).

The enterprise viewed under vision system as a complex system exceeds the analytical approach which examines in detail and thorough parties to a narrow scope of reality, losing the overview. Under the systems approach are elaborated models used in making business decisions and manageable systems that allow simplify systems to operational dimensions. The enterprise as system is related to its environment, which receives inputs in the form of human resources, financial, material, etc., that by suitable transformation allows to obtain results in the form of products and / or services as system outputs.

Computer applications in the enterprise have been helpful in achieving competitiveness making more efficient its management, example of this is the office tools, data warehousing, accounting, decision support systems, e-commerce solutions, Enterprise Resource Planning (ERP), social networks, etc.

The architecture of an e-commerce solution in the context of Web 2.0, you must consider the elements of environments as investors, suppliers, competitors, distribution channels and regulatory entities that allow external customer satisfaction, with an organizational structure coordinated (internal customers) aimed at creating value for customers and shareholders. The business structure is composed by the subsystems management, production, human talent, financial, and commercial.

This architecture cannot get away from the concept of Enterprise Resource Planning (ERP) and its advantages for being a proposed integrative, flexible, scalable and easy to capacity planning decision making (Leon, 2008). A key element is the technological infrastructure that must be managed with their most important active, people, connectivity, hardware, applications and Web portal. This infrastructure should be directed to Customer Relationship Management (CRM) (Raab, Ajami, Gargeya, & Goddard, 2008) using the potential of Internet e-CRM.

The architecture should address key issues in functionality in the context of Web 2.0, social networks pursuant to dynamic interaction possibilities with customers and stakeholders (Yu & Kong, 2011), Web analytics as a tool for decision making based on indicators of Web accessibility (Carmona et al., 2012), Online marketing, cloud computing like technological infrastructure available with moderate investment (Marston, Li, Bandyopadhyay, Zhang, & Ghalsasi, 2011), social media, business rules and processes and knowledge management (Öztayşi & Kaya, 2011). Figure 2 shows the schematic of the proposed architecture for e-business solutions in Web 2.0.

Is important to note that the implementation of innovative processes supported by the proposed e-commerce model, it is necessary for companies to appropriate knowledge management models that allow the previous experience in the use of technological resources and tools that facilitate the appropriation of concepts and procedures outlined in this document (Tarazona, Rodriguez, Pelayo-Garcia, & Sanjuan, 2012).

Subprocesses of an Integrated E-Commerce Solution: Metamodel Elements

Figure 3 shows the elements of Proposed Metamodel based on the subprocesses developed in an integrated e-commerce solution.

Implementation of E-Commerce Site: Result of Technology strategic aligned with business strategy to deploy the Web site ensuring content management capacity for e-commerce.

Customer Interaction with E-Commerce Site: With the implementation of a platform for user-friendly design is achieved customer interaction with the portal overcoming barriers psychological safety and electronics to achieve an actual sale.

Selection and Purchase Order Product/ Service: The customer browses the catalog of products or services, select the one that interests and generates the purchase order.

Online Payment: The e-commerce site contains an electronic payment manager that facilitates online payment process.

Generating Sales Order and Customer Registration: Order is generated and managed in The

Figure 2. Architecture for e-business solutions in web 2.0

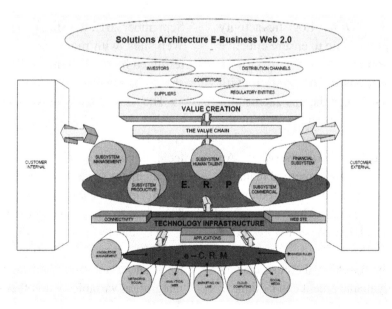

Figure 3. Flow diagram for an integrated solution e-commerce

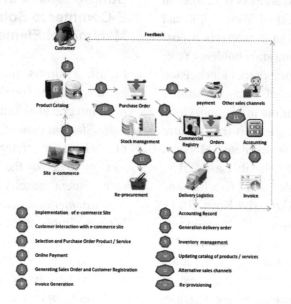

repositories and accounting modules and carry out a customer data storage, with the goals of feeding recommendation systems.

Invoice Generation: It generates support purchase accounting (invoice) with taxes and discounts.

Accounting Record: The integration of electronic sales with the accounting applications must be provided in order to update the required information.

Generation Delivery Order: Logistics activity begins with the report of sale to ensure effective delivery to the customer.

Inventory Management: Integration with inventory module facilitates the management of them recording available units and facilitating the process of re-order.

Updated Catalog of Products/Services: An adequate update facilitates commercial management, accounting, and inventory of the company.

Alternative Sales Channels: The company can have alternative channels like physical stores, other distributors, etc.

Re-Provisioning: Based on the customer information Resupply management can be done.

STUDY OF E-COMMERCE PLATFORMS

To guide the construction of the metamodel, main solutions and content management of electronic commerce available in the market were reviewed.

To select the electronic commerce platforms were considered two recent studies. Quantcast Corp. and research firm Internet marketing infoAnalytica Consulting Pvt. Ltd., published in September 2012 statistics of the best e-commerce Web sites, with more than a million hits as determined by the volume of data traffic. Figure 4 shows the results.

The second study by wappalyzer.com in December 2012 evaluates market share. Wappalyzer is a tool available online to discover the technologies used on Websites. It detects content management systems, Web shops, Web servers, JavaScript frameworks, analytical tools and more. Their results are shown in Figure 5.

We selected platforms Magento, Prestashop and RBS change. Evaluation variables were defined and associated features. For example, the integration variables with other information sys-

Figure 4. E-commerce solutions in the top 1 million hits

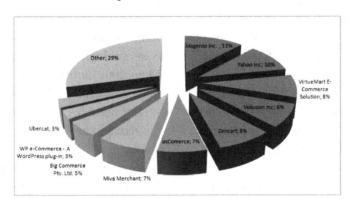

Figure 5. Market share

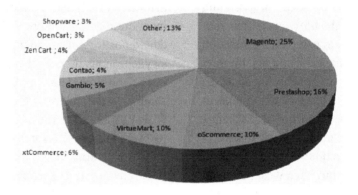

tems has the characteristics of Integration / file sharing, Web Services, Api, Real Time, Complexity of Data Migration. The same procedure was followed for the variables mobile version, fidelity, sales promotion, product and store information, payment, inventory management and geolocation.

These e-commerce solutions are developed on free platforms and are available to users, versions without costs have basic functionality if you want get better functionality service and support should assume a cost.

To install PrestaShop 1.5 is required A Web-host providing the following: PHP 5.2 or later,MySQL 5.0 or later. Better if: Unix hosting, Apache Web Server 1.3 or later, at least 64 Mb of RAM. (Prestashop, 2013)Access codes to FTP server and MySQL database (provided by your Web-host)., a text editor, a FTP client and a Web browser.

Magento is built on Zend Framework, to ensure that the code is safe and scalable basis (Allen, 2013). Zend Framework 2 is an open source framework for developing Web applications and services using PHP 5.3+. it uses 100% object-oriented code and utilises most of the new features of PHP 5.3, namely namespaces, late static binding, lambda functions and closures.

Magento was built with three basic principles in mind: Flexibility. The code allows customization Magento adequate. Upgradeable: Separating the kernel code, the community and customizations (X Commerce, 2013); Magento can be customized easily without losing the ability to upgrade. Speed and Security: The coding standards used by developers, follow best practices to maximize the efficiency of the software and provide a secure online showcase.

The CMS, of RBS Change, is developed using a framework object-oriented PHP 5 allows (RBS-CHANGE, 2013). An abstraction of object DBMS-R, any data is "document", described in XML Exchange handles the creation of SQL schema simple API query object documents database, complex queries on trees, joints Inheritance between documents as PHP objects, documents support inheritance factorization of code, maintainability increased

Managing document versions: archiving different versions, collision detection between editors, lifecycle standardized documents: from "draft" to "archived" through "published" or "Pending validation" (workflow), the life cycle is clear, automatic and customizable transitions Organization tree structures: trees manage documents. Imports XML easily populate your database using XML configurable flow .Cache instance documents at the request PHP and between queries, Change implements strategies to collect heavy loads.

The platforms analyzed have performed well in its core functionality but have weaknesses in other variables related to the integration with other systems, product and store information (product catalog), the availability of mobile operation aspects. These weaknesses hinder interoperability and the reuse what is the challenge we must overcome the proposed metamodel.

DEFINING SEMANTICS PROCESS INDEPENDENT OF THE PLATFORM

The ontology definition of e-business processes are developed to be deployed later on any platform using transformations based models. ontologies are models for specifying the semantics of concepts used by various heterogeneous sources in a well defined and unambiguous way (Selma et al., 2012). On the other hand, Ontologies exist in various domains (E-commerce, Engineering, Tourism, etc.) and are used to increase interoperability between sources. They may be used to improve communication between decision makers and users collaborating together, by specifying the semantics of the used concepts. A useful approach is of ontologies for services (Silva, Viamonte, & Maio, 2009) aimed at overcoming interoperability in e-commerce applications.

In Figure 6 shows an ontology that supports the metamodel based on the proposed by (Sun & Wang, 2012). It has been adapted taking into account the criteria specified in the evaluation of e-commerce solutions documented in this chapter.

The ontology proposal focuses on the definition of specific rules aimed to characterize the activities of product catalog management. The interaction of customers and suppliers with the data repository of products and services must be a synchronous process that enables to efficiency of the solution. The supplier has a pre-indexed catalog to a database which should be updated online to facilitate the comparison process and recovery that classifies and deployment the results. Protégé is proposed as a tool for data processing, it facilitates extract metadata. The reasoning engine could be JENA, application development Java libraries semantic code. Data Indexing is relational using SQL, the output is the ontology using the OWL language.

DEVELOPMENT TOOLS METAMODEL

We will use the framework EMF (Eclipse Modeling Framework) (Eclipse Foundation, 2012) which is a framework that works on eclipse, its main uses are modeled through class models and source code generation (Kehn, Fairbrother, & Le, 2002). This proposal is consistent with the vision of using MDE tools. The purpose is to automatically generate source code.

Model Ecore is required, it is a manual editor operates as a navigation tree for the creation model based on Ecore (Eclipse Foundation, 2013a). Other tool required is Ecore Diagram, which is a

Figure 6. Ontology proposed for product catalog

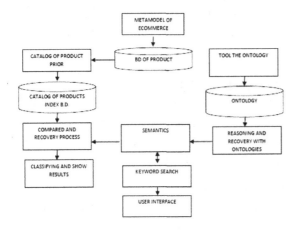

graphical editor similar to the tools for creating class diagrams UML. Generates a file XMI (XML Metadata Interchange) which is a specification for sharing diagrams.

CONSTRUCTION OF THE DSL MODEL

As you are working under Eclipse, to build the editor or DSL is used GMF Tooling (Graphical Modeling Framework Tooling) (Eclipse Foundation, 2013b) makes part of the GMP (Graphical Modeling Project). The diagram obtained as a result of using the DSL editor, will be associated with a file that XMI syntax based on the metamodel created. Figure 7 presents a preliminary metamodel.

For the generation of code, there are several technologies that are integrated into Eclipse, such as Acceleo, Jet, Xpand and MOFScript (Eclipse Foundation, 2013c) all use the same principle, the creation of transformation rules based a metamodel. These rules will be applied to the model to generate code in the language required, these technologies are called M2T or Model to Text. The transformation from one model to another is called M2M or Model to Model, tools such as ATL or OperationalQVT, perform this task. Finally applying transformational technolo-

Figure 7. Preliminary metamodel

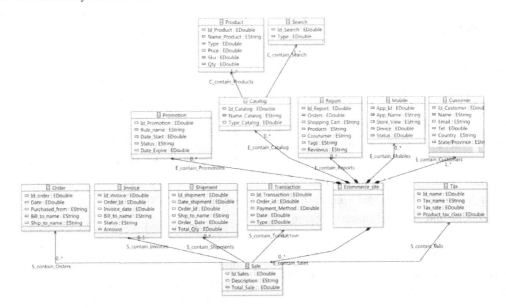

gies on the model you get the code in the format defined for deployment.

The DSL build software in HTML, JavaScript and PHP and maintaining the persistence characteristics of a MySQL database. Therefore all generated code will be Web, allowing to be accessed from any operating system and the only software requirement is a Web browser.

FUTURE RESEARCH DIRECTIONS

- Ontology development and proposal requires adjustment to improve the taxonomy of e-commerce processes.
- The metamodel development and implementation require an evaluation of their results.
- It requires the construction of a functional prototype of the proposed elements that make use of the tools provided by the model driven engineering.
- The e-commerce solutions are subject to constant changes in the business environment monitoring their performance and new features are a constant challenge for research.

CONCLUSION

- This chapter describes the research aimed at resolving the challenges in integrating e-commerce solutions. Describes a proposal developed from the evaluation of existing solutions seeking to overcome their weaknesses.
- A detailed analysis of the existing platforms oriented functional requirements metamodel and the preliminary design of the ontology.
- Using the tools provided by MDA and development environments that support it are useful in solving the problem.

- The proposed metamodel does meet the expectations of interoperability and reuse provided for in research objectives.

REFERENCES

Allen, R. (2013). *Getting started with zend framework 1.11*. Retrieved January 6, 2013, from http://akrabat.com/zend-framework-tutorial/

Bakaev, M., & Avdeenko, T. (2010). Ontology to support web design activities in e-commerce software development process. In Y. Shokin, I. Bychkov, & O. Potaturkin (Eds.), *Proceedings of IASTED ACIT2010* (pp. 241–248). ACTA Press. Retrieved from http://www.iasted.org/conferences/sessionpapers-691.html

Carmona, C., Ramírez-Gallego, S., Torres, F., Bernal, E., del Jesus, M. J., & García, S. (2012). Web usage mining to improve the design of an e-commerce website: OrOliveSur.com. *Expert Systems with Applications, 39*(12), 11243–11249. doi:10.1016/j.eswa.2012.03.046.

Commerce, X. I. (2013). *Magento documentation*. Retrieved January 6, 2013, from http://docs.magentocommerce.com/

Eclipse Foundation. (2013a). *Ecore tools*. Retrieved from http://wiki.eclipse.org/index.php/Ecore_Tools

Eclipse Foundation. (2013b). *Graphical modeling framework (GMF) tooling*. Retrieved from http://www.eclipse.org/projects/project.php?id=modeling.gmp.gmf-tooling

Eclipse Foundation. (2013c). *MOFScript documentation*. Retrieved from http://www.eclipse.org/gmt/mofscript/doc/

Faroughian, F. F., Kalafatis, S. P., Ledden, L., Samouel, P., & Tsogas, M. H. (2012). Value and risk in business-to-business e-banking. *Industrial Marketing Management, 41*(1), 68–81. doi:10.1016/j.indmarman.2011.11.012.

Garcia, A., Ruiz, B., Lopez, J. L., & Gonzalez, I. (2011). Semantic model for knowledge representation in e-business. *Knowledge-Based Systems*, *24*(2), 282–296. doi:10.1016/j.knosys.2010.09.006.

González, R., Martinez, O. S., Cueva, J., Garcia-Bustelo, B. C., Gayo, J. E. L., & Ordoñez, P. (2011). Recommendation system based on user interaction data applied to intelligent electronic books. *Computers in Human Behavior*, *27*(4), 1445–1449. doi:10.1016/j.chb.2010.09.012.

Grandon, E., & Pearson, M. (2004). Electronic commerce adoption: An empirical study of small and medium US businesses. *Information & Management, 42*(1), 197–216. Retrieved fromhttp://dx.doi.org/10.1016/j.im.2003.12.010

Huang, C.-Y., Tzeng, G.-H., & Ho, W.-R. J. (2011). System on chip design service e-business value maximization through a novel MCDM framework. *Expert Systems with Applications*, *38*(7), 7947–7962. doi:10.1016/j.eswa.2010.12.022.

Kauremaa, J., Nurmilaakso, J.-M., & Kari, T. (2010). E-business enabled operational linkages: The role of RosettaNet in integrating the telecommunications supply chain. *International Journal of Production Economics*, *127*(2), 343–357. doi:10.1016/j.ijpe.2009.08.024.

Kehn, D., Fairbrother, S., & Le, C.-T. (2002). *How to internationalize your eclipse plug-in.* Retrieved from http://www.eclipse.org/articles/Article-Internationalization/how2I18n.html

Leon, A. (2008). *Enterprise resource planning.* Retrieved from http://books.google.es/books?hl=es&lr=&id=pTGDy2GX_sUC&oi=fnd&pg=PT20&dq=ENTERPRISE+RESOURCE+PLANNING&ots=Apu7El9-p3&sig=0x5rNgyVcMhCeYNgwnywc0IZGKE

Marston, S., Li, Z., Bandyopadhyay, S., Zhang, J., & Ghalsasi, A. (2011). Cloud computing — The business perspective. *Decision Support Systems*, *51*(1), 176–189. doi:10.1016/j.dss.2010.12.006.

Nurmilaakso, J.-M. (2008). EDI, XML and e-business frameworks: A survey. *Computers in Industry*, *59*(4), 370–379. doi:10.1016/j.compind.2007.09.004.

Nurmilaakso, J.-M., & Kotinurmi, P. (2004). A review of XML-based supply-chain integration. *Production Planning and Control, 15*(6), 608–621. doi:10.1080/09537280412331283937.

Öztayşi, B., & Kaya, T. (2011). Performance comparison based on customer relationship management using analytic network process. *Expert Systems with Applications, 38*(11), 9788–9798. doi:http://dx.doi.org/10.1016/j.eswa.2011.01.170

Prestashop. (2013). *Prestashop.* Retrieved from http://www.prestashop.com/blog/en/upgrade-your-online-store-to-prestashop-v1-4-9/

Qingfeng, Z., Wenbo, C., & Lihua, H. (2008). E-business transformation: An analysis framework based on critical organizational dimensions. *Tsinghua Science and Technology, 13*(3), 408–413. doi:10.1016/S1007-0214(08)70065-8.

Raab, G., Ajami, R., Gargeya, V., & Goddard, G. J. (2008). *Customer relationship management: A global perspective.* Retrieved from http://books.google.es/books?id=MCKX_5Ur5rEC&printsec=frontcover&dq=customer+relationship&hl=es&sa=X&ei=kbzdUJWQFMu6hAeV0YC4BA&ved=0CF8Q6AEwBg

RBS-CHANGE. (2013). *Guide du développeur.* Retrieved January 7, 2013, from http://wiki.rbschange.fr/devguide:start

Selma, K., Ilyès, B., Ladjel, B., Eric, S., Stéphane, J., & Baron, M. (2012). Ontology-based structured web data warehouses for sustainable interoperability: Requirement modeling, design methodology and tool. *Computers in Industry, 63*(8), 799 – 812. Retrieved fromhttp://dx.doi.org/10.1016/j.compind.2012.08.001

Silva, N., Viamonte, M. J., & Maio, P. (2009). Agent-based electronic market with ontology-services. In *Proceedings of the 2009 IEEE International Conference on e-Business Engineering*, (pp. 51–58). IEEE. doi:10.1109/ICEBE.2009.17

Soto, P., & Meroño, A. (2009). Evaluating internet technologies business effectiveness. *Telematics and Informatics*, 26(2), 211–221. doi:10.1016/j.tele.2008.01.004.

Sun, J., & Wang, L. (2012). Research on e-commerce data management based on semantic web. In *Proceedings of the 2012 IEEE 14ᵗʰ International Conference on High Performance Computing and Communication & 2012 IEEE 9ᵗʰ International Conference on Embedded Software and Systems*, (pp. 925–928). IEEE. doi:10.1109/HPCC.2012.133

Tarazona, G. M., Rodriguez, L., & Pelayo-Garcia, C., & Sanjuan. (2012). Model innovation of process based on the standard e-commerce international GS1. *International Journal of Interactive Multimedia and Artificial Intelligence*, 1(7), 70. doi:10.9781/ijimai.2012.178.

von Bertalanffy, L. (2006). *Teoría general de los sistemas: Fundamentos, desarrollo, aplicaciones* (Económica, F. de C., Ed.). Mexico: Segunda.

Yu, Y., & Kong, K. (2011). The research of enterprise boundary from the perspective of social network. *E-Business and E-Government (ICEE), 2011*. Retrieved from http://ieeexplore.ieee.org/xpls/abs_all.jsp?arnumber=5887220

Zhao, L., Macaulay, L., Adams, J., & Verschueren, P. (2008). A pattern language for designing e-business architecture. *Journal of Systems and Software*, 81(8), 1272–1287. doi:10.1016/j.jss.2007.11.717.

Zou, Z., & Deng, Y. (2011). The evaluation model of e-business based on process. *Energy Procedia*, 13, 5601–5608. doi:10.1016/j.egypro.2011.12.208.

Zwass, V. (1996). Electronic commerce. *Structures and Issues, 1*(1).

KEY TERMS AND DEFINITIONS

B2B (Business-to-Business): On the Internet, also known as e-biz, is the exchange of products, services, or information between businesses rather than between businesses and consumers.

Business to Customer (B2C): Through the network, the company offers its products to customers who accessed the quantity you need, do hereby numerous products currently marketed.

Business to Government (B2G): Here are the transactions carried out between different companies and government organizations, such as paying taxes, even though this is true in its infancy.

Customer to Customer (C2C): It was one of the first e-business practices appeared in the early 90's Web pages are little known and specialized. Your maximum evolution came with the popularization of e-bay that gives the possibility of direct sales between its users.

Customer to Government (C2G): Here the user would communicate with state agencies to make their tax payments or social assistance, although this is not instituted yet, it's about time it is.

Operation (Order Management): The fulfillment of customer orders from sale to shipping, which include handling returns and supporting orders and warranties backed by customer support.

Regulatory Entities: Government agencies or legally exert social control and audit of the business transactions in shares and seeks to safeguard the interests of users.

T-Commerce: The idea is to let users buy products over the Internet but through their interactive television, instead of over a phone (m-commerce) or through a PC or PDA.

Chapter 8
Process for the Validation of System Architectures against Requirements

André Pflüger
SOPHIST GmbH, Germany

Wolfgang Golubski
University of Applied Sciences of Zwickau, Germany

Stefan Queins
SOPHIST GmbH, Germany

ABSTRACT

The development of systems consisting of hardware and software is a challenging task for the system architect. On the one hand, he has to consider an increasing number of system requirements, including the dependencies between them for designing the system architecture; on the other hand, he has to deal with a shortened time-to-market period and requirements changes of the customers up to the implementation phase. This chapter presents a process that enables the architect to validate the system architecture against the architecture-relevant requirements. The process is part of the system design phase and can be integrated in the iterative design of the system architecture. In order to keep track of all requirements, including their dependencies, the architect clusters the requirements according to architecture-specific aspects, the so-called validation targets. For each target he defines examinations processes and check criteria to define the validation status. If all targets are valid, i.e., all check criteria are met by the result of the examination processes, the system architecture itself is valid. Instead of formal validation techniques like model checking, the approach prefers simulations for the examination processes. The approach uses model-based documentation based on the Unified Modeling Language (UML). All data required for the simulations is part of an UML model and extracted to configure and run the simulations. Therefore, changes in the model affect the validation result directly. The process supports the architect in building a system architecture that fulfills the architecture-relevant requirements, and it supports the architect in analyzing the impacts after requirements or architecture changes. A tool facilitates the work effort of the architect by partly automating the major process steps.

DOI: 10.4018/978-1-4666-4217-1.ch008

MOTIVATION

One major challenge in developing products consisting of hardware and software components is to create an architecture, which is consistent with the requirements. Such products or systems are specified by a continually growing amount of requirements, which are additionally linked to one another. This creates an increasing system complexity that the system architect has to deal with. The markets demand the system's customer to react flexible on changing conditions. As a consequence, the customer wants to influence the system development not only up to the system analysis but also up to implementation. These continually changing requirements make it difficult for the system architect to create and maintain the system architecture.

Although the architecture is the foundation of the system and changing it in a later development phase causes much effort and therefore money, architecture validation, i.e. checking if all architecture-relevant requirements are met, is often part of the system development in name only. According to our experiences, if anything, the validation is performed only once and almost at the end of the design phase. One reason might be that it is a time- and work-consuming task for the architect that has to be repeated each time requirements change. Another reason might be the often applied informal techniques, e.g. reviews, which are tedious and rely on human interpretation

and subjectivity. These techniques do not generate reproducible validation results or provide automation possibilities. Therefore, they are not suitable for a system development with ever-changing requirements. Formal techniques like model checking are more suited for this task. Nevertheless, despite of their capability, the acceptance and usage in industry is very low (Woodcock, Larsen, Bicarregui, & Fitzgerald, 2009).

To support the architect in validating the system architecture under the conditions described above, we developed a validation process for system architectures using dynamic validation techniques like simulations (Debabbi, Hassaine, Jarraya, Soeanu, & Alawneh, 2010) based on the Unified Modeling Language (UML). It can be integrated into the iterative process of creating system architectures and is therefore part of the system design phase. Figure 1 shows the validation process in the context of the first system development phase's system analysis and system design. The results of the system analysis are input for the system design whereas the results of the design phase are also input for the system analysis. Both phases and the architecture validation process need the system requirements. The architect creates a system architecture using the results of the system analysis and the requirements. It is validated by using the architecture-relevant requirements and validation-specific information. The validation process provides the architect an architecture-specific view on the requirements enabling him

Figure 1. Validation process in the context of system analysis and design

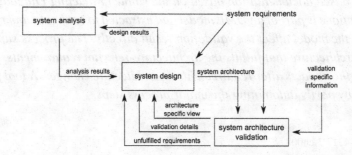

to handle the amount of requirements including their interconnections. This view is created by identifying validation targets which describe an architecture-specific aspect. A target is linked to all aspect-specific requirements reducing the amount of elements which have to be taken into account by the architect for the architecture validation. The architecture in its entirety is valid if all targets are valid. The validation statuses of the targets are checked by examination processes which use the information modeled in UML for their configuration. If the system architecture is invalid, the process provides the requirements which are not fulfilled and detailed information about the examination processes for problem analysis. After modifications of the architecture or requirements the architect reruns the validation process. The process provides automation possibilities to minimize the effort which can be done by machine.

Section *Description of the Validation Process* provides an overview over the validation process including the definitions of some basic terms. Section *Example of Use* applies the process on an example from the area of embedded systems and section *Support Tool* introduces the support tool and describes the application possibilities. Section *Detailed Process Description* provides a detailed description of the validation process followed by our experiences with this approach and a list of the benefits in section *Benefits and Experiences*. Section *Related Work* describes the related work for the introduced approach before section *Conclusion* concludes the chapter.

DESCRIPTION OF THE VALIDATION PROCESS

There are many definitions of the terms validation and verification in literature (Boehm, 1981; Endres, & Rombach, 2003; Grady, 1997; INCOSE, 2011; Pohl, 2010; Navy Modeling and Simulation Management Office, 2004). The differences

between them range from marginal to an inverse meaning of the terms. For our work we generally define validation as a process performed during or at the end of a development phase to check the resulting artifact(s) against the corresponding requirements specified prior to the phase. Verification is a process performed for approval of system parts or the entire system. The main differences are the checked artifacts and the point of time in system engineering at which the process is applied.

Figure 2 illustrates a simplified validation process by an UML activity diagram containing all relevant process steps. It serves as a starting point for the process description. A detailed description is given in section *Detailed Process Description*. All terms introduced and explained in this section are part of the term model in Figure 3 providing an overview of the terms and their connections. The acting person for the whole process is the system architect.

In the first step the system architect must *determine the validation targets* from the system requirements. A validation target sums up all requirements of one architecture-specific aspect and can be associated to other targets if these targets are depending on each other. It contains no check criteria required for the validation directly. These are part of the associated requirements (see Figure 3). A *check criterion* contains a comparative value and a logical operator. A good starting point for identifying validation targets are the non-functional requirements. Examples for validation targets are *performance* and *energy consumption* from the example described in section *Example of Use*. The target performance is connected to the requirement "The system shall provide tracks for fed in test data after 320ms." The target energy consumption is connected to the requirement "The system shall consume less than 220W." The check criteria for these requirements are "after 320ms" and "less than 220W." The two targets are connected to each other because the performance influences the energy consumption and vice versa.

Figure 2. Validation process for system architectures

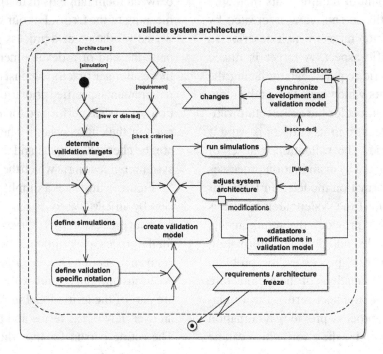

One validation target can be connected to many architecture-relevant requirements. An architecture-relevant requirement is a requirement which has influence on the architecture in

one way or another. It can be functional or non-functional. This excludes requirements dealing with the project itself, e.g. constraining project activities or describing deliverables such as

Figure 3. Overview of the basic terms of the validation process

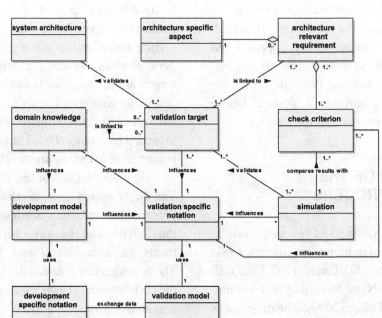

manuals or training documentation. A validation target is valid if all associated requirements are met by the system architecture. To check this, the architect has to *define simulations* in the next step. A simple simulation for the example target performance would be the sum up of all execution times required for providing tracks. The simulation result would have to fulfill the check criterion *<= 320ms*. A similar simulation could be defined for the target energy consumption.

To perform these simulations several data like the execution time of the software components and their execution order or the energy consumption of the hardware components are required. In our approach the simulations use the information modeled in an UML model as data source that is why the architect has to define the semantics of the UML elements allowing the simulation to extract the required values from the model. This definition of the semantic, the validation specific notation, are done by using the UML profile mechanism. The architect adds the stereotype *software* extending the UML meta-class Component to the profile of the validation target performance and adds the tagged value *executionTime* to this stereotype. By this tagged value the architect can add the execution time of each software component. The execution order can be modeled with the help of an activity diagram whereas the activities are connected to the software components. Assuming that only software components are used to provide tracks, all data required for this simulation is available in the UML model. For validating the target energy consumption the architect defines the stereotype *hardware* extending the UML meta-class Component and adds the tagged value *energyConsumption*.

Using the defined profiles the architect *creates the validation model* in the next step and adds all information required for running the simulations. For this step the architect can utilize the information already modeled in the development model. It contains all development-specific information whereas the validation model contains all struc-tural as well as behavioral information about the architecture required for the validation. This information is used on the one hand for configuration data and on the other hand as input parameter for the simulations. After running the simulations and evaluating their results, either the architect has to adjust the system architecture if at least one target validation failed or he has to synchronize the information in the validation and development model if all target validations succeeded. If any *changes* occur to *requirements*, *simulations* or the *architecture*, the architect has to rerun at least parts of the process. Due to the validation targets, the architect only has to rerun the simulations if requirements changes are limited to the check criteria. The whole validation process terminates with the *requirements or architecture freeze*.

EXAMPLE OF USE

The example in this chapter is reused from a previous experiment (Pflüger, Golubski, & Queins, 2011) but extended for the purpose of demonstrating the support tool that is not described in the previous work (Pflüger et al., 2011). We also use an improved simulation technique. Section *Domain Description* gives a brief introduction in the radar domain. Section *Apply the Validation Process* applies the validation process on the radar example and section *Requirement Change* describes how the change of a requirement is handled by the process.

Domain Description

The example is from the area of embedded systems: a simplified radar system. It receives echoes of electro-magnetic signals from an antenna, processes these data in real-time and provides visible · tracks on a radar display. Figure 4 illustrates the activities for processing radar signals. It shows that in a radar processor the data processing is almost sequential. It is only separated by data processing

Figure 4. Processing of radar signals

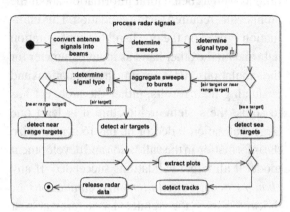

variants due to different types of signals which are in our example: sea targets, air targets and near range targets. These signals are characterized by different electro-magnetic wave forms and processing algorithms allowing the radar engineer to detect objects in a short or far away distance with different resolutions. E.g. objects on surface of the water are usually not very fast in comparison with missiles in the air and therefore they have to be treated differently. The overall goal is to filter out signals reflected by objects in radar range which the radar engineer does not want to see on his radar display. These tracks depend on the field of usage; e.g. air surveillance radars at airports need to detect not only planes but also groups of birds because they are a threat to airplane engines. The system processes a continuous stream of data so that the computing performance for data of a certain point in time is influenced by the processing of past and future signals.

Apply the Validation Process

In our example, there are three hardware boards (UML components with the stereotype *hardware*) with two processing units, one microprocessor and one Field Programmable Gate Array (FPGA), each. They are illustrated in the deployment view of the development model in Figure 5. In this example, the processing units are also modeled by an

UML component with stereotype *hardware*. The software component interfaces are mapped to the physical ones represented by ports on hardware components, e.g. *BV_Beams* of *beam forming* on port *Ethernet_2* of *Board_1*. This allows the architect to trace data flow on the hardware and to overview dependencies between the boards. In the development model each software component (UML component with stereotype *software*) has to have a dependency connection with stereotype *executedOn* to a hardware component indicating its execution environment, e.g. the software component *beam forming* is executed on the *FPGA* named *Board_1* (see Figure 5).

According to the first step in the validation process (see Figure 2) the architect detects validation targets from system requirements. For that reason he identifies the following six architecture relevant requirements:

- The system shall provide tracks for fed in test data after 320ms. (A1)
- The system shall provide plots for fed in test data after 280ms. (A2)
- The system shall be able to compute 3500 MiBit/s data received from antenna. (A3)
- The system shall consume less than 220W. (A4)
- The temperature of each FPGA shall be less than 50°C. (A5)
- The temperature of each microprocessor shall be less than 70°C. (A6)

The first three non-functional requirements can be assigned to two validation targets (VT). A1 and A2 deal with the processing time of the system (VT1), A3 with the communication infrastructure (VT2). A4 can be assigned to the aspect energy consumption (VT3) and A5 and A6 to hardware temperature (VT4). The next steps are to define the examination simulation and the validation specific notation for each target. Figure 6 shows the UML profile used for the validation specific notation. The processing time to provide tracks

Figure 5. Deployment view of the radar processor in the development model

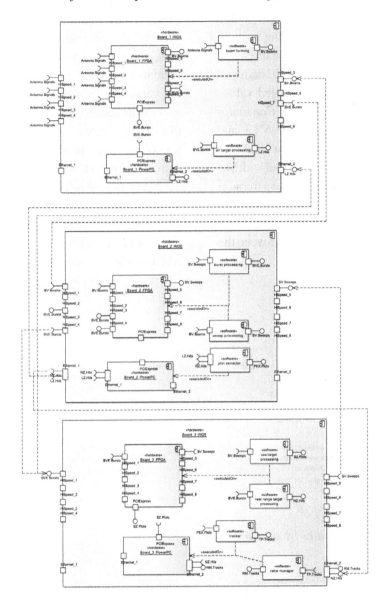

and plots is calculated by required floating point operations of the software components. That is why the stereotype *software* has the tagged value *complexity* specifying needed floating point operations for the software component. The stereotype *hardware* has the tagged value *performance* providing the performance of processing units in *MFlop/s*. Software and hardware components are connected by a dependency with the stereotype *executedOn*. The execution order of the software components are evaluated by the activities assigned to the software components (see Figure 7). Therefore, the notation includes the stereotype *realize* extending the UML metaclass Dependency. In order to calculate system's processing time we have to consider the amount of parallel processed software components on the same processing unit influencing the performance available for assigned software components. If we assume linear energy consumption and linear temperature rising for processing units in combination with a basic value, these data can be calculated by using processing unit load deduced by VT1's simulation. We add the tagged values *energyConsumption* and *basicEnergyConsumption* to the stereotype *hardware* for VT3 and *temperature* and *basicTemperature* for VT4 (see Figure 6). For VT2's simulation the band width of the communication device from antenna to radar system is required. We add the stereotype *communication* with tagged value *bandWidth* to the association representing physical link between the

board and the hardware component executing the first software component in the processing chain.

After the determination of the validation targets, their corresponding simulations and the validation specific notation, the architect creates the validation model using the support tool described in section *Support Tool*. The tool loads the development model, lists all available elements according to the model tree and enables the architect to select validation relevant structural (e.g. hardware and software components, *executedOn* and *realize* dependencies) and behavioral elements (e.g. activities) to transform them into the validation model. After transformation the architect can add missing validation-specific data (e.g. amount

Figure 6. Validation specific notation

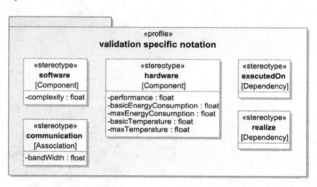

Figure 7. Realization of activities by software components

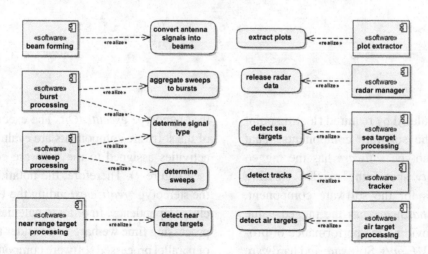

Figure 8. Deployment view in the validation model

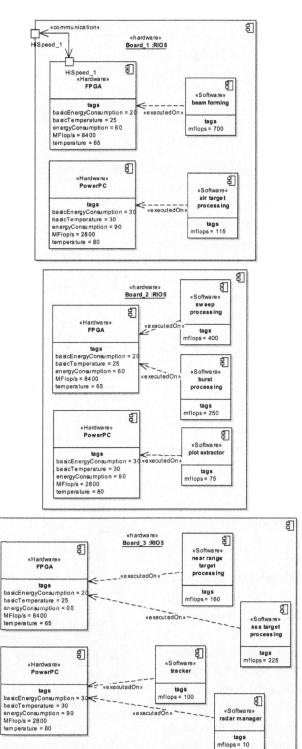

of flops required by software components) by using the UML profiles. Figure 8 shows the deployment view of the resulting validation model. The results of the system architecture validation, i.e. of the four validation targets, are shown in Table 1 to Table 3.

Requirement Change

In the course of system development requirements are changing. In our example the customer changes requirement A1: Tracks shall be provided after 310ms instead of 320ms. This modification causes no change to the validation targets itself because they are defined independently from specific values. By evaluating the structure of validation targets and requirements (A1 is connected to VT1 and VT1 is connected to VT3) the architect can divine that the requirement change could affect the performance and the energy consumption of the system. According to the validation process (see Figure 2) the next step is *run simulations*. The architecture validation fails because VT1 cannot be validated: 313ms is greater than 310ms. The architect has to change the architecture in order to fulfill the new requirement. He tries to increase performance by assigning the software component *sweep processing* to the *PowerPC* of *Board_2*. This modification is memorized because it has to be transferred to the development model in case of a successful validation.

Although VT1 is valid after this architecture modification, the validation fails due to energy consumption. The detailed results of the simulation are shown in Table 4 and Table 5.

By analyzing the data of all performed simulations the architect is able to identify the problem. Details on analyzing the simulation data with the help of the support tool are described in section *Support Tool*. The processing unit load of the *PowerPC* on *Board_2* increased due to raising energy consumption which cannot be compensated by decreasing energy consumption of the *FPGA* on *Board_2*. The architect restores the

Table 1. Results first simulation VT1

Data	Processing Time [ms]
Tracks	313
Plots	277

Table 2. Results first simulation VT2

Communication Line	Band Width [MiBit/s]
Antenna – Radar processor	5200

Table 3. Results first simulation VT3 and VT4

Processing Unit	Processor Load [%]	Temperature [°C]	Energy [W]
Board_1:FPGA	86	47	34
Board_1:PowerPC	8	52	38
Board_2:FPGA	84	45	33
Board_2:PowerPC	8	52	38
Board_3:FPGA	17	38	26
Board_3:PowerPC	23	67	48
Total energy consumption			217

Table 4. Results second simulation VT1

Data	Processing Time [ms]
Tracks	306
Plots	270

Table 5. Results second simulation VT3 and VT4

Processing Unit	Processor Load [%]	Temperature [°C]	Energy [W]
Board_1:FPGA	86	47	34
Board_1:PowerPC	8	52	38
Board_2:FPGA	66	40	30
Board_2:PowerPC	28	69	52
Board_3:FPGA	15	36	25
Board_3:PowerPC	21	60	47
Total energy consumption			226

former architecture in the validation model, exchanges the software components *burst processing* and *near range target processing* and reruns architecture validation. The validation for each target succeeds resulting in transferring the modifications, i.e. the changed *extecutedOn* dependencies of the two software components, to the development model. The resulting deployment view of the development model is illustrated in Figure 9.

Figure 9. Deployment view in the development model after requirement change

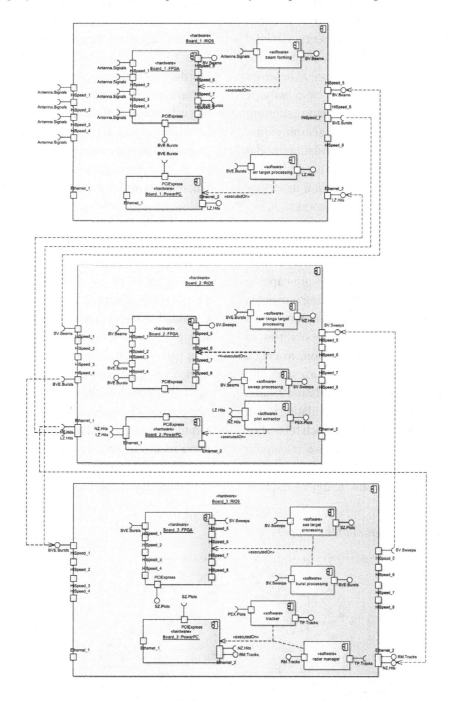

SUPPORT TOOL

Figure 10 shows the five use cases of the support tool available for the *architect*. Section *Validation Target Management* goes into detail for the uses cases *manage validation targets*, *support impact analysis* and *import requirements*. The support tool does not manage the requirements this is why the support tool imports them from an external *Requirement Management Tool*. Section *Model Transformation Support* addresses the use case *model transformations* and section *Simulation Management* focuses on the use case *manage simulations*. This does not only include assigning simulations to validation targets but also providing modeled information from the validation model and importing their results in order to validate the targets. Section *Software Architecture* describes the software architecture of the support tool.

Validation Target Management

Applications like Rational DOORS are capable of managing requirements. By adding attributes it could be possible to manage validation targets in some manner. However, the possibilities to directly start the assigned simulation, to check the simulation results against the corresponding criteria, to persist and restore validation results and to evaluate requirements and validation target dependencies are not available in such tools. For these reasons we developed our own managing tool for validation targets enabling the architect to handle the targets and the assigned require-

ments. The architect can import requirements from an external requirements management tool by a XML (e.g. the standardized Requirements Interchange Format [Object Management Group, 2011]) or spread sheet interface into an empty or existing set of requirements and validation targets. If existing requirements are changed by importing a requirements file, the requirements and the assigned targets are highlighted. The architect can manage validation targets including the associations to the architecture-relevant requirements. For the validation targets he has to choose check criteria and simulations. The architect can start the validation of the entire architecture or even for single targets. The tool presents the results in a graphical overview (see Figure 11). The validation targets are color-coded due to their validation status whereas red means invalid, green means valid and yellow means undefined. The latter is active for a target either if it has not been validated yet or changes occur after the last validation.

Several filters enable the architect to handle the amount of requirements and their interconnections. Requirements without an association to a validation target can be filtered and displayed. It is possible to show all assigned requirements of a selected validation target as well as all assigned validation targets of one selected requirement. Furthermore the tool lists all indirect connected validation targets by analyzing the assigned requirements and evaluating their connections to other requirements. If those requirements are assigned to another validation target than the selected one it is displayed by the tool including the

Figure 10. Use case diagram of the support tool

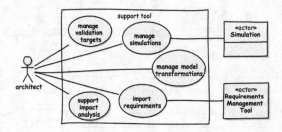

Figure 11. Software architecture of the support tool

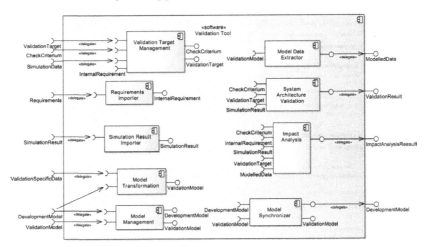

associated requirements. This architecture-specific view supports the architect to identify complex dependencies between validation targets and helps to realize the impact of certain requirements on the system architecture.

Model Transformation Support

The support tool does not only manage the files of the development and validation models but also provides model synchronization and transformation of elements between them. Development and validation information are separated in our validation process to avoid information overkill in the development model and to enable the disengagement of data in the validation model from data in the development model. Thus, the validation relevant data is independent from changes in the development model caused by development progress. These advantages come at the price of extra effort for creating the validation model, for synchronizing the data and for checking consistency. The effort can be reduced by using the meta-model based modeling language UML for documentation. If development and validation model are based on the same meta-model, modeled data can be transformed from one model to an existing or new one without great effort (e.g.

using Xpand of the Eclipse Modeling Project [The Eclipse Foundation, 2012]). Figure 12 illustrates the selection of modeled elements which will be transformed from the development model to a new validation model. The elements of the development model are displayed as a tree allowing the architect to navigate through the elements in the same way as it is provided in common modeling tools. The architect can see detailed information about the selected element on the right side of the window. The red round icon with the X in the middle indicates that this element will not be transformed. In Figure 12 the elements not transformed are ports which have not been named (name of the UML element is <<NO_NAME>>).

Modeled data can be checked against self-defined rules to ensure consistency and it can be synchronized by analyzing, comparing and merging model content (e.g. using Eclipse Modeling Framework [EMF] Compare [The Eclipse Foundation, 2012]).

Simulation Management

The support tool manages the simulations of the validation targets and provides an interface for reading data from the validation model. This data can be utilized by the simulations as data source for

Figure 12. Color-coded validation target overview according to validation status

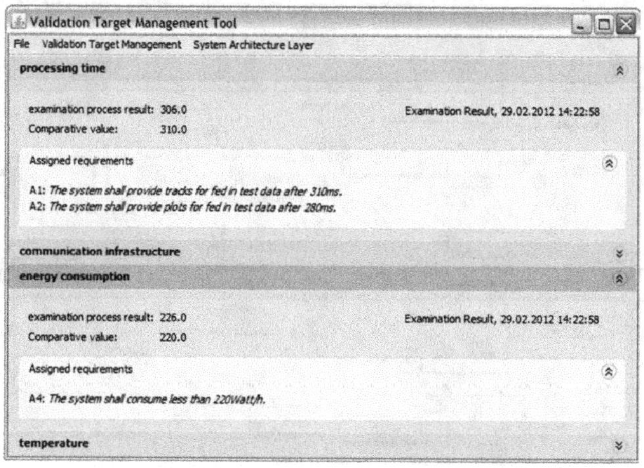

their algorithms on the one hand and to configure the simulation, e.g. the hardware infrastructure or the software-hardware mapping, on the other hand. The simulations provide their results over a universal result interface whereby the tool updates the validation status of the targets and the whole architecture accordingly. The tool has also access to the simulation interim data and can display them either raw or in a special format, e.g. as a coordinate system. Figure 13 shows the development of the processor load of the six processing units during the simulation.

These interfaces enable the architect to use simulations suitable for the level of detail in the current development status and to modify the architecture without reprogramming the simulations. For the radar system, we developed a simulation considering multiple validation targets. Although the level of detail is not high, even domain experts cannot foresee the simulation results because there are too many influencing factors.

Software Architecture

The architecture of the support tool is illustrated in Figure 14. The software is composed of nine software components realizing the main use cases

shown in Figure 10. Whereas some realizations of the use cases are obvious due to the names of the software components, e.g. *import requirements* is realized by *Requirements Importer* or *support impact analysis* is realized by *Impact Analysis*, other are not immediately obvious. The use case *manage validation targets* is realized by the software components *Validation Target Management* and *System Architecture Validation*. The use case

Figure 13. Element selection for the model-to-model transformation

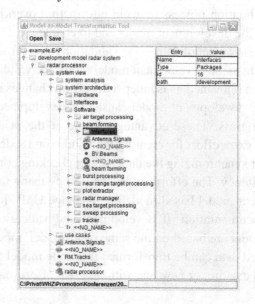

Figure 14. Development of processor load during the simulation

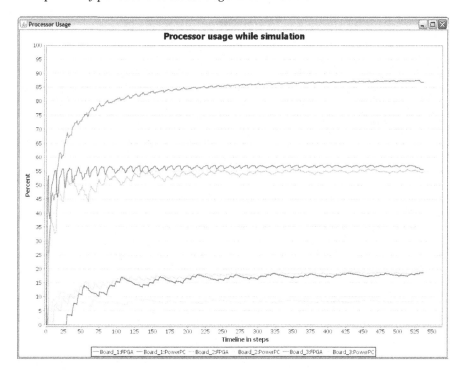

manage simulations is realized by *Validation Target Management*, the component *Simulation Result Importer* and *Model Data Extractor*. The use case *manage model transformations* is realized by the components *Model Management, Model Transformation* and *Model Synchronizer*.

Detailed Process Description

The activity diagram describing the validation process (see Figure 2 in section *Description of the Validation Process*) acts as a starting point to present the validation process. It contains all essential steps but leaves out some interesting details like the basic profiles or the detailed handling of changes. This detailed version of the process is illustrated in Figure 15. Instead of the term simulation we use the generic term examination process because the process basically enables the usage of other validation techniques, e.g. formal techniques, instead of dynamic ones. This is quite helpful if the validation process should be applied

in a project in which examination processes are already available. However, the authors prefer simulations.

After determining the validation targets in the first step the architect adds dependencies between targets and requirements as well as between targets. The dependencies between targets enable the architect to analyze the static impacts of architecture and requirement changes. At this place, static impacts involve identifying targets and requirements which may be affected by changes. To be sure which targets and requirements are affected the examination processes have to be executed. Thus, the dependencies enable the architect to identify potential impacts without running the examination processes.

The completeness of identified targets and the dependencies have to be checked, e.g. by a review with the project staff. The first three steps have to be repeated if either targets or dependencies are incomplete, otherwise the architect can continue with defining the examination processes for the

Figure 15. Detailed UML activity diagram for the architecture validation process

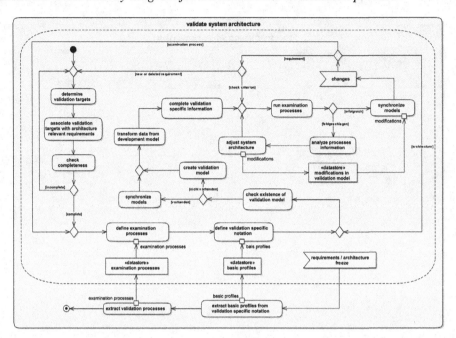

validation targets. The architect is supported in this process step by an examination process database containing processes used in former projects. After choosing the processes, the architect is able to define the validation specific notation. During this step he is also supported by a database which contains UML basic profiles. Basic profiles are generalized profiles, which are independent of project-specific information. Those generalized profiles can be integrated by creating a stereotype in the project-specific profile, which inherits from basic profile stereotypes. Those databases support transferring knowledge and experiences from other projects and reusing processes and profiles.

After defining the notation, the system architect can start to add all validation-relevant information into the validation model. If there is no such model available, the architect creates a new one. If a validation model exists, the architect synchronizes the development and validation model to ensure that the existing elements in the validation model are up-to-date. Elements of the development model which do not exist in the validation

model are added by the architect in the next step. Those process steps – creating the validation mode, synchronizing development and validation model and transferring elements from development into validation model – can be supported by the tool described in section *Support Tool*. The following step, adding the missing validation-specific information, can also be supported by a tool if this information is available in a computer readable format, e.g. hardware or software information in a database. Otherwise, the architect has to add this information manually.

By defining the targets, the examination processes and the validation specific notation as well as creating the validation model, the architect created the foundation for running all examination processes (*run examination processes*). The processes are able to use the information in the validation model to configure the process, e.g., adopt the architecture from the validation model in the simulation, and to provide at least parts of the input parameter for the process. Input parameter for example can be the energy consumption of a hardware device or the required floating-point operations or the execution time of a software component. Managing the processes including starting and importing their results is supported by the described tool. It also provides the system architect to analyze the process results to identify the parts of the architecture which could lead to validation errors (*analyze processes information*).

If at least one target cannot be validated, the system architecture has to be adjusted by the architect in order to fulfill also the associated requirements of this target (*adjust system architecture*). If all targets are valid, possible changes in the validation model are synchronized with the development model (*synchronize models*). This can be supported by a tool, e.g. displaying the differences of the two models and enabling the architect to choose which changes should be transformed to the development model. At this point a valid architecture exists which can only become invalid if *changes* occur. We consider three types of changes:

- Changes to requirements.
- Changes to examination processes.
- Changes to the architecture.

If at least one requirement has been changed, two cases can be distinguished: First, the requirement change just involves the change of check criteria. In this case, the architect just has to rerun the examination processes to ensure that the architecture is still valid. If it is not, he has to adjust the architecture. If it is still valid, the architect does not have to do anything. Before running the processes, he could also perform a static impact analysis to get a first impression of possible impacts. If requirements are added or deleted, the architect has to start over identifying new validation targets using the already available data. If an examination process is changed, the architect starts again at the process step *define examination processes* using the data already available (e.g., targets, notation, or examination processes). Changes to the architecture require transforming the changes, which are relevant for the validation from the development model to the validation model. Based on the changed validation model the architect has to rerun the examination processes in order to check the validation status of the architecture.

The whole validation process terminates if the requirements or the architecture are defined as complete. The point of time in the development process when this occurs can be very different and is among other things depending on the project conditions and the cost-benefit analysis. It could either be after the system design phase or even after the software design phase. It is also possible to just use the validation process for getting an overview at project start.

Benefits and Experiences

We developed the approach on the basis of industrial projects of the SOPHIST GmbH and the experience from developments of embedded systems. The project scopes are up to about 40 processing units and 70 software components. The used examination processes are essentially similar to the introduced example. According to our experience applying the approach the extra work caused by the process amortizes within several iterations of system architecture designs and requirement changes. The architects are open to try some design ideas by e.g. replacing hardware boards just to check if there is more than one valid system architecture. The approach has been road-tested with two separated groups composed of experienced (nine and more years) system engineers on the one hand and post-graduate's students on the other hand. Those field trials indicate that the approach can be learned within a one day workshop for experienced system engineers and within a two or three day workshop for beginners.

The benefits of our approach can be outlined as followed:

- The approach defines a model-driven system architecture validation process for the architect which can be integrated into iterative architecture design.
- The required time and effort for system architecture validation can be reduced by automation of examination processes and of validation process' tasks.
- The validation targets create an architecture-specific view allowing the architect to keep track of all architecture-relevant requirements and their dependencies, direct and indirect.
- The system architect can analyze the impacts of requirement changes on the system architecture via their connections to the validation targets.
- The validation process indicates also secondary effects of architecture changes.
- Separation of validation and development information allows independent working on both models.
- Model-based documentation allows transferring data between models reducing extra effort caused by model separation.
- Choosing UML as modeling language allows usage of tools like EMF for implementation of tools for data extraction and transformation.
- UML profile mechanism enables the architect to add arbitrary validation-specific data without much effort and independently from other notations.
- Using different level of details the system architect can take advantage of the validation process to estimate development cost and time during and even before project start.

Related Work

The elicitation of requirements in particular non-functional requirements is not part of our approach. Nevertheless, non functional requirements are con-

siderable for architecture design and therefore we require a preferably complete set of non-functional requirements satisfying basic quality properties like testability or unambiguousness. An example for a suitable approach is described in (Dörr, 2010). This systematic elicitation process allows finding inconsistent and conflicting requirements based on a requirements meta-model. This model could also be supportive for indentifying architecture-relevant requirements to determine validation targets and examination processes.

According to (Debabbi et al., 2010) the simulations used in our approach can be classified as dynamic validation technique in contrast to formal techniques like model checking or theorem proofing. The simulations are evaluating the system behavior based on data modeled in UML. This semi-formal modeling language does not have the accuracy of the mathematical models normally used by formal verification techniques. (Schamai, Helle, Fritzson, & Paredis, 2010) describe a system design verification approach using the object-oriented equation-based modeling language Modelica. The data required for verification is added to an UML model by the ModelicaML UML profile. The formalized requirements are observed by violation monitors, roughly comparable to the validation targets. The main target of the approach is the detection of design errors whereas our approach answers the question: Could it be possible to satisfy the requirements? Similar approaches due to the main target are e.g. (Hall, 2008) dealing with hard real-time systems, (Aydal, Paige, Utting, & Woodcock, 2009) using modeled data for system testing and (Holtmann, Meyer, & Meyer, 2011) providing a development approach for the automotive domain. The focus of the latest lies on software rather than on system architectures using AUTomotive Open System Architecture (AUTOSAR).

Adding information to the model is done by using default UML elements and elements provided by domain specific profiles like Modeling and Analysis of Real Time and Embedded systems

(MARTE) (Object Management Group, 2012), System Modeling Language (SysML) (Object Management Group, 2012), Architecture Analysis & Design Language (AADL) (Carnegie Mellon University, 2012) or Electronic Architecture and Software Technology – Architecture Description Language (EAST-ADL) (EAST-ADL Association, 2012). However, these profiles do neither provide a process for architecture validation nor allow adding arbitrary data. Therefore, our approach uses the UML profile mechanism to create validation specific profiles to add data which cannot be added by existing profiles.

Scenario-based analysis methods for software architectures like Software Architecture Analysis Method (SAAM) or Architecture Tradeoff Analysis Method (ATAM) (Clements, Kazman, & Klein, 2001) can also be applied on system architectures (Carnegie Mellon University, 2012). Nevertheless, they are evaluating a set of architectures according to chosen quality properties to select the one that fits best. Our approach focuses on finding valid architectures which could be analyzed by those methods afterwards.

There is a validation and verification component for the tool Simulink (MathWorks, 2012). It requires detailed information about the developed system which is not necessarily available at system design level. Although it would be possible to validate the entire architecture even in an early development phase using the harness model, the main focus of Simulink is on developing single parts, e.g. FPGAs, of the system. Nevertheless, Simulink does not use UML for modeling and the mentioned component is restricted to functional and security requirements.

The project System Architecture Virtual Integration (SAVI) (Feiler, Wrage, & Hansson, 2010) initiated by the Aerospace Vehicle Systems Institutes is based on three key concepts: a reference model, a model repository with model bus and a model based development process. Models using e.g. UML, AADL or SysML and mapped to the reference model can be compared with the content of a requirements repository. In theory a validation of system architectures against requirements would be possible but the overhead would be high because this is not the projects intention. Furthermore, the project only exists in the description of a feasibility study.

The support tool is highly specific to the validation process. It provides a model-driven simulation to deal with heavily dependent validation targets. (Gray, & Audsley, 2011) describes an approach to distribute simulation code to different processing units by changing the virtual machine code leaving the simulation code unmodified. This could be used for a radar simulation based on a detailed system architecture. However, there is no radar simulation available which can be configured by an UML model and adjusted to different level of details.

CONCLUSION

System development has to deal with a rising complexity and evolving conditions challenging the system architect who has to design and document the system architecture. Its design cannot be done according to the book; it is a kind of art and involves human decisions (Maier, & Rechtin, 2009). Therefore it is error prone and requires validation against the corresponding requirements. The evolving conditions cause recurring requirement changes whose impact on the architecture has to be analyzed by the architect. The architecture validation and impact analysis are time and work consuming tasks mostly done without a defined process leading to hardly reproducible results.

The introduced approach defines a model-driven validation process integrated into iterative development of system architectures. Validation targets form an architecture-specific view supporting the architect to keep track of all architecture-relevant requirements and dependencies. For each validation target the architect has to define at least one examination process whose results decide on the validation status of the target. The entire system architecture is valid if all targets are valid. The examination processes use the model-based documentation as data source for their configuration and their data input. The approach focuses on dynamic validation techniques but is not limited to them.

To achieve independent working on development and validation and to avoid information overkill, information is separated into two models. To add arbitrary validation-specific information, validation specific notations are created by using UML profile mechanism. It enables the architect to apply several stereotypes on one UML element containing different data without having dependencies between the notations. Databases for basic profiles and applied examination processes enable the architect to transfer validation knowledge from one project to another.

The automation possibilities of our approach demonstrated by the prototypes do not only reduce the extra effort caused by the validation process itself but also the total amount of work for architecture validation and impact analysis. According to our experiences the extra effort to apply the approach amortizes after few iterations of system architecture design and requirement changes.

REFERENCES

Aydal, E. G., Paige, R. F., Utting, M., & Woodcock, J. (2009). Putting formal specifications under the magnifying glass: Model-based testing for validation. In *Proceedings of the Second International Conference on Software Testing, Verification and Validation* (pp. 131-140). Denver, CO: IEEE Computer Society.

Boehm, B. W. (1981). *Software engineering economics*. New York: Prentice Hall.

Carnegie Mellon University. (2012a). *Architecture analysis and design language*. Retrieved November 4, 2012, from http://www.aadl.info

Carnegie Mellon University. (2012b). *System and software architecture tradeoff analysis method*. Retrieved November 4, 2012, from http://www.sei.cmu.edu/architecture/tools/evaluate/systematam.cfm

Clements, P., Kazman, R., & Klein, M. (2001). *Evaluating software architectures: Methods and case studies*. Amsterdam: Addison-Wesley Longman.

Debabbi, M., Hassaine, F., Jarraya, Y., Soeanu, A., & Alawneh, L. (2010). *Verification and validation in systems engineering - Assessing UML/SysML design models*. Berlin: Springer. doi:10.1007/978-3-642-15228-3.

Dörr, J. (2010). *Elicitation of a complete set of non-functional requirements*. (Doctoral Dissertation). University of Kaiserslautern. Stuttgart: Fraunhofer Verlag.

EAST-ADL Association. (2012). *Electronic architecture and software technology – Architecture description language*. Retrieved November 4, 2012, from http://www.east-adl.info

Eclipse Foundation. (2012a). *EMF compare project*. Retrieved November 4, 2012, from http://www.eclipse.org/emf/compare

Eclipse Foundation. (2012b). *Eclipse modeling project*. Retrieved November 4, 2012, from http://www.eclipse.org/modeling/

Endres, A., & Rombach, D. (2003). *A handbook of software and systems engineering*. Amsterdam: Addison-Wesley Longman.

Feiler, P., Wrage, L., & Hansson, J. (2010). *System architecture virtual integration: A case study*. Retrieved from http://www.erts2010.org

Grady, J. O. (1997). *System validation and verification*. Boca Raton, FL: CRC Press.

Gray, I., & Audsley, N. C. (2011). Targeting complex embedded architectures by combining the multicore communications API (MCAPI) with compile-time virtualisation. In *Proceedings of the ACM SIGPLAN/SIGBED Conference on Languages, Compilers, and Tools for Embedded Systems* (pp. 51-60). Chicago, IL: ACM.

Hall, R. J. (2008). Validating real time specifications using real time event queue modeling. In *Proceedings of the 23rd IEEE/ACM International Conference on Automated Software Engineering* (pp. 79-88). L'Aquila, Italy: IEEE.

Holtmann, J., Meyer, J., & Meyer, M. (2011). A seamless model-based development process for automotive systems. In *Proceedings of Software Engineering 2011 Workshops including Doctoral Symposium* (pp. 79-88). Karlsruhe, Germany: Bonner Köllen Verlag.

International Council on System Engineering. (2011). *INCOSE systems engineering handbook, version 3.2.2*. Retrieved from http://www.incose.org

Maier, M. W., & Rechtin, E. (2009). *The art of systems architecting*. Boca Raton, FL: CRC Press.

MathWorks. (2012). *Simulink's verification, validation and test module*. Retrieved November 4, 2012, from http://www.mathworks.com/verification-validation

Navy Modeling and Simulation Management Office. (2004). *Modeling and simulation verification, validation and accreditation implementation handbook*. Washington, DC: Department of the Navy.

Object Management Group. (2011). *Requirements interchange format, version 1.0.1*. Retrieved November 4, 2012, from http://www.omg.org/spec/ReqIF

Object Management Group. (2012a). *Modeling and analysis of real-time and embedded systems*. Retrieved November 4, 2012, from http://www.omg.org/omgmarte

Object Management Group. (2012b). *Systems modeling language*. Retrieved November 4, 2012, from http://www.sysml.org

Pflüger, A., Golubski, W., & Queins, S. (2011). Model driven validation of system architecture. In *Proceedings of the 13th IEEE International Symposium on High-Assurance Systems Engineering* (pp. 25-28). Boca Raton, FL: IEEE Computer Society.

Pohl, K. (2010). *Requirements engineering - Fundamentals, principles, and techniques*. Berlin: Springer. doi:10.1007/978-3-642-12578-2.

Schamai, W., Helle, P., Fritzson, P., & Paredis, C. J. J. (2010). Virtual verification of system designs against system requirements. In *Proceedings of Models in Software Engineering - Workshops and Symposia at MODELS 2010* (pp. 75–89). Oslo, Norway: Springer.

Woodcock, J., Larsen, P., Bicarregui, J., & Fitzgerald, J. (2009). Formal methods: Practice and experience. *ACM Computing Surveys, 4*(41), 1–36. doi:10.1145/1592434.1592436.

Chapter 9
Demystifying Domain Specific Languages

Abdelilah Kahlaoui
École de Technologie Supérieure, Canada

Alain Abran
École de Technologie Supérieure, Canada

ABSTRACT

Domain Specific Languages (DSLs) provide interesting characteristics that align well with the goals and mission of model-driven software engineering. However, there are still some issues that hamper widespread adoption. In this chapter, the authors discuss two of these issues. The first relates to the vagueness of the term DSL, which they address by studying the individual terms: domain, specificity, and language. The second is related to the difficulty of developing DSLs, which they address with a view to making DSL development more accessible via processes, standards, and tools.

INTRODUCTION

The concept of Domain Specific Languages (DSLs) is not new, and the advantages to using them have long been highlighted in the literature:

We must develop languages that the scientist, the architect, the teacher, and the layman can use without being computer experts. The language for each user must be as natural as possible to her/ him. The statistician must talk to his terminal in the language of statistics. The civil engineer must use the language of civil engineering. When a man learns his profession he must learn the problem-oriented languages to go with that profession (Martin, 1967, p. 89).

We must constantly turn to new languages in order to express our ideas more effectively. Establishing new languages is a powerful strategy for controlling complexity in engineering design; we can often enhance our ability to deal with a complex problem by adopting a new language that enables us to describe (and hence to think about) the problem in a different way, using primitives, means of combination, and means of abstraction that are particularly well suited to the problem at hand (Abelson, Sussman, & Sussman, 1996, pp. 359-360).

The use of DSLs is not limited to information technology, as they are used in many other areas as well, such as finance (Arnold, Van Deursen, & Res, 1995), chemistry (Murray-Rust, 1997), biology (Hucka et al., 2003), music (Boulanger, 2000),

DOI: 10.4018/978-1-4666-4217-1.ch009

for example. Among the DSLs most commonly used in computer science today are the Structured Query Language (SQL) (Chamberlin & Boyce, 1974; ISO, 2008), the regular expression language for manipulating strings (Friedl, 2006), Microsoft Office Excel (Microsoft, 2011), and the eXtensible Markup Language (XML) (ISO, 1986).

A DSL is usually designed to solve a specific class of problems in a particular domain. The focus of DSLs on a particular domain facilitates the creation of languages that best represent the domain concepts. This convergence between problem domain and solution domain has many benefits, in terms of the expressiveness and precision (semantics) of the DSL. In addition, DSLs have also shown good potential in terms of productivity, reusability, and reliability (Kelly & Tolvanen, 2008; Kleppe, 2008).

In this chapter, we discuss the concept of DSLs (section 1), and present the types of DSLs (section 2) and the tools used to develop them (section 3). Section 4 presents some of the standards that can be used as a foundation for developing DSLs. Section 5 describes the development process itself. Finally, we summarize this work in section 6.

BACKGROUND

As mentioned earlier, DSLs have been a part of the computing world for decades. SQL and the UNIX languages *awk* and *make* are a few examples. These languages were developed by specialists with solid language development skills and good knowledge of the DSL domain. However, the emergence of the model driven approach and the need for languages capable of producing precise models that can be processed by machines, has opened up new horizons for DSLs. In the future, these languages could play a central role in the software development cycle, which would take DSLs from the arena of specialists to that of software developers.

However, software developers generally do not have the skills required to develop DSLs, and so an effort must be made to make DSL development more accessible. Only two areas have been addressed up to now to achieve this: DSL tooling, and DSL development. On the one hand, tooling has been driven by the likes of IBM, Microsoft, and Metacase (see section 3 for further details about DSL tools). These companies offer tools designed to support most of the activities of the DSL development cycle. Unfortunately, these tools remain immature. On the other hand, there has been significant progress on individual aspects of DSL development. For example, (Mernik, Heering, & Sloane, 2005) have identified a set of patterns for the decision, analysis, design, and implementation phases of DSL development; (Tolvanen, 2006) provides guidelines and steps on how to create a DSL; (Deursen, Klint, & Visser, 2000) discuss DSL design methodology and provide a list of related publications, and (Thibault, Marlet, & Consel, 1999) propose a framework for designing and implementing DSLs.

Although this work helps demystify DSL development, it does not describe a well defined DSL development process that covers all its major aspects, namely: what process to follow, what products to use, what tools are required, and who is involved. So far, the research effort has mainly focused on DSL development phases and activities. For (Deursen, et al., 2000), a DSL development process comprises three phases: analysis, implementation, and use, while (Mernik, et al., 2005) identify five phases: decision, analysis, design, implementation, and deployment.

To improve the DSL development experience, three areas need to be considered: 1) processes to provide a disciplined approach to DSL development; 2) tools to support language development and maintenance; and 3) standards to allow these languages and their supporting tools to be built in a unified and interoperable way.

Process: Analysis of the state of the art suggests that DSLs have been developed in an ad hoc manner up to now: there are no well defined methods for managing the DSL development cycle, and the quality of the DSLs developed often depends on the competence, creativity, and intuition of their developers. According to (Bezivin & Heckel, 2004), languages (i.e. programming and modeling languages), like software, need an engineering discipline to support their development. This discipline should provide support for the definition, implementation, and validation of these languages.

Tools: DSLs are specialized languages characterized by their own syntax and semantics. This specialization allows a DSL to express the solution in the most suitable way for the problem at hand. However, the use of DSLs requires the creation of specialized tools with which to edit, analyze, compile, and debug models. Yet the development of such tools is complex and costly. Therefore, the creation of an infrastructure that will make the construction of these tools cheaper, as well as more accessible, will be a major step towards the democratization of DSLs.

Standards: The current incompatibility between tools, stemming from the fact that different metamodels are used to define them, affects the portability of DSLs (Bézivin, 2004), making it a real challenge; for example, Microsoft uses its own metamodel (meta-metamodel), Eclipse EMP uses Ecore, and MetaEdit+ uses GOPPRR. To address the problem of portability, and hence interoperability, standards are needed to form a foundation for the development of these tools, and tool builders must comply with these standards.

The remainder of this chapter presents the state of the art in the three areas mentioned above.

1. WHAT IS A DSL?

It is difficult to find a definition that is applicable to all DSLs, as each definition in the literature is given from a specific point of view. These differences even affect the naming of these languages; thus, DSLs are also referred to as Little Languages, Micro Languages, Domain Modeling Languages (DML), Domain Specific Modeling Languages (DSML), Domain Specific Visual Languages (DSVL) (Sprinkle & Karsai, 2004), Domain Specific Visual Modeling Languages (DSVML), Domain Specific Embedded Languages (DSEL), etc.

One approach to introducing the concept of DSLs is by describing the three terms: *Domain*, *Specificity*, and *Language*.

1.1. Domain

It is difficult to define a DSL, largely because of the vagueness of the term *domain*, as every community has developed its own perception of the term and formulated its own definition. Sometimes, several definitions can be found within the same community. In this subsection, we present the concept of the domain as perceived in different software fields.

In the context of software product lines, a domain can be seen as "a specialized body of knowledge, an area of expertise, or a collection of related functionality" (Northrop, 2002, p. 2).

In the context of generative programming, Czarnecki and Eisenecker define a *domain* as:

An area of knowledge:

- Scoped to maximize the satisfaction of the requirements of its stakeholders.
- Including a set of concepts and terminology understood by practitioners in that area.
- Including knowledge of how to build software systems (or parts of software systems) in that area (Czarnecki & Eisenecker, 2000, p. 754).

In the domain analysis community, a rather flexible view of the term has been adopted, since domain analysis is used in various contexts and by many other communities as well. According to (Kang, et al., 1990), "a domain is a more general concept which may be stretched to apply to most any potential class of systems" (p. 8).

It is important to note that the definition varies among domain analysis methods, even within this same community (e.g. the domain analysis community):

In Feature-Oriented Domain Analysis (FODA), a domain is "a set of current and future applications which share a set of common capabilities and data" (Kang, et al., 1990, p. 2). In Domain-Specific Software Architecture (DSSA), it is "a set of common problems or functions that applications in that domain can solve/do" (Kaisler, 2005, p. 210).

In Family-Oriented Abstraction, Specification, and Translation (FAST), a domain is a product family (Weiss, 1998), that is, a set of software products that share a common set of features. According to Ardis and Weis, there are no rules that allow easy identification of a family, because of the vagueness of the concept (Ardis & Weiss, 1997). Parnas (1976) considers "a set of programs to constitute a family whenever it is worthwhile to study programs from the set by first studying the common properties of the set and then determining the special properties of the individual family members" (p. 1).

Concerning the Organization Domain Modeling (ODM) method, Simos et al. (1996) say the following:

A domain in the ODM context can be any field of inquiry or realm of discourse that has a common, defining categorical definition and a set of elements that are evaluated to be members of the domain by virtue of sharing those defining features (p. 21).

The concept of domain as used in different communities and in different fields (linguistics, artificial intelligence, object-oriented technology, and software reuse) was studied in (Simos, et al., 1996). Two broad categories of domain were distinguished: the *real-world* domain, and the domain as *a set of systems*.

1. **Real-world domain:** This understanding of the term has mainly been adopted by the knowledge engineering, artificial intelligence, and object oriented modeling communities. In this context, domain knowledge is primarily developed based on the problem domain rather than the solution domain.

2. **Domain as a set of systems:** This understanding of the term is primarily supported by the software reuse community. In this community, analysts are particularly concerned with the creation of models that facilitate the design of reusable software. Therefore, the domain knowledge should be relevant to the construction of a family of software systems.

The domain as a set of systems can be further divided into two subcategories: the domain as a collection of systems and the domain as a class of systems. The former does not necessarily take into account the consistency of the characteristics of its component systems. The latter is governed by a set of rules and/or criteria which determine the systems to include or exclude.

In real world domains, practitioners usually play the role of domain experts; whereas in domains defined as a set of systems, this role is played by the engineers who developed the systems for the domain.

ODM also distinguishes between the following types of domains: vertical vs. horizontal, native vs. innovative, and diffused vs. encapsulated. Vertical domains are large-scale domains and cover systems in their entirety. They are usually business domains, such as education, insurance, telecommunications, etc. Horizontal domains are smaller scale technical domains that handle a part of a system's functionality. User interface construction, database access, and emailing are examples of such domains.

A horizontal domain may be diffused or encapsulated. A diffused horizontal domain defines functionality that is global within a system. An encapsulated horizontal domain defines a functional domain, the features of which are clustered in a single component of the system.

Native domains are familiar to practitioners, and are easily identified by domain experts. They generally correspond to functional domains within a business domain (e.g. sales, inventory, supplies, etc.). An *innovative* domain is defined from the perspective of innovation, in terms of creating new opportunities and solutions for the system in question.

1.2. Specificity

Specificity is the condition of being peculiar to a particular domain. This feature should determine the capacity of a DSL to solve the problems of a particular domain in the most natural way for its users. Mernik, et al. (2005) state that domain specificity is a matter of degree. A DSL with a high degree of specificity should provide constructs and features that are consistent with the daily tasks of domain experts. These experts must be able to understand the DSL and work with it without the need for special technical skills.

However, given that most domains change and evolve continuously to meet changing needs in the industry, maintaining the specificity of a DSL is a challenge. It requires that the DSL have a powerful ability to adapt and evolve, in order to easily accommodate the changes and transformations in the domain. The difficulty arises when trying to retain the expressiveness and the high level of abstraction of a DSL while responding to changes in the domain. A DSL must also ensure backward compatibility, so that the new version of the DSL continues to support the models developed with previous versions.

1.3. Language

In very general terms, a language consists of syntax and semantics: the syntax defines the form of valid expressions used in the language, while the semantics is concerned with the meaning of those expressions.

Generally, we distinguish two types of language: human language, and computer language. Human language is used by humans to express themselves or to communicate thoughts and ideas. These languages are difficult for computers to process. Computer language is more formal, in the sense that it is specifically designed to be processed by computers.

Software engineering and computer science are more concerned with computer languages. These languages can be classified based on many criteria; for example: formal vs. informal, programming vs. modeling, textual vs. graphical, imperative vs. declarative, general purpose vs. domain specific, executable vs. non executable, etc.

In light of the foregoing, a DSL may be considered as a small executable programming or modeling language characterized by:

- An operational domain, usually a horizontal one. A vertical domain is too broad to be used for a DSL. Often, in practice, many DSLs are required to implement a business domain.
- A syntax and a semantics specific to the domain.
- An expressive notation familiar to domain experts. The notation can be textual or graphical, and is often a combination of the two.

As mentioned previously, it is difficult to find a definition that fits all aspects and features of a DSL. The definition that we propose summarizes our view of the DSL, which is based on the definition proposed in (Deursen et al., 2000):

A DSL is a small language that offers, through appropriate notations and abstractions, a power of expression to improve the performance of stakeholders in a particular domain.

This definition highlights some of the characteristics that we believe are important in a DSL. It is a small language restricted in its syntax and its semantics. Unlike a general purpose language, a DSL must contain only the constructions that are essential to solving problems in the domain (Wile, 2004).

It is also characterized by expressiveness and a high level of abstraction. Raising the level of abstraction yields significant gains in productivity and quality (Mernik et al., 2005). In fact, offering abstractions and notations familiar to domain experts and hiding the implementation details make the development process easier and safer. The use of expressive abstractions makes it easy for domain experts to verify and validate the proposed solutions. They may even participate in designing these solutions.

Another important consideration is the stakeholders and their needs. As already seen, very few definitions explicitly mention these as an integral part of the domain concept (Czarnecki & Eisenecker, 2000). We believe that if a DSL is to be useful to its users it must take into account the organizational roles, experiences, and skills of its stakeholders (Wile, 2004).

2. TYPES OF DSLS

Fowler (2011) classifies DSLs into two categories: internal DSLs, and external DSLs. An internal DSL is a domain specific language defined within another language, usually a general purpose language, called the host language. It is a kind of extension of the host language that defines a dialect specific to the domain in question. The main advantage of this approach is that it does not require prior knowledge of language development.

DSL developers do not need to define a grammar or create tools to support internal DSLs. Among the most popular languages used for developing this kind of DSL are Ruby (Hansson, 2011), Lisp (McCarthy, 1965; Steele, 1990), Haskell (Jones, 2002), and Groovy (Strachan & McWhirter, 2011).

An external DSL is a language that is independent of the main application language. This type of DSL offers more flexibility in terms of grammar and notation. Some examples are SQL, XML, and CSS (Cascading Style Sheets). The major drawback of this type of DSL is the cost associated with the development of their supporting tools (generators, compilers, editors, etc.).

Tables 1 and 2 show the advantages and disadvantages of these two types of DSL.

Table 1. Advantages and disadvantages of internal DSLs

Advantages	Disadvantages
• Take advantage of the host language's capabilities and tools. • Their developers focus more on functionality from a high level of abstraction, while the host language handles low level details. • Do not require prior knowledge of language development.	• Their grammar and notation are driven by the host language. • Their efficiency is dependent on the capabilities of the host language. • Experience difficulty expressing something that has no equivalent in the host language.

Table 2. Advantages and disadvantages of external DSLs

Advantages	Disadvantages
• No grammatical or syntactical constraints. • Total control of syntax, grammar, model validation, etc.	• More difficult to design and implement. • Their developers must build all the supporting tools (e.g. compilers, editors, debuggers, etc.) • Require language development expertise (grammar definition, parsing, etc.) • Their users have a new language to learn.

In addition to the classification established by Fowler, DSLs can also be categorized based on their notation and specification style.

2.1. Notation

DSL models can be expressed in either textual or graphical notation, and sometimes a combination of the two is used. It is important to mention here the common misconception that textual notation is associated with programming languages, and graphical notation with modeling languages (Greenfield & Short, 2004a). It is entirely permissible, and even in some cases more appropriate, to define a graphical programming DSL, and vice versa.

2.2. Specification Style

DSL statements can be imperative or declarative (Greenfield & Short, 2004b). Imperative statements describe instructions to be executed without describing the expected result. In contrast, declarative statements describe the expected result without describing how it is obtained (Liberty & Horovitz, 2008).

3. DSL DEVELOPMENT TOOLS

DSL development tools are software utilities that support the creation of DSLs. These tools can generate, a specific integrated environment from a DSL specification, providing numerous facilities for DSL users.

In this section, we present some of the DSL development tools used in practice to show that the processes adopted by these tools are closely similar.

3.1. Eclipse Modeling Project (EMP)

The Eclipse Modeling Project was created to bring together all the sub projects under way in the Eclipse modeling community. It is aimed at creating a unified set of frameworks, tools, and standards to support model driven development.

The main components of the eclipse modeling project are: Abstract Syntax Development, Concrete Syntax Development, and Model Transformation technologies.

3.1.1. Abstract Syntax Development

The Abstract Syntax Development component handles the definition of abstract syntax for general purpose modeling languages and DSLs. It is supported by the Eclipse Modeling Framework (EMF) and its underlying technologies. EMF provides tools for defining models and building tools based on these definitions. Technically, EMF consists of three parts: Ecore, a meta-metamodel for the definition of metamodels, a simulator to simulate the behavior of the defined models, and a generator for generating a java implementation of these models.

3.1.2. Concrete Syntax Development

The Concrete Syntax Development component handles the creation of textual and graphical concrete syntax, in addition to editors for DSLs. This is supported by two main projects: Graphical Modeling Project (GMP), and Textual Modeling Framework (TMF). GMP provides a set of tools for building graphical editors based on EMF and GEF (Graphical Editing Framework). TMF provides tools for building textual syntaxes and editors for DSLs based on EMF.

3.1.3. Model Transformation Technologies

Model Transformation technologies handle model-to-model and model-to-text transformations. They are supported by two main projects: Model to Model Transformation (M2M), and Model to Text Transformation (M2T).

3.2. MetaEdit+ from Metacase

MetaEdit+ is a domain specific modeling environment that supports the building of domain specific languages. It is composed of two main tools: MetaEdit+ Workbench and MetaEdit+ Modeler. MetaEdit+ Workbench provides tooling for designing DSLs and building their specific modeling environments. MetaEdit+ Modeler provides the operating environment for the DSL, as defined by the MetaEdit+ Workbench.

3.2.1. MetaEdit+ Workbench

Mainly designed for domain experts and architects, this tool provides an integrated environment for defining and implementing DSLs. It includes an object editor for defining concepts, a property editor for defining the attributes of concepts, and a relationship editor for defining the relations between concepts. The environment also provides a symbol editor for defining the concrete syntax of the DSL and a generator editor for developing generators.

3.2.2. MetaEdit+ Modeler

MetaEdit+ Modeler provides modeling tools that support a DSL defined in MetaEdit+ Workbench. These tools include graphical editors for creating and editing DSL models, and browsers for viewing and managing resources.

Developing a DSL using MetaEdit+ consists of the following:

1. **Abstract syntax definition:** Specification of DSL concepts, their relations, and their constraints, using the tool MetaEdit+ Workbench.
2. **Concrete syntax definition:** Description of DSL notation, using the symbol editor offered by the MetaEdit+ Workbench.
3. **Generator construction:** Building of the generator(s) implementing the DSL. MetaEdit+ provides a generator editor for developing, debugging, and testing generators. These generators are written in a specific language that allows the manipulation of model information and the generation of code from a reference implementation.

3.3. Visual Studio Visualization and Modeling SDK (VMSDK)

Visual Studio Visualization and Modeling SDK (VMSDK) is the successor of the DSL tools launched by Microsoft in 2004. It is a software development kit that comes with Visual Studio, which allows the creation of a customized design environment in Visual Studio from modeling business concepts (metamodel).

Developing a DSL using Visual Studio 2010 and VMSDK consists of the following:

1. **Solution creation:** Creating a solution using a domain specific language template.
2. **DSL template selection:** Choosing, from a list of templates, the template that most resembles the desired DSL. Each DSL template defines a basic working DSL that can be edited to meet the developer's own requirements.
3. **Abstract and concrete syntax definition:** Using the DSL definition interface diagram. This interface defines the domain classes that define the DSL concepts and the relations that bind them. This diagram also shows the shapes and connectors used to display the DSL concepts (classes).

4. **Mapping:** Linking the concepts of the DSL with the elements of the concrete syntax.
5. **Code Generation:** Generating code from text models using text template transformation. A text model is a text file containing directives and commands that the template transformation engine runs to generate the final code.
6. **DSL deployment:** A DSL can be installed on the local computer or on other computers. Two methods are possible: VSX (Visual Studio eXtension), or MSI (Microsoft Installer). The first method is easy to use, but requires that Visual Studio be installed on each machine. The second method creates an MSI file that can be opened from Windows Explorer.

4. INDUSTRY STANDARDS

The DSL development tools presented in the previous section use either proprietary technologies or adapted versions of technologies known as standards (e.g. MOF, QVT, OCL, etc.). This variety of technologies affects the interoperability of tools and the portability of DSLs, and the standards are aimed at alleviating these problems.

The Object Management Group (OMG) standards appear to be the de facto standards for modeling and metamodeling. They cover many of the needs expressed when defining DSLs, and several tools rely on these standards to develop their functionality.

Below is a brief description of these standards:

4.1. Meta Object Facility (MOF)

This is a metamodeling language that was adopted by the OMG for the first time in 1997 to meet the needs of metamodel creation. In 2005, MOF specification 1.4.1 was adopted as an ISO standard – ISO/IEC 19502:2005. In version 2.0, MOF specification defines two variants: *Essential* MOF (EMOF), which is a subset containing only the essential concepts for defining simple metamodels, and *Complete* MOF (CMOF), which is a more comprehensive specification for defining more complex metamodels (OMG, 2008).

As a self-defined language, MOF sits on top of the four layer metamodeling architecture of the OMG. However, it should be noted that MOF is better at defining the structure of languages (abstract syntax), and does not support the definition of the operational semantics.

4.2. Object Constraint Language (OCL)

OCL is a constraint language used to specify expressions on UML models. These expressions include pre- and post-conditions on operations and methods, queries on objects, and invariants on classes and types. This type of expression does not have any side-effects. When an OCL expression is evaluated, it simply returns a value without altering the state of the system (OMG, 2006a). However, OCL also provides expressions that specify operations and actions that do alter the state of the system.

4.3. Query, View, Transformation (QVT)

QVT is a model transformation specification. Version 1.1 of this specification is composed of two parts: declarative, and imperative. The declarative part is defined by the languages *Relations* and *Core*. *Relations* allows the expression of declarative specifications for relations between MOF models. This language is characterized by its ability to handle complex pattern matching. Its concrete syntax can be textual or graphical. *Core* is simpler than *Relations*. It is defined using slight extensions of EMOF and OCL. Because of this minimalist approach, the missing features must be programmed manually, which can make the specification of transformations wordy and complex (OMG, 2008).

The imperative part is defined by the *Operational Mappings* language. This language is used to write imperative transformation specifications using a concrete syntax similar to that of imperative languages. A transformation entirely written using *Operational Mappings* is called an operational transformation.

In addition to these languages, QVT introduces a feature called *BlackBox* to invoke transformation functions written in external languages like XSLT and XQuery.

4.4. XML Metadata Interchange (XMI)

XMI is the OMG specification for describing and sharing models using XML format (OMG, 2005). In 2005, the 2.0.1 version of the XMI specification was accepted as an ISO standard (ISO/IEC 19503:2005) (ISO, 2005).

Since XMI is unable to represent the graphical part of models, the OMG has defined the Diagram Interchange (DI), a specification that extends the UML metamodel with an additional metamodel for representing graphical information. This specification also provides a mechanism for converting XMI to SVG (Scalable Vector Graphics) to achieve interoperability with graphical tools (OMG, 2006b).

5. DSL DEVELOPMENT PROCESS

Although DSLs have been used for a long time, they still lack well defined processes and methods that can manage the whole DSL development cycle (Mernik, Heering, & Sloane, 2005; Thibault, Marlet, & Consel, 1999). The literature (Cleaveland, 1988; Consel & Marlet, 1998; Deursen, Klint, & Visser, 2000; Mernik, Heering, & Sloane, 2005; Tolvanen, 2006; Van Deursen & Klint, 1998) shows that a typical DSL development cycle involves the following four phases: decision, analysis, design, and implementation.

5.1. Decision

DSL development is not a simple task. Becoming involved in the development of a DSL is usually the result of a decision made after examining other options, such as the use of a general purpose language, the purchase of an off-the-shelf DSL, etc.

The idea of developing a DSL usually follows an attempt to developing a great many applications for the domain using general purpose languages. For a domain where little knowledge is available, a new DSL makes little sense. It makes more sense if the domain knowledge is strong enough and when other alternatives fail to meet all the requirements. In (Mernik et al., 2005), a set of patterns has been identified that summarizes situations where the use of DSLs has been shown to be viable in the past.

5.2. DSL Analysis

The DSL Analysis phase focuses on the identification and organization of domain knowledge (Prieto-Diaz, 1990). Several domain analysis methods are available to help perform domain analysis, but, according to Prieto-Diaz (1990), this process is often conducted in an ad hoc way, and therefore relies closely on the expertise of the domain analyst. According to (America, Thiel, Ferber, & Mergel, 2001), domain analysis consists of two main activities: domain scoping and domain modeling.

5.2.1. Domain Scoping

Domain scoping defines the boundaries of the DSL domain. In this step, the DSL analyst focuses on defining the problem space targeted by the DSL and on the specification of the features to include or exclude from the DSL (Cleaveland, 1988).

Defining the right domain scope is crucial (Schmid, 2002; van der Linden, 2002). If the scope is too broad, the development of the DSL becomes more costly and the DSL will tend to use more generic concepts, which will have a negative effect on its expressiveness. In contrast, if the scope is too narrow, the DSL will be too specific, which will reduce its possibilities.

A good definition of DSL scope starts with a precise definition of its problem domain. After all, a DSL is a language designed to meet specific requirements of a particular problem in a given domain. Therefore, a precise definition of the problem domain helps to better define the boundaries of the DSL.

Another technique is to define the scope of the DSL based on the concept of viewpoints. According to Tolvanen (2006), creating a DSL often starts from a particular viewpoint, which defines the perspective from which the problem or the solution, or both, is specified or modeled. First, the analyst defines the domain viewpoints, and then, for each viewpoint, he determines the DSLs that can support it. Viewpoints are an effective way to separate and organize stakeholder concerns: viewpoint driven DSLs are more likely to meet the needs of their users.

In (Simos, 1995; Simos et al., 1996), a discussion of the domain concept is given, and some techniques for defining domain scope are presented.

5.2.2. Domain Modeling

In domain modeling, domain knowledge is organized into domain models. There is no specific model for this activity (America et al., 2001). Each domain analysis method specifies its own set of models to produce. Yet, two models are particularly important for DSL analysis: the conceptual model, also called the information model, and the model of commonalities and variations.

5.2.2.1. Conceptual Model

The objective of conceptual modeling is to identify and organize DSL concepts and their relations. A conceptual model may take the form of an entity-relationship model, a semantic network, or any other form that can express domain knowledge in a clear and precise manner.

5.2.2.2. Commonality and Variability Models

Commonality and variability models are used to present the common features and variations in a software product family. Commonality analysis identifies characteristics and assumptions that are common to all members of the family (Weiss, 1998). Variability analysis identifies characteristics and assumptions that are not common to all members of the family. According to Weiss (1998), commonality and variability analysis can be used as input to the DSL design process. Commonalities define the parts that can be implemented as reusable components by all members of the family, while the variations help to formalize the grammar and notation of DSLs.

In variability analysis, two main activities are performed: identification of variation points, and definition of variation parameters.

5.2.2.2.1. Variation Points

Variation points identify locations where variations can take place (Ivar, Martin, & Patrik, 1997). Each of these locations represents a design decision to be made for each member of the family. A variation point is characterized by a type specifying the nature of the variation, and a set of relations defining its dependencies and interactions with other variations (a more detailed discussion on dependency types can be found in (Bühne, Halmans, & Pohl, 2003)). According to Bachmann and Bass (2001), there are three types of variation: *an optional variation, an alternative variation*, and *a set of alternative variations* (see also (Muthig & Atkinson, 2002)). A variation is optional if the underlying functionality is optional for the family member. It is alternative if the member must implement one instance from the alternatives offered by the variation point. If the member must implement one or more of the alternatives, then the variation is *a set of alternatives*.

5.2.2.2.2. Variation Parameters

Variation parameters are used to parameterize variations (Coplien, Hoffman, & Weiss, 1998). A variation parameter is a variable characterized by a type and a range of values. Thus, the configuration of a family member is actually a definition of a subset of the range of values defined for the family.

Feature Modeling is one of the most commonly used techniques for capturing and managing commonalities and variations (Antkiewicz & Czarnecki, 2004; Czarnecki, Helsen, & Eisenecker, 2004; Lee, Kang, & Lee, 2002). The common and variable features of the family are organized into feature diagrams. These diagrams have a tree-like structure, where the root represents a concept and the leaves represent its features and sub features.

5.3. Design

Designing a DSL consists in defining its abstract syntax, concrete syntax, and semantics. These three activities are introduced in the following sections, along with the tools and techniques for performing them.

5.3.1. Abstract Syntax

The abstract syntax defines the concepts and their relations and the grammatical rules of the DSL. These three components define the core vocabulary and grammar of the DSL (Clark, Sammut, & Willans, 2008). The concepts define the types of elements handled by the DSL. The relations and grammatical rules define how these elements can be combined to form valid models (Greenfield & Short, 2004b).

The relevance of the concepts defined depends strongly on the working level of abstraction. According to (Tolvanen, 2006), the most important part in the design process of a DSL is to find the right abstractions.

Abstraction is the process of the mind by which we eliminate the less relevant concepts and consider only those that are more relevant for the subject at hand (Office québécois de la langue française, 2002). To perform this activity, the level of abstraction must be carefully specified. If it is too abstract, the DSL will not be able to

provide all the necessary information in its models. However, an overly detailed level of abstraction will likely increase the complexity of the DSL. The question that arises is how to define the right abstractions. According to Kramer (2007), doing so depends on the ability to perform abstract thinking. The author states that the level and the value of an abstraction are generally determined by its purpose. This implies that the purpose of the abstraction process must be clearly defined at the outset.

Two approaches are generally used to define the abstract syntax (Greenfield & Short, 2004b): context-free grammar (CFG), and metamodeling. CFG is better suited to describing textual languages, due to its text processing capabilities, whereas the metamodeling approach lends itself better to describing graphical modeling languages.

5.3.1.1. Context-Free Grammar

In 1956, Noam Chomsky proposed a hierarchy for classifying the types of formal grammars used to describe languages. According to this classification, non contextual grammars are second in the hierarchy of types (Chomsky, 1956, 1959). A context-free grammar is a formal grammar consisting of a set of productions of the form $A{\rightarrow}B$, where A is a non terminal symbol which may be substituted by any string of the vocabulary, and B is a terminal or a non terminal symbol. A non terminal symbol is a composite element, the internal structure of which can be described with other symbols (terminal or non terminal). A non terminal symbol must appear on the left side of at least one production. A terminal symbol is a sequence of one or more characters forming an irreducible element of the language (ISO, 1996).

There are various notations for representing a context-free grammar. The best known of these are the BNF notation (Backus Normal Form/ Backus-Naur Form) and ISO/IEC 14977 that defines a syntactical notation based on the BNF and its popular extensions (ISO, 1996):

5.3.1.1.1. BNF

Originally called the Backus Normal Form, after its inventor John Backus, who developed this notation to describe the grammar of ALGOL (**ALGO**rithmic **L**anguage), this is an imperative programming language created in the late 1950s to algorithmically describe programming problems. It later became the Backus-Naur Form, after Peter Naur had improved it (Knuth, 1964). There are currently several variants of this notation is use. Extended BNF (EBNF), Augmented BNF (ABNF), and Reduced BNF (RBNF) are some examples.

5.3.1.1.2. ISO/IEC 14977: 1996 – EBNF

The notation described in ISO/IEC 14977 is based on the EBNF notation proposed by Niklaus Wirth (ISO, 1996). It is characterized by its adoption of a syntax similar to that of regular expressions. This syntax facilitates the description of aspects such as repetition and the grouping of blocks. This makes building compilers easier, because parsers can be generated automatically using a compiler-compiler (Garshol, 2010).

5.3.1.2. Metamodeling

Since its use in the definition of UML, metamodeling has become the preferred approach for defining modeling languages (Greenfield & Short, 2004b). Its use for defining DSLs offers many advantages. The most important of these is the unification of the development process. Metamodeling allows DSLs to be defined in a unified way using the same metamodeling language to develop nearly all the components of a DSL (e.g. abstract syntax, concrete syntax, and semantics). Added to this is the use of an intuitive notation that facilitates communication of the designer's intentions.

Metamodeling can be defined as the process of defining metamodels. A metamodel is a model of a model. It is written in a metalanguage and defines the language used to build models. In this regard, a model is an instance of the metamodel that was used to define its modeling language. This model instantiation mechanism is at the heart of the metamodeling approach, and can be extended across multiple levels of abstraction.

There are many frameworks for defining metamodels. The most popular of these is the four-layer metamodeling architecture of the OMG, which adopts a strict metamodeling approach. That is, if a model M_0 is an instance of another model M_1, then each element in M_0 must be an instance of some element in M_1. For example, the UML metamodel is regarded as an instance of the MOF meta-metamodel. So, every UML element is an instance of an element of the MOF metamodel (OMG, 2009). Strict metamodeling also suggests that the various layers have strict limits and cannot be crossed by any relation other than the *instance of* relation. In addition, such a relation is only permissible between two immediately adjacent layers (Atkinson & Kühne, 2002).

The strict metamodeling approach helps simplify the process of metamodeling. However, it has some drawbacks (Álvarez, Evans, & Sammut, 2001; Atkinson & Kühne, 2002). For example, according to Atkinson et al. (2002), there is no clear description of the precise meaning of the *instance of* relation, which may give rise to many possible interpretations. The authors propose the following definition:

In an n-level modeling architecture, $M_0, M_1, \ldots, M_{n-1}$, every element of an M_m level model must be an instance-of exactly one element of an M_{m+1} level model, for all $0 <= m < n-1$, and any relationship other than the instance-of relationship between two elements X and Y implies that level(X) = level(Y). (Atkinson & Kühne, 2002)

5.3.1.3. Abstract Syntax Definition

Regardless of the approach adopted for defining the abstract syntax, the process remains typically the same (see Clark, et al., 2008, for further details). This process consists of concept identification and grammatical rules definition.

5.3.1.3.1. Concept Identification

The first step in defining the abstract syntax is to identify the concepts to be used by the DSL. First, the output of the abstraction process, initiated in the domain analysis phase, is sorted and filtered. In this step, only the concepts relevant to the vocabulary of the DSL are considered. The concepts related to the concrete syntax or the semantics are left aside.

Here are some practical steps that can help manage this process.

5.3.1.3.1.1. Identification of the Level of Abstraction

Working at the right level of abstraction is crucial for the success of a DSL (Tolvanen, 2006), because this directly affects its expressiveness. Usually, the level of abstraction is determined by its purpose (Kramer, 2007), which helps manage the relevance of abstractions. In the case of DSLs, the abstraction level should be determined respecting two criteria: 1) the expressiveness of the DSL, and 2) the ability to generate code from DSL models.

5.3.1.3.1.2. Building of a List of Candidate Concepts

Preparing a list of the most significant concepts for the DSL is an art, and depends largely on the skills and expertise of the analysts. We highlight below some of the techniques and practices that can help in this process.

According to Tolvanen (2006), concept identification often starts from a particular viewpoint, the most commonly used viewpoints in this process being the following:

- **Physical product structure:** This viewpoint is particularly useful when modeling physical objects. The concepts then focus on describing the physical structure of the object being modeled.
- **Look and feel of the system:** Concepts are identified from the viewpoint of the end us-

ers' interfaces, navigation, and interaction with the system;
- **Variability space:** Concepts are identified based on the variability space of the software product family. DSLs defined in this way are primarily used to parameterize family members;
- **Domain expert concepts:** Concepts are identified based on the viewpoint of the domain experts. DSLs defined based on domain expert concepts are likely to offer a higher level of expressiveness;
- **Generation output:** Concepts are identified based on the generation target. For example, if this target is an XML file, then the XML schema can be used as a source for identifying DSL concepts.

Having determined the appropriate viewpoint, the analyst can use the usual analysis and design techniques to identify the concepts of the DSL (Fontoura, Prec, & Rumpe, 2000; Larman, 2004). Useful techniques are briefly described as follows:

- **Reuse:** It is preferable to check whether or not any domain analysis has been performed for the domain in question before starting to identify concepts, in order to avoid reinventing the wheel and to benefit from the experience of others;
- **Iterative approach:** This approach is particularly useful when not enough is known about either the problem or the solution domain. The iterations make it possible to learn more about both. The number of iterations generally depends on the size and complexity of the domain;
- **Names and nominal sentences:** This technique was proposed in (Abbott, 1983), and is based on the extraction of names and nominal phrases that appear in the domain description. The extracted names and phrases constitute a list of candidate concepts that will have to be refined to keep

only the concepts relevant to the DSL. The refinement activity is necessary because of the ambiguity created by natural language;

- **Archetype driven approach:** This approach consists of identifying domain concepts based on the archetypes defined in (Coad, de Luca, & Lefebvre, 1999). According to the authors, all domain concepts belong to one of the following four archetypes: Moment-Interval, Role, Party, or Description. These archetypes define the attributes, operations, and interactions that are typical for a class or a set of classes of a given category (Peter Coad, 1992; Coad, North, & Mayfield, 1997). Each of the archetypes is presented in a different color. This technique is called layering, and, according to Coad et al., is used to express additional layers of information and provide better readability for models. The colors give an immediate indication of the content of the model by allowing the reader to instantly divide the model into four visual layers (Coad et al., 1999).

The four archetypes are the following:

1. **Moment-interval (Pink):** An event or activity that occurs at a particular time, or during an interval of time. For example, borrowing a book from a library occurs during an interval of time, whereas the sale of a book occurs at a moment in time;
2. **Role (Yellow):** The participation in an event or activity of a party (an individual, a group, or an organization, for example), a place, or a thing;
3. **Description (Blue):** Description of a party, a place, or a thing. It can be used as an entry in a catalog, for example;
4. **Party, place, or thing (Green):** An entity that plays one or more roles.

In the same context, Larman has proposed a list of a large number of categories of classes, which, according to the author, are generally used by developers (see (Larman, 2004) for further details). Analysis patterns, such as those proposed in (Fowler, 1997) can also be used to identify concepts.

5.3.1.3.2. Definition of the Grammatical Rules

The second step in the process of defining the abstract syntax is to define the grammatical rules that determine the validity of models, and is particularly useful when it comes to implementing tools to verify the correctness and validity of DSL models. In this case, these rules should be expressed with a formal language like OCL. However, in practice, they are often expressed informally using natural language (Clark, et al., 2008).

5.3.2. Concrete Syntax

While the abstract syntax focuses on the description of the vocabulary and grammar of the DSL, the concrete syntax deals with the specification of the notation used to represent the elements used in the DSL models (Greenfield & Short, 2004b). The concrete syntax can take various forms. It can be textual or graphical, or a combination of the two. A textual concrete syntax is used primarily for programming languages, while a graphical concrete syntax is used for modeling languages. Languages that combine both forms of notation usually use the graphical notation to represent views at a higher level of abstraction and the textual notation to capture more detailed information (Clark, et al., 2008).

5.3.2.1. Textual Concrete Syntax

The textual concrete syntax defines DSL models (programs) as textual structures that represent declarations of data structures, and either expressions or statements that use and control the flow of execution of these structures. The main advantage of a textual syntax is its ability to capture complex expressions. However, beyond a certain number of lines, these textual expressions become difficult to understand and maintain.

Usually, a textual concrete syntax is specified using a notation from the BNF family. There are some advantages to using a BNF-like notation, the most important being that this formalism is supported by many of the tools used for generating lexers and parsers. Lexers are software components that perform the lexical analysis of a program, which is the process of converting a sequence of characters into a sequence of tokens. Parsers, in contrast, convert these sequences of tokens into an abstract syntax tree (AST).

5.3.2.2. Graphical Concrete Syntax

Little work has been devoted to the rigorous definition of graphical concrete syntaxes (Greenfield & Short, 2004b). This type of syntax is often defined informally (Fondement & Baar, 2005), and describes the graphical elements (symbols) used to represent the elements in DSL models and to determine their geometrical layering. It provides a graphical user interface for working with the concepts of the DSL. Each element (concept, relation, etc.) to be represented in a model is associated with a graphical symbol. The main advantage of this type of syntax is its ability to express information in a clear and an intuitive way (Clark et al., 2008). However, its weakness is that it can express the information only at a certain level of abstraction. Beyond that level, the syntax becomes too complex and difficult, if not impossible, to understand.

5.3.3. Semantics

Generally, the abstract syntax does not contain enough information to define the meaning of the constructs of the DSL. The goal of semantics is to capture and organize all this information in semantic models.

Understanding the meaning of DSL constructs is essential for defining executable DSLs, the models of which are easy for machines to analyze and process. Transformation and code generation techniques depend heavily on the clarity and precision of the DSL semantics. Every syntactically valid DSL expression must have a precise and unambiguous meaning (Harel & Rumpe, 2000), so that the models are clearly understood and the risk of misinterpretation is minimized (Clark et al., 2008).

The semantics of a language in general and of a DSL in particular consists of two parts: the semantic domain, and the semantic mapping (Harel & Rumpe, 2000). The semantic domain defines the set of possible meanings that can be given to the various DSL expressions and statements, and the semantic mapping sets the relationships between the expressions/statements defined in the syntactical domain, and their meanings in the semantic domain.

In practice, the same approaches used to define the semantics of programming languages can be used to define the semantics of DSLs. However, we must distinguish between programming and modeling DSLs. The semantics of modeling DSLs is considered to be the more challenging task, and may require different approaches and techniques.

Among the styles used to define the semantics of DSLs are the following:

- **Algebraic semantics:** Consists of an algebraic specification of the elements of the language. This style of semantics is usually used to specify abstract data types, such as data structures (Slonneger & Kurtz, 1995).
- **Operational semantics:** Describes the dynamic behavior of the elements of a DSL by specifying how a program is interpreted in terms of its execution steps.
- **Denotational semantics:** Originally called mathematical semantics (Slonneger & Kurtz, 1995), this approach describes the meaning of a language through the construction of mathematical objects called

denotations. Unlike operational semantics, denotational semantics focuses on the effect of the program rather than its execution steps.

- **Translational semantics:** Involves translating the expressions of one language (source) into expressions in another language (target), the semantics of which is known. In the case of DSLs, this approach is used to translate the expressions of a DSL into expressions in another DSL or in a general purpose language.

5.4. Implementation

Implementing a DSL consists in developing the tools to perform model transformation and code generation. Mernik et al. (2005) have identified seven patterns for implementing DSLs and a set of guidelines to help choose the most appropriate implementation technique to meet the requirements.

In practice, two classes of technique are used: techniques for external DSLs and techniques for internal DSLs (see section 2).

5.4.1. Implementation of External DSLs

External DSLs are usually implemented by creating supporting tools, such as compilers, interpreters, and code generators. These tools are created using compiler-compilers, such as Lex (Lesk, 1975), Yacc (Johnson, 1974), Flex (Paxson, 1988), Bison (Free Software Foundation, 2009), and ANTLR (Parr, 2007). These tools can automatically generate code for lexical analysis, parsing, and error handling based on a formal description of a DSL (DSL grammar). Other implementation activities, such as semantic analysis, are left to the developer of the DSL.

5.4.2. Implementation of Internal DSLs

Unlike external DSLs, implementing an internal DSL does not require the creation of compilers

or translators, since the syntax of internal DSLs must conform to the syntax of their host language. Therefore, internal DSLs benefit from the support tools of the host language. However, as with external DSLs, the implementation of the semantics is left to the DSL developer.

The techniques used for implementing internal DSLs depend on the characteristics and capabilities provided by the host language. For example, C++ is well known for its mechanism of template meta-programming, operator overloading, and macros. Lisp is known for its macro system, which facilitates the extension of its syntax. The Ruby language is characterized by its flexible syntax, macro support, dynamic typing, and closure. DSL developers are compelled to work with the possibilities provided by the host language. Therefore, selection of the right host language becomes a key factor in the success of the DSL.

Below is a list of features and techniques commonly used in the implementation of internal DSLs:

Meta-programming: This is the task of writing meta-programs, which are programs that can analyze, generate, and manipulate other programs. Meta-programming is implemented by programming languages in various ways:

Macro: A mechanism by which some of the code is generated using text substitution. The use of this mechanism involves three steps: 1) macro-definition, to associate an identifier with the replacement text; 2) macro-instruction, to call the macro; and 3) macro-expansion, to substitute the macro with the replacement text.

The system of macros in Lisp shows the power and potential of this text substitution technique. It is commonly used to extend the syntax of Lisp, and can be useful for developing DSLs.

Template: A means to generically represent the overall structure of the code with parameters that will be substituted at runtime.

Operator overloading: The ability of a language to overload its predefined operators. This feature is widely used in C++ to change the semantics of its predefined operators.

Reflexivity: The feature of a programming language that can create programs capable of examining and modifying their structure (structural reflection) and behavior (behavioral reflection). Structural reflection allows manipulation of program code and abstract data types during execution. Behavioral reflection allows a program to obtain information about its implementation, and eventually reorganize itself to adapt to its execution context. The ability of a programming language to dynamically intervene and change the behavior of a program provides a number of possibilities for implementing DSLs. In fact, reflexivity can be used to generate specific code and integrate it automatically into the running program.

Syntax flexibility: The ability of a language to extend its syntax to adapt to a particular domain. This feature allows the compiler to take over new syntaxes without altering any of its components. Lisp, Smalltalk, and Ruby are examples of languages that use this capability to extend their syntax and build DSLs.

Syntactic Sugar: The ability of a language to make its syntax more succinct, more elegant, and more expressive. Ruby is an example of this type of language.

This list of features is not exhaustive. In fact, every language stands out for its own set of characteristics that differentiates it from others. Also effective for developing DSLs are features like closures and string evaluation statements (e.g. javascript's *eval* statement). It is therefore recommended that a preliminary analysis be performed to examine the potential and possibilities of a general purpose language before using it as a host language for a DSL.

6. SUMMARY

A domain specific language is a small language that offers, through appropriate notations and abstractions, a power of expression to improve the performance of stakeholders in a particular domain. These languages are used in various fields to help domain experts design solutions using concepts and notations that are familiar to them. But organizations have hurdles to overcome if they want to adopt DSLs on a wider scale.

The first hurdle to overcome is the development of DSLs. Up to now, DSLs have been developed in an ad hoc manner; there are no well defined methods for managing the DSL development cycle. DSL developers must have strong language development skills and good domain knowledge.

In spite of the advantages of DSLs, developing a new DSL is not always a good choice. Before becoming involved in the development of a DSL, an examination of other options such as the use of a general purpose language, the purchase of an off-the-shelf DSL has to be made. The idea of developing a DSL usually follows an attempt to developing a great many applications for the domain using general purpose languages.

Once the decision for the development of a new DSL is made and the type of DSL is determined (internal or external), the most suitable DSL development environment (i.e. development team, DSL development tools for external DSLs, host language for internal DSL, etc.) must be chosen to begin the development process which, typically, consists of three phases: analysis, design and implementation.

The DSL Analysis phase focuses on the identification and organization of domain knowledge. Several domain analysis methods are available to help perform domain analysis. Typically, the output of domain analysis consists of: domain scope, abstraction model, commonalities and variabilities.

Designing a DSL consists in defining its abstract syntax, concrete syntax and semantics. A key point in this design process is to find the right abstractions. The level of abstraction must be carefully specified so that it is not too broad or too narrow. The abstract syntax can then be defined using context free grammar or metamodeling techniques. The concrete syntax is defined using DSL development tools that offer utilities for defining concrete syntax elements and mapping them to the abstract syntax elements. Usually, these tools permit the specification of textual and graphical concrete syntax. After defining the syntax aspect of the DSL comes the definition of its semantics which determines the effect of the execution of DSL models.

Implementing a DSL consists in developing the tools to perform model transformation and code generation. External DSLs are usually implemented by creating supporting tools such as compilers, interpreters and generators. Implementing an internal DSL does not require the creation of compilers or translators, since the syntax of internal DSLs must conform to the syntax of their host language; however it requires careful selection of the host language.

REFERENCES

Abbott, R. (1983). Program design by informal English descriptions. *Communications of the ACM, 26*(11), 882–894.

Abelson, H., Sussman, G., & Sussman, J. (1996). *Structure and interpretation of computer programs* (2nd ed.). Cambridge, MA: MIT Press.

America, P., Thiel, S., Ferber, S., & Mergel, M. (2001). *Introduction to domain analysis. ESAPS Project.* Engineering Software Architectures, Processes, and Platforms for System Families.

Antkiewicz, M., & Czarnecki, K. (2004). *FeaturePlugin: Feature modeling plug-in for Eclipse.* Paper presented at the 2004 OOPSLA Workshop on Eclipse Technology eXchange. Vancouver, Canada.

Ardis, M., & Weiss, D. (1997). *Defining families: The commonality analysis.* Paper presented at the 19th International Conference on Software Engineering. Boston, MA.

Arnold, B., Van Deursen, A., & Res, M. (1995). *An algebraic specification of a language for describing financial products.* Paper presented at the IEEE Workshop on Formal Methods Application in Software Engineering. Seattle, WA.

Atkinson, C., & Kühne, T. (2002). Rearchitecting the UML infrastructure. *ACM Transactions on Modeling and Computer Simulation, 12*(4), 290–321.

Bachmann, F., & Bass, L. (2001). Managing variability in software architectures. *ACM SIGSOFT Software Engineering Notes, 26*(3), 126–132.

Bézivin, J. (2004). In search of a basic principle for model driven engineering. *The European Journal for the Informatics Professional, 5*(2), 21–24.

Bézivin, J., & Heckel, R. (2004). *Language engineering for model-driven software development.* Paper presented at the Dagstuhl Seminar. Dagstuhl, Germany.

Boulanger, R. (2000). *The Csound book: Perspectives in software synthesis, sound design, signal processing, and programming.* Cambridge, MA: MIT press.

Bühne, S., Halmans, G., & Pohl, K. (2003). *Modelling dependencies between variation points in use case diagrams.* Paper presented at the 9th Workshop in Requirements Engineering – Foundations for Software Quality. Klagenfurt, Austria.

Chamberlin, D., & Boyce, R. (1974). *SEQUEL: A structured English query language.* Paper presented at the 1974 ACM SIGFIDET (now SIGMOD) Workshop on Data Description, Access and Control. New York, NY.

Chomsky, N. (1956). Three models for the description of language. *I.R.E. Transactions on Information Theory, 2*(3), 113–124.

Chomsky, N. (1959). On certain formal properties of grammars. *Information and Control, 2*(2), 137–167.

Clark, T., Sammut, P., & Willans, J. (2008). *Applied metamodelling: A foundation for language driven development* (2nd ed.). CETEVA.

Cleaveland, J. C. (1988). Building application generators. *IEEE Software, 5*(4), 25–33.

Coad, P. (1992). Object-oriented patterns. *Communications of the ACM*, *35*(9), 152–159.

Coad, P., de Luca, J., & Lefebvre, É. (1999). *Java modeling color with UML: Enterprise components and process*. Upper Saddle River, NJ: Prentice Hall PTR.

Coad, P., North, D., & Mayfield, M. (1997). *Object models: Strategies, patterns, and applications* (2nd ed.). Upper Saddle River, NJ: Prentice Hall.

Coplien, J., Hoffman, D., & Weiss, D. (1998). Commonality and variability in software engineering. *IEEE Software*, *15*, 37–45.

Czarnecki, K., & Eisenecker, U. (2000). *Generative programming: Methods, tools, and applications*. Boston: Addison Wesley.

Czarnecki, K., Helsen, S., & Eisenecker, U. (2004). Staged configuration using feature models. *Lecture Notes in Computer Science*, *3154*, 266–283.

Deursen, Λ. V., Klint, P., & Visser, J. (2000). Domain-specific languages: An annotated bibliography. *ACM SIGPLAN Notices*, *35*(6), 26–36.

Fondement, F., & Baar, T. (2005). Making metamodels aware of concrete syntax. *Lecture Notes in Computer Science*, *3748*, 190–204.

Fontoura, M., Pree, W., & Rumpe, B. (2000). *The UML profile for framework architectures*. Boston, MA: Addison-Wesley Longman Publishing Co..

Fowler, M. (1997). *Analysis patterns reusable object models*. Boston, MA: Addison-Wesley Longman Publishing Co., Inc..

Fowler, M. (2011). Domain specific languages. *Martin Fowler*. Retrieved August 13, 2012, from http://martinfowler.com/bliki/DomainSpecificLanguage.html

Free Software Foundation. I. (2009). Bison -- GNU parser generator. *The GNU Operating System*. Retrieved August 10, 2012, from http://www.gnu.org/software/bison/

Friedl, J. (2006). *Mastering regular expressions* (3rd ed.). Sebastopol, CA: O'Reilly Media, Inc..

Garshol, L. (2010). *BNF and EBNF: What are they and how do they work?* Retrieved August 16, 2012, from http://www.garshol.priv.no/download/text/bnf.html

Greenfield, J., & Short, K. (2004a). *Software factories: Industrialized software development*. Retrieved August 20, 2012, from http://www.softwarefactories.com/index.html

Greenfield, J., & Short, K. (2004b). *Software factories: Assembling applications with patterns, models, frameworks, and tools*. Indianapolis, IN: Wiley Publishing Inc..

Hansson, D. (2011). *Ruby on rails*. Retrieved August 20, 2012, from http://rubyonrails.org

Harel, D., & Rumpe, B. (2000). *Modeling languages: Syntax, semantics and all that stuff, part I: The basic stuff*. Israel: Weizmann Science Press of Israel.

Hucka, M. et al. (2003). The systems biology markup language (SBML): A medium for representation and exchange of biochemical network models. *Bioinformatics (Oxford, England)*, *19*(4), 524–531. PMID:12611808.

ISO. (1986). *Standard generalized markup language (SGML)* (Vol. []. International Organization for Standardization.]. *ISO*, *8879*, 155.

ISO. (1996). Syntactic metalanguage -- Extended BNF (Vol. ISO/IEC 14977:1996, pp. 12). International Organization for Standardization.

ISO. (2005). XML metadata interchange (XMI) (Vol. ISO/IEC 19503:2005, pp. 115). International Organization for Standardization.

ISO. (2008). Database languages -- SQL -- Part 2: Foundation (SQL/foundation) (Vol. ISO/IEC 9075:2008, pp. 1317). International Organization for Standardization.

Ivar, J., Martin, G., & Patrik, J. (1997). *Software reuse: Architecture, process and organization for business success.* New York, NY: ACM Press/Addison-Wesley Publishing Co..

Johnson, S. (1979). YACC-yet another compiler-compiler. In *UNIX Programmer's Manual.* AT&T Bell Laboratories.

Jones, S. (2002). *Haskell 98 language and libraries: The revised report.* Retrieved August 20, 2012, from http://www.haskell.org/onlinereport/

Kaisler, S. H. (2005). *Software paradigms.* Hoboken, NJ: John Wiley & Sons.

Kang, K., Cohen, S., Hess, J., Novak, W., & Peterson, A. (1990). *Feature-oriented domain analysis (FODA) feasibility study (Online No. CMU/SEI-90-TR-021).* Pittsburgh, PA: Carnegie Mellon University Software Engineering Institute.

Kelly, S., & Tolvanen, J. (2008). *Domain-specific modeling.* Hoboken, NJ: John Wiley & Sons, Inc..

Kleppe, A. (2008). *Software language engineering: Creating domain-specific languages using metamodels.* Reading, MA: Addison-Wesley Professional.

Knuth, D. (1964). Backus normal form vs. Backus naur form. *Communications of the ACM, 7*(12), 735–736.

Kramer, J. (2007). Is abstraction the key to computing? *Communications of the ACM, 50*(4), 36–42.

Larman, C. (2004). *Applying UML and patterns: An introduction to object-oriented analysis and design and iterative development* (3rd ed.). Upper Saddle River, NJ: Prentice Hall.

Lee, K., Kang, K., & Lee, J. (2002). *Concepts and guidelines of feature modeling for product line software engineering.* Paper presented at the 7th International Conference on Software Reuse: Methods, Techniques, and Tools. Austin, TX.

Lesk, M. (1975). *Lex: A lexical analyzer generator.* Murray Hill, NJ: Bell Laboratories.

Liberty, J., & Horovitz, A. (2008). *Programming: NET 3.5.* O'Reilly Media, Inc..

Martin, J. (1967). *Design of real-time computer systems.* Upper Saddle River, NJ: Prentice-Hall, Inc..

McCarthy, J. (1965). *LISP 1.5 programmer's manual.* Cambridge, MA: The MIT Press.

Mernik, M., Heering, J., & Sloane, A. M. (2005). When and how to develop domain-specific languages. *ACM Computing Surveys, 37*(4), 316–344.

Microsoft. (2011). *Microsoft Excel 2010.* Microsoft.

Murray-Rust, P. (1997). Chemical markup language. *World Wide Web Journal, 2*(4), 135–147.

Muthig, D., & Atkinson, C. (2002). *Model-driven product line architectures.* Paper presented at the 2nd International Conference on Software Product Lines. San Diego, CA.

Northrop, L. M. (2002). SEI's software product line tenets. *IEEE Software, 19*(4), 32–40.

Office Québécois de la Langue Française. (2002). *Grand dictionnaire terminologique.* Author.

OMG. (2005). *XML metadata interchange V 2.1* (online no. formal/2009-02-04). OMG.

OMG. (2006a). *Object constraint language V2.0* (online no. formal/2006-05-01). OMG.

OMG. (2006b). *Unified modeling language: Diagram interchange v 2.0* (online). OMG.

OMG. (2008). *Query/view/transformation, v1.0* (online). OMG.

OMG. (2009). *UML 2.2 infrastructure specification (online).* OMG.

Parnas, D. (1976). On the design and development of program families. *IEEE Transactions on Software Engineering, 2*(1), 1–9.

Parr, T. (2007). The definitive ANTLR reference: Building domain-specific languages. In *The pragmatic programmers* (p. 369). Raleigh, NC: Pragmatic Bookshelf.

Paxson, V. (1988). *Flex-fast lexical analyzer generator*. Free Software Foundation.

Prieto-Diaz, R. (1990). Domain analysis: An introduction. *SIGSOFT Software Engineering Notes, 15*(2), 47–54.

Schmid, K. (2002). *A comprehensive product line scoping approach and its validation*. Paper presented at the 24th International Conference on Software Engineering. Orlando, FL.

Selic, B. (2007). *A systematic approach to domain-specific language design using UML*. Paper presented at the 10th IEEE International Symposium on Object and Component-Oriented Real-Time Distributed Computing (ISORC '07). Santorini Island, Greece.

Simos, M. (1995). *Organization domain modeling (ODM): Formalizing the core domain modeling life cycle*. Paper presented at the 1995 Symposium on Software Reusability. Seattle, WA.

Simos, M., Creps, D., Klingler, C., Levine, L., & Allemang, D. (1996). *Organization domain modeling (ODM) guidebook, version 2.0 (No. STARS-VC-A025/001/00). Software Technology For Adaptable, Reliable Systems*. STARS.

Slonneger, K., & Kurtz, B. (1995). *Formal syntax and semantics of programming languages*. Reading, MA: Addison-Wesley.

Sprinkle, J., & Karsai, G. G. (2004). A domain-specific visual language for domain model evolution. *Journal of Visual Languages and Computing, 15*(3-4), 291–307.

Steele, G. (1990). *Common LISP: The language* (2nd ed.). Digital Press.

Strachan, J., & McWhirter, B. (2011). *Groovy: An agile dynamic language for the Java platform*.

Thibault, S. A., Marlet, R., & Consel, C. (1999). Domain-specific languages: From design to implementation application to video device drivers generation. *IEEE Transactions on Software Engineering, 25*(3), 363–377.

Tolvanen, J. (2006). *Domain-specific modeling: How to start defining your own language*. Retrieved April 13, 2012, from http://www.devx.com/enterprise/Article/30550

van der Linden, F. (2002). Software product families in Europe: the Esaps & Cafe projects. *IEEE Software, 19*(4), 41–49.

Weiss, D. (1998). *Commonality analysis: A systematic process for defining families*. Paper presented at the Second International ESPRIT ARES Workshop on Development and Evolution of Software Architectures for Product Families. Las Palmas de Gran Canaria, Spain.

Wile, D. (2004). Lessons learned from real DSL experiments. *Science of Computer Programming, 51*(3), 265–290.

Chapter 10

A Model–Based Approach to Aligning Business Goals with Enterprise Architecture

Tony Clark
Middlesex University, UK

Balbir Barn
Middlesex University, UK

ABSTRACT

Modern organizations need to address increasingly complex challenges including how to represent and maintain their business goals using technologies and IT platforms that change on a regular basis. This has led to the development of modelling notations for expressing various aspects of an organization with a view to reducing complexity, increasing technology independence, and supporting analysis. Many of these Enterprise Architecture (EA) modelling notations provide a large number of concepts that support the business analysis but lack precise definitions necessary to perform computer-supported organizational analysis. This chapter reviews the current EA modelling landscape and proposes a simple language for the practical support of EA simulation including business alignment in terms of executing a collection of goals against prototype execution.

INTRODUCTION

Business and IT alignment has remained an on-going concern for organizations since the 1980s (Luftman, 2000). Throughout this period, researchers have addressed the importance of alignment and in particular the need for congruence between business strategy and IT strategy (Chan & Reich, 2007). While there are multiple definitions for Business and IT Alignment (BIA) including integration, linkage, bridge, fusion or even fit, most

are consistent with the definition derived from the *Strategic Alignment Model* (SAM) (Henderson & Venkatraman, 1993). They state that alignment is the degree of fit and integration among business strategy, IT strategy, business infrastructure, and IT infrastructure.

Enterprise Architecture (EA) aims to capture the essentials of a business, its IT and its evolution, and to support analysis of this information: *it is a coherent whole of principles, methods, and models that are used in the design and realization of an enterprise's organizational structure, business processes, information systems and infrastructure.*

DOI: 10.4018/978-1-4666-4217-1.ch010

(Lankhorst, 2009). In addition to presenting a coherent explanation of the *what*, *why* and *how* of a business, EA aims to support specific types of business analysis including: alignment between business functions and IT systems, and business change describing the current state of a business (as-is) and a desired state of a business (to-be). Thus EA has the potential to serve as the basis of machinery that can be used to address BIA (Wang, Zhou & Jiang, 2008; Pereira & Sousa, 2005).

Various informal frameworks have been proposed for expressing EA, business goals and BIA including SAM, TOGAF, ArchiMate, BMM, KAOS and i*. In general these methods and technologies support a wide range of business facing modelling concepts that are appropriate for the business analyst, but that present problems in terms of a precise analysis of business alignment.

In general, BIA involves comparing business goals with business design. Goals express the *why* of an organization in terms of requirements, motivations, policies, and regulations. Business designs express the *how* of an organization either in terms of business processes and information structures, or in terms of configurations of software components. As such, BIA can be viewed as verifying that the operational aspects of a business are correct with respect to the required behaviour.

The view of BIA raises similar issues to software verification where a system implementation must be shown to be correct with respect to a system requirement. Many formal and informal techniques have been developed over the last 40 years that aim to support this process for software development. Our proposal is that these techniques are appropriate for BIA; however, they must be modified in order to accommodate the broader nature of organizational architecture.

In particular, it would be interesting to leverage the precise nature of software requirements expressed in formal logic. A significant problem with such an approach is that EA model tend to be discursive and business facing and therefore lack a precise semantics would be necessary for

a logic-based language to be used to express the goals. Our proposal is to provide a small and well-defined collection of modelling concepts into which the business concepts can be mapped (Clark, Barn & Oussena, 2012). Given such a precise basis, business goals can then be expressed using a formal language.

Business goals fall into two different areas: behavioural requirements for an organization and non-functional requirements. Our claim is that a precise basis for an EA model is necessary to facilitate definitions and analysis of both of these types of goal. In order to effectively express non-functional business goals, the organizational model must be both precise and provide a means to measure a given non-functional property as a function of the model (or its semantics). For example, a quality based attribute such as reliability requires that the model associate each structural and behavioural feature of the organization with a reliability function such that a goal can be expressed in terms of an invariant over the value of the function, or a relative change in the case of an as-is and to-be business change. This chapter does not address non-functional goals, however our approach is described in (Barn & Clark, 2012).

Behavioural goals express a required behaviour for an organization. Work on intentional systems development such as KAOS has proposed a formal language for expressing behavioural goals similar to that used for specifying the dynamic behaviour of software systems. Having expressed the behavioural goal, the question arises: how to achieve BIA?

Having represented the goal in a precise way, it follows that the organizational architecture must be represented in a precise way to support BIA. However, there is a lack of consensus regarding a precise language for EA since, as described above, current EA languages tend to be business facing and to provide a rich collection of (often overlapping) business modelling concepts.

Furthermore, having such a precise basis for both what and how in EA does not guarantee an effective method for automatic BIA since computer based formal verification is notoriously difficult to scale. There are two important reasons for this related to the size of the search space generated by non-trivial system definitions. Firstly, in order to control a search engine that seeks out an alignment proof, the human engineer requires great skill in expressing the verification criteria. Often the results of a verification proof need to be interpreted by an expert. Secondly, in general automatic verification is undecidable which means in practice that it is not possible to know a priori whether an automatic proof system will terminate or not. Whilst formal verification techniques may be very successful for very specific areas, it is difficult to see how they could be applied to current BIA problems in general. Although fully automatic verification may not be immediately applicable for BIA, partial techniques may be useful.

Our approach, called LEAP, provides such a precise basis for both goals and architectures. Rather than providing an automated proof that the goals and architecture are aligned, LEAP supports the construction of executable models of a system such that the goals can be measured against a prototype simulation. As the simulation is executed using concrete data, the goals are discharged thereby providing a trace of the system execution including evidence that the system is behaving correctly. Incorrect behaviour shows up as an unsatisfied goal and can be traced back through the simulation.

Our contribution is to provide a precise basis for both goals and architectures and an approach to BIA based on simulation. This chapter reviews technologies for EA and for intentional modelling, introduces LEAP and the mechanisms for BIA and shows how the approach works using a simple case study.

BACKGROUND

Enterprise Architecture

Enterprise Architecture (EA) aims to capture the essentials of a business, its IT and its evolution, and to support analysis of this information. A key objective of EA is being able to provide a holistic understanding of all aspects of a business, connecting the business drivers and the surrounding business environment, through the business processes, organizational units, roles and responsibilities, to the underlying IT systems that the business relies on. In addition to presenting a coherent explanation of the *what*, *why* and *how* of a business, EA aims to support specific types of business analysis including (Ekstedt, Johnson, Plazaola, Silva, & Lilieskold, 2004; Reige & Aier, 2009; Niemann, 2006; Butcher, Fischer, Kurpjuweit, & Winter, 2006): *alignment* between business functions and IT systems; *business change* describing the current state of a business (*as-is*) and a desired state of a business (*to-be*); *maintenance* the de-installation and disposal, upgrading, procurement and integration of systems including the prioritization of maintenance needs; *quality* by managing and determining the quality attributes for aspects of the business such as security, performance to ensure a certain level of quality to meet the needs of the business; *acquisition and mergers* describing the alignment of businesses and the effect on both when they merge; *compliance* in terms of a regulatory framework, e.g. Sarbanes-Oxley; *strategic planning* including corporate strategy planning, business process optimization, business continuity planning, IT management.

EA has its origins in Zachman's original EA framework (Zachman, 1999) while other leading examples include the Open Group Architecture Framework (TOGAF) (Spencer, 2004) and the framework promulgated by the Department of Defense (DoDAF) (Wisnosky & Vogel, 2004). In addition to frameworks that describe the nature of models required for EA, modelling languages specifically designed for EA have also emerged. One leading architecture modelling language is ArchiMate (Lankhorst, Proper, & Jonkers, 2010).

A modern enterprise can be thought of as being constructed of three key layers and three key aspects as shown in Figure 1 (Jonkers, Lankhorst, Buuren, Bonsangue & Van Der Torre, 2004). The business layer contains intentional features such as business goals, the essential information required by the organization and the high-level structure of the organizational units. The application layer describes the data, resources and functionality necessary to realize the business directives, and the infrastructure layer describes the physical systems on which the organization runs.

EA Modelling

The analysis of modern organizations is supported by the construction of EA models that describe various features of the organization shown in Figure 1. Figure 2 shows an idealized EA model that includes many features supported by current technologies. Intentional modeling is used to capture the goals of an organization and is shown in Figure 2 as a goal decomposition tree. Each goal refers to models of the information, resources and organization structure necessary to express the requirements.

The goal tree is rooted at the high-level requirements of the CXO including the view of the organization information and structures that are

appropriate at this level. As the goal tree is decomposed, the requirements become more specific and detailed. The detail increases until the goals become operational in the form of business processes that initially span the organizational structure, but are increasingly refined until they are localized within specific technology units.

The models shown in Figure 2 are idealized in the sense that they are intended to cover all aspects of the organization from top-level management to the operational systems that run the business. The intention is that each level of decomposition represents a view of the business. They are interdependent so that information from the technology layer can be reported back to the CXO in terms that reflect the goals that the CXO initially expressed.

The rest of this section provides an overview of the current technologies for EA modeling.

ArchiMate

ArchiMate (Lankhorst, Proper & Jonkers, 2010) is a standard managed by the Open Group[1]. It consists of a framework of layers and aspects similar to the Zachman framework (Zachman, 1999) that defines a theory or `world view' about the way enterprises are structured. The aspects are described using a set of modelling concepts that constitute a DSML for EA. The framework is described in Figure 3 and is taken from (Engelsman, Quartela, Jonkers & van Sinderen, 2010). The framework distinguishes between the business layer (concerned with products and services offered to customers), the application layer (concerned with the application services that the company implements internally), and the technology layer (concerned with the infrastructure services necessary to run the applications). To model each layer, ArchiMate provides modelling concepts in each of the three layers:

1. **Business:** Actor; role; collaboration; interface; object; process; function; interaction;

Figure 1. Enterprise architecture concepts

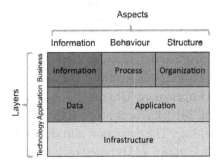

Figure 2. A model-driven enterprise

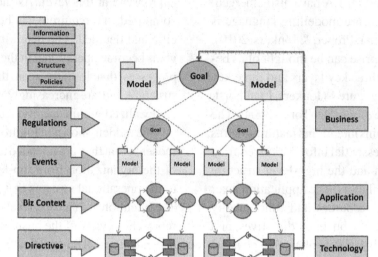

Figure 3. ArchiMate structure

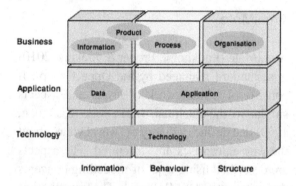

event; service; representation; meaning; value; product; contract.

2. **Application:** Component; collaboration; interface; object; function; interaction; service.

3. **Technology:** Node; device; network; communication path; interface; software; service; artifact.

Clearly, there is a great deal of overlap between the modelling concepts in the different layers; for example, *interface* occurs in all three layers, and *function* occurs in the first two. There are con-

cepts whose meaning would seem to overlap, for example *process*, *service* and *function*. Archimate provides a notation for each of the modelling concepts. The notation has a syntax definition in the form of well-formedness constraints, however there is no semantics in the sense of axiomatic, denotational or operational definitions.

There is a proposal for a UML profile for ArchiMate (Iacob, Jonkers & Wiering, 2004). An overview of the proposal is shown in Figure 4 where the business layer is modelled using class diagrams, the application layer using component diagrams and the technology layer using deployment diagrams. However this does not constitute a semantics since UML itself does not have a precise semantics. The lack of semantics makes it difficult to compare model elements for similarity, difference and redundancy. Furthermore, the lack of semantics makes it difficult to determine the meaning of extensions to the language as proposed below.

The original definition of ArchiMate did not support business motivation. The ARMOR language (Engelsman, Quartela, Jonkers, & van Sinderen, 2010) has been proposed as an extension to ArchiMate. The extension introduces goals as shown in Figure 5 and is based on languages such

Figure 4. UML profile for ArchiMate

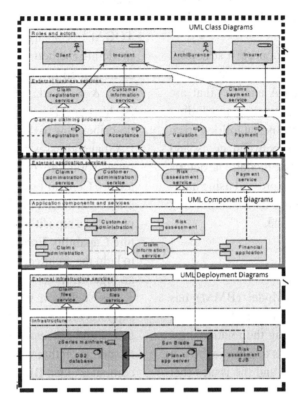

Figure 5. ARMOR extension to ArchiMate

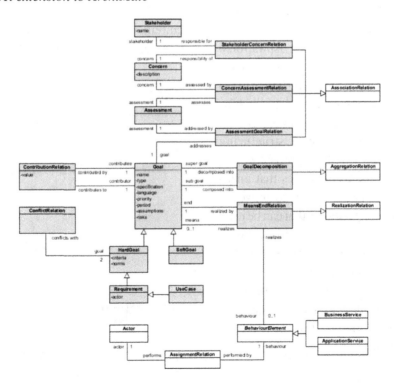

as KAOS, i*, and BMM described below. As the model shows, the extension is based on adding goals to use-case actors.

The ARMOR language supports a structural representation of business goals. The authors describe several forms of EA analysis that are supported by the ArchiMate extension including traceability and impact analysis that follows from the structural relationships between goals and other aspects of the ArchiMate model. The details of the goals themselves are expressed using natural language and as such have no semantics that can be processed by a machine.

BMM

The Business Motivation Model (BMM) has been developed by the Business Rules Group[2]. It provides a way of capturing the relationships between what a business aims to achieve, how it proposes to achieve its aims and the issues that will influence the outcome in a positive and negative way. The BMM is essentially an ontology of terms and relationships that would be used by a business analyst when structuring the aspirations and planned behavior for an organization. For example it distinguishes between aspirational terms such as *ends*, *visions*, *goals* and *objectives*; planning terms such as *means*, *missions*, *strategies* and *tactics*; and influencing terms such as *opportunities*, *threats*, *strengths* and *weaknesses*.

The BMM provides a useful structuring mechanism for other modeling approaches (for example it is one of the technologies that influences the ARMOR language described above). It is a useful structuring mechanism that can be used as the basis of structural analysis of intentional aspects of EA modeling, for example an *end* is *realized* by a *means* and is *impacted* by a *weakness*. However, there is no precisely defined meaning to these terms and relationships: the detail is left to the individual BMM application, or is left up to user interpretation.

TOGAF

TOGAF[3] is a large-scale EA meta-model and modeling method that consists of six main parts as described in Figure 6 (Ernst, Matthes, Ramache, & Schweda, 2009). TOGAF includes the Architecture Development Method (ADM) that describes how to derive an organization-specific EA that addresses business architecture. Various frameworks are provided including the Architecture Content Framework that describes deliverables, artifacts; the Enterprise Continuum that provides a repository for EA reuse; the Architecture Capability Framework containing resources to help the architect establish EA practice within an organization.

As such is a huge integrated resource that supports all aspects of the EA process. The language and processes are very detailed, but lack the precision that would be necessary to perform computer aided BIA.

KAOS

KAOS[4] is a language for expressing system requirements. It is organized as a goal decomposition tree where the goals are linked to agents that

Figure 6. TOGAF architectural develoment method cycle

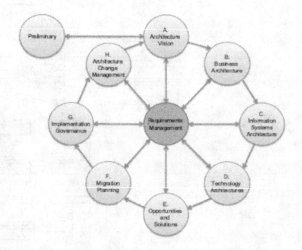

Figure 7. An example KAOS model

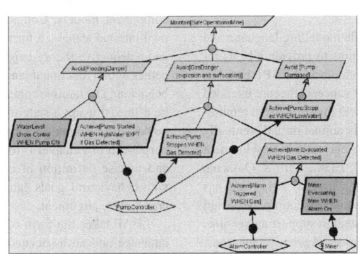

are responsible for achieving their functional and non-functional specifications. Like BMM, KAOS includes a representation for conflicting goals and issues such as obstacles to goal satisfaction.

KAOS has an associated tool called Objectiver that can be used to construct KAOS models and to analyse various structural properties. Figure 7 shows an example KAOS model (Ponsard & Devroey, 2011). The model shows a goal decomposition tree rooted at the Maintain[SafeOperationofMine] goal. The goals are linked to agents (for example the PumpController) that are responsible for achieving or maintaining the requirements expressed by the goal.

The authors (Ponsard & Devroey, 2011) observe that many behavioural goals can be expressed using temporal logic that expresses constraints over the ongoing behavior of the agents. Although KAOS does not provide explicit support for any formal languages, the authors show how temporal logic formulas can be added to KAOS models and subsequently translated into the B language that provides support for formal verification. This is a very attractive approach since the B language and its associated tooling is mature and supports a wide range of analysis. However, this approach seems to be related to systems requirements and

works at the general level. It is not clear how this approach will scale as over large EA models.

i*

i* (Liu, Yu & Myopoulos, 2003) is a goal-oriented requirements engineering notation and method that, unlike KAOS above, includes a description of who interacts with a system and answers the question: *what do they want to achieve?* Each actor in a system has goals that they want to achieve (unlike KAOS where there is a single goal that is decomposed and linked to agents that are responsible for achieving the leaf goals). Like KAOS, goals may be hard or soft meaning that they either refer to system behaviour or refer to non-functional requirements such as system quality attributes. Like KAOS, i* goals are decomposed and ultimately linked to tasks that are responsible for accomplishing the goal.

Like the other modeling approaches described above, i* supports structural analysis that shows which actors are related to which tasks, which actors are involved in the system, their interdependencies and what their respective expectations are.

LEAP

LEAP is an executable modelling language and associated tool that aims to provide a basis for component-based development. LEAP is based on a collection of simple concepts that are intended to span the development life-cycle from requirements through analysis, animation and eventually deployment. LEAP is currently in development (Clark & Barn, 2012; Clark, Barn & Oussena, 2012; Clark, Barn & Oussena, 2011) and has been applied to case studies including the design of an information system to support universities comply with UK Border Agency regulations, organizational change in universities in order to achieve non-functional requirements, and modelling of a crisis management system[5].

Our aim with LEAP is to support both enterprise models and system models using the same collection of features. Our view is that such systems can be represented as hierarchically organized collaborating components expressed using a suitable collection of modelling languages. Therefore, a specification language is provided that expresses

conditions over static and dynamic features of component models. Components manage their own internal state as a form of *knowledge base* and a deductive theory language is provided together with a functional language for expressing behaviour. Declarative component behaviour can be achieved using a state-machine language together with a language for event driven rules. Our purpose in this chapter is to show how a simple and precise definition of components together with behavioural goals can provide a basis for architecture alignment.

LEAP takes the form of a textual modeling language and an associated tool. Figure 8 is a snapshot of the tool that shows the key features. The top-left panel is a view of the elements in a LEAP model that has been loaded into the tool. The user can browse models, edit properties, and invoke tool functionality from this panel. The bottom left panel shows a view of the file system showing LEAP source code. A LEAP model consists of one or more source files that can be loaded from this panel.

Figure 8. LEAP tool

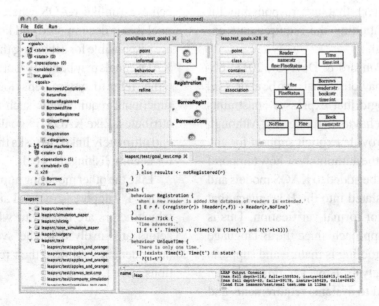

Two top-right panels show diagram views of the loaded model. The left diagram panel shows goals and the right diagram panel shows an information model. Below that is a text editor panel that contains the source code of part of the LEAP model. The editor provides syntax support for the LEAP language. Below the editor is a property editor for LEAP model elements and a console window for output.

LEAP models are organized as one or more components. A component has a message interface and can consume messages sent to its input ports and produce messages on its output ports. Connectors from output ports to input ports are used to link components together. Components are viewed as black boxes that independently consume and produce messages.

Internally, components manage a state that consists of a list of data terms. Message handlers can change the state of a component and produce output messages. Rules monitor the state of a component and fire actions when rule-patterns are satisfied. Messages are handled using either state machines (when the behaviour lends itself to such a structure) or a collection of operations (when behaviour is complex).

Components are used to describe system architecture. In the degenerate case, a system can be viewed as a single LEAP component whose message interface implements the system functionality and its observable outputs. Multiple components can be used to represent a system at increasing levels of detail, where each component represents groupings such as logical system functionality, physical IT systems, organizational units, people, etc.

The state of a component is expressed in terms of a collection of data terms that are instances of an information model owned by the component. An information model consists of classes and associations. The model is a data type for a collection of data values that are *terms*. A term is equivalent to a row in a relational database table and the intention is that LEAP will be able to interface to databases in the future. The information model defines a structure over the database tables so that the list of raw terms can be viewed as structured data.

The behaviour of a component is implemented in a number of ways, the least structured of which is as an operation. An operation is a named function that will be invoked when a message with the same name is processed. The body of the function can access and update the state of the component and can produce output messages.. The state of a component is available to an operation as a list of terms and therefore LEAP provides a rich collection of list-processing expressions including list-comprehensions for implementing operation bodies.

The required behaviour of a component is specified using goals. Like other systems for intentional modelling, LEAP goal models are organized as a decomposition tree where the leaves of the tree are specific requirements that must be achieved by components. LEAP supports non-functional and functional goals. This chapter deals only with functional goals.

Functional goals can be expressed using a temporal logic that places constraints on the behaviour of components. Each component is a self-contained black box that processes messages received at input ports and produces messages at output ports. Multiple components are connected so that messages sent to their output ports are transferred to the input ports of one or more target components. Messages are processed from the input port one at a time. Operations, state machines or data driven rules can control the behaviour of a component. The examples in this chapter use operations to control a component and the principles apply to all other modes of behaviour definition.

When a message is processed, it is removed from the input queue and matched against an operation with the same name. The operation arguments are bound from the contents of the message and the body of the operation is performed. The operation body has access to the internal state of the component and may change it and may produce output messages. An output message may be *synchronous* or *asynchronous*. A synchronous message causes the active component to halt and wait for the response from the message; an asynchronous message is added to the output queue and execution continues without waiting for the result. All operations produce a result. In the case of an asynchronous message the result is ignored. In the case of a synchronous message, the source of the message is a component whose execution is resumed.

A functional goal is a condition on the behaviour of a component. The behaviour is a sequence of state transitions that are caused by messages being consumed and produced. We use a temporal logic that can express properties over sub-sequences of behaviour; allowing, for example, the condition that after a given message is processed then the component will eventually achieve a satisfactory state. The rest of this section introduces the key features of LEAP using some simple examples.

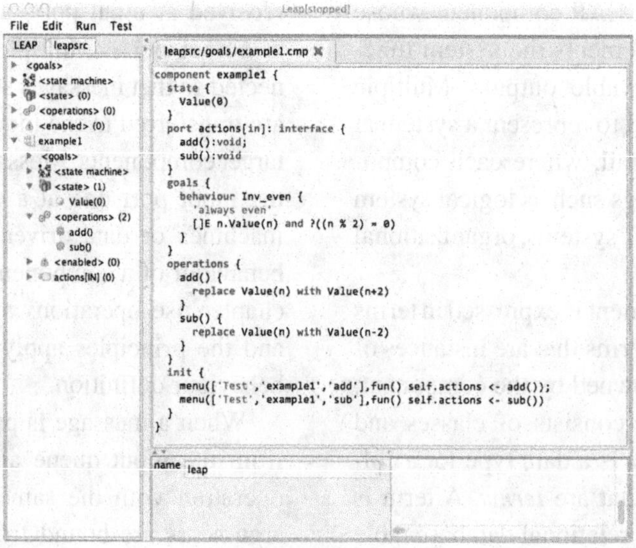

Invariants

Figure 9 shows a simple example of a goal being used to define an invariant over the state of a component. A component definition consists of a collection of optional sub-clauses that contain different aspects of the component. The example initialises the state of the component to contain a single term of the form Value(0). Each term has a type (in this case Value) and some argument values (in this case 0). The tree-view on the left shows the model after it is loaded and the state contains the single term.

A component defines any number of input and output ports. In the example there is a single input port called actions. A port has an interface that defined the type signatures of the messages that can be processed by the port. In this case there are two asynchronous messages called add and sub respectively.

The example goals clause defines the functional requirements for the component. In this case it is an invariant that requires the state of the component to contain an event integer. We know it is an invariant because of the form of the logical

Figure 9. Example invariant

```
File   Edit   Run   Test

LEAP   leapsrc              leapsrc/goals/example1.cmp

▶ <goals>                   component example1 {
▶ <state machine>            state {
▶ <state> (0)                  Value(0)
▶ <operations> (0)           }
▶ <enabled> (0)              port actions[in]: interface {
▼ example1                     add():void;
  ▶ <goals>                    sub():void
  ▶ <state machine>          }
  ▼ <state> (1)              goals {
      Value(0)                 behaviour Inv_even {
  ▼ <operations> (2)             'always even'
      add()                      []E n.Value(n) and ?((n % 2) = 0)
      sub()                    }
  ▶ <enabled> (0)            }
  ▶ actions[IN] (0)          operations {
                               add() {
                                 replace Value(n) with Value(n+2)
                               }
                               sub() {
                                 replace Value(n) with Value(n-2)
                               }
                               init {
                                 menu(['Test','example1','add'],fun() self.actions <- add());
                                 menu(['Test','example1','sub'],fun() self.actions <- sub())
                               }
                             }

                             name  leap
```

expression: []P. The [] operator applies to a logical statement P and states that P must hold *at all times from this time on*. Time is measured in terms of message processing, when a component handles a message it moves from one time frame to the next. If a statement holds at all times from now on then it must hold no matter what messages are processed. Since the goal named Inv_even has no qualifier before the [] operator then it holds at time 0, therefore it always holds, i.e. it is an *invariant*.

The operations clause defines the behaviour of the component. A component should define operations for all messages that it can handle, but may also define auxiliary operations that are used as helpers. In this case the component defines operations that add and subtract 2 from the integer value in its local state. The body of the operations use a *replace* command (an expression whose value is ignored) to remove the current value and add a new value.

LEAP uses pattern matching to process lists of values. The state of a component is managed as a list of terms and a replace command uses a pattern Value(n) to match against the list and to extract the value n. Operationally, the pattern is matched against every term in the list until a match is found. In this case the component's state is always a list with a single element.

The final clause is used to initialize the component. It is evaluated when the component is loaded. In this case it is used to add two items to the LEAP tool menu bar that allow us to test the component by sending it messages. The function menu takes two arguments: a list of strings that name the menu item using nested menus and a function to be called when the menu item is selected. In both cases the function sends a message to an input port, where self is used by a component to refer to itself.

Figure 10 shows a screenshot after the message add (selected via the menu Test) is processed. The state change can be seen in the browser window on the left. In addition to processing the message, LEAP has applied the goals to the simulation. This is shown in the output window in the bottom right where the message delivery is recorded and the reduction of the invariant is shown.

Initially, each goal is in an *outstanding* state. This means that the goal has yet to be satisfied or *discharged*. When a message is processed a state change occurs. All outstanding goals are processed by checking that they hold with respect to the state change. If a goal is fully satisfied by the state change then it becomes *discharged* and will take not further part in the component execution. If the goal is false then it *fails*, which means that the component cannot satisfy its initial set of goals. Otherwise, it may be the case that the goal cannot be fully satisfied because it needs to know about future state changes. If this is the case then the goals is *reduced* by transforming it into a simpler form that is then outstanding with respect to future message processing.

Consider the Inv_even goal. It has the form [] P which means that it must hold for the current state change. In order to work out how to apply this goal, it is transformed into the following equivalent form P and @[]P. Which states that P must hold now and in the next state change []P must hold. The temporal logic operator @ applies to condition Q and requires Q to hold in the next state change.

In order to check P and @[]P we can check each half of the conjunction separately. In this case P is the formula E n.Value(n) and ?((n % 2) = 0). A formula of the form E n.Q is used to require that the variable n is completely new and cannot be confused with any other variable called n in Q. The formula Q is a conjunction that can be tested in the current state change. The term Value(n) requires that there is a term that matches the pattern in the state before the change occurs. The formula ?((n % 2) = 0) requires that the value of n is even. Given the current state of the component is Value(0) before the state change, the left hand of the conjunction is discharged.

That leaves the other half of the conjunction: @[]P. Since this formula starts with an @, it is not

Figure 10. Processing a message

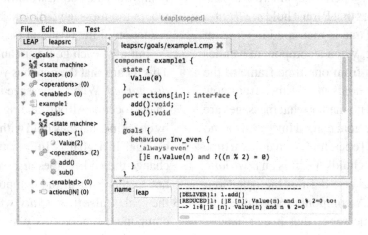

possible to check it with respect to the first state change. Therefore the formula @[]P is reduced to []P as shown in the LEAP output console. This is the original goal, therefore it will be checked in the next and all subsequent state changes, requiring that the component always contains an even value. Testing via the menu operations will verify that no matter ow many add and sub messages are sent to the component the formula Value(n) and ?((n % 2) = 0) is always satisfied. If we modify the definition one of the operations to be incorrect then the console will flag this up:

Actions: Pre- and Post-Conditions

Components perform state changes in response to handling messages. A behavioural goal that expresses a condition in terms of such a change is a formula of the form <m>P -> Q where m is a pattern that matches the message that is being handled, P is a pre-condition and Q is post-condition. Generally, a pre-condition is a formula that relates m to the state of the component before the corresponding operation is invoked. A post-condition is a formula that expresses a condition on the state of the component after the operation has completed. If a pre-post condition holds at all times then the formula has the form []<m>P-> Q.

Figure 11 shows an example of a behavioural goal that specifies a single operation. The goal Pre_post_add contains a formula of the form []<m>P -> Q where m is the message pattern add(), P is a state pattern Value(n) and Q is a conjunction Value(m) in state' and ?(m=n+1). The formula applies every time the component processes an add() message. The pre-condition requires that there is a value n in the state and the post-condition requires that the value has increased by 1. A state formula has the complete form p in e where p is a pattern and e is an expression that evaluates to produce a list of values. The formula is true when the pattern matches a value in the list. There are two special expressions that denote lists of values: state and state'. They both denote the list of terms that is the state of the immediately enclosing component. A goal is checked each time a state transition occurs in a component and the expression state refers to the component's state before the operation is performed and state' refers to the state after the operation has completed. Therefore the formula Value(m) in state' and ?(m=n+1) requires that there is a new value m that is 1 greater than n after the operation add has completed.

Figure 11 shows the state of the component after two messages have been processed. The first message is add() and therefore the goal is checked

264

Figure 11. Actions with pre- and post-conditions

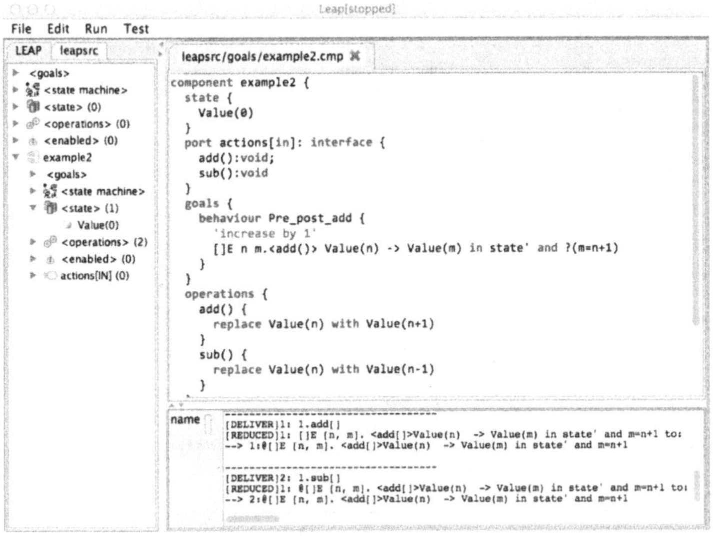

and reduced. The second message is sub() in which case the goal does not apply to the transition, however it is still reduced because of the operator [].

The Future

The previous sections have shown how behavioural goals express formulas that must always hold and which hold over a single state transition in a component. Sometimes an action will occur in a situation where we require a situation to be achieved *at some time in the future*. A formula that can express such a condition has the form <>P. In this case the formula P may hold immediately, may hold after the next state transition, after two more state transitions etc. Once P is achieved, the formula <>P is discharged.

Suppose that we want a component that manages a numeric value that is increased and decreased in response to messages. For each increase we would like to ensure that the value is eventually decreased to return to its current value. Figure 12 shows an example of a goal that requires each add() message to be followed by a sub() message at some time in the future. The formula takes the form of a pre-post condition, there the

post-condition is @(<>Value(n)) meaning that in the next state (i.e. not immediately), after any number of state transitions, the integer managed by the component will return to its current value n.

The goal can be seen in action via the LEAP console window. The component is sent two add() messages and then two sub() messages. After each sub() message the outstanding goals are discharged.

Duration

The previous section has shown how a formula can be required to hold at some time in the future. It is useful to be able to express that a formula holds during the interim. This requires the ability to express time durations. The formula P U Q requires that P holds *until* Q holds (after which we do not care whether P holds or not).

Figure 13 shows an example of a formula that, like example 3, requires the value in the component to increase and then return to its original value. The added requirement is that in the interim, the value must always be greater than n, i.e. the value cannot skip over n to become less and then approach n from below.

Figure 12. Expressing conditions that eventually hold

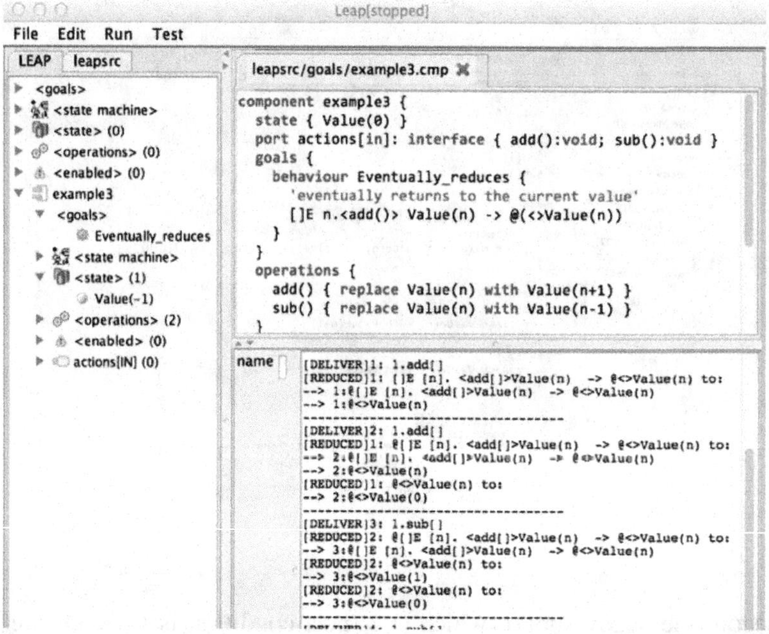

Figure 13. Time duration

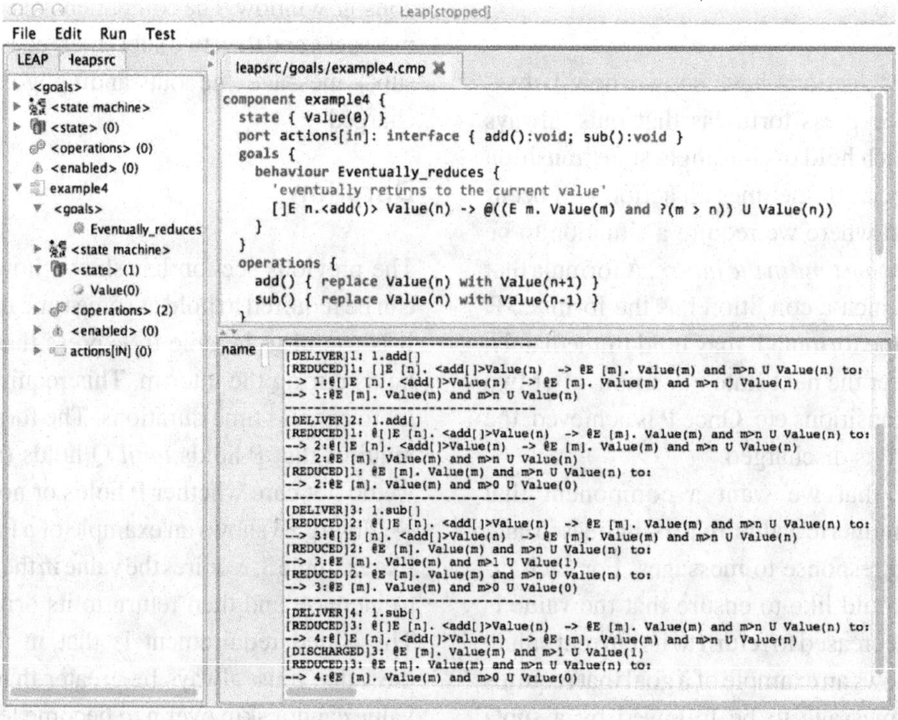

Output Messages

Component state transitions involve an input message that is matched to an operation. When the operation is invoked the internal state of the component may change and some output messages may be produced. A goal may with to specify a condition on the output messages. The formula [m] requires that the message pattern m matches an output message in the current time frame. The message pattern may be asynchronous in which case it specifies no return value or synchronous in which case it has the form [p=m] where p is a pattern that is required to match the value returned by the target component.

Figure 14 shows an example of a component that manages an integer value and which specifies a limit on the value. The value may be incremented until the limit is reached when an event is raised by sending a message to the output port named events. The console window shows the result of three increments. The component implementation does not match its specification (shown by printing a message instead of raising the event) and the goal fails.

Nested Components

The examples given above have used goals to specify the behaviour of single components. In general, an enterprise will be organized as a hierarchically decomposed collection of interrelated components. In addition, there needs to be a development method for constructing executable models for organizations. One such method is to start with a single high-level component that uses a single information model to capture the essential features of the organization and then to develop a more sophisticated model by step-wise refinement. This method leads to a requirement for parent goals to place constraints on the behaviour of their children. Furthermore, if we are use LEAP to address the 3-layers for an organization described in Figure 1 then the business layer must be able to control the behaviour of components defined at the technology layer.

Each LEAP goal is owned by a component and may refer to the component's children. Any state change in a child causes the goals of its parent (transitively) to be checked. A parent can refer to the state of its children by name. If a child is

Figure 14. Asynchronous output messages

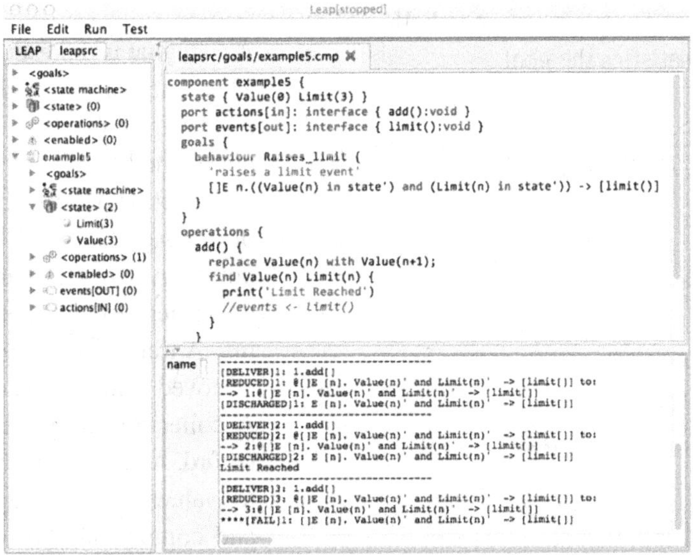

called c then the parent may refer to its pre-state as c.state and its post-state as c.state'.

Consider a simple example that requires a parent component to keep two children in sync. Each child maintains a counter and the parent can change each child independently by sending it messages. This example also provides an opportunity to explain another feature of LEAP: higher-order components. Although the parent component has two children, they have the same structure and behaviour. Therefore it makes sense to have a single definition for a child component that is parameterized with respect to the differences.

Figure 15 shows an example LEAP function definition. The function maps a component name and returns a new component. The supplied name is used as a menu label. The component that is returned manages a single integer value and provides a single operation that is used to increment the value.

Figure 16 shows the definition of a component that uses the mk_child template function. The behavioural goal expresses a condition that whenever the state of the parent or the children changes, the value in child2 eventually becomes the same value as that in child1. To complete the specification we should also add a goal that states that if the value in child2 changes, the value in child1 eventually synchronizes. The implementation of the inc operation sends a message to both children and thereby satisfies the goal.

Figure 15. A component template

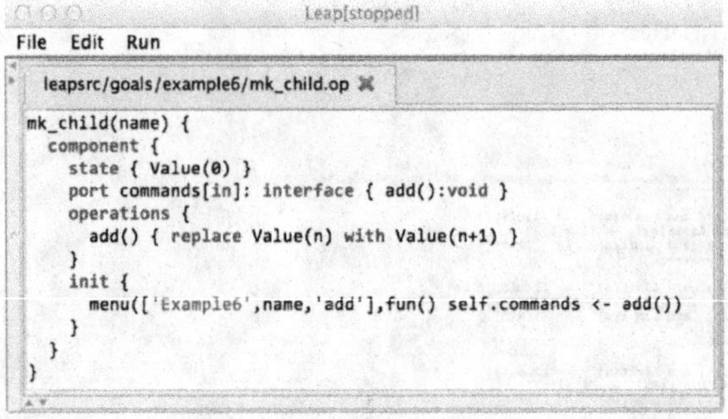

```
⦿⦿⦿                    Leap[stopped]
File   Edit   Run

  leapsrc/goals/example6/mk_child.op ✖

mk_child(name) {
  component {
    state { Value(0) }
    port commands[in]: interface { add():void }
    operations {
      add() { replace Value(n) with Value(n+1) }
    }
    init {
      menu(['Example6',name,'add'],fun() self.commands <- add())
    }
  }
}
```

Figure 16. A parent goal

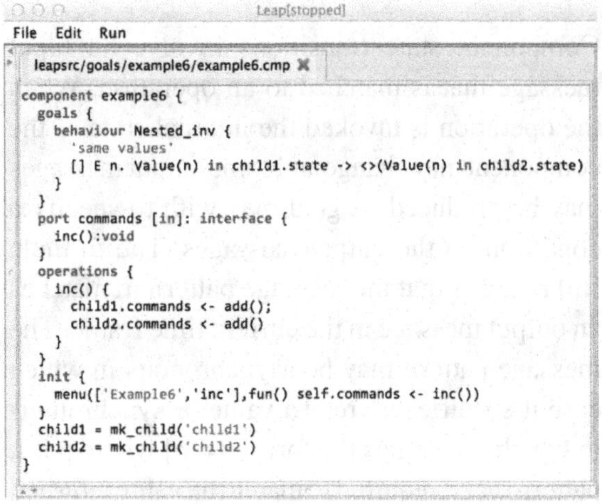

```
⦿⦿⦿                    Leap[stopped]
File   Edit   Run

  leapsrc/goals/example6/example6.cmp ✖

component example6 {
  goals {
    behaviour Nested_inv {
      'same values'
      [] E n. Value(n) in child1.state -> <>(Value(n) in child2.state)
    }
  }
  port commands [in]: interface {
    inc():void
  }
  operations {
    inc() {
      child1.commands <- add();
      child2.commands <- add()
    }
  }
  init {
    menu(['Example6','inc'],fun() self.commands <- inc())
  }
  child1 = mk_child('child1')
  child2 = mk_child('child2')
}
```

IMPLEMENTATION

LEAP is implemented as a Java engine that constructs component models and executes them. This section provides a brief overview of the Java classes that are used to represent and execute the models including how BIA is achieved by executing goals against running simulations.

Figure 17 shows part of the LEAP component model. The class Value is used to represent all values that can be denoted in user-models. A component is a value that consists of the following elements:

- A state that is represented as a list of terms. The state can be modified by adding and removing terms, but individual terms cannot be modified.
- A collection of ports. Each port has a queue of messages and is either used for input or output. At any given time, a component has a number of input messages that are pending. A transition occurs when a message is removed from the head of the input queue.
- A collection of definitions contained in a record. A record is a value that maps names to values via bindings. Both operations and components are values and therefore

Figure 17. LEAP implementation model

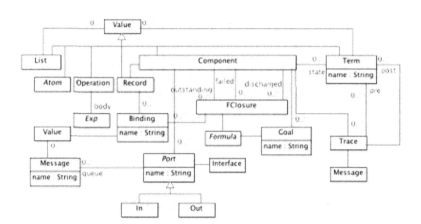

a component contains its children and the operations that implement its messages via the record. Note that components may contain any types of value in its record. The abstract class Atom is the root of a collection of classes that define basic value types such as integer. Note also that the body of an operation is defined by the abstract class Exp that is the root of a class of expression syntax classes.

- A component manages a trace consisting of a sequence of transitions. Each transition records the state change that occurs when a message is processed from one of the input queues.

- A component contains a collection of goals. A goal consists of a formula that defines a constraint over the trace of the component. Each formula may contain *free variables* that can take values from elements in the trace. A formula together with bindings for each of its free variables is called an *fclosure*. A component manages three collections of fclosures: *outstanding* that are formulas yet to be established; *failed* that are formulas that have evaluated to false; *discharged* that are formulas each of which have evaluated to true.

An evaluation step at a component is described by the following algorithm:

The reduction step uses unification over values in the trace to calculate the variable bindings. Where the reduction involves choice the fclosure records the choice point in case backtracking is required at a later stage. An fclosure can be fully reduced if there are no temporal operators that require more trace than is available. For example a formula @P requires access to the next step in the trace. If this is available then the formula reduction can continue, otherwise the formula reduces to P and the algorithm will add it to the collection of outstanding fclosures.

CASE STUDY

This section provides a simple example of a single module application to show how goals can specify the behavior of an IT component. The application is a library in which time limits are imposed on borrowings so that a fine must be paid if a borrowing exceeds the limit.

Figure 18 shows the required IT component and its interfaces. A reader must register before using the library and subsequently may borrow and return books. At regular intervals a clock ticks and time advances. The results interface

Figure 18. Library component

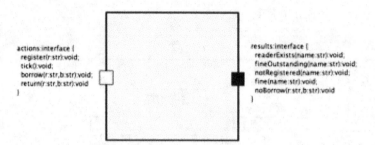

shows events that are raised in response to library state changes. Registering the same reader twice results in a readerExists event, attempting to use the library when the reader has a fine results in a fineOutstanding event, attempting to use the library before registering results in a notRegistered event, attempting to return a book that the reader has not borrowed results in a noBorrow event.

The information model used to represent the state of the library is shown in Figure 19. In LEAP an information model defines a collection of term types such that the state of the component consists of lists of terms of the declared types. Associations, such as fine, represent nested terms and are shown both as an association and a property of the type.

The specification of the library is shown in Figure 20. The goal Registration requires that new readers are added to the state. The goal Tick is interesting because it specifies that time must be increasing: given time currently at t, it will stay at t until it increases by 1 time unit. The goal UniqueTime requires that there can be no two time terms with different values in any given state. The goals BorrowRegistered, BorrowedFine, returnRegistered and ReturnFine all define situations where illegal actions are attempted that consequently that lead to events being raised. The final goal, BorrowedCompletion specifies that if a book is successfully borrowed by a reader then eventually the reader will return the book or a fine event will be raised.

The implementation of the library is defined in Figure 21. Having defined both the goals and the design for the software component, LEAP allows the alignment to be checked by running the goals against a simulation of the design. This provides confidence that the goals and the IT design are aligned.

FUTURE RESEARCH DIRECTIONS

The LEAP tool supports the design of goals and executable designs, and has been used to construct models of systems including alignment of business goals from the UK Higher Education sector and engineering crisis management. Goal alignment is achieved by simultaneously checking the goals against a running prototype of the system in terms of the models. There are several areas for future development:

Figure 19. Library information model

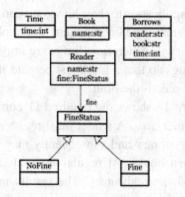

Figure 20. Library specification

```
goals {
  behaviour Registration {
    'When a new reader is added the database of readers is extended.'
    [] E r f. (<register(r)> !Reader(r,f)) -> Reader(r,NoFine)'
  }
  behaviour Tick {
    'Time advances.'
    [] E t t'. Time(t) -> (Time(t) U (Time(t') and ?(t'=t+1)))
  }
  behaviour UniqueTime {
    'There is only one time.'
    [] !exists Time(t), Time(t') in state' {
      ?(t!=t')
    }
  }
  behaviour BorrowRegistered {
    'To borrow a book the reader must be registered.'
    [] E r b s. (<borrow(r,b)> !Reader(r,s)) -> [notRegistered(r)]
  }
  behaviour BorrowedFine {
    'To borrow a book the reader must be fine free.'
    [] E r b. (<borrow(r,b)> Reader(r,Fine)) -> [fineOutstanding(r)]
  }
  behaviour ReturnRegistered {
    'To return a book the reader must be registered.'
    [] E r b s. (<return(r,b)> !Reader(r,s)) -> [notRegistered(r)]
  }
  behaviour ReturnFine {
    'To return a book the reader must be fine free.'
    [] E r b. (<return(r,b)> Reader(r,Fine)) -> [fineOutstanding(r)]
  }
  behaviour BorrowedCompletion {
    'After borrowing successfully, return or fine.'
    [] E t. (<borrow(r,b)> and Borrow(r,b,t)') ->
       <>(<return(r,b)> or [fine(r)])
  }
}
```

Figure 21. Library implementation

```
operations {
  register(r) {
    find Reader(r,_) in state {
      results <- readerExists(r)
    } else new Reader(r,NoFine)
  }
  tick() {
    replace Time(t) with Time(t+1);
    for Borrow(r,_,t') when (time()) = t' + 3 {
      results <- fine(r);
      replace Reader(r,_) with Reader(r,Fine)
    }
  }
  borrow(r,b) {
    find Reader(r,s) {
      case s {
        Fine -> results <- fineOutstanding(r);
        NoFine -> new Borrow(r,b,time())
      }
    } else results <- notRegistered(r)
  }
  time() {
    find Time(t) {
      t
    } else 0
  }
  return(r,b) {
    find Reader(r,s) {
      case s {
        Fine -> results <- fineOutstanding(r);
        NoFine -> find Borrow(r,b,t) {
          delete Borrow(r,b,t)
        } else results <- noBorrow(r,b)
      }
    } else results <- notRegistered(r)
  }
}
```

- LEAP systems consist of collections of components. A suitable development method is step-wise refinement of components starting with a single component with a high-level information model and developing the system through a number of elaborations involving increasing numbers of collaborating components and increasingly complex information models. Each layer developed by such an approach will be linked to the previous layer via a refinement relationship. For the approach to be practical, support must be provided for recording the refinement relationship and checking that it holds.

- The LEAP goal language provides temporal operators that are based on the notion of future that involves an arbitrary number of steps. Many applications require a specific notion of time (albeit relativized to each individual component) and the ability to express conditions such as *within the next 10 time units P must hold*. Indeed the library example shown above uses an explicit representation of time to achieve this kind of condition. The goal language can be extended to systematically encode time as part of the temporal operators.

- As it stands, LEAP goals can only be shown to hold against specific execution of the models. This choice was made because more general approaches such as model checking and theorem proving do not scale well. However, these techniques may be useful for specific types of application or in restricted circumstances, in which case more general properties of LEAP models can be established.

- LEAP provides a technology for linking to external applications. The LEAP system is written in Java and provides a Java interface definition that allows any Java program to be integrated as a LEAP component. This mechanism can be used to link to external IT systems such as databases and provide a route to linking LEAP goals with existing systems.

- The LEAP language for expressing executable models is simple and has been designed to allow analysis and transformation. Once a LEAP system model has been developed and checked and aligned with the system goals should be possible to run the LEAP models against the systems in an organization and thereby show that the organization is aligned with the LEAP model.

Corporate-level information systems provide services that help an organization meet corporate goals. As such systems cover more of an organization's functions it inevitably becomes more complex leading to challenging system evolution problems that may inhibit the organization's ability to adapt. A vision that addresses this problem is the Model Driven Organization (MDO) that uses modeling technologies to represent key aspects of a business and thereby present different views to appropriate stakeholders and to facilitate EA use-cases such as goal alignment, regulatory compliance, acquisition and merger etc. MDA techniques can be used to generate parts of infrastructure from the models. In the limit, this approach leads to a situation where an organization is completely represented in terms of models and is executed in terms of the models: *the models are the business*. MDO represents an emerging area that we believe to be fruitful for model-driven software engineering and the work presented in this chapter is a contribution to this vision.

CONCLUSION

This chapter has reviewed the need for business alignment and the current state of the art in Enterprise Architecture modelling languages. Our claim is that these languages are generally business facing and provide good support for the business analyst, but otherwise provide little or no support for precise analysis that is required to establish alignment. Systems that aim to provide such support are often based around requirements definition and do not contain modelling elements suitable for architectural definition. Furthermore, systems that provide support for precise analysis of alignment tend to be limited in scope of application because of the state space explosion.

LEAP has been designed to provide a simple basis for constructing executable architectural models and has been shown elsewhere to support many of the features defined by EA modelling languages. As such it is proposed as a basis for EA modelling. LEAP includes a language for expressing both behavioural and non-functional goals and as such is proposed as a basis for testing architectural alignment. The approach taken is not to establish global system properties because of the limitation of current approaches, but to provide confidence in alignment by running goals against the executable system models and to record the successes and failures.

This chapter has provided an overview of the LEAP language and toolset in terms of the different types of goals that can be expressed. We have defined the alignment algorithm used by LEAP and given a simple standard example in terms of the ubiquitous library information system.

Our aim is to provide a precise practical basis for EA analysis including alignment and LEAP is the technology platform we are currently developing. Further work is needed to integrate with existing technologies for EA and to strengthen the analysis provided by LEAP.

REFERENCES

Barn, B., & Clark, T. (2012). Goal based alignment of enterprise architectures. In *Proceedings of the 7th International Conference on Software Paradigm Trends* (pp. 230-236). SciTePress.

Butcher, T., Fischer, R., Kurpjuweit, S., & Winter, R. (2006). Analysis and application scenarios of enterprise architecture: An exploratory study. In *Proceedings of the 10th IEEE International Enterprise Distributed Object Computing Conference Workshops EDOCW'06*. IEEE.

Chan, Y. E., & Reich, B. H. (2007). IT alignment: What have we learned? *Journal of Information Technology*, 22(4), 297–315. doi:10.1057/palgrave.jit.2000109.

Clark, T., & Barn, B. (2012). A common basis for modelling service-oriented and event-driven architecture. In *Proceedings of the 5th Annual India Software Engineering Conference, ISEC 2012*. ACM.

Clark, T., Barn, B., & Oussena, S. (2011). LEAP: A precise lightweight framework for enterprise architecture. In *Proceedings of the 4th Annual India Software Engineering Conference, ISEC 2011*. ACM.

Clark, T., Barn, B., & Oussena, S. (2012). A method for enterprise architecture alignment. In *Proceedings of the 4th Working Conference on Practice-Driven Research on Enterprise Transformation, PRET 2012* (pp. 48-76). Springer.

Ekstedt, M., Johnson, P., Plazaola, L., Silva, E., & Lilieskold, J. (2004). Consistent enterprise software system architecture for the CIO - A utility-cost based approach. In *Proceedings of the 37th Annual Hawaii International Conference on System Sciences* (pp. 8-8). IEEE.

Engelsman, W., Quartela, D., Jonkers, H., & van Sinderen, M. (2010). Extending enterprise architecture modelling with business goals and requirements. *Journal of Enterprise Information Systems*, 5(1), 9–36. doi:10.1080/17517575.2010.491871.

Ernst, M., Matthes, F., Ramacher, R., & Schweda, C. (2009). Using enterprise architecture management patterns to complement TOGAF. In *Proceedings of the Enterprise Distributed Object Computing Conference, EDOC 2009*. IEEE.

Henderson, J. C., & Venkatraman, N. (1993). Strategic alignment: Leveraging information technology for transforming organizations. *IBM Systems Journal*, 32(1), 4–16. doi:10.1147/sj.382.0472.

Iacob, M., Jonkers, H., & Wiering, M. (2004). *Towards a UML profile for the ArchiMate language*. Retrieved from https://doc.telin.nl/dscgi/ds.py/Get/File-47276

Jonkers, H., Lankhorst, M., Buuren, R., Bonsangue, M., & Van Der Torre, L. (2004). Concepts for modeling enterprise architectures. *International Journal of Cooperative Information Systems*, 13, 257–287. doi:10.1142/S0218843004000985.

Lankhorst, M. (2009). *Introduction to enterprise architecture*. Berlin: Springer-Verlag.

Lankhorst, M., Proper, E., & Jonkers, J. (2010). The anatomy of the ArchiMate language. *International Journal of Information System Modeling and Design, 1*(1). doi:10.4018/jismd.2010092301.

Liu, L., Yu, E., & Myopoulos, J. (2003). Security and privacy requirements analysis with a social setting. In *Proceedings of the 11th IEEE International Conference on Requirements Engineering*. IEEE.

Luftman, J. (2000). Assessing business-IT alignment maturity. *Strategies for Information Technology Governance, 4*(14), 99.

Niemann, K. (2006). *From enterprise architecture to IT governance: Elements of elective IT management*. Vieweg+ Teubner Verlag.

Pereira, C. M., & Sousa, P. (2005). Enterprise architecture: Business and IT alignment. In *Proceedings of the 2005 ACM Symposium on Applied Computing* (pp. 1345). ACM.

Ponsard, C., & Devroey, X. (2011). Generating high-level event-B system models from KAOS requirement models. In *Proceedings of Actes du XXIX eme Congres INFORSID*. INFORSID.

Reige, C., & Aier, S. (2009). A consistency approach to enterprise architecture method engineering. In Proceedings of Service-Oriented Computing, ICSOC Workshops (pp. 388-399). Springer.

Spencer, J. (2004). TOGAF enterprise Ed. Version 8.1.

Wang, X., Zhou, X., & Jiang, L. (2008). A method of business and IT alignment based on enterprise architecture. In *Proceedings of the IEEE International Conference on Service Operations, Logistics and Informatics,* (vol. 1, pp. 740-745). IEEE.

Wisnosky, D. E., & Vogel, J. (2004). *DoDAF wizdom: A practical guide to planning, managing and executing projects to build enterprise architectures using the department of defense architecture framework*. DoDAF.

Zachman, J. (1999). A framework for information systems architecture. *IBM Systems Journal, 38*(2/3), 454–470. doi:10.1147/sj.382.0454.

ENDNOTES

1. http://www.opengroup.org/archimate.
2. http://www.businessrulesgroup.org/. http://www.opengroup.org/architecture/togaf9-doc/arch/index.html.
4. http://www.objectiver.com/fileadmin/download/documents/KaosTutorial.pdf.
5. http://cserg0.site.uottawa.ca/cma2012/CaseStudy.pdf.

Chapter 11
Towards Public Services and Process Integration:
A Domain–Specific Modeling Approach

Guillermo Infante Hernández
Universidad de Oviedo, Spain

Aquilino A. Juan Fuente
Universidad de Oviedo, Spain

Benjamín López Pérez
Universidad de Oviedo, Spain

Edward Rolando Núñez-Valdéz
Universidad de Oviedo, Spain

ABSTRACT

Software platforms for e-government transactions may differ in developed functionalities, languages and technologies, hardware platforms, and operating systems that support them. Those differences can be found among public organizations that share common processes, services, and regulations. This scenario hinders interoperability between these organizations. Hence, to find a technique for integrating these platforms becomes a necessity. In this chapter, a rule-based domain-specific modeling environment for public services and process integration is suggested, which consists of common identified public service elements and a set of process integration rules. This approach provides the needed integration or interoperability pursued in this domain. Furthermore a service and process model is proposed to formalize the information needed for integration of both. A set of integration rules is also presented as part of the modeling environment. This set of integration rules completes the proposed model to meet the business requirements of this domain.

DOI: 10.4018/978-1-4666-4217-1.ch011

INTRODUCTION

Governments worldwide are becoming more dependent on Information and Communication Technologies (ICT) in their everyday transactions. This results in an increased study of e-government in recent years and the development of theoretical and conceptual models to understand its different aspects (Dawes, Pardo, & Cresswell, 2004; Gilgarcia & Pardo, 2005; Gupta, 2003). Although, there is not any global accepted definition of the e-government concept as argued in (Halchin, 2004). Some of the most relevant definitions are provided by (Means & Schneider, 2000; Abramson & Means, 2001; Fountain, 2001).Only with the purpose to understand this domain, one of the most generic and accepted approaches must be mentioned in this chapter. Despite the encountered differences, an overall definition of e-government can be defined *as the use of technology, especially Web-based applications to enhance access to and efficiently deliver government information and services*. Furthermore in (Abramson & Means, 2001) there is a classification of three major categories or relationships called Government-to-Government (G2G), Government-to-Citizen (G2C), and Government-to-Business (G2B). This chapter mainly focuses on G2G relationship where the information sharing between Public Administrations' (PAs) processes and services takes place. These information interchanges or interoperability between PA organizations have been classified as a relevant subject and a critical prerequisite for the adequate performance of PA systems (Klischewski, 2004; Peristeras, Loutas, Goudos, & Tarabanis, 2007; Tambouris, Manouselis, & Costopoulou, 2007).

The European Interoperability Framework for Pan-European e-Government Services (EIF) (Overeem, Witters, & Peristeras, 2007) of the European Commission defines interoperability as the ability of Information and Communication Technology (ICT) systems and of the business processes they support to exchange data and to enable sharing of information and knowledge.

EIF defines three interoperability types such as the technical level, semantic level and organizational level where this chapter focuses on. The interaction among different business processes and services is addressed. At this level the following aspects are covered:

1. **Domain specific integration modeling:** This includes the definition of the metamodel that contains common processes and services elements to undertake their integration.
2. **Business rules integration:** This describes the construction of the integration knowledge base used to validate instances of the defined model both in modeling time and runtime.
3. **Domain specific modeling editor development:** This address the description of the necessary steps to undertake the development of a domain specific modeling tool as proof of concept for the proposals introduced in this chapter.

BACKGROUND

Process modeling has gained a lot of attention over the past decade involving process reengineering and innovation (Wang & Wang, 2006). The use of Service Orientated Architectures (SOAs) has changed the process orientation to service orientation modeling approach. These architectures are mainly dedicated to issues related to advertise, discover, invoke, compose and monitor services available from multiple providers over the Web. This change resulted in the development of the Web Services (Alonso, Casati, Kuno, & Machiraju, 2004; Moitra & Ganesh, 2005).

There are discussions on different approaches to undertake process-service integration modeling. The workflow and SOA approaches are discussed in (Gortmaker, Janssen, & Wagenaar, 2005) presenting two reference models: Workflow

Reference Model (Eder & Liebhart, 1996) and the SOA reference model (Papazoglou & Georgako-poulos, 2003). Relevancy of these models in the implementation of service-process integration in e-government is questioned. According to (Gort-maker et al., 2005), the workflow reference model is mainly focused on technology and therefore fails to address the non-technical integration issues. Instead the SOA reference model manages to address several of these issues in a rather descriptive way. Hence the SOA model manages the required functionality but does not indicate how this should be implemented. Therefore, the conclusion from this works is that a new domain specific process-service integration model is needed to facilitate process integration in e-government context.

There are a number of generic process models proposed for e-government domain. Amongst this models can be found the Federal Enterprise Archi-tecture Business Reference Model (Chief, 1999) and the SAP Public Sector Solution Map (Draijer & Schenk, 2004). These models represent generic representations of e-government domain and do not address the process-service integration issue.

By the other hand the IMPULSE project (IM-PULSE, 2002) addresses public administration services integration based on processes distributed over different information and workflow systems. These kinds of services are usually composed by a number of available processes which reside on single PA managed workflow systems. Some authors (Pasic, Diez, & Espinosa, 2002) argue that this approach is more suitable for virtual enterprises and similar applications, and less to PAs with hierarchical structures of rationalized procedures. There is a need therefore to build new models for the integration of various kinds of PA systems from the process modeling perspective where the internal workflow implementation details are transparent to other PAs systems. A process-service integration metamodel is sug-gested in this chapter to address this deficit.

DOMAIN SPECIFIC PROCESS-SERVICE MODELING INTEGRATION

A successful approach to reduce the development complexity of large software systems is the use of abstraction of the underlying system into models (Fowler, 2010; Selic, 2003). These models can be used as documentation to the underlying system, but these abstractions may become outdated as the system changes. Model-Driven Development (MDD) fosters the use of models as first-class citizens in the development process, where the system may be automatically generated from its model (Selic, 2003). Modeling is particularly beneficial for rapidly-evolving domains, as a modeled system is less sensitive to the changes in its underlying platforms. When a system is ef-fectively modeled against a well-defined modeling language, the model may also be used to predict the behavior of the system, and at a significantly lower cost than the implementation of the mod-eled system (Selic, 2003).

These modeling benefits can be taken into e-government domain to formalize this very chang-ing context and to gain an abstract representation of repetitive tasks in order to automatize them. Figure 1 describes an activity diagram that depicts a common notification process in an e-government transaction. As shown in Figure 1 there are some repeated actions that implicitly encapsulates an external service call, e.g. (Sign Publication or Notification calls an electronic signature service to perform the action). However the single use of models in this context may not be completely suitable to address all the changes caused by dif-ferent policies, regulations and laws enactments. One of the alternatives to address this issue is to use validation tools to show design errors in model instances so they can be fix it. The drawback of validation is that there is not a simple way to get the big picture of the entire design quality corre-sponding to defined constraints. These constraints

Figure 1. UML activity diagram of a common notification process

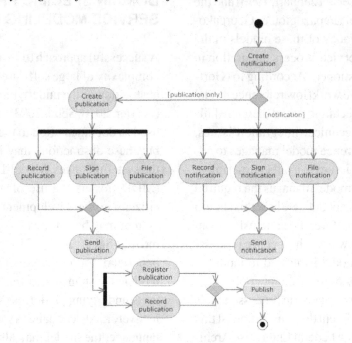

in e-government domain come from the mentioned public regulations and may significantly vary from one territory, organization or country to another. As the variations on process model requirements takes place, the services that support their transactions over the Web must be adapted to guarantee a proper interoperability functioning. There is a need then to count on an updating or self-constructing integrated mechanism that evaluates the process model instances and adapt external services integration into modeled processes. This mechanism is called in this chapter as *model adapting* and is described below as a component.

Service Integration Metamodel

This section includes the definition of the service integration metamodel (ServInt) that contains common processes and services elements to undertake their interoperation. The idea behind the definition of the metamodel in this context is to provide the binding elements amongst processes and services that can be used to ease the integra-

tion of both. This point of view places the domain expert at the modeler role when defining process models, this way it can use its knowledge of the e-government domain without been aware of the services needed for the transactions execution in the modeled process. Figure 2 describes a fragment of the proposed metamodel.

Here is a brief description of the main metamodel elements:

- **Transaction:** Represents the containment element of all the modeled processes. A transaction, e.g. (a driving license application) represents a specific process or set of them to achieve a final result.
- **Process:** Central element into a transaction formed by a set of related input actions which execution determines its final result or output.
- **Action:** Represents an operation performed to attain a specific goal. It is the triggering element for service integration.

Figure 2. Process-service integration metamodel excerpt

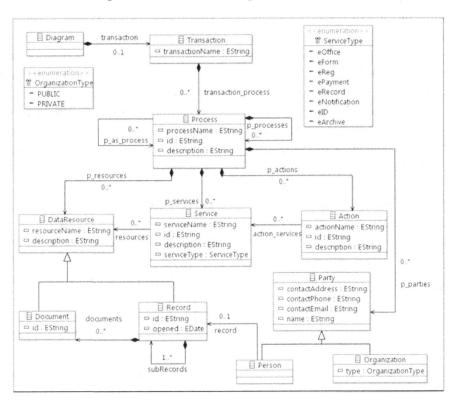

- **Service:** Exposed and external technology intended to process incoming requests that gives a correspondent response. In this context, this element takes the form of a public Web service offered by some PA or government, e.g. (electronic ids, payments, signatures, etc.).
- **Data Resource:** Any data used in process transactions. It can be a Document that belongs to some Person's or Organization's Record.

Interoperation Modeling

The definition of domain models is an effort intensive activity that requires coordination amongst different backgrounds and skills: from modeling experts to master model driven environments and resources; and from the domain experts to deepen into the application domain as stated in

(Bertolino, De Angelis, Di Sandro, & Sabetta, 2011). The definition of models is also a critical activity. Since models usually are the starting point for many subsequent transformations, faults that are possibly introduced in this stage can have detrimental impacts. Therefore, ensuring that the model is correct becomes of crucial importance. In the case of e-government domain models (e.g. process transaction models), the accuracy which they have been defined determines for example the compliance with a specific regulation or mandate as the context of their usage is usually the public sector. Therefore, the models validation becomes of crucial importance in this domain since it can prevent from failing in unlawful procedures. As mentioned before this approach places the domain expert in the modeler role. The idea is to have an editor with semiautomatic model validation to model processes that can be integrated with the services they need to function properly. The implementation of the editor involves the development and integration of two components: model adapting and service integration, as well as the underlying model instances and ServInt metamodel itself. An overall summary of these components and their integration is provided in Figure 3 as an UML component diagram.

The ServInt metamodel component is implemented as a single component using Eclipse Modeling Framework (EMF) (Steinberg, Budinsky, Paternostro, & Merks, 2008). This component internally depends on two external components to provide the metamodels for XSD and Ecore.

Figure 3. UML component diagram of the proposed implementation

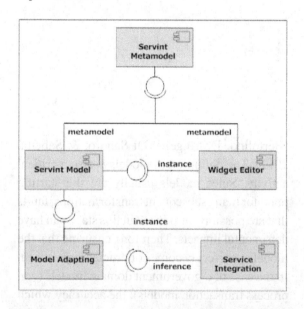

Figure 4. ServInt model UML component diagram

The decomposition of the ServInt model component is provided in Figure 4. This component is made up of two sub-components: a model instance component and a model transformation component. The former component provides the functionality to store, interact and serialize a given ServInt model instance, with respect to the ServInt metamodel; and the latter component provides the functionality to transform model instances between different metamodel versions.

The *model instance component* interacts with all other components in the system as they all use ServInt model instances to function. The implementation of this component, however, is simply the generated source code from EMF from the given Ecore-based metamodel. As described by (Steinberg et al., 2008), this involves automatically creating a genmodel model for a given metamodel source and then using this genmodel instance to generate the relevant source codes. ServInt model instances are therefore stored as XMI representations within *servint* files. The *model transformation component* is implemented with the single purpose of testing the implementation with existing model instances according to changes in the underlying ServInt metamodel.

Domain Specific Integration Modeling Editor

As mentioned before, to exploit domain expert's knowledge at modeling time along with the usabil-

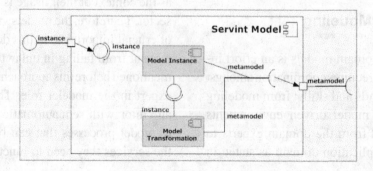

ity of a visual editor that *speaks* his/her language, a domain specific integration modeling editor is proposed. The UML component diagram of the developed Widget Editor is shown in Figure 5.

Part of the implementation of EMF is EMF. Edit Support, which provides a basic user interface for editing model instances, by combining the generated model plugin with the Eclipse UI Framework JFace (Steinberg, et al., 2008). An Edit plugin may be generated automatically from the genmodel model instance.

This generated plugin includes a tree-based or widget-based viewer of a model instance derived automatically from the metamodel structure, and a properties-based element viewer allowing a model instance developer to modify the attributes and references of selected model elements. Although

the generated implementation of this component is fairly incomplete, it can be the start point to extend its behavior and implement a rapid prototyping editor, also is a necessary requirement for future diagram editor construction. The extended implementation of a widget-based editor for editing ServInt model instances is shown in Figure 6.

As discussed earlier in this chapter there is a need of updating or self-constructing integrated mechanism that evaluates the process model instances and adapts external services integration into modeled processes. This mechanism called *model adapting* is implemented as a component and is described in Figure 7. The model adapting component defines the implementation of the model adapting process, based on the argumentation proposed by (Wright & Dietrich, 2010).

Figure 5. Widget editor UML component diagram

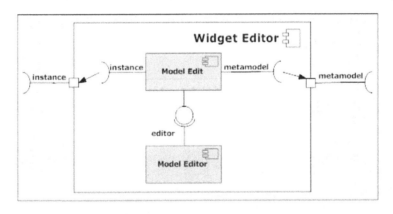

Figure 6. Implementation of a widget-based editor for ServInt model instances using EMF

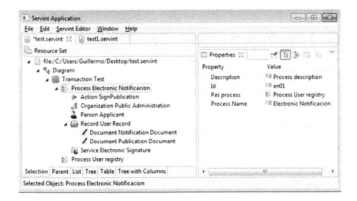

The underlying rule engine behind the implementation of model adapting in ServInt model instances is Drools (Sottara, Mello, & Proctor, 2010). Drools, also known as JBoss Rules, is an open source business rule management system and inference rule engine implemented in Java that supports an implementation of the JSR-94 specification. Inference rules are evaluated using an enhanced implementation of the Rete algorithm (Sottara et al., 2010). Drools natively provides an expressive textual language for defining inference rules, but also supports the integration of a custom rule DSL to improve the productivity of defining rules within certain domains.

The underlying model that Drools operates within is simple POJOs, making it easy to integrate into an existing Java-based software system, this structure do not need to be defined as part of the rule base; this means that all metamodel properties and operations are always accessible to

a Drools rule. Alternatively, metamodel reflection is possible using the EMF API. A model adapting rule is implemented in Drools to adapt a modeled process as described in Figure 8.

FUTURE RESEARCH DIRECTIONS

There are some research lines related to this work that needs to be mentioned. Model driven engineering has gained a lot of attention from the research community and its applications nowadays may vary significantly from different domains. E-government domain can be one of the contexts where MDE can be successfully applied as argued in this chapter due to its straightforward methods to transform domain models in executable software. The code generation of e-government application platforms as a way to achieve standardization in respect to interoperability issues can be a promis-

Figure 7. Model adapting UML component diagram

Figure 8. Model adapting rule implemented in drools

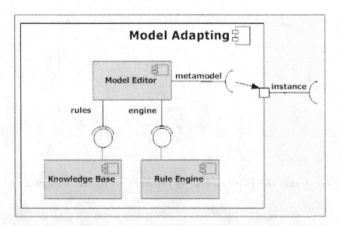

```
rule "Adapt process to interoperate with eNotification"
    no-loop
    when
        $service: Service(serviceType == ServiceType.ENOTIFICATION)
        $action: Action(action_services contains $service)
        $process: Process(p_actions contains $action)
    then
        modify($process){
    getP_services().add($service)
    }
end
```

ing research field. Also the administrative process modeling with graphical editors in order to improve the understanding of the modeled processes semantics from domain experts constitute a viable research direction. Another interesting direction of research can be the use of standards like SBVR (OMG & Specification, 2008) along with MDE model transformation techniques in order to obtain semantically enriched e-government specifications.

CONCLUSION

In this chapter, a rule-based domain-specific modeling environment for public services and process integration is proposed. This environment is composed by the definition of the ServInt metamodel where the most relevant elements involved in e-government transactions domain were formalized. This formalization was taken as a starting point to gain an abstract representation of repetitive tasks in order to automatize them, as well as the information structure needed to integrate administrative processes and services. A known issue related to this integration is also argued in this chapter, the one referring to the constant changes in this domain caused by different policies, regulations, and laws enactments. These variations on process model requirements have to deal with the corresponding changes in services interoperation mechanisms that support their transactions over the Web. As a solution to this issue this work suggests a *model adapting component* as part of the proposed solution that evaluates the process model instances and adapts external services integration into modeled processes to guarantee a proper interoperability functioning. Along with model adapting there is another important use of rules integration in the modeling environment: the model instance validation that in this domain can be used to prevent from failing in unlawful procedures. Finally,

this chapter places the domain expert in modeler role and proposed a domain specific modeling editor as a proof of concept implementation that encompasses all previous argumentations. It can be considered that this proposal eases the task of modeling public processes performed by public employees without been aware of the intrinsic mechanisms to achieve that task and in a friendly environment that *speaks* his/her language. Can be concluded also that this work aids the interoperation of public processes and services since it provides a mechanism that tackles the semantics of this integration in a form of a rule based knowledge base that can be changed without affecting the information contained in both processes and services structures.

REFERENCES

Abramson, M. A., & Means, G. E. (2001). *E-government 2001*. London: Rowman & Littlefield Publishers.

Alonso, G., Casati, F., Kuno, H., & Machiraju, V. (2004). *Web services: Concepts, architectures and applications*. Berlin: Springer.

Bertolino, A., De Angelis, G., Di Sandro, A., & Sabetta, A. (2011). Is my model right? Let me ask the expert. *Journal of Systems and Software, 84*(7), 1089–1099. Retrieved October 15, 2012, from http://dx.doi.org/10.1016/j.jss.2011.01.054

Chief, T. (1999, September). Federal enterprise architecture framework. *Architecture (Washington, D.C.), 80*. Retrieved from http://www.cio.gov/documents/fedarch1.pdf.

Dawes, S. S., Pardo, T. A., & Cresswell, A. M. (2004). Designing electronic government information access programs: A holistic approach. *Government Information Quarterly, 21*(1), 3–23. Retrieved from http://www.sciencedirect.com/science/article/B6W4G-4B71BC0-1/2/0ffcef06875aa7c64fdf9b510e62466b doi:10.1016/j.giq.2003.11.001.

Draijer, C., & Schenk, D. (2004). Best practices of business simulation with SAP R/3. *Journal of Information Systems Education, 15*(3), 261. Retrieved from http://findarticles.com/p/articles/mi_qa4041/is_200410/ai_n9464918/pg_5/.

Eder, J., & Liebhart, W. (1996). Workflow transactions. In *Workflow Handbook 1997* (pp. 195–202). New York: John Wiley & Sons, Inc. Retrieved from http://citeseerx.ist.psu.edu/viewdoc/summary?doi=10.1.1.21.7110

Fountain, J. E. (2001). Building the virtual state: Information technology and institutional change. *Information Systems Research, 7*, xii. Retrieved from http://isr.journal.informs.org/cgi/content/abstract/7/1/22.

Fowler, M. (2010). Domain specific languages. *International Journal of Computers and Applications, 1*, 39–60. Retrieved from http://martinfowler.com/dslwip/.

Gilgarcia, J., & Pardo, T. (2005). E-government success factors: Mapping practical tools to theoretical foundations. *Government Information Quarterly, 22*(2), 187–216. Retrieved July 3, 2011, from http://linkinghub.elsevier.com/retrieve/pii/S0740624X05000158

Gortmaker, J., Janssen, M., & Wagenaar, R. W. (2005). Towards requirements for a reference model for process orchestration in e-government. In M. Böhlen, J. Gamper, W. Polasek, & M. A. Wimmer (Eds.), *EGovernment Towards Electronic Democracy* (Vol. 3416, pp. 169–180). Springer. Retrieved from http://springerlink.metapress.com/(hgp11niu3o1t4b552xj3zy55)/app/home/contribution.asp?referrer=parent&backto=issue,16,28,journal,526,3824,linkingpublicationresults,1:105633,1

Gupta, M. (2003). E-government evaluation: A framework and case study. *Government Information Quarterly, 20*(4), 365–387. Retrieved July 11, 2011, from http://linkinghub.elsevier.com/retrieve/pii/S0740624X03000790

Halchin, L. E. (2004). Electronic government: Government capability and terrorist resource. *Government Information Quarterly, 21*(4), 406–419. Retrieved from http://www.sciencedirect.com/science/article/B6W4G-4DTKPJW-1/2/f6b-622cecc53f2d033cfc84e8827b67d doi:10.1016/j.giq.2004.08.002.

IMPULSE. (2002). *Project IST-1999-21119.* Retrieved from http://cordis.europa.eu/search/index.cfm?fuseaction=proj.document&PJ_LANG=PL&PJ_RCN=4850507&pid=270&q=D67BEC82A602A23FF8B013B7DA527238&type=pro

Klischewski, R. (2004). Information integration or process integration? How to achieve interoperability in administration. *Electronic Government, 3183*, 57–65. Retrieved from http://www.springerlink.com/index/cndhp3plq6pt05x3.pdf

Means, G., & Schneider, D. (2000). *Meta-Capitalism: The e-business revolution and the design of 21st-century companies and markets.* New York: Wiley. Retrieved from http://www.amazon.ca/exec/obidos/redirect?tag=citeulike09-20&amp,path=ASIN/0471393355

Moitra, D., & Ganesh, J. (2005). Web services and flexible business processes: Towards the adaptive enterprise. *Information & Management*, *42*(7), 921–933. Retrieved from http://linkinghub.elsevier.com/retrieve/pii/S0378720604001338 doi:10.1016/j.im.2004.10.003.

OMG & Specification. (2008). *Semantics of business vocabulary and business rules*. OMG.

Papazoglou, M. P., & Georgakopoulos, D. (2003). Service-oriented computing. *Communications of the ACM*, *46*(10), 24–28. Retrieved from http://ieeexplore.ieee.org/lpdocs/epic03/wrapper.htm?arnumber=1607964 doi:10.1145/944217.944233.

Pasic, A., Diez, S., & Espinosa, J. (2002). IMPULSE: Interworkflow model for e-government. In R. Traunmüller & K. Lenk (Eds.), Electronic Government (Vol. 2456, pp. 53–79). Springer. Retrieved from http://dx.doi.org/ doi:10.1007/3-540-46138-8_77.

Peristeras, V., Loutas, N., Goudos, S., & Tarabanis, K. (2007). Semantic interoperability conflicts in pan-European public services. In H. Österle, J. Schelp, & R. Winter (Eds.), *15th European Conference on Information Systems ECIS 2007* (pp. 2173–2184). University of St. Gallen. Retrieved from http://is2.lse.ac.uk/asp/aspecis/20070128.pdf

Selic, B. (2003). The pragmatics of model-driven development. *IEEE Software*, *20*, 19–25. Retrieved from http://ieeexplore.ieee.org/lpdocs/epic03/wrapper.htm?arnumber=1231146 doi:10.1109/MS.2003.1231146.

Sottara, D., Mello, P., & Proctor, M. (2010). A configurable rete-OO engine for reasoning with different types of imperfect information. *IEEE Transactions on Knowledge and Data Engineering*, *22*, 1535–1548. doi:10.1109/TKDE.2010.125.

Steinberg, D., Budinsky, F., Paternostro, M., & Merks, E. (2008). EMF: Eclipse modeling framework. In *Engineering* (p. 744). Reading, MA: Addison-Wesley Professional. Retrieved from http://portal.acm.org/citation.cfm?id=1197540

Tambouris, E., Manouselis, N., & Costopoulou, C. (2007). Metadata for digital collections of e-government resources. *The Electronic Library*, *25*(2), 176–192. Retrieved from http://www.emeraldinsight.com/10.1108/02640470710741313 doi:10.1108/02640470710741313.

van Overeem, A. V. O. A., Witters, J. W. J., & Peristeras, V. P. V. (2007). An interoperability framework for pan-european e-government services (PEGS). In *Proceedings of the 2007 40th Annual Hawaii International Conference on System Sciences HICSS07* (Vol. 2009, p. 7). IEEE. Retrieved from http://ieeexplore.ieee.org/lpdocs/epic03/wrapper.htm?arnumber=4076384

Wang, M., & Wang, H. (2006). From process logic to business logic—A cognitive approach to business process management. *Information & Management*, *43*(2), 179–193. Retrieved from http://linkinghub.elsevier.com/retrieve/pii/S0378720605000479 doi:10.1016/j.im.2005.06.001.

Wright, J. M., & Dietrich, J. B. (2010). Non-monotonic model completion in web application engineering. In *Proceedings of the 2010 21st Australian Software Engineering Conference*, (pp. 45–54). IEEE. Retrieved December 3, 2012, from http://ieeexplore.ieee.org/lpdocs/epic03/wrapper.htm?arnumber=5475055

ADDITIONAL READING

Alpar, P., & Olbrich, S. (2005). Legal requirements and modelling of processes in e-government. *Electronic. Journal of E-Government*, *3*(3), 107–116. Retrieved from http://www.ejeg.com/volume-3/vol3-iss3/v3-i3-art2.htm.

Badri, M., & Alshare, K. (2008). A path analytic model and measurement of the business value of e-government: An international perspective. *International Journal of Information Management, 28*(6), 524–535. doi:10.1016/j.ijinfomgt.2006.10.004.

Buhl, H. U., & Löffler, M. (2011). *The role of business and information systems engineering in e-government.* Business & Information Systems Engineering. doi:10.1007/s12599-011-0182-4.

Gilgarcia, J., & Pardo, T. (2005). E-government success factors: Mapping practical tools to theoretical foundations. *Government Information Quarterly, 22*(2), 187–216. doi:10.1016/j.giq.2005.02.001.

Indiharstemberger, M., & Jaklic, J. (2007). Towards e-government by business process change—A methodology for public sector. *International Journal of Information Management, 27*(4), 221–232. doi:10.1016/j.ijinfomgt.2007.02.006.

Karagiannis, D., Utz, W., Woitsch, R., & Leutgeb, A. (2008). Business processes and rules an egovernment case-study. *Artificial Intelligence, 5.*

Muller, P.-A., Fondement, F., Baudry, B., & Combemale, B. (2010). Modeling modeling modeling. *Software & Systems Modeling.* doi:doi:10.1007/s10270-010-0172-x.

Murzek, M., & Specht, G. (2010). *Model-driven development of interoperable, inter-organisational business processes. interoperability in digital.* doi:10.4018/978-1-61520-887-6.ch007

Norman Andersen, K. (2010). *Electronic government and the information systems perspective.* Paper presented at the First International Conference, EGOVIS 2010. Bilbao, Spain.

Peristeras, V., Tarabanis, K., & Goudos, S. K. (2009). Model-driven egovernment interoperability: A review of the state of the art. *Computer Standards & Interfaces, 31*(4), 613–628. doi:10.1016/j.csi.2008.09.034.

Riss, U. V., Weber, I., & Grebner, O. (2009). Business process modelling, task management, and the semantic link. In K. Hinkelmann (Ed.), *AAAI Spring Symposium AI Meets Business Rules and Process Management* (pp. 99–104). AAAI Press. Retrieved from https://www.aaai.org/Papers/Symposia/Spring/2008/SS-08-01/SS08-01-013.pdf

Salhofer, P., & Stadlhofer, B. (2012). Semantic MDA for e-government service development. In *Proceedings of the 2012 45th Hawaii International Conference on System Sciences.* IEEE. Retrieved from http://ieeexplore.ieee.org/lpdocs/epic03/wrapper.htm?arnumber=6149279

Shareef, M. A., Kumar, V., Kumar, U., & Dwivedi, Y. K. (2011). e-Government adoption model (GAM): Differing service maturity levels. *Government Information Quarterly, 28*(1), 17–35. doi:10.1016/j.giq.2010.05.006.

Zampou, E., & Eliakis, S. (2010). Measuring the benefit of interoperability: A business process modelling approach. In Interoperability in Digital, (pp. 321–338). doi: doi:10.4018/978-1-61520-887-6.ch017.

KEY TERMS AND DEFINITIONS

Domain Specific Modeling Language (DSML): Modeling language of limited expressiveness focused on a particular domain.

E-Government: Use of technology, especially Web-based applications to enhance access to and efficiently deliver government information and services.

Interoperability: Ability of ICT systems and of the business processes they support to exchange data and to enable sharing of information and knowledge.

Model-Driven Development (MDD): Approach that promotes the idea that models should be adopted as part of systems development using the essentials of models automation and modeling standards.

Public Administrations: Organizations that delivers public services to citizens, other administrations and businesses.

Service Oriented Architecture (SOA): Software architecture that defines the usage of services to support business requirements.

Web Service: Technology that uses a set of protocols and standards to exchange data among applications that differs in programing languages, platforms, and operating systems.

Chapter 12
Architecture–Driven Modernization for Software Reverse Engineering Technologies

Liliana Martinez
Universidad Nacional del Centro de la Provincia de Buenos Aires, Argentina

Liliana Favre
Universidad Nacional del Centro de la Provincia de Buenos Aires, Argentina & Comisión de Investigaciones Científicas de la Provincia de Buenos Aires, Argentina

Claudia Pereira
Universidad Nacional del Centro de la Provincia de Buenos Aires, Argentina

ABSTRACT

Modernization of legacy systems is a new research area in the software industry that is intended to provide support for transforming an existing software system to a new one that satisfies new demands. Software modernization requires technical frameworks for information integration and tool interoperability that allow managing new platform technologies, design techniques, and processes. The new OMG (Object Management Group) initiative for modernization aligned with this requirement is Architecture-Driven Modernization (ADM). Reverse engineering techniques play a crucial role in system modernization. In this chapter, the authors describe the state-of-the-art in the model-driven modernization area, reverse engineering in particular, and discuss about existing tools and future trends. In addition, they describe a framework to reverse engineering models from object-oriented code that distinguishes three different abstraction levels linked to models, metamodels, and formal specifications. As an example, this chapter shows how to reverse engineering use case diagrams from Java code in the ADM context focusing on transformations at metamodel level. The authors validate their approach by using Eclipse Modeling Framework.

DOI: 10.4018/978-1-4666-4217-1.ch012

INTRODUCTION

In the last years, software modernization, understood as technological and functional evolution of legacy systems, has become a new area of research in the software industry whose aim is to provide principles, methods, techniques and tools to support the transformation from an existing software system to a new one that satisfies new demands. The growing demand for modernization is due, among others, to several factors:

- New methods and modeling languages such as UML (UML, 2011a, 2011b) and RUP, new platforms, Internet-related technologies, and new architectures such as SOA (Service-Oriented Architecture) and MDA (Model-Driven Architecture) (MDA, 2012), the OMG proposal for MDD (Model-Driven Development), have encouraged the modernization of legacy systems in order to achieve competitive advantages for organizations.

- The emergence of the Cloud computing paradigm is leading to the migration of traditional desktop applications into the Cloud due to the benefits obtained for both consumers and providers of IT services.

- The great technological advance in mobile technologies, such as improved processing power and data storage, Internet access, video and audio players, office applications, makes mobile devices resemble a personal computer. Then, many existing software system needs to be migrated to these mobile platforms.

To meet new demands, existing systems must constantly evolve. However, some systems can not be modified or adapted to incorporate the new requirements. A number of solutions have been proposed to deal with this problem. These solutions fall generally into three categories: redevelopment, which rewrites existing applications; wrapping, which wraps an existing component in a new and more accessible software component; and migration, which moves the existing system to a more flexible environment, while retaining the original system data and functionality (Bisbal, Lawless, Wu, & Grimson, 1999). Each of these solutions have a greater or lesser degree of impact on the system, and consequently in the organization. The best solution should be to restore the value of the existing system, extracting and exploiting investment and knowledge to migrate to a new system that incorporates the new requirements and/or new technologies. However, the lack of both standardization of legacy artifacts and automated processes supported by CASE (Computer Aided Software Engineering) tools are the most important limitations in this approach. MDD techniques such as metamodeling and model transformation can be used to evolve existing systems (Favre, 2010). These techniques can help reduce software evolution costs by automating many basic activities, including code manipulation. In this context, a new approach known as Architecture-Driven Modernization (ADM) (ADM, 2012) has emerged complementing OMG standards such as MDA. The outstanding ideas behind MDA are separating the specification of the system functionality from its implementation on specific platforms, managing the software evolution from abstract models to implementations.

The ADM approach has established a set of solutions for information system modernization. ADM is defined as "the process of understand and evolve existing software assets for the purpose of software improvement, modifications, interoperability, refactoring, restructuring, reuse, porting, migration, translation, integration, service-oriented architecture deployment" (ADM, 2012). The OMG ADM Task Force (ADMTF) is developing a set of standards (metamodels) to facilitate interoperability between modernization tools. To date, ADMTF has published the standards KDM (Knowledge Discovery Metamodel), ASTM (Abstract Syntax Tree Metamodel) and

SMM (Software Metrics Metamodel) (KDM, 2011; ASTM, 2011; SMM, 2012).

The modernization process includes three stages: reverse engineering, restructuring and forward engineering. Reverse engineering, the process of analyzing available software artifacts in order to extract information and provide high-level views of the system, has become a crucial stage within the system modernization. In the ADM context, the reverse engineering goal is to discover the knowledge of the existing solution and produce models at different levels of abstraction. These models are the starting point for the restructuring process and generation of the new system (forward engineering). The success of ADM approach depends on the existence of CASE tools that make a significant impact on the automation of each stage of the modernization processes. Commercial tools have recently begun to emerge. The current techniques available in these tools provide forward engineering and limited facilities for reverse engineering.

This chapter describes the state of the art in the model-driven modernization area, reverse engineering in particular. We expose some related work, existing tools and future trends. Also, we analyze a reverse engineering proposal using a combination of ADM, traditional static and dynamic analysis and formal specification. The core of the chapter describes how to reverse models that represent an abstract view of existing systems from its code. These models provide a uniform representation of the system in the ADM standard context. To support model discovery we propose an adaptation of traditional software engineering techniques to the ADM context. The idea is to extract Platform Independent Models (PIMs) from existing systems in order to use them in the modernization process. We describe reverse engineering of PIMs expressed in terms of UML diagrams such as Class Diagrams, State Diagrams, Use Case Diagrams and Activity Diagrams. We propose the use of OMG standards (including ASTM and KDM) and the MoDisco

(Model Discovery) Platform (MoDisco, 2012) to validate our approach. It is worth considering that currently MoDisco can only recover UML class diagram from Java code.

BACKGROUND

Software industry constantly evolves to satisfy new demands. Nowadays, there is an increased demand for software migration as well as modernization of legacy systems that are still business-critical in order to extend their useful lifetime. The success of system modernization depends on the existence of technical frameworks for information integration and tool interoperability. In this section, we present work related to software modernization, particularly reverse engineering. Next, we discuss the limitations of the CASE tools to support ADM. Finally, we describe OMG standards for Modernization.

Related Work

Many works have contributed to reverse engineering object-oriented code. Tonella and Potrich (2005) provide a relevant overview of techniques that have been recently investigated and applied in the field of reverse engineering of object-oriented code. Authors describe the algorithms involved in the recovery of UML diagrams, such as class diagrams, state diagrams, and sequence diagrams, from code. This proposal is based on static and dynamic analysis. Canfora and Di Penta (2007) compare existing work in the reverse engineering area, discuss success stories and main achievements, and provide a road map for possible future developments in this area. Angyal, Lengyel, and Charaf (2006) introduce the importance of the model-based development and present an overview of the state of the art of reverse engineering methods and tools. Also, they state that the model-based development approaches without comprehensive tools are hardly usable in practice.

Many works are linked to MDD-based reverse engineering. MacDonald, Russell, and Atchison (2005) report on a project that assessed the feasibility of applying MDD to the evolution of a legacy system. Deissenboeck and Ratiu (2006) show the first steps towards the definition of a metamodel that unifies a conceptual view on programs with the classical structure-based reverse engineering metamodels. Reus, Geers and van Deursen (2006) describe a feasibility study in reengineering legacy systems based on grammars and metamodels. Fleurey, Breton, Baudry, Nicolas, and Jézéquel (2007) report on the use of MDE as an efficient, flexible and reliable approach for a software migration process. This process, developed at Sodifrance, includes automatic analysis of the existing code, reverse engineering of abstract high-level models, model transformation to target platform models and code generation. Authors detail different metamodels and transformations that are produced for the automation of these steps. Sodifrance has developed a tool suite for model manipulation called Model-In-Action (MIA) that is used as a basis for automating the migration. Cánovas Izquierdo and García Molina (2009a) analyze the difficulties encountered when using existing solutions for model extraction in the software modernization context and propose a language called Gra2MoL (Grammar To Model Transformation Language), which was designed to address the problem of model extraction. This provides a query language for concrete syntax trees, and specifies mappings between source grammar elements and target metamodel elements by rules whose structure is similar to those provided in model transformation languages, such as ATL. Gra2MoL has been used to extract models from Java and PL/SQL code. Favre, Martinez, and Pereira (2009) describe a reverse engineering approach MDA compliant which integrate techniques that come from compiler theory, metamodeling and formal specification. Authors describe a process that combines static and dynamic analysis for generating MDA models, show how MOF and

QVT metamodels can be used to drive model recovery processes and depict how metamodels and transformations can be integrated with formal specifications in an interoperable way. In that work, reverse engineering of class diagram and state diagram at Platform Specific Model (PSM) level from Java code is exemplified.

With the emergence of ADM, new approaches and tools are being developed. Cánovas Izquierdo and García Molina (2009b) present a process to extract models that conform to the KDM metamodel. First, a grammar-to-model transformation language called Gra2MoL is used to extract models that conform to the ASTM metamodel. Next, these models are transformed in KDM models by using RubyTL, a model-to-model transformation language. An example of migration from Struts to JSF is presented. Barbier, Deltombe, Parisy, and Youbi (2011) describe a model driven reverse engineering method based on metamodeling and model transformation, two core notions of MDE. The method was implemented in the BLU AGE® Reverse module, an Eclipse IDE plugin. In this approach, a textual Domain-Specific Language (a specific grammar) is constructed to later describe source code as formal KDM models. Next, these KDM models are transformed to UML PIMs. Authors explain the actions to be performed to generalize this method by extending KDM along with an implementation of the Abstract Syntax Tree Metamodel (ASTM) standard. Authors state that the link between KDM and ASTM is not clear even confusing.

CASE Tools and Software Modernization

The success of approaches such as ADM and MDA depend on the existence of CASE tools that make a significant impact on software processes such as forward engineering and reverse engineering processes (Favre, Pereira, & Martinez, 2009).

All of the MDA tools are partially compliant to MDA features. They provide good support for modeling and limited support for automated transformation in reverse engineering. They generally support MDD from the PIM level and use UML class diagrams for designing PIMs. As an example we can mention ArcStyler, one of the first products to embrace MDA using the relevant technology standards and providing model transformation. The main MDA Case tools and their facilities are described in (CASE MDA, 2012).

Techniques that currently exist in MDA CASE tools provide little support for validating models in the design stages. Reasoning about models of systems is well supported by automated theorem provers and model checkers, however these tools are not integrated into CASE tools environments. Another problem is that as soon as the requirements specifications are handed down, the system architecture begins to deviate from specifications. Only research tools provide support for formal specification and deductive verification. As an example, we can mention USE 3.0 (USE, 2011) that is a system for specification of information systems in OCL (Object Constraint Language) (OCL, 2012). USE allows snapshots of running systems can be created and manipulated during an animation checking OCL constraints to validate the specification against non-formal requirements.

Many CASE tools support reverse engineering, however, they only use more basic notational features with a direct code representation and produce very large diagrams. Reverse engineering processes are facilitated by inserting annotations in the generated code. These annotations are the link between the model elements and the language. As such, they should be kept intact and not be changed. It is the programmer responsibility to know what he or she can modify and what he or she can not modify.

With the emergence of ADM new tools need to be developed. In order to be ADM compliant, these tools should provide the following features:

- Support for modeling.
- Interoperability and standardization: tools should be able to import and export data between them by using standards such as XML Metadata Interchange (XMI) (XMI, 2011). Also, tools should provide implementation of ADM standards such as KDM and ASTM.
- Automated transformations for both forward engineering and reverse engineering and access to the definition of these transformations.
- Support for verification and validation of models: mechanisms for determining the correctness and accuracy of the model.
- Support for reverse engineering of PIM including not only class diagrams but also use cases diagrams, state diagrams, activity diagrams, and so on.
- Support for traceability: mechanism that keeps record of links between the source and target model elements in the model transformation context.

Today, the most complete technology that supports ADM is MoDisco, a Generative Modeling Technology (GMT) component for model-driven reverse engineering. Because of the heterogeneity of legacy systems, there are numerous ways to extract models from such systems. MoDisco provides a generic and extensible framework to facilitate the development of tools to extract models from legacy systems and use them on use cases modernization. As an Eclipse component, MoDisco can be integrated with plug-ins or technologies available in the Eclipse environment such as Eclipse Modeling Project, Eclipse Modeling Framework (EMF), model-to-model transformation and Graphical Modeling Framework (GMF).

The MoDisco project is working in close collaboration with the ADMTF. To facilitate reuse of components between several modernization solutions, MoDisco is organized in three layers:

- Infrastructure layer contains generic components independent from any legacy technology such us:
  - EMF implementations of the Abstract Syntax Tree Metamodel core (GASTM) and Knowledge Discovery Metamodel (KDM).
  - KDM Source discoverer.
  - KDM to UML converter, which is a plug-in that allows transforming KDM models into UML models.
- Technology layer contains component dedicated to one legacy technology, for instance:
  - Metamodels for the Java language, Java AST and XML standard.
  - Java Discoverer that allows creating models from Java source code contained in a Java project.
  - Discoverer to create XML models from XML files.
- Use-cases layer contains components providing a solution for a specific modernization use-case.

Bruneliere, Cabot, and Dupé (2012) state that the MoDisco approach is used as a solid base for real applications, however, some important improvements on model driven reverse engineering techniques are still needed. They affirm that important research issues to be addressed within the context of the MoDisco should include: scalability of model manipulation techniques, advanced composition of heterogeneous models and traceability during the whole life cycle of a project.

Tools and Languages for Model Transformation

QVT (Query, View, Transformation) (QVT, 2011) is a metamodel from the OMG for expressing transformation in MDA-based processes. The QVT specification has a hybrid declarative/imperative nature. The declarative part is split into a two-level architecture, Relations and Core languages, that represent the same semantics at two different levels of abstraction. On the other hand, the imperative part includes one standard language, Operational Mapping, and one non-standard Black-Box.

Few MDA-based CASE tools support QVT or at least, any of the QVT languages. As an example, IBM Rational Software Architect and Spark System Enterprise Architect do not implement QVT. Other tools partially support QVT, for instance Together allows defining and modifying transformations Model-to-Model (M2M) and Model-to-Text (M2T) that are QVT-Operational compliant. Medini QVT partially implements QVT (Medini, 2012). It is integrated with Eclipse and allows the execution of transformations expressed in the QVT-Relation language.

The MMT (Model-to-Model Transformation) Eclipse project, originally known as the M2M project, is a subproject of the top-level Eclipse Modeling Project that provides a framework for model-to-model transformation languages. Transformations are executed by transformation engines that are plugged into the Eclipse Modeling infrastructure. There are three transformation engines that are developed in the scope of that project: ATL, QVTo, QVTd:

- ATL is a model transformation language and toolkit developed by ATLAS INRIA & LINA research group (ATL, 2012). In the field of MDE, ATL provides ways to produce a set of target models from a set of source models. The ATL Integrated Development Environment (IDE) provides a number of standard development tools (syntax highlighting, debugger, etc.) that aims to facilitate the development of ATL transformations.

- QVT Operational (QVTo) component is a partial implementation of the Operational Mappings Language defined by the OMG standard specification MOF 2.0 Query/View/Transformation. In long term, it aims to provide a complete implementation of the operational part of the standard.

- The QVT Declarative (QVTd) component is a partial implementation of the Core and Relations languages defined by the OMG standard specification MOF 2.0 Query/View/Transformation. To date, the QVT declarative component is in its "incubation" phase and provides only editing capabilities to support the QVT declarative language.

Standards for Modernization: KDM and ASTM

The key motivation for the establishment of standards for the interchange of software models within the ADMTF context is to facilitate interoperability between the tools and services of the adherents of the standard (ADM, 2012). The purpose of standardization is to achieve well-defined interfaces and well-defined formats for interchange of information about software models used by the software modernization tools. This will enable a new generation of solutions to benefit the whole industry and encourage collaboration among complementary vendors. ADMTF is developing a set of standards to facilitate interoperability between modernization tools. We are interested in KDM and ASTM in particular.

KDM and ASTM are two complementary modeling specifications (ASTM, 2011). KDM establishes a specification that allows representing semantic information about a software system, whereas ASTM establishes a specification for representing the syntax of the source code by means of abstract syntax trees. ASTM acts as the lowest level foundation for modeling of software within the OMG ecosystem of standards, whereas

KDM serves as a gateway to the higher-level OMG models. ASTM complement KDM by providing a continuous framework for mapping between low-level software models that are represented in ASTM and higher-level conceptual views of software that are represented by KDM another OMG modeling standards, such as UML.

Knowledge Discovery Meta-Model (KDM)

The Knowledge Discovery Metamodel is designed as the OMG foundation for software modernization. Its main goal is to provide a common interchange format that allows interoperability between tools for maintenance, evolution, assessment and modernization. KDM is defined via Meta-Object Facility (MOF) (MOF, 2011) and determines the interchange format via the XMI.

KDM is a metamodel for knowledge discovery in software that allows representing information related to existing software assets, their associations, and operational environments regardless of the implementation programming language and runtime platform. KDM represents entire enterprise software systems, not just code. The metamodel represents the physical and logical software assets at various levels of abstraction as entities and relations. Its extensibility mechanism allows addition of domain-, application- and implementation-specific knowledge.

KDM separates knowledge about existing systems into several orthogonal facets known as Architecture Views. The KDM specification is organized into the following 4 layers, each layer is further organized into packages which define a set of metamodel elements whose purpose is to represent a certain independent facet of knowledge related to existing software systems (KDM, 2011):

- **Infrastructure Layer:** It specifies a small set of concepts used throughout the entire specification. This layer consists of 3 packages: Core, *kdm* and Source. The Core package provides basic constructs for creating and describing metamodel classes in all specific KDM packages. The *kdm* package describes several infrastructure elements that are present in each KDM instance. The Source package represents the physical artifacts of an existing system as KDM entities and specifies the mechanism of traceability links that provide associations between KDM elements and their "original" language-dependent representation in the source code of the existing software system. *kdm* package together with the elements defined in the Core package constitutes the so-called KDM Framework.

- **Program Elements Layer:** It provides a language-independent intermediate representation for constructs determined by common programming languages. This Layer defines a single KDM Model, called CodeModel, and consists of Code and Action packages. The Code package represents code items which are programming elements as determined by programming languages, such as data types, classes, methods and variables, and structural relations between them. The Action package captures the low level behavior elements that determine the control flow and data flow between code items.
- **Runtime Resource Layer:** This layer represents the operational environment of the existing software system and consists of four packages. Platform package represents runtime platform resources, such as inter-process communication, the use of registries and data management. UI package represents the knowledge related to the user interfaces. Event package represents the knowledge related to events and state transition behavior. Data package represents the artifacts related to persistent data, such as indexed files and relational databases.

- **Abstractions Layer:** It represents domain and application abstractions as well as artifacts related to the build process of the existing software system. This layer consists of three packages. Conceptual package provides constructs for creating a conceptual model during the analysis phase of knowledge discovery from existing code. Structure package represents the logical organization of the software system into subsystems, layers and components. Build package represents the engineering view of the software system, the facts involved in its build process.

Abstract Syntax Tree Metamodel (ASTM)

In the MDD context, Abstract Syntax Trees (ASTs) are used as a model of the source code. OMGTF has defined ASTM, a specification for modeling elements to express AST in a representation that facilitates the interchange of software models among tools (ASTM, 2011).

ASTM describes the elements used for composing AST models. An AST is a model of how the statements of a software asset are structured reflecting the grammar of the particular programming language. In order to provide for uniformity as well as a universal framework for extension, the ASTM specification is composed of:

- **The Generic Abstract Syntax Metamodel (GASTM):** It represents a generic set of language modeling elements common across numerous languages that establishes a common core for language modeling.
- **The Specialized Abstract Syntax Metamodels (SASTMs):** It represents a set of complementary specifications that extend the core for particular languages such as Ada, C, Fortran, Java, that are modeled in MOF or MOF compatible forms and expressed as the GASTM along with

modeling element extensions sufficient to capture the language.

- **Propietary Abstract Syntax Tree Metamoldels (PASTM):** It expresses ASTs for languages such as Ada, C, COBOL, modeled in formats inconsistent with MOF, GSATM, or SASTM.

A FRAMEWORK FOR ADM-BASED REVERSE ENGINEERING

To reverse engineering models from object-oriented code, we propose a framework based on the integration of ADM, traditional static and dynamic analysis and formal specification. This framework distinguishes three different abstraction levels linked to models, metamodels and formal specifications (Figure 1). We describe how to reverse models that represent an abstract view of existing systems from its code. These models provide a uniform representation of the system in the ADM standard context.

In the MDD context, the reverse engineering stage extracts elements from existing systems and represents them into a Platform Specific Model (PSM), and subsequently Platform Independent Models (PIMs) are obtained from the PSMs. In the ADM context, KDM is the support for representing PSMs by using ASTM as intermediate representation of a software system. The models at PIM level are built from PSM by means of transformation (formal mappings) between KDM and UML.

The model level includes code, PIMs, PSMs and ISMs (Implementation Specific Models). PIMs are expressed in UML and OCL and include use case diagrams, activity diagrams, interaction diagrams to model system processes and state diagrams to model lifecycle of the system entities. PSMs are expressed as KDM models. An ISM is a specification of the existing system that is expressed by means of the code and its abstract representation (AST).

At model level, transformations are based on classical compiler construction techniques. They involve processes with different degrees of automation which range from totally automatic static analysis to processes that require human intervention to dynamically analyze the resultant models. All the algorithms that deal with reverse engineering share an analysis framework. The basic idea is to describe source code or models by an abstract language and perform a propagation analysis in a data-flow graph called in this context object-data flow (Tonella & Potrich, 2005). The static analysis is complemented with dynamic analysis supported by tracer tools.

The metamodel level includes metamodels defined via Meta-Object Facility (MOF), such as UML, KDM, and ASTM, which describe the transformations at model level. A metamodel is an explicit model of the constructs and rules needed to construct specific models. MOF metamodels use an object modeling framework that is essentially a subset of UML. The modeling concepts are classes that model MOF metaobjects, associations that model binary relations between metaobjects, data types that model other data, and packages

Figure 1. Framework for MDA-based reverse engineering

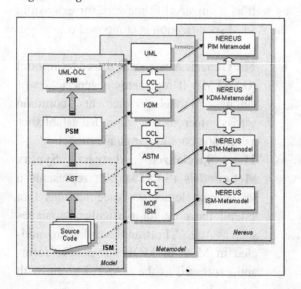

that modularize the models. The metamodel level includes the UML metamodel that describes families of PIMs, the KDM metamodel that describes families of PSM models and the ASTM metamodel that describes ASTM models. Metamodel transformations are specified as OCL contracts between a source metamodel and a target metamodel. MOF metamodels "control" the consistency of these transformations.

The level of formal specification includes specifications of MOF metamodels and metamodel-based transformations in the metamodeling language NEREUS that can be used to connect them with different formal and programming languages (Favre, 2006). NEREUS is suited for specifying metamodels such as MOF that are based on the concepts of entity, association, and system. Favre (2009) defines a bridge between MOF metamodels and NEREUS and shows how to integrate NEREUS with CASL (Bidoit and Mosses, 2004).

To sum up, in the level of models, instances of ISM, PSM and PIM are generated by applying static and dynamic analysis. Static analysis builds an abstract model of the state and determines how the program executes to this state. Dynamic analysis operates by executing a program and evaluating the execution trace of the program. Contracts based on MOF-metamodels "control" the consistency of these transformations and NEREUS facilitates the connection of the metamodels and transformations with different formal languages.

This chapter focuses on reverse engineering of PIMs from object-oriented code at metamodel level. A process for the recovery of use case diagrams from Java code is analyzed and specified as metamodel-based transformations.

SPECIFYING REVERSE ENGINEERING IN ADM

A metamodeling technique is used to specify reverse engineering in ADM. MOF metamodels

are used to describe the transformations at model level. For each transformation, source and target metamodels are specified. A source metamodel defines the family of source models to which transformations can be applied. A target metamodel characterizes the generated models.

The reverse engineering process at metamodel level consists of two major steps:

1. The first step is to analyze the source code of the existing system in order to discover its corresponding PSM model that conforms to KDM metamodel. This process is carried out in two consecutive transformations:
    a. **Code-to-Model transformation:** The source code is transformed into an abstract syntax tree (AST) that conforms to the ASTM metamodel in order to preserve the interoperability. To reach this aim, a discoverer for the programming language corresponding to the source code that executes this code-to-model transformation must be built.
    b. **Model-to-Model transformation:** The AST is transformed into a KDM model. This process is carried out by means of a KDM discover implemented as an ATL model-to-model transformation that takes as input a model conforming to the ASTM metamodel and produces as output a model conforming to the KDM metamodel.
2. In the second step, the KDM model is transformed into PIM-UML models by means of a KDM-to-UML Converter, implemented as an ATL model-to-model transformation that takes as input a model conforming to the KDM metamodel and produces as output a model conforming to the UML metamodel.

Model-to-model transformations are implemented in ATL that is a model transformation language in the field of MDE that is developed on top of the Eclipse platform. It is a hybrid language that provides a mix of declarative and imperative constructs. ATL mainly focuses on the model-to-model transformations which can be specified by means of ATL modules. An ATL module is composed of the following elements:

- A header section that defines the names of the transformation module and the variables of the source and target metamodels.
- An optional import section that enables to import some existing ATL libraries
- A set of helpers that can be used to define variables and functions.
- A set of rules that defines how source model elements are matched and navigated to create and initialize the elements of the target models.

All models obtained in this chain of transformations are saved in the interchange format XMI, an OMG standard that combines XML, MOF and UML for integrating tools, repositories, and applications in distributed heterogeneous environments.

STUDY CASE: SPECIFYING REVERSE ENGINEERING OF USE CASES

Reverse engineering of use case diagrams is exemplified in terms of the same study case used in Tonella and Potrich (2005), the Java program *eLib* that support the main library functions. Tonella and Potrich (2005) describe a reverse engineering approach at model level of object-oriented code based on classical compiler techniques and abstract interpretation to obtain UML diagrams from Java code, particularly class, object, interaction, state and package diagrams. That work does not reverse engineering neither use case diagrams nor activity diagrams.

In this section, we exemplify a reverse engineering process at metamodel level to recover use case

diagrams from code by using the program *eLib*. The Java code is partially depicted in Figure 2. It supposes an archive of documents of different categories, properly classified. The documents are of different kinds, including books, journals and technical reports. Each of them has specific functionality. Each document can be uniquely identified and library users can request document for loan. In order to borrow a document, a user must be identified by the librarian. As regards the loan management, users can borrow documents up to a maximum number. While books are available for loan to any user, journals can be borrowed only by internal users, and technical reports can be consulted but not borrowed. A detailed description may be found at Tonella and Potrich (2005). Next, we describe the reverse engineering process that was implemented in Eclipse using OMG standards, KDM and UML in particular.

Figure 2. eLib program

```java
public class Library {
    Map documents = new HashMap ();
    Map users = new HashMap ();
    Collection loans = new LinkedList();
    final int MAX_NUMBER_OF_LOANS = 20;

    public boolean addUser(User user) {...}

    public boolean removeUser(int userCode) {...}

    private void addLoan(Loan loan) {...}

    public boolean borrowDocument(User user, Document doc) {
        if (user == null || doc == null)
            return false;
        if (user.numberOfLoans() < MAX_NUMBER_OF_LOANS &&
            doc.isAvailable() && doc.authorizedLoan(user)) {
            Loan loan = new Loan(user, doc);
            addLoan(loan);
            return true;    }
        return false;
    }
class User {...
    int userCode; Collection loans = new LinkedList();
    public int numberOfLoans() { return loans.size();  }
    public boolean authorizedUser() {return false;}
... }

class InternalUser extends User {
    public boolean authorizedUser() {return true; }
}

class Document {
    Loan loan = null;
    public boolean isAvailable() {return loan == null;}
    public boolean authorizedLoan(User user) {return true;}
...}

class Journal extends Document {
    public boolean authorizedLoan(User user) {
        return user.authorizedUser();    }
...}

class Book extends Document { ...}

class TechnicalReport extends Document { ...}
```

Recovering KDM Model

As above-mentioned, the first step of the reverse engineering process at metamodel level consists in the transformation of the existing software system into PSM models which are instance of KDM metamodel. This metamodel is partially shows in Figure 3. The main metaclasses are *Segment*, *KDMModel*, *KDMEntity* and *KDMRelationship*. *Segment* is a container for meaningful information about an existing software system. Each segment may include one or more *KDMModel* instances that represent one architectural view of the system. A *KDMModel* instance owns entities. A KDM entity is a named model element that represents an artifact of existing software systems, such as packages, methods and classes. A KDM entity owns elements and relationships. *KDMRelationship* element is an abstraction that specifies relationships between KDM entities.

Each concrete instance of *KDMRelationship*, such as *ImplementationOf*, *Extends* and *Calls*, has exactly one target and exactly one origin.

The *eLib* program is written in Java language, for this reason we use MoDisco discoverers to obtain its corresponding KDM model which is partially depicted in Figure 4. It consists of one Segment that contains the meaningful information about *eLib* program. The segment owns three models (instances of *KDMModel*), each representing one architectural view of the system. The model *eLibrary* owns one instance of the metaclass Package called *LibraryPackage*. This package contains eight instances of *UnitClass* that represent user-defined classes in the program *eLib* such as Library, User and Document. The *ClassUnit Library* owns *StorableUnits* that represent variables and *MethodUnits* that represent member functions. The *MethodUnit borrowDocument* owns one *Signature* that represents the procedure signature

Figure 3. KDM metamodel

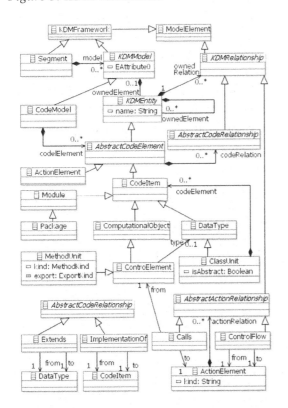

Figure 4. KDM model of the eLib program

and one *BlockUnit* that represents logically and physically related blocks of *ActionElements* (basic unit of behavior), for instance blocks of statements. The *BlockUnit* contain *ActionElements* such as *if*, *method invocation* and *return* statements.

Recovering PIM Model

The second step of the reverse engineering process is the transformation of the KDM model into UML models at PIM level. In this stage, the KDM model of the *eLib* program is used as the starting point to recover PIMs models by means of a KDM-to-UML converter. This converter was implemented as an ATL model-to-model transformation that takes as input a model conforming to the KDM metamodel and produces as output a model conforming to the UML metamodel.

The source metamodel correspond to the KDM metamodel that is partially depicted in Figure 3. The target metamodel correspond to the UML metamodel of use cases. Figure 5 partially shows its main metaclasses. *UseCase* is a kind of behaviored classifier that specifies some behavior that the subject can perform in collaboration with one or more actors. A use case may be related to others through generalization, extend or include relationships.

The model-to-model transformation specified in ATL is partially depicted in Figure 6. The module *KDM2UseCases* that corresponds to the transformation specifies the way to produce use cases diagrams (target model) from KDM model (source model). Both source and target models must conform to their respective metamodel. MM corresponds to KDM and MM1 correspond to UML metamodel.

The module is composed of helpers and rules that allow discovering elements of the use case diagrams, such us use cases, generalizations and dependences (UML, 2011b):

- **Use case:** It is a description of a set of sequences of actions that a system performs to provide an observable result of value to an actor. Basic use cases are extracted analyzing public methods.

- **Generalization:** It is a relationship where the child use case inherits the behavior and meaning of the parent use case; the child may add to or override the behavior of its parent. The child may be substituted in any place that the parent appears. For each pair of methods with a relation of implementation between them, a generalization between use cases corresponding to these methods is generated. To determine the right kind of the relationship, either re-

Figure 5. UML metamodel of use case diagram

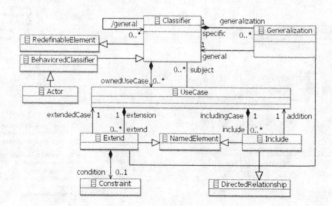

Figure 6. KDM2UseCases transformation

```
-- @nsURI MM=http://www.eclipse.org/MoDisco/kdm/code
-- @nsURI MM1=http://www.eclipse.org/uml2/3.0.0/UML

module KDM2useCases;
create OUT : MM1 from IN : MM;

--------------------------- Helpers ---------------------------
--get_Method() return the method that contains the self element
helper context MM!Element def:  get_Method() : MM!MethodUnit =
    ... ;
--in_publicMethod()returns a boolean stating whether self is into a public method
helper context MM!Calls  def : in_publicMethod() : Boolean =
    ... ;
--is_publicMethod() returns a boolean stating whether self is a public method
helper context MM!MethodUnit
    def : is_publicMethod(): Boolean =
        self.kind = #method and self.export = #public
    ... ;
--get_MethodUnit() returns the public methods contained in a package
helper context MM!Package
    def : get_MethodUnit() : Sequence(MM!MethodUnit) =
    ... ;

--------------------------- Rulers ---------------------------

rule KDMPackage2UMLPackage{
    from p:MM!Package
    to UMLpackage:MM1!Package (
        name <- p.name ,
        packagedElement <- p.get_MethodUnit()
        )
}
rule MethodUnit2UseCase1{
    from method:MM!MethodUnit
        (method.kind = #method and method.export = #public
            and method.codeRelation.oclIsUndefined() )
    to useCase:MM1!UseCase (
        name <-  method.refImmediateComposite().name+ '_' + method.name
        )
}
rule MethodUnit2UseCase2{
    from method:MM!MethodUnit
        (method.kind = #method and method.export = #public
            and  not method.codeRelation.oclIsUndefined())
    to useCase:MM1!UseCase (
        name <-  method.refImmediateComposite().name + '_' + method.name,
        general <- method.codeRelation ->collect(relation | relation.to)
        )
}
rule Calls2Dependency{
    from call:MM!Calls ( call.to.is_publicMethod() and call.in_publicMethod() )
    to use_case_dependency :MM1!Dependency (
        name <- 'from_' + call.get_Method().name + '_to_' + call.to.name,
        supplier <- call.to ,
        client <- call.get_Method()
        )
}
```

define or enrichment, the expertise of the software engineer is needed.

- **Dependency:** It is a using relationship between two use cases in which a change to one (the independent use case) of them may affect the semantics of the other (the dependent use case). For each public method of a class, the method calls are analyzed to extract dependence relationships between basic use cases. The kind of relationship, include or extend, may be inferred by a dynamic analysis.

The actors cannot be automatically inferred. They represent a coherent set of roles that users of use cases play when interacting with these use cases. Actors can be human or they can be automated systems. Although the actors are used in the models, they are not actually part of the system. They live outside the system.

The rules that carry out the transformation are the followings:

- The rule *KDMPackage2UMLPackage* transforms each KDM package into an UML package that contains use cases (packaged elements).

- The rule *MethodUnit2UseCase1* transforms each public method that does not redefine inherited method into a basic use case that can only have dependences. The name of the use case is formed by the name of the method preceded by the name of the class that owns that method.

- The rule *MethodUnit2UseCase2* transforms each public method that redefines an inherited method into a basic use case that has generalizations and can have dependences. The name of the use case is formed by the name of the method preceded by the name of the class that owns that method.

- The rule *Calls2Dependency* transforms each relationship Calls between two public methods into a dependency between the use cases corresponding to these methods.

Figure 7.a partially shows the target model resulting from the transformation *KDM2UseCases* when it is applied to the KDM Model corresponding to *eLib* program (Figure 3). Figure 7.b partially shows the use case diagram corresponding to the uses cases depicted in Figure 7a.

The proposed recovery process allows obtaining use case diagrams that correspond to a low-level functional view. To obtain higher-level views, use cases may be clustered in single abstract use cases by applying simple heuristics (Di Lucca, Fasolino, & De Carlini, 2000) implemented as ATL transformation:

- A group of use cases where one of them includes exclusively the remaining ones will be clustered in a single more abstract use case shown in a separate diagram.

- A group of use cases where a use case is extended by the remaining ones will be clustered in a single more abstract use case shown in a separate diagram.

Considering the use case diagram shown in Figure 7.b, if the use case *Library_borrowDocument* included exclusively the use cases U*ser_numberOfLoans*, *Documet_isAvailable* and *Documet_authorizedLoan*, the group of use cases would be clustered in a single more abstract use case called *Library_borrowDocument*.

FUTURE RESEARCH DIRECTIONS

Reverse engineering techniques are used as a mean to design software systems by evolving existing ones based on new requirements or technologies. In particular, reverse engineering is an integral part of the modernization of legacy systems whose aging can or will have a negative impact on the economy, finance and society.

To date, software industry evolves to tackle new approaches that are aligned with Internet, object orientation and distributed components. However, the majority of the large information systems running today in many organizations were developed many years ago with technology that is now obsolete. Many large systems remain in use after more than 20 years; they may be written for mainframe hardware which is expensive to maintain and which may not be aligned with current organizational politics. There is a high risk in replacing legacy systems that are still business-critical. That is the reason for the increased demand of reengineering techniques of legacy system to extend their useful lifetime.

The success of legacy system modernization depends on the existence of technical frameworks like ADM to cope with the diversity of languages

Figure 7. Target model resulting from the KDM2UseCases transformation

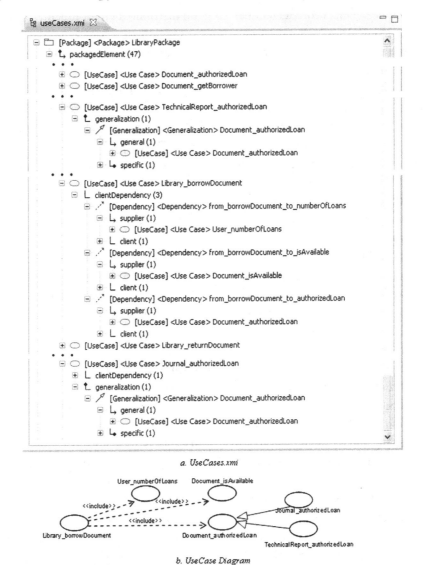

a. UseCases.xmi

b. UseCase Diagram

and technologies used to develop a single software system. Besides, the existing CASE tools must incorporate new functionality that make a significant impact on the automation of reverse engineering processes.

Most CASE tools can reverse engineering static diagrams, however there is a lack of tool support for the extraction of dynamic diagrams and also OCL pre- and post-conditions. One of the major challenges of reverse engineering is to deal with the high dynamicity. For example, object-oriented languages introduce the concept of reflection. This affects the static analysis then, future tasks in reverse engineering should promote a high integration of human feedbacks into automatic reverse engineering processes.

Refactoring is an important step for evolving models in reverse engineering processes; however CASE tools do not provide support for model refactoring, these tools only provide limited facilities for refactoring on source code through an explicit selection made for the designer. Formal techniques are needed in order to ensure behavioral properties of the software involved in the refactoring.

Another research trend of reverse engineering is design pattern identification to understand the design considerations promoting reuse and quality of different software artifacts. Pattern identification allows measuring quality of software reverse engineering, pattern and anti-pattern can help to discover weakness of code or models.

There is a need to develop tools for new software architecture that have characteristics of being highly distributed, self-configurable and heterogeneous. Besides, a new generation of extremely dynamic tools that insure consistency of variety of artifacts representing different dimensions should emerge. For instance, new tools can help to determine what information need to be collected at run time for both, checking that the contracts are satisfied when the program run and inferring constraints that may be added to the artifact specification. Among others, an interesting research direction would be treat the notion of change in programming and modeling languages as a first-class entity and provide support for multi language systems.

Existing formal methods provide a poor support for evolving specifications and incremental verification approaches. Particularly with the existing verification tools, simple changes in a system require to verify its complete specification again making the cost of the verification proportional to its size. To use formal methods that place change and evolution in the center of the software development process is another challenge (Canfora & Di Penta, 2007).

The integration between ontologies (that are essentially CIMs) will occupy a central place in ADM. A new type of tools that do a more intelligent job will arise in light of the evolution of ADM standards such as KDM. Probably, the next generation of tools might be able to recover the behavior of software systems in terms of domain

models and translate it into executable programs on distributed environment.

In summary, a lot remains to be done to provide support for ADM-based processes:

- Research on formalisms and theories to increase understanding of reverse engineering and software evolution processes.
- Development of methods, techniques and heuristics to provide support for software changes.
- New verification tools that embrace change and evolution as central in software development processes.
- Development of new sophisticated tools to develop industrial size software systems.
- Definition of standards to evaluate the quality of evolved artifacts/systems.

CONCLUSION

The reverse engineering has become a crucial stage within the system modernization process. Its role is to analyze existing software in order to extract information exploiting investment and knowledge in order to provide high-level views of the system. This chapter presents a framework ADM compliant to reverse engineering models from object-oriented code based on the integration of static and dynamic analysis, metamodeling and formal specification. The framework distinguishes three different abstraction levels linked to models, metamodels and formal specifications. In this chapter we focus on reverse engineering at metamodel level. We propose a metamodeling technique based on MOF metamodels and transformation. In order to be compliant with ADM, the technique is implemented by using OMG standards, such as ASTM, KDM and UML, all of them are defined via Meta-Object Facility. ATL was selected as the language to implement transformations. We implement and validate our approach by using the Eclipse Modeling Framework and the MoDisco platform. Although we analyze the reverse engineering of Java code, the bases of our approach can be easily applied to other object-oriented language.

Also, we present the state of the art in the modernization area, reverse engineering in particular. Some of these works are linked to MDD-based reverse engineering whereas others are linked to ADM. We discuss about existing tools and mention the needed features to be ADM compliant.

To date, MoDisco can only recover UML class diagram from Java code, we are working on the recovery of other diagrams corresponding at the level PIM such us use cases diagrams, state diagrams, interaction diagrams and activity diagrams. We foresee integrate our result in Eclipse.

REFERENCES

ADM. (2012). *Architecture-driven modernization task force*. Retrieved September 24, 2012, from http://www.omgwiki.org/admtf/doku.php

Angyal, L., Lengyel, L., & Charaf, H. (2006). An overview of the state-of-the-art reverse engineering techniques. In *Proceedings of the 7th International Symposium of Hungarian Researchers on Computational Intelligence* (pp. 507-516). Budapest, Hungary: Hungarian Research.

ASTM. (2011). *Abstract syntax tree metamodel, version 1.0*. Retrieved September 24, 2012, from http://www.omg.org/spec/ASTM

ATL. (2012). *AtlasTransformation language (ATL) documentation*. Retrieved September 24, 2012, from http://www.eclipse.org/atl/documentation/

Barbier, F., Deltombe, G., Parisy, O., & Youbi, K. (2011). Model driven engineering: Increasing legacy technology independence. In *Proceedings of Second India Workshop on Reverse Engineering (IWRE, 2011) in The 4th India Software Engineering Conference* (pp. 5-10).Thiruvanantpuram, India: CSI.

Bidoit, M., & Mosses, P. (2004). *CASL user manual- Introduction to using the common algebraic specification language (LNCS) (Vol. 2900)*. Heidelberg, Germany: Springer-Verlag.

Bisbal, J., Lawless, D., Wu, B., & Grimson, J. (1999). Legacy information systems: Issues and directions. *IEEE Software*, *16*(5), 103–111. doi:10.1109/52.795108.

Bruneliere, H., Cabot, J., & Dupé, G. (2012). How to deal with your IT legacy: What is coming up in MoDisco? *ERCIM News, 88*, 43-44. Retrieved September 24, 2012, from http://ercim-news.ercim.eu/images/stories/EN88/EN88-Web.pdf

Canfora, G., & Di Penta, M. (2007). New frontiers of reverse engineering. In Proceedings of Future of Software Engineering, 2007, FOSE '07 (pp. 326-341). IEEE Press.

Cánovas Izquierdo, J., & García Molina, J. (2009a). A domain specific language for extracting models in software modernization. In *Proceedings of Model Driven Architecture - Foundations and Applications (LNCS) (Vol. 5562*, pp. 82–97). Berlin: Springer-Verlag. doi:10.1007/978-3-642-02674-4_7.

Cánovas Izquierdo, J., & García Molina, J. (2009b). Extracción de modelos en una modernización basada en ADM. *Actas de los Talleres de las Jornadas de Ingeniería de Software y BBDD, 3*(2), 41-50. Retrieved September 24, 2012, from http://www.sistedes.es/ficheros/actas-talleres-JISBD/Vol-3/No-2/DSDM09.pdf

CASE MDA. (2012). *Committed companies and their products*. Retrieved September 24, 2012, from www.omg.org/mda/committed-products.htm

Deissenboeck, F., & Ratiu, D. (2006). A unified metamodel for concept-based reverse engineering. In *Proceedings of 3rd International Workshop on Metamodels, Schemes, Grammars, and Ontologies for Reverse Engineering*. Retrieved September 24, 2012, 2011 from http://planet-mde.org/atem2006/atem06Proceedings.pdf

Di Lucca, G., Fasolino, A., & De Carlini, U. (2000). Recovering use case models from object-oriented code: A thread-based approach. In *Proceedings of the Seventh Working Conference on Reverse Engineering (WCRE 2000)*, (pp. 108-117). WCRE.

Favre, L. (2006). A rigorous framework for model driven development. In Siau, K. (Ed.), *Advanced Topics in Database Research* (*Vol. 5*, pp. 1–27). Hershey, PA: Idea Group Publishing. doi:10.4018/978-1-59140-935-9.ch001.

Favre, L. (2009). A formal foundation for metamodeling. In *Proceedings of Reliable Software Technologies, ADA Europe 2009 (LNCS)* (*Vol. 5570*, pp. 177–191). Heidelberg, Germany: Springer-Verlag. doi:10.1007/978-3-642-01924-1_13.

Favre, L. (2010). *Model driven architecture for reverse engineering technologies: Strategic directions and system evolution*. Hershey, PA: IGI Global. doi:10.4018/978-1-61520-649-0.

Favre, L., Pereira, C., & Martinez, L. (2009). Foundations for MDA case tools. In Khosrow-Pour, M. (Ed.), *Encyclopedia of Information Science and Technology* (2nd ed., pp. 159–166). Hershey, PA: IGI Global.

Favre, L. Martinez, L., & Pereira, C. (2009). MDA-based reverse engineering of object-oriented code. In *Proceedings EMMSAD 2009* (LNBIP), (Vol. 29, pp. 251-263). Berlin: Springer-Verlag.

Fleurey, F., Breton, E., Baudry, B., Nicolas, A., & Jézéquel, J. (2007). Model-driven engineering for software migration in a large industrial context. In Engels, G., Opdyke, B., Schmidt, D. C., & Weil, F. (Eds.), *MoDELS 2007 (LNCs)* (*Vol. 4735*, pp. 482–497). Berlin: Springer-Verlag. doi:10.1007/978-3-540-75209-7_33.

KDM. (2011). *Knowledge discovery metamodel, version 1.3*. OMG Document Number: formal/2011-08-04. Retrieved September 24, 2012, from http://www.omg.org/spec/KDM/1.3

MacDonald, A., Russell, D., & Atchison, B. (2005). Model driven development within a legacy system: An industry experience report. In *Proceeding of 2005 Australian Software Engineering Conference ASWEC 05* (pp. 14-22). IEEE Press.

MDA. (2012). *The model-driven architecture*. Retrieved September 24, 2012, from http://www.omg.org/mda/

Medini. (2012). *Medini QVT*. Retrieved September 24, 2012, from http://projects.ikv.de/qvt

MoDisco. (2012). *Model discovery*. Retrieved September 24, 2012, from http://www.eclipse.org/MoDisco

MOF. (2011). *Meta object facility (MOF) core specification version 2.4.1*. OMG Document Number: formal/2011-08-07. Retrieved September 24, 2012, from http://www.omg.org/spec/MOF/2.4.1

OCL. (2012). *OCL: Object constraint language: Version 2.3.1*. OMG Document Number: formal/2012-01-01. Retrieved September 24, 2012, from http://www.omg.org/spec/OCL/2.3.1/

QVT. (2011). *QVT: MOF 2.0 query, view, transformation: Version 1.1*. OMG Document Number: formal/2011-01-01. Retrieved September 24, 2012, from http://www.omg.org/spec/QVT/1.1/

Reus, T., Geers, H., & van Deursen, A. (2006). Harvesting software system for MDA-based re-engineering. *Lecture Notes in Computer Science*, *4066*, 220–236. doi:10.1007/11787044_17.

SMM. (2012). *Software metrics meta-model, version 1.0*. OMG Document Number: formal/2012-01-05. Retrieved September 24, 2012, from http://www.omg.org/spec/SMM/1.0/

Sommerville, I. (2004). *Software engineering* (7th ed.). Reading, MA: Addison Wesley.

Tonella, P., & Potrich, A. (2005). *Reverse engineering of object oriented code*. Heidelberg, Germany: Springer-Verlag.

UML. (2011a). *Unified modeling language: Infrastructure version 2.4.1*. OMG Specification formal/2011-08-05. Retrieved September 24, 2012, from http://www.omg.org/spec/UML/2.4.1/

UML. (2011b). *Unified modeling language: Superstructure version 2.4.1*. OMG Specification: formal/2011-08-06. Retrieved September 24, 2012, from http://www.omg.org/spec/UML/2.4.1/

USE. (2011). *A UML-based specification environment*. Retrieved September 24, 2012, from http://sourceforge.net/apps/mediawiki/useocl/

XMI. (2011). *OMG MOF 2 XMI mapping SpecificationOMG*. Document Number: formal/2011-08-09. Retrieved September 24, 2012, from http://www.omg.org/spec/XMI/2.4.1

KEY TERMS AND DEFINITIONS

Abstract Syntax Tree Metamodel (ASTM): A metamodel from the Object Management Group (OMG) that describes the elements used for composing Abstract Syntax Trees (AST).

Architecture Driven Modernization (ADM): The process of understanding and evolving existing software assets of a system of interest in the context of the Model Driven Architecture (MDA).

Atlas Transformation Language (ATL): A model transformation language and toolkit developed on top of the Eclipse platform that provides ways to produce target models from source models.

Computer Aided Software Engineering (CASE) Tool: A tool to aid in analysis and design of software systems.

Knowledge Discovery Metamodel (KDM): A metamodel from the Object Management Group (OMG) for representing existing software, its elements, associations and operational environments that is related to software assurance and modernization.

Metamodel: A special kind of model that defines the language for expressing a model.

Model Driven Architecture (MDA): An initiative of the Object Management Group (OMG) for the development of software systems based on the separation of business and application logic from underlying platform technologies. It is an evolving conceptual architecture to achieve cohesive model-driven technology specifications.

MOF (Meta-Object Facility): A meta-metamodel from the Object Management Group (OMG) that defines a common way for capturing the diversity of modeling standards and interchange constructs involved in MDA.

Query, View, Transformation (QVT): A metamodel from the Object Management Group for expressing transformations in MDA-based processes.

Reverse Engineering: The process of analyzing and comprehending available software artifacts, such as requirements, design, architectures and code in order to extract information and provide high-level views of the system.

Chapter 13
Adaptive Software based on Correct-by-Construction Metamodels

Franck Barbier
LIUPPA, France

Pierre Castéran
LaBRI, France

Eric Cariou
LIUPPA, France

Olivier le Goaer
LIUPPA, France

ABSTRACT

Despite significant research efforts in the last decade, UML has not reached the status of being a high-confidence modeling language. This is due to unsound foundations that result from the insufficiently formal structuring of metamodels that define the MOF/UML Infrastructure. Nowadays, UML-related metamodels are implemented in computing environments (e.g., EMF) to play the role of metadata when one seeks adaptation at runtime. To properly instrument metamodel-based adaptation, this chapter re-formalizes the core of the MOF/UML Infrastructure along with giving formal proofs that avoid ambiguities, contradictions, or redundancies. A (meta-)class creation mechanism (either by instantiation or inheritance) is based on inductive types taken from the constructive logic. Inherent proofs based on the Coq automated prover are also provided. This chapter's contribution is aligned with a previously established metamodeling framework named "Matters of (meta-)modeling."

INTRODUCTION

In recent years, Model Driven Development (MDD) has been considered as a suitable software engineering technology to make software potentially and really adaptive at runtime (Zhang & Cheng, 2006). This gave rise to the notion of models at runtime (Fleurey & Solberg, 2009; Morin et al., 2009). Models at runtime are embedded models within the system during its execution and aim to express adaptation policies, conditions, and rules on models representing the system under execution. On another hand, research contributions

DOI: 10.4018/978-1-4666-4217-1.ch013

on MDD-based software admit the unavoidable need for executable modeling languages.

Model execution consists in interpreting the model through a dedicated execution engine instead of executing a code based on, or generated from, the model. In this context, the adaptation deals with directly modifying and acting on the model under execution (Cariou *et al.*, 2012).

Practically, based on its meta-meta-model Ecore (an implementation of the MOF) and its reflection capabilities (a.k.a. metadata), the Eclipse Modeling Framework (EMF) (Steinberg *et al.*, 2008) has become the reference platform for developing MDD tools. EMF has then played a great role in implementing executable modeling languages. For instance, Kermeta (www. kermeta.org), an action language relying on Ecore metamodels, facilitates the development of execution engines. Such executable modeling languages can be defined from scratch, following the concept of DSML (Domain-Specific Modeling Language).

Executable modeling languages can also be based on an effort to make existing languages like UML (or some of its constituents) executable. In this scope, SCXML (State Chart XML) and PauWare (Barbier, 2008) are two tools that offer the possibility of executing Harel's Statecharts.

SCXML is a standard (www.w3.org/TR/scxml). Its most well-known implementation is that of the Apache foundation: Commons SCXML (commons.apache.org/scxml). SCXML possesses its own metamodel based on a lightweight XML notation, which is independent of EMF and UML in general. Differently, PauWare (www.PauWare.com) is a Java library that is properly aligned with UML State Machine Diagrams.

In contrast with EMF-based executable modeling languages defined for instance with Kermeta, SCXML models may be embedded in applications' components and interpreted in real-time. For efficiency, PauWare prefers a Java-based representation of models that requires very little memory and an accelerated models' interpretation. For instance, a PauWare-based application may be embedded in a tiny device (an Android or Java ME device for instance) where SCXML requires more space because of XML. PauWare code may indifferently be generated from XMI (State Machine Diagrams sub-component of UML) or from the SCXML notation. In (Ballagny *et al.*, 2009), we proposed an adaptation-enabled version of PauWare named MOCAS (sourceforge.net/projects/mocasengine).

The common point of all these adaptation techniques and tools is that they are based on the usage of models such as UML State Machine Diagrams. Unfortunately, the continuous enhancement of MOCAS stumbles over the unsound structure of the UML Superstructure metamodel relating to state machines. A systematic restructuring of this metamodel was therefore required. A sample of a revised metamodel for state machines is proposed (in the "Example" section of this chapter) along with a method to formally prove that revisions are well-founded. This occurred by means of the Coq automated theorem prover (coq.inria.fr) to express metatypes as inductive types that come from the constructive type logic. In this chapter, we propose a more ambitious method based on the same logic that leads to build from scratch a Domain-Specific Modeling Language (DSML) dedicated to software adaptation. The definition of this DSML requires to have at one's disposal a metamodeling framework allowing to formally define a model conforming to a metamodel.

The key issue is the definition of a minimal kernel of metatypes and metarelationships that may serve as bootstrap for the rest of the language to be defined. Precisely, adaptation requires reflective capabilities that are embodied by metacircularity in the language's kernel. We illustrate this problem with the *Class* and *Property* metatypes of the UML Infrastructure metamodel (Figure 1). Namely, classes are structurally composed of properties (black diamond notation in UML). Chronologically speaking, mutual dependencies in definitions show cycles, namely *Class* is defined from *Property*, which is defined from

Figure 1. Core of the UML Infrastructure metamodel

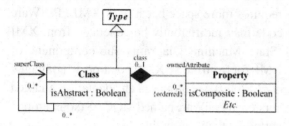

Class. There are also recursions, namely *Class* is defined from itself.

We solve this problem in the chapter. Concretely, we express in Coq such a metamodel kernel based on a recognized metamodeling theoretical framework (Kühne, 2006). We verify the kernel's consistency and its completeness: no contradiction (incompatible logical properties), no redundancy (logical properties that may be derived from each others) and no silence (missing logical properties which let too much interpretation latitude). In the chapter, we comment on the proofs written and executed within the Coq automated prover.

Once this kernel built, the MOF (or its Ecore version) meta-meta-model can be formally implemented in Coq. This will allow the formally definition of the UML metamodel or any DSML based on the fact that they conform to the MOF. Notably, we may design metatypes and metarelationships specific to adaptation actions (see "Example" section). Models resulting from these metatypes and metarelationships enable adaptation at runtime. We show at this end of this chapter an existing UML metamodel piece relating to state machines, which is proven "wrong". As such, it is replaced by a new metamodel piece being part of a DSML for adaptation. Some code illustrates how to use the DSML at the implementation level.

BACKGROUND

The Unified Modeling Language (UML) has popularized metamodeling (Atkinson & Kühne, 2002; Kühne, 2006). UML models represent business systems created by software engineers. Metamodels aim at embodying UML modeling constructs that are domain concepts for UML. New languages called DSMLs, standing for Domain-Specific Modeling Languages, can be created from scratch based on the principle of metamodeling. They can also be created from the Meta-Object Facility (MOF)/UML Infrastructure. In this latter case, one may benefit from many environments/platforms respecting this widespread standard. This is a choice made in this chapter.

Inspired by the traditional class-instance dichotomy of object-oriented programming, models are instances of metamodels (Another characterization is: "models conform to metamodels"). The generalization of this principle leads to the fact that metamodels are also instances of models, called meta-metamodels. An infinite regression is avoided by creating a meta-circularity relationship: the meta-metamodel is an instance of itself. In this context, UML has adopted a four-layer metamodel hierarchy (Figure 2):

- M0 this level corresponds to the set of non-instantiable entities.
- M1 this level corresponds to users' models; objects at the M0 level are instances of classes that are subject to various design constraints at M1.
- M2 this metamodel level corresponds to the UML language itself or *Superstructure* (OMG, Superstructure, 2010); entities at this level are classes (also called metaclasses) for the classes belonging to M1.

Figure 2. The UML four-layer metamodel hierarchy (note that properties at M2 are instances of the property meta-metaclass at M3)

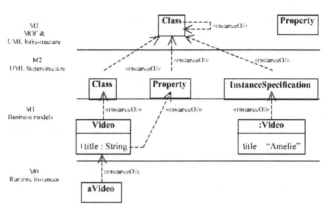

- M3 this metamodel level called *Infrastructure* (OMG, Infrastructure, 2010) corresponds to a set of meta-meta-classes. These are classes for the classes at M2, which are in turn classes for those at M1. For historical reasons, there are two strongly interlaced metamodels at M3: the *Meta Object Facility* (MOF) (OMG, MOF, 2006) and the *InfrastructureLibrary*. Both often serve as backbone when creating new DSMLs. They were originally designed to embody the UML Infrastructure and the UML Superstructure (the DSML defining UML). It is backed up by the UML Infrastructure, and thus the MOF.

Research on metamodeling seeks to make metamodels generative and executable in computing environments. In essence, instantiating a metamodel produces models, which in turn are instantiated. This is the generative facet. Having anomalies or errors in a metamodel leads to having problems in its instances at an exponential scale. Despite numerous initiatives to re-formalize the metamodels of the UML universe (*Meta Object Facility, Infrastructure,* and *Superstructure*), UML still has an unsound basis. In this context, this chapter considers the calculus of inductive constructions as an appropriate theory because the

MOF/UML kernel relies on recursive and mutually dependent definitions of bootstrap entities. So, a complete proven formalization of these entities in the Coq automated prover (Bertot & Castéran, 2004) that supports this calculus is covered.

The "Related Work" section compares this chapter's approach with similar initiatives and tries to justify its own originality. Furthermore, metamodels are implemented in computing environments to play the role of metadata at runtime. This is the executable facet. The Eclipse Modeling Framework (EMF) (Steinberg *et al.*, 2008) is the most well-known tool in this area, which uses Java as the action language to manage any kind of model. So, persistent metamodels written with the help of Ecore, the meta-metalanguage of EMF, act as a reflection support for virtual machines of "models at runtime" (Morin *et al.*, 2009).

Motivation

Since birth, UML has been subject to clarifications and even corrections (Broy & Cengarle, 2011). Lightweight corrections include the restructuring of key metaclasses (creations, suppressions and updates); this comprises the corrected/new metarelationships between them. Such an approach often involves a set-centric textual language like OCL (Object Constraint Language), a UML add-on, or Z (Milicev, 2007). Heavyweight corrections are based on the assessment and the use of recognized theoretical frameworks (*e.g.*, graph theories, category theories, classical/non-classical logics or the calculus of inductive constructions in this chapter). In this case, out of the existing reformulations of the UML core, we found no solution that concomitantly addresses the following issues:

- Expressing UML mathematically is not enough. In effect, we found no ready-to-use and extensible specification realization of the UML kernel in an automated theorem prover that fundamentally creates higher confidence in the proposed (re)-formalization. This remark excludes automated proofs on UML business models only, *e.g.*, (Egea, 2005; Kyas *et al.*, 2005): proofs in these two research works do not apply to metamodels or their kernels.
- In essence, specifying the core of UML requires a characterization of the *Class* metaclass at M2 (Figure 2). What is the class of *Class* at M2? This imposes the formal definition of *Class* and *Property* at M3 (*i.e.*, classes are structurally composed of properties). Chronologically speaking, mutual dependencies in definitions show cycles, namely *Class* is defined from *Property*, which is defined from *Class*. There are also recursions, namely *Class* is defined from itself.
- A way to solve the infinite regression problem in the definition of UML has to be explicitly found. In this context, many pioneering contributions underestimate this issue (Bézivin & Gerbé, 2001).
- A minimal set of metaclasses must serve as bootstrap for the rest of UML. So any UML metaclass must be created from existing ones based on a well-formed instantiation process, as is proposed in this chapter (see section "Constructing New Metaclasses").

We try to demonstrate in this chapter that the constructive logic in conjunction with an implementation of the proposed formalization within the Coq automated theorem prover are able to treat the four items listed above. This chapter's specification realization in Coq is downloadable (and testable) from www.FranckBarbier.com/Coq.

Constructive Logic

In this chapter, core UML metaclasses are rewritten as inductive types in the sense of the constructive logic. More precisely, we re-formalize core classes of the MOF, which are also shared with the *InfrastructureLibrary*). Similar to the object-oriented programming standpoint, inductive types have constructors. Inductive types are also associated with an induction principle: proving a property about a type leads to dividing the proof into sub-proofs for each constructor of this type. In addition, an inductive type can be defined "alone" (*e.g.*, the *Living_organism* type below). In contrast, several mutually inductive types can be defined "together" (typically, *Class* and *Property* in the core of UML). So, specifying an inductive type in Coq is as follows:

```
Inductive Living_organism: Type:= (*
Type is a predefined Coq sort over
Type, Set and Prop *)
| DNA (* first constructor *)
| cons: Living_organism -> Living_or-
ganism. (* second constructor *)
```

DNA and *cons* are the names of the two chosen constructors for the *Living_organism* type along with their signatures. Common functions are defined as follows:

```
Definition constituent(lo: Living_or-
ganism): Living_organism:= match lo
with
| cons source => source (* constitu-
ent lo is equal to source when con-
```

```
structed as follows: cons source *)
| _ => DNA (* result is DNA for the
remaining constructor(s); underscore
sign means "any" in Coq *)
end.
```

Proofs are carried out by means of "tactics" (*simpl* and *trivial* below) indicating how to converge towards the goal from both initial and intermediate (computed) assumptions:

```
Theorem Circularity: (constituent
DNA) = DNA.
Proof. (* generated goal is: (con-
stituent DNA) = DNA *)
simpl. (* (constituent DNA) = DNA is
simplified as DNA = DNA by applying
the constituent function *)
trivial. (* no other step required *)
Save. (* Circularity proof completed
*)
```

Expected Results

In Barbier and Ballagny (2010), we discussed the benefits for implementing metamodels in applications in order to support software adaptation. Adaptation amounted to changing models dynamically, more specifically executable UML state machines embedded in applications (see also "Example" section).

In fact, metamodels guide adaptation actions in the sense that models must always conform to metamodels.

So, this chapter capitalizes on this idea by looking for a generalization: one seeks a reliable formalization of foundation metaclasses, namely *Class*, *Property* (this chapter's focus), *Generalization* (which characterizes inheritance in UML)… We have the possibility of disambiguating metamodel pieces having persistent anomalies or errors. We have also the possibility of better integrating OCL constraints. The proven specification in this chapter indeed supports the seamless integration of UML and OCL, *i.e.*, any OCL assertion is easily expressible in Coq. Once done, the support of a generative approach is provided: from the re-formalized core UML, new DSMLs through new metaclasses/metarelationships can be introduced. New domain-oriented proofs can be optionally developed for strengthening domain semantics associated with DSMLs.

Metamodeling

The meta-metamodel in Figure 1 means (for conciseness, some aspects of the original UML model are omitted, *e.g.*, the *name* attribute for *Class*):

- A *Class* instance is composed of (black diamond) either zero or several *Property* instances (*ownedAttribute* role). A given *Property* instance belongs to at most one *Class* instance (*class* role). There is no sharing, meaning that a given *Property* object cannot belong to distinct *Class* objects.
- In UML, attributes inside classes and compositions (black diamonds) have the same "semantics". For example, the *isAbstract* Boolean attribute of *Class* is semantically equivalent to a composition link from *Class* to Boolean with the *1..1* cardinality and the *isAbstract* role both being right next to Boolean drawn in a box.
- A *Class* instance is linked to either zero or several *Class* instances that have the *superClass* role (this association embodies *direct* inheritance only, *i.e.*, it does not represent all of the super classes of a class (transitive closure)). Interpreting this in the reverse order means that a *Class* instance either has or does not have direct descendant classes. This metarelationship conceptualizes inheritance links at the immediately lower metamodeling level.
- *Class* inherits from *Type*.
- Classes are either abstract or not. When abstract, their name is written in italics.

For instance, the *Type* metaclass is abstract. Moreover, the *Class* metaclass has a *Boolean* attribute named *isAbstract*. This means that any instance of *Class* owns this attribute with a value among true or false. Namely, *Type* is an instance of *Class* (this instantiation link does not appear in Figure 1 since links that cross metamodeling layers are not represented in common practice) with the value true for this attribute. In object orientation, an abstract class has no direct instances. This means, in terms of metamodeling, one cannot create a new metaclass (since *Type* belongs to the M3 level, such a hypothetical metaclass would belong to the M2 level) as a direct instance of *Type*.

In this context, Kühne proposes in (Kühne, 2006, pp. 377-378) a large-scope characterization of metamodeling. A relationship on classes christened as "metaness" is introduced as follows: acyclicity, antitransitivity and level-respecting. This characterization is hotly debated and softly refuted in (Hesse, 2006) with answers and arguments in (Kühne bis, 2006). Hesse especially shows that these three discriminating properties are probably necessary, yet they remain insufficient for metaness, *i.e.*, some acyclic/antitransitive/level-respecting real-world relationships are inappropriate candidates for embodying metaness. This chapter considers metaness within the UML context only. This means that we do not deal with multi-instantiation. The absence of multi-instantiation is named "strict metamodeling" in either (Atkinson & Kühne, 2002) or in (Asikainen, T. & Männistö, 2009). Multi-instantiation is such that an instance *i* may straightforwardly conform to many classes: for instance, one creates *i* from A and B at the same time. Differently, *i* conforms to A if *i* has been directly instantiated from A, and to B as well if A inherits from B: this latter case is just called conformance and has no relation with multi-instantiation. Further discussion on these issues is in section "Level-respecting".

Next Steps

Next section revisits the current UML kernel organization in constructive logic. We show why *Class* and *Property* are the necessary and sufficient classes for bootstrapping UML. Accordingly, section "Proven Metamodel Kernel for UML" offers an associated re-formalization along with proofs based on Atkinson & Kühne's metaness characterization. An "Example" section shows to run the proposed method to construct adaptive software. To close, section "Related Work" is an overview of similar contributions, while section "Conclusion" draws conclusions and sketches perspectives.

Organization of the UML Metamodel Kernel in Constructive Logic

In (OMG, Infrastructure, 2010, p. 16), it is written: "A metamodel is an instance of a meta-metamodel, meaning that every element of the metamodel is an instance of an element in the meta-metamodel (...) (in effect, each UML metaclass is an instance of an element in *InfrastructureLibrary*)." Conforming to this precept, we lay down that:

- The *Class* element is an instance of itself. In UML, there is a *Class* element at the M2 level, which is an instance of a *Class* element at the M3 level (Figure 2). Conceptually speaking, there is no reason to differentiate between *M3::Class* and *M2::Class*. So, if *M3::Class = M2::Class*, then *Class* must be configured as an instance of itself (meta-circularity).
- The *Type* and *Property* elements are instances of *Class*. By convention, the two Instantiation links are not represented in Figure 1.

- The *isAbstract* attribute of *Class* at M3 is an instance of *Property* from the immediately upper level with *isComposite = true*. So, this internal attribute is similar to a *Composition* link with *1..1* being right next to Boolean drawn in a box.
- The *isComposite* attribute of *Property* at M3 is an instance of *Property* with *isComposite = true*.
- The *Composition* link from *Class* to *Property* at M3 is an instance of *Property* with *isComposite = true*.
- The *Association* link from *Class* to *Class* at M3 (*superClass* role) is an instance of *Property* with *isComposite = false*.
- Finally, the *Generalization* link from *Class* to *Type* at M3 is an instance of the *Association* link from *Class* to *Class*.

UML Core Metaclasses as Inductive Types

We specify *Class* at the meta-metamodel level (M3 in Figure 2) as an inductive type. We specify *Property* at the same time. In this case, *Class*, *Property* and *NonAbstractClass* (*NonAbstractClass* is necessary for preventing abstract classes to be instantiated) are mutually dependent inductive types. It is also shown how the *isAbstract* and *isComposite* attributes (Figure 1) are implemented in Coq:

```
Inductive Class: Type:=
  BBoolean | (* UML Boolean *)
  CClass | (see Table 1)
  PProperty | (see Table 1)
  instantiate: NonAbstractClass ->
Property -> Property -> Class |
  inheritsFrom: Property -> Property
-> Property -> Class

with Property: Type:=
  Null | (* Null is introduced in the
```

Table 1. Equivalence of terms between UML and Coq

UML world	Coq world
CClass	Class (inductive type)
TType	Type (preexisting sort in Coq)
PProperty	Property (inductive type)

```
MOF documentation, p. 11 *)
  set_isAbstract: Property |
  set_isComposite: Property |
  set_ownedAttribute: string -> Class
-> nat -> nat -> Property -> Property
| (* attribute name, attribute type,
lower bound, upper bound, isComposite
or not *)
  set_superClass: Class -> Property
(*   inheritance *)
with NonAbstractClass: Type:=
  instantiate2: Class -> NonAbstract-
Class.
```

In this Coq text, *Class*, *Property*, *NonAbstractClass* and *Type* are Coq types while *BBoolean*, *CClass*, *PProperty* and *TType* are UML elements (*i.e.*, Coq constants).

Constructing New Metaclasses

The generative nature of the above specification allows the creation of UML core concepts through two processes. The former amounts to instantiating a Coq *Class* object (which is equivalent to a UML *CClass* object), for example:

```
Definition Object: Class:= instanti-
ate (instantiate' CClass) Null Null.
(* the Object metaclass appears in
the MOF documentation, p. 15 *)
```

Here, the first *Null* occurrence means that *Object* is not abstract, while the second means that it has no "owned attribute" (note that simplified instantiate methods may be provided to avoid using *Null*). By convention, the signature of instantiate (*instantiate: NonAbstractClass -> Property -> Property -> Class*) is ordered so that one expects as first argument the Coq *Class* object to be instantiated; as second argument, the abstract nature (a *Property* object) of the constructed Coq Class object and, as third argument, its "owned attribute" (a *Property* object as well). To deal with multiple values, another instantiation process uses the *list Property* Coq type. The fourth and last parameter ("returned value") is the type of the constructed Coq *Class* object.

The second process allows the creation of UML concepts by inheritance, *e.g.*, the *Element* class (it appears in the MOF documentation, p. 15) that inherits from *Object*:

```
Definition Element: Class:= inher-
itsFrom (set_superClass Object)
set_isAbstract Null. (* the Element
metaclass appears in the MOF documen-
tation p. 15 *)
```

The *inheritsFrom* signature (*inheritsFrom: Property -> Property -> Property -> Class*) allows the creation of a Coq *Class* object (see *Element* above) from properties only. Here, *Null* means that *Element* has no "owned attribute".

A Proven Version of the UML "instanceOf" Relationship

To solve the problem of assigning an instantiation class to *CClass* (meta-circularity), we specify the recursive class function over the Class inductive type as follows:

```
Fixpoint class(c: Class): Class:=
match c with
| instantiate (instantiate2 c')  _ _
=> c'
| inheritsFrom (set_superClass super)
_ _ => class super
```

```
| _ => CClass (* BBoolean => CClass
| CClass => CClass | PProperty =>
CClass *) end.
```

So, the assigned class of a newly created *Class* entity is:

The first argument of the *instantiate2* constructor;

The class of the entity used in the *inheritsFrom* constructor, e.g., if *Element* inherits from *Object* (see above) then the class of *Object* is assigned as instantiation class to *Element*;

CClass for the remaining cases (in Coq, underscore symbol is used for that purpose).

Consequently, the UML «*instanceOf*» relationship can be easily derived from the class function as follows:

```
Inductive instanceOf(c': Class):
Class -> Prop:= (* e.g., instanceOf
CClass Object *)
def: forall c, c' = class c -> in-
stanceOf c' c.
```

This Coq text is a formal characterization of the *Instantiation* relationship in the form of an inductive predicate (*def* constructor above). Such a characterization is totally absent from UML, despite its critical role. Indeed, Instantiation creates an impassable separation between modeling levels. In other words, if *c* is an instance of *c'*, the *Mc* model to which *c* belongs is an instance of that of *Mc'*. Unlike *Instantiation* links, *Generalization*, *Composition* and *Association* objects are intended to appear at the same modeling level. Another point is that the *Instantiation* relationship is quasi-irreflexive, *i.e.*, no element is an instance of itself except *CClass*. The strength of Coq is its ability to express and prove this lemma as follows:

```
Lemma Instantiation_quasi_irreflexiv-
ity: forall c: Class, c = class c ->
c = CClass.
```

To prove *Instantiation_quasi_irreflexivity*, two intermediate "technical" lemmas are required to bypass the problem of proving that recursive constructors are acyclic in constructive logic (McBride *et al.*, 2006). Roughly speaking, the result of instantiating an already existing *c* class cannot lead to *c* (*No_loop* lemma below) or any other preexisting entity in general (acyclicity). The *No_loop'* lemma seeks the same goal when creating entities by means of inheritance.

```
Lemma No_loop: forall c: Class,
forall p p': Property, instantiate
(instantiate2 c) p p' <> c.
Lemma No_loop': forall c: Class,
forall p p': Property, inheritsFrom
(set_superClass c) p p' <> class c.
```

PROVEN METAMODEL KERNEL FOR UML

Metaness

Kühne lays down in (Kühne, 2006) the principle of composition of the class function for expressing the metaness relationship. In (Kühne, 2006), metaness is viewed "as a two-level detachment of the original".

In Coq, we put forward the possibility of recursively computing the metaiclass of any UML element e for any *i* natural number with $meta_0class$ $e = e$ and $meta_iclass$ $e = class$ e (the *i* index materializes levels in metamodeling):

```
Fixpoint metaness(n: nat) (c: Class):
Class:= match n with
| 0 => c
| S m => class (metaness m c) (* S
m is the successor of m for natural
numbers in Coq *)
end.
```

Figure 3. Metaness acyclicity

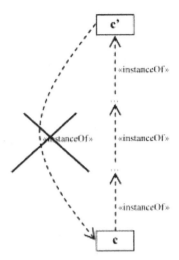

So, *metaness 0 c* is the *c* entity itself, while *metaness 1 c* is the direct class of *c*. *metaness 2 c* is the class of the class of *c*, namely the metaclass of *c*, etc. An interesting lemma to be proven is, when *n* is not equal to 0, *c* = *metaness n c* is only possible when *c* = *CClass*. By definition, *S n* (the successor of any *n*) is not equal to 0. We thus have:

```
Lemma Metaness_majorant: forall c:
Class, forall n: nat, c = metaness (S
n) c -> c = CClass.
```

The method for proving this lemma is similar to *Instantiation_quasi_irreflexivity* with, again, the problem exposed in (McBride *et al.*, 2006). This complex proof is viewable from www.FranckBarbier.com/Coq.

Metaness Acyclicity

The proof of metaness acyclicity is based on the following Coq theorem:

```
Theorem Metaness_acyclicity: forall c
c': Class, forall n: nat, c <> CClass
-> c' = metaness n c -> c <> class
c'.
```

Figure 4. Metaness antitransitivity

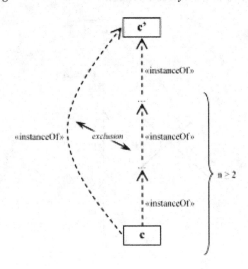

This theorem is illustrated through Figure 3. Contrary to the previous lemmas, the proof of this theorem is fairly concise in Coq:

```
intros. (* c, c' & n are introduced
as context variables with H: c <>
CClass and H0: c' = metaness n c *)
intro H1. (* the goal c <> class c'
is changed in False and c = class c'
becomes the H1 hypothesis in the
context *)
elim H. (* the current goal becomes c
= CClass *) clear H. (* no more use
of H *)
rewrite H0 in H1. (* c = class c'
becomes c = class (metaness n c) *)
clear H0.
change (class (metaness n c)) with
(metaness (S n) c) in H1.
generalize Metaness_
majorant;firstorder. (* the Metan-
ess_majorant lemma above is used to
solve the proof *)
```

Comments in this Coq text show how the proof proceeds by simply applying *metaness (class (metaness n c) = metaness (S n) c)* and by reusing the *Metaness_majorant* lemma. As a result, this

paper's specification of metaness with inductive types (section "Metaness" above) is acyclic as advocated by Kühne.

Metaness Antitransitivity

The proof of metaness antitransitivity is based on the following Coq theorem:

```
Theorem Metaness_anti_transitivity:
forall c c': Class, forall n: nat, c
<> CClass -> c' = metaness (S (S n))
c -> c' = class c -> c' = CClass.
```

The second part of this theorem may be advantageously rewritten in relation to what is depicted in Figure 4:

```
c <> CClass /\ n >= 2 -> c' = metan-
ess n c -> c' = class c -> c' =
CClass.
```

The proof of metaness antitransitivity relies on the following lemma:

```
Lemma Metaness_foundation: forall c:
Class, forall n: nat, metaness (S n)
c = metaness n (class c).
```

Intuitively, this lemma states that if *y* is the metaclass of *x* at level *i* then *class y* is the metaclass of *x* at level *i + 1*. Using this *Metaness_foundation* lemma and *Metaness_majorant*, the proof of metaness antitransitivity is straightforward:

```
intros.
subst c'. rewrite H1. (* this leads
to introducing H1: metaness (S (S n))
c = class c and to proving class c =
CClass *)
```

```
assert (H4:= Metaness_foundation c (S
n)). (* this leads to introducing H4:
```

Figure 5. A UML metamodel and a model conforming to it

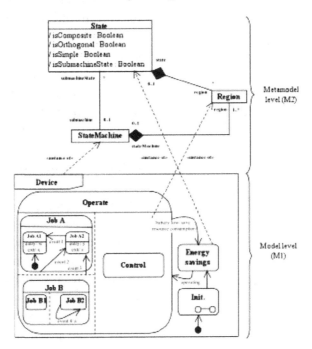

Figure 6. Adaptation leading to a dynamical model modification

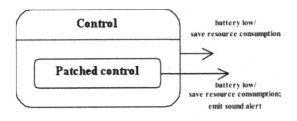

```
metaness (S (S n)) c = metaness (S n)
(class c) *)
rewrite H4 in H1. clear H4. (* H1
hypothesis becomes H1: metaness (S n)
(class c) = class c; H4 is no longer
needed *
generalize (Metaness_majorant n
(class c));firstorder. (* the Metan-
ess_majorant lemma is used to solve
the proof *)
```

Level-Respecting

In Kühne (2006, p. 378), the level-respecting property is intended to ensure that all metaness paths from one class to another have the same length. The reason is that Kühne deals at the same time with several kinds of metaness (linguistic versus ontological). In fact, the UML linguistic style of metamodeling leads to having a stronger characterization of level-respecting in this paper. Namely, this means that there is a unique path from a c class to a c' class when $c' = $ *metaness n c*.

The proof of level-respecting is based on the following Coq theorem:

```
Theorem Metaness_level_respecting:
forall n m: nat, c <> CClass -> c' <>
CClass -> c' = metaness n c -> c' =
metaness m c -> n = m.
```

Due to its complexity, here is an intuitive version of the level-respecting proof:

Figure 7. Corrected version of the UML metamodel in Figure 5

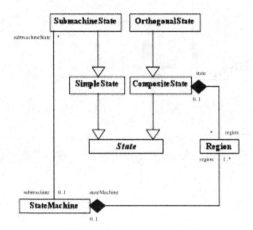

```
c' = metaness n
c' = metaness m c
```

If *n = S m* then we have:

```
class (metaness m c) = metaness m c
(* ∀ m *)
metaness m c = CClass (* ∀ m *)
```

This leads to *c = CClass* by applying the *Metaness_majorant* lemma. This contradicts *c <> CClass*. So, *n <> S m*. By generalization, *n* can be computed through the composition of the *S* function on *m: n = S(... S(S m) ...)*. Consequently, the only way to have *c' = metaness n c* and *c' = metaness m c* is to have *n = m*.

To sum up, this paper's formalization provides a proven demonstration of Atkinson & Kühne's metamodeling framework within the context of UML.

EXAMPLE

In this section, we provide a simplified workflow sketching how to put into practice the method promoted in this chapter. In the example, Figure 5 shows a model (bottom of figure, state machine) that conforms to a small subset of the original UML metamodel (top of figure).

The adaptation protocol (Figure 6) consists in dynamically injecting a *Patched control* state with an appropriate outgoing transition so that the *battery low* event is now managed by means of *Patched control* instead of *Control*. Effectively, in the UML semantics, transitions associated with inner states override (*i.e.*, hide) that of outer states. The *PauWare* model execution engine implements this semantics. The MOCAS extension (see "Introduction" section) offers a support for linking at runtime new states and transitions to state machines in general.

The key problem of metamodel-based adaptation is the fact that model modifications must lead to models that continue to obey to metamodels. Above all, metamodels that exist at runtime must be error-free. Unfortunately, this is not the case for the UML metamodel in Figure 5. More precisely, we are able to demonstrate with Coq that the *SubmachineState* is a great source of contradiction: it may be set to *true* while the state having this value *is not* actually a submachine. The complete proof appears in (Barbier & Ballagny, 2010). Figure 7 is the corrected metamodel that is required at runtime. This metamodel is a reliable support to carry out the adaptation shown in Figure 6. The EMF implementation (Java) is as follows:

```
public class SubmachineState extends
SimpleState {
        private org.eclipse.uml2.uml.
StateMachine submachine;
    ...
```

The PauWare/MOCAS implementation follows up:

```
private State Control = new
SubmachineState("Control"); // allow
adaptation by overriding
private State Patched_control = new
SimpleState("Patched control");
    ...
```

RELATED WORK

Researchers agree about the need for a mathematical foundation for UML. There have been several attempts in literature to rephrase UML into well-defined mathematical spaces (e.g., graphs, algebras) along with an implementation in related automated provers like Maude (Boronat & Meseguer, 2010), PVS (Paige *et al.*, 2007) or Coq in this chapter. To that extent, researchers have designed UML-like metamodeling frameworks (and some that are unlike UML too) from mathematical roots. This is the case of the Meta-Modeling Language (MML) (Clark *et al.*, 2001), which is based on a dedicated calculus that goes beyond Abadi and Cardelli's $\varsigma - $ calculus (Abadi & Cardelli, 1996).

In our opinion, contributions can be divided into three categories: re-thinking, re-formalization or simply revisiting UML.

Rethinking the MOF/UML and/or metamodeling at large: Clark *et al.* in (Clark *et al.*, 2001) and, more recently, Boronat and Meseguer in (Boronat & Meseguer, 2010) offer metamodeling theories. Jackson and Sztipanovits do the same in (Jackson & Sztipanovits, 2009) with a meta-metamodel agnostic approach; *i.e.*, it is independent of the MOF and UML to fabricate any formal metamodel-based DSML. While Clark *et al.* built a metamodeling calculus, Boronat and Meseguer defined a fully self-contained metamodeling framework based on the membership equational logic (MEL). Besides, they offer MOMENT2, an EMF tool that almost acts as a gateway between Maude (a tool to exercise MEL in an automated way) and the EMF world. In the same line of reasoning, Jackson and Sztipanovits use Horn logic with stratified negation ("a non-monotonic extension of Horn logic") as the basis of their proposal. They are also concerned with the operationalization of their metamodeling framework within the FORMULA automated prover and Model Integrated Computing (MIC) tool suite. Like us, Poernomo in (Poernomo, 2008) observes the appropriateness of the constructive logic for metamodeling. He lays the foundation for having metaclasses as constructive types (reused in this chapter). Nonetheless, the focus is on model-transformations-as-proofs. In this paper, metaness is not the focus. There is also no discussion on prover implementation and experimentation, except a UML-to-SQL transformation that is trivial.

(Re-)formalizing the MOF/UML and/or a general-purpose metamodeling language: This chapter falls in this category by viewing relationships between a metamodel and its models as instantiations in the OO sense. More generally, the broad-scope and open characterization of metamodeling by Kühne in (Kühne, 2006) assimilates the MOF and UML as a practice of linguistic instantiation (as opposed to ontological instantiation): "linguistic instantiation is a relation between model and language elements where the former play the role of instance and the latter that of class or type." (Asikainen, T. & Männistö, 2009). In this second category, existing mathematics are reused to redesign the MOF and UML, thus seeking compatibility with the well-established and widespread view of metamodeling provided by Kühne. Similar to this chapter, NIVEL is a partial realization of Kühne's framework based on the Weight Constraint Programming Language (WCRL). Since NIVEL has not sought compliance with the MOF and UML, it has its own semantics and notation. Beyond that, in contrast with this chapter, there is no focus on meta-circularity when defining NIVEL, *i.e.*, there are no proofs to reinforce its formal nature. In the same line of reasoning, Alanen and Porres in (Alanen & Porres, 2008) propose a set-centric re-formalization of a small UML part that focuses on multiplicity constraints and related properties; namely the *{subset}* and *{union}* UML adornments on association ends. This work is similar to (Milicev, 2007) which relies on Z. Paige *et al.* in (Paige *et al.*, 2007) have great interest in the BON metamodeling framework, which was initially dedicated to the Eiffel programming language. They compare PVS and Eiffel as supports for expressing metamodels in general and the BON metamodel in particular. They demonstrate how models may be accordingly checked in an Eiffel-like fashion. Using PVS is comparable to the use of Coq in this chapter due to the possibility of carrying out proofs in PVS.

Revisiting UML: works in this category do not really stress any improvement in the semantics of the MOF and UML. Instead, they single out small generative kernels of metaconstructs (for example, *eClass*, *eReference*… in EMF) in order to support metalanguages in popular tools. For example, similar to Ecore, a direct implementation of the MOF in Smalltalk is described in (Ducasse *et al.*, 2009). This is the case for KM3 (Jouault & Bézivin, 2006), which was inspired by the pioneering work of Bézivin and Gerbé (Bézivin & Gerbé, 2001). Kermeta (Morin *et al.*, 2009) is another EMF-compliant meta-metalanguage. Contrary to others, it has a rich Eiffel-like semantics to manipulate metamodels. Kermeta creates the junction with category 2, mostly with the Paige *et al.* contribution, in which they implement their vision of metamodeling for both Eiffel and PVS. Category 3 differs from 1 and 2 because of its focus on the notion of "model transformation" (Kuske *et al.*, 2009; Ehrig *et al.*, 2009), which deals with an issue that only remotely relates to this chapter.

Discussion: categories 1 and 2 raise the problem of justifying, why choose one mathematical support over another? In category 1, papers discuss the appropriateness of a custom-made mathematical support in absolute terms; *i.e.*, without comparisons and alternatives. These papers capitalize on existing mathematical theories to invent metamodeling-based extensions (*e.g.*, Horn logic extension, Abadi and Cardelli's ς − calculus extension, MEL add-on). As observed by Jackson and Sztipanovits (Jackson & Sztipanovits, 2009, p. 472), category 1 is free from the historical "instance semantics" of the MOF and UML, while both this chapter and NIVEL rely on it. In this chapter, the proposed instantiation protocol guarantees by construction that new objects are po-

tential classes to be instantiated. In contrast with other works, building a model is not subject to checking that requires a model to conform to its metamodel. So, this property is provided by construction in this chapter's specification and by being accomplished in Coq.

Orthogonally, some papers in categories 1 and 2 emphasize the accomplishments of their rethinking/(re-)formalization of the MOF and UML in automated provers (*e.g.*, Maude, FORMULA, PVS, Coq). In this chapter, we single out the explicit writing of the UML kernel in constructive logic (the metaness relationship in particular), as well as the explicit writing of Coq proofs and their justifications with the help of Coq tactics. Even though most papers provide a similarly explicit expression of UML metamodels in their chosen mathematical space, no unequivocal proofs are offered along with their comprehensive and traceable progress in the preferred prover.

CONCLUSION

The need for making metamodels (MOF and UML Infrastructure) more robust, results from designing DSMLs on top of these metamodels. Research contributions use metamodeling in a more or less formal way to develop UML-like metamodeling frameworks. Moreover, the direct operationalization of metamodels in dedicated (computing) environments (*e.g.*, EMF) increases the expected quality of runtime models and their runtime verification (Cariou *et al.*, 2011). In this scope, this chapter is an attempt to construct high-confidence metamodels based on the constructive logic, along with inherent proofs. The key contribution is a generative approach to construct new metaclasses from existing ones: the entire MOF can be described with this technique. New proofs may also be introduced by reusing (or not) foundation lemmas/theorems. In this context, we pursue the following goals:

- Proofs about particular concepts like the *Composition* relationship may definitely make the UML semantics reliable. We aim at introducing this key concept as a new metaclass and proving local properties, like unsharing or coincident lifetime. Typically, coincident lifetime supposes the concomitant birth and death of the composite and component elements, preventing the sharing of components with other composites.

- **Scalability:** No scalability issues are discussed in this chapter but a key objective is to fully specify the UML Infrastructure and Superstructure with presumably slight difficulties in maintaining the current organization of metamodels and the OCL constraints that rule these metamodels. Metanavigations along with redefinitions or unions or projections constitute an important challenge in this area.

- The final goal is the creation of a virtual machine of executable models on the top of EMF (and thus Java). We do not target (even in the future) any automatic translation from Coq to Ecore/Java. Although Coq already supports a bridge to the CAML programming language, an automatic translation to Ecore/Java is tricky due to the conceptual gap between Java and the constructive logic. Coq functions are free from performance concerns, whereas it is a key expectation when programming in Java. So, we will only stress a manual translation to Ecore/Java while taking care of performance in a pragmatic way.

REFERENCES

Abadi, M., & Cardelli, L. (1996). *A theory of objects*. Berlin: Springer. doi:10.1007/978-1-4419-8598-9.

Alanen, M., & Porres, I. (2008). A metamodeling language supporting subset and union properties. *Software & Systems Modeling, 7*(1), 103–124. doi:10.1007/s10270-007-0049-9.

Asikainen, T., & Männistö, T. (2009). Nivel: A metamodeling language with a formal semantics. *Software & Systems Modeling, 8*(4), 521–549. doi:10.1007/s10270-008-0103-2.

Atkinson, C., & Kühne, T. (2002). Model-driven development: A metamodeling foundation. *IEEE Software, 20*(5), 5–22.

Ballagny, C., Hameurlain, N., & Barbier, F. (2009). MOCAS: A state-based component model for self-adaptation. In *Proceedings of the Third IEEE International Conference on Self-Adaptive and Self-Organizing Systems* (pp. 206-215). IEEE Computer Society Press.

Barbier, F. (2008). Supporting the UML state machine diagrams at runtime. In *Proceedings of the European Conference on Model-Driven Architecture* (LNCS), (vol. 5095, pp. 339-349). Berlin: Springer.

Barbier, F., & Ballagny, C. (2010). Proven metamodels as backbone for software adaptation. In *Proceedings of the 12th IEEE International High Assurance Systems Engineering Symposium* (pp. 114-121). IEEE Computer Society Press.

Bertot, Y., & Castéran, P. (2004). *Interactive theorem proving and program development – Coq'Art: The Calculus of inductive constructions*. Berlin: Springer. doi:10.1007/978-3-662-07964-5.

Bézivin, J., & Gerbé, O. (2001). Towards a precise definition of the OMG/MDA framework. In *Proceedings of Automated Software Engineering* (pp. 273–280). IEEE Computer Society Press. doi:10.1109/ASE.2001.989813.

Boronat, A., & Meseguer, J. (2010). An algebraic semantics for MOF. *Formal Aspects of Computing, 22*(3-4), 269–296. doi:10.1007/s00165-009-0140-9.

Broy, M., & Cengarle, M. V. (2011). UML formal semantics: Lessons learned. *Software & Systems Modeling*, *10*(4), 441–446. doi:10.1007/s10270-011-0207-y.

Cariou, E., Ballagny, C., Feugas, A., & Barbier, F. (2011). Contracts for model execution verification. In *Proceedings of the 7th European Conference on Modeling Foundations and Applications* (LNCS), (vol. 6698, pp. 3-18). Berlin: Springer.

Cariou, E., Barbier, F., & Le Goaer, O. (2012). Model execution adaptation? In *Proceedings of the 7th International Workshop on Models@run.time*. MoDELS.

Clark, T., Evans, A., & Kent, S. (2001). The metamodelling language calculus: Foundation semantics for UML. In *Proceedings of the 4th International Conference on Fundamental Approaches to Software Engineering* (pp. 17-31). ACM Press.

Ducasse, S., Girba, T., Kuhn, A., & Renggli, L. (2009). Meta-environment and executable meta-language using Smalltalk: An experience report. *Software & Systems Modeling*, *8*(1), 5–19. doi:10.1007/s10270-008-0081-4.

Egea, M. (2005). *ITP/OCL: A theorem prover-based tool for UML+OCL class diagrams*. (Master Thesis). Departamento de Sistemas Informáticos y Programación, Universidad Complutense de Madrid, Madrid, Spain.

Ehrig, K., Küster, J. M., & Taentzer, G. (2009). Generating instance models from meta models. *Software & Systems Modeling*, *8*(4), 479–500. doi:10.1007/s10270-008-0095-y.

Fleurey, F., & Solberg, A. (2009). A domain specific modeling language supporting specification, simulation and execution of dynamic adaptive systems. In *Proceedings of MODELS 2009* (LNCS), (vol. 5795, pp. 606-621). Berlin: Springer.

Hesse, W. (2006). More matters on (meta-)modeling: Remarks on Thomas Kühne's matters. *Software & Systems Modeling*, *5*(4), 387–394. doi:10.1007/s10270-006-0033-9.

Jackson, E., & Sztipanovits, J. (2009). Formalizing the structural semantics of domain-specific modeling languages. *Software & Systems Modeling*, *8*(4), 451–478. doi:10.1007/s10270-008-0105-0.

Jouault, F., & Bézivin, J. (2006). KM3: A DSL for metamodel specification. [LNCS]. *Proceedings of Formal Methods for Open Object-Based Distributed Systems*, *4037*, 171–185. doi:10.1007/11768869_14.

Kühne, T. (2006a). Matters of (meta-) modeling. *Software & Systems Modeling*, *5*(4), 369–385. doi:10.1007/s10270-006-0017-9.

Kühne, T. (2006b). Clarifying matters of (meta-) modeling: An author's reply. *Software & Systems Modeling*, *5*(4), 395–401. doi:10.1007/s10270-006-0034-8.

Kuske, S., Gogolla, M., Kreowski, H.-J., & Ziemann, P. (2009). Towards an integrated graph-based semantics for UML. *Software & Systems Modeling*, *8*(3), 403–422. doi:10.1007/s10270-008-0101-4.

Kyas, M., Fecher, H., de Boer, F., Jacob, J., Hooman, J., & van der Zwaag, M. et al. (2005). Formalizing UML models and OCL constraints in PVS. *Electronic Notes in Theoretical Computer Science*, *115*, 39–47. doi:10.1016/j.entcs.2004.09.027.

McBride, C., Goguen, H., & McKinna, J. (2006). A few constructions on constructors. *Lecture Notes in Computer Science*, *3839*, 186–200. doi:10.1007/11617990_12.

Milicev, D. (2007). On the semantics of associations and association ends in UML. *IEEE Transactions on Software Engineering*, *33*(4), 238–251. doi:10.1109/TSE.2007.37.

Morin, B., Barais, O., Jézéquel, J.-M., Fleurey, F., & Solberg, A. (2009). Models@Run.time to support dynamic adaptation. *IEEE Computer*, *42*(10), 44–51. doi:10.1109/MC.2009.327.

Paige, R., Brooke, P., & Ostroff, J. (2007). Metamodel-based model conformance and multiview consistency checking. *ACM Transactions on Software Engineering and Methodology*, *16*(3). doi:10.1145/1243987.1243989.

Poernomo, I. (2008). Proofs-as-model-transformations. In *Proceedings of the International Conference on Model Transformations* (LNCS), (vol. 5063, pp. 214-228). Berlin: Springer.

Steinberg, D., Budinsky, F., Paternostro, M., & Merks, E. (2008). *EMF - Eclipse modeling framework* (2nd ed.). Reading, MA: Addison-Wesley.

Zhang, J., & Cheng, B. (2006). Model-based development of dynamically adaptive software. In *Proceedings of the International Conference on Software Engineering* (pp. 371-380). ACM Press.

Compilation of References

(2010). *Webster's New World College Dictionary*. Cleveland, OH: Wiley Publishing, Inc..

Abadi, M., & Cardelli, L. (1996). *A theory of objects*. Berlin: Springer. doi:10.1007/978-1-4419-8598-9.

Abbott, R. (1983). Program design by informal English descriptions. *Communications of the ACM, 26*(11), 882–894.

Abelson, H., Sussman, G., & Sussman, J. (1996). *Structure and interpretation of computer programs* (2nd ed.). Cambridge, MA: MIT Press.

Abramson, M. A., & Means, G. E. (2001). *E-government 2001*. London: Rowman & Littlefield Publishers.

ADM. (2012). *Architecture-driven modernization task force*. Retrieved September 24, 2012, from http://www.omgwiki.org/admtf/doku.php

Ågerfalk, P. J. (2010). Getting pragmatic. *European Journal of Information Systems, 19*(3), 251–256. doi:10.1057/ejis.2010.22.

Ågerfalk, P. J., & Fitzgerald, B. (2006). Exploring the concept of method rationale: A conceptual tool for method tailoring. In Siau, K. (Ed.), *Advanced Topics in Database Research* (*Vol. 5*). Hershey, PA: Idea Group. doi:10.4018/978-1-59140-935-9.ch004.

Ahmad, A. (2004). *A performance analysis approach based on the UML class diagram*. Paper presented at the International Workshop on Software and Performance. New York, NY.

Alanen, M., & Porres, I. (2008). A metamodeling language supporting subset and union properties. *Software & Systems Modeling, 7*(1), 103–124. doi:10.1007/s10270-007-0049-9.

Alexander, V., Timo, S., Oliver, B., & Wolfgang, R. (2006). *Formal performance analysis and simulation of UML/SysML models for ESL design*. Paper presented at the e Conference on Design, Automation and Test in Europe. London, UK.

Ali, S., Briand, L. C., Hemmati, H., & Panesar-Walawege, R. K. (2010). A systematic review of the application and empirical investigation of search-based test-case generation. *IEEE Transactions on Software Engineering, 36*(6), 742–762. doi:10.1109/TSE.2009.52.

Allen, R. (2013). *Getting started with zend framework 1.11*. Retrieved January 6, 2013, from http://akrabat.com/zend-framework-tutorial/

Alonso, G., Casati, F., Kuno, H., & Machiraju, V. (2004). *Web services: Concepts, architectures and applications*. Berlin: Springer.

Alsumait., et al. (2003). Use case maps: A visual notation for scenario-based requirements. In *Proceedings of the 10th International Conference on Human-Computer Interaction*. IEEE.

Álvarez, J., Evans, A., & Sammut, P. (2001). Mapping between levels in the metamodel architecture. In M. Gogolla, & C. Kobryn (Eds.), *Proc. UML 2001 – The Unified Modeling Language: Modeling Languages, Concepts and Tools* (LNCS), (vol. 2185, pp. 34-46). Berlin: Springer-Verlag.

America, P., Thiel, S., Ferber, S., & Mergel, M. (2001). *Introduction to domain analysis. ESAPS Project*. Engineering Software Architectures, Processes, and Platforms for System Families.

Anastasakis, K., Bordbar, B., Georg, G., & Ray, I. (2010). On challenges of model transformation from UML to alloy. *Software Systems Modelling, 9*(1).

Andre, D. A., & Paolo, B. (2007). *A model-driven approach to describe and predict the performance of composite services.* Paper presented at the 6th International Workshop on Software and Performance. New York, NY.

Andrea, D. A. (2005). *A model transformation framework for the automated building of performance models from UML models.* Paper presented at the 5th International Workshop on Software and Performance. New York, NY.

Angyal, L., Lengyel, L., & Charaf, H. (2006). An overview of the state-of-the-art reverse engineering techniques. In *Proceedings of the 7th International Symposium of Hungarian Researchers on Computational Intelligence* (pp. 507-516). Budapest, Hungary: Hungarian Research.

Anil, S. J. (2000). *UML diagrams to object Petri net models: An approach for modeling and analysis.* Paper presented at the 12th International Conference on Software Engineering and Knowledge Engineering. Chicago, IL.

Antkiewicz, M., & Czarnecki, K. (2004). *FeaturePlugin: Feature modeling plug-in for Eclipse.* Paper presented at the 2004 OOPSLA Workshop on Eclipse Technology eXchange. Vancouver, Canada.

Ardis, M., & Weiss, D. (1997). *Defining families: The commonality analysis.* Paper presented at the 19th International Conference on Software Engineering. Boston, MA.

Aristotle. in Translation. (1984). Complete works. (J. Barnes, Ed.). Princeton, NJ: Princeton University Press.

Armstrong, D. M. (1989). *Universals: An opinionated introduction.* Westview Press.

Arnold, B., Van Deursen, A., & Res, M. (1995). *An algebraic specification of a language for describing financial products.* Paper presented at the IEEE Workshop on Formal Methods Application in Software Engineering. Seattle, WA.

Asikainen, T., & Männistö, T. (2009). Nivel: A metamodeling language with a formal semantics. *Software & Systems Modeling, 8*(4), 521–549. doi:10.1007/s10270-008-0103-2.

Asimov, I. (1988). *Prelude to foundation.* London: Grafton Books.

Aßmann, U., Zschaler, S., & Wagner, G. (2006). Ontologies, meta-models, and the model-driven paradigm. In Calero, C., Ruiz, F., & Piattini, M. (Eds.), *Ontologies for Software Engineering and Software Technology.* Berlin: Springer. doi:10.1007/3-540-34518-3_9.

ASTM. (2011). *Abstract syntax tree metamodel, version 1.0.* Retrieved September 24, 2012, from http://www.omg.org/spec/ASTM

Atkinson, C. (1997). Metamodelling for distributed object environments. In *Proceedings of the First International Enterprise Distributed Object Computing Workshop (EDOC'97).* Brisbane, Australia: IEEE Computer Society.

Atkinson, C., & Kühne, T. (2000a). Strict profiles: why and how. In *Proceedings Third International Conference on the Unified Modeling Language,* (LNCS), (vol. 1939, pp. 309-322). Berlin: Springer-Verlag.

Atkinson, C. (1999). Supporting and applying the UML conceptual framework. In Bézivin, J., & Muller, P.-A. (Eds.), *The Unified Modeling Language «UML» 1998: Beyond the Notation (LNCS) (Vol. 1618,* pp. 21–36). Berlin: Springer-Verlag. doi:10.1007/978-3-540-48480-6_3.

Atkinson, C., Gutheil, M., & Kennel, B. (2009). A flexible infrastructure for multilevel language engineering. *IEEE Transactions on Software Engineering, 35*(6), 742–755. doi:10.1109/TSE.2009.31.

Atkinson, C., Kennel, B., & Goß, B. (2011). The level-agnostic modeling language. In Malloy, B., Staab, S., & van den Brand, M. (Eds.), *SLE 2010 (LNCS) (Vol. 6563,* pp. 269–275). Berlin: Springer-Verlag.

Atkinson, C., & Kühne, T. (2001a). The essence of multilevel metamodelling. In Gogolla, M., & Kobryn, C. (Eds.), *UML»2001 – The Unified Modeling Language. Modeling Languages, Concepts and Tools, (LNCS) (Vol. 2185,* pp. 19–33). Berlin: Springer-Verlag. doi:10.1007/3-540-45441-1_3.

Atkinson, C., & Kühne, T. (2001b). Processes and products in a multi-level metamodelling architecture. *International Journal of Software Engineering and Knowledge Engineering, 11*(6), 761–783. doi:10.1142/S0218194001000724.

Atkinson, C., & Kühne, T. (2002). Model-driven development: A metamodeling foundation. *IEEE Software, 20*(5), 5–22.

Atkinson, C., & Kühne, T. (2002). Rearchitecting the UML infrastructure. *ACM Transactions on Modeling and Computer Simulation, 12*(4), 290–321.

Atkinson, C., & Kühne, T. (2003). Model-driven development: a metamodelling foundation. *IEEE Software, 20*, 36–41. doi:10.1109/MS.2003.1231149.

Atkinson, C., & Kühne, T. (2005). Concepts for comparing modeling tool architectures. In *Model Driven Engineering Languages and Systems, (LNCS)* (Vol. 3713, pp. 398–413). Berlin: Springer-Verlag. doi:10.1007/11557432_30.

Atkinson, C., & Kühne, T. (2008). Reducing accidental complexity in domain models. *Software & Systems Modeling, 7*(3), 345–359. doi:10.1007/s10270-007-0061-0.

ATL. (2012). *Atlas Transformation language (ATL) documentation*. Retrieved September 24, 2012, from http://www.eclipse.org/atl/documentation/

Austin, J. L. (1962). *How to do things with words*. Oxford, UK: Oxford University Press.

Aydal, E. G., Paige, R. F., Utting, M., & Woodcock, J. (2009). Putting formal specifications under the magnifying glass: Model-based testing for validation. In *Proceedings of the Second International Conference on Software Testing, Verification and Validation* (pp. 131-140). Denver, CO: IEEE Computer Society.

Baader, F., & Nutt, W. (2002). Basic description logics. In Baader, F., Calvanese, D., McGuinness, D. L., Nardi, D., & Patel-Schneider, P. F. (Eds.), *Description Logic Handbook*. Cambridge, UK: Cambridge University Press.

Baar, T., & Markovic, S. (2007). A graphical approach to prove the semantic preservation of UML/OCL refactoring rules.[LNCS]. *Proceedings of the Perspectives of Systems Informatics, 4378*, 70–83. doi:10.1007/978-3-540-70881-0_9.

Bachmann, F., & Bass, L. (2001). Managing variability in software architectures. *ACM SIGSOFT Software Engineering Notes, 26*(3), 126–132.

Bakaev, M., & Avdeenko, T. (2010). Ontology to support web design activities in e-commerce software development process. In Y. Shokin, I. Bychkov, & O. Potaturkin (Eds.), *Proceedings of IASTED ACIT 2010* (pp. 241–248). ACTA Press. Retrieved from http://www.iasted.org/conferences/sessionpapers-691.html

Ballagny, C., Hameurlain, N., & Barbier, F. (2009). MOCAS: A state-based component model for self-adaptation. In *Proceedings of the Third IEEE International Conference on Self-Adaptive and Self-Organizing Systems* (pp. 206-215). IEEE Computer Society Press.

Banerjee, I., Nguyen, B., Garousi, V., & Memon, A. (2012). Graphical user interface (GUI) testing: Systematic mapping and repository. *Information and Software Technology*.

Barbier, F. (2008). Supporting the UML state machine diagrams at runtime. In *Proceedings of the European Conference on Model-Driven Architecture* (LNCS), (vol. 5095, pp. 339-349). Berlin: Springer.

Barbier, F., & Ballagny, C. (2010). Proven metamodels as backbone for software adaptation. In *Proceedings of the 12th IEEE International High Assurance Systems Engineering Symposium* (pp. 114-121). IEEE Computer Society Press.

Barbier, F., Deltombe, G., Parisy, O., & Youbi, K. (2011). Model driven engineering: Increasing legacy technology independence. In *Proceedings of Second India Workshop on Reverse Engineering (IWRE, 2011) in The 4th India Software Engineering Conference* (pp. 5-10). Thiruvanantpuram, India: CSI.

Barbier, G., Flusin, J., Cucchi, V., Pinet, F., & Hill, D. R. C. (2013). *Vine model design using a domain-specific modeling language*. Paper presented at the European Simulation and Modeling Conference. Essen, Germany.

Barbier, G., Pinet, F., & Hill, D. R. C. (2011). MDE in action: First steps towards a crop model factory. In *Proceedings of the ESM 2011 European Simulation and Modeling Conference* (pp. 130-137). Guimarães, Portugal: ESM.

Barn, B., & Clark, T. (2012). Goal based alignment of enterprise architectures. In *Proceedings of the 7th International Conference on Software Paradigm Trends* (pp. 230-236). SciTePress.

Beddall, B. G. (1968). Wallace, Darwin, and the theory of natural selection. *Journal of the History of Biology, 1*(2), 261–323. doi:10.1007/BF00351923.

Bennett, A. J. (2004). *Performance engineering with the UML profile for schedulability, performance and time: A case study.* Paper presented at the IEEE Computer Society's 12th Annual International Symposium on Modeling, Analysis, and Simulation of Computer and Telecommunications Systems. New York, NY.

Bennett, A. J., & Murray, W. C. (2004). *Experimental evaluation of the uml profile for schedulability, performance, and time.* Paper presented at the International Conference on the Unified Modeling Language. New York, NY.

Bergez, J.-E., Chabrier, P., Gary, C., Jeuffroy, M. H., Makowski, D., & Quesnel, G. et al. (2013). An open platform to build, evaluate and simulate integrated models of farming and agro-ecosystems. *Environmental Modelling & Software.* doi:10.1016/j.envsoft.2012.03.011.

Bernstein, R. J. (2010). *The pragmatic turn.* Cambridge, UK: Polity Press.

Bertolino, A. (2002). *Real-time UML-based performance engineering to aid manager's decisions in multi-project planning.* Paper presented at the 3rd International Workshop on Software and Performance. Rome, Italy.

Bertolino, A., De Angelis, G., Di Sandro, A., & Sabetta, A. (2011). Is my model right? Let me ask the expert. *Journal of Systems and Software, 84*(7), 1089–1099. Retrieved October 15, 2012, from http://dx.doi.org/10.1016/j.jss.2011.01.054

Bertot, Y., & Castéran, P. (2004). *Interactive theorem proving and program development – Coq'Art: The Calculus of inductive constructions.* Berlin: Springer. doi:10.1007/978-3-662-07964-5.

Bezemer, C., & Zaidman, A. (2010). Multi-tenant SaaS applications: Maintenance dream or nightmare? In *Proceedings of the Joint ERCIM Workshop on Software Evolution (EVOL) and International Workshop on Principles of Software Evolution (IWPSE) (IWPSE-EVOL '10)*, (pp. 88-92). New York: ACM.

Bézivin, J., & Gerbé, O. (2001). Towards a precise definition of the OMG/MDA framework. In *Proceedings of the 16th IEEE International Conference on Automated Software Engineering (ASE 2001)* (pp. 273-280). San Diego, CA: IEEE Computer Society.

Bézivin, J., & Heckel, R. (2004). *Language engineering for model-driven software development.* Paper presented at the Dagstuhl Seminar. Dagstuhl, Germany.

Bézivin, J., Joualt, F., & Valduriez, P. (2004). On the need for megamodels. In *Proceedings of Workshop on Best Practices for Model-Driven Software Development at the 19th Annual ACM Conference on Object-Oriented Programming, Systems, Languages, and Applications.* ACM Press.

Bézivin, J. (2004). In search of a basic principle for model driven engineering. *The European Journal for the Informatics Professional, 5*(2), 21–24.

Bézivin, J., & Gerbé, O. (2001). Towards a precise definition of the OMG/MDA framework. In *Proceedings of Automated Software Engineering* (pp. 273–280). IEEE Computer Society Press. doi:10.1109/ASE.2001.989813.

Bhathal, R. (2012). Australia and the transit of Venus. *Astronomy & Geophysics, 53*(3), 3.22-3.24.

Bidoit, M., & Mosses, P. (2004). *CASL user manual- Introduction to using the common algebraic specification language (LNCS) (Vol. 2900).* Heidelberg, Germany: Springer-Verlag.

Bisbal, J., Lawless, D., Wu, B., & Grimson, J. (1999). Legacy information systems: Issues and directions. *IEEE Software, 16*(5), 103–111. doi:10.1109/52.795108.

Blouin, A., Combemale, B., Baudry, B., & Beaudoux, O. (2011). *Modeling model slicers.* Paper presented at the MODELS 2011. New York, NY.

Bock, C., & Odell, J. J. (1994). A foundation for composition. *Journal of Object-Oriented Programming, 7*(6), 10–14.

Boehm, B. W. (1981). *Software engineering economics.* New York: Prentice Hall.

Borkar, V. S. (1998). There's no such thing as a free lunch: The bias-variance dilemma. *Resonance -. Journal of Science Education, 3*(6), 40–51.

Boronat, A., & Meseguer, J. (2010). An algebraic semantics for MOF. *Formal Aspects of Computing, 22*(3-4), 269–296. doi:10.1007/s00165-009-0140-9.

Boulanger, R. (2000). *The Csound book: Perspectives in software synthesis, sound design, signal processing, and programming*. Cambridge, MA: MIT press.

Bouman, B. A. M., Van Keulen, H., van Laar, H. H., & Rabbinge, R. (1996). The 'school of de wit' crop growth simulation models: A pedigree and historical review. *Agricultural Systems, 52*(2/3), 171–198. doi:10.1016/0308-521X(96)00011-X.

Brachman, R. J. (1985). I lied about the trees' or, defaults and definitions in knowledge representation. *AI Magazine, 6*(3), 80–93.

Brentano, F. (1874). *Psychologie vom empirischen standpunkt*. Leipzig, Germany: Verlag von Duncker & Humblot.

Brisson, N., Launay, M., & Beaudoin, N. (2009). *Conceptual basis, formalisations and parameterization of the STICS crop model*.

Brown, A. (2004). Oops! Coping with human error in IT. *ACM Queue – System Failures, 2*(8), 34-41.

Broy, M. (2011, October). Can practitioners neglect theory and theoreticians neglect practice? *IEEE Software*, 19–24.

Broy, M., & Cengarle, M. V. (2011). UML formal semantics: Lessons learned. *Software & Systems Modeling, 10*(4), 441–446. doi:10.1007/s10270-011-0207-y.

Brucker, A., & Wolff, B. (2008). HOL-OCL: A formal proof environment for UML/OCL. In *Proceedings of FASE 2008* (LNCS), (vol. 4961). Berlin: Springer.

Bruneliere, H., Cabot, J., & Dupé, G. (2012). How to deal with your IT legacy: What is coming up in MoDisco? *ERCIM News, 88*, 43-44. Retrieved September 24, 2012, from http://ercim-news.ercim.eu/images/stories/EN88/EN88-Web.pdf

Bühne, S., Halmans, G., & Pohl, K. (2003). *Modelling dependencies between variation points in use case diagrams*. Paper presented at the 9th Workshop in Requirements Engineering – Foundations for Software Quality. Klagenfurt, Austria.

Bunge, M. (1977). Treatise on basic philosophy: *Vol. 3. Ontology I: The furniture of the world*. Boston: Reidel.

Bunge, M. (1979). Treatise on basic philosophy: *Vol. 4. Ontology II: A world of systems*. Boston: Reidel.

Butcher, T., Fischer, R., Kurpjuweit, S., & Winter, R. (2006). Analysis and application scenarios of enterprise architecture: An exploratory study. In *Proceedings of the 10th IEEE International Enterprise Distributed Object Computing Conference Workshops EDOCW'06*. IEEE.

Butterfield, H. (1957). *The origins of modern science, 1300-1800*. London: G. Bell.

Buttner, F., Cabot, J., & Gogolla, M. (2011). On validation of ATL transformation rules by transformation models. In Proceedings of MoDeVVa 2011. MoDeVVa.

Cabot, J., Clariso, R., Guerra, E., & De Lara, J. (2010). Verification and validation of declarative model-to-model transformations through invariants. *Journal of Systems and Software*. doi:10.1016/j.jss.2009.08.012.

Cabot, J., Clariso, R., & Riera, D. (2007). UMLtoCSP: A tool for the verification of UML/OCL models using constraint programming.[ACM Press.]. *Proceedings of Automated Software Engineering, 07*, 547–548.

Canevet, C. (2004). *Analysing UML 2.0 activity diagrams in the software performance engineering process*. Paper presented at the 4th International Workshop on Software and Performance. New York, NY.

Canevet, C. (2003). Performance modelling with the unified modelling language and stochastic process algebras. *IEE Proceedings. Computers and Digital Techniques, 150*(2), 107–120. doi:10.1049/ip-cdt:20030084.

Canfora, G., & Di Penta, M. (2007). New frontiers of reverse engineering. In Proceedings of Future of Software Engineering, 2007, FOSE '07 (pp. 326-341). IEEE Press.

Cánovas Izquierdo, J., & García Molina, J. (2009b). Extracción de modelos en una modernización basada en ADM. *Actas de los Talleres de las Jornadas de Ingeniería de Software y BBDD, 3*(2), 41-50. Retrieved September 24, 2012, from http://www.sistedes.es/ficheros/actas-talleres-JISBD/Vol-3/No-2/DSDM09.pdf

Cánovas Izquierdo, J., & García Molina, J. (2009a). A domain specific language for extracting models in software modernization. In *Proceedings of Model Driven Architecture - Foundations and Applications (LNCS)* (*Vol. 5562*, pp. 82–97). Berlin: Springer-Verlag. doi:10.1007/978-3-642-02674-4_7.

Cardelli, L. (1988). Structural subtyping and the notion of power type. In J. Ferrante, & P Mager (Eds.), *Proceedings Fifteenth Annual ACM Symposium on Principles of Programming Languages*. ACM Press.

Cariou, E., Ballagny, C., Feugas, A., & Barbier, F. (2011). Contracts for model execution verification. In *Proceedings of the 7th European Conference on Modeling Foundations and Applications* (LNCS), (vol. 6698, pp. 3-18). Berlin: Springer.

Cariou, E., Barbier, F., & Le Goaer, O. (2012). Model execution adaptation? In *Proceedings of the 7th International Workshop on Models@run.time*. MoDELS.

Carmichael, A. (1994). Towards a common object-oriented meta-model for object development. In Carmichael, A. (Ed.), *Object Development Methods* (pp. 321–333). New York: SIGS Books.

Carmona, C., Ramírez-Gallego, S., Torres, F., Bernal, E., del Jesus, M. J., & García, S. (2012). Web usage mining to improve the design of an e-commerce website: OrOliveSur.com. *Expert Systems with Applications*, *39*(12), 11243–11249. doi:10.1016/j.eswa.2012.03.046.

Carnap, R. (1947). *Meaning and necessity: A study in semantics and modal logic*. Chicago, IL: University of Chicago Press.

Carnegie Mellon University. (2012a). *Architecture analysis and design language*. Retrieved November 4, 2012, from http://www.aadl.info

Carnegie Mellon University. (2012b). *System and software architecture tradeoff analysis method*. Retrieved November 4, 2012, from http://www.sei.cmu.edu/architecture/tools/evaluate/systematam.cfm

CASE MDA. (2012). *Committed companies and their products*. Retrieved September 24, 2012, from www.omg.org/mda/committed-products.htm

Cengarle, M., & Knapp, A. (2009). Interactions. In Lano, K. (Ed.), *UML 2 Semantics and Applications*. New York: Wiley.

Cetinkaya, D., Verbraeck, A., & Seck, M. S. (2011). *MDD4MS: A model driven development framework for modeling and simulation*. Paper presented at the 2011 Summer Computer Simulation Conference. Hague, Netherlands.

Chamberlin, D., & Boyce, R. (1974). *SEQUEL: A structured English query language*. Paper presented at the 1974 ACM SIGFIDET (now SIGMOD) Workshop on Data Description, Access and Control. New York, NY.

Chambers, R. (1844). *Vestiges of the natural history of creation*. London, W: R Chambers.

Chan, Y. E., & Reich, B. H. (2007). IT alignment: What have we learned? *Journal of Information Technology*, *22*(4), 297–315. doi:10.1057/palgrave.jit.2000109.

Chief, T. (1999, September). Federal enterprise architecture framework. *Architecture (Washington, D.C.)*, *80*. Retrieved from http://www.cio.gov/documents/fedarch1.pdf.

Chimia-Opoka, J., Felderer, M., Lenz, C., & Lange, C. (2008). Querying UML models using OCL and prolog: A performance study.[IEEE Press.]. *Proceedings of ICSTW*, *2008*, 81–88.

Chomsky, N. (1956). Three models for the description of language. *I.R.E. Transactions on Information Theory*, *2*(3), 113–124. doi:10.1109/TIT.1956.1056813.

Chomsky, N. (1959). On certain formal properties of grammars. *Information and Control*, *2*(2), 137–171. doi:10.1016/S0019-9958(59)90362-6.

Christoph, L., Axel, T., Alexander, K., & Marco, L. (2002). *Performance analysis of time-enhanced UML diagrams based on stochastic processes*. Paper presented at the 3rd International Workshop on Software and Performance. Rome, Italy.

Clark, T., & Barn, B. (2012). A common basis for modelling service-oriented and event-driven architecture. In *Proceedings of the 5th Annual India Software Engineering Conference, ISEC 2012*. ACM.

Clark, T., Barn, B., & Oussena, S. (2011). LEAP: A precise lightweight framework for enterprise architecture. In *Proceedings of the 4th Annual India Software Engineering Conference, ISEC 2011*. ACM.

Clark, T., Barn, B., & Oussena, S. (2012). A method for enterprise architecture alignment. In *Proceedings of the 4th Working Conference on Practice-Driven Research on Enterprise Transformation, PRET 2012* (pp. 48-76). Springer.

Clark, T., Evans, A., & Kent, S. (2001). The metamodelling language calculus: Foundation semantics for UML. In *Proceedings of the 4th International Conference on Fundamental Approaches to Software Engineering* (pp. 17-31). ACM Press.

Clark, T., Sammut, P., & Willans, J. (2008). *Applied metamodelling: A foundation for language driven development* (2nd ed.). CETEVA.

ClearSy. (2012). *Atelier B*. Retrieved from http://www.atelierb.eu

Cleaveland, J. C. (1988). Building application generators. *IEEE Software, 5*(4), 25–33.

Clements, P., Kazman, R., & Klein, M. (2001). *Evaluating software architectures: Methods and case studies*. Amsterdam: Addison-Wesley Longman.

Coad, P. (1992). Object-oriented patterns. *Communications of the ACM, 35*(9), 152–159.

Coad, P., de Luca, J., & Lefebvre, É. (1999). *Java modeling color with UML: Enterprise components and process*. Upper Saddle River, NJ: Prentice Hall PTR.

Coad, P., North, D., & Mayfield, M. (1997). *Object models: Strategies, patterns, and applications* (2nd ed.). Upper Saddle River, NJ: Prentice Hall.

Cockburn, A. (2001a). *Writing effective use cases*. Reading, MA: Addison-Wesley.

Cockburn, A. (2001b). *Agile software development*. Reading, MA: Addison-Wesley Professional.

Commerce, X. I. (2013). *Magento documentation*. Retrieved January 6, 2013, from http://docs.magentocommerce.com/

Copernicus, N. (1543). *De revolutionibus orbium coelestium*. Nuremburg.

Coplien, J., Hoffman, D., & Weiss, D. (1998). Commonality and variability in software engineering. *IEEE Software, 15*, 37–45.

Czarnecki, K., & Eisenecker, U. (2000). *Generative programming: Methods, tools, and applications*. Boston: Addison Wesley.

Czarnecki, K., Helsen, S., & Eisenecker, U. (2004). Staged configuration using feature models. *Lecture Notes in Computer Science, 3154*, 266–283.

Dahchour, M., & Pirotte, A. (2002). Materialization and its metaclass implementation. *IEEE Transactions on Knowledge and Data Engineering, 14*(5), 1078–1094. doi:10.1109/TKDE.2002.1033775.

Dalle, O., Ribault, J., & Himmelspach, J. (2009). Design considerations for M&S software. In M. D. Rosseti, R. R. Hill, B. Johansson, A. Dunkin, & R. G. Ingalls (Eds.), *Proceedings of the WSC 2009 Winter Simulation Conference* (pp. 944-955). Austin, TX: WSC.

Daniel, P. (2012). *13 reasons for UML's descent into darkness*. Retrieved from http://littletutorials.com/2008/05/15/13-reasons-for-umls-descent-into-darkness/

Dardenne, A., van Lamsweerde, A., & Fickas, S. (1991). Goal-directed requirements acquisition. *Science of Computer Programming, 20*(1-2), 3–50. doi:10.1016/0167-6423(93)90021-G.

Darimont, R., & Lemoine, M. (2006). Goal-oriented analysis of regulations. In *Proceedings of the International Workshop on Regulations Modelling and their Validation and Verification, REMO2V'06*, (pp. 838-844). REMO2V.

Darwin, C. (1859). *On the origin of species*. London: John Murray.

Darwin, C., & Wallace, A. R. (1858). On the tendency of species to form varieties, and on the perpetuation of varieties and species by natural means of selection. *Journal of the Proceedings of the Linnean Society of London Zoology, 3*, 46–50. doi:10.1111/j.1096-3642.1858.tb02500.x.

Davis, J., & Chang, E. (2011a). Lifecycle and generational application of automated updates to MDA based enterprise information systems. In *Proceedings of the Second Symposium on Information and Communication Technology (SoICT '11)*, (pp. 207-216). ACM.

Davis, J., & Chang, E. (2011b). Variant logic meta-data management for model driven applications applications - Allows unlimited end user configuration and customization of all meta-data EIS application features. In *Proceedings of the 13th International Conference on Enterprise Information Systems (ICEIS 2011)*, (pp. 395-400). SciTePress.

Davis, J., & Chang, E. (2011c). Temporal meta-data management for model driven applications - Provides full temporal execution capabilities throughout the meta-data EIS application lifecycle. In *Proceedings of the 13th International Conference on Enterprise Information Systems (ICEIS 2011)*, (pp. 376-379). SciTePress.

Davis, J., & Chang, E. (2011d). Automatic application update with user customization integration and collision detection for model driven applications. In *Proceedings of the World Congress on Engineering and Computer Science 2011*, (pp. 1081-1086). Newswood Limited.

Davis, J., Tierney, A., & Chang, E. (2004). Meta data framework for enterprise information systems specification - Aiming to reduce or remove the development phase for EIS systems. In *Proceedings of the 6th International Conference on Enterprise Information Systems (ICEIS 2004)*, (pp. 451-456). SciTePress.

Dawes, S. S., Pardo, T. A., & Cresswell, A. M. (2004). Designing electronic government information access programs: A holistic approach. *Government Information Quarterly*, *21*(1), 3–23. Retrieved from http://www.sciencedirect.com/science/article/B6W4G-4B71BC0-1/2/0ffcef06875aa7c64fdf9b510e62466b doi:10.1016/j.giq.2003.11.001.

De Alwis, B., & Sillito, J. (2009). Why are software projects moving from centralized to decentralized version control systems? In *Proceedings of the 2009 ICSE Workshop on Cooperative and Human Aspects on Software Engineering*, (pp. 36-39). IEEE Computer Society.

Debabbi, M., Hassaine, F., Jarraya, Y., Soeanu, A., & Alawneh, L. (2010). *Verification and validation in systems engineering - Assessing UML/SysML design models*. Berlin: Springer. doi:10.1007/978-3-642-15228-3.

Deissenboeck, F., & Ratiu, D. (2006). A unified meta model for concept-based reverse engineering. In *Proceedings of 3rd International Workshop on Metamodels, Schemes, Grammars, and Ontologies for Reverse Engineering*. Retrieved September 24, 2012, 2011 from http://planet-mde.org/atem2006/atem06Proceedings.pdf

deLara, J., & Vangheluwe, H. (2002). AToM3: A tool for multi-formalism and meta-modelling. In Kutsche, R.-D., & Weber, H. (Eds.), *Fundamental Approaches to Software Engineering* (pp. 174–188). Berlin: Springer.

DenHaan, J. (2008). *8 reasons why model-driven aproaches (will) fail*. Retrieved September, 2012, from http://www.infoq.com/articles/8-reasons-why-MDE-fails

Denning, P. J., Dennis, J. B., & Qualitz, J. E. (1978). *Machines, languages, and computation*. Englewood Cliffs, NJ: Prentice-Hall.

Descartes, R. (1637). *Discours de la méthode*.

Descartes, R. (1644). *Principia philosophiae*.

Deursen, A. V., Klint, P., & Visser, J. (2000). Domain-specific languages: An annotated bibliography. *ACM SIGPLAN Notices*, *35*(6), 26–36.

Di Lucca, G., Fasolino, A., & De Carlini, U. (2000). Recovering use case models from object-oriented code: A thread-based approach. In *Proceedings of the Seventh Working Conference on Reverse Engineering (WCRE 2000)*, (pp. 108-117). WCRE.

Di Marco, A., & Mirandola, R. (2006). *Model transformation in software performance engineering*. Paper presented at the International Conference on Quality of Software Architectures. New York, NY.

Distefano, S. (2005). *Software performance analysis in uml models*. Paper presented at the Workshop on Techniques, Methodologies and Tools for Performance Evaluation of Complex System. New York, NY.

Dörge, F. C. (2004). *Illocutionary acts: Austin's account and what Searle made of it. Inaugural-Dissertation zur Erlangung des Grades eines Doktors der Philosophie*. Eberhard-Karls-Universität Tübingen.

Dorin, P., & Murray, W. (2002). *Software performance models from system scenarios in use case maps*. Paper presented at the 12th International Conference on Computer Performance Evaluation, Modelling Techniques and Tools. London, UK.

Dorina, P. D. (2000). *Deriving performance models from UML models by graph transformations*. Paper presented at the Tutorials, Workshop on Software and Performance. New York, NY.

Dörr, J. (2010). *Elicitation of a complete set of non-functional requirements*. (Doctoral Dissertation). University of Kaiserslautern. Stuttgart: Fraunhofer Verlag.

Draijer, C., & Schenk, D. (2004). Best practices of business simulation with SAP R/3. *Journal of Information Systems Education, 15*(3), 261. Retrieved from http://findarticles.com/p/articles/mi_qa4041/is_200410/ai_n9464918/pg_5/.

Ducasse, S., Girba, T., Kuhn, A., & Renggli, L. (2009). Meta-environment and executable meta-language using Smalltalk: An experience report. *Software & Systems Modeling, 8*(1), 5–19. doi:10.1007/s10270-008-0081-4.

EAST-ADL Association. (2012). *Electronic architecture and software technology – Architecture description language*. Retrieved November 4, 2012, from http://www.east-adl.info

Eclipse Foundation. (2012a). *EMF compare project*. Retrieved November 4, 2012, from http://www.eclipse.org/emf/compare

Eclipse Foundation. (2012b). *Eclipse modeling project*. Retrieved November 4, 2012, from http://www.eclipse.org/modeling/

Eclipse Foundation. (2013a). *Ecore tools*. Retrieved from http://wiki.eclipse.org/index.php/Ecore_Tools

Eclipse Foundation. (2013b). *Graphical modeling framework (GMF) tooling*. Retrieved from http://www.eclipse.org/projects/project.php?id=modeling.gmp.gmf-tooling

Eclipse Foundation. (2013c). *MOFScript documentation*. Retrieved from http://www.eclipse.org/gmt/mofscript/doc/

Eder, J., & Liebhart, W. (1996). Workflow transactions. In *Workflow Handbook 1997* (pp. 195–202). New York: John Wiley & Sons, Inc. Retrieved from http://citeseerx.ist.psu.edu/viewdoc/summary?doi=10.1.1.21.7110

Egea, M. (2005). *ITP/OCL: A theorem prover-based tool for UML+OCL class diagrams*. (Master Thesis). Departamento de Sistemas Informáticos y Programación, Universidad Complutense de Madrid, Madrid, Spain.

Egea, M., & Rusu, V. (2010). Formal executable semantics for conformance in the MDE framework. *Innovations in System Software Engineering, 6*(1-2), 73–81. doi:10.1007/s11334-009-0108-1.

Egginton, W., & Sandbothe, M. (2004). *The pragmatic turn in philosophy: Contemporary engagements between analytic and continental thought*. State Albany, NY: University of New York Press.

Ehrig, K., Küster, J. M., & Taentzer, G. (2009). Generating instance models from meta models. *Software & Systems Modeling, 8*(4), 479–500. doi:10.1007/s10270-008-0095-y.

Ekstedt, M., Johnson, P., Plazaola, L., Silva, E., & Lilieskold, J. (2004). Consistent enterprise software system architecture for the CIO - A utility-cost based approach. In *Proceedings of the 37th Annual Hawaii International Conference on System Sciences* (pp. 8-8). IEEE.

Elberzhager, F., Münch, J., & Nha, V. T. N. (2012). A systematic mapping study on the combination of static and dynamic quality assurance techniques. *Information and Software Technology, 54*, 1–15. doi:10.1016/j.infsof.2011.06.003.

Elena, G.-M., & Jose, M. (2005). *A software performance engineering tool based on the UML-SPT*. Paper presented at the International Conference on the Quantitative Evaluation of Systems. New York, NY.

Elena, G.-M., & José, M. (2006). *ArgoSPE: Model-Based software performance engineering*. Paper presented at the International Conference on Applications and Theory of Petri Nets and Other Models of Concurrency. New York, NY.

Endres, A., & Rombach, D. (2003). *A handbook of software and systems engineering*. Amsterdam: Addison-Wesley Longman.

Engelsman, W., Quartela, D., Jonkers, H., & van Sinderen, M. (2010). Extending enterprise architecture modelling with business goals and requirements. *Journal of Enterprise Information Systems*, *5*(1), 9–36. doi:10.1080/175 17575.2010.491871.

Eric, W., Robert, L., & Victor, R. (2011). An assessment of systems and software engineering scholars and institutions (2003–2007 and 2004–2008). *Journal of Systems and Software*, *84*(1), 162–168.

Eriksson, O., Henderson-Sellers, B., & Ågerfalk, P. J. (2013). *Ontological and linguistic metamodelling revisited – A language use approach*. Unpublished.

Eriksson, O., & Ågerfalk, P. J. (2010). Rethinking the meaning of identifiers in information infrastructures. *Journal of the Association for Information Systems*, *11*(8), 433–454.

Ernst, M., Matthes, F., Ramacher, R., & Schweda, C. (2009). Using enterprise architecture management patterns to complement TOGAF. In *Proceedings of the Enterprise Distributed Object Computing Conference, EDOC 2009*. IEEE.

Eugster, P. T., Damm, C. H., & Guerraoui, R. (2004). Towards safe distributed application development. In *Proceedings of the 26th International Conference on Software Engineering (ICSE '04)*, (pp. 347-356). IEEE Computer Society.

Evgeni, D., Andreas, S., & Reiner, D. (2002). UML-based performance engineering possibilities and techniques. *IEEE Software*, *19*(1), 74–83. doi:10.1109/52.976944.

Fabrício Gomes, D. F., & Jerffeson Teixeira, D. S. (2011). *Ten years of search based software engineering: A bibliometric analysis*. Paper presented at the International Symposium on Search-Based Software Engineering. New York, NY.

Falbo, R., Guizzardi, G., & Duarte, K. C. (2002). An ontological approach to domain engineering. In *Proceedings of the International Conference on Software Engineering and Knowledge Engineering SEKE'02*. Ischia, Italy: ACM Press.

Faroughian, F. F., Kalafatis, S. P., Ledden, L., Samouel, P., & Tsogas, M. H. (2012). Value and risk in business-to-business e-banking. *Industrial Marketing Management*, *41*(1), 68–81. doi:10.1016/j.indmarman.2011.11.012.

Favre, J.-M. (2004). Foundations of meta-pyramids: Languages vs. metamodels: Episode II: Story of Thotus the baboon. In *Proceedings of Dagstuhl Seminar 04101 ''Language Engineering for Model-Driven Software Development''*. Dagstuhl.

Favre, L. Martinez, L., & Pereira, C. (2009). MDA-based reverse engineering of object-oriented code. In *Proceedings EMMSAD 2009* (LNBIP), (Vol. 29, pp. 251-263). Berlin: Springer-Verlag.

Favre, J. M., Bézivin, J., & Bull, I. (2006). Evolution, rétro-ingénierie et IDM: Du code aux modèles. In *L'ingénierie dirigée par les modèles* (pp. 185–215). Hermes Science.

Favre, J.-M., & NGuyen, T. (2005). Towards a megamodel to model software evolution through transformations. *Electronic Notes in Theoretical Computer Science*, *127*(3), 59–74. doi:10.1016/j.entcs.2004.08.034.

Favre, L. (2006). A rigorous framework for model driven development. In Siau, K. (Ed.), *Advanced Topics in Database Research* (Vol. 5, pp. 1–27). Hershey, PA: Idea Group Publishing. doi:10.4018/978-1-59140-935-9.ch001.

Favre, L. (2009). A formal foundation for metamodeling. In *Proceedings of Reliable Software Technologies, ADA Europe 2009 (LNCS)* (Vol. 5570, pp. 177–191). Heidelberg, Germany: Springer-Verlag. doi:10.1007/978-3-642-01924-1_13.

Favre, L. (2010). *Model driven architecture for reverse engineering technologies: Strategic directions and system evolution*. Hershey, PA: IGI Global. doi:10.4018/978-1-61520-649-0.

Favre, L., Pereira, C., & Martinez, L. (2009). Foundations for MDA case tools. In Khosrow-Pour, M. (Ed.), *Encyclopedia of Information Science and Technology* (2nd ed., pp. 159–166). Hershey, PA: IGI Global.

Feiler, P., Wrage, L., & Hansson, J. (2010). *System architecture virtual integration: A case study*. Retrieved from http://www.erts2010.org

Firesmith, D. G. (2005). Are your requirements complete? *Journal of Object Technology, 4*(1), 27–43. doi:10.5381/jot.2005.4.1.c3.

Firesmith, D., Henderson-Sellers, B., & Graham, I. (1997). *OPEN modeling language (OML) reference manual.* New York: SIGS Books.

Flatscher, R. G. (2002). Metamodeling in EIA/CDIF – Meta-metamodel and metamodels. *ACM Transactions on Modeling and Computer Simulation, 12*(4), 322–342. doi:10.1145/643120.643124.

Fleurey, F., & Solberg, A. (2009). A domain specific modeling language supporting specification, simulation and execution of dynamic adaptive systems. In *Proceedings of MODELS 2009* (LNCS), (vol. 5795, pp. 606-621). Berlin: Springer.

Fleurey, F., Breton, E., Baudry, B., Nicolas, A., & Jézéquel, J. (2007). Model-driven engineering for software migration in a large industrial context. In Engels, G., Opdyke, B., Schmidt, D. C., & Weil, F. (Eds.), *MoDELS 2007 (LNCs) (Vol. 4735,* pp. 482–497). Berlin: Springer-Verlag. doi:10.1007/978-3-540-75209-7_33.

Fondement, F., & Baar, T. (2005). Making metamodels aware of concrete syntax. *Lecture Notes in Computer Science, 3748,* 190–204.

Fontoura, M., Pree, W., & Rumpe, B. (2000). *The UML profile for framework architectures.* Boston, MA: Addison-Wesley Longman Publishing Co..

Fountain, J. E. (2001). Building the virtual state: Information technology and institutional change. *Information Systems Research, 7,* xii. Retrieved from http://isr.journal.informs.org/cgi/content/abstract/7/1/22.

Fowler, M. (2011). Domain specific languages. *Martin Fowler.* Retrieved August 13, 2012, from http://martinfowler.com/bliki/DomainSpecificLanguage.html

Fowler, M. (1997). *Analysis patterns reusable object models.* Boston, MA: Addison-Wesley Longman Publishing Co., Inc..

Fowler, M. (2010). Domain specific languages. *International Journal of Computers and Applications, 1,* 39–60. Retrieved from http://martinfowler.com/dslwip/.

France, R., & Rumpe, B. (2007). Model-driven development of complex software: A research roadmap. In *Proceedings of Future of Software Engineering (FOSE 2007),* (pp. 37-54). IEEE Computer Society.

Free Software Foundation. I. (2009). Bison -- GNU parser generator. *The GNU Operating System.* Retrieved August 10, 2012, from http://www.gnu.org/software/bison/

Frege, G. (1892a). Über sinn und bedeutung. In Zeitschrift für Philosophie und philosophische Kritik, 100, 25-50.

Frege, G. (1892b). Über begriff und gegenstand. In Vierteljahrsschrift für Wissenschaftliche Philosophie, 16, 192-205.

Frege, G. (1884). *Die grundlagen der arithmetik.* Breslau.

Frege, G. (1950). *The foundations of arithmetic* (Austin, J. L., Trans.). Oxford, UK: Basil Blackwell.

Fried, H. (2000). *Using UML models for performance calculation.* Paper presented at the 2nd International Workshop on Software and Performance. Ottawa, Canada.

Friedl, J. (2006). *Mastering regular expressions* (3rd ed.). Sebastopol, CA: O'Reilly Media, Inc..

Fuentes, J. M., Quintana, V., Llorens, J., Génova, G., & Prieto-Diaz, R. (2003). Errors in the UML metamodel? *ACM SIGSOFT Software Engineering Notes, 28*(6), 3. doi:10.1145/966221.966236.

Galilei, G. (1610). *Sidereus nuncius.*

Galilei, G. (1632). *Dialogue concerning the two chief world systems.*

Garcia, A., Ruiz, B., Lopez, J. L., & Gonzalez, I. (2011). Semantic model for knowledge representation in e-business. *Knowledge-Based Systems, 24*(2), 282–296. doi:10.1016/j.knosys.2010.09.006.

Gargantini, A., Riccobene, E., & Scandurra, P. (2009). A semantic framework for metamodel-based languages. *Journal of Automated Software, 16*(3-4), 415–454. doi:10.1007/s10515-009-0053-0.

Garousi, V. (2011). Classification and trend analysis of UML books (1997-2009). *Journal on Software & System Modeling.*

Garousi, V., Krishnamurthy, D., & Shahnewaz, S. (2012). *UML-driven software performance engineering: A systematic mapping.* Paper presented at the http://www.softqual.ucalgary.ca/projects/SM/UML_SPE

Garousi, V., Mesbah, A., Betin-Can, A., & Mirshokraie, S. (2012). A systematic mapping of web application testing. *Information and Software Technology.*

Garousi, V., & Varma, T. (2010). A bibliometric assessment of Canadian software engineering scholars and institutions (1996-2006). *Canadian Journal on Computer and Information Science, 3*(2), 19–29.

Garshol, L. (2010). *BNF and EBNF: What are they and how do they work?* Retrieved August 16, 2012, from http://www.garshol.priv.no/download/text/bnf.html

Gaynor, M., & Bradner, S. (2004). A real options framework to value network, protocol, and service architecture. *SIGCOMM Computer Communications Review, 34*(5), 31–38. doi:10.1145/1039111.1039121.

Genova, G. (2010). Is computer science truly scientific? *Communications of the ACM, 53*(7), 37–39. doi:10.1145/1785414.1785431.

Gilgarcia, J., & Pardo, T. (2005). E-government success factors: Mapping practical tools to theoretical foundations. *Government Information Quarterly, 22*(2), 187–216. Retrieved July 3, 2011, from http://linkinghub.elsevier.com/retrieve/pii/S0740624X05000158

Glass, R. L. (1995). An assessment of systems and software engineering scholars and institutions (1993-1994). *Journal of Systems and Software, 31*(1), 3–6. doi:10.1016/0164-1212(95)00058-9.

Glass, R. L., & Chen, T. Y. (2001). An assessment of systems and software engineering scholars and institutions (1996-2000). *Journal of Systems and Software, 59*(1), 107–113. doi:10.1016/S0164-1212(01)00052-8.

Glass, R. L., & Chen, T. Y. (2002). An assessment of systems and software engineering scholars and institutions (1997-2001). *Journal of Systems and Software, 64*(1), 79–86. doi:10.1016/S0164-1212(02)00023-7.

Goethals, F., Vandenbulcke, J., & Lemahieu, W. (2004). Developing the extended enterprise with the FADEE. In *Proceedings of the 2004 ACM Symposium on Applied Computing (SAC '04),* (pp. 1372-1379). ACM.

Gogolla, M., Bohling, J., & Richters, M. (2005). Validating UML and OCL models in USE by automatic snapshot generation. *Software & Systems Modeling, 4*(4), 386–398. doi:10.1007/s10270-005-0089-y.

Gonzalez-Perez, C., & Henderson-Sellers, B. (2006). A powertype-based metamodelling framework. *Software & Systems Modeling, 5*(1), 72–90. doi:10.1007/s10270-005-0099-9.

Gonzalez-Perez, C., & Henderson-Sellers, B. (2007). Modelling software development methodologies: A conceptual foundation. *Journal of Systems and Software, 80*(11), 1778–1796. doi:10.1016/j.jss.2007.02.048.

Gonzalez-Perez, C., & Henderson-Sellers, B. (2008). *Metamodelling for software engineering.* Chichester, UK: John Wiley & Sons.

González, R., Martinez, O. S., Cueva, J., Garcia-Bustelo, B. C., Gayo, J. E. L., & Ordoñez, P. (2011). Recommendation system based on user interaction data applied to intelligent electronic books. *Computers in Human Behavior, 27*(4), 1445–1449. doi:10.1016/j.chb.2010.09.012.

Gortmaker, J., Janssen, M., & Wagenaar, R. W. (2005). Towards requirements for a reference model for process orchestration in e-government. In M. Böhlen, J. Gamper, W. Polasek, & M. A. Wimmer (Eds.), *EGovernment Towards Electronic Democracy* (Vol. 3416, pp. 169–180). Springer. Retrieved from http://springerlink.metapress.com/(hgp11niu3o1t4b552xj3zy55)/app/home/contribution.asp?referrer=parent&backto=issue,16,28,journal,526,3824,linkingpublicationresults,1:105633,1

Grady, J. O. (1997). *System validation and verification.* Boca Raton, FL: CRC Press.

Graham, I. M., Bischof, J., & Henderson-Sellers, B. (1997). Associations considered a bad thing. *Journal of Object-Oriented Programming, 9*(9), 41–48.

Grandon, E., & Pearson, M. (2004). Electronic commerce adoption: An empirical study of small and medium US businesses. *Information & Management, 42*(1), 197–216. Retrieved from http://dx.doi.org/10.1016/j.im.2003.12.010

Gray, I., & Audsley, N. C. (2011). Targeting complex embedded architectures by combining the multicore communications API (MCAPI) with compile-time virtualisation. In *Proceedings of the ACM SIGPLAN/SIGBED Conference on Languages, Compilers, and Tools for Embedded Systems* (pp. 51-60). Chicago, IL: ACM.

Greenfield, J., & Short, K. (2004a). *Software factories: Industrialized software development.* Retrieved August 20, 2012, from http://www.softwarefactories.com/index.html

Greenfield, J., & Short, K. (2004b). *Software factories: Assembling applications with patterns, models, frameworks, and tools.* Indianapolis, IN: Wiley Publishing Inc..

Gu Gordon, P. (2002). *XSLT transformation from UML models to LQN performance models.* Paper presented at the 3rd International Workshop on Software and Performance. Rome, Italy.

Gu Gordon, P., & Petriu, D. C. (2005). *From UML to LQN by XML algebra-based model transformations.* Paper presented at the International Workshop on Software and Performance. New York, NY.

Guarino, N. (1998). Formal ontology and information systems. In N. Guarino (Ed.), *Formal Ontology in Information Systems: Proceedings of the International Conference on Formal Ontology and Information Systems (FOIS).* IOS Press.

Guarino, N., & Welty, C. (2000). A formal ontology of properties. In R. Dieng & O. Corby (Eds.), *Proceedings 12th International Conference on Knowledge Engineering and Knowledge Management,* (LNCS), (vol. 1937, pp. 97-112). Berlin: Springer-Verlag.

Guarino, N., & Welty, C. (2001). Identity and subsumption: LADSEB-CNR internal report 01/2001. In Green, R., Bean, C. A., & Myaeng, S. H. (Eds.), *The Semantics of Relationships: An Interdisciplinary Perspective.* Dordrecht, The Netherlands: Kluwer.

Guerra, E., de Lara, J., Kolovos, D., Paige, R., & Marchi dos Santos, O. (2010). transML: A family of languages to model model transformations. In *Proceedings of MODELS 2010* (LNCS), (vol. 6394). Berlin: Springer-Verlag.

Guizzardi, G. (2005). *Ontological foundations for structural conceptual models.* CTIT PhD Thesis Series, No. 05-74, Enschede, The Netherlands.

Guizzardi, G. (2006). Agent roles, qua individuals and the counting problem. In Garcia, Choren, Pereira de Lucena, Giorgini, Holvoet, & Romanovky (Eds.), Software Engineering for Multi-Agent Systems IV, Research Issues and Practical Applications (LNCS), (vol. 3914, pp. 143-160). Berlin: Springer-Verlag.

Guizzardi, G., Wagner, G., Guarino, N., & van Sinderen, M. (2004). An ontologically well-founded profile for UML conceptual models. In A. Persson & J. Stirna (Eds.), *16th International Conference on Advances in Information Systems Engineering (CAiSE'04),* (LNCS), (vol. 3084, pp. 122-126). Berlin: Springer-Verlag.

Guizzardi, G., & Wagner, G. (2005). Towards ontological foundations for agent modelling concepts using the unified foundational ontology (UFO). In Bresciani, P., Giorgini, P., Henderson-Sellers, B., Low, G., & Winikoff, M. (Eds.), *Agent-Oriented Information Systems II (LNAI)* (*Vol. 3508,* pp. 110–124). Berlin: Springer-Verlag. doi:10.1007/11426714_8.

Gupta, M. (2003). E-government evaluation: A framework and case study. *Government Information Quarterly, 20*(4), 365–387. Retrieved July 11, 2011, from http://linkinghub.elsevier.com/retrieve/pii/S0740624X03000790

Guy, W. (2012). *Ranting about UML tools.* Retrieved from http://www.cs.bgu.ac.il/~gwiener/software-engineering/ranting-about-uml-tools-part-1/

Habermas, J. (1979). What is universal pragmatics? In Habermas, J. (Ed.), *Communication and the Evolution of Society* (McCarthy, T., Trans.). London: Heinemann.

Hagen, C., & Brouwers, G. (1994). Reducing software life-cycle costs by developing configurable software. In *Proceedings of the Aerospace and Electronics Conference,* (vol. 2, pp. 1182-1187). IEEE Press.

Hakojarvi, M., Hautala, M., Ahokas, J., Oksanen, T., Maksimow, T., & Aspiala, A. et al. (2010). Platform for simulation of automated crop production. *Agronomy Research*, 8(1), 797–806.

Halchin, L. E. (2004). Electronic government: Government capability and terrorist resource. *Government Information Quarterly*, 21(4), 406–419. Retrieved from http://www.sciencedirect.com/science/article/B6W4G-4DTKPJW-1/2/f6b622cecc53f2d033cfc84e8827b67d doi:10.1016/j.giq.2004.08.002.

Hall, R. J. (2008). Validating real time specifications using real time event queue modeling. In *Proceedings of the 23rd IEEE/ACM International Conference on Automated Software Engineering* (pp. 79-88). L'Aquila, Italy: IEEE.

Halpin, T. (2005). Higher order types and information modeling. In Siau, K. (Ed.), *Advanced Topics in Database Research*. Hershey, PA: Idea Group. doi:10.4018/978-1-59140-471-2.ch010.

Halpin, T., & Bloesch, A. (1999). Data modeling in UML and ORM: A comparison. *Journal of Database Management*, 10(4), 4–13. doi:10.4018/jdm.1999100101.

Hansson, D. (2011). *Ruby on rails*. Retrieved August 20, 2012, from http://rubyonrails.org

Harel, D., & Kugler, H. (2002). Synthesizing state-based object systems from LSC specifications. *Foundation of Computer Science*, 13(1), 5–51. doi:10.1142/S0129054102000935.

Harel, D., & Rumpe, B. (2000). *Modeling languages: Syntax, semantics and all that stuff, part I: The basic stuff*. Israel: Weizmann Science Press of Israel.

Hassan, G. (2000). Performance engineering of component-based distributed software systems. In *Performance Engineering, State of the Art and Current Trends* (pp. 40–55). London: Springer-Verlag.

Hayat Khan, R., & Heegaard, P. E. (2010). *Translation from UML to SPN model: A performance modeling framework*. Paper presented at the International Conference on Computer Design and Applications. New York, NY.

Henderson, J. C., & Venkatraman, N. (1993). Strategic alignment: Leveraging information technology for transforming organizations. *IBM Systems Journal*, 32(1), 4–16. doi:10.1147/sj.382.0472.

Henderson-Sellers, B., & Edwards, J. M. (1994). booktwo of object-oriented knowledge: The working object. New York: Prentice-Hall.

Henderson-Sellers, B., & Gonzalez-Perez, C. (2005). The rationale of powertype-based metamodelling to underpin software development methodologies. *Australian Conferences in Research and Practice in Information Technology, 43*, 7-16.

Henderson-Sellers, B., & Gonzalez-Perez, C. (2006). On the ease of extending a powertype-based methodology metamodel. In Proceedings of Meta-Modelling and Ontologies WoMM 2006. WoMM.

Henderson-Sellers, B. (1994). Methodologies - Frameworks for OO success. *American Programmer*, 7(10), 2–11.

Henderson-Sellers, B. (2006). Method engineering: theory and practice. In Karagiannis, D., & Mayr, H. C. (Eds.), *Information Systems Technology and its Applications (LNI)*. Bonn: Gesellschaft für Informatik.

Henderson-Sellers, B. (2011a). Bridging metamodels and ontologies in software engineering. *Journal of Systems and Software, 84*, 301–313. doi:10.1016/j.jss.2010.10.025.

Henderson-Sellers, B. (2011b). Random thoughts on multi-level conceptual modelling. In Delcambre, L., & Kaschek, R. (Eds.), *The Evolution of Conceptual Modeling (LNCS)* (Vol. 6520, pp. 93–116). Berlin: Springer-Verlag. doi:10.1007/978-3-642-17505-3_5.

Henderson-Sellers, B. (2012). *On the mathematics of modelling, metamodelling, ontologies and modelling languages*. Berlin: Springer. doi:10.1007/978-3-642-29825-7.

Henderson-Sellers, B., & Bulthuis, A. (1998). *Object-oriented metamethods*. New York: Springer. doi:10.1007/978-1-4612-1748-0.

Henderson-Sellers, B., & Unhelkar, B. (2000). *OPEN modeling with UML*. Reading, MA: Addison-Wesley.

Hesse, W. (2006). More matters on (meta-)modeling: Remarks on Thomas Kühne's matters. *Software & Systems Modeling, 5*(4), 387–394. doi:10.1007/s10270-006-0033-9.

Hillyer, C., Bolte, J., van Evert, F., & Lamaker, A. (2003). The ModCom modular simulation system. *European Journal of Agronomy, 18*, 333–343. doi:10.1016/S1161-0301(02)00111-9.

Hoare, C. (1985). *Communicating sequential processes.* New York: Prentice-Hall International.

Holtmann, J., Meyer, J., & Meyer, M. (2011). A seamless model-based development process for automotive systems. In *Proceedings of Software Engineering 2011 Workshops including Doctoral Symposium* (pp. 79-88). Karlsruhe, Germany: Bonner Köllen Verlag.

Huang, C.-Y., Tzeng, G.-H., & Ho, W.-R. J. (2011). System on chip design service e-business value maximization through a novel MCDM framework. *Expert Systems with Applications, 38*(7), 7947–7962. doi:10.1016/j.eswa.2010.12.022.

Hucka, M. et al. (2003). The systems biology markup language (SBML): A medium for representation and exchange of biochemical network models. *Bioinformatics (Oxford, England), 19*(4), 524–531. PMID:12611808.

Hui, B., Liaskos, S., & Mylopoulos, J. (2003). Requirements analysis for customisable software: A goals-skills-preferences framework. In *Proceedings of the 11th IEEE International Requirements Engineering Conference,* (pp. 117-126). IEEE Press.

Hui, S. (2005). *Performance analysis of UML models using aspect-oriented modeling techniques.* Paper presented at the 8th International Conference on Model Driven Engineering Languages and Systems. Montego Bay, Jamaica.

Hume, D. (1739). *A treatise of human nature.* Oxford, UK: Oxford University Press.

Husserl, E. (1900). *Logische untersuchungen: Erster teil: Prolegomena zur reinen logik.*

Husserl, E. (1901). *Logische untersuchungen: Zweiter teil: Untersuchungen zur phänomenologie und theorie der erkenntnis.*

Husserl, E. (1939). Erfahrung und urteil: Untersuchungen zur genealogie der logik (experience and judgment). (J.S. Churchill & K. Amerika, Trans.). Lodnon: Routledge.

Iacob, M., Jonkers, H., & Wiering, M. (2004). *Towards a UML profile for the ArchiMate language.* Retrieved from https://doc.telin.nl/dscgi/ds.py/Get/File-47276

IEC. (2012). *IEC 61508: Functional safety of electrical/electronic/programmable electronic safety-related systems.* IEC.

IMPULSE. (2002). *Project IST-1999-21119.* Retrieved from http://cordis.europa.eu/search/index.cfm?fuseaction=proj.document&PJ_LANG=PL&PJ_RCN=4850507&pid=270&q=D67BEC82A602A23FF8B013B7DA527238&type=pro

International Council on System Engineering. (2011). *INCOSE systems engineering handbook, version 3.2.2.* Retrieved from http://www.incose.org

ISO. (1986). *Standard generalized markup language (SGML)* (Vol.[]. International Organization for Standardization.]. *ISO, 8879,* 155.

ISO. (1996). Syntactic metalanguage -- Extended BNF (Vol. ISO/IEC 14977:1996, pp. 12). International Organization for Standardization.

ISO. (2005). XML metadata interchange (XMI) (Vol. ISO/IEC 19503:2005, pp. 115). International Organization for Standardization.

ISO. (2008). Database languages -- SQL -- Part 2: Foundation (SQL/foundation) (Vol. ISO/IEC 9075:2008, pp. 1317). International Organization for Standardization.

ISO/IEC. (1995). *Software life cycle processes ISO/IEC 12207.* Geneva: International Standards Organization/International Electrotechnical Commission.

ISO/IEC. (2007). *Software engineering - Metamodel for development methodologies, ISO/IEC 24744.* Geneva: International Organization for Standardization/International Electrotechnical Commission.

ITU. (2008). *Formal description techniques (FDT) – User requirements notation recommendation Z.151 (11/08).* Retrieved September 3, 2012, from http://www.itu.int/rec/T-REC-Z.151-200811-I/en

Ivar, J., Martin, G., & Patrik, J. (1997). *Software reuse: Architecture, process and organization for business success.* New York, NY: ACM Press/Addison-Wesley Publishing Co..

Jackie, F. (1995). *When to leap on the hype cycle.* Gartner Inc..

Jackson, E., & Sztipanovits, J. (2009). Formalizing the structural semantics of domain-specific modeling languages. *Software & Systems Modeling, 8*(4), 451–478. doi:10.1007/s10270-008-0105-0.

Jagudin, E., Remar, A., Pop, A., & Fritzson, P. (2006). OpenModelica MDT eclipse plugin for modelica development, code browsing, and simulation. In *Proceedings of the 47th Conference on Simulation and Modelling.* Helsinki, Finland: IEEE.

Jallas, E. (1998). *Improved model-based decision support by modeling cotton variability and using evolutionary algorithms. (Unpublished PhD).* Mississippi: Mississippi State University.

James, S., & Wolfgang, E. (2003). *A model-driven approach to non-functional analysis of software architectures.* Paper presented at the 18th IEEE International Conference on Automated Software Engineering. New York, NY.

James, S., & Wolfgang, E. (2004). *Model driven performance analysis of enterprise information systems.* Paper presented at the International Workshop on Test and Analysis of Component Based Systems. Warsaw, Poland.

Jamieson, P. D., Semenov, M. A., Brooking, I. R., & Francis, G. S. (1998). Sirius: A mechanistic model of wheat response to environmental variation. *European Journal of Agronomy, 8*, 161–179. doi:10.1016/S1161-0301(98)00020-3.

Jansen, S., Brinkkemper, S., & Helms, R. (2008). Benchmarking the customer configuration updating practices of product software vendors. In *Proceedings of the 7th International Conference on Composition Based Software Systems* (pp. 82-91). IEEE Computer Society.

Jensen, K. (1997). *Coloured Petri nets: Basic concepts, analysis methods, and practical use.* Berlin: Springer Verlag. doi:10.1007/978-3-642-60794-3.

Jill, J., Lydia, M., & Fiona, L. (2011). *Doing your literature review: Traditional and Systematic techniques.* Thousand Oaks, CA: SAGE Publications.

Jing, X., Murray, W., & Dorina, P. (2003). *Performance analysis of a software design using the uml profile for schedulability, performance, and time.* Paper presented at the 13th International Conference on Modelling Techniques and Tools for Computer Performance Evaluation. Urbana, IL.

Johansson, I. (2005). Qualities, quantities, and the endurant-perdurant distinction in top-level ontologies. In Althoff, K.-D., Dengel, A., Bergmann, R., Nick, M., & Roth-Berghofer, T. (Eds.), *WM 2005: Professional Knowledge Management Experiences and Vision.* DFKI.

Johnson, S. (1979). YACC-yet another compiler-compiler. In *UNIX Programmer's Manual.* AT&T Bell Laboratories.

Jones, S. (2002). *Haskell 98 language and libraries: The revised report.* Retrieved August 20, 2012, from http://www.haskell.org/onlinereport/

Jonkers, H., Lankhorst, M., Buuren, R., Bonsangue, M., & Van Der Torre, L. (2004). Concepts for modeling enterprise architectures. *International Journal of Cooperative Information Systems, 13*, 257–287. doi:10.1142/S0218843004000985.

Jose, M., Javier, C., & Eduardo, M. (2000a). *A pattern-based approach to model software performance.* Paper presented at the 2nd International Workshop on Software and Performance. Ottawa, Canada.

Jose, M., Javier, C., & Eduardo, M. (2000b). *A Pattern-based approach to model software performance using UML and Petri nets: Application to agent-based systems.* Paper presented at the International Workshop on Software and Performance. New York, NY.

Jose, M., Javier, C., & Eduardo, M. (2000c). *A pattern-based approach to model software performance using UML and Petri nets: Application to agent-based systems.* Paper presented at the 2nd International Workshop on Software and Performance. Ottawa, Canada.

Jose, M., Javier, C., & Eduardo, M. (2000d). *Performance evaluation for the design of agent-based systems: A Petri net approach.* Paper presented at the Workshop on Software Engineering and Petri Nets, within the 21st International Conference on Application and Theory of Petri Nets. Aarhus, Denmark.

Jose, M., Javier, C., Simona, B., & Susanna, D. (2002). *A compositional semantics for UML state machines aimed at performance evaluation.* Paper presented at the Sixth International Workshop on Discrete Event Systems. New York, NY.

José, M., & Javier, C. (2003). Software performance modeling using UML and petri nets. In Calzarossa, M. A. G. (Ed.), *Performance Tools and Applications to Networked Systems (LNCS)* (Vol. 2965, pp. 265–289). Berlin: Springer.

Jouault, F., & Bézivin, J. (2006). KM3: A DSL for metamodel specification.[LNCS]. *Proceedings of Formal Methods for Open Object-Based Distributed Systems, 4037*, 171–185. doi:10.1007/11768869_14.

Kaisler, S. H. (2005). *Software paradigms.* Hoboken, NJ: John Wiley & Sons.

Kang, K., Cohen, S., Hess, J., Novak, W., & Peterson, A. (1990). *Feature-oriented domain analysis (FODA) feasibility study (Online No. CMU/SEI-90-TR-021).* Pittsburgh, PA: Carnegie Mellon University Software Engineering Institute.

Kaschek, R. (2011). Introduction: Issues of a conceptual modeling agenda. In Kaschek, R., & Delcambre, L. (Eds.), *The Evolution of Conceptual Modeling (LNCS)* (Vol. 6520, pp. ix–xv). Berlin: Springer. doi:10.1007/978-3-642-17505-3.

Kauremaa, J., Nurmilaakso, J.-M., & Kari, T. (2010). E-business enabled operational linkages: The role of RosettaNet in integrating the telecommunications supply chain. *International Journal of Production Economics, 127*(2), 343–357. doi:10.1016/j.ijpe.2009.08.024.

Kaur, P., & Singh, H. (2009). Version management and composition of software components in different phases of the software development life cycle. *ACM Sigsoft Software Engineering Notes, 34*(4), 1–9. doi:10.1145/1543405.1543416.

Kavakli, E. (2002). Goal-oriented requirements engineering: A unified framework. *Requirements Engineering, 6*(4), 237–251. doi:10.1007/PL00010362.

KDM. (2011). *Knowledge discovery metamodel, version 1.3.* OMG Document Number: formal/2011-08-04. Retrieved September 24, 2012, from http://www.omg.org/spec/KDM/1.3

Kehn, D., Fairbrother, S., & Le, C.-T. (2002). *How to internationalize your eclipse plug-in.* Retrieved from http://www.eclipse.org/articles/Article-Internationalization/how2I18n.html

Kelly, S., & Pohjonen, R. (2009). Worst practices for domain-specific modeling. *Software, 26*(4), 22–29. doi:10.1109/MS.2009.109.

Kelly, S., & Tolvanen, J. (2008). *Domain-specific modeling.* Hoboken, NJ: John Wiley & Sons, Inc..

Kendra, C., Lirong, D., Yi, D., & Jing, D. (2003). *Modeling performance as an aspect: A UML based approach.* Paper presented at the 4th AOSD Modeling With UML Workshop. San Francisco, CA.

Kendra, C., Lirong, D., & Yi, D. (2004). Performance modeling and analysis of software architectures: An aspect-oriented UML based approach. *Science of Computer Programming, 57*(1), 89–108.

Kent, S., Evans, A., & Rumpe, B. (1999). UML semantics FAQ. In Moreira, A., & Demeyer, S. (Eds.), *ECOOP'99 Workshops (LNCS)* (Vol. 1743, pp. 33–56). Berlin: Springer-Verlag.

Kepler, (1627). *Rudolphine tables.*

Kepler, J. (1596). *Mysterium cosmographicum.*

Kepler, J. (1609). *Astronomia nova.*

Kepler, J. (1617-1621). *Epitome of Copernican astronomy.*

Kitchenham, B., Brereton, O. P., Budgen, D., Turner, M., Bailey, J., & Linkman, S. (2009). Systematic literature reviews in software engineering – A systematic literature review. *Information and Software Technology, 51*(1), 7–15. doi:10.1016/j.infsof.2008.09.009.

Kitchenham, B., & Charters, S. (2007). *Guidelines for performing systematic literature reviews in software engineering.* Evidence-Based Software Engineering.

Kleppe, A. (2007). *A language description is more than a metamodel.* Paper presented at ATEM2007 (part of MoDELS2007). IEEE.

Kleppe, A. (2008). *Software language engineering: Creating domain-specific languages using metamodels.* Reading, MA: Addison-Wesley Professional.

Klischewski, R. (2004). Information integration or process integration? How to achieve interoperability in administration. *Electronic Government, 3183,* 57–65. Retrieved from http://www.springerlink.com/index/cndhp3plq6pt05x3.pdf

Knuth, D. (1964). Backus normal form vs. Backus naur form. *Communications of the ACM, 7*(12), 735–736.

Koegel, M., Herrmannsdoerfer, M., von Wesendonk, O., & Helming, J. (2010). Operation-based conflict detection. In *Proceedings of the 1st International Workshop on Model Comparison in Practice (IWMCP '10),* (pp. 21-30). ACM.

Kolahdouz-Rahimi, S., Lano, K., Pillay, S., Troya, J., & Van Gorp, P. (2012). Goal-oriented measurement of model transformation methods. *Science of Computer Programming.*

Kolovos, D. S., Rose, L. M., Abid, S. B., Paige, R. F., Polack, F. A. C., & Botterweck, G. (2010). EuGENia: Taming EMF and GMF using model transformation. In *Proceedings of the 13th International Conference, MODELS 2010, Model Driven Engineering Languages and Systems* (pp. 211-225). Oslo, Norway: Springer.

Kornecki, A. J., & Johri, S. (2006). Automatic code generation: Model-code semantic consistency. In H. R. Arabnia & H. Reza (Eds.), *Proceedings of the 2006 International Conference on Software Engineering and Practice SERP'06* (pp. 191-197). Las Vegas, NV: SERP.

Kramer, J. (2007). Is abstraction the key to computing? *Communications of the ACM, 50*(4), 36–42.

Kühne, T. (2007). *Making modeling languages fit for model-driven development.* Paper presented at ATEM2007 (part of MoDELS2007). IEEE.

Kühne, T. (2009). Contrasting classification with generalization. In M. Kirchberg & S. Link (Eds.), *Proceedings of the Sixth Asia-Pacific Conference on Conceptual Modelling,* (pp. 71-78). IEEE.

Kühne, T. (2006). Matters of (meta-)modeling. *Software & Systems Modeling, 5,* 369–385. doi:10.1007/s10270-006-0017-9.

Kühne, T. (2006a). Matters of (meta-) modeling. *Software & Systems Modeling, 5*(4), 369–385. doi:10.1007/s10270-006-0017-9.

Kühne, T. (2006b). Clarifying matters of (meta-) modeling: An author's reply. *Software & Systems Modeling, 5*(4), 395–401. doi:10.1007/s10270-006-0034-8.

Kuhn, T. (1962). *The structure of scientific revolutions.* Chicago, IL: University of Chicago Press.

Kurtev, I., Bézivin, J., Joualt, F., & Valduriez, P. (2006). Model-based DSL frameworks. In *Proceedings of OOPSLA'06: Companion to the 21st ACM SIGPLAN Conference on Object-Oriented Programming Systems, Languages, and Applications.* ACM.

Kuske, S., Gogolla, M., Kreowski, H.-J., & Ziemann, P. (2009). Towards an integrated graph-based semantics for UML. *Software & Systems Modeling, 8*(3), 403–422. doi:10.1007/s10270-008-0101-4.

Kyas, M., Fecher, H., de Boer, F., Jacob, J., Hooman, J., & van der Zwaag, M. et al. (2005). Formalizing UML models and OCL constraints in PVS. *Electronic Notes in Theoretical Computer Science, 115,* 39–47. doi:10.1016/j.entcs.2004.09.027.

Laarman, A., & Kurtev, I. (2010). Ontological metamodelling with explicit instantiation. In van den Brand, M., Gašević, D., & Gray, J. (Eds.), *SLE2009 (LNCS) (Vol. 5969,* pp. 174–183). Berlin: Springer-Verlag.

Lakoff, G. (1987). *Women, fire, and dangerous things: What categories reveal about the mind.* Chicago, IL: University of Chicago Press. doi:10.7208/chicago/9780226471013.001.0001.

Lamarck, J.-B. (1809). *Philosophie zoologique, ou exposition des considérations relatives à l'histoire naturelle des animaux.* Paris.

Lankhorst, M. (2009). *Introduction to enterprise architecture.* Berlin: Springer-Verlag.

Lankhorst, M., Proper, E., & Jonkers, J. (2010). The anatomy of the ArchiMate language. *International Journal of Information System Modeling and Design, 1*(1). doi:10.4018/jismd.2010092301.

Lano, K., & Kolahdouz-Rahimi, S. (2010a). Specification and verification of model transformations using UML-RSDS. In *Proceedings of IFM 2010* (LNCS), (vol. 6396, pp. 199-214). Berlin: Springer.

Lano, K., & Kolahdouz-Rahimi, S. (2010b). Migration case study using UML-RSDS. In *Proceedings of TTC 2010*. Malaga, Spain: TTC.

Lano, K., & Kolahdouz-Rahimi, S. (2011a). Model-driven development of model transformations. In *Proceedings of ICMT 2011*. ICMT.

Lano, K., & Kolahdouz-Rahimi, S. (2011c). Specification of the GMF migration case study. In *Proceedings of TTC 2011*. TTC.

Lano, K., & Kolahdouz-Rahimi, S. (2011c). Specification of the hello world case study. In *Proceedings of TTC 2011*. TTC.

Lano, K., Kolahdouz-Rahimi, S., & Clark, T. (2012). Comparison of verification techniques for model transformations. In *Proceedings of Modevva Workshop, MODELS 2012*. MoDeVVa.

Lano, K. (2009). A compositional semantics of UML-RSDS. *SoSyM, 8*(1), 85–116. doi:10.1007/s10270-007-0064-x.

Lano, K. (Ed.). (2009). *UML 2 semantics and applications*. New York: Wiley. doi:10.1002/9780470522622.

Lano, K., & Kolahdouz-Rahimi, S. (2011b). Slicing techniques for UML models. *Journal of Object Technology, 10*, 1–49. doi:10.5381/jot.2011.10.1.a11.

Larman, C. (2004). *Applying UML and patterns: An introduction to object-oriented analysis and design and iterative development* (3rd ed.). Upper Saddle River, NJ: Prentice Hall.

Lee, K., Kang, K., & Lee, J. (2002). *Concepts and guidelines of feature modeling for product line software engineering*. Paper presented at the 7th International Conference on Software Reuse: Methods, Techniques, and Tools. Austin, TX.

Leon, A. (2008). *Enterprise resource planning*. Retrieved from http://books.google.es/books?hl=es&lr=&id=pTGDy2GX_sUC&oi=fnd&pg=PT20&dq=ENTERPRISE+RESOURCE+PLANNING&ots=Apu7El9-p3&sig=0x5rNgyVcMhCeYNgwnywc0IZGKE

Lesk, M. (1975). *Lex: A lexical analyzer generator*. Murray Hill, NJ: Bell Laboratories.

Letier, E. et al. (2008). Deriving event-based transition systems from goal-oriented requirements models. *Automated Software Engineering, 15*(2), 175–206. doi:10.1007/s10515-008-0027-7.

Lewis, D. (1971). Counterparts of persons and their bodies. *The Journal of Philosophy, 68*, 203–211. doi:10.2307/2024902.

Liberty, J., & Horovitz, A. (2008). *Programming: NET 3.5*. O'Reilly Media, Inc..

Liskov, B. (1987). Data abstraction and hierarchy. In *Addendum to the Proceedings OOPSLA (Addendum)*. ACM.

Liu, L., Yu, E., & Myopoulos, J. (2003). Security and privacy requirements analysis with a social setting. In *Proceedings of the 11th IEEE International Conference on Requirements Engineering*. IEEE.

Liu, H. H. (2011). *Software performance and scalability: A quantitative approach*. New York: John Wiley & Sons. doi:10.1002/9781118135532.

Locke, J. (1975). *An essay concerning human understanding*. Oxford, UK: Oxford University Press.

Louarn, G. (2009). *Analyse et modélisation de l'organogénèse et de l'architecture d'un rameau de vigne (vitis vinifiera l.)*. (Unpublished PhD). Ecole nationale supérieure agronomique de Montpellier, Montpellier, France.

Lowe, E. J. (2001). *The possibility of metaphysics: Substance, identity and time*. Oxford, UK: Oxford University Press. doi:10.1093/0199244995.001.0001.

Luftman, J. (2000). Assessing business-IT alignment maturity. *Strategies for Information Technology Governance, 4*(14), 99.

Lukas, P., Simon, S., Michael, G., Peter, M., & Volker, D. (2009). A practical approach for performance-driven UML modelling of handheld devices – A case study. *Journal of Systems and Software*, *82*(1), 75–88. doi:10.1016/j.jss.2008.03.065.

Ma, X., Baresi, L., Ghezzi, C., Panzica, V., Manna, L., & Lu, J. (2011). Version-consistent dynamic reconfiguration of component-based distributed systems. In *Proceedings of the 19th ACM SIGSOFT Symposium and the 13th European Conference on Foundations of Software Engineering (ESEC/FSE '11)* (pp. 245-255). ACM.

MacBride, F. (2011). Impure reference: A way around the concept *horse* paradox. *Philosophical Perspectives*, *25*(1), 297–312. doi:10.1111/j.1520-8583.2011.00217.x.

MacDonald, A., Russell, D., & Atchison, B. (2005). Model driven development within a legacy system: An industry experience report. In *Proceeding of 2005 Australian Software Engineering Conference ASWEC 05* (pp. 14-22). IEEE Press.

Maier, M. W., & Rechtin, E. (2009). *The art of systems architecting*. Boca Raton, FL: CRC Press.

Margolis, E., & Laurence, S. (2012). Concepts. In E. N. Zaltz (Ed.), *The Stanford Encyclopedia of Philosophy*. Retrieved from http://plato.stanford.edu/archives/fall2012/entries/concepts/

Marston, S., Li, Z., Bandyopadhyay, S., Zhang, J., & Ghalsasi, A. (2011). Cloud computing — The business perspective. *Decision Support Systems*, *51*(1), 176–189. doi:10.1016/j.dss.2010.12.006.

Martin-Clouaire, R., & Rellier, J.-P. (2009). Modelling and simulating work practices in agriculture. *International Journal of Metadata. Semantics and Ontologies*, *4*(1/2), 42–53. doi:10.1504/IJMSO.2009.026253.

Martin, J. (1967). *Design of real-time computer systems*. Upper Saddle River, NJ: Prentice-Hall, Inc..

Martin, J., & Odell, J. J. (1992). *Object-oriented analysis and design*. Englewood Cliffs, NJ: Prentice-Hall.

Martin, J., & Odell, J. J. (1995). *Object-oriented methods: A foundation*. Upper Saddle River, NJ: Prentice Hall.

Martin, J., & Odell, J. J. (1998). *Object-oriented methods: A foundation*. Upper Saddle River, NJ: Prentice Hall.

Masolo, C., Guizzardi, G., Vieu, L., Bottazzi, E., & Ferrario, R. (2005). Relational roles and qua-individuals. In *Proceedings AAAI Fall Symposium on Roles, an Interdisciplinary Perspective,* (pp. 103-112). AAAI.

Mathias, F., Hugo, B., & Bert, V. (2009). *Applying megamodelling to model driven performance engineering*. Paper presented at the IEEE International Conference and Workshop on the Engineering of Computer Based Systems. New York, NY.

Mathias, F., Wasif, G., Christoph, F., Ivor, S., Peter, K., & John, B. (2008). *Towards utilizing model-driven engineering of composite applications for business performance analysis*. Paper presented at the 4th European Conference on Model Driven Architecture: Foundations and Applications. Berlin, Germany.

Mathias, F., & Jendrik, J. (2008). Putting performance engineering into model-driven engineering: Model-driven performance engineering. In Giese, H. (Ed.), *Models in Software Engineering* (pp. 164–175). Berlin: Springer-Verlag.

MathWorks. (2012). *Simulink's verification, validation and test module*. Retrieved November 4, 2012, from http://www.mathworks.com/verification-validation

McBride, C., Goguen, H., & McKinna, J. (2006). A few constructions on constructors. *Lecture Notes in Computer Science*, *3839*, 186–200. doi:10.1007/11617990_12.

McBride, T., & Henderson-Sellers, B. (2011). A method assessment framework. In Ralyté, J., Mirbel, I., & Deneckère, R. (Eds.), *Engineering Methods in the Service-Oriented Context*. Berlin: Springer. doi:10.1007/978-3-642-19997-4_7.

McCarthy, J. (1965). *LISP 1.5 programmer's manual*. Cambridge, MA: The MIT Press.

McGregor, J. D., & Korson, T. (1993). Supporting dimensions of classification in object-oriented design. *Journal of Object-Oriented Programming*, *5*(9), 25–30.

McNeile, A., & Roubtsova, E. (2007). Protocol modelling semantics for embedded systems. In *Proceedings of the Special Session on Behavioural Models for Embedded Systems at the IEEE Second International Symposium on Industrial Embedded Systems, SIES'2007*. Lisbon, Portugal: IEEE.

McNeile, A., & Roubtsova, E. (2008). CSP parallel composition of aspect models. In *Proceedings of the International Workshop on Aspect-Oriented Modelling, AOM'08*. ACM Press.

McNeile, A., & Simons, N. (2011). *Modelscope*. Retrieved September 3, 2012, from http://www.metamaxim.com

McNeile, A., & Roubtsova, E. (2010). Aspect-oriented development using protocol modeling. *Transactions on Aspect-Oriented Software Development, 7*, 115–150.

McNeile, A., & Simons, N. (2006). Protocol modelling: A modelling approach that supports reusable behavioural abstractions. *Software & Systems Modeling, 5*(1), 91–107. doi:10.1007/s10270-005-0100-7.

MDA. (2012). *The model-driven architecture*. Retrieved September 24, 2012, from http://www.omg.org/mda/

Means, G., & Schneider, D. (2000). *MetaCapitalism: The e-business revolution and the design of 21st-century companies and markets*. New York: Wiley. Retrieved from http://www.amazon.ca/exec/obidos/redirect?tag=citeulike09-20&amp,path=ASIN/0471393355

Medini. (2012). *Medini QVT*. Retrieved September 24, 2012, from http://projects.ikv.de/qvt

Merilinna, J., & Pärssinen, J. (2010). *Verification and validation in the context of domain-specific modelling*. Paper presented at the DSM'10 10th Workshop on Domain-Specific Modelling. Reno, NV.

Mernik, M., Heering, J., & Sloane, A. M. (2005). When and how to develop domain-specific languages. *ACM Computing Surveys, 37*(4), 316–344.

Merseguer, J., & Campos, J. (2003). *Exploring roles for the UML diagrams in software performance engineering*. Paper presented at the International Conference on Software Engineering Research and Practice. New York, NY.

Meyer, B. (1988). *Object-oriented software construction*. Hemel Hempstead, UK: Prentice-Hall.

Microsoft. (2011). *Microsoft Excel 2010*. Microsoft.

Microsoft. (2012). *Z3 theorem prover*. Retrieved from http://research.microsoft.com/en-us/um/redmond/projects/z3/

Miguel, D., Thomas, L., Mehdi, H., Stéphane, B.-B., & Sophie, P. (2000). *UML extensions for the specification and evaluation of latency constraints in architectural models*. Paper presented at the 2nd International Workshop on Software and Performance. Ottawa, Canada.

Milicev, D. (2007). On the semantics of associations and association ends in UML. *IEEE Transactions on Software Engineering, 33*(4), 238–251. doi:10.1109/TSE.2007.37.

Milne, A. A. (1926). In which pooh goes visiting and gets into a tight place. In *Winnie-the-Pooh*. London: Methuen & Co. Ltd., London.

Ministry of Defence. (1997). Defence standard 00-55: Requirements for safety-related software in defence equipment. Ministry of Defence.

Mirco, T., & Stephen, G. (2008). *Automatic extraction of PEPA performance models from UML activity diagrams annotated with the MARTE profile*. Paper presented at the International Workshop on Software and Performance. New York, NY.

MoDisco. (2012). *Model discovery*. Retrieved September 24, 2012, from http://www.eclipse.org/MoDisco

MOF. (2011). *Meta object facility (MOF) core specification version 2.4.1*. OMG Document Number: formal/2011-08-07. Retrieved September 24, 2012, from http://www.omg.org/spec/MOF/2.4.1

Mohagheghi, P., Gilani, W., Stefanescu, A., Fernandez, M. A., Nordmoen, B., & Fritzsche, M. (2011). Where does model-driven engineering help? Experiences from three industrial cases. *Software & Systems Modeling*, 1–21.

Moitra, D., & Ganesh, J. (2005). Web services and flexible business processes: Towards the adaptive enterprise. *Information & Management, 42*(7), 921–933. Retrieved from http://linkinghub.elsevier.com/retrieve/pii/S0378720604001338 doi:10.1016/j.im.2004.10.003.

Monarchi, D., Booch, G., Henderson-Sellers, B., Jacobson, I., Mellor, S., Rumbaugh, J., & Wirfs-Brock, R. (1994). Methodology standards: help or hindrance? *ACM SIGPLAN, 29*(10), 223–228. doi:10.1145/191081.191115.

Moreno, M., & Simonetta, B. (2004). *UML-PSI: The UML performance simulator*. Paper presented at the Quantitative Evaluation of Systems, First International Conference. Torino, Italy.

Morin, B., Barais, O., Jézéquel, J.-M., Fleurey, F., & Solberg, A. (2009). Models@Run.time to support dynamic adaptation. *IEEE Computer, 42*(10), 44–51. doi:10.1109/MC.2009.327.

Muller, P.-A., Fleurey, F., & Jézéquel, J.-M. (2005). *Weaving executability into object-oriented meta-languages*. Paper presented at the MODELS 2005. Montego Bay, Jamaica.

Murray, W., Hui, S., Toqeer, I., & Jose, M. (2005). *Performance by unified model analysis (PUMA)*. Paper presented at the 5th International Workshop on Software and Performance. Palma, Spain.

Murray-Rust, P. (1997). Chemical markup language. *World Wide Web Journal, 2*(4), 135–147.

Muthig, D., & Atkinson, C. (2002). *Model-driven product line architectures*. Paper presented at the 2nd International Conference on Software Product Lines. San Diego, CA.

Nariman, M., & Vahid, G. (2008). *A UML-based conversion tool for monitoring and testing multi-agent systems*. Paper presented at the IEEE International Conference on Tools with Artificial Intelligence. New York, NY.

Navy Modeling and Simulation Management Office. (2004). *Modeling and simulation verification, validation and accreditation implementation handbook*. Washington, DC: Department of the Navy.

Neumayr, B., Schrefl, M., & Thalheim, B. (2011). Modeling techniques for multi-level abstraction. In Kaschek, R., & Delcambre, L. (Eds.), *The Evolution of Conceptual Modeling, (LNCS) (Vol. 6520*, pp. 68–92). Berlin: Springer. doi:10.1007/978-3-642-17505-3_4.

Newton, I. (1687). *Philosophiæ naturalis principia mathematica*.

Niemann, K. (2006). *From enterprise architecture to IT governance: Elements of elective IT management*. Vieweg+ Teubner Verlag.

Nitu. (2009). Configurability in SaaS (software as a service) applications. In *Proceedings of the 2nd India Software Engineering Conference (ISEC '09)* (pp. 19-26). ACM.

Noonan, H. (2011). Identity. In E. N. Zaltz (Ed.), *The Stanford Encyclopedia of Philosophy*. Retrieved from http://plato.stanford.edu/archives/win2011/entries/identity/

Northrop, L. M. (2002). SEI's software product line tenets. *IEEE Software, 19*(4), 32–40.

Nurmilaakso, J.-M. (2008). EDI, XML and e-business frameworks: A survey. *Computers in Industry, 59*(4), 370–379. doi:10.1016/j.compind.2007.09.004.

Nurmilaakso, J.-M., & Kotinurmi, P. (2004). A review of XML-based supply-chain integration. *Production Planning and Control, 15*(6), 608–621. doi:10.1080/095372 80412331283937.

Object Management Group (OMG). (1999). *RFP for scheduling, performance, and time*. OMG document number ad/99-03-13.

Object Management Group (OMG). (2003). *UML profile for schedulability, performance and time (SPT), version 1.0*. Retrieved from http://www.omg.org/spec/SPTP/1.0/

Object Management Group (OMG). (2005a). *RFP for UML profile for modeling and analysis of real-time and embedded systems (MARTE)*. OMG document: real-time/05-02-06.

Object Management Group (OMG). (2005b). *UML profile for schedulability, performance and time (SPT), version 1.1*. Retrieved from http://www.omg.org/spec/SPTP/1.1/

Object Management Group (OMG). (2011). *UML profile for MARTE: Modeling and analysis of real-time embedded systems, version 1.1*. Retrieved from http://www.omg.org/spec/MARTE/1.1

Object Management Group (OMG). (2012). *UML metamodel superstructure specification*. Retrieved from http://www.omg.org/spec/UML/2.4.1/Superstructure/PDF

Object Management Group. (2006). *Meta-object facility (MOF) core specification*. OMG document formal/06-01-01.

Object Management Group. (2009). *UML superstructure, version 2.3*. OMG document formal/2010-05-05.

Object Management Group. (2011). *Requirements interchange format, version 1.0.1*. Retrieved November 4, 2012, from http://www.omg.org/spec/ReqIF

Object Management Group. (2012a). *Modeling and analysis of real-time and embedded systems*. Retrieved November 4, 2012, from http://www.omg.org/omgmarte

Object Management Group. (2012b). *Systems modeling language*. Retrieved November 4, 2012, from http://www.sysml.org

OCL. (2012). *OCL: Object constraint language: Version 2.3.1*. OMG Document Number: formal/2012-01-01. Retrieved September 24, 2012, from http://www.omg.org/spec/OCL/2.3.1/

Odell, J. (1994). Power types. *Journal of Object-Oriented Programming, 7*(2), 8–12.

OED. (1942). *The pocket oxford dictionary of current English* (Fowler, F. G., & Fowler, H. W., Eds.). 4th ed.). Oxford, UK: Clarendon Press.

Office Québécois de la Langue Française. (2002). *Grand dictionnaire terminologique*. Author.

Ogden, C. K., & Richards, I. A. (1923). *The meaning of meaning*. New York: Harcourt, Brace and World.

Oliveira, F. M. (2007). *Performance testing from UML models with resource descriptions*. Paper presented at the Brazilian Workshop on Systematic and Automated Software Testing. Sao Paolo, Brazil.

OMG & Specification. (2008). *Semantics of business vocabulary and business rules*. OMG.

OMG. (1997). *UML notation: Version 1.1*. OMG document ad/97-08-05.

OMG. (2000). *Request for proposal: UML 2.0 infrastructure RFP*. OMG Document Number ad/2000-08-08.

OMG. (2002). *Unambiguous UML (2U) submission to UML 2 infrastructure RFP*. OMG Document number ad/2002-06-07.

OMG. (2003). *Unified modeling language specification*. OMG document formal/03-03-01.

OMG. (2005). *XML metadata interchange V 2.1* (online no. formal/2009-02-04). OMG.

OMG. (2006). *Unified modeling language: Infrastructure: Version 2.0*. OMG Document Number formal/05-07-05.

OMG. (2006a). *Object constraint language V2.0 (online no. formal/2006-05-01)*. OMG.

OMG. (2006b). *Unified modeling language: Diagram interchange v 2.0* (online). OMG.

OMG. (2008). *Query/view/transformation, v1.0 (online)*. OMG.

OMG. (2009). *UML 2.2 infrastructure specification (online)*. OMG.

OMG. (2010). *OMG unified modeling language™ (OMG UML): Infrastructure version 2.3*. OMG Document Number formal/2010-05-03.

OMG. (2011a). *OMG unified modeling language™ (OMG UML): Infrastructure version 2.4.1*. OMG Document Number: formal/2011-08-05.

OMG. (2011b). *OMG unified modeling language™ (OMG UML): Superstructure version 2.4.1*. OMG Document Number: formal/2011-08-06.

OMG. (2012). OMG model driven architecture. *The Architecture of Choice for a Changing World*. Retrieved May 13, 2012, from http://www.omg.org/mda/

Opdahl, A., & Henderson-Sellers, B. (2004). A template for defining enterprise modelling constructs. *Journal of Database Management, 15*(2), 39–73. doi:10.4018/jdm.2004040103

Orejas, F., Guerra, E., de Lara, J., & Ehrig, H. (2009). Correctness, completeness and termination of pattern-based model-to-model transformation.[CALCO.]. *Proceedings of CALCO, 2009*, 383–397.

Öztayşi, B., & Kaya, T. (2011). Performance comparison based on customer relationship management using analytic network process. *Expert Systems with Applications, 38*(11), 9788–9798. doi:http://dx.doi.org/10.1016/j.eswa.2011.01.170

Pablo, L.-G. J., Jose, M., & Javier, C. (2002). *Performance engineering based on UML & SPN's: A software performance tool.* Paper presented at the 7th International Symposium on Computer and Information Sciences. Orlando, FL.

Pablo, L.-G. J., José, M., & Javier, C. (2004). *From UML activity diagrams to stochastic Petri nets: Application to software performance engineering.* Paper presented at the International Workshop on Software and Performance. New York, NY.

Paige, R., Brooke, P., & Ostroff, J. (2007). Metamodel-based model conformance and multiview consistency checking. *ACM Transactions on Software Engineering and Methodology, 16*(3). doi:10.1145/1243987.1243989.

Paley, W. (1809). *Natural theology: Or, evidences of the existence and attributes of the deity* (12th ed.). London: Printed for J. Faulder.

Papazoglou, M. P., & Georgakopoulos, D. (2003). Service-oriented computing. *Communications of the ACM, 46*(10), 24–28. Retrieved from http://ieeexplore.ieee.org/lpdocs/epic03/wrapper.htm?arnumber=1607964 doi:10.1145/944217.944233.

Papazoglou, M. P., & Heuvel, W. J. (2007). Service oriented architectures: approaches, technologies and research issues. *The VLDB Journal, 16*(3), 389–415. doi:10.1007/s00778-007-0044-3.

Parnas, D. (1976). On the design and development of program families. *IEEE Transactions on Software Engineering, 2*(1), 1–9.

Parnas, D. L. (1972). A technique for software module specification with examples. *Communications of the ACM, 15*(5), 330–336. doi:10.1145/355602.361309.

Parr, T. (2007). The definitive ANTLR reference: Building domain-specific languages. In *The pragmatic programmers* (p. 369). Raleigh, NC: Pragmatic Bookshelf.

Partridge, C. (2002). *Note: A couple of meta-ontological choices for ontological architectures.* Technical Report 06/02, LADSEB-CNR, Padova, Italy.

Partridge, C. (1996). *Business objects: Re-engineering for re-use.* Oxford, UK: Butterworth Heineman.

Pasic, A., Diez, S., & Espinosa, J. (2002). IMPULSE: Interworkflow model for e-government. In R. Traunmüller & K. Lenk (Eds.), Electronic Government (Vol. 2456, pp. 53–79). Springer. Retrieved fromhttp://dx.doi.org/doi:10.1007/3-540-46138-8_77.

Pastor, O., Levin, A. M., Celma, M., Casamayor, J. C., Virrueta, A., & Eraso, L. E. (2011). Model-based engineering applied to the interpretation of the human genome. In Kaschek, R., & Delcambre, L. (Eds.), *The Evolution of Conceptual Modeling, (LNCS)* (Vol. 6520, pp. 306–330). Berlin: Springer. doi:10.1007/978-3-642-17505-3_14.

Paxson, V. (1988). *Flex-fast lexical analyzer generator.* Free Software Foundation.

Peacocke, C. (1992). *A study of concepts.* Cambridge, MA: MIT Press.

Peirce, C. (1898). *Reasoning and the logic of things: The Cambridge conference lectures of 1898.* Harvard.

Pekka, K. (2001). UML-based performance modeling framework for component-based distributed systems. In *Performance Engineering, State of the Art and Current Trends* (pp. 167–184). London: Springer-Verlag.

Pennebaker, J. W., Mehl, M. R., & Niederhoffer, K. G. (2003). Psychological aspects of natural language use: Our words, our selves. *Annual Review of Psychology, 54,* 547–577. doi:10.1146/annurev.psych.54.101601.145041 PMID:12185209.

Pereira, C. M., & Sousa, P. (2005). Enterprise architecture: Business and IT alignment. In *Proceedings of the 2005 ACM Symposium on Applied Computing* (pp. 1345). ACM.

Peristeras, V., Loutas, N., Goudos, S., & Tarabanis, K. (2007). Semantic interoperability conflicts in pan-European public services. In H. Österle, J. Schelp, & R. Winter (Eds.), *15th European Conference on Information Systems ECIS 2007* (pp. 2173–2184). University of St. Gallen. Retrieved from http://is2.lse.ac.uk/asp/aspecis/20070128.pdf

Pete, M., & Rob, H. (2000). *PEPA performability modelling using UML statecharts.* Paper presented at the UK Performance Engineering Workshop. Durham, UK.

Peter, K., & Rob, P. (2000). *Derivation of Petri net performance models from UML specifications of communications software.* Paper presented at the International Conference on Computer Performance Evaluation: Modelling Techniques and Tools. New York, NY.

Petersen, K., Feldt, R., Mujtaba, S., & Mattsson, M. (2008). *Systematic mapping studies in software engineering.* Paper presented at the 12th International Conference on Evaluation and Assessment in Software Engineering (EASE). New York, NY.

Petri, K., & Marko, H. (2005). *Performance modeling and reporting for the UML 2.0 design of embedded systems.* Paper presented at the International Symposium on System-on-Chip. Tampere, Finland.

Petriu, D. B., & Murray, W. (2004). *A metamodel for generating performance models from UML designs.* Paper presented at the 7th International Conference on Modelling Languages and Applications. New York, NY.

Petriu, D. C., & Hui, S. (2002). *Applying the UML performance profile: Graph grammar-based derivation of LQN models from UML specifications.* Paper presented at the International Conference on Computer Performance Evaluation, Modelling Techniques and Tools. New York, NY.

Petriu, D. C., & Xin, W. (2000). *From UML descriptions of high-level software architectures to LQN performance models.* Paper presented at the International Workshop on Applications of Graph Transformations with Industrial Relevance. New York, NY.

Petriu, D. B., & Murray, W. (2007). An intermediate metamodel with scenarios and resources for generating performance models from UML designs. *Journal of Software and Systems Modeling, 6*(2), 163–184. doi:10.1007/s10270-006-0026-8.

Peurbach, G., & Regiomontanus, J. (1496). *Epitome of Ptolemy's almagest.*

Pflüger, A., Golubski, W., & Queins, S. (2011). Model driven validation of system architecture. In *Proceedings of the 13th IEEE International Symposium on High-Assurance Systems Engineering* (pp. 25-28). Boca Raton, FL: IEEE Computer Society.

Ping, G. G. (2003). *Early evaluation of software performance based on the UML performance profile.* Paper presented at the Conference of the Centre for Advanced Studies on Collaborative Research. New York, NY.

Pirotte, A., Zimányi, E., Massart, D., & Yakusheva, T. (1994). Materialization: A powerful and ubiquitous abstraction pattern. In J. Bocca, M. Jarke, & C. Zaniolo (Eds.), *20th International Conference on Very Large Data Bases* (pp. 630-641). Academic Press.

Poernomo, I. (2008). Proofs-as-model-transformations. In *Proceedings of the International Conference on Model Transformations* (LNCS), (vol. 5063, pp. 214-228). Berlin: Springer.

Poernomo, I., & Terrell, J. (2010). Correct-by-construction Model Transformations from Spanning tree specifications in Coq, *ICFEM 2010*.

Pohl, K. (2010). *Requirements engineering - Fundamentals, principles, and techniques.* Berlin: Springer. doi:10.1007/978-3-642-12578-2.

Ponsard, C., & Devroey, X. (2011). Generating high-level event-B system models from KAOS requirement models. In *Proceedings of Actes du XXIX eme Congres INFORSID*. INFORSID.

Pradal, C., Dufour-Kowalski, S., Boudon, F., Fournier, C., & Godin, C. (2008). OpenAlea: A visual programming and component-based software for plant modeling. *Functional Plant Biology, 35*(9-10), 751–760. doi:10.1071/FP08084.

Prestashop. (2013). *Prestashop.* Retrieved from http://www.prestashop.com/blog/en/upgrade-your-online-store-to-prestashop-v1-4-9/

Prieto-Diaz, R. (1990). Domain analysis: An introduction. *SIGSOFT Software Engineering Notes, 15*(2), 47–54.

Ptolemy, C. (150). *Almagest, originally entitled mathematike syntaxis.*

Qingfeng, Z., Wenbo, C., & Lihua, H. (2008). E-business transformation: An analysis framework based on critical organizational dimensions. *Tsinghua Science and Technology, 13*(3), 408–413. doi:10.1016/S1007-0214(08)70065-8.

Quesnel, G., Duboz, R., & Ramat, E. (2009). The virtual laboratory environment - An operational framework for multi-modelling, simulation and analysis of complex dynamical systems. *Simulation Modelling Practice and Theory, 17*(4), 641–653. doi:10.1016/j.simpat.2008.11.003.

Quine, W. V. O. (1953). *From a logical point of view*. Boston: Harvard University Press.

Quine, W. V. O. (1960). *Word and object*. Cambridge, MA: MIT Press.

Quine, W. V. O. (1969). *Ontological relativity and other essays*. New York: Columbia University Press.

QuYang. K. J., Juha-Pekka, S., & Kari, T. (2006). *Layered UML workload and SystemC platform models for performance simulation*. Paper presented at the International Forum on Specification and Design Languages. Darmstadt, Germany.

QVT. (2011). *QVT: MOF 2.0 query, view, transformation: Version 1.1*. OMG Document Number: formal/2011-01-01. Retrieved September 24, 2012, from http://www.omg.org/spec/QVT/1.1/

Raab, G., Ajami, R., Gargeya, V., & Goddard, G. J. (2008). *Customer relationship management: A global perspective*. Retrieved from http://books.google.es/books?id=MCKX _5Ur5rEC&printsec=frontcover&dq=customer+relatio nship&hl=es&sa=X&ei=kbzdUJWQFMu6hAeV0YC4 BA&ved=0CF8Q6AEwBg

Raffaela, M., & Vittorio, C. (2000). *UML-based performance modeling of distributed systems*. Paper presented at the 3rd International Conference on the Unified Modeling Language. York, UK.

Rajkovic, P., Jankovic, D., Stankovic, T., & Tosic, V. (2010). Software tools for rapid development and customization of medical information systems. In *Proceedings of 12th IEEE International Conference on e-Health Networking Applications and Services* (pp. 119-126). IEEE Computer Society.

Rasha, T., & Dorina, P. (2008). *Integrating performance analysis in the model driven development of software product lines*. Paper presented at the International Conference on Model Driven Engineering Languages and Systems. New York, NY.

RBS-CHANGE. (2013). *Guide du développeur*. Retrieved January 7, 2013, from http://wiki.rbschange.fr/ devguide:start

Regev, G., & Wegmann, A. (2011). Revisiting goal-oriented requirements engineering with a regulation view. *Lecture Notes in Business Information Processing, 109*.

Reige, C., & Aier, S. (2009). A consistency approach to enterprise architecture method engineering. In Proceedings of Service-Oriented Computing, ICSOC Workshops (pp. 388-399). Springer.

Reiner, D., Claus, R., Andreas, S., & Andre, S. (Eds.). (2001). *Performance engineering: State of the art and current trends*. Berlin: Springer.

Ren, Y., Xing, T., Quan, Q., & Zhao, Y. (2010). Software configuration management of version control study based on baseline. In *Proceedings of 3rd International Conference on Information Management, Innovation Management and Industrial Engineering*, (Vol. 4, pp. 118-121). IEEE Press.

Rensink, A., & Kuperus, J.-H. (2009). Repotting the geraniums: On nested graph transformation rules. In *Proceedings of GT-VMT 2009*. EASST.

Respect-IT. (2007). *A KAOS-tutorial*. Retrieved September 3, 2012, from http://www.objectiver.com/fileadmin/ download/documents/KaosTutorial.pdf

Reus, T., Geers, H., & van Deursen, A. (2006). Harvesting software system for MDA-based reengineering. *Lecture Notes in Computer Science, 4066*, 220–236. doi:10.1007/11787044_17.

Richters, M., & Gogolla, M. (1998). On formalising the UML object constraint language OCL. In *Proceedings of the 17th International Conference on Conceptual Modelling* (LNCS). Berlin: Springer.

Ritchey, T. (2012). Outline for a morphology of modelling methods: Contributions to a general theory of modelling. *Acta Morphologica Generalis, 1*(1), 1–20.

Rob, P. (1998). *Using UML to derive stochastic process algebra models*. Paper presented at the 15th UK Performance Engineering Workshop, Department of Computer Science. Bristol, UK.

Robinson, S. (2007). Editorial: The future's bright the future's... conceptual modelling for simulation! *Journal of Simulation, 1*, 149–152. doi:10.1057/palgrave.jos.4250026.

Robinson, S. (2008). Conceptual modelling for simulation part I: Definition and requirements. *The Journal of the Operational Research Society, 59*(3), 278–290. doi:10.1057/palgrave.jors.2602368.

Roubtsova, E. E. (2011). Reasoning on models combining objects and aspects. *Lecture Notes in Business Information Processing, 109*, 1–18. doi:10.1007/978-3-642-29788-5_1.

RTCA. (2012). *RTCA/EUROCAE DO-178C standard software considerations in airborne systems and equipment certification*. RTCA.

Runeson, P., Runeson, P., Rainer, A., & Regnell, B. (2012). *Case study research in software engineering: Guidelines and examples*. New York: John Wiley & Sons. doi:10.1002/9781118181034.

Sabri, P., & Thomas, F. (2002a). *On customizing the UML for modeling performance-oriented applications*. Paper presented at the 5th International Conference on The Unified Modeling Language. Dresden, Germany.

Sabri, P., & Thomas, F. (2002b). *UML-based modeling of performance oriented parallel and distributed applications*. Paper presented at the Winter Simulation Conference. San Diego, CA.

Sabri, P., & Thomas, F. (2005). *Performance prophet: A performance modeling and prediction tool for parallel and distributed programs*. Paper presented at the 2005 International Conference on Parallel Processing Workshops. Oslo, Norway.

Sacha, R., Andreas, M., & Klaus, P. (2006). *A reuse technique for performance testing of software product lines*. Paper presented at the International Workshop on Software Product Line Testing. New York, NY.

Salvatore, D., Daniele, P., Antonio, P., & Marco, S. (2004). *UML design and software performance modeling*. Paper presented at the 19th International Symposium on Computer and Information Sciences. Kemer-Antalya, Turkey.

Sanchez Cuadrado, J., de Lara, J., & Guerra, E. (2012). Bottom-up meta-modelling: An interactive approach. In R.B. France, J. Kazmeier, R. Breu, & C. Atkinson (Eds.), *Model Driven Engineering Languages and Systems: 15th International Conference, MODELS 2012*, (LNCS), (vol. 7590, pp. 3-19). Berlin: Springer-Verlag.

Schamai, W., Helle, P., Fritzson, P., & Paredis, C. J. J. (2010). Virtual verification of system designs against system requirements. In *Proceedings of Models in Software Engineering - Workshops and Symposia at MODELS 2010* (pp. 75–89). Oslo, Norway: Springer.

Scheidgen, M. (2008). *Textual modelling embedded into graphical modelling*. Paper presented at the EC-MDAFA'08 4th European Conference on Model Driven Architecture - Foundations and Applications. London, UK.

Schmid, K. (2002). *A comprehensive product line scoping approach and its validation*. Paper presented at the 24th International Conference on Software Engineering. Orlando, FL.

Schmidt, D. (2006). Introduction: Model-driven engineering. *IEEE Computer Science, 39*(2), 25–31. doi:10.1109/MC.2006.58.

Schmietendorf, A., & Dimitrov, E. (2001). Possibilities of performance modeling with UML. In *Performance Engineering, State of the Art and Current Trends* (pp. 78–95). Berlin: Springer.

Schuff, D., & St. Louis, R. (2001). Centralization vs. decentralization of application software. *Communications of the ACM, 44*(6), 88–94. doi:10.1145/376134.376177.

Searle, J. R. (1969). *Speech acts: An essay in the philosophy of language*. Cambridge, UK: Cambridge University Press. doi:10.1017/CBO9781139173438.

Searle, J. R. (1995). *The construction of social reality*. New York: The Free Press.

Seidewitz, E. (2003). What models mean. *IEEE Software, 20*, 26–31. doi:10.1109/MS.2003.1231147.

Selic, B. (2007). *A systematic approach to domain-specific language design using UML*. Paper presented at the 10th IEEE International Symposium on Object and Component-Oriented Real-Time Distributed Computing (ISORC '07). Santorini Island, Greece.

Selic, B. (2003). The pragmatics of model-driven development. *IEEE Software*, *20*, 19–25. Retrieved from http://ieeexplore.ieee.org/lpdocs/epic03/wrapper.htm?arnumber=1231146doi:10.1109/MS.2003.1231146.

Selic, B. (2011). The theory and practice of modeling language design for model-based software engineering – A personal perspective. In Fernandes, J. M., Läm-mel, R., Visser, J., & Saraiva, J. (Eds.), *Generative and Transformational Techniques in Software Engineering III International Summer School, GTTSE 2009, (LNCS)* (*Vol. 6491*, pp. 390–321). Berlin: Springer-Verlag. doi:10.1007/978-3-642-18023-1_7.

Selic, B. (2012). What will it take? A view on adoption of model-based methods in practice. *Software & Systems Modeling*, 1–14.

Selic, B. (2012b). What will it take? A view on adoption of model-based methods in practice. *Software & Systems Modeling*, *11*, 513–526. doi:10.1007/s10270-012-0261-0.

Selma, K., Ilyès, B., Ladjel, B., Eric, S., Stéphane, J., & Baron, M. (2012). Ontology-based structured web data warehouses for sustainable interoperability: Requirement modeling, design methodology and tool. *Computers in Industry, 63*(8), 799 – 812. Retrieved fromhttp://dx.doi.org/10.1016/j.compind.2012.08.001

Sengupta, B., & Roychoudhury, A. (2011). Engineering multi-tenant software-as-a-service systems. In *Proceedings of the 3rd International Workshop on Principles of Engineering Service-Oriented Systems (PESOS '11)*, (pp. 15-21). ACM.

Shan, L., & Zhu, H. (2012). Unifying the semantics of models and meta-models in the multi-layered UML meta-modelling hierarchy. *International Journal of Software Informatics*, *6*(2), 163–200.

Sider, T. (2003). *Four dimensionalism: An ontology of persistence and time*. Oxford, UK: Oxford University Press.

Silva, N., Viamonte, M. J., & Maio, P. (2009). Agent-based electronic market with ontology-services. In *Proceedings of the 2009 IEEE International Conference on e-Business Engineering*, (pp. 51–58). IEEE. doi:10.1109/ICEBE.2009.17

Simona, B., Susanna, D., & Jose, M. (2002). *From UML sequence diagrams and statecharts to analysable petri net models*. Paper presented at the International Workshop on Software and Performance. New York, NY.

Simona, B., & Jose, M. (2007). Performance evaluation of UML design with stochastic well-formed nets. *Journal of Systems and Software*, *80*(11), 1843–1865. doi:10.1016/j.jss.2007.02.029.

Simonetta, B., & Marta, S. (2011). *On transforming UML models into performance models*. Paper presented at the Workshop on Transformations in the Unified Modeling Language. Genova, Italy.

Simonetta, B., & Moreno, M. (2003a). *A simulation-based approach to software performance modeling*. Paper presented at the European Software Engineering Conference. Berlin, Germany.

Simonetta, B., & Moreno, M. (2003b). *Towards performance evaluation of mobile systems in UML*. Paper presented at the The European Simulation and Modelling Conference. Naples, Italy.

Simonetta, B., & Moreno, M. (2005). *Performance evaluation of UML software architectures with multiclass queueing network models*. Paper presented at the 5th International Workshop on Software and Performance. Palma, Spain.

Simonetta, B., Mattia, G., & Moreno, M. (2003). *Towards simulation-based performance modeling of UML specifications* (Technical Report CS-2003-2). Mestre, Italy: Dipartimento di Informatica, Universit`a Ca' Foscari di Venezia.

Simonetta, B., Di Marco, A., & Inverardi, P. (2004). Model-based performance prediction in software development: A survey. *IEEE Transactions on Software Engineering*, *30*(5), 295–310. doi:10.1109/TSE.2004.9.

Simos, M. (1995). *Organization domain modeling (ODM): Formalizing the core domain modeling life cycle*. Paper presented at the 1995 Symposium on Software Reusability. Seattle, WA.

Simos, M., Creps, D., Klingler, C., Levine, L., & Allemang, D. (1996). *Organization domain modeling (ODM) guidebook, version 2.0 (No. STARS-VC-A025/001/00). Software Technology For Adaptable, Reliable Systems*. STARS.

Slonneger, K., & Kurtz, B. (1995). *Formal syntax and semantics of programming languages.* Reading, MA: Addison-Wesley.

Smith, B. (2004). Beyond concepts: Ontology as reality representation. In A. Varzi & L. Vieu (Eds.), *Proceedings FOIS 2004: International Conference on Formal Ontology and Information Systems.* IOS Press.

Smith, C. U., Vittorio, C., & Di, M. A. (2005). *From UML models to software performance results: An SPE process based on XML interchange formats.* Paper presented at the International Workshop on Software and Performance. New York, NY.

Smith, B. (1997). On substances, accidents and universals: In defence of a constituent ontology. *Philosophical Papers, 27,* 105–127. doi:10.1080/05568649709506558.

SMM. (2012). *Software metrics meta-model, version 1.0.* OMG Document Number: formal/2012-01-05. Retrieved September 24, 2012, from http://www.omg.org/spec/SMM/1.0/

Soloway, E., Lampert, R., Letovsky, S., Littman, D., & Pinto, J. (1988). Designing documentation to compensate for delocalized plans. *Journal of Communication of the ACM, 31*(11), 1259–1267. doi:10.1145/50087.50088.

Sommerville, I. (2004). *Software engineering* (7th ed.). Reading, MA: Addison Wesley.

Song, C.-Y., & Baik, D.-K. (2003). A layered metamodel for hierarchical modeling in UML. *International Journal of Software Engineering and Knowledge Engineering, 13*(2), 191–214. doi:10.1142/S0218194003001263.

Soto, P., & Meroño, A. (2009). Evaluating internet technologies business effectiveness. *Telematics and Informatics, 26*(2), 211–221. doi:10.1016/j.tele.2008.01.004.

Sottara, D., Mello, P., & Proctor, M. (2010). A configurable rete-OO engine for reasoning with different types of imperfect information. *IEEE Transactions on Knowledge and Data Engineering, 22,* 1535–1548. doi:10.1109/TKDE.2010.125.

Sovran, Y., Power, R., Aguilera, M. K., & Li, J. (2011). Transactional storage for geo-replicated systems. In *Proceedings of the Twenty-Third ACM Symposium on Operating Systems Principles (SOSP '11),* (pp. 385-400). ACM.

Spencer, J. (2004). TOGAF enterprise Ed. Version 8.1.

Spiteri, S. T. (2008). *Intuitive mapping of UML 2 activity diagrams into fundamental modeling concept Petri net diagrams and colored Petri nets.* Paper presented at the 15th IEEE International Conference and Workshops on the Engineering of Computer-Based Systems. Seoul, Korea.

Sprinkle, J., & Karsai, G. G. (2004). A domain-specific visual language for domain model evolution. *Journal of Visual Languages and Computing, 15*(3-4), 291–307.

SRI. (2012). *Yices SMT solver.* Retrieved from http://yices.csl.sri.com/

Steele, G. (1990). *Common LISP: The language* (2nd ed.). Digital Press.

Steffen, B., Heiko, K., & Ralf, R. (2008). The Palladio component model for model-driven performance prediction. *Journal of Systems and Software, 82*(1), 3–22.

Steimann, F. (2000). On the representation of roles in object-oriented and conceptual modelling. *Data & Knowledge Engineering, 35,* 83–106. doi:10.1016/S0169-023X(00)00023-9.

Steinberg, D., Budinsky, F., Paternostro, M., & Merks, E. (2008). EMF: Eclipse modeling framework. In *Engineering* (p. 744). Reading, MA: Addison-Wesley Professional. Retrieved from http://portal.acm.org/citation.cfm?id=1197540

Steinholtz, B., & Walden, K. (1987). Automatic identification of software system differences. *IEEE Transactions on Software Engineering, 13*(4), 493–497. doi:10.1109/TSE.1987.233186.

Stephen, G., & Leila, K. (2005). A unified tool for performance modelling and prediction. *Reliability Engineering & System Safety, 89*(1), 17–32. doi:10.1016/j.ress.2004.08.004.

Stocks, J. L. (1922). *Translation of Aristotle's De Caelo.*

Strachan, J., & McWhirter, B. (2011). *Groovy: An agile dynamic language for the Java platform.*

Sun, J., & Wang, L. (2012). Research on e-commerce data management based on semantic web. In *Proceedings of the 2012 IEEE 14th International Conference on High Performance Computing and Communication & 2012 IEEE 9th International Conference on Embedded Software and Systems*, (pp. 925–928). IEEE. doi:10.1109/HPCC.2012.133

Swerdlow, N., & Neugebauer, O. (1984). *Mathematical astronomy in Copernicus's de revolutionibus*. New York: Springer-Verlag. doi:10.1007/978-1-4613-8262-1.

Swoyer, C., & Orilia, F. (2011). Properties. In E. N. Zalta (Ed.), *The Stanford Encyclopedia of Philosophy*. Retrieved from http://plato.stanford.edu/archives/win2011/entries/properties/

Tambouris, E., Manouselis, N., & Costopoulou, C. (2007). Metadata for digital collections of e-government resources. *The Electronic Library*, *25*(2), 176–192. Retrieved from http://www.emeraldinsight.com/10.1108/02640470710741313 doi:10.1108/02640470710741313.

Tarazona, G. M., Rodriguez, L., & Pelayo-Garcia, C., & Sanjuan. (2012). Model innovation of process based on the standard e-commerce international GS1. *International Journal of Interactive Multimedia and Artificial Intelligence*, *1*(7), 70. doi:10.9781/ijimai.2012.178.

Theelen, B. D., & der, P. P. H. A. v. (2003). *Using the SHE method for UML-based performance modeling*. Paper presented at the Forum on Specification and Design Language. Marseille, France.

Thibault, S. A., Marlet, R., & Consel, C. (1999). Domain-specific languages: From design to implementation application to video device drivers generation. *IEEE Transactions on Software Engineering*, *25*(3), 363–377.

Tolvanen, J. (2006). *Domain-specific modeling: How to start defining your own language*. Retrieved April 13, 2012, from http://www.devx.com/enterprise/Article/30550

Tonella, P., & Potrich, A. (2005). *Reverse engineering of object oriented code*. Heidelberg, Germany: Springer-Verlag.

Touraille, L., Traoré, M. K., & Hill, D. R. C. (2011). A model-driven software environment for modeling, simulation and analysis of complex systems. In *Proceedings of the Spring Simulation Multiconference - Symposium on Theory of Modeling and Simulation (TMS/DEVS)*, (pp. 229-237). Boston: TMS.

Tse, T. H., Chen, T. Y., & Glass, R. L. (2006). An assessment of systems and software engineering scholars and institutions (2000-2004). *Journal of Systems and Software*, *79*(6), 816–819. doi:10.1016/j.jss.2005.08.018.

Tversky, A., & Simonson, I. (1993). Article. *Management Science*, *39*(10), 1179–1189. doi:10.1287/mnsc.39.10.1179.

Ullmann, S. (1972). *Semantics: An introduction to the science of meaning*. Oxford, UK: Basil Blackwell.

UML. (2011a). *Unified modeling language: Infrastructure version 2.4.1*. OMG Specification formal/2011-08-05. Retrieved September 24, 2012, from http://www.omg.org/spec/UML/2.4.1/

UML. (2011b). *Unified modeling language: Superstructure version 2.4.1*. OMG Specification: formal/2011-08-06. Retrieved September 24, 2012, from http://www.omg.org/spec/UML/2.4.1/

UML2.OMG. (2007). *Unified modeling language: Superstructure version 2.1.1*. Formal/2007-02-03.

USE. (2011). *A UML-based specification environment*. Retrieved September 24, 2012, from http://sourceforge.net/apps/mediawiki/useocl/

Vahid, G. (2008a). *A formalism for arrival time analysis of real-time tasks based on UML models*. Paper presented at the Canadian Conference on Electrical and Computer Engineering. Toronto, Canada.

Vahid, G. (2008b). *Empirical analysis of a genetic algorithm-based stress test technique for distributed real-time systems*. Paper presented at the Annual Conference on Genetic and Evolutionary Computation. New York, NY.

Vahid, G. (2008c). *Traffic-aware stress testing of distributed real-time systems based on UML models in the presence of time uncertainty*. Paper presented at the International Conference on Software Testing, Verification, and Validation. Lillehammer, Norway.

Vahid, G. (2010c). *UML model-driven detection of performance bottlenecks in concurrent real-time software.* Paper presented at the IEEE International Symposium on Performance Evaluation of Computer Telecommunication Systems. Ottawa, Canada.

Vahid, G., & Yvan, L. (2006). *Traffic-aware stress testing of distributed systems based on UML models.* Paper presented at the 28th International Conference on Software Engineering. Shanghai, China.

Vahid, G., Briand, L. C., & Yvan, L. (2005). *A unified approach for predictability analysis of real-time systems using UML-based control flow information.* Paper presented at the GHHS. New York, NY.

Vahid, G. (2010a). A genetic algorithm-based stress test requirements generator tool and its empirical evaluation. *IEEE Transactions on Software Engineering, 36*(6), 778–797. doi:10.1109/TSE.2010.5.

Vahid, G. (2010b). Experience and challenges with UML-driven performance engineering of a distributed real-time system. *Information and Software Technology, 52*(6), 625–640. doi:10.1016/j.infsof.2010.01.003.

Vahid, G. (2011). Fault-driven stress testing of distributed real-time software based on UML models. *Software Testing. Verification & Reliability, 21*(2), 101–124. doi:10.1002/stvr.418.

Vahid, G., & Yvan, L. (2008). Traffic-aware stress testing of distributed real-time systems based on UML models using genetic algorithms. *Journal of Systems and Software, 81*(2), 161–185. doi:10.1016/j.jss.2007.05.037.

Vahid, G., & Yvan, L. (2009). A UML-based quantitative framework for early prediction of resource usage and load in real-time systems. *Journal of Software and System Modeling, 8*(2), 275–302. doi:10.1007/s10270-008-0099-7.

van Amstel, M., Bosems, S., Kurtev, I., & Pires, L. F. (2011). Performance in model transformations: Experiments with ATL and QVT. In *Proceedings of ICMT 2011* (LNCS), (vol. 6707, pp. 198-212). Berlin: Springer.

van der Linden, F. (2002). Software product families in Europe: the Esaps & Cafe projects. *IEEE Software, 19*(4), 41–49.

van Lamsweerde, A. (2004). Goal-oriented requirements engineering: A roundtrip from research to practice. In *Proceedings of the 12th IEEE International Requirements Engineering Conference.* Kyoto, Japan: IEEE.

van Overeem, A. V. O. A., Witters, J. W. J., & Peristeras, V. P. V. (2007). An interoperability framework for pan-european e-government services (PEGS). In *Proceedings of the 2007 40th Annual Hawaii International Conference on System Sciences HICSS07* (Vol. 2009, p. 7). IEEE. Retrieved from http://ieeexplore.ieee.org/lpdocs/epic03/wrapper.htm?arnumber=4076384

Van, H. T., et al. (2004). Goal-oriented requirements animation. In *Proceedings of RE'04: 12th IEEE International Requirements Engineering Conference,* (pp. 218-228). IEEE.

Verheul, J., & Roubtsova, E. (2011). An executable and changeable reference model for the health insurance industry. In *Proceedings of the 3rd International Workshop on Behavioural Modelling - Foundations and Applications.* ACM.

Vincenzo, G., & Raffaela, M. (2001). *UML modelling and performance analysis of mobile software architectures.* Paper presented at the 4th International Conference on The Unified Modeling Language, Modeling Languages, Concepts, and Tools. New York, NY.

Vincenzo, G., & Raffaela, M. (2002). *PRIMAmob-UML: A methodology for performance analysis of mobile software architectures.* Paper presented at the 3rd International Workshop on Software and Performance. Rome, Italy.

Vittorio, C., & Maurizio, G. (2004). *Performance modeling and validation of a software system in a RT-UML-based simulative environment.* Paper presented at the International Symposium on Object-Oriented Real-Time Distributed Computing. Vienna, Austria.

Vittorio, C., & Raffaela, M. (2000). *Deriving a queueing network based performance model from UML diagrams.* Paper presented at the International Workshop on Software and Performance. New York, NY.

Vittorio, C., Michele, G., & Marco, P. (2004). *Xprit: An XML-based tool to translate uml diagrams into execution graphs and queueing networks.* Paper presented at the Quantitative Evaluation of Systems, First International Conference. Enschede, The Netherlands.

Vittorio, C., Antinisca, D. M., & Paola, I. (2011). *Model-based software performance analysis.* Berlin: Springer.

Vittorio, C., Katerina, G.-P., & Kalaivani, A., R., Ahmed, H., Rania, E., et al. (2005). Model-based performance risk analysis. *IEEE Transactions on Software Engineering, 31*(1), 3–20. doi:10.1109/TSE.2005.12.

Vittorio, C., & Raffaela, M. (2002). PRIMA-UML: A performance validation incremental methodology on early UML diagrams. *Science of Computer Programming, 44*(1), 101–129. doi:10.1016/S0167-6423(02)00033-3.

Völter, M. (2011). MD/DSL best practices[from http://www.voelter.de/publications/index.html]. *Update,* (March): 2011. Retrieved September 27, 2012

von Bertalanffy, L. (2006). *Teoría general de los sistemas: Fundamentos, desarrollo, aplicaciones* (Económica, F. de C., Ed.). Mexico: Segunda.

Wallace, A. R. (1855). On the law which has regulated the introduction of new species. *Annals & Magazine of Natural History, 16,* 184–196. doi:10.1080/037454809495509.

Wand, Y., & Weber, R. (1993). On the ontological expressiveness of information systems analysis and design grammars. *Journal of Information Systems, 3,* 217–237. doi:10.1111/j.1365-2575.1993.tb00127.x.

Wand, Y., & Weber, R. (1995). On the deep structure of information systems. *Information Systems Journal, 5,* 203–223. doi:10.1111/j.1365-2575.1995.tb00108.x.

Wang, X., Zhou, X., & Jiang, L. (2008). A method of business and IT alignment based on enterprise architecture. In *Proceedings of the IEEE International Conference on Service Operations, Logistics and Informatics,* (vol. 1, pp. 740-745). IEEE.

Wang, M., & Wang, H. (2006). From process logic to business logic—A cognitive approach to business process management. *Information & Management, 43*(2), 179–193. Retrieved from http://linkinghub.elsevier.com/retrieve/pii/S0378720605000479 doi:10.1016/j.im.2005.06.001.

Weiping, L. (2009). An analysis of new features for workflow system in the SaaS software. In *Proceedings of the 2nd International Conference on Interaction Sciences: Information Technology, Culture and Human (ICIS '09),* (pp. 110-114). ACM.

Weiss, D. (1998). *Commonality analysis: A systematic process for defining families.* Paper presented at the Second International ESPRIT ARES Workshop on Development and Evolution of Software Architectures for Product Families. Las Palmas de Gran Canaria, Spain.

Wet, N. D., & Pieter, K. (2005). Using UML models for the performance analysis of network systems. *The International Journal of Computer and Telecommunications Networking - Telecommunications and UML Languages, 49*(5), 627 - 642.

Whitmire, S. A. (1997). *Object oriented design measurement.* New York: John Wiley & Sons, Inc..

Wieringa, R. (2011). Real-world semantics of conceptual models. In Kaschek, R., & Delcambre, L. (Eds.), *The Evolution of Conceptual Modeling (LNCS)* (Vol. 6520, pp. 1–20). Berlin: Springer. doi:10.1007/978-3-642-17505-3_1.

Wieringa, R., de Jonge, W., & Spruit, P. (1995). Using dynamic classes and role classes to model object migration. *Theory and Practice of Object Systems, 1*(1), 31–83.

Wikipedia. (2012). *Edmund Husserl.* Retrieved from http://www.en.wikipedia.org/wiki/Edmund_Husserl

Wile, D. (2004). Lessons learned from real DSL experiments. *Science of Computer Programming, 51*(3), 265–290.

Wisnosky, D. E., & Vogel, J. (2004). *DoDAF wizdom: A practical guide to planning, managing and executing projects to build enterprise architectures using the department of defense architecture framework.* DoDAF.

Wittgenstein, L. (1921). *Tractatus logico-philosophicus.* London: Routledge and Kegan Paul.

Wittgenstein, L. (1953). *Philosophical investigations.* New York: Macmillan.

Wittgenstein, L. (1958). *Philosophical investigations* (2nd ed.). Oxford, UK: Basil Blackwell.

Wohlin, C., Runeson, P., Höst, M., Ohlsson, M. C., Regnell, B., & Wesslén, A. (2000). *Experimentation in software engineering: An introduction.* Dordrecht, The Netherlands: Kluwer Academic Publishers. doi:10.1007/978-1-4615-4625-2.

Woodcock, J., Larsen, P., Bicarregui, J., & Fitzgerald, J. (2009). Formal methods: Practice and experience. *ACM Computing Surveys*, *4*(41), 1–36. doi:10.1145/1592434.1592436.

Wright, J. M., & Dietrich, J. B. (2010). Non-monotonic model completion in web application engineering. In *Proceedings of the 2010 21st Australian Software Engineering Conference*, (pp. 45–54). IEEE. Retrieved December 3, 2012, from http://ieeexplore.ieee.org/lpdocs/epic03/wrapper.htm?arnumber=5475055

Wu, B., Deng, S., Li, Y., Wu, J., & Yin, J. (2011). Reference models for SaaS oriented business workflow management systems. In *Proceedings of the 2011 IEEE International Conference on Services Computing (SCC '11)*, (pp. 242-249). IEEE Computer Society.

XMI. (2011). *OMG MOF 2 XMI mapping Specification-OMG*. Document Number: formal/2011-08-09. Retrieved September 24, 2012, from http://www.omg.org/spec/XMI/2.4.1

Yu, E. (1995). *Modelling strategic relationships for process reengineering*. (Ph.D. Thesis). Dept. of Computer Science, University of Toronto, Toronot, Canada.

Yu, Y., & Kong, K. (2011). The research of enterprise boundary from the perspective of social network. *E-Business and E-Government (ICEE), 2011*. Retrieved from http://ieeexplore.ieee.org/xpls/abs_all.jsp?arnumber=5887220

Zachman, J. (1999). A framework for information systems architecture. *IBM Systems Journal*, *38*(2/3), 454–470. doi:10.1147/sj.382.0454.

Zave, P., & Jackson, M. (1997). Four dark corners of requirements engineering. *ACM Transactions on Software Engineering and Methodology*, *6*(1), 1–30. doi:10.1145/237432.237434.

Zhang, J., & Cheng, B. (2006). Model-based development of dynamically adaptive software. In *Proceedings of the International Conference on Software Engineering* (pp. 371-380). ACM Press.

Zhao, L., Macaulay, L., Adams, J., & Verschueren, P. (2008). A pattern language for designing e-business architecture. *Journal of Systems and Software*, *81*(8), 1272–1287. doi:10.1016/j.jss.2007.11.717.

Zhu, X., & Wang, S. (2009). Software customization based on model-driven architecture over SaaS platforms. In *Proceedings of International Conference on Management and Service Science* (pp. 1-4). CORD.

Zou, Z., & Deng, Y. (2011). The evaluation model of e-business based on process. *Energy Procedia*, *13*, 5601–5608. doi:10.1016/j.egypro.2011.12.208.

Zwass, V. (1996). Electronic commerce. *Structures and Issues*, *1*(1).

About the Contributors

Vicente García Díaz is an associate professor in the Computer Science Department of the University of Oviedo. He has a PhD from the University of Oviedo in computer engineering. His research interests include model-driven engineering, domain specific languages, technology for learning and entertainment, project risk management, software development processes and practices. He graduated in Prevention of Occupational Risks and is a Certified Associate in Project Management through the Project Management Institute.

Juan Manuel Cueva Lovelle became a mining engineer from Oviedo Mining Engineers Technical School in 1983 (Oviedo University, Spain). He has a PhD from Madrid Polytechnic University, Spain (1990). From 1985 he has been a professor at the languages and computers systems area in Oviedo University (Spain), and is an ACM and IEEE voting member. His research interests include object-oriented technology, language processors, human-computer interface, Web engineering, modeling software with BPM, DSL, and MDA.

Begoña Cristina Pelayo García-Bustelo is a lecturer in the Computer Science Department of the University of Oviedo. She has a PhD from the University of Oviedo in computer engineering. Her research interests include object-oriented technology, Web engineering, eGovernment, modeling software with BPM, DSL and MDA.

Oscar Sanjuán Martínez is a lecturer in the Computer Science Department of the Carlos III University of Madrid. He has a PhD from the Pontifical University of Salamanca in computer engineering. His research interests include object-oriented technology, Web engineering, software agents, modeling software with BPM, DSL, and MDA.

* * *

Alain Abran holds a Ph.D. in Electrical and Computer Engineering (1994) from École Polytechnique de Montréal (Canada) and master degrees in Management Sciences (1974) and Electrical Engineering (1975) from University of Ottawa. He is a professor at the École de Technologie Supérieure (ETS) – Université du Québec (Montréal, Canada). He has over 15 years of experience in teaching in a university environment as well as more than 20 years of industry experience in information systems development and software engineering. His research interests include software productivity and estimation models, software engineering foundations, software quality, software functional size measurement, software risk management, and software maintenance management. He has published over 300 peer-reviewed publications and he is the author of the book *Software Metrics and Software Metrology* and a co-author of the book *Software Maintenance Management* (Wiley Interscience Ed. & IEEE-CS Press). Dr. Abran is co-editor of the *Guide to the Software Engineering Body of Knowledge* – SWEBOK (see ISO 19759 and www.sWebok.org) and he is the chairman of the Common Software Measurement International Consortium (COSMIC) – www.cosmicon.com.

Pär J. Ågerfalk (Ph.D., Linköping University, Sweden) is a (full) Professor in the Department of Informatics and Media at Uppsala University where he holds the Chair in Information Systems. His work has appeared in a number of leading Information Systems journals, including *MIS Quarterly*, *Information Systems Research*, and *Journal of Information Technology*. He recently stepped down as co-editor of the *Scandinavian Journal of Information Systems* and is currently editor of the *European Journal of Information Systems*. Dr. Ågerfalk is the founding chair of the AIS Special Interest Group on Pragmatist IS Research (AIS SIGPrag) and is currently a guest co-editor for a special issue of *MIS Quarterly* on Information Systems for Symbolic Action – Social Media and Beyond. He is the Dean of the Swedish Research School of Management and Information Technology and Chairman of the Swedish Information Systems Academy.

Franck Barbier (detailed vitæ at www.FranckBarbier.com): (CS) Ph.D. in 1991 (University of Chambéry, France), French higher (CS) Ph.D. (a.k.a. HDR) in 1998 (University of Nantes, France); associate professor from '91 to '98 at the University of Nantes, visiting researcher at the University of Sydney from '98 to '99 and full professor (University of Pau, France) from 2000; Director of the CS Research Department of the University of Pau (LIUPPA) from 2000 to 2004. Deputy head of the ICT sector at the French Research Agency (2009-2012). His research activities and interests are object/component/service modeling through UML, model driven engineering, software design, test, and runtime management for mobile and distributed systems, software adaptation through built-in test, executable models and models at runtime; 100 published papers in refereed journals/books/conferences including 5 books (2 as editor and 3 as full author).

Guillaume Barbier is a PhD student since March 2010. He is employed by ITK (http://itkWeb.com/?lang=en) and supervised by Dr. François Pinet and Pr. David R.C. Hill. He graduated both in computer science and theoretical ecology (M.Sc. AgroParisTech), respectively in 2001 and 2005. Using his working knowledge of software engineering and mathematical modeling, his work aims at bridging the gap between software engineers and crop modelers by providing a visual and textual tool for crop model design.

Balbir S. Barn, BSc, PhD, is Deputy Dean, and Professor of Software Engineering at Middlesex University, UK. Balbir's research career has spanned commercial research at Texas Instruments and Sterling Software where he was part of the research and design team of leading software products such as the IEF. His academic research is focused on applied approaches to software engineering, for example to use model driven approaches as language abstractions for enterprise architecture. He has led numerous externally funded projects on cross-disciplinary themes aimed at developing and deploying mobile applications in areas as diverse as social work and criminology. One further key strand of research activity includes exploring the integration of practices from analytical philosophy, such as Toulmin's Argumentation model to theory building activities in conceptual modelling for Information Systems design.

Eric Cariou obtained its Ph.D. in computer science from the University of Rennes 1 and Télécom Bretagne in 2003. Then, he got a post-doctorate position at the University of Lille 1. Since 2005, he is associate professor at the University of Pau. His research interests deal with software architecture and model-driven engineering. He worked on software components dedicated to the communication between components and the integration of component and agent approaches through services. Concerning MDE, he has developed techniques for contract-based verification. They have been applied to verifying model transformations and model execution. He is also working on software adaptation through models@runtime principles and more precisely on the adaptation of executed models.

Pierre Castéran is an associate professor at the University of Bordeaux 1, LaBRI since 1984, and member of the Formal Methods research team at LaBRI. He is a specialist of interactive proof assistants, mainly for obtaining "correct by construction" software. He is presently developing a library, written for the Coq proof assistant for the formal proof of properties of distributed systems. This library is based on a formal semantics of such systems expressed in terms of labeled graph transformations, aims to be used in teaching theoretical aspects of distributed software: correctness, termination detection, certified program transformations. He participates also in the dissemination of the Coq proof assistant technology through summer schools, Websites, and tutorials. He is the co-author with Yves Bertot (INRIA) of the first reference book on the Coq system: *Interactive Theorem Proving and Program Development* published in 2004 by Springer.

Tony Clark is Professor of Informatics and Head of the Computer Science Department in the School of Science and Technology at Middlesex University. Tony has experience of working in both Academia and Industry on a range of software projects and consultancies. While at Marconi Research Ltd (1985-1994), he worked in both Software Engineering and Knowledge Based Systems, and was responsible for designing novel systems for recognising aircraft behaviour and fusing sonar data, and for designing and implementing an AI Toolkit, the first of its kind in the UK. From 1994-2003 Tony was an academic firstly at Bradford University and then at King's College London. During this time, he worked on languages for Object-Oriented specification and design including contributing to a range of Industry standards (UML 2.0, MDA, QVT, MOF) through participation in the Object Management Group (OMG). During this time Tony's group at King's College London developed tooling for object-oriented language development. This tooling work together with the development of a novel approach to meta-modelling and language design on the UML 2.0 standard led to a spin-out company which Tony co-founded in 2003 and served as Technical Director 2003-2008. The company sold UML-based meta-tools and acted as consultant to a number of blue-chip companies. Tony is an editorial board member of the *SoSyM Journal*, has edited several special issues including *IEEE Software and SoSyM*, and was co-chair of the MODELS conference in 2011. He is the author of over 80 articles including contributions to industry standards (UML 2.0, QVT) and an influential e-book on meta-modelling. Further information can be found at http://www.eis.mdx.ac.uk/staffpages/tonyclark/.

Véronique Cucchi is an agronomist at ITK society since March 2011. She received both a PhD in Forest Science (INRA/Bordeaux 1 University) and a M.Sc in Computer Science (Montpellier 2 University), respectively in 2004 and 2010. Her fields concern models in agronomy and decision support systems (DSS).

Jon Davis has over 25 years of industry and academic experience. For many years, he has been developing software solutions for the heavy engineering, manufacturing and mining industries, plus the public and university sector, his main focus being on software modelling and reusability. He is also a project management specialist lecturing to university, public and private sector organisations. In recent years, he has paid special attention to research in the scope of generic models for Enterprise Information Systems definition, in which he has analyzed the advantages of using model-driven automated application generation and led the development of a new model and framework publishing numerous papers in the field. Jon Davis graduated in Science then Mathematics at Melbourne and Newcastle University, followed by an Honours degree in Computer Science at Newcastle University and is currently in the final stages of completing a PhD at Curtin University.

Owen Eriksson is a Senior Lecturer of Information Systems in the Department of Informatics and Media at Uppsala University and an Associate Professor of Informatics in the Department of Management and Engineering at Linköping University. He received his Ph.D. from Linköping University and has held positions at Dalarna University, University of Borås and the Viktoria Institute. His main research fields are conceptual modeling and database design based on language/action theories, e-infrastructures, and Intelligent Transport Systems (ITS). His research is action-oriented and design-oriented and he has been the research leader of a number of externally funded research projects in close co-operation with authorities and industry. His work has appeared in journals such as *European Journal of Information, Systems, Journal of Information Technology,* and *Journal of the Association of Information Systems.*

Liliana Favre is a full professor of Computer Science at Universidad Nacional del Centro de la Provincia de Buenos Aires in Argentina. She is also a researcher of CIC (Comisión de Investigaciones Científicas de la Provincia de Buenos Aires). Her current research interests are focused on model driven development, model driven architecture, and formal approaches, mainly on the integration of algebraic techniques with MDA-based processes. She has been involved in several national research projects about formal methods and software engineering methodologies. Currently she is research leader of the Software Technology Group at Universidad Nacional del Centro de la Provincia de Buenos Aires. She has published several book chapters, journal articles, and conference papers. She has acted as editor of the book *UML and the Unified Process.* She is the author of the book *Model Driven Architecture for Reverse Engineering Technologies: Strategic Directions and System Evolution.*

Vahid Garousi is an Associate Professor of Software Engineering at the University of Calgary, leading the software quality engineering research group. Vahid received a PhD in Software Engineering from Carleton University in 2006. His MSc degree was in Electrical and Computer Engineering from the University of Waterloo in 2003. Vahid usually serves in the program or organization committees of many international, IEEE and ACM conferences. He is a member of the IEEE and the IEEE Computer Society, and is a registered professional engineer in Canada. His research interests include model-driven software development, software testing and quality assurance, and applications of optimization and evolutionary computation to software testing. He won an Alberta Ingenuity new faculty award in June 2007. Vahid was recently selected a Distinguished Visitor (speaker) for the IEEE Computer Society's Distinguished Visitors Program (DVP) for the period of 2012-2014.

Wolfgang Golubski received the Dr.rer.nat. degree from the University of Bochum, Germany, in 1992. From 1994 to 2003, he worked in the Computer Science Departments at the Universities of Münster and Siegen, Germany, as a research assistant. In 1997, he qualified as university lecturer (habilitation) at the University of Siegen in 1997. He is currently a Professor of Computer Science at the Zwickau University of Applied Sciences. His work spans many areas of computer science. The research interests include model-driven software development, software architecture, middleware, and requirements engineering.

César González-Pérez leads the Semantic Technologies research line at the Institute of Heritage Sciences (Incipit), Spanish National Research Council (CSIC), where he focuses on co-research in software engineering and cultural heritage. His ultimate goal is to develop the necessary theories, methods, and technologies to improve the way in which we ascribe meaning to information in the cultural heritage realm. Prior to this Cesar worked at a variety of research organisations, both in academia and industry, in the areas of conceptual modelling, metamodelling, and development methodologies. Cesar is also the founder and research advisor to Neco, a company based in Spain specialising in software development support services, and founder and technical consultant to Cobase Ltd., a UK-based company providing cloud services for the construction industry. Cesar is also a co-editor of the ISO/IEC 24744 International Standard for software development methodologies, and author of over 50 peer-reviewed publications.

David R. C. Hill was Vice President of Blaise Pascal University (2008-2012). Professor Hill is also past director of the Inter-Univeristy Computing Center (CIRI) (2008-2010). From August 2005 to August 2007, he was deputy director of ISIMA Computer Science & Modeling Institute (French Grande Ecole d'Ingénieur) where he managed various departments before 2005. Professor Hill is now head of the Software Engineering Department at ISIMA and head of the Regional Computing Mesocenter. Since 1990, he has authored or co-authored more than two hundred papers and he has also published many text books. His Web page is www.isima.fr/~hill.

Brian Henderson-Sellers is Director of the Centre for Object Technology Applications and Research and Professor of Information Systems at the University of Technology, Sydney (UTS). He is author of over a dozen books on object and agent technologies and is well known for his work in OO methodologies (MOSES, COMMA, OPEN, OOSPICE) and in OO metrics. Brian is the Chief Editor of the journal *International Journal on Agent-Oriented Software Engineering* and on the Editorial Board of several IT journals including *Software and Systems Modelling*. In 1999, he was voted number 3 in the Who's Who of Object Technology (*Handbook of Object Technology*, CRC Press, Appendix N). He has been a member of the Review Panel for the OMG's SPEM and UML standards. Brian was General Chair of the IFIP WG8.1 Working Conference on Method Engineering (Geneva, 2007) and is Co-Editor of the ISO/IEC 24744 International Standard. In July 2001, Professor Henderson-Sellers was awarded a Doctor of Science (DSc) from the University of London for his research contributions in object-oriented methodologies and, in 2010, the Consensus IT Professionals Award.

Guillermo Infante Hernández, Accounting and Finances degree 2006 from University of Holguin, Cuba. Web Master Engineering degree 2010, from University of Oviedo. He has been working as research fellow in University of Holguin from 2006 to 2010 as part of the Computer-Aided Design and Computer-Aided Manufacture (CAD/CAM) research department team. His work in this department lead him to a research stay in Faculty of Engineering of the University of Porto in 2008 to work on manufacturing optimization algorithms using neural networks. From 2010 to the present, he has been working on his doctoral thesis at the Computer Science Department of University of Oviedo. Some of the research interests he is working on include Model Driven Engineering applied to e-government domain, Rule driven software development and Web Engineering amongst others.

Aquilino Adolfo Juan Fuente, Lecturer of Computer Sciences at the University of Oviedo (Spain). He received PhD in Computer Engineering in 2002. His research interests are Software Architecture, Web engineering and e-learning Architectures. He has published more than 30 books and papers in refereed scientific journals and conferences, and he has taken part in more than 20 research projects.

Abdelilah Kahlaoui holds a Ph.D. in Software Engineering (2011) from École de Technologie Supérieure – Université du Québec (Canada). He has more than 15 years of experience in the IT industry. He has worked on many projects involving domain-specific languages and code generation techniques. His current research interests include Model Driven Engineering, Domain-Specific Language design and application, and software product quality.

Diwakar Krishnamurthy is an associate professor with the department of electrical and computer engineering at the University of Calgary. He received his PhD from Carleton University in 2004. His research interests are focused on software performance engineering. Diwakar is currently involved in industry-funded projects related to performance management and modeling of enterprise application systems.

Kevin Lano is Reader in Software Engineering at King's College London. He has worked for over 20 years in the fields of system specification and verification. A co-founder of the Precise UML group in 1996, he produced some of the first research on model transformation specification and verification and subsequently has developed techniques for the correct-by-construction software engineering of model transformations and for the verification of transformations. He is the author of the UML-RSDS toolset for precise model-based development.

Olivier Le Goaer holds a Ph.D. from the University of Nantes, France. He is an associate professor at the University of Pau since 2010, and member of the MOVIES research team at LIUPPA. His research activities and interests are all related to software evolution—at design-time or at run-time—leaning on model-driven engineering practices. He is also particularly interested in mobile programming and stays abreast of the newest Web technologies.

Benjamín López Pérez, Ph.D. on Computer Science Engineering from the University of Oviedo. Tenured Associate Professor at the Computer Science Department of the University of Oviedo. Computer Science Engineer from the University of Malaga in 1991. Research interests are Computational reflection, Aspect Oriented Software Development, Meta-level systems and meta-object protocols, Web Engineering and software architecture applied to e-government domain. He has participated in several research projects funding for Microsoft Research, Spanish Department of Science and Innovation, and Regional Government. He has held various positions. He is currently Director of the Computer Science Engineering School in University of Oviedo.

Liliana Martinez is an assistant professor in computer science area at the Facultad de Ciencias Exactas, Universidad Nacional del Centro de la Provincia de Buenos Aires (UNCPBA), Tandil, Argentina. She is a member of the Software Technology Group, which develops its activities at the INTIA Research Institute at the UNCPBA. She has a Master degree in Software Engineering from Universidad Nacional de La Plata, Argentina. Her research interests are focused on system modernization, reverse engineering in particular. She has published book chapters, journal articles, and conference papers. She has been member of the program committee of international conferences related to software engineering.

Edward Rolando Núñez-Valdéz, Ph.D. from the University of Oviedo in Computer Engineering. Master and DEA in Software Engineering from the Pontifical University of Salamanca and B.S. in Computer Science from Autonomous University of Santo Domingo. He has participated in several research projects. He has taught Mathematics and Computer science at various schools and universities and has worked in software development companies and IT Consulting as IT consultant and application developer. He has published several articles in international journals and conferences. Currently working as researcher at the University of Oviedo. His research interests include Object-Oriented technology, Web Engineering, recommendation systems, Modeling Software with DSL and MDA.

Claudia Pereira is an assistant professor in computer science area at the Facultad de Ciencias Exactas, Universidad Nacional del Centro de la Provincia de Buenos Aires (UNCPBA), Tandil, Argentina. She is a member of the Technology Software Group at the INTIA Research Institute at the UNCPBA. She has a Master degree in Software Engineering from Universidad Nacional de La Plata, Argentina. Her main research interests are focused on system modernization, refactoring in particular. She has published book chapters, journal articles, and conference papers. She has been member of the program committee of international conferences related to software engineering.

André Pflüger graduated from the University of Applied Sciences Zwickau and received his diploma in 2007 and his master's degree in 2009 in the field of Computer Science. His research topics were the analysis of operational and performance data in manufacturing and the Model Driven Software Development (MDSD) for Java Enterprise applications. He continues his MDSD research as a member of the GeneSEZ research group. Since 2009, he has been a PhD student at the Otto-Friedrich University of Bamberg. The topic of his thesis is the model driven validation of system architectures against system requirements using UML, which has been developed in cooperation with the SOPHIST GmbH in Nuremberg. He works as a consultant and trainer in the area of requirements engineering, system analysis, and design for the SOPHIST GmbH.

François Pinet (http://www.irstea.fr/pinet) received his M.Sc in Computer Science in 1997 (ENS – Lyon) and his PhD in Computer Science in 2002 (INSA Lyon, France). He is currently a research director at the French Institute for Agricultural and Environmental Engineering (Irstea – Clermont-Ferrand). His field of research is in software engineering, environmental information systems, and geomatics.

Stefan Queins completed his informatics degree, and then he obtained his doctorate (Dr. Ing.) from the University of Kaiserslautern, Germany. His doctoral thesis covered the topic of "How to Exploit the Application's Subject to Adapt the Development Process." As a consultant at the SOPHIST GmbH in Nuremberg, he uses object-oriented methods and notations in the fields of system analysis and architecture of technical-oriented systems. Besides that, he is involved in the introduction of customized process models in development projects. He also provides his knowledge in training sessions dealing with that. His interest in the fields of practical research continued after his doctorate and he applies the knowledge gained therein to his projects.

Shekoufeh Kolahdouz Rahimi is a doctoral candidate in Computer Science at Kings College London. Her PhD is in the area of Model Driven Engineering and particularly Model Transformation. As a member of Software Modelling and Applied Logic group at KCL with Dr Kevin Lano, she has defined a transformation quality framework based on the ISO/IEC 9126 international software quality standard. The framework is validated on different transformation languages using diverse case studies. The evaluation procedure provides clear guidelines for suitability of selected transformation approaches on specific transformation problem by identifying the advantage and disadvantage of each approach. In addition, she has involved in development of UML-RSDS a hybrid specification language for defining system data by UML class diagrams and OCL constraints. She received her MSc in Computing and Internet Systems from the King College London, UK, and her BSc in Hardware Engineering in her home town Esfahan, Iran. Her research interest includes Model Driven development, Model Driven Architecture, Constraint-Driven Development, Specification and Verification of Model Transformation, Composition of Model Transformation, Measurement of Model Transformation and Semantics of Model Transformation.

Luz Andrea Rodriguez is a PhD student in Computer Engineering in the University of Oviedo, Asturias, Spain, Master Engineering and Website Design (2012), Specialization in hygiene and occupational health (2010), Industrial Engineer, Francisco José de Caldas District University, Bogota, DC (2008). She is Full Time Professor Foundation Liberators University (August 2011- May 2012) Area Production. She is full professor in occupational health at INPAHU (August 2010-May 2011). Director project Research "Strategies for Strengthening of Information System Tourism Health in Bogota."

Ella Roubtsova obtained her engineering degree with honours at Yaroslavl State Technical University, Russia (http://www.ystu.ru/), and her PhD at the Institute for Control Theory, Academy of Science, Moscow, Russia (http://www.ipu.ru/en). She worked as lecturer at the Yaroslavl State University (Russia) (http://www.uniyar.ac.ru/), as research fellow at Technical University of Delft (The Netherlands) (http://home.tudelft.nl/), and as researcher at Technical University Eindhoven (The Netherlands) (http://www.win.tue.nl/~ella/). She was also Honorary Fellow of Munich University of Applied Sciences (Germany) (http://www.hm.edu/en/index.en.html). Now Dr. Roubtsova works in the master program at the Open University of the Netherlands (http://www.ou.nl/). She is a senior member of the Institute of Electrical and Electronics Engineers, IEEE, the author of more than 80 scientific publications, seven university courses, and reviewer of scientific journals. Her interest in systems development is stimulated by industrial projects and by her students' work as system developers and software architects.

Shawn Shahnewaz is a thesis-based M.Sc. student at the department of Electrical and Computer Engineering (ECE) at University of Calgary, Canada. He has also completed his M.Sc. in Computer Science and Engineering from Islamic University of Technology (IUT) in Bangladesh. His research interests include automated software engineering, optimized software maintenance, data mining, and Web technologies.

Giovanny Tarazona, Doctoral candidate in systems and computer services for Internet in the Oviedo University, Asturias, Spain (2012) – diploma of advanced studies November 2007 Pontifical Salamanca University in campus Madrid Spain, Specialization in computer project (2006), Specialization in engineering software (1999). He is Industrial engineer, Francisco José de Caldas District University, Bogota, DC, (1998). He is Full Time Professor Francisco José de Caldas District University – Faculty of Engineering since July 2003. He is founding member of KAIZEN PBT GROUP Ltda, legal representative, director of several projects, Bogotá, DC, 1996 – December 2011. Coordinator Specialization Computer Project in Francisco José de Caldas District University (July 2011 – December 2011), Coordinator Specialization Computer Automatic Industry (February 2009 – July 2011), Director Institute Of Extension And Non Formal Education IDEXUD (March 2007 – December 2007), Coordinator Industrial Engineering (January 2006 – March 2007), Coordinator Internship Unit Faculty of Engineering (June – December 2005). Director Research Group on Electronic Commerce Colombian GICOECOL Francisco José de Caldas District University, Director of several research projects.

Index